DAVID BUSCH'S
SONY® α
a6400/ILCE-6400

GUIDE TO DIGITAL PHOTOGRAPHY

David D. Busch

rockynook

David Busch's Sony® α a6400/ILCE-6400
Guide to Digital Photography
David D. Busch

Project Manager: Jenny Davidson
Series Technical Editor: Michael D. Sullivan
Layout: Bill Hartman
Cover Design: Mike Tanamachi
Indexer: Valerie Haynes Perry
Proofreader: Mike Beady

ISBN: 978-1-68198-519-0
1st Edition (1st printing, October 2019)

© 2019 David D. Busch

All images © David D. Busch unless otherwise noted

Rocky Nook, Inc.
1010 B Street, Suite 350
San Rafael, CA 94901
USA
www.rockynook.com

Distributed in the UK and Europe by Publishers Group UK
Distributed in the U.S. and all other territories by Ingram Publisher Services

Library of Congress Control Number: 2019931625

This book is printed on acid-free paper.
Printed in Korea

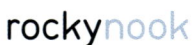

For Cathy

Acknowledgments

Thanks to everyone at Rocky Nook, including Scott Cowlin, managing director and publisher, for the freedom to let me explore the amazing capabilities of the Sony Alpha a6400 camera in depth. I couldn't do it without my veteran production team, including project manager, Jenny Davidson, and series technical editor, Mike Sullivan. Also thanks to Bill Hartman, layout; Valerie Hayes Perry, indexing; Mike Beady, proofreading; Mike Tanamachi, cover design; and my agent, Carole Jelen, who has the amazing ability to keep both publishers and authors happy. Special thanks to Kristy Steeves at www.kristysteevesphotography.com for my new back cover portrait.

About the Author

With more than 2.5 million books in print, **David D. Busch** is the world's #1 bestselling camera guide author, and the originator of popular series like *David Busch's Compact Field Guides* and *David Busch's Quick Snap Guides*. He has written more than 100 hugely successful guidebooks for Sony and other digital camera models, including the all-time #1 bestsellers for several different cameras, as well as many popular books devoted to photography, including *Mastering Mirrorless Photography*. As a roving photojournalist for more than 20 years, he illustrated his books, magazine articles, and newspaper reports with award-winning images. He's operated his own commercial studio, suffocated in formal dress while shooting weddings, and shot sports for a daily newspaper and an upstate New York college. His photos and articles have appeared in *Popular Photography, Rangefinder, Professional Photographer*, and hundreds of other publications. He's also reviewed dozens of digital cameras for CNet and other CBS publications.

When About.com named its top five books on Beginning Digital Photography, debuting at the #1 and #2 slots were Busch's *Digital Photography All-In-One Desk Reference for Dummies* and *Mastering Digital Photography*. He has had as many as 18 books listed in the Top 100 of Amazon.com's Digital Photography Bestseller list—simultaneously! Busch's 250-plus other books published since 1983 include bestsellers like *Digital SLR Cameras and Photography for Dummies*.

Busch is a member of the Cleveland Photographic Society (www.clevelandphoto.org), which has operated continuously since 1887. Visit his website at http://www.sonyguides.com.

Contents

Chapter 2
Sony a6400 Roadmap

Chapter 3
Camera Settings I Menu

Chapter 4
Camera Settings II Menu   133

Chapter 5
Network and Playback Menus   175

Chapter 6
Setup Menu and My Menu   199

Chapter 7
Nailing the Optimum Exposure   223

Chapter 8
Mastering Autofocus Options   279

Chapter 9
Advanced Shooting   307

Chapter 10
Movie Making

333

Chapter 11
Working with Lenses

363

Chapter 12
Working with Flash   387

Preface

In the mirrorless world, Sony has become the leader by providing innovative technology in a lineup of cameras that are smaller, lighter, faster to focus, and loaded with cutting-edge features that many of us have been dreaming about. So, it's no wonder you're excited about your new Sony a6400/ ICLE-6400, a compact mirrorless camera with full-sized features, including what is currently one of the fastest autofocus systems in the world, an improved sensor, rugged all-magnesium alloy body, and Ultra High Definition 4K video. With all these features at your disposal, you don't expect to take good pictures with such a camera—you demand and anticipate *outstanding* photos.

However, your gateway to pixel proficiency is dragged down by the limited instructions provided by Sony. Over the years, Sony has reduced the amount of useful information included in its printed guidebooks, often to a scant few pages, and relegated more detailed instructions to online HTML-based guides and PDF versions that are difficult to navigate. And, sad to say, not everything you need to know is included.

What you really need is a guide that explains the purpose and function of the cameras' basic controls, how you should use them, and *why*. That's what I am giving you in this book. If you want a quick introduction to focus controls or which exposure modes are best, this book is for you. If you can't decide on what basic settings to use with your camera because you can't figure out how changing ISO or white balance or focus defaults will affect your pictures, you need this guide.

Introduction

The innovative "real-time tracking" autofocus feature in the Sony Alpha a6400/ILCE-6400 is the most significant upgrade from this model's predecessor, the a6300/ILCE-6300. The bold step of providing blazing-fast follow-focus—which includes face detection, eye detection (you can choose left or right eye!), and animal eye detection demonstrates that Sony doesn't play it safe. Since the company entered the digital photography arena, it hasn't been satisfied with the old paradigms and technology. At a time when the top dogs in the digital camera world are still mired in the race to produce the best single lens reflex models, Sony has concentrated on non-dSLR cameras, including mirrorless models like the Sony Alpha a6400/ILCE-6400. (For simplicity, I'll generally refer to this camera as the a6400 throughout the book.)

Sony has packaged up the most alluring features of advanced digital cameras and stuffed them into a compact, highly affordable body, which has some features you won't find on other cameras. The a6400/ILCE-6400 boasts a body that is, minus your choice of lens, more compact than any digital SLR. But, tucked inside is a large 24-megapixel sensor with the same size, light-gathering power, and resolution of those found in the typical digital SLR. As I mentioned, the amazing new autofocus system provides "real-time tracking" and the ability to lock in focus based on detection of your human or animal subjects' eyes, a current feature not available with similar precision outside the Sony world. Add in the ability to use an expanding roster of interchangeable E-mount lenses and a reasonably affordable price tag, and you have a compact camera that sacrifices nothing in terms of features and capabilities. The original products in the Alpha lineup were great, and the new camera is even better. Indeed, this shooter has many of the advanced features of the top-of-the-line Alpha a7 III-series models!

You'll find your new camera is loaded with facilities that few would have expected to find in such a basic camera. Indeed, the a6400 retains the ease of use that smoothes the transition for those new to digital photography. For those just dipping their toes into the digital pond, the experience is warm and inviting. The Sony Alpha a6400 isn't a snapshot camera—it is a point-and-shoot (if you want to use it in that mode) for the thinking photographer.

Of course, once you've confirmed that you made a wise purchase, the question comes up, *how do I use this thing?* All those cool features can be mind-numbing to learn, if all you have as a guide is the mediocre manual furnished with the camera. Basic functions and options are explained, but there's really very little about *why* you should use particular settings or features, and the organization may make it difficult to find what you need. Multiple cross-references may send you flipping back and forth between two or three sections of the book to find what you want to know. The basic manual is also hobbled by black-and-white line drawings and tiny pictures that aren't very good examples of what you can do.

Help is on the way. I sincerely believe that this book is your best bet for learning how to use your new camera, and for learning how to use it well. I've tried to make *David Busch's Sony Alpha a6400/ ILCE-6400 Guide to Digital Photography* comprehensive, but easy to comprehend. The roadmap sections use large, color pictures to show you where all the buttons and dials are, and the explanations of what they do are longer and more detailed. I've tried to avoid overly general advice, including the checklists you'll find in other manuals on how to take a "sports picture" or a "portrait picture" or a "travel picture." If you want to know where you should stand to take a picture of a quarterback dropping back to unleash a pass, there are plenty of books that will tell you that. This one concentrates on teaching you how to select the best autofocus mode, shutter speed, f/stop, or flash capability to take, say, a great sports picture under any conditions.

What You'll Learn

This book is aimed at Sony veterans as well as newcomers to digital photography. Both groups can be overwhelmed by the options the a6400 offers, while underwhelmed by the explanations they receive in their user's manual, which some suspect was written by a Sony employee who last threw together instructions on how to operate a camcorder or DVD player. Does a manual that repeatedly refers to the a6400 as "the product" turn you off as it did me?

Given the number of pages allotted by Rocky Nook to this book, from necessity I will emphasize *still photography.* However, I *will* devote a lot of space to helping you get up to speed on using the camera's video capabilities. After all, even though small in size, it is fully capable of shooting awesome, professional-level movies. But detailed advice about choosing between Internal UHD 4K30 and 1080p/120 fps recording, or technical information about S-Log3 gamma, display assist functions, and other pro-level features are beyond the scope of this book. Given that I expect that only a relatively small—albeit important—segment of the readers of this book want or require such information, I'm going with Vulcan philosopher Spock Prime's observation early in *The Wrath of Khan* that "Logic clearly dictates that the needs of the many outweigh the needs of the few."

Who Am I?

After spending many years as the world's most successful unknown author, I've become slightly less obscure in the past few years, thanks to a horde of camera guidebooks and other photographically oriented tomes. You may have seen my photography articles in *Popular Photography, Rangefinder, Professional Photographer*, and dozens of other photographic publications. But, first, and foremost, I'm a photojournalist and made my living in the field until I began devoting most of my time to writing books. Although I love writing, I'm happiest when I'm out taking pictures, which is why I spend many winters ensconced in the Florida Keys, dividing my time between writing books and taking photographs. You'll find images of many of these visual treats within the pages of this guide.

Like all my digital photography books, this one was written by someone with an incurable photography bug. I've worked as a sports photographer for an Ohio newspaper and for an upstate New York college. I've operated my own commercial studio and photo lab, cranking out product shots on demand and then printing a few hundred glossy 8 × 10s on a tight deadline for a press kit. I've served as a photo-posing instructor for a modeling agency. People have actually paid me to shoot their weddings and immortalize them with portraits. I even prepared press kits and articles on photography as a PR consultant for a formerly dominant (and now vestigial) Rochester, NY company. My trials and travails with imaging and computer technology have made their way into print in book form an alarming number of times, including hundreds of volumes on photographic topics. I teach classes, and have branched out into online training courses.

Like you, I love photography for its own merits, and I view technology as just another tool to help me get the images I see in my mind's eye. But, also like you, I had to master this technology before I could apply it to my work. This book is the result of what I've learned, and I hope it will help you master your Sony a6400/ILCE-6400.

I'd like to ask a special favor: let me know what you think of this book. If you have any recommendations about how I can make it better, visit my website at www.sonyguides.com, click on the E-Mail Me tab, and send your comments, suggestions on topics that should be explained in more detail, or, especially, any typos. (The latter will be compiled on the Errata page you'll also find on my website.) I really value your ideas, and I appreciate it when you take the time to tell me what you think! Some of the content of the book you hold in your hands came from suggestions I received from readers like you. If you found this book especially useful, tell others about it. Visit http://www.amazon.com/dp/1681985195 and leave a positive review. Your feedback is what spurs me to make each one of these books better than the last, and if enough of you like what I've done, Rocky Nook may be moved to ask me to follow up with a new book the next time Sony introduces one of its photographic innovations. Thanks!

1

Getting Started with Your Sony a6400

Don't panic if you opened this book to the "Getting Started..." chapter and realized that you've already taken several hundred or a thousand (or two) photos. The information in this chapter is designed to get the rawest beginner up and running with the a6400 quickly. However, you'll find that the advice I'm about to offer is useful for those who have already become somewhat comfortable with this well-designed (yet complex) camera. You can zip right through the basics, and then dive into learning a few things you probably didn't know about your a6400.

Fortunately, this very sophisticated camera is incredibly easy to use in many aspects, right out of the box. In fact, it was designed to allow even the novice to start taking great pictures with about five seconds of effort. Just flick the power switch to On; it's concentric with the shutter release button on top of the camera. Then, rotate the mode dial located just aft of the switch to select the green Auto icon. (See Figure 1.1.) Frame the subject on the monitor (the rear LCD screen) or by looking through the viewfinder. Press the shutter release button when you're ready to take your first shot.

Preparing for those steps by charging the battery, mounting a lens, and inserting a formatted Secure Digital card isn't exactly rocket science, either. If you already have some experience with cameras designed for enthusiasts, you can jump from Auto mode directly to a scene (SCN) mode (which makes settings for you suitable for various types of subjects, such as portraits or landscapes), or one of the semi-automatic modes, including P (Program), A (Aperture Priority), or S (Shutter Priority). When you rotate the mode dial to any position, the camera displays an icon at the upper-left corner of the LCD monitor screen and in the viewfinder indicating the current mode. With the mode dial set to the SCN position, you can rotate the control dial (located to the immediate right of the mode dial) to select an appropriate scene mode. Icons representing the scene mode you've selected will be displayed at upper left, as well.

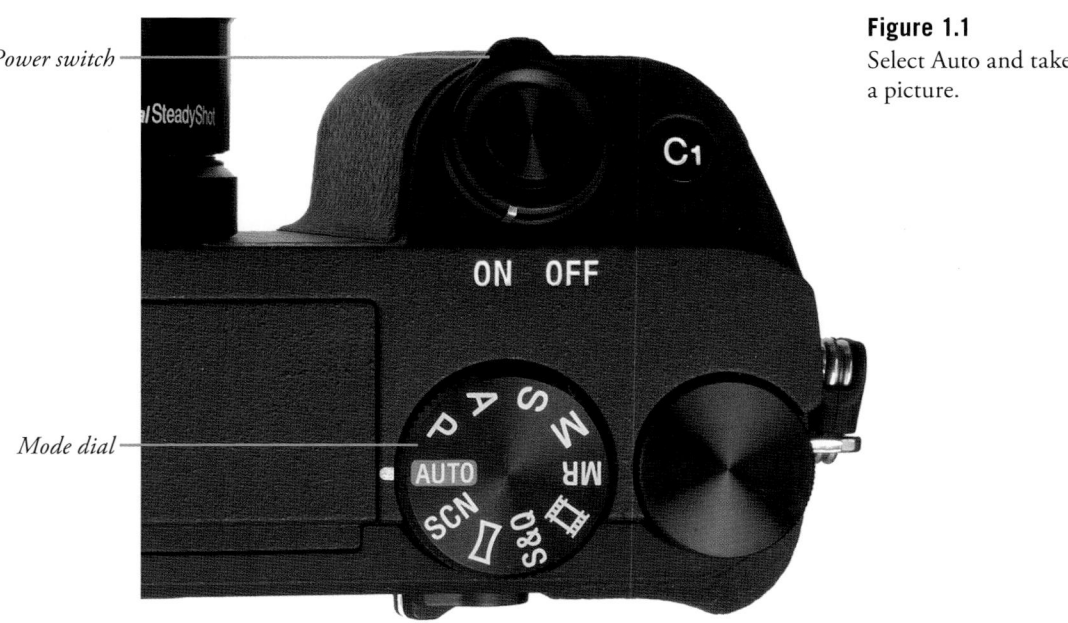

Figure 1.1

Select Auto and take a picture.

Power switch

Mode dial

Auto mode (represented by a green Auto label on the mode dial) makes virtually all the settings for you; semi-auto modes calculate the best exposure; and scene modes automatically make camera settings for excellent shots of people, landscapes, flowers, night scenes, and more. (You can also set the a6400 to produce a Mode Dial Guide screen with additional information on each mode; I'll show you how to activate this optional help later in this book.)

WAIT FOR IT...

I'll explain the basic controls later in this chapter. Your a6400 has a lot of them, some with similar names. For example, the control *dial* next to the mode dial is different from the control *wheel* on the back panel of the camera. I'll tell you what each does in this chapter and the next.

So, budding photographers are likely to muddle their way through getting the camera revved up and working well enough to take a bunch of pictures without the universe collapsing. Eventually, though, many may turn to this book when they realize that they can do an even better job with a little guidance.

Also, I realize that most of you didn't buy this book at the same time you purchased your Sony a6400. As much as I'd like to picture thousands of avid photographers marching out of their camera stores with an a6400 box under one arm, and my book in hand, I know that's not going to happen *all* the time. A large number of you had your camera for a week, or two, or a month, became comfortable with it, and sought out this book in order to learn more. So, a chapter on "setup" seems like too little, too late, doesn't it?

In practice, though, it's not a bad idea, once you've taken a few orientation pictures with your camera, to go back and review the basic operations of the camera from the beginning, if only to see if you've missed something. This chapter is my opportunity to review the setup procedures for the camera for those among you who are already veteran users, and to help ease the more timid (and those who have never before worked with an interchangeable-lens camera) into the basic pre-flight checklist that needs to be completed before you really spread your wings and take off. For the uninitiated, as easy as it is to use initially, your Sony a6400 *does* have some dials, buttons, and menu items that might not make sense at first, but will surely become second nature after you've had a chance to review the instructions in this book.

But don't fret about wading through a manual to find out what you must know to take those first few tentative snaps. I'm going to help you hit the ground running with this chapter (or keep on running if you've already jumped right in). If you *haven't* had the opportunity to use your a6400 yet, I'll help you set up your camera and begin shooting in minutes. You won't find a lot of detail in this chapter. Indeed, I'm going to tell you just what you absolutely *must* understand, accompanied by some interesting tidbits that will help you become acclimated. I'll go into more depth and even repeat some of what I explain here in later chapters, so you don't have to memorize everything you see. I'll save some of the a6400's more advanced features—including the cool touch screen controls—for Chapter 2 and beyond. For now, just relax, follow a few easy steps, and then go out and begin taking your best shots—ever.

Your Out-of-Box Experience

Your Sony a6400 comes in an attractive box filled with stuff, including a multi-purpose USB/charging cable, basic instructions, some pamphlets, and a few other items. The most important components are the camera and lens, battery/AC adapter, and, if you're the nervous type, the neck strap. You'll also need a Secure Digital card, as one is not included.

The first thing to do is to carefully unpack the camera and double-check the contents with the checklist on one side of the box. While this level of setup detail may seem as superfluous as the instructions on a bottle of shampoo, checking the contents *first* is always a good idea. It's better to know *now* that something is missing so you can seek redress immediately, rather than discover a few days later before an important family event that the USB cable—essential for battery charging—was never in the box.

So, check the box at your earliest convenience, and make sure you have (at least) the following:

- **Sony a6400 body.** This is hard to miss. The camera is the main reason you laid out the big bucks, and it is tucked away inside a nifty protective envelope you should save for re-use in case the camera needs to be sent in for repair. It almost goes without saying that you should check out the camera immediately, making sure the color LCD on the back isn't scratched or cracked, the battery compartment and connection terminal doors open properly, and, when a charged battery is inserted and lens mounted, the camera powers up and reports for duty. Out-of-the-box defects in these areas are rare, but they can happen. It's probably more common that your dealer played with the camera or, perhaps, it was a customer return. That's why it's best to buy your camera from a retailer you trust to supply a factory-fresh camera.

- **Lens.** You may be able to buy the a6400 with or without a lens, although many retailers may stock only the "kit" form that includes the 16-50mm f/3.5-5.6 OSS retractable zoom, the most popular option with the a6400. It's unusually compact when the camera is powered off and offers two valuable benefits: an image stabilizer (Optical SteadyShot or OSS) to help compensate for camera shake and a cool power zooming feature. Because I was upgrading from my original a6000, I already owned this lens, so I took advantage of a package deal that mated the body with a separately packaged Zeiss Vario-Tessar T* E 16-70mm f/4 ZA OSS lens. I'll discuss your many lens options in detail in Chapter 11.

  My recommendation: If you plan to use your a6400 to shoot movies, the 16-50mm power zoom lens is a good choice for smooth, relatively quiet zooming. However, it is known primarily for its compactness and zoom feature, rather than optimum image quality. Although the 16-70mm Zeiss lens's (roughly) $1,000 price tag approaches that of the a6400 itself, it is a much sharper lens at all focal lengths, a zoom range that takes you out to 70mm, and a constant f/4 aperture that doesn't change as you zoom in.

- **Eyepiece cup.** This item fits snugly against your eye, and prevents extraneous light from entering the electronic viewfinder window. It can be attached by lining up the underside of the cup with the bottom of the viewfinder frame, and swiveling it forward until it snaps in place. You may need to remove the cup temporarily for better access to the diopter adjustment dial (described later) or when using some larger accessories that attach to the multi interface (flash) shoe on top of the camera.

- **InfoLithium NP-FW50 battery.** The power source for your Sony camera is packaged separately. It should be charged as soon as possible (as described next) and inserted in the camera.

  My recommendation: With the a6400, it's smart to have more than one battery pack. Although tiny in size, this camera gulps power, and, even with the generous standards Sony cites in its literature, each is likely to last for no more than 290 to 340 still shots or roughly 95 minutes of video. If you are a heavy user of the LCD monitor for review, expect even less longevity. Buy *more*, and stick to Sony-brand products; third-party batteries have been known to fail quickly, sometimes in potentially destructive ways. I have eight of these, but, then, I also own a Sony a6000 and a5000 that use the same batteries.

■ **AC Adapter AC-UB10C/D.** This is the device (shown in Figure 1.2) that you'll use to charge the battery with household power; the USB cable plugs into it and the adapter plugs into a wall socket. This eliminates the need to have a computer powered up to charge the battery.

My recommendation: Charging the battery while it's in the camera means your a6400 is tied up while you're recharging. I prefer the option of slipping a new battery into my camera and having the depleted battery recharge while I continue to shoot. You can buy an optional Sony BC-VW1 external charger (see Figure 1.3), or the BC-TRW Quick Charger; the latter makes charging the battery a much faster process. Either allows you to recharge one battery while another is ensconced in your camera as you continue shooting.

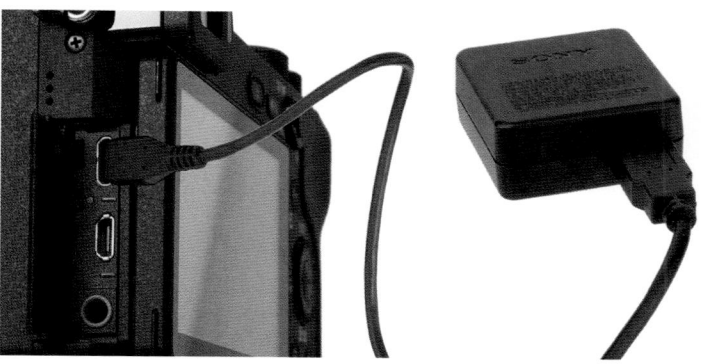

Figure 1.2 The AC Adapter AC-UB10C/D takes several hours to provide a normal charge to a battery pack that was completely depleted.

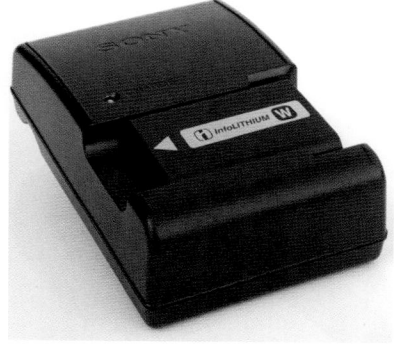

Figure 1.3 The optional Sony BC-VW1 charger allows rejuvenating your battery outside the camera, so you can keep shooting with a spare battery.

■ **Micro B USB 2.0 cable.** Use this cable to link your Sony to a computer when you need to transfer pictures but don't have an optional card reader accessory handy. While the camera is connected with the cable, the battery inside the body will also be charging, so you can actually rejuvenate your battery using any powered USB terminal. In addition, you'll definitely need to make that USB connection between the a6400 and a computer when you have occasion to upgrade the camera's firmware. The USB cable can also be connected to the included AC adapter if you want to charge the battery using household power.

My recommendation: Sony stuck with USB 2.0 instead of the faster USB 3.0 protocol because the latter wouldn't allow charging the battery through the USB cable. I don't use this cable much. Instead, as I mentioned earlier, I prefer an external charger, instead, and like to copy images to my computer with a USB 3.0 card reader, rather than the slower USB cable connection.

■ **Shoulder strap.** Sony provides a suitable neck or shoulder strap, with the Sony logo subtly worked into the design.

My recommendation: While I am justifiably proud of owning a fine Sony camera, I never attach the factory strap to my camera, and instead opt for a more serviceable strap from UPstrap (www.upstrap-pro.com). If you carry your camera over one shoulder, as many do, I particularly recommend UPstrap (shown in Figure 1.4). It has a patented non-slip pad that offers reassuring traction and eliminates the contortions we sometimes go through to keep the camera from slipping off. I know several photographers who refuse to use anything else. If you do purchase an UPstrap, be sure to tell photographer-inventor Al Stegmeyer that I sent you hence.

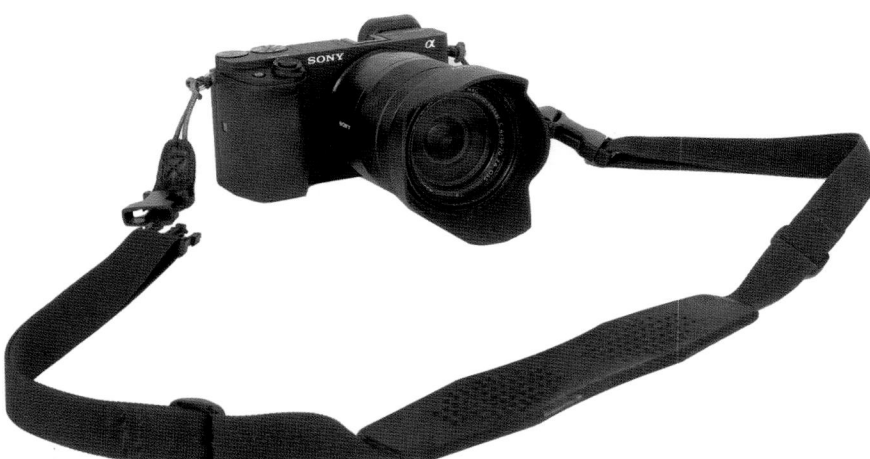

Figure 1.4
Third-party neck straps, like this UPstrap model, are often preferable to the Sony-supplied strap.

■ **Shoe cap.** This plastic piece slides into the camera's multi interface shoe on top (what we used to call a "hot shoe") and protects the contacts from dirt, moisture, and damage when you don't have an electronic flash, microphone, or other accessory attached.

My recommendation: Because of the extra contacts located at the front of the multi interface shoe, it's possible to damage those contacts inadvertently. If you use an external flash or microphone as much as I do, you can remove this piece and leave it off when not shooting. It's easy to lose this cap, however, so I have purchased inexpensive replacements (both regular and with a bubble level) which you can obtain from my web page at www.laserfairepress.com for a few bucks.

■ **Application software.** Sony no longer includes a software CD in the package. The first time you power up the camera, it will display the current URL for your country where you can download imaging software for the a6400, such as the Imaging Edge utility, which replaced the earlier PlayMemories Home software.

- **Printed instruction manual.** The camera comes with a brief printed instruction booklet and a Wi-Fi/NFC connection guide; a longer guide to the camera's operation can be accessed from Sony's esupport.sony.com website. There will also be assorted pamphlets listing available accessories, lenses, as well as warranty and registration information.
- **Body cap.** This accessory will probably already be attached to the camera body if you purchase your a6400 without a lens. It fits onto the body to cover the lens mount opening when no lens is attached, protecting your sensor.

Initial Setup

The initial setup of your Sony a6400 is fast and easy. Basically, you just need to charge the battery, attach a lens (if that hasn't already been done), and insert a memory card. I'll address each of these steps separately, but if you already feel you can manage these setup tasks without further instructions, feel free to skip this section entirely. You should probably at least skim its contents, however, because I'm going to list a few options that you might not be aware of.

Battery Included

Your Sony a6400 is a sophisticated hunk of machinery and electronics, but it needs a charged battery to function, so rejuvenating the NP-FW50 lithium-ion battery pack should be your first step. A fully charged power source should be good for approximately 360 shots under normal temperature conditions when using the electronic viewfinder, and roughly 410 shots if you compose your shots primarily with the less power-hungry LCD monitor on the back of the camera. These estimates are based on standard tests defined by the Camera & Imaging Products Association (CIPA). If you often use the camera's Wi-Fi feature (discussed later), you can expect to take fewer shots before it's time for a recharge. This is an Info-Lithium battery so the camera can display the approximate power remaining with a graphic indicator.

Remember that all rechargeable batteries undergo some degree of self-discharge just sitting idle in the camera or in the original packaging. Lithium-ion power packs of this type typically lose a small amount of their charge every day, even when the camera isn't turned on. Li-ion cells lose their power through a chemical reaction that continues when the camera is switched off. So, it's very likely that the battery purchased with your camera, even if charged at the factory, has begun to poop out after the long sea voyage on a banana boat (or, more likely, a trip by jet plane followed by a sojourn in a warehouse), so you'll want to revive it before going out for some serious shooting.

My recommendation: As I mentioned earlier, I own eight NP-FW50 batteries, and keep one in the camera at all times. Nevertheless, I always check battery status before I go out to shoot, as some juice may have been siphoned off while the camera sat idle. I go to the Network 1 menu and turn Airplane Mode on (as described in Chapter 5) when I don't need Wi-Fi features.

Charging the Battery

When you're ready to charge the battery, turn the camera Off. Then, plug one end of the USB cable (with the smaller connector) into the top terminal under the door in the left end of the a6400; it will fit only when in the proper orientation. Plug the other end (with the familiar USB connector) into a computer's USB terminal. Turn the camera On and you'll see a note on the LCD screen, USB Mode; this confirms that the connection has been made. As discussed earlier, you can also connect the camera to the AC adapter and plug that into a wall socket.

Whether you charge from a computer's USB terminal or household power, a Charge light next to the USB/charging terminal glows yellow-orange, without flashing. It continues to glow until the battery completes the charge and the lamp turns off. In truth, the full charge is complete about one hour *after* the charging lamp turns off, so if your battery was really dead, don't remove it from the charger until the additional time has elapsed. Be sure to plan for charging time before your shooting sessions, because it takes about 150 minutes in a warm environment to fully restore a completely depleted battery. (With the optional Quick Charger BC-TRW accessory, that should take a little less time; it sells for about $50 through major online photo retailers in the US.)

If the charging lamp flashes after you insert the battery into the camera, that indicates an error condition. Make sure you have the correct model number of battery; remove it and re-insert it. To insert/remove it, slide the latch on the bottom of the camera, open the battery door, and press the blue lever in the battery compartment that prevents the pack from slipping out when the door is opened; then, ease the battery out. To insert it, do so with the three contact openings facing down into the compartment (see Figure 1.5).

Fast flashing that can't be stopped by re-inserting the battery indicates a problem with the battery. Slow flashing (about 1.5 seconds between flashes) means the ambient temperature is too high or low for charging to take place.

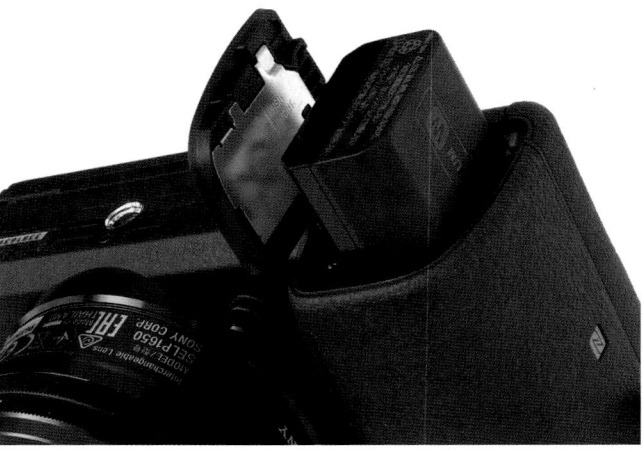

Figure 1.5
Insert the battery in the camera; it only fits one way.

Final Steps

Your Sony a6400 is almost ready to fire up and shoot. You'll need to select and mount a lens (if not previously done) and insert a memory card. Each of these steps is easy, and if you've used any similar camera in the past, such as a Sony or other model, you already know exactly what to do. I'm going to provide a little extra detail for those of you who are new to the Sony or interchangeable-lens camera worlds.

Mounting the Lens

Most buyers purchase the camera in a kit including a lens, but you may have bought it as a "body-only" configuration; that allows you to select any compatible (Sony E-mount) lens that you already own, as with any interchangeable-lens camera. In any event, sooner or later you're likely to want to switch to a different lens for other photographic uses, so it's important to know how to do so.

As you'll see, my recommended lens-mounting procedure emphasizes protecting your equipment from accidental damage, and minimizing the intrusion of dust. If your camera has no lens attached, select the lens you want to use and loosen (but do not remove) the rear lens cap. I generally place the lens I am planning to mount vertically in a slot in my camera bag, where it's protected from mishaps but ready to pick up quickly. By loosening the rear lens cap, you'll be able to lift it off the back of the lens at the last instant, so the rear element of the lens is covered until then.

After that, remove the body cap that protects the camera's exposed sensor by rotating the cap toward the shutter release button. You should always mount the body cap when there is no lens on the camera, because it helps keep dust out of the interior of the camera, where it potentially can find its way onto the sensor. This is a particular issue with the a6400, because, unlike dSLRs, there are no intermediate items protecting the sensor from exposure, such as the mirror that provides the dSLR with its view through the viewfinder or the shutter.

By the way, when buying my first Sony camera a few years ago, I found that a body cap was not included because the lens was already mounted on the camera. If your camera didn't come with a body cap, you should try to locate one through Sony or another vendor (they're available from www.laserfairepress.com) if you possibly can; a camera body should never be left with its sensor exposed.

Once the body cap has been removed, remove the rear lens cap from the lens, set the cap aside, and then mount the lens on the camera by matching the raised white alignment indicator on the lens barrel with the white dot on the camera's lens mount (see Figure 1.6). Rotate the lens away from the shutter release button until it seats securely and clicks into place. (Don't press the lens release button during mounting.) Some lenses ship with a hood. If that accessory is included, and if it's bayoneted on the lens in the reversed position (which makes the lens/hood combination more compact for transport), twist it off and remount with the rim facing outward (see Figure 1.7). A lens hood protects the front of the lens from accidental bumps, and reduces flare caused by extraneous light arriving at the front element of the lens from outside the picture area.

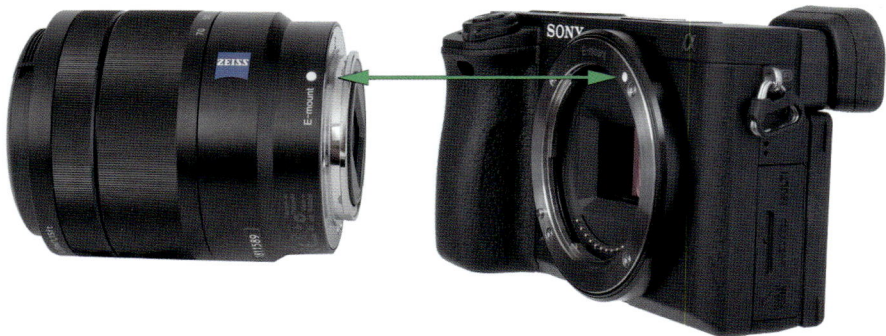

Figure 1.6
Match the raised white dot on the lens with the white dot on the camera mount to properly align the lens with the bayonet mount.

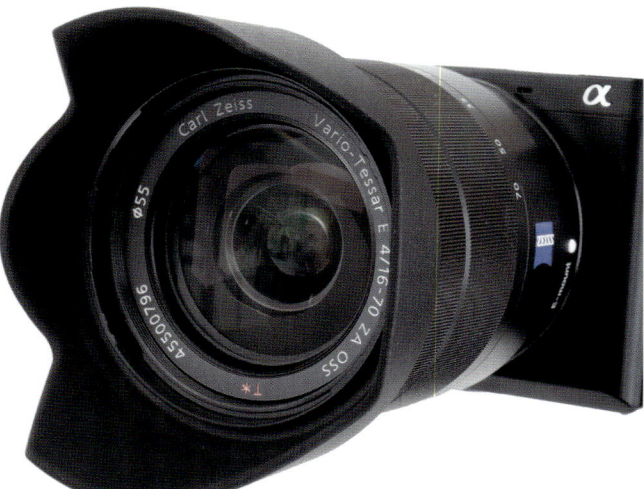

Figure 1.7
A hood protects the lens from extraneous light and from accidental bumps, but not all lenses include this accessory.

Turn on the Power

Locate the On/Off power switch that is wrapped around the shutter release button and rotate it to the On position. The LCD display will be illuminated. If you bring the viewfinder up to your eye, a sensor will detect that action and switch the display to the built-in electronic viewfinder instead. (You can disable this automatic switching in the Camera Settings II-06 menu, as I'll describe in Chapter 4.) After one minute of idling, the a6400 goes into standby mode to save battery power. Just tap the shutter release button to bring it back to life. (The one-minute time is the default setting. You can select a longer time before power-save mode kicks in through the menu system, as I discuss in Chapter 6.)

When the camera first powers up, you may be asked to set the date and time. The procedure is fairly self-explanatory (although I'll explain it in detail in Chapter 6). You can use the left/right directional buttons to navigate among the date, year, time, date format, and daylight savings time indicator, and use the up/down buttons to enter the correct settings. When finished, press the center button to confirm the settings and return to the menu system. If you need to change the date or time later, you can find the option in the Setup 5 menu.

Once the Sony a6400 is satisfied that it knows what time it is, you will be viewing a live view of the scene in front of the lens—on the LCD screen or in the viewfinder when that is held up to your eye—whenever you turn the camera on. The view is superimposed with many items of data over the display; these provide a quick method for checking many current camera settings, including current shutter speed and aperture (f/stop), shooting mode, ISO sensitivity, and other parameters. You can show/hide the information displays by pressing the Disp. (up directional) button.

Adjusting the Diopter Setting

The a6400 is equipped with a built-in electronic viewfinder or EVF, a small high-resolution OLED (organic light-emitting diode) screen that can be used instead of the LCD screen for framing your photos or movies. A sensor detects your eye at the viewfinder and shuts off power to the LCD when you are using the EVF. Usually, when you're learning to use the camera's many features, you'll rely on the LCD screen's display, but when you're actually taking photos, you'll sometimes want to use the EVF instead. You can also use it to review your photos or video clips.

If you wear glasses and want to use the EVF without them, or if you find the viewfinder needs a bit of correction, rotate the diopter adjustment dial located to the right of the viewfinder window, as shown in Figure 1.8, left. For easiest access to the dial, pull the eyepiece cup back until it pops off. Then, adjust the dial while looking through the viewfinder until the image appears sharpest. Replace the eyepiece cup; for the most part it will prevent accidentally changing the setting as you use the camera.

Figure 1.8
Diopter adjustment
dial (left); inserting
a memory card
(right).

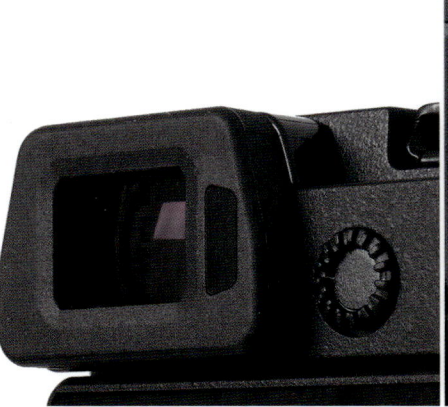
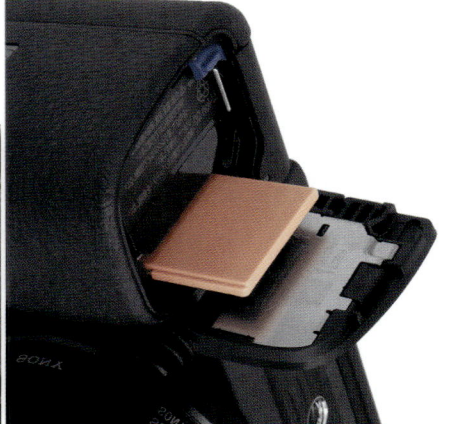

Inserting a Memory Card

You can't take actual photos without a memory card inserted in your Sony camera. If you don't have a card installed, the camera will sound as if it's taking a photo and it will display that "photo." However, the image is only in temporary memory and not actually stored; you'll get a reminder about that with a flashing orange NO CARD warning at the upper left of the LCD. If you go back later and try to view that image, it will not be there. So, be sure you have inserted a compatible card with adequate capacity before you start shooting stills or videos.

The a6400 accepts Secure Digital (SD), Secure Digital High Capacity (SDHC), Secure Digital Extra Capacity (SDXC), and Sony Memory Stick Pro Duo (Pro-HG Duo) cards. The newest type of SD card, the super-high-capacity (and super-fast) SDXC type, at this writing, is available in capacities as high as 512GB.

Whichever card you decide on, it fits in the single slot underneath the battery compartment door on the bottom of the camera. You should remove the memory card only when the camera is switched off. Insert an SD card with the label facing toward the left side of the camera (as you hold it in shooting position, and shown at right in Figure 1.8.), or away from the lens if inserting any type of Memory Stick Pro card. In either case, the metal contacts go into the slot first; the card simply will not fit into the slot if it is incorrectly oriented.

Close the door, and your pre-flight checklist is done! (I'm going to assume you'll remember to remove the lens cap when you're ready to take a picture!) When you want to remove the memory card later, just press down on the card edge that protrudes from the slot, and the card will pop right out.

My recommendation: If you already own an old-school Memory Stick, go ahead and use it, but if you're buying a memory card specifically for this camera, I recommend buying a 64GB Secure Digital SDXC card instead. It's likely that you won't be able to use the Memory Stick in any other non-Sony device, whereas the SDXC card should be compatible with many other devices you own. A 64GB SDXC card won't quickly become obsolete, and will be compatible with the a6400's 4K movie-making capabilities in the future, even if you don't plan to use that feature right away.

Formatting a Memory Card

There are three ways to create a blank SD Pro card for your Sony a6400, and two of them are at least partially wrong. Here are your options, both correct and incorrect:

- **Transfer (move) files to your computer.** You'll sometimes decide to transfer (rather than copy) all the image files to your computer from the memory card (either using a direct cable transfer or with a card reader and appropriate software, as described later in this chapter). When you do so, the image files on the card can be erased leaving the card blank. Theoretically. Unfortunately, this method does *not* remove files that you've labeled as Protected (by choosing Protect from the Playback menu during playback), nor does it identify and lock out parts of your card that have become corrupted or unusable since the last time you formatted the card.

Therefore, I recommend always formatting the card, rather than simply moving the image files, each time you want to make a blank card. The only exception is when you *want* to leave the protected/unerased images on the card for a while longer, say, to share with friends, family, and colleagues.

■ **(Don't) Format in your computer.** With the memory card inserted in a card reader or card slot in your computer, you can use Windows or Mac OS X to reformat the memory card. Don't even think of doing this! The operating system won't necessarily arrange the structure of the card the way the camera likes to see it (in computer terms, an incorrect *file system* may be installed). In particular, cards larger than 32GB must be initialized using the exFAT format, and while your computer may offer exFAT as an option, it may default to a different scheme. The only way to ensure that the card has been properly formatted for your camera is to perform the format *in the camera itself.* The only exception to this rule is when you have a seriously corrupted memory card that your camera refuses to format. Sometimes it is possible to revive such a corrupted card by allowing the operating system to reformat it first, then trying again in the camera to restore the proper exFAT system.

My recommendation: Use the Setup menu method to format a memory card in the camera. I'll describe the procedure next.

To format a memory card, just follow these steps:

1. **Press the MENU button.** The a6400's menu screen appears, with six tabs, each containing multiple screens of entries. (If you've enabled the "tile" menu screen, as described in Chapter 6, it will appear instead; it's disabled by default.) (See Figure 1.9.)

2. **Select Setup.** If the tile menu is visible, use the left/right directional buttons (the left/right edges of the control *wheel*) or use the control *dial* (next to the mode button) to navigate to the Setup menu (a wrench/toolbox icon), and press the center button (located in the middle of the control wheel) to open up the menu. (If you've disabled the tile menu, the conventional menu system will appear immediately, without the intermediate Step 2.)

Figure 1.9
Choose Setup in the tile menu (if it's enabled).

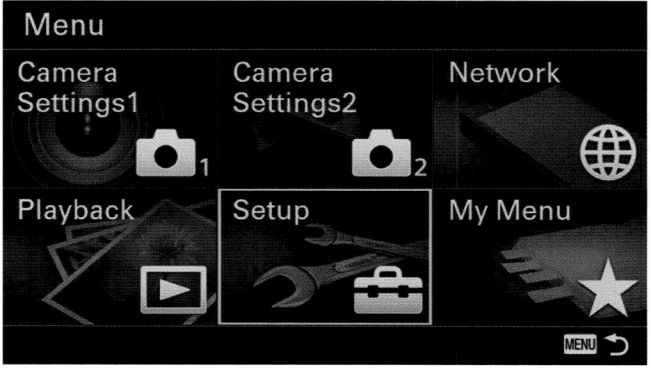

3. **Navigate to the Setup 5 tab.** Once in the conventional menu, use the directional buttons or control dial to move to the Setup icon (a toolbox) at the far right of the menu tabs. Then, press the down button to move into the Setup tab, followed by the left/right buttons to select Setup 5. (See Figure 1.10.)

4. **Choose Format.** Rotate the control wheel on the back of the camera to highlight Format and press the center button.

5. **Confirm.** A display will appear asking if you want to delete all data. If you're sure you want to do so, press up/down to choose OK, and press the center button to confirm your choice. This will begin the formatting process.

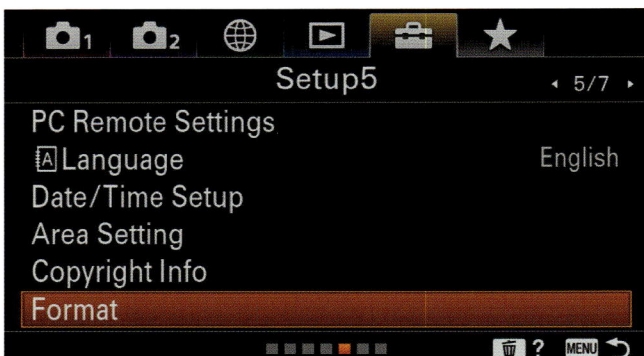

Figure 1.10
Navigate to the Setup 5 menu and select Format.

HOW MANY SHOTS?

The Sony a6400 provides a fairly accurate estimate of the number of shots that your memory card will hold. This number is visible near the top-left corner of the LCD (next to the memory card icon) in standard live view. It is only an estimate, because the actual number will vary, depending on the capacity of your memory card, the aspect ratio (proportions) of the image (the a6400 can use both traditional 3:2 proportions and 16:9—HDTV—aspect ratios), and the content of the image itself. (Some photos may contain large areas that can be more efficiently squeezed down to a smaller size.) If you change the file format (from JPEG to RAW or from a large JPEG to a small JPEG, for example), the number will change. The Display Media Info setting in the Setup 6 menu will show you how many images you can capture at your current settings, and how much movie-shooting time you can squeeze out of your memory card.

Table 1.1 shows the typical number of shots you can expect using a medium-sized 32GB memory card. Take those numbers, double them if you're using a 64GB card, and cut them in half if you're using a 16GB card. The numbers shown may differ from what you read in the camera's manual. I obtained them by formatting my own 32GB SDHC card and writing down the number of shots available at each setting. Although the a6400 can shoot more than 10,000 images with a high-capacity card, the maximum number of recordable images displayed on the LCD or viewfinder will never exceed 9,999.

Table 1.1 Typical Shots with a 32GB Memory Card

	Format	Large	Medium	Small
3:2 Aspect Ratio	JPEG Standard	5609	8366	11336 (9999)
	JPEG Fine	3441	6065	8903
	JPEG Extra Fine	1696	2788	4371
	RAW	1248	N/A	N/A
	RAW+JPEG Standard	1021	1086	1125
	RAW+JPEG Fine	916	1035	1095
	RAW+JPEG Extra Fine	716	861	971
16:9 Aspect Ratio	JPEG Standard	6261	8985	11890 (9999)
	JPEG Fine	3929	6692	9608
	JPEG Extra Fine	1972	3192	4926
	RAW	1241	N/A	N/A
	RAW+JPEG Standard	1035	1090	1123
	RAW+JPEG Fine	943	1046	1099
	RAW+JPEG Extra Fine	761	893	991
1:1 Aspect Ratio	JPEG Standard	8366	11901 (9999)	12367 (9999)
	JPEG Fine	5162	8985	11234 (9999)
	JPEG Extra Fine	2540	4165	6513
	RAW	1261	N/A	N/A
	RAW+JPEG Standard	1096	1145	1173
	RAW+JPEG Fine	1014	1106	1152
	RAW+JPEG Extra Fine	843	968	1057

Selecting a Shooting Mode

When it comes time to select the shooting mode and other settings on the a6400 camera, you may start to fully experience the "feel" of the user interface. Thanks to the mode dial shown earlier in Figure 1.1, it's simple and quick to set a shooting mode. There are actually two approaches to selecting a shooting mode—the default mode and a prompted mode, which includes additional on-screen help.

The default method assumes you have already learned what each shooting mode does. It offers a minimum of guidance. When you rotate the mode dial to one of these positions, an indicator appears in the upper-left corner of the electronic viewfinder and LCD monitor representing the selected mode:

- **Auto.** This position is actually two modes in one: Intelligent Auto and Superior Auto. You can select which of the two will be activated using the Auto Mode entry in the Camera Settings I-03 menu. (I'll cover all Camera Settings menu options in Chapter 3.)

  - **Intelligent Auto.** When Intelligent Auto is active, the a6400 examines your subject and selects an appropriate scene mode. (Scene modes are described next.) The camera makes the settings of aperture and shutter speed for you; it will fire flash in low light if appropriate and the flash is in the up position. You still can make some decisions on your own, though, such as whether to use single shots or continuous shooting through a drive mode setting, whether to use the flash, and whether to use autofocus or manual focus.

  - **Superior Auto.** Fully automatic like Intelligent Auto, this mode provides an extra benefit. In low-lighting conditions, with backlit scenes (in which most of the illumination comes from behind your subject), and scenes that include extremely bright areas as well as shadow areas, the camera can capture multiple images and create an optimized composite photo. I'll explain this mode, and some restrictions that apply to it, in Chapter 7.

MAKING THE SCENE

Note that the scenes recognized by Intelligent Auto and Superior Auto are not exactly the same as those you can individually specify using the Scene Selection option described next. The Auto modes can choose Portrait, Night Portrait, Night Scene, Landscape, Hand-Held Twilight, and Macro modes (also found under Scene Selection), but can call on additional Infant, Backlight Portrait, Backlight, Spotlight, Low Light, and Night Scene/Tripod modes.

■ **Scene Selection.** The SCN position on the dial lets you choose any of nine different scene modes, each suited for a different type of subject or lighting condition. When the dial is in the SCN position, the individual scene modes are chosen by rotating the control dial on the far right shoulder of the a6400. In scene modes, you do not get to control any aspect of the camera, except for the choice of autofocus or manual focus and flash. As mentioned earlier, flash will not fire when certain scene modes are in use. Here's a brief summary of the nine options.

● **Portrait.** This is the first of the nine scene modes, selected as sub-choices under the SCN heading on the shooting mode dial. With the Portrait setting, the camera uses settings to blur the background and sharpen the view of the subject, while using soft skin tones. Flash will fire in low light if you have popped it into the up position.

● **Sports Action.** Use this mode to freeze fast-moving subjects. The camera uses a fast shutter speed if possible; in a dark arena, for example, it simply won't be able to set a fast shutter speed so it will not be able to freeze the motion. The camera will fire continuously while the shutter button is held down. Flash will never fire in this mode.

● **Macro.** This mode is helpful when you are shooting close-up pictures of a subject such as a flower, insect, or other small object. Flash will fire in low light if you have popped it into the up position, but the flash may be too bright for a subject that's very close to the camera.

● **Landscape.** Select this scene mode when you want a maximum range of sharpness (instead of a blurred background) as well as vivid colors of distant scenes. Flash will never fire in this mode.

● **Sunset.** This is a great mode to accentuate the warm (red/orange) colors of a sunrise or sunset. Flash will never fire in this mode.

● **Night Scene.** This mode is for night scenes, using slower shutter speeds to provide a useful exposure, but without using flash. You should use a tripod to avoid the effects of camera shake that can be problematic with a slow shutter speed.

● **Hand-held Twilight.** This special mode is designed for use in low light. The camera will set a high ISO (sensitivity) level to enable it to use a fast shutter speed to minimize the risk of blurring caused by camera shake. (In extremely dark conditions however, the shutter speed may still be quite long.) When you press the shutter release button, the camera takes six shots in succession. The processor then composites them into one after discarding most of the digital noise (graininess) that is common in conventional photos made at high ISO. It provides one image that's of surprisingly fine quality. Flash is never fired in this mode.

● **Night Portrait.** Choose this mode when you want to illuminate a subject in the foreground with flash, but still allow the background to be exposed properly by the available light. Be prepared to use a tripod or to rely on the SteadyShot feature to reduce the effects of camera shake. If there is no foreground subject that needs to be illuminated by the flash, you may do better by using the Anti Motion Blur, discussed next. Remember that you must pop the flash into the up position before taking a shot if you want the flash to fire.

- **Anti Motion Blur.** Similar to Hand-held Twilight, this mode is also designed for use indoors or in low lighting, but it's more effective at reducing blurring that might be caused by a subject's motion or by a shaky camera. That's because the camera sets an even higher ISO level to be able to use an even faster shutter speed so you should not need to use a tripod. (Of course, in an extremely dark location, the shutter speed may still be a bit long.) Again, it fires a series of six shots and composites them into one with minimal digital noise.

> **TIP**
>
> The camera will never fire flash in certain scene modes where flash would be inappropriate, such as Landscape, Sunset, Night Scene, Sports, etc. Hence, it won't let you use the pop-up flash if you have set such a scene mode. If you had previously popped the flash up while using some other mode, it simply won't fire it when you take a shot, no matter how dark the scene might be.

- **Sweep Panorama.** This special mode lets you "sweep" the camera across a scene that is too wide for a single image. The camera takes multiple pictures while you move it; after taking a series of shots, its processor combines them into a single, wide (or long) panoramic final product.
- **Movie.** Allows shooting movie clips.
- **MR (Memory Recall 1 and 2).** These aren't actually exposure modes, but, instead, let you choose from any of two different groups of settings that you've previously stored in an internal memory storage "slot" numbered 1 and 2. You can use Memory Recall to set up the a6400 for specific types of shooting scenes, and then retrieve those settings from the mode dial. As I'll discuss in Chapter 3, you can actually store four additional groups of settings on your memory card and load them into slot 1 or slot 2 using a pair of Camera Settings I-04 entries.

If you have more photographic experience, you might want to opt for one of the semi-automatic or manual modes, selecting it from the mode dial. These, too, are described in more detail in Chapter 7. These modes, which let you apply more creativity to your camera's settings, are indicated by the letters P, A, S, and M. All overrides are available and flash will always fire if it's in the up position in any of the following:

- **P (Program auto).** This mode allows the a6400 to make the basic exposure settings, but you can still override the camera's settings to fine-tune your image.
- **A (Aperture Priority).** Choose this mode when you want to use a particular lens opening (called an aperture or f/stop), especially to control how much of your image is in focus. The camera will set the appropriate shutter speed after you have set your desired aperture using the control dial that's around the mode dial.

- **S (Shutter Priority).** This mode is useful when you want to use a particular shutter speed to stop action or produce creative blur effects. You dial in your chosen shutter speed with the control dial, and the camera will set the appropriate aperture (f/stop) for you.

- **M (Manual).** Select this mode when you want full control over the shutter speed and the aperture (lens opening), either for creative effects or because you are using a studio flash or another flash unit not compatible with the camera's automatic flash metering. You also need to use this mode if you want to use the Bulb setting for a long exposure, as explained in Chapter 7. You select both the aperture (with the control dial) and the shutter speed (with the control wheel on the camera back). There's more about this mode, and the others, in Chapter 7.

Getting Instant Help

If you want some extra information when choosing a shooting mode, you can activate this additional help by enabling the Mode Dial Guide in the Setup 2 menu. Once the Mode Dial Guide is enabled, the a6400 displays information about each of the modes when a mode is selected with the dial. Henceforth, when you rotate the mode dial to a position, a description of what that shooting mode does appears, as you can see at left in Figure 1.11. You then have these options:

- **Program, Aperture Priority, Shutter Priority, Manual.** After reviewing the descriptive information, press the center button to remove the help from the display.

- **SCN.** Press the center button, and a description of the scene mode appears, as you can see at right in Figure 1.11. You can then press the up/down buttons or rotate the control dial to scroll through the available scene modes. Press the center button again to confirm your scene mode.

- **Auto.** Press the center button, and use the up/down buttons to toggle between Intelligent Auto and Superior Auto. Or just press the center button a second time to confirm the current setting.

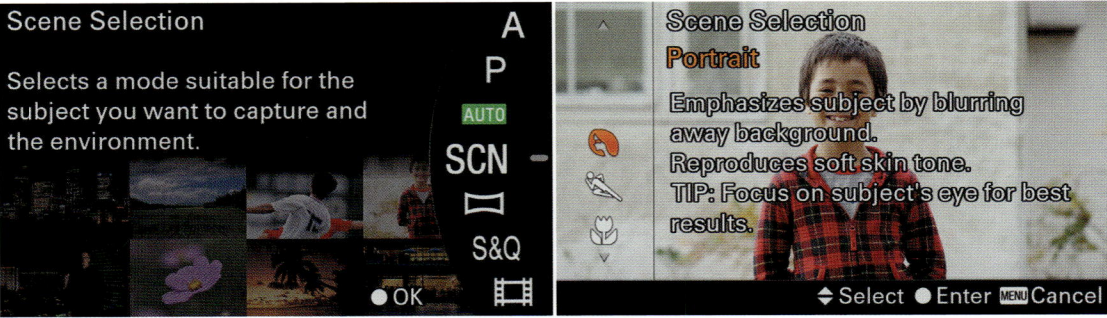

Figure 1.11 A help screen appears detailing functions of the selected shooting mode (left); scene modes can be chosen when the mode dial is in the SCN position.

- **Movie.** Press the center button, and you can select the movie version of the P, A, S, and M exposure modes described earlier. You can have a different exposure mode selected for movies and stills.

- **Sweep Panorama.** Press the center button and the panorama screen appears. You can rotate the control dial to choose the direction of panning, as described in Chapter 3.

- **MR.** In the Memory Recall position, when you press the center button, you can view the current memory settings and/or switch to a different saved memory register, as I'll describe in Chapter 3.

Choosing a Metering Mode

You might want to select a particular exposure metering mode for your first shots, although the default high-tech Multi (short for multi-zone or multi-segment) metering is probably the best choice while getting to know your camera. When using scene modes, Superior Auto, or Intelligent Auto, the camera uses Multi metering and that cannot be changed. In other modes, to change the metering mode, press the MENU button and navigate to the Camera Settings menu (upper-left corner in Figure 1.9, if the Tile Menu is active), and thence to the Camera Settings I-08 menu to the Metering Mode entry. Press the center button, then scroll up/down with the directional buttons to reach Multi, Center (for center weighted), Spot, Entire Screen Averaging, or Highlight selections. Press the center button to confirm your choice and return the camera to shooting mode. The metering options are as follows:

- **Multi metering.** In this standard metering mode, the camera attempts to intelligently classify your image and choose the best exposure based on readings from 1,200 different zones or segments of the scene. You can read about this so-called "evaluative" metering concept, as well as the other options, in Chapter 7.

- **Center metering.** The camera meters the entire scene, but gives the most emphasis (or weighting) to the central area of the frame.

- **Spot metering.** The camera considers only the brightness in a very small central spot so the exposure is calculated only based on that area. When this choice is highlighted, you can press the left/right buttons to switch from Standard size spot to Large, and back again.

- **Entire Screen Averaging.** The camera gives equal weight to all areas of the frame, averaging them together to produce the exposure.

- **Highlight.** This setting tries to maintain detail in highlights, possibly underexposing some of the shadow detail. It's especially useful when shadow detail isn't as important.

OPTION OPTIONS

You'll soon find that your a6400 gives you multiple ways to select options. In this Quick Start chapter, I'll show you just one of them. For example, you can select a metering mode using the Camera Settings I-08 menu, as described, or you can press the Fn button and specify the metering method from the 12-item Function menu that pops up. Alternatively, when the "Quick Navi" screen is shown on the LCD monitor, you can press the Fn button to change the metering mode as well as most of the other shooting settings. I'll show you how to use the other selection options in Chapter 2.

Choosing a Focus Mode

The Camera Settings I menu also has entries to allow you to choose Focus Mode and Focus Area (both in Camera Settings I-05), and are accessed using the same navigation steps described earlier. Focus Mode is the easiest to understand; it determines *when* focus is established.

If you're using a scene mode or one of the two Auto modes, you do not get any options under Autofocus Mode; in fact, it is grayed out since it's not available in these modes. The choices that are available when using P, A, S, or M mode are as follows:

- **Single-shot AF (AF-S).** This mode, sometimes called *single autofocus*, sets focus after you touch the shutter release button and the camera beeps to confirm focus (unless you've turned the beeps off). The active focus point(s) are shown in green on the screen and a green dot appears in the bottom-left corner of the display. The focus will remain locked as long as you maintain contact with the shutter release button, or until you take the picture. If the autofocus system is unable to achieve sharp focus (because the subject is too close to the camera, for example), the focus confirmation circle will blink. This mode is best when your subject is relatively motionless as when you're taking a portrait or landscape photo.

- **Continuous AF (AF-C).** This mode, sometimes called *continuous servo* or *continuous tracking focus* by photographers, sets focus when you partially depress the shutter button, but continues to monitor the frame and refocuses if the distance between the camera and the subject changes. (This allows it to continuously focus on a person walking toward you, for example.) No beep sound is provided. Instead of the green focus confirmation dot, a green dot surrounded by two brackets (curved lines) appears to indicate that the camera is not having a problem achieving and maintaining focus. If the camera should fail to acquire focus, the green dot and the brackets will blink. Continuous AF is a useful mode for photographing moving subjects.

- **Automatic AF (AF-A).** Starts autofocus using AF-S, but switches to AF-C if your subject is moving.

- **DMF (Direct Manual Focus).** Allows you to manually adjust focus after autofocus has been confirmed, using the focus ring on the lens.

- **Manual Focus.** Focus by rotating the focus ring on the lens. The a6400 offers magnification and Focus Peaking as aids to manual focus. I'll describe their use in Chapter 3.

Selecting a Focus Area

The Sony a6400 is equipped with a hybrid autofocus system that I'll explain in detail in Chapter 8. In scene modes, the focus area that will set focus is selected automatically by the camera; in other words, the AF system decides which part of the scene will be in sharpest focus. In the semi-automatic P, A, and S mode, and in the manual M mode, you can allow the camera to select the focus point automatically, or you can specify which focus point should be used with the Focus Area feature.

Set the camera to one of the four autofocus modes mentioned above (AF-S, AF-C, AF-A, or DMF), and select Focus Area from the Camera Settings I-05 menu. By default, it will be set to Wide (multi-point autofocus). Scroll up/down until you reach the option you want to use and press the center button to confirm your selection. Here's a brief overview of the options.

- **Wide.** The a6400 automatically chooses the appropriate focus area or areas; often several subjects will be the same distance from the camera as the primary subject. The active AF area or areas are then displayed in green on the LCD or in the viewfinder, depending on which display you're using.

- **Zone.** In this mode, a grid consisting of nine focus areas appears on the LCD while you're shooting. You can move this grid around the frame with the directional buttons, press the center button to lock it in, and the camera will select which of the focus areas to use to focus.

- **Center.** The camera always uses the focus area in the center of the frame, so it will focus on the subject that's closest to the center in your composition.

- **Flexible Spot.** After you select this option from Focus Area, you can use the left/right directional buttons to specify Small, Medium, or Large focus areas. Then, while viewing your subject, you can use the directional controls to move the focus frame (rectangle) around the screen to your desired location. Move the frame so it covers the most important subject in the scene; then press the center button to lock it into place. I'll discuss this topic in more detail in Chapter 8.

- **Expand Flexible Spot.** If the camera is unable to lock in focus using the selected focus point, it will also use the eight adjacent points to try to achieve focus.

- **Tracking.** In this mode, the camera locks focus onto the subject area that is under the selected focus spot when the shutter button is depressed halfway. Then, if the subject moves (or you change the framing in the camera), the camera will continue to refocus *on that subject*. You can select this mode only when the focus mode is set to Continuous AF (AF-C). You can activate it for any of the five focus area options described above. That is, once you've highlighted Tracking on the selection screen, you can then press the left/right directional button and choose Wide, Zone, Center, Flexible Spot, or Expand Flexible Spot.

Other Settings

There are a few other settings you can make if you're feeling ambitious, but don't feel bad if you postpone using these features until you've racked up a little more experience with your Sony a6400. By default, these camera features will be at Auto so the camera will make a suitable setting.

Adjusting White Balance and ISO

If you like, you can custom-tailor your white balance (overall color balance) and the ISO level (sensitivity) as long as you're not using one of the Auto or SCN modes. To start out, it's best to leave the white balance (WB) at Auto, and to set the ISO either to Auto or (if you prefer a fixed ISO value) to ISO 200 for daylight photos or to ISO 400 for pictures on a dark, overcast day or indoors when you'll be shooting with flash. You'll find complete recommendations for both camera features in Chapter 7. You can adjust white balance with the White Balance entry in the Camera Settings I-11 menu; the ISO can be set after pressing the ISO section of the control wheel (the right directional button). After accessing either feature, navigate (scroll) to make the desired setting with the directional buttons or by rotating the control wheel.

Using the Self-Timer

If you want to have time to get into the photo before the tripod-mounted camera takes the actual shot, the self-timer is what you need. You can get to this feature by pressing the drive mode button (the left directional button of the control wheel) and then scrolling up or down. The drive mode can also be selected from the Camera Settings menu, but it's quicker to use the direct access button.

When the Drive Mode screen is visible, scroll up/down through the various options until you reach the Self-timer 10 Sec. option, which will provide a ten-second delay. Press the center button to confirm your choice and a self-timer icon will appear on the live view display. Press the shutter release to lock focus and exposure and to start the timer. The self-timer lamp will blink and the beeper will sound (unless you've silenced it in the menu) until the final two seconds when the lamp remains on and the beeper beeps more rapidly until the picture is taken.

There are a few options you can select to vary the operation of the self-timer. When the self-timer option is first highlighted, press the left/right keys to choose among 10-second, 5-second, and 2-second options. Also, on the Drive Mode screen, just below the self-timer, there is an option labeled C3/C5; scroll to it and you'll see it's called Self-timer (Cont.), and you can select 2-, 5-, or 10-second intervals, with 3 or 5 Img (image) options after each delay time. That means the camera will take three or five images after the self-timer's 2-, 5-, or 10-second delay has run out. The multiple image option is handy if you are taking family group pictures with a few known inveterate blinkers to be pictured. Note that the self-timer setting is "sticky" and will still be in effect for multiple shots, even if you turn the camera off and power up again. When you're done using the self-timer, reset the camera to one of the other Drive Mode options.

In addition to the Self-timer, Continuous shooting, and Single-shot choices in the Drive menu, there also are exposure/white balance/dynamic range optimization bracketing options, discussed in Chapter 3.

Using the a6400's Flash

Working with the built-in flash unit (see Figure 1.12) deserves a chapter of its own, and I'm providing one in Chapter 12. In basic operation, the a6400's flash is easy enough to work with that you can begin using it right away, either to provide the main lighting for a scene or as supplementary illumination to fill in (brighten) the shadows. The a6400 will automatically balance the amount of light emitted from the flash so that it illuminates the shadows nicely, without overwhelming the highlights and producing a glaring "flash" look. (Think *Baywatch* when they're using too many reflectors on the lifeguards!)

Now, as you may have noticed, in producing its mirrorless cameras, Sony has marched to the beat of a different drummer. This camera is quite different from non-mirrorless models, in its construction, appearance, extensive use of menus, and the like. When designing the built-in flash unit, Sony has continued its trend toward the unconventional with a complex design for the mechanism. In many cases, you won't need it, because the camera is equipped with strong tools for shooting in low light, including ISO settings that go all the way up to 32000 (and "boostable" to the equivalent of ISO 102400) and the Anti Motion Blur and Hand-held Twilight modes. In both of those modes, the camera takes six shots in rapid succession to enhance its ability to capture images in low light that are not ruined by excessive visual noise (graininess or mottled color specks). However, there always will be occasions when flash is at least worthy of consideration as an option (as I'll explain in Chapter 12).

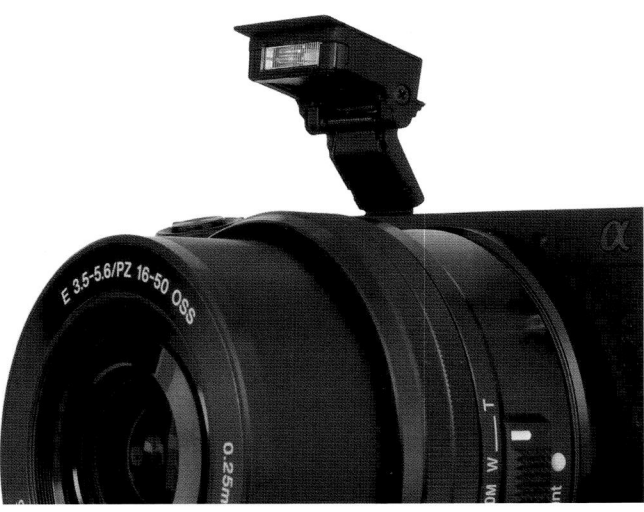

Figure 1.12
The Sony a6400
includes a small
built-in flash unit.

To elevate the flash, press the flash pop-up button located on the back of the camera, just to the left of the MENU button. You may need to press it for a second or more. If it still won't elevate, allow the camera to focus first and beep in confirmation; afterward, press the button for up to a full second, and the mechanism should respond. Sometimes you'll need to keep it depressed for longer or press it several times if it balks. The flash will refuse to pop up when the camera is set for Sports Action scene mode because flash will never fire in this mode. Surprisingly, it will pop up when you're in other scene modes where flash will not actually fire, such as Anti Motion Blur and Hand-held Twilight mode, if you are persistent in pressing the button.

Once raised, the flash will automatically charge itself using the camera's internal battery. The Flash Mode item in the Camera Settings I-10 menu provides options for using the flash, but these differ depending on the mode the camera is set to. For example, in Intelligent Auto or Superior Auto mode, you can choose to have the flash Off, or set to Auto flash, so the camera decides when to fire it, or to Fill-flash so flash will fire for every shot even on a sunny day. The same options are available in two of the scene modes: Portrait and Macro. In the other scene modes, you have only one or two flash options.

In the less automatic P, A, S, and M modes, you also get the Fill-flash option and two others: Slow Sync and Rear Sync, to be discussed in Chapter 12. In those shooting modes, you don't get the Off option or the Auto flash option. That's not a problem. If you don't want flash to fire, simply push it down into its storage position; when you want it to fire, pop it up and it will provide a burst of extra light for every photo.

An Introduction to Movie Making

I'm going to talk in more detail about your movie-making options with the a6400 camera in Chapter 10. For now, though, I'll give you enough information to get started, in case a cinematic subject wanders into your field of view before you get to that chapter. The overrides you have set for certain aspects while shooting still photos will apply to the video clip that you'll record; these include exposure compensation, white balance, any Picture Effect, and even the aperture if the camera is in A mode or the shutter speed if it's in S mode. You also get access to the settings for the movie file formats (XAVC S HD, XAVC S 4K, and AVCHD) and the resolution in the Record Setting item of the Camera Settings II section of the menu.

After you start recording you can change the aperture or the shutter speed; either step will make your movie brighter or darker as you'll notice while making the change. However, you can also set plus or minus exposure compensation for that purpose while filming. The a6400 provides an effective Continuous Autofocus in Movie mode and sound is recorded in stereo with the built-in mics located on the front of the camera above the lens.

Let's save the discussion of those aspects for Chapter 10. For the moment, let's just make a basic movie. With the camera turned on, aim at your subject and locate the red Movie record button in the upper-right corner of the body. (You don't have to switch to Movie mode using the mode dial; Movie mode simply gives you access to more movie-shooting controls.)

Compose as you wish and press that button once to start the recording, and again to stop it; don't hold the button down. You can record for up to about 29 minutes consecutively if you have sufficient storage space on your memory card and charge in your battery. The camera will adjust the focus and exposure automatically, and you can zoom while recording, if you have a zoom lens attached to the camera.

After you finish recording a video clip, you can view it by pressing the Playback button located below the control wheel. While a movie is being played back, you can press the bottom directional button to pop up a list of a DVR-style operation panel at the bottom of the screen, allowing pausing, fast forward, reverse, frame display, sound volume adjustment, and so forth.

Reviewing the Images You've Taken

The Sony a6400 has a broad range of playback and image review options. I'll cover them in more detail in Chapter 2. Initially, you'll want to learn just the basics for viewing still photos, so I'll assume you have taken only such images. After shooting some JPEG and/or RAW photos, here's how to view them, using controls shown in Figure 1.13:

- Press the Playback button to display the most recently taken image on the LCD. (It's the small button with a right-pointing triangle symbol below the control wheel.)
- Press the left directional button, or scroll the control dial to the left, to view a previous image.

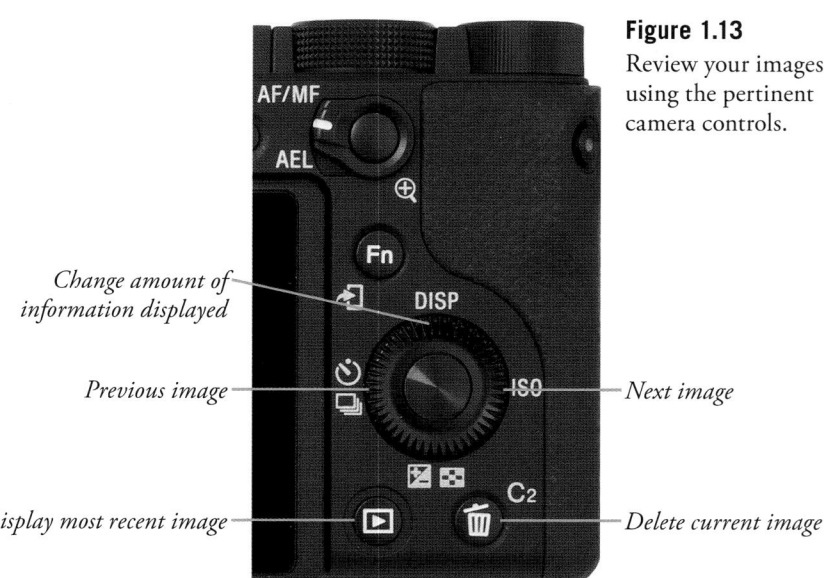

Figure 1.13
Review your images using the pertinent camera controls.

Change amount of information displayed

Previous image

Next image

Display most recent image

Delete current image

- Press the right directional button, or scroll the control dial to the right, to view the next image.

- While viewing a photo, press the DISP button (top directional button) repeatedly to cycle among the available displays: views that have no recording data, full recording data (f/stop, shutter speed, image quality/size, etc.), and a thumbnail image with histogram display. (I'll explain all these in Chapter 2.)

- Press the lower right button, marked with a C2 (Custom 2) label and trash can icon, and follow the prompt to delete the currently displayed image.

- While the image is displayed, press the MENU button and from the Playback 1 menu, select Rotate (at the bottom of the screen), followed by pressing the center button, to rotate the image on the screen 90 degrees. Successive presses of the center button rotate the image 90 degrees each time. (You won't likely need this feature unless you have disabled automatic rotation, which causes the camera to display your vertically oriented pictures already rotated. I'll explain how to activate/deactivate automatic rotation in Chapter 6.)

- Press the Zoom/AEL button located to the right of the MENU button to zoom into the image. Rotating the control wheel on the back of the camera allows you to zoom in and out. You can also scroll around inside the image using the directional buttons. To exit this screen and return to normal view, press the MENU button.

- While in Playback mode using Folder view mode (described in Chapter 6), press the down button to display an index screen showing 12 or 30 thumbnail images (select the number using the Image Index option in the Playback 3 menu). Keep scrolling downward to view the thumbnails of the next images (assuming you have shot lots of photos). Scroll to the thumbnail of the photo you want to view and press the center button; the photo will then fill the screen. The a6400 can arrange index images by Date View, Folder View (Still), AVCHD View, XAVC S HD View, and XAVC S 4K View, so you can view only certain types of images/videos, or those taken on a specific date. I'll explain those options in more detail in Chapter 6.

Transferring Files to Your Computer

The final step in your picture-taking session will be to transfer the photos and/or movies you've taken to your computer for printing, further review, or editing. (You can also take your memory card to a retailer for printing if you don't want to go the do-it-yourself route.) Your a6400 allows you to specify images to print, and to create print orders right in the camera. It also offers an option for selecting which images to transfer to your computer.

For now, you'll probably want to transfer your images by either using the USB cable from the camera to the computer or by removing the memory card from the a6400 and transferring the images with a card reader. The latter option is ordinarily the best, because it's usually much faster and doesn't deplete the camera's battery. However, you might need to use a cable transfer when you have the cable and a computer but no card reader. (You might be using the computer at a friend's home or the one at an Internet café, for example.)

Here's how to transfer images from a memory card to the computer using a card reader:

1. Turn off the camera.

2. Slide open the battery compartment door, and press on the card, which causes it to pop up so it can be removed from the slot.

3. Insert the memory card into a memory card reader accessory that is plugged into your computer. Your installed software detects the files on the card and offers to transfer them. The card can also appear as a mass storage device on your desktop; in that case, you can open that and then drag and drop the files to your computer.

To transfer images from the camera to a computer using the USB cable:

1. Turn off the camera.

2. Open the terminal door on the left side of the camera (the upper door, marked with the candelabra-like USB symbol) and plug the USB cable furnished with the camera into the USB terminal inside that door. (See Figure 1.14.)

3. Connect the other end of the USB cable to a USB terminal on your computer.

4. Turn on the camera. From this point on, the method is the same as the card reader instructions above.

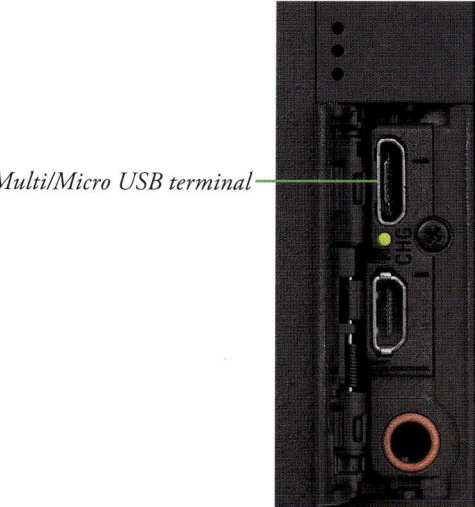

Multi/Micro USB terminal

Figure 1.14
Images can be transferred to your computer using a USB cable plugged into the USB terminal.

Wireless File Transfer

Your a6400 is also equipped with built-in Wi-Fi, which provides many options, including a method for wireless transfer of image files to a Mac or Windows computer when connected to a wireless network. This is a multi-faceted topic, so I won't begin to discuss it here; instead, you'll find full coverage in Chapter 5.

2

Sony a6400 Roadmap

The tiny black-and-white drawings in the official Sony manuals—impaled with dozens of call-outs—can be confusing. At times, looking for information about a specific feature seems a lot like being presented with a world globe when what you really want is to find the capital of Brazil!

In this book, rather than bewilder you with a satellite view, I'm going to give you a street-level map that includes close-up, full-color photos of your a6400 from several angles, with labels clearly pointing to each individual component, accompanied by a description of exactly what it does. And, I don't force you to flip back and forth among dozens of pages to get a basic overview of what a particular button or dial does. Each photo is accompanied by a brief description that summarizes the control, so you can begin using it right away. Only when a particular feature deserves a lengthy explanation do I direct you to a more detailed write-up later in the book.

So, if you're wondering what the left directional button on the control wheel does, I'll tell you up front, rather than have you flip to several pages. This book is not a scavenger hunt. But after I explain how to use the drive mode button to select continuous shooting, I *will* provide a cross-reference to a longer explanation later in the book that clarifies the use of the various drive modes, the self-timer, and the several varieties of bracketing. Some readers write and complain about even my minimized cross-reference approach; they'd like to open the book to one page and read *everything* there is to know about bracketing, for example. Unfortunately, it's impossible to understand some features without having a background in what related features do. So, my strategy is to provide you with these introductions in the earlier chapters, covering simple features completely, and relegating some of the really in-depth explanations to later chapters. I think this kind of organization works best for a camera as sophisticated as the Sony a6400.

By the time you finish this chapter, you'll have a good understanding of every control and of the various roles it can take on. I'll provide a lot more information about items in the menus and sub-menus in Chapters 3, 4, 5, and 6, but the following descriptions should certainly satisfy the button pusher and dial twirler in you.

Front View

When thinking about any given camera, we always imagine the front view. That's the view that your subjects see as you snap away, and the aspect that's shown in product publicity and on the box. The frontal angle is, essentially, the "face" of a camera like the Sony a6400. But, not surprisingly, most of the "business" of operating the camera happens *behind* it, where the photographer resides. The front of the a6400 actually has very few controls and features to worry about. These few controls are most obvious in Figure 2.1:

- **Power switch.** Turn the camera on by rotating this switch to the On position.

- **Shutter release button.** Angled on top of the hand grip is the shutter release button. Touch it gently to activate the camera's circuits and, after composing a photo, maintain slight pressure on it to lock exposure and focus. (Focus lock is available in Single-shot autofocus mode—the one you would use for a subject that's not moving.) The a6400 assumes that when you tap or depress the shutter release, you are ready to take a picture, so the release can be tapped to activate the exposure meter or to exit from most menus.

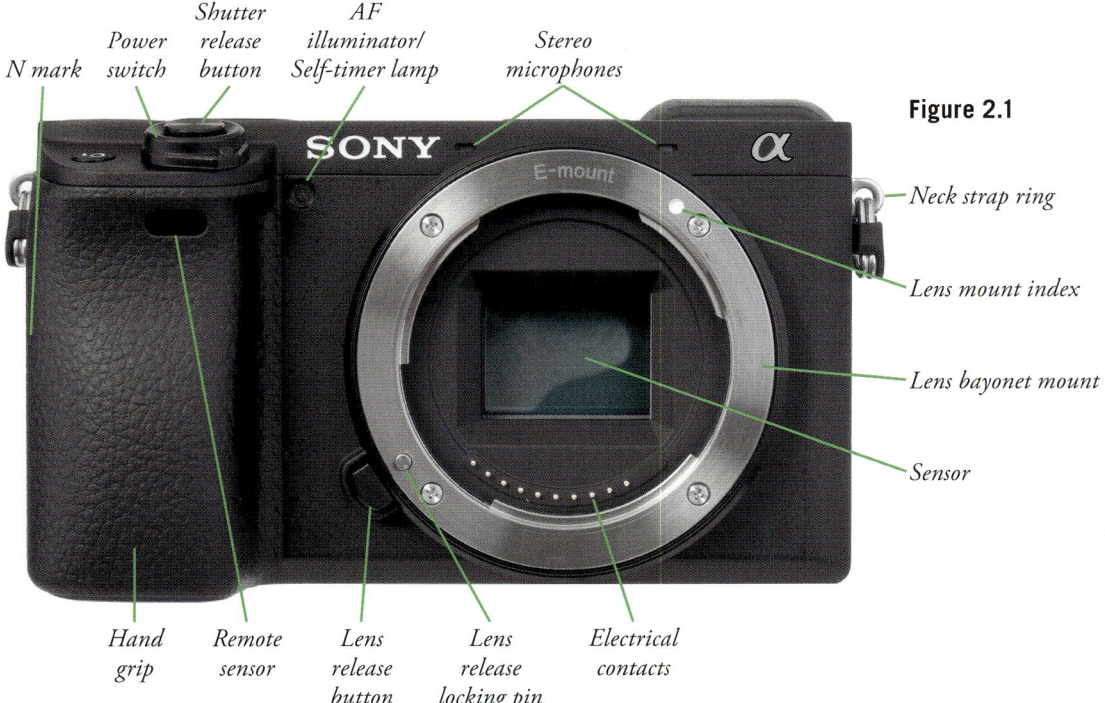

Figure 2.1

- **AF illuminator/Self-timer lamp.** This bright LED flashes while your camera counts down the 2-second, 5-second, or 10-second self-timer. In 5- and 10-second modes, the lamp blinks at a measured pace, off and on at first, then switches to a constant glow in the final moments of the countdown. When the self-timer is set to 2 seconds, the lamp stays lit throughout the countdown. It also serves as the AF (autofocus) illuminator, emitting its red-orange glow in dark conditions to help the camera's autofocus system achieve sharp focus.

- **Remote sensor.** Detects infrared signals from the RMT-DSLR1 or RMT-DSLR2 Wireless Remote Commanders to take still pictures and (with the RMT-DSLR2 model only) to start/stop movie recording. I'll show you how to adjust the various remote control options in Chapter 6.

  Note that this sensor is not needed when using the Sony RMT-P1BT Wireless Remote Commander, which operates by Bluetooth radio signals rather than infrared. You must have the Version 2.0 firmware upgrade released in June 2019 to use that device.

- **Stereo microphones.** These microphones capture sound during movie shooting, including any noise emanating from their immediate surroundings, such as your lens's autofocus motor. To avoid that, you can connect an external microphone using the multi interface connector on top of the camera or the microphone jack on the side (both discussed later).

- **Hand grip.** This provides a comfortable hand-hold, and also contains the a6400's battery and memory card compartments.

- **Lens release button.** Press and hold this button to unlock the lens so you can rotate it in order to remove the lens from the camera.

- **Lens release locking pin.** Retracts when the release button is pressed, to allow removing the lens.

- **Lens mount index mark.** Match this recessed, white index button with a similar white indicator on the camera's lens mount to line the two up for attaching the lens to the a6400.

- **Lens bayonet mount.** Grips the matching mount on the rear of the lens to secure the lens to the camera body.

- **Electrical contacts.** These metal contact points match up with a similar set of points on the lens, allowing for communication with the camera about matters such as focus and aperture.

- **Neck strap ring.** Attach the strap that comes with your a6400 to this ring and its counterpart on the other side of the camera, or use a third-party strap of your choice.

- **Sensor.** This fairly ordinary-looking little rectangle is the heart and soul of your digital camera. On the Sony camera, the Exmor sensor is a CMOS (complementary metal-oxide semiconductor) device, 23.5mm × 15.6mm in size. This sensor, with a very respectable resolution of just over 24 megapixels, ensures that you'll get extremely high quality still and video pictures. Sony has upgraded the sensor since the original a6000 model; this one has more efficient copper wiring that allows the sensor to move data into the camera's memory buffer and thence onto your memory card much more quickly.

- **N Mark (on side of camera).** Although you can't see the N Mark in this view, it's emblazoned on the side of the camera, and indicates the touch point for connecting the a6400 with an NFC (Near Field Communication) device, such as an Android smartphone (at present, Apple devices use NFC only for ApplePay). When linked, the two devices can communicate directly using short-range wireless technology, as I'll describe later in the book.

In Figure 2.2 you can see the a6400's built-in pop-up flash and the terminal cover that provides a modicum of protection from dust and moisture for the components inside.

- **Pop-up flash.** Press the button on the back of the camera (shown in Figure 2.3) to release the flash. Note that the flash is hinged, so you can, theoretically, adjust its angle to, say, provide bounce flash. Unless you're bouncing the flash off of a piece of white cardboard or some other nearby surface, the meager output of this unit is unlikely to provide much bounce for your buck. In Chapter 12, I'll show you how to use more powerful flash units that can be plugged into the multi interface shoe (a special type of "hot shoe") on top of the camera.

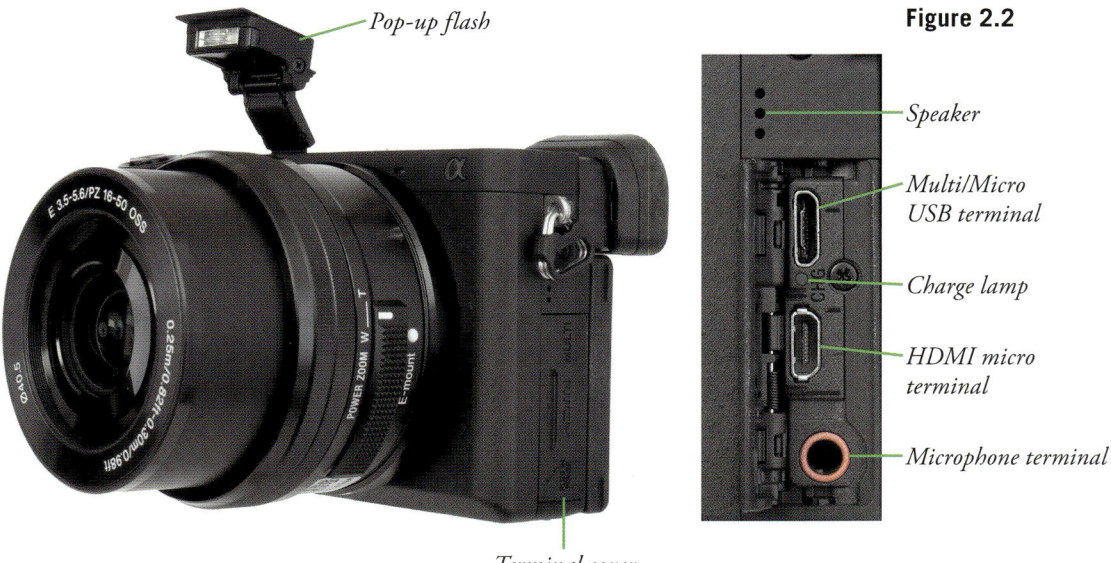

Pop-up flash

Figure 2.2

Speaker

Multi/Micro USB terminal

Charge lamp

HDMI micro terminal

Microphone terminal

Terminal cover

- **Speaker.** Sounds emanating from your a6400 are produced by this speaker.

- **Terminal cover.** Fold back this cover to reveal the three terminals and the charge lamp described next.

- **Multi/Micro USB terminal.** Connect the a6400 to your computer using this terminal, with the USB cable that's supplied with the camera. That connection can be used to upload images to the computer, to charge the battery while it's in the camera, and to upgrade the firmware to the latest version available for the a6400, using a file downloaded from the Sony support website (http://esupport.sony.com/).

  The same terminal serves as a charging port when the USB cable is connected to the included AC adapter, or plugged into a powered USB port. You can use the camera while it is charging, which means constant power can be supplied during long shoots and when recording time lapse images over a matter of hours (or days). As you'll learn in Chapter 5, Sony has added a great Time Lapse capability to the a6400 (replacing a clumsy PlayMemories app offered for earlier models). It allows you to shoot blossoms opening up, the march of the sun across the sky during the day, and other types of scenes.

- **Charge lamp.** This yellow LED flashes while battery charging is underway.

- **HDMI micro terminal.** If you'd like to see the images from your camera on a television screen, you'll need to buy an HDMI cable (not included with the camera) to connect this terminal to an HDTV set or monitor. Be sure to get a Type D cable; it has a male micro-HDMI connector at the camera end and a standard male HDMI Type A connector at the TV end. Once the cable is connected, you can not only view your stored images on the TV in Playback mode, you can also see what the camera sees by viewing your TV screen. So, in effect, you can use your HDTV set as a large monitor to help with composition, focusing, and the like.

  One unfortunate point is that the camera no longer supports video output to an old-style TV's yellow composite video jack. If for some reason it's *really* important to you to connect the camera to one of those inputs, you'll need to find a device that can "downscale" the HDMI signal to composite video. I have done this successfully with a device by Gefen called the HDMI to Composite Scaler, which costs somewhat more than $200 to $300 at newegg.com, svideo.com, and other sites.

  The good news is that if you own a TV that supports Sony's Bravia sync protocol, you can use your Bravia remote control to control image display, mark images for printing, switch to index view, or perform other functions.

- **Microphone terminal.** Allows connecting an external microphone to provide better audio recording than the a6400's own built-in microphones.

The Sony a6400's Business End

The back panel of the Sony is where most of the camera's physical controls reside. There aren't that many of them, but, as I noted earlier, some of them can perform several functions, depending on the context.

Most of the controls on the back panel of the a6400 are clustered on the right side of the body, with several located on the top edge. The key components labeled in Figure 2.3 include:

- **Viewfinder.** Look into this window to activate the eye-level electronic viewfinder (EVF), an internal OLED (organic LED) display with 2,359,296 dots of resolution (a significant upgrade from the 1.4 million dots found in the a6000). It shows 100 percent of the frame at .71X magnification (with a 50mm lens) or 1.07X magnification (with a 35mm lens), making it virtually the equal of the optical viewfinders found in traditional digital SLR cameras. As I'll show you in Chapter 4, you can adjust the viewfinder's "refresh" rate from the default 60/50 fps rate to a smoother 120/100 fps, albeit with a slight loss of resolution, using an entry in the Camera Settings II-06 menu.

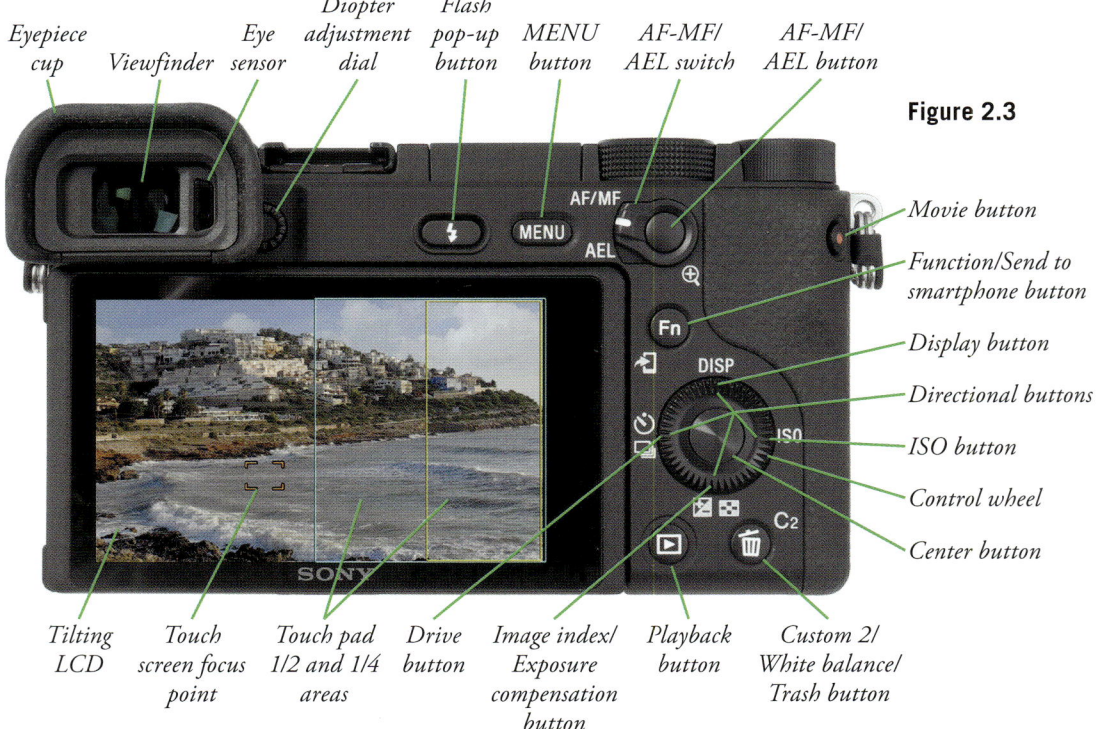

Eyepiece cup   Viewfinder   Eye sensor   Diopter adjustment dial   Flash pop-up button   MENU button   AF-MF/ AEL switch   AF-MF/ AEL button

Figure 2.3

Movie button

Function/Send to smartphone button

Display button

Directional buttons

ISO button

Control wheel

Center button

Tilting LCD   Touch screen focus point   Touch pad 1/2 and 1/4 areas   Drive button   Image index/ Exposure compensation button   Playback button   Custom 2/ White balance/ Trash button

I actually like the a6400's EVF better than an optical viewfinder in some circumstances, such as when shooting in dim light. The view is quite bright, and, as a bonus, the a6400's focus peaking feature (discussed in Chapter 8) makes it easier to achieve sharp focus manually. You can frame your composition and see the information on the electronic viewfinder's display.

While some a6400 owners will use the LCD for framing their photos instead of the electronic viewfinder, the latter offers some benefits. On sunny days, when the LCD display is often obliterated by glare, the EVF is definitely preferable. You might also want to use it for reviewing your images and video clips in Playback mode. Holding the camera pressed up against your face helps provide extra steadiness to reduce camera shake (and image blurring) at slow shutter speeds. (The SteadyShot stabilizer in some lenses is not a panacea and is more effective when the camera is at least somewhat stable.) When taking several pictures in succession, the EVF and camera held at eye-level provide a familiar shooting platform. Most sports photos, for example, are best captured with the camera pressed tightly to your eye.

- **Eye sensor.** This solid-state device detects when you (or anything else, unfortunately) approach the viewfinder; the camera then triggers a switch that turns off the back panel LCD, activates the viewfinder screen, and starts the autofocus system. You can enable or disable both automatic switching and Eye-Start AF, as I will explain in Chapter 4.

- **Eyepiece cup.** This soft rubber frame seals out extraneous light when pressing your eye tightly up to the viewfinder, and it also protects your eyeglass lenses (if worn) from scratching. It easily snaps on or off. I remove mine when I make diopter adjustments (described next).

- **Diopter adjustment dial.** As described in Chapter 1, you can spin this to adjust the built-in diopter correction to suit your vision. Since it's right beside the viewfinder window, it's a bit difficult to change the diopter setting while your eye is at the EVF, but it's worth taking the time to adjust it.

- **Flash pop-up button.** Press this button to elevate the built-in electronic flash unit. You'll find that the flash will sometimes refuse to pop up. In that case, allow the camera to focus first and beep in confirmation; then, press the button for up to a full second, or press it several times, and the flash should elevate. The flash will pop up even when the camera is set to some SCN modes where flash will never fire, such as Anti Motion Blur and Hand-held Twilight mode, if you are persistent in pressing the button. Use caution when the flash is up, and when retiring it back into the camera. It doesn't appear to have the most rugged mechanism I've seen.

- **MENU button.** Press to enter the a6400's menu system. This button also serves to exit many functions, including menu settings and playback zoom. A Menu/Exit label will appear in the viewfinder or LCD in that case.

■ **AF-MF/AEL switch/button.** Rotate this switch to change the function of the button located in the center of the switch. Note that, as I'll explain in Chapter 4, you can redefine the functions of the button (as well as other buttons and controls) using several different entries in the Custom Settings II-08 menu.

- **AF/MF position.** With the switch in this position, pressing and holding the button changes the focus method to the opposite method temporarily. If the camera is set for autofocus, holding the button switches to manual focus; if the camera is set for manual focus, holding the button down switches to autofocus and locks the focus. In Chapter 4, I'll show you how to adjust the behavior of this button so it simply toggles between AF and MF, without the need to hold the button down.

- **AEL position.** Rotating the switch to the AEL position and pressing *and holding* the button locks exposure by default. An asterisk appears in the lower-right corner of the LCD or viewfinder to show you exposure has been locked. If you keep it depressed, you can then recompose and the exposure will not change; it will remain optimized for your primary subject. The Custom Key (Shoot.) entry in the Custom Settings II-08 menu has an AEL Button option that allows you to turn the button into a toggle switch, so you will not need to hold it down to maintain autoexposure lock.

  Since the AEL button is customizable, that menu item also allows you to change its purpose entirely, so it activates shooting tips or one of many other camera functions instead of providing autoexposure lock. If you use a certain function very often, you might want to program the AEL button to activate the screen to set the desired option of that camera feature: Auto Portrait Framing, Soft Skin Effect, or DRO (Dynamic Range Optimizer) and Auto HDR (High Dynamic Range), for example. (I won't list all of the options of the menu item here, but will do so in Chapter 4.) Of course, you will need to remember the purpose you have assigned to the AEL button, but that won't be difficult unless you change its behavior often in the menu.

- **In Playback mode (zoom).** When you're reviewing images, the position of the switch doesn't matter; when you press the AF-MF/AEL button, the camera will always activate the zoom feature of the image display. While reviewing pictures, pressing the Playback button activates the zoom in feature. You can press the button multiple times to progressively zoom in on your image, or rotate the control wheel (on the back of the camera) clockwise to zoom in. Zoom out by rotating the control wheel counterclockwise. To exit zooming, press the MENU button.

Tip

Many buttons on the a6400 can be redefined to some other action, allowing you to tailor the camera's operation so it best suits your needs, as I'll describe in Chapter 4. However, keep in mind that customizing your camera's behavior can be confusing—both for you and for others you may allow to use the camera.

■ **Function/Send to Smartphone button.** In Shooting mode, press the Fn button to produce a screen with shooting setting options, as seen in Figure 2.4. By default, the 12 functions shown are displayed. However, as I'll describe in Chapter 4, you can choose exactly which functions you'd like to display, and you aren't locked into 12. If you prefer, you can define a single row of six favorite functions, or include some other number/combination of choices. To adjust any of the functions, just follow these steps:

1. **Access Fn menu.** Press the Fn button and use the directional keys to highlight one of the options.

2. **Make adjustment.** When your setting is highlighted, you can rotate the control wheel *or* the control dial to cycle through the available choices, which will appear one by one as you spin. Optionally, when the function is highlighted, you can press the center button to produce an adjustment screen with all the choices shown. Use the directional buttons to select the one you want. Note that with either method, some choices are accompanied by a right-pointing arrow that indicates there are additional sub-options (such as Level 1, 2, or 3 with the Dynamic Range Optimizer). Press the right button to access these extra options.

3. **Confirm.** Press the center button to confirm your choice and return to the Function menu.

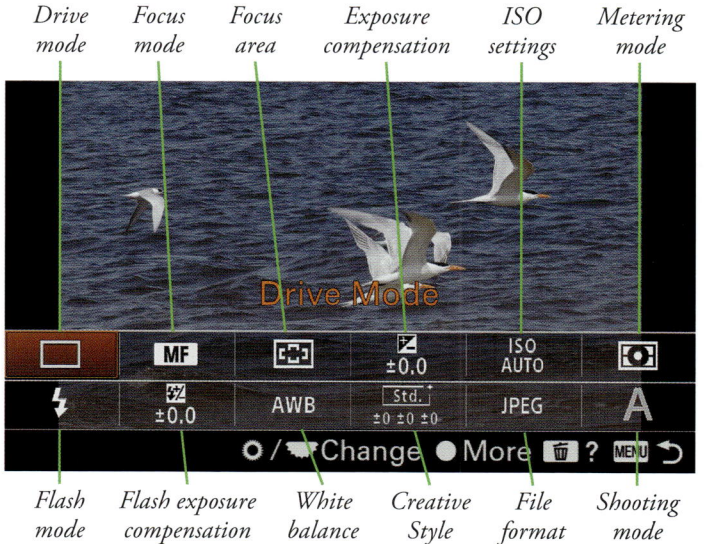

Figure 2.4

Up to 12 user-selectable choices are available in the Function menu. This is the default layout.

Drive mode   Focus mode   Focus area   Exposure compensation   ISO settings   Metering mode

Flash mode   Flash exposure compensation   White balance   Creative Style   File format   Shooting mode

- **Movie button.** Another handy feature, this button with a central red dot is located on the right rear corner of the body. The recessed design was intended to minimize the risk of inadvertently recording a video clip. When you want to make a movie, there is no need to change the Shooting mode, or to fiddle with menu systems, as with some other cameras. Simply press the record button; when you're finished, press it again to stop recording. Movie making can be initiated from any Shooting mode; however, if you rotate the mode dial to the Movie position, you get access to additional options, which I'll discuss in Chapter 10.

- **Playback button.** Displays the last picture taken. Thereafter, you can move back and forth among the available images by pressing the left/right directional buttons or spinning the control wheel (on the back of the camera) or control dial (on top of the camera) to advance or reverse one image at a time. To quit playback, press this button again. The a6400 also exits Playback mode automatically when you press the shutter release button halfway (so you'll never be prevented from taking a picture on the spur of the moment because you happened to be viewing an image).

- **Center button.** The center button functions as the selection button; press it to select or confirm a choice from a menu screen.

- **Custom 2/White Balance/Trash button.** This button has different functions, depending on mode and how you may have redefined it.

  - **Shooting mode.** This button produces the White Balance settings screen.

  - **Playback mode.** In Playback mode, the button serves as a delete key to trash the current image.

- **Control wheel.** This ridged dial, which surrounds the large center button, also has multiple functions, depending on the camera's mode. In both Shooting and Playback modes it can be useful for navigating menu screens to get to the item or option you want to use.

  The control wheel performs several important functions and is the only control on the camera that can be activated in two different ways: you can turn the ridged part of the wheel to perform certain actions (such as navigation or setting exposure controls), and you can press in on the various edges at top, bottom, left, and right. In that mode the edges serve as directional buttons that are incorporated into the north, east, south, and west positions of the wheel while navigating through menu screens, for example.

  - **Playback mode.** When an image is magnified in Playback mode, all four buttons can be used to move the viewing area around within a magnified image and within index screens during playback. When the image is not magnified, the left/right buttons move to the previous/next image on your memory card in Playback mode.

- **Shooting mode.** When the camera is in Shooting mode, rotating the control wheel changes shutter speed in Manual and Shutter Priority modes, and changes the aperture in Aperture Priority mode. If you're using Program mode, the control wheel produces different combinations of shutter speed and aperture that produce the same exposure (*program shift*). The four directional buttons are used to make adjustments. For example, when the Autofocus Area is set to Flexible Spot, you can use all four of the directional buttons to move the focus bracket to any of its available positions on the screen.

■ **Tilting LCD/Touch screen.** This screen can be used to preview images, view them afterward, and to display/navigate menus. The LCD monitor has 16:9 proportions, which is perfect for previewing/shooting/reviewing movie clips. When you're shooting still photos using the default 3:2 aspect ratio, black bars appear at the left and right of the screen.

You can set the LCD monitor brightness with an item in the Setup menu, to be discussed in Chapter 6; there's a special feature that provides a super-bright display, useful on bright days when the screen would otherwise be difficult to view. The monitor swivels upward to provide a waist-level view (see Figure 2.5, left) up to a full 180 degrees so that it faces in the same direction as the lens making it ideal for vloggers, taking selfies, or for giving your subject a preview of the photo you'll be taking. In that position, the eyepiece cup protrudes on the screen area, but if you find that distracting, you can remove it, as I did for Figure 2.5, right. The camera helpfully inverts the image so it is presented right-side up when the screen is tilted forward. With the LCD tilted downward, you can hold the a6400 overhead for a "periscope view."

I'll explain how to use the touch screen in the next section.

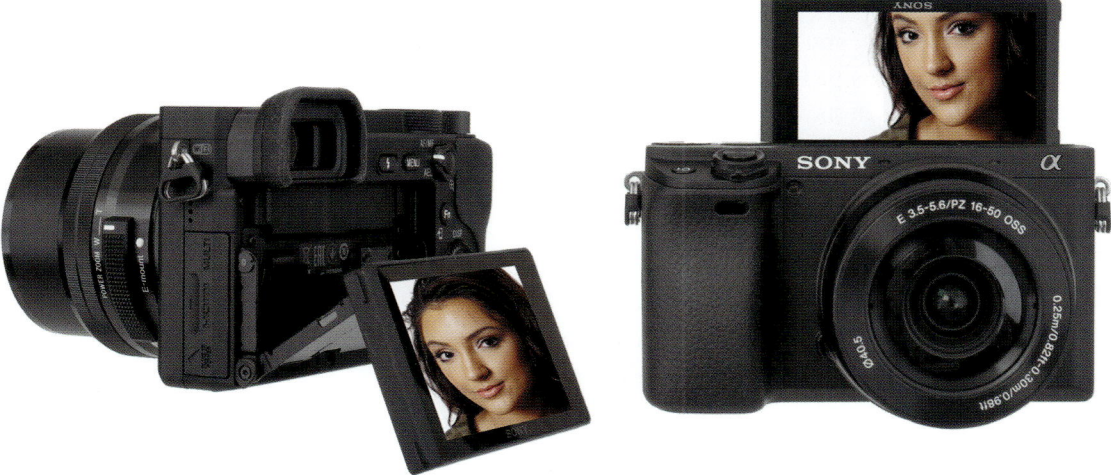

Figure 2.5 Tilting LCD.

Using the Touch Screen/Pad

Compact cameras like the a6400 are generally unencumbered by the large buttons and dials found on bulkier digital SLRs. Small size and light weight are one of the key attractions of digital cameras, after all. Fortunately, even though your camera's controls are squeezed into a smaller space, Sony has added valuable tools—including the a6400's touch screen/touch pad—to streamline many of the most frequent operations. The dual *screen/pad* nomenclature is applied to the LCD monitor because the touch features of this camera can be used in three different ways. Only one can be active at one time, and can be specified using the Function of Touch Operation entry in the Camera Settings II-09 menu, as described in Chapter 4.

> **TIP**
>
> In this chapter, I'm going to show you how to *use* each of the three functions; descriptions for the settings for these and other options for the a6400's menu entries are collected in the three menu reference chapters, Chapters 4, 5, and 6, rather than scattered throughout the book.

Your first step is to enable Touch Operations. Visit the Setup 3 menu, select Touch Operation, and choose On. Then, access the Camera Settings II-09 menu, navigate to the Function of Touch Operation entry, and select one of these three functions: (If you need help navigating the a6400's menu system, you'll find directions at the beginning of Chapter 4.)

- **Touch shutter.** If you select Touch Shutter in the Function of Touch Operation entry of the Camera Settings II-09 menu, when you compose your images using the LCD monitor to compose your photos, you can tap the screen to specify the focus point. The camera will then immediately take a picture. While Touch Shutter is enabled, you can activate it or deactivate it by tapping the icon shown at upper right in Figure 2.6. When the feature is activated, an orange bar appears to the left of the icon.

  The Touch Shutter feature is useful for capturing bursts of images when Drive Mode is set to Continuous Shooting, and for bracketing when Continuous Bracketing is enabled. Just keep touching the screen during the burst, and remove your finger to stop capture. Touch Shutter is unavailable when using the viewfinder, or Movie, S&Q Motion, Sweep Panorama, Smile Shutter, or Manual Focus modes; when using Digital or Clear Image Zoom; and when Focus Area is set to Digital or Clear Image Zoom.

Figure 2.6
Tap or slide your finger across the screen to focus; tap the cancel icon (at upper right) to turn off Touch Focus.

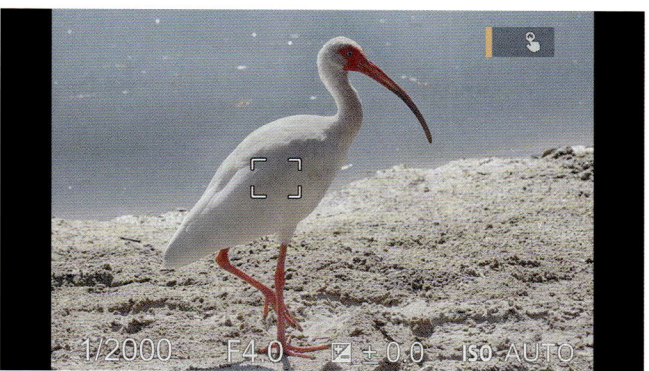

■ **Touch Focus.** When you select Touch Focus in the Function of the Touch Operation entry, you can tap the LCD screen to select a focus point or zone anywhere that the a6400 is able to achieve autofocus (that is, most of the frame other than the edges).

• **If using the LCD monitor to compose:** Tap the screen or hold down your finger and slide the focus area around within the frame. The camera will focus at that point.

• **If using the viewfinder to compose:** Touch the LCD screen and move the focus point around while looking through the viewfinder. The a6400 will focus on the point you select.

• **When using manual focus:** Double-tap the LCD to activate the focus magnifier.

In any case, the focus area will remain at that position, and the a6400 will focus when you press the shutter release down halfway. You can deactivate touch focus by pressing the Center button (described in the next section), or by tapping the "cancel focus" icon (a pointing finger with an X next to it) that appears at upper right on the screen. A quick tap may not register; this function requires a firm press. I'll explain the various AF-area modes in Chapter 8.

Note: Touch Focus is not available when Focus Area is set to Flexible Spot or Expand Flexible Spot. However, you can still move the focus frame around. In Movie mode, Spot Focus can be used, but only when working with the LCD. Touch Focus is not available when using Sweep Panorama, Digital Zoom, or with A-mount lenses when using the LA-EA2 or LA-EA4 adapters.

■ **Touch Tracking.** With the Function of Touch Operation set to Touch Tracking, you can specify a subject that will be tracked by tapping the LCD monitor. Tracking will start and continue until you press the Center button or tap the Cancel Tracking icon in the upper-right corner of the LCD monitor. The camera will focus on the tracked subject when you press the shutter release down halfway. Note that this feature is not available with Hand-held Twilight and Anti-Motion Blur Scene modes (which each capture multiple images and combine them); when using Sweep Panorama or Manual Focus modes; with Smart, Clear Image, or Digital zoom features; and when using the LA-EA2 or LA-EA4 lens adapters. It is also disabled in Movie mode when Record Setting is set to 120p/100p.

Touch Panel or Touch Pad?

The LCD monitor can function in one of two modes—or you can activate both modes at the same time. The options are available from the Touch Panel/Pad entry of the Setup 3 menu.

- **Touch Panel+Pad.** When you select this option, the a6400 switches between the two modes described next; when you are composing your image on the LCD monitor, the screen functions as a Touch Panel. If you bring the camera up to your eye, the screen switches to Touch Pad mode. This gives you the flexibility of using either mode if you decide both might be useful in a given shooting session. The descriptions of the panel and pad modes that follow will help you choose.

- **Touch Panel Only.** When touch panel mode is active and you're using the LCD monitor to compose, you can touch the LCD monitor screen to specify the focus area (similarly to Touch Focus, described earlier).

- **Touch Pad Only.** When touch pad mode is active and you're using the electronic viewfinder to compose, you can touch the LCD monitor screen to specify the focus area. You don't have to tap the exact area (actually, that's impossible, because you're not actually looking at the LCD) if you use Relative Positioning, described in the next section. Instead, when you touch the pad, a focus point appears in the viewfinder *relative to the location on the LCD.* As I'll explain shortly, that mode is useful because you can change the size of the sensitive area of the LCD screen. Once the focus area is specified (shown as cyan and yellow brackets in Figure 2.3, earlier), keep your finger on the screen and slide it around to the position you want, using your view through the EVF as your reference.

Before you wax ecstatic about these touch features, you'll want to know that they are limited to the ability to specify a focus point when shooting stills and videos. You can't select menu entries, type in text, scroll through playback views, or pinch/expand with your fingertips to zoom in and out during image review. However, the focusing features are quite useful, especially when shooting movies, as they allow selecting a focus area with a gentle tap. You have additional options for the touch pad, discussed next.

Touch Pad Options

Three touch pad options are available from the Setup 3 menu. Here, is an overview of the adjustments you can make, and why you might want them.

- **Operation in Vertical Orientation.** Here you can specify whether touch controls are available when the camera is oriented in the vertical position (On), or only when the camera is held in horizontal orientation (Off). The touch feature can be a little awkward to use when rotated vertically, so some prefer to disable touch control for that mode.

■ **Touch Position Mode.** Choose Absolute Position, to allow you to quickly move the focusing frame to a distant position on the LCD. This setting automatically changes the Operation Area (described next) to encompass the full screen. Use Relative Position to move the focus point relative to the location on the LCD. That is, if you tap the center of the sensitive area, the focus point appears in the center; tap to the right or left, and the focus area appears to the right or left side.

■ **Operation Area.** By default, the entire touch pad is sensitive when using the EVF, and that works well for most people. However, if your left eye is dominant (i.e., you're "left-eyed"), your nose will touch the screen, and the a6400 registers that as a finger press. You can select Whole Screen if you want to make the entire LCD sensitive to touch pad operations.

To *limit* the sensitive area, you can choose the right or left 1/2 or 1/4 of the screen, or upper/lower right or left corners. The "relative" orientation remains the same, but it is limited to that reduced area. As noted, if you selected Absolute Position above, the entire screen is used, regardless of your setting here.

Directional Button Functions

Each directional button also has a default specific purpose that activates when pressed, and that function is labeled on the area outside the wheel itself. You can also redefine any of these keys using the Custom Keys entry in the Custom Settings II-08 menu, as described in Chapter 4.

■ **Directional Buttons.** The Up, Down, Left, and Right buttons have default definitions:

• **Up key: DISP.** The Up button is labeled as DISP, for Display Contents, and it provides display-oriented functions, which vary depending on your Shooting/Playback mode:

◆ **Shooting mode.** When the camera is in Shooting mode, press the DISP button repeatedly to cycle among the five screens that display data in the electronic viewfinder display or the six screens that display information about current settings on the LCD screen.

The default display for the LCD is called Display All Info. (See Figure 2.7.) This provides a full information display with a great deal of data overlaid over the live preview to show the settings in effect. The data provided when the camera is in a SCN mode or either Auto mode is quite limited; use P, A, S, or M mode to view all of the available data in each display option. Not all the information shown in the figure will be displayed at all times.

When you keep pressing the DISP button, the a6400 LCD cycles through other viewing modes, including No Display Info, which actually provides a few bits of data, a Graphic Display that shows the shutter speed and aperture on two related scales along with some recording information, and a basic display with a histogram in the bottom right of the screen. There is also a For Viewfinder text information screen that omits the thumbnail and shows only shooting information. You can enable/disable each of these information displays using the Custom Settings II-01 menu, as I'll explain in Chapter 4.

◆ **Playback mode.** In Playback mode, the DISP button offers different display options, as you would expect. When viewing still images in playback, press the DISP button to cycle among the three available playback screens: Display Info (full recording data); Histogram with recording data; and No recording data. When displaying a movie on the screen, the DISP button produces only two screens: with or without recording information. There is no histogram display available.

• **Down key: Exposure compensation/Index/Movie Playback.** This button has several functions, which differ depending on the mode you're using.

   ◆ **Shooting mode.** When the mode dial is set to Program, Aperture Priority, Shutter Priority, or Sweep Panorama, pressing this button reveals the exposure compensation display. Scroll up/down among the plus and minus options by rotating the control dial, the control wheel, or by pressing the directional buttons of the wheel. I'll discuss exposure compensation and other exposure-related topics in Chapter 7. This button has no function in either of the two Auto modes, nor in any scene mode.

   ◆ **Playback mode.** Press the down button to activate an index view, which shows thumbnails in any of several different varieties, depending on how you have set the View Mode in the Playback 3 menu. The view can consist of 12 or 30 thumbnail images, and you can choose from Date View, Folder View (Still), AVCHD View, XAVCS HD View, or XAVC S 4K View. See Chapter 6 for instructions on choosing among these modes.

If you're viewing a movie clip, press the down button to invoke a series of controls at the bottom of the screen that allow you to play, pause, fast forward/rewind/slow playback, skip to next or previous movie, and adjust volume.

• **Left key: Drive mode.** One press of this button in a compatible shooting mode leads to a series of options that let you set the self-timer, enable the camera to shoot one frame at a time or continuously at a fast or very fast rate, or set up exposure bracketing. The latter causes the camera to automatically take a series of shots, varying the exposure for each to ensure you get the best exposure possible.

When you scroll to the Self-timer or Bracketing item, you can press the right key to adjust options for those drive modes, as discussed in Chapter 7. I'll discuss continuous shooting and the self-timer in Chapter 9 and Bracket (exposure bracketing) in Chapter 7.

• **Right key: ISO.** When not helping you navigate to the right through menus and other screens, this button lets you activate the ISO screen in a compatible Shooting mode. You can then scroll up/down among the options by rotating the camera's control dial or control wheel or by pressing the wheel's directional buttons.

LCD Panel Data Displays

The Sony a6400 provides a tilting and expansive 3-inch color LCD with high resolution to display everything you need to see, from images to a collection of informational data displays. Some of the data is shown only when you are viewing the Display All Info screen, but even then, not every item of data will be available all the time. When shooting movies or still photos using the 16:9 aspect ratio, the screen is laid out as shown in Figure 2.7 (when capturing stills using the default 3:2 proportions, black bars "crop" the image at right and left). As discussed earlier, the electronic viewfinder display options provide much less data in order to avoid cluttering the live preview with numerals and icons during serious photography. Shown in the figure are the most important icons that the camera can display in the LCD in Display All Info when it's set for P, A, S, or M mode; less data is available in other display modes and when other shooting modes are being used. Additional icons appear for some settings not shown, such as Airplane Mode. The For Viewfinder/ Quick Navi text-only display (described next) that is shown only on the LCD monitor and not in the viewfinder is shown in Figure 2.8.

- **Shooting mode.** Shows whether you're using Program auto, Aperture Priority, Shutter Priority, Manual, Panorama, one of the scene modes, or one of the two Auto modes.

- **Memory card/Uploading status.** Indicates whether a memory card is in the camera. (If you remove the card, a blinking NO CARD indicator will appear instead.) If the camera is connected using Wi-Fi, the indicator will display icons representing the upload status.

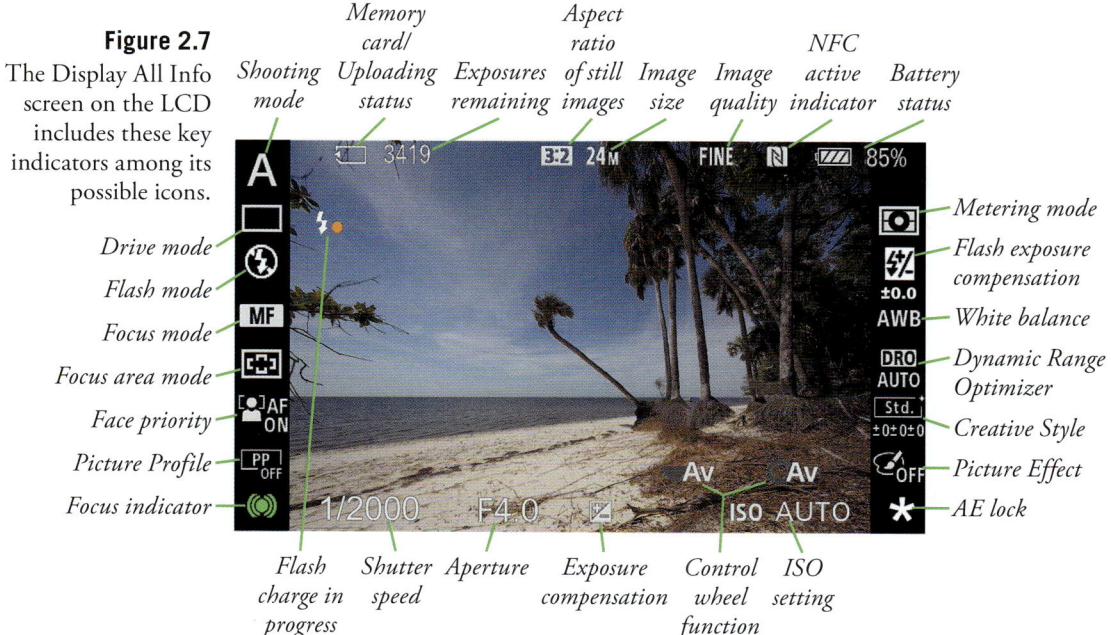

Figure 2.7
The Display All Info screen on the LCD includes these key indicators among its possible icons.

- **Exposures remaining.** Shows the approximate number of shots available to be taken on the memory card, assuming current conditions, such as image size and quality. When shooting a movie, the recordable time remaining is shown instead.

- **Aspect ratio of still images/Image size.** Shows whether the a6400 is set for the 3:2 aspect ratio or wide-screen 16:9 aspect ratio (the image size icon changes to a "stretched" version when the aspect ratio is set to 16:9) and whether you're shooting Large, Medium, or Small resolution images. If you're shooting only RAW photos, not RAW & JPEG, there is no symbol shown, because there are no options for RAW photo size. In addition, when the camera is set to the 16:9 aspect ratio, the display has black bands at the top and the bottom, as you would expect with the longer/narrower format vs. the 3:2 aspect ratio, which is closer to square in shape.

- **Image quality.** Your image quality setting (JPEG Fine, JPEG Standard, RAW, or RAW & JPEG) is displayed.

- **NFC active indicator.** Shows when your a6400 is linked to another device using Near Field Communications.

- **Battery status.** The remaining battery life (in percent) is indicated by this icon.

- **Metering mode.** The icons represent Multi, Center, or Spot metering. (See Chapter 7 for more detail.)

- **Flash exposure compensation.** This icon is shown whenever flash is active to indicate the level of flash exposure compensation, if any, that you have set.

- **White balance.** Shows current white balance setting. The choices are Auto White Balance, Daylight, Shade, Cloudy, Incandescent, Fluorescent, Flash, Color Temperature, and Custom. I'll discuss white balance settings and adjustments in Chapter 3.

- **Dynamic Range Optimizer (DRO).** Indicates the type of dynamic range optimization (highlight/shadow detail enhancement) in use: Off, Auto DRO, levels 1–5 of DRO, or the special Auto HDR feature, all described in Chapter 7.

- **Creative Style.** Indicates which of the Creative Style settings (Standard, Vivid, Portrait, Landscape, Sunset, or Black-and-White) is being applied. I'll discuss the use of these settings in Chapter 9.

- **Picture effect.** Shows which of the special effects, such as Toy Camera, Pop Color, or Posterization is being applied. I'll explain these options in Chapter 3.

- **Control wheel function.** This icon lets you know the function of the control dial in the Shooting mode in use, such as aperture control in A mode. This icon disappears when the zoom magnification scale appears; that scale—not shown here because it's visible for only two seconds after you zoom the lens—depicts the focal length currently set or the amount of digital zoom in effect.

- **Flash charge in progress.** This lightning bolt icon appears on the screen when the flash unit is active; a solid orange dot beside it indicates the flash has recycled (charged) and is ready to fire.

- **Flash mode.** Provides flash mode information when flash is active. The possible choices are Flash Off, Auto Flash, Fill-Flash, Slow Sync, Rear Curtain, and Wireless. Not all of these choices are available at all times. I'll discuss flash options in more detail in Chapter 12.

- **Drive mode.** Shows whether the camera is set for Single-shot, Continuous shooting, Speed Priority Continuous shooting, Self-timer, Self-timer with continuous shooting, or Exposure bracketing. There is one additional option available: Remote Commander, which sets up the camera to be controlled by an infrared remote control.

- **AE lock.** Appears when autoexposure has been locked at the current setting.

- **ISO setting.** Indicates the sensor ISO sensitivity currently set, either Auto ISO or a numerical value. I'll discuss this camera feature in Chapter 7.

- **Exposure compensation.** This indicator shows the amount of exposure compensation, if any, currently set.

- **Shutter speed.** Shows the current shutter speed, either as set by the camera's autoexposure system or, in Manual or Shutter Priority mode, as set by the user. If the camera's Graphic display is used, the screen illustrates that faster shutter speeds are better for action and slower speeds are fine for scenes with less movement.

- **Aperture.** Displays the current f/stop set by the camera or, in Manual or Aperture Priority mode, as set by the user. If you're viewing the Graphic display, icons indicate that wider apertures produce less depth-of-field (a "blurry" background) while smaller apertures provide a greater range of acceptable sharpness (increasing the odds of a more distinct background).

- **Focus indicator.** Flashes while focus is underway, and turns a solid green when focus is confirmed.

- **Focus mode.** Shows the currently selected focus mode, such as AF-S, AF-C, DMF (Direct Manual Focus), or MF (Manual Focus), as explained in Chapter 8.

- **Focus area mode.** Displays the active focus area mode, such as Wide, Zone, Center, or Flexible Spot, as explained in Chapter 8.

- **Picture Profile status.** Picture Profiles are used to adjust some parameters when shooting movies, as I will explain in Chapter 10.

Some of the same items of data are also available when other display options are selected with the DISP button, as discussed earlier in this chapter. When the Graphic Display option is used, the camera provides an illustration of the value of a small or wide aperture, and a fast or slow shutter speed, as discussed in the previous section.

Using the Quick Navi Function Menu

If you select the Quick Navi screen by pressing the DISP button until it appears, the LCD monitor shows the For Viewfinder/Quick Navi display, with only the shooting data and a live histogram displayed, but no live view of the scene, as you can see in Figure 2.8. When the Quick Navi screen is shown, press the Fn button, and you can then use the left/right/up/down directional buttons to highlight any of the settings that are not grayed out. (See Figure 2.9.)

Once an option is highlighted, you can rotate the control wheel to change its settings quickly, or press the center button to produce a screen with all the options. Use directional buttons and the center button to select the option you want. The Quick Navi screen is, in effect, a more fully featured Function menu. When the Quick Navi display is visible on the LCD monitor, you must compose images using the electronic viewfinder.

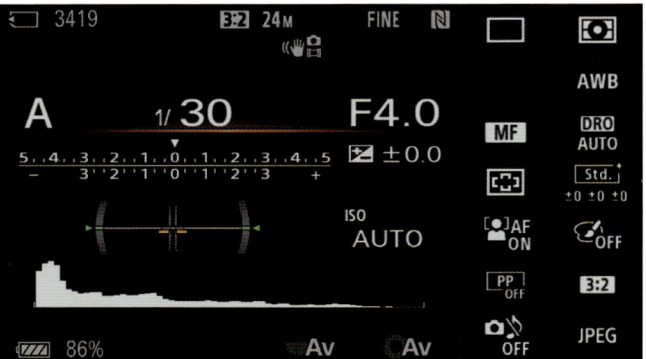

Figure 2.8
The For Viewfinder/Quick Navi information screen is available only for the LCD monitor and is not shown in the viewfinder.

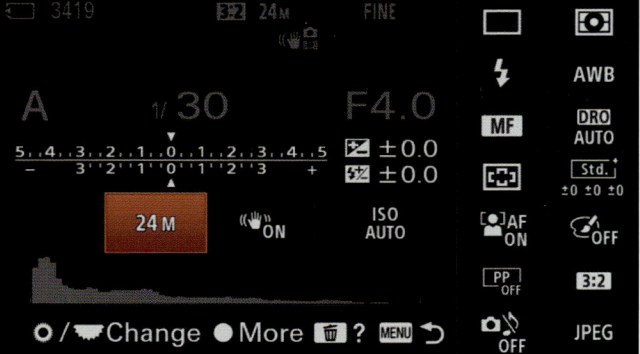

Figure 2.9
Press the Fn button and then use the directional buttons to highlight the settings.

Going Topside

The top surface of the a6400 has several frequently accessed controls of its own. They are labeled in Figure 2.10:

■ **Sensor focal plane.** Precision macro and scientific photography sometimes requires knowing exactly where the focal plane of the sensor is. The symbol etched on the top of the camera marks that plane.

■ **Multi interface shoe.** This "standard" accessory shoe is used for electronic flash units, and contains extra electrical contacts for use with Sony-brand microphones, such as the Sony ECM-XYSTM1 microphone, and other accessories, such as an adapter for pro-quality XLR mics. However, this shoe is also compatible with the ISO-518 hot shoe used by virtually all other camera manufacturers. Electronic flash that are not designed specifically for Sony cameras, especially older units, may use a triggering voltage that is too high and could damage your camera's circuitry.

The multi interface shoe replaces the non-standard Minolta-style proprietary "iISO" used by Sony for many of its cameras until about 2012. The older shoe required adapters to use non-Sony accessories. The new multi interface connector can still be used with older Sony flash units and accessories, but requires an adapter of its own for backward compatibility. If you own no older Sony electronic flash or accessories, you can simply move forward and purchase gear for the new, more standard hot shoe.

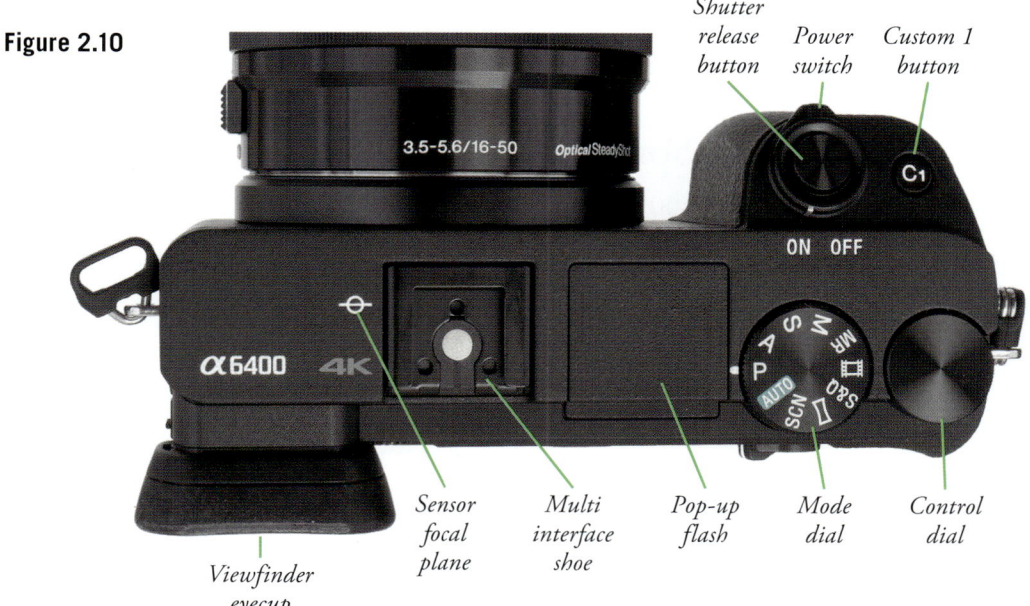

Figure 2.10

Shutter release button — *Power switch* — *Custom 1 button*

Viewfinder eyecup — *Sensor focal plane* — *Multi interface shoe* — *Pop-up flash* — *Mode dial* — *Control dial*

- **Pop-up flash.** The top surface of the pop-up flash fits flush with the top of the camera so it's not visible until you elevate it.

- **Mode dial.** Rotate to select Shooting modes including Manual exposure, Shutter Priority, Aperture Priority, Program Auto, Auto (Superior Auto and Intelligent Auto), SCN modes, Panorama, Movie mode, and Memory Recall 1 and Memory Recall 2.

- **Control dial.** Don't confuse this with the control *wheel* on the back of the camera. (Sony should not have given them such similar names: main dial/sub dial would have been much better.) It's used, often in conjunction with the control wheel to provide additional options. For example, in Manual exposure mode, the control *dial* adjusts the aperture, while the control *wheel* sets the shutter speed.

- **Power switch.** Rotate to the right to turn on the camera; to the left to switch it off.

- **Shutter release button.** Partially depress this button to lock in exposure and focus. Press it all the way to take the picture. Hold this button down to take a continuous stream of images when the drive mode is set for Continuous shooting. Tapping the shutter release when the camera's power save feature has turned off the autoexposure and autofocus mechanisms reactivates both. When a review image or menu screen is displayed on the LCD, tapping this button removes that display returning the camera to the standard view and reactivating the autoexposure and autofocus mechanisms.

- **Custom 1 button.** This button can be defined to perform any of several different functions, such as drive mode, focus mode, flash mode, flash compensation, focus area, exposure compensation, and 37 other behaviors. You can also select Not Set to deactivate it entirely. In Chapter 4 I'll show you how to redefine this button in the Custom Key Settings entry of the Camera Settings II-08 menu.

Underneath Your Sony a6400

The bottom panel of your a6400 has only a few components, illustrated in Figure 2.11.

- **Tripod socket**. Attach the camera to a vertical grip, flash bracket, tripod, monopod, or other support using this standard receptacle. The socket is positioned roughly behind the optical center of the lens, a decent location when using a tripod with a pan (side rotating) movement, compared to an off-center orientation. For most accurate panning, the socket would ideally be placed a little forward (actually in *front* of the camera body) so the pivot point is located *under* the optical center of the lens, but you can't have everything. There are special attachments you can use to accomplish this if you like.

- **Battery/memory card compartment door.** Open the door to access the battery and memory card.

Figure 2.11

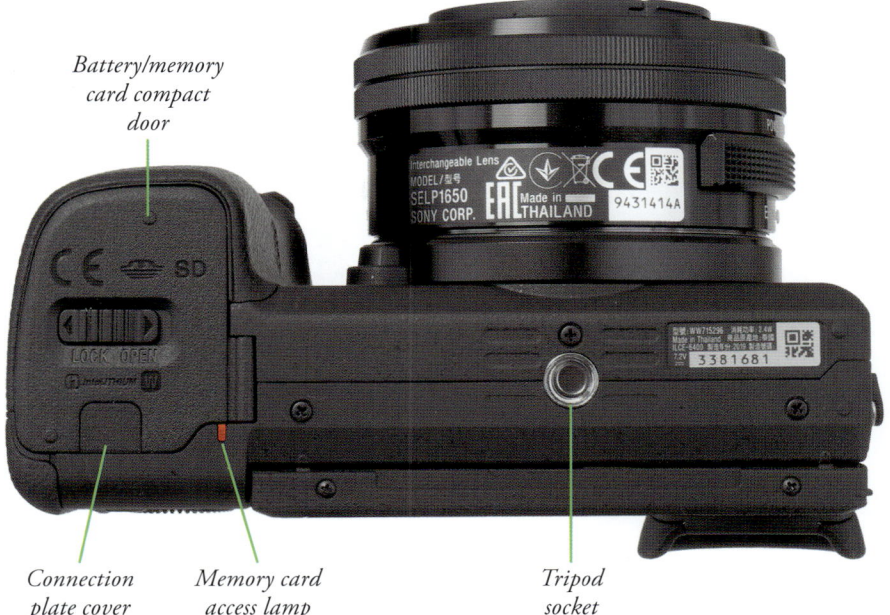

Battery/memory card compact door

Connection plate cover   *Memory card access lamp*   *Tripod socket*

- **Memory card access lamp.** Flashes red while the memory card is being written to. This lamp's location on the underside of the camera is not ideal. (I like to view the access lamp as a confirmation that a camera is actually taking pictures and saving them to the memory card.) However, it is located next to the battery/memory card cover door you must open before removing a memory card, so you should notice its red glow *before* you make the mistake of changing cards before the current image(s) are safely stored on your card.

- **Connection plate cover.** This opening allows the cable for the optional AC adapter to exit the camera.

3

Camera Settings I Menu

The a6400 has a remarkable number of features and options you can use to customize the way your camera operates. Not only can you change settings used at the time the picture is taken, but you can adjust the way your camera behaves. This chapter and the three that follow will help you sort out the settings for all of the menus. These include the Camera Settings I, Camera Settings II, Network, Playback, Setup, and My menus. This chapter details options with the Camera Settings I menu; you'll find Camera Settings II in Chapter 4, Network menus in Chapter 5, and Playback, Setup, and My Menu discussed in Chapter 6. This chapter covers the Camera Settings I's still photo adjustments; you'll find the movie-oriented settings in Chapter 10.

Why four entire chapters just on the menus, when other sources may have just a single chapter with a line or two about each menu entry explaining what they do? As you're discovering, the a6400 is an incredibly versatile camera with a mind-numbing number of different menu entries, many of which have submenus and multiple options. Even if you're a Sony veteran or an advanced photo enthusiast, you want more than just a brief explanation of what all the menu options do. You also need to know what they *don't* do, *when* to use each one, and, most importantly, when *not* to use them.

And, I'll bet, you purchased this book because you also wanted to know *my* personal preferences for settings and how I use these features. When I share what I know in person at workshops and other sessions with groups of photographers, I always tell them my informal motto: *I make terrible mistakes, so you don't have to!* I like to push cameras to their limits and, in the process, discover exactly what they can do, and what they can't.

So, like most of the rest of this book, Chapters 3 to 6 will cover both aspects in some detail. I'm not going to waste a lot of space on some of the more obvious menu choices in these chapters, especially those with only On/Off or Enable/Disable options. Instead, I'll concentrate on the more complex aspects of setup, such as autofocus. I'll start with an overview of using the camera's menus themselves.

Anatomy of the Menus

The menu system is quite easy to navigate. Press the MENU button and a tile menu with icons for each of the six main menu headings may appear. (See Figure 3.1.) That screen is essentially useless, as the only thing you can do with it is move to the conventional menu system. When your camera left the factory, it was turned off by default. If it appears, I recommend you immediately eliminate the extra step, using the Setup 1 menu's Tile Menu setting to disable it, described in Chapter 6.

Pressing the MENU button takes you to a screen like the one shown in Figure 3.2. Rotate the control dial (located at the top-right corner of the camera) to move from one top-level main menu or tab to the next. Each tab is assigned a color: Camera Settings I (red), Camera Settings II (purple), Network (green), Playback (blue), Settings (yellow), and My Menu (gray). When a tab is active its highlight color will be bright, and the hues of the other tabs more subdued, as you can see in the figure.

To navigate among menu entries:

- **Change main tabs.** When only the tab is highlighted (that is, none of its entries are highlighted in orange), you can quickly move from one main menu tab to the next by using the control *dial* or the control *wheel's* left/right directional buttons.

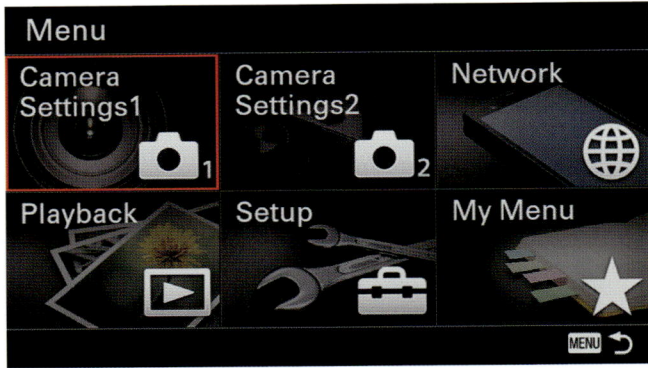

Figure 3.1
Although it is disabled by default, your camera has a redundant tile menu, which displays icons representing the six menu categories.

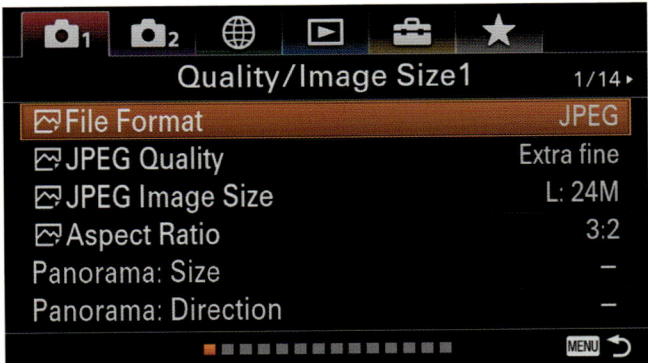

Figure 3.2
You can bypass the tile menu and go directly to the a6400's conventional menu system.

- **Select a menu entry.** To choose a specific menu entry within a main menu tab, use the up/down controls of the control wheel's directional buttons to highlight a specific menu entry.

- **Change menu pages.** Each main menu tab has multiple pages. When any entry in a main menu tab is highlighted you can move from one page within that tab to the next using the left/right controls. When you reach the last page of a tab's menus, additional movement wraps over to the first page of the next tab. The current page within a tab is shown by a numeric value (such as 1/14) and by a series of boxes at the bottom of the screen (you'll find both in Figure 3.2).

  For example, if you are using the Camera Settings I menu, the right key will take you from Camera Settings I-01 to Camera Settings I-02, and thence onward to the Camera Settings I-03 to I-14 tabs. Pressing the right key an additional time takes you onward to the Camera Settings II-1 page.

- **Make adjustments.** When a menu entry is highlighted, press the control wheel's center button to view options. After making adjustments, press the button again to confirm and exit, or MENU to cancel.

Tip

Note that each of the main tabs may have several pages: the Camera Settings I menu has tabs 1 to 14; Camera Settings II menu has pages 1 to 9; Network has two pages; the Playback menu has 3; and the Setup menu boasts pages 1 to 7. Your customizable My Menu starts out with one page, but can expand to include up to 30 menu entries. The advantage to having so many menu pages is that all the entries for a given page can be shown on a single screen, with no downward scrolling (past the maximum of six that can appear on a given page)required.

Of course, not everything has to be set using these menus. The a6400 has some convenient direct setting controls, such as the buttons of the control wheel that provide quick access to the drive modes, display information, and the ISO options. These and other buttons can be assigned other direct access functions—more than 50 different functions in all. These control features allow you to bypass the multi-paged menus for many of the most commonly used camera functions.

There is also a Function menu that appears when you press the Fn button, with a set of shooting setting options, as I described in Chapter 2. Although the Fn menu has a default set of 12 functions, you can redefine those entries as well. Your a6400 offers a remarkable degree of customization.

FINAL REMINDER: CONTROL DIAL vs CONTROL WHEEL

Remember that the control *dial* is the control in the upper right corner of the a6400, and the control *wheel* is the control located on the back of the camera, surrounding the center button.

At times you will notice that some lines on various menu screens are "grayed out;" you cannot select them given the current camera settings. For example, if you decide to shoot a panorama photo, you may find that the Panorama: Size and Panorama: Direction choices are grayed out. Want to know why? Scroll to the grayed out item and press the center button. The camera then displays a screen that explains why this feature is not available: because the feature is not available when Shutter Priority mode is active, in this example. Unfortunately, that's not very helpful. The screen *should* have instead told you that the Panorama settings are not available when the Shooting mode is anything *other* than Sweep Panorama. Given the incomplete information (and lacking this book), you might have spent several frustrating minutes switching to other Shooting modes, still to find that no Panorama settings are possible. In addition, there are many grayed out menu entries with advice that boils down to "Not Available" with no reason given. Thanks, Sony!

ABOUT THOSE ICONS

Menu entries are preceded by an icon, such as the "mountain" icon shown next to the File Format, JPEG Quality, JPEG Image Size, and Aspect Ratio entries in Figure 3.2. A mountain icon indicates that the particular menu entry applies *only* to still photography; an icon resembling a film frame shows that the menu entry applies *only* to movie making. Presumably, entries without any icon can be used with both. The three Enlarge entries in the Playback menu and Language entry in the Setup menu are preceded by magnifying glass and text icons, respectively, and apparently used just for decorative purposes.

Improved Menu System

If you're migrating from an earlier Sony Alpha camera, particularly the a6000 and a6300, you'll see some dramatic changes in the menu arrangement, most of them for the better. Right off the bat you'll notice that the former Custom menu has been renamed Camera Settings 2. (In this book, I will use the Roman numerals I and II for the two Camera Settings menus in order to differentiate between the menu number and the page number, which I refer to with Arabic numerals.)

In addition, each of the six main menu tabs has been assigned a color to help orient you to your position within the maze of entries. As you navigate between them, the tab at the top changes from red (Camera Settings I), to purple (Camera Settings II), green (Network), blue (Playback), yellow (Setup), and gray (My Menu). As a further navigational aid, the two Camera Settings menus are divided into sub-sections, with labels that let you know which sub-section you're currently using. Such fine-tuning is necessary, because Sony has, finally, relocated most menu entries in a more logical fashion. With the a6400, you'll find related settings within the same menu tab, and usually grouped close together.

While the new menu arrangement is an improvement, it still provides a daunting array of 36 individual menu pages, including 23 in the Camera Settings I and II menus alone, some with just one or two entries apiece.

Of course, not everything has to be set using these menus. The a6400 has some convenient direct setting controls, such as the buttons of the control wheel that provide quick access to the drive modes, display information, and the ISO options. These and other buttons can be assigned other direct access functions—more than four dozen different functions in all. These control features allow you to bypass the multi-tabbed menus for many of the most commonly used camera functions.

There is also a Function menu that appears when you press the Fn button, with a set of shooting setting options, as I described in Chapter 2. Although the Fn menu has a default set of 12 functions, you can redefine those entries as well. Your a6400 offers a remarkable degree of customization.

Camera Settings I Menu

Figure 3.2, shown earlier, shows the first screen of the Camera Settings I menu. As you can see, at most only a half dozen items are displayed at one time. The items found in this menu include:

Quality/Image Size (Pages 01-02)
- File Format (Stills)
- JPEG Quality (Stills)
- JPEG Image Size (Stills)
- Aspect Ratio (Stills)
- Panorama: Size
- Panorama: Direction
- Long Exposure Noise Reduction (Stills)
- High ISO Noise Reduction (Stills)
- Color Space (Stills)
- Lens Compensation

Shooting Mode/Drive Modes (Pages 03-04)
- Auto Mode
- Scene Selection
- Superior Auto Image Extract
- Drive Mode
- Bracket Settings
- Interval Shooting Functions
- Memory Recall
- Memory
- Register Custom Shooting Settings

Autofocus (Pages 05-07)
- Focus Mode
- Priority Setting in AF-S
- Priority Setting in AF-C
- Focus Area
- Focus Area Limit
- Switch Vertical/Horizontal AF Area (Stills)
- AF Illuminator (Stills)
- Face/Eye AF Settings
- AF with Shutter (Stills)
- Pre-AF (Stills)
- Eye-Start AF (Stills)
- AF Area Registration (Stills)
- Delete Registered AF Area (Stills)
- AF Area Auto Clear
- Display Continuous AF Area
- Circulation of Focus Point
- AF Micro Adjustment

Exposure (Pages 08-09)
- Exposure Compensation
- ISO Setting
- Metering Mode
- Face Priority in Multi Metering
- Spot Metering Point
- Exposure Step
- Autoexposure Lock with Shutter (Stills)
- Exposure Standard Adjustment

Flash (Page 10)
- Flash Mode
- Flash Compensation
- Exposure Compensation Settings
- Wireless Flash
- Red Eye Reduction

Color/White Balance/Image Processing (Pages 11-12)
- White Balance
- Priority Setting in Auto White Balance
- DRO/Auto HDR
- Creative Style
- Picture Effect
- Picture Profile
- Soft Skin Effect (Stills)
- Shutter Auto White Balance Lock (Stills)

Focus Assist (Page 13)
- Focus Magnifier
- Focus Magnification Time
- Initial Focus Magnification (Stills)
- Autofocus in Focus Magnification (Stills)
- Manual Focus Assist (Stills)
- Peaking Setting

Shooting Assist (Page 14)
- Face Registration
- Registered Faces Priority
- Smile Shutter
- Auto Object Framing (Stills)
- Self-portrait/-Timer

File Format (Stills)

Options: RAW, RAW & JPEG, JPEG

Default: JPEG

My preference: RAW & JPEG

This menu item lets you choose the file format setting that will be used by the a6400 to store its still photo files. You have three options: RAW, RAW & JPEG, and JPEG. The two entries that follow this one allow you to specify the RAW file type (compressed or uncompressed), and JPEG quality (Extra Fine, Fine, and Standard).

Should you select RAW, JPEG, or both? You can elect to store only JPEG versions of the images you shoot, or you can save your photos as "unprocessed" RAW files, which consume several times as much space on your memory card. Or, you can store both file types at once as you shoot. Note that to open a RAW file, you must have an image editor or RAW processor capable of converting the RAW file to editable form. The free Sony Imaging Edge software can do this for you; Photoshop, Lightroom, Photoshop Elements, and other programs compatible with Adobe Camera Raw (ACR) can also make the conversion for you.

Many photographers elect, as I do, to shoot *both* a JPEG and a RAW file (RAW & JPEG), so they'll have a JPEG version that might be usable as-is, as well as the original "digital negative" RAW file in case they will later want to make some serious editing of the photo with imaging software for reasons discussed shortly. If you use the RAW & JPEG option, the camera will save two different versions of the same file to the memory card: one with a .JPG extension, and one with the .ARW extension that signifies Sony's proprietary ARW 2.3 RAW format that consists of raw data.

For Users of Older Photoshop Versions

Adobe stopped upgrading its ACR software for the stand-alone (non-Creative Cloud/CC version) of Photoshop with Photoshop CS6. If that is your primary image editor, you'll need to use an external RAW processor, Adobe's free DNG Converter, or, my preference, MetaRAW ($49.95), which is available for both Windows and MacOS from www.thepluginsite.com. MetaRAW seamlessly "updates" the previous versions of Adobe Camera RAW by adding Adobe DNG converter capabilities to it when needed. As you import an "unsupported" RAW file, MetaRAW invisibly ushers the file through a DNG converter (which must also be installed on your computer), and thence to ACR, where you can use Camera Raw's adjustments. You can use Adobe Camera Raw, Adobe DNG Converter and MetaRaw's own converter for opening camera raw files. If one does not support a certain raw file, one of the others is used automatically.

JPEG vs. RAW

You'll sometimes be told that RAW files are the "unprocessed" image information your camera produces, before it's been modified. That's nonsense. RAW files are no more unprocessed than old-school camera film is after it's been through the chemicals to produce a negative or transparency. A lot can happen in the developer that can affect the quality of a film image—positively and negatively—and, similarly, your digital image undergoes a significant amount of processing before it is saved as a RAW file. Sony even applies a name (BIONZ) to the digital image processor used to perform this magic in Sony cameras.

A RAW file is closer in concept to a film camera's processed negative. It contains all the information, with no compression, no sharpening, no application of any special filters or other settings you might have specified when you took the picture. Those settings are stored with the RAW file, so they can be applied when the image is converted to JPEG or another format compatible with your favorite image editor. However, using RAW converter software such as Adobe Camera Raw (in Photoshop, Elements, or Lightroom) or Sony's Imaging Edge or the Sony Image Data Converter (available for download from various Sony websites worldwide), you can override a RAW photo's settings (such as White Balance and Saturation) by applying other settings in the software. You can make essentially the same changes there that you might have specified in your camera before taking a photo.

Making changes to settings such as White Balance is a non-destructive process in a RAW converter since the changes are made before the photo is fully processed by the software program. Making a change in settings does not affect image quality, except for changes to exposure, highlight or shadow detail, and saturation; the loss of quality is minimal however, unless the changes you make for these aspects are significant. The RAW format exists because sometimes we want to have access to all the information captured by the camera, before the camera's internal logic has processed it and converted the image to a standard file format.

Note that RAW files are generally recorded using 14 bits per pixel ("bit depth"), except when using Long Exposure Noise Reduction, Silent Shooting, Continuous Shooting in Superior Auto mode, and for Bulb exposures. In those cases, the RAW files are stored using 12 bits per pixel. Two bits may not sound like much (unless you're getting a shave-and-a-haircut), but it translates into many more colors available to render your image with a wider dynamic range. I'll explain bit depth in more detail under the Color Space entry later in this chapter.

A RAW photo does take up more space than a JPEG and preserves all the information captured by your camera after it's been converted from analog to digital form. Since we can make changes to settings after the fact while retaining optimal image quality, errors in the settings we made in-camera are much less of a concern than in JPEG capture. When you shoot JPEGs, any modification you make in software is a destructive process; there is always some loss of image quality, although that can be minimal if you make only small changes or are skilled with the use of adjustment layers.

JPEG provides smaller files by compressing the information in a way that loses some image data. The lost data is reconstructed when you open a JPEG in a computer, but this is not a perfect process. If you shoot JPEGs at the highest quality (Extra Fine) level (JPEG Quality choices are explained below), the compression (and loss of data) is minimal; you might not be able to tell the difference between a photo made with RAW capture and a Large/Fine JPEG. If you use the lower quality level, you'll usually notice a quality loss when making big enlargements or after cropping your image extensively.

So, why don't we always use RAW? Although some photographers do save only in RAW format, it's more common to use either RAW plus the JPEG option or to just shoot JPEG and eschew RAW altogether. While RAW is overwhelmingly helpful when an image needs to be modified, working with a RAW file can slow you down significantly. The RAW images take longer to store on the memory card, so you cannot shoot as many in a single burst. Also, after you shoot a series, the camera must pause to write them to the memory card, so you may not be able to take any shots for a while (or only one or two at a time) until the RAW files have been written to the memory card. When you come home from a trip with numerous RAW files, you'll find they require more post-processing time and effort in the RAW converter, whether you elect to go with the default settings in force when the picture was taken or make minor adjustments.

Those who often shoot long series of photos in one session, or want to spend less time at a computer, may prefer JPEG over RAW. Wedding photographers, for example, might expose several thousand photos during a bridal affair and offer hundreds to clients as electronic proofs on a DVD. Wedding shooters take the time to make sure their in-camera settings are correct, minimizing the need to post-process photos after the event. Given that their JPEGs are so good, there is little need for them to get bogged down working with RAW files in a computer. Sports photographers also avoid RAW files because of the extra time required for the camera to record a series of shots to a memory card and because they don't want to spend hours in extra post-processing. As a bonus, JPEG files consume a lot loss memory in a hard drive.

My recommendation: When shooting sports, I'll switch to shooting Large/Extra Fine JPEGs (with no RAW file) to minimize the time it takes for the camera to write a series of photos to the card; it's great to be able to take another burst of photos at any time, with little or no delay. I also appreciate the fact that I won't need to wade through long series of photos taken in RAW format.

In most situations however, I shoot virtually everything as RAW & JPEG. Most of the time, I'm not concerned about filling up my memory cards, as I usually carry at least three 64GB or 128GB memory cards with me. If I know I may fill up all those cards (say, on a long trip), I'll also carry my notebook computer and an external 2 terabyte hard drive to back up my files.

JPEG Quality (Stills)

Options: Extra Fine, Fine, Standard

Default: Fine

My preference: Extra Fine

To reduce the size of your image files and allow more photos to be stored on a given memory card, the camera's processor uses JPEG compression to squeeze the images down to a smaller size. This compacting reduces the image quality a little, so you're offered your choice of Extra Fine, Fine, and Standard compression. Standard compression is quite aggressive; the camera discards a lot of data. While Fine is, well, just fine, you'll find that Extra Fine provides even better results, so it should really be your *standard* when shooting JPEG photos.

For most work, extra compression (or lower resolution, described next) is false economy. You never know when you might need that extra bit of picture detail. Your best bet is to have enough memory cards to handle all the shooting you want to do until you have the chance to transfer your photos to your computer or a personal storage device.

JPEG Image Size (Stills)

Options: L, M, S

Default: L

My preference: L

Here you can choose between the a6400's Large, Medium, and Small settings for JPEG still pictures. The larger the size that's selected, the higher the resolution: the images are composed of more megapixels. If you select RAW or RAW & JPEG for File Format, you'll find that the Image Size option is still available, but will be applied only to recorded JPEG files; RAW files are always stored in Large format.

As you scroll among the options, you'll note that the size for Large, Medium, and Small is shown in megapixels, as shown for the a6400 in Table 3.1. The number of pixels will vary, depending on the *aspect ratio* you've chosen. For example, with the a6400, you'll get 24MP in Large mode using the 3:2 aspect ratio, and 20MP in Large mode using the 16:9 aspect ratio.

As I noted earlier, there are some limited advantages to using the Medium and Small resolution settings, and similar space-saving benefits accrue to the Standard JPEG compression setting. All these options help stretch the capacity of your memory card, so you can shoehorn quite a few more pictures onto a single card. That can be useful when you're away from home and are running out of storage, or when you're shooting non-critical work that doesn't require full resolution (such as photos taken for real estate listings, web page display, photo ID cards, or similar applications).

Table 3.1 Image Sizes Available

Image Size	3:2 Aspect Ratio	16:9 Aspect Ratio	1:1 Aspect Ratio
Large (L)	24MP 6000 × 4000 pixels	20MP 6000 × 3376 pixels	16MP 4000 × 4000 pixels
Medium (M)	12MP 4240 × 2832 pixels	10MP 4240 × 2400 pixels	8MP 2832 × 2832 pixels
Small (S)	6MP 3008 × 2000 pixels	5.1MP 3008 × 1688 pixels	4MP 2000 × 2000 pixels

Scroll to this Image Size menu item, press the center button, and scroll to the desired option: L, M, or S. Then press the center button to confirm your choice. As I noted, the actual size of the images depends on the aspect ratio you have chosen in the subsequent menu item (discussed below), either the standard 3:2, the wide-screen 16:9 format, or square 1:1 format.

There are few reasons to use a size other than Large with this camera, even if reduced resolution is sufficient for your application, such as photo ID cards or web display. Starting with a full-size image gives you greater freedom for cropping and fixing problems with your image editor. An 800 × 600–pixel web image created from a full-resolution (large) original often ends up better than one that started out as a small JPEG.

Of course, the Medium and Small settings make it possible to squeeze more pictures onto your memory card. The smaller image sizes might come in handy in situations where your memory cards are almost full, and/or you don't have the opportunity to offload the pictures you've taken to your computer. For example, if you're on vacation and plan to make only 4 × 6–inch snapshot prints of the photos you shoot, setting a lower resolution will stretch your memory card's capacity. Even then, it makes more sense to simply buy and carry memory cards with higher capacity and use your a6400 camera at its maximum resolution.

Aspect Ratio (Stills)

Options: 3:2, 16:9, 1:1 aspect ratios

Default: 3:2

My preference: 3.2; you can always crop to 16:9 in your image editor

The aspect ratio is simply the proportions of your image as stored in your image file. The standard aspect ratio for digital photography is approximately 3:2; the image is two-thirds as tall as it is wide, as shown by the outer green rectangle in Figure 3.3. These proportions conform to those of the most common snapshot size in the USA, 4 × 6 inches. Of course, if you want to make a standard 8 × 10–inch enlargement, you'll need to trim some of the length of the image area since this format is closer to square; you (or a lab) would need 8 × 12–inch paper to print the full image area. The 3:2 aspect ratio was also the norm in photography with 35mm film.

If you're looking for images that will "fit" a wide-screen computer display, or a high-definition television screen, you can use this menu item to switch to a 16:9 aspect ratio, which is much wider than it is tall. The camera performs this magic by cutting off the top and bottom of the frame (as illustrated by the yellow boundaries in Figure 3.3) and storing a reduced resolution image (as shown in Table 3.1). Your 24MP image becomes a 20MP shot if you set the camera to shoot in 16:9 aspect ratio instead of using the default 3:2 option. If you need the widescreen look, this menu option will save you some time in image editing, but you can achieve the same proportions (or any other aspect ratio) by trimming a full-resolution image with your software. The 16:9 option is most useful if you plan to take a *lot* of photos that will work best in that format. Only the JPEG version of a shot is cropped; the RAW file retains its full image area, which will be trimmed by your RAW converter when you import the image into your image editor. The 1:1 option represented by the red square in the figure is the ratio used for Instagram and many "instant" photo digital cameras.

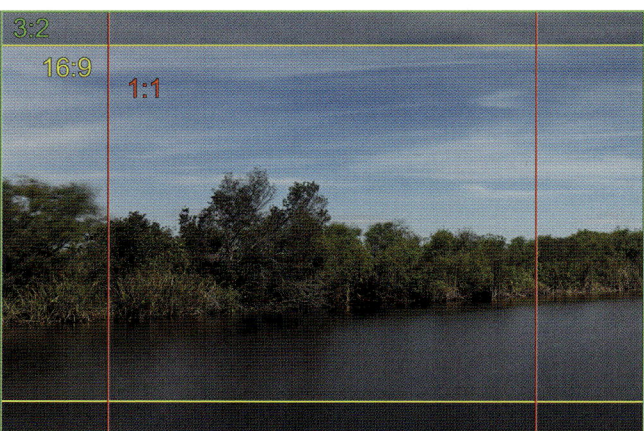

Figure 3.3

The 3:2 aspect ratio is shown by the outer green box. The yellow bars indicate the 16:9 aspect ratio (achieved either in-camera or later by cropping in software). The red box represents 1:1 proportions.

Panorama: Size

Options: Standard, Wide

Default: Standard

My preference: Wide! If you're shooting panoramas, go for it.

This item is available only when the Shooting mode is set to Sweep Panorama mode (usually abbreviated as Panorama). This item offers only two options: the default Standard and the optional Wide, which can produce a longer/taller panorama photo.

With the Standard setting, if you are shooting a horizontal panorama, the size of your images will be 8192 × 1856 pixels. If your Standard panorama photos are vertical, the size will be 3872 × 2160 pixels. (The options for panorama direction are covered in the next section.) If you activate the Wide option instead, horizontal panoramas will be at a size of 12416 × 1856 pixels, and vertical panoramas will be 5536 × 2160 pixels. Of course, vertically panned panorama photos are actually "tall" rather than wide regardless of the option you select.

Panorama: Direction

Options: Right, Left, Up, Down

Default: Right

My preference: Right

When the Shooting mode is set to Sweep Panorama, this menu item gives you four options for the direction in which the camera will prompt you to pan: right, left, up, or down. Note that when the live view screen is displayed on the LCD or EVF, you can cycle among the four shooting directions by rotating the control dial.

The camera actually is processing the image pieces you have already captured *as you continue to shoot,* so you have to select one of these directions so the camera will know ahead of time how to perform this processing of the many JPEGs you'll shoot while panning. Within seconds of finishing the capture, all your shots will be aligned and stitched together into the final panorama photo. The default, right, is probably the most natural way to sweep the camera horizontally, at least for those of us who read from left to right. Of course, you may have occasions to use the other options, depending on the scene to be photographed; for a panorama photo of a very tall building, for example, you'd want to use one of the vertical options (up or down).

Table 3.2 shows the size and resolution of Wide and Standard panoramas in both horizontal and vertical camera orientations.

With the camera held in the horizontal (landscape) orientation and panned *left to right* or *right to left*, the resulting panorama proportions are shown in Figure 3.4 for Standard (top) and Wide (bottom) options. Both versions are 1856 pixels tall, but measure 8192 and 12416 pixels wide, respectively.

If you hold the camera in the horizontal orientation and pan *up* or *down*, different proportions result, as seen in Figure 3.5. Standard and Wide versions are each 2160 pixels wide, but measure 3872 and 5536 pixels tall, respectively. In practice, your a6400 gives you four different panorama proportions.

Table 3.2 Sweep Panorama Image Sizes Available

a6400 Mode	Megapixels	Resolution
Standard Panorama—Horizontal	15M	8192 × 1856
Wide Panorama—Horizontal	23M	12416 × 1856
Standard Panorama—Vertical	8.4M	2160 × 3872
Wide Panorama—Vertical	12M	2160 × 5536

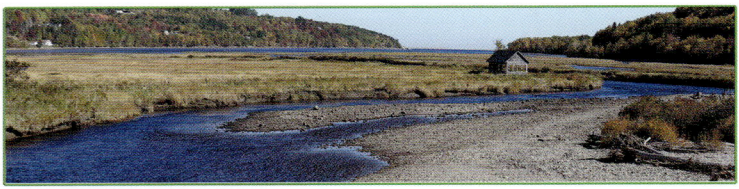

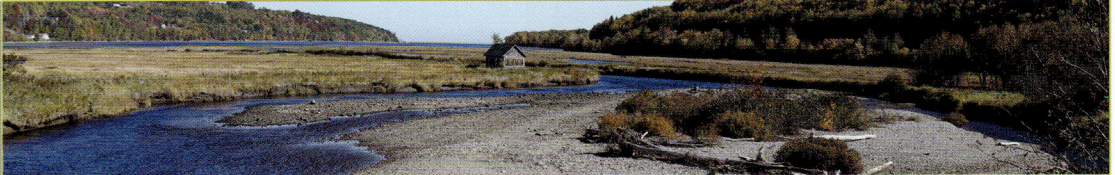

Figure 3.4 Horizontal standard format (green box) and wide format (yellow box), produced by panning left or right.

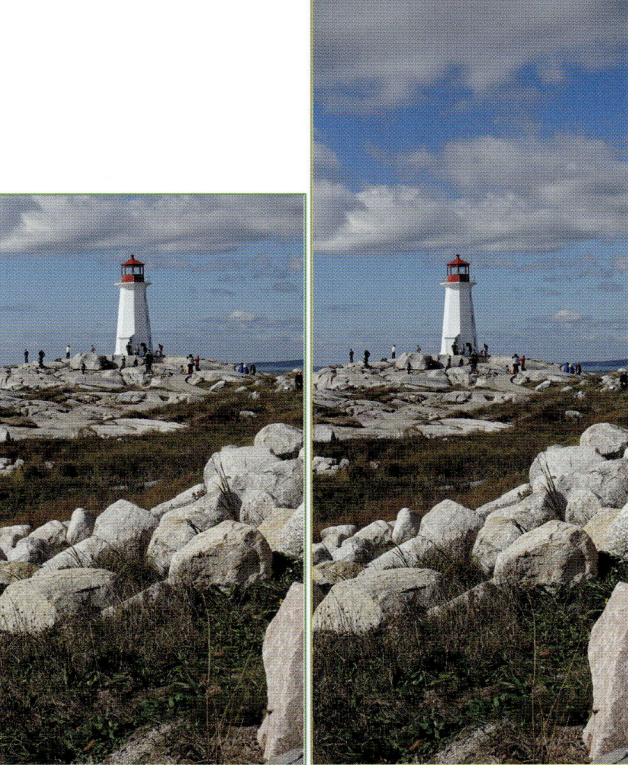

Figure 3.5
Vertical standard format (green box) and wide format (yellow box), produced by panning up or down.

Vertical Orientation for Horizontal or Vertical Pans

There are actually two more techniques for shooting panoramas. You can rotate your camera to the *vertical* (portrait) orientation and pan left or right, or up or down. I find the former technique most useful: vertical camera orientation, but left/right horizontal pan. Because each frame that is captured has a 2:3 aspect ratio, rather than the standard 3:2 aspect ratio, you'll end up with a pano that's less wide, and encompasses more of the scene vertically. Simply set Panorama: Direction to Down and pan left to right, or Up and pan right to left when the camera has been rotated 90 degrees counterclockwise. You'll end up with a different aspect ratio that is less widescreen in appearance, as you can see in Figure 3.6, which compares the normal Standard pan with the camera held horizontally and the Standard pan with the camera rotated vertically.

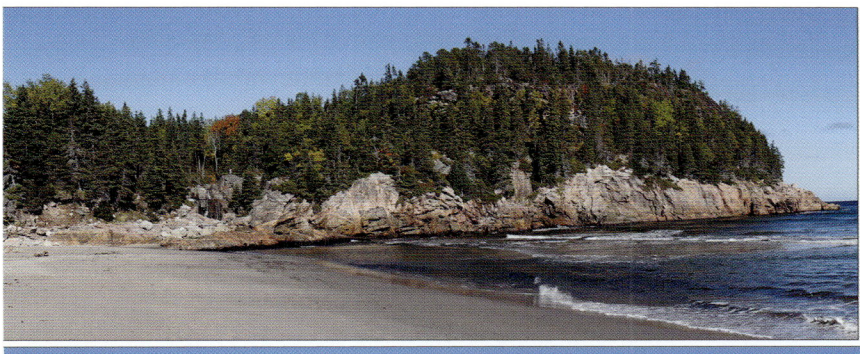

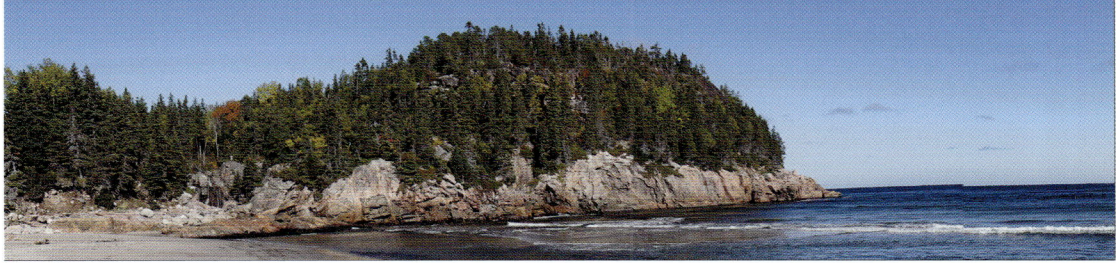

Figure 3.6 Horizontal panorama with the camera rotated to vertical orientation, and Panorama: Size set to Standard (top); at bottom is a Standard horizontal panorama.

Shooting Panoramas

I spend many weeks shooting scenics, and expend a lot of time taking panoramas with this camera, as you can see from the illustrations, all from a recent visit to Nova Scotia. While the process is simple in concept, it can be frustrating in execution, chiefly because it's easy for your "sweeping" motion to be too fast or too slow, and you may be 80 percent through the process when the camera informs you that your movement was at the wrong pace.

Here's a procedure that will help you minimize the frustration.

1. **JPEG only.** Know that if your camera is set to RAW or RAW & JPEG, the camera will temporarily switch to JPEG mode for the panorama (panos cannot be shot using RAW format), but will restore your original setting when you rotate the mode dial out of the Panorama position.

2. **Avoid incompatible features.** Some functions and settings are not available when capturing panoramas. They include Smile Shutter, Face Priority Multi Metering, Auto Object Framing, DRO/HDR, Picture Effects, Picture Profiles, Soft Skin Effect, AF tracking, digital zoom features, Drive Mode options, and Bright Monitoring. (What these features do are all explained in Chapters 3 to 6.)

3. **Take your position.** Your "wide" panorama will encompass roughly 220 degrees, so plant your feet firmly such that the center of your picture is straight in front of you. Keep the camera as near to your body as possible (use the EVF—please don't shoot panos with the LCD monitor!) so that the rotation point as your body twists is as close as possible to the sensor plane. Technically, the pivot point should be located underneath the center point of the lens, but it's easier to use the back of the camera as a reference.

4. **Set focus and exposure.** Lock focus and exposure before you start shooting, as the camera doesn't adjust once capture begins. The Focus Area is locked at the Wide setting and cannot be changed, and Face Priority AF is turned off. Electronic flash is disabled, and ISO is fixed at ISO Auto (to allow the individual panorama shots to maintain the same exposure). High ISO is set to Normal and Long Exposure Noise Reduction is not available.

5. **Twist and shout.** With your feet securely anchored, twist your body as far as you can toward the angle you'll use for the beginning of the exposure. That is, if you choose Right, twist as far as you can to the right.

6. **Unwind.** While viewing through the electronic viewfinder, begin shooting, slowly "untwisting" to pan the camera until you're facing forward again.

7. **Speed kills.** Continue twisting smoothly toward the finish position. It's important to keep a constant speed.

8. **View your progress.** As you shoot, the camera will provide a highlighted view of the area currently being captured, as it takes a series of overlapping shots. An arrow is shown on the screen to indicate the direction you should be moving.

9. **Follow through.** If you rotate too slowly or too quickly, a message that the camera could not shoot the panorama will appear, advising you to move more slowly or more quickly.

10. **Cross the finish line.** You'll finish twisted all the way in the opposite direction from your initial position. When you have successfully captured a panorama, the screen will blank for a few seconds while the camera stitches your exposures together. It will then display your finished shot.

11. **View your results.** The preview shows a reduced-size version of the entire panorama; press the center button to see a scrolling display of the entire shot.

There are a couple aspects of panorama shooting that you might not have considered:

- **"Multiple" exposures.** Panoramas are best rendered with subjects that do not move. If something is in motion as you sweep the camera, you may get multiple renditions of that subject.

- **Collateral "damage" from cropping.** Avoid including very important information at the very top and bottom of your frames (when shooting in left/right mode, for example). Because you probably won't hold the camera perfectly level as you pan, the camera will automatically try to align your images as they are stitched together, and there will often be some "excess" image above and/or below that is cropped out to produce a seamless image.

Long Exposure NR/High ISO NR (Stills)

Long Exposure NR: **Options:** On/Off **Default:** On

High ISO NR: **Options:** Normal, Low, Off **Default:** Normal

My preference: Off for both

These are the first entries in the Camera Settings I-02 (Quality/Image Size 2) menu. (See Figure 3.7.) I've grouped these two menu options together because they work together, each under slightly different circumstances. Moreover, the causes and cures for noise involve some overlapping processes. Digital noise is that awful graininess that shows up as multicolored specks in images, and these menu items help you manage it. In some ways, noise is like the excessive grain found in some high-speed photographic films. However, while photographic grain is sometimes used as a special effect, it's rarely desirable in a digital photograph.

The visual noise-producing process is something like listening to a CD in your car, and then rolling down all the windows. You're adding sonic noise to the audio signal, and while increasing the CD player's volume may help a bit, you're still contending with an unfavorable signal-to-noise ratio that probably mutes tones (especially higher treble notes) that you really want to hear.

The same thing happens when the analog signal is amplified: You're increasing the image information in the signal, but boosting the background fuzziness at the same time. Tune in a very faint or distant AM radio station on your car stereo. Then turn up the volume. After a certain point,

Figure 3.7

The Camera Settings I-02 (Quality/Image Size2) menu.

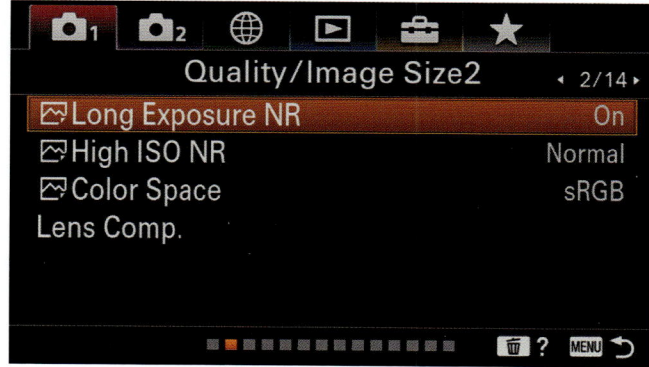

turning up the volume further no longer helps you hear better. There's a similar point of diminishing returns for digital sensor ISO increases and signal amplification as well.

Your a6400 can reduce the amount of grainy visual noise in your photo with noise reduction processing. That's useful for a smoother look, but NR processing does blur some of the very fine detail in an image along with blurring the digital noise pattern. These two menu items let you choose whether or not to apply noise reduction to exposures of longer than one second and how much noise reduction to apply (Normal or Low) when shooting at a high ISO level (at roughly ISO 1600 and above).

High ISO NR is grayed out when the camera is set to shoot only RAW format photos. The camera does not use this feature on RAW format photos since noise reduction—at the optimum level for any photo—can be applied in the software you'll use to modify and convert the RAW file to JPEG or TIFF. (If you shoot in RAW & JPEG, the JPEG images, but not the RAW files, will be affected by this camera feature.) As well, High ISO Noise Reduction is never applied when the camera is set to Sweep Panorama, Continuous Shooting, or Continuous Bracketing modes; when using Sports Action, Hand-held Twilight, and Anti Motion Blur scene modes; or when the ISO is set to Multi Frame Noise Reduction.

Digital noise is also created during very long exposures. Extended exposure times allow more photons to reach the sensor, but increase the likelihood that some photosites will react randomly even though not struck by a particle of light. Moreover, as the sensor remains switched on for the longer exposure, it heats up, and this heat can be mistakenly recorded as if it were a barrage of photons. To minimize the digital noise that can occur during long exposures, the a6400 uses a process called "dark frame subtraction." After you take the photo, the camera fires another shot, at the same shutter speed, with the shutter closed to make the so-called dark frame. The processor compares the original photo and the dark frame photo and identifies the colorful noise speckles and "hot" pixels. It then removes (subtracts) them so the final image saved to the memory card will be quite "clean."

Context-Sensitive

The a6400 has a novel "context-sensitive" noise reduction algorithm that examines the image to identify smooth tones, subject edges, and textures, and apply different NR to each. This processing works best with areas with continuous tones and subtle gradations, and does a good job of reducing noise while preserving detail. Because the BIONZ X digital processing chip is doing so much work, you may see a message on the screen while NR is underway. You cannot take another photo until the processing is done and the message disappears. If you want to give greater priority to shooting, set Long Exposure NR and High ISO NR to Off.

Long Exposure NR works well but it causes a delay; roughly the same amount of time as the exposure itself. That would be a long ten seconds after a 10-second exposure. During this delay, the camera locks up so you cannot take another shot. You may want to turn this feature off to eliminate that delay when you need to be able to take a shot at any time. This feature is Off by default in Continuous Shooting, Bracketing, Panorama mode and two scene modes, Sports Action and Handheld Twilight.

You might want to turn off noise reduction for long exposures and set it to a weak level for high ISO photos in order to preserve image detail. (NR processing blurs the digital noise pattern, but it can also blur fine details in your images.) Or, you simply may not need NR in some situations. For example, you might be shooting waves crashing into the shore at ISO 200 with the camera mounted on a tripod, using a neutral-density filter and long exposure to cause the pounding water to blur slightly. To maximize detail in the non-moving portions of your photos, you can switch off long exposure noise reduction.

Color Space (Stills)

Options: sRGB, Adobe RGB
Default: sRGB
My preference: sRGB

The Sony a6400's Color Space option gives you two different color spaces (also called *color gamuts*), named Adobe RGB (because it was developed by Adobe Systems in 1998), and sRGB (supposedly because it is the *standard* RGB color space). These two color gamuts define a specific set of colors that can be applied to the images your a6400 captures.

You're probably surprised that the Sony a6400 doesn't automatically capture *all* the colors we see. Unfortunately, that's impossible because of the limitations of the sensor and the filters used to capture the fundamental red, green, and blue colors, as well as that of the phosphors used to display those colors on the LEDs in your camera and computer monitors. Nor is it possible to *print* every color our eyes detect, because the inks or pigments used don't absorb and reflect colors perfectly.

On the other hand, the a6400 does capture quite a few more colors than we need. A 14-bit RAW image contains a possible 281 *trillion* different hues (16,384 colors per red, green, or blue channel), which are condensed down to a mere 16.8 million possible colors when converted to a 24-bit (eight bits per channel) image.

The set of colors, or gamut, that can be reproduced or captured by a given device (scanner, digital camera, monitor, printer, or some other piece of equipment) is represented as a color space that exists within the larger full range of colors. That full range is represented by the odd-shaped splotch of color shown in Figure 3.8, as defined by scientists at an international organization back in 1931. The colors possible with Adobe RGB are represented by the black triangle in the figure, while the sRGB gamut is represented by the smaller white triangle. The location of the corners of each triangle represent the position of the primary red, green, and blue colors in the gamut.

A third color space, ProPhoto RGB, represented by the yellow triangle in the figure, has become more popular among professional photographers as more and more color printing labs support it. While you cannot *save* images using the ProPhoto gamut with your a6400, you can convert your photos to 16-bit ProPhoto format using Adobe Camera RAW when you import RAW photos into an image editor. ProPhoto encompasses virtually all the colors we can see (and some we can't), giving advanced photographers better tools to work with in processing their photos. It has richer reds,

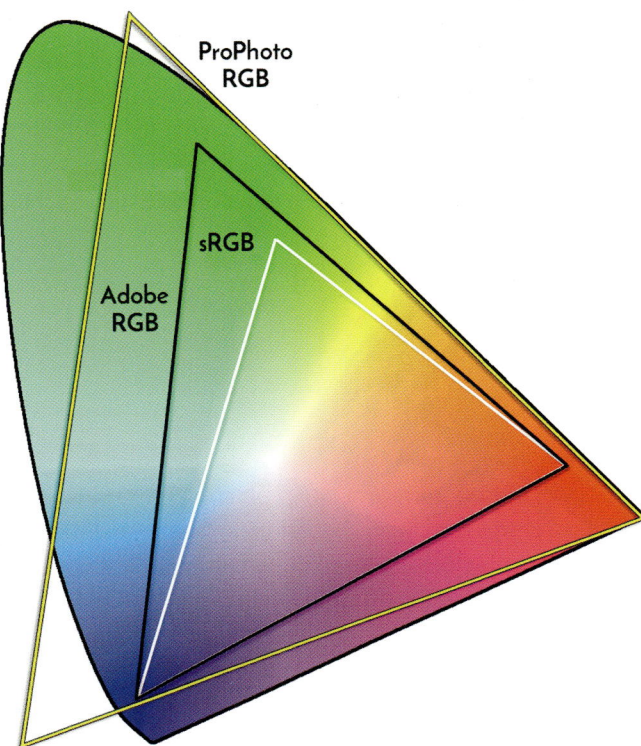

Figure 3.8
The outer curved figure shows all the colors we can see; the outlines show the boundaries of Adobe RGB (black triangle), sRGB (white triangle), and ProPhoto RGB (yellow triangle).

greens, and blues, although, as you can see from the figure, its green and blue primaries are imaginary (they extend outside the visible color gamut). Those with exacting standards need not use a commercial printing service if they want to explore ProPhoto RGB: many inkjet printers can handle cyans, magentas, and yellows that extend outside the Adobe RGB gamut.

Regardless of which triangle—or color space—is used by the a6400, you end up with some combination of 16.8 million different colors that can be used in your photograph. (No one image will contain all 16.8 million! Think about it: the only way a 24-megapixel image could include that many colors would be if two-thirds of the pixels were each a unique hue!) But, as you can see from the figure, the colors available will be *different*.

Adobe RGB, like ProPhoto RGB, is an expanded color space useful for commercial and professional printing, and it can reproduce a wider range of colors. It can also come in useful if an image is going to be extensively retouched, especially within an advanced image editor, like Adobe Photoshop, which has sophisticated color management capabilities that can be tailored to specific color spaces. As an advanced user, you don't need to automatically "upgrade" your a6400 to Adobe RGB, because images tend to look less saturated on your monitor and, it is likely, significantly different from what you will get if you output the photo to your personal inkjet. (You can *profile* your monitor for the Adobe RGB color space to improve your on-screen rendition using widely available color calibrating hardware and software.)

While both Adobe RGB and sRGB can reproduce the exact same 16.8 million absolute colors, Adobe RGB spreads those colors over a larger portion of the visible spectrum, as you can see in the figure. Think of a box of crayons (the jumbo 16.8 million crayon variety). Some of the basic crayons from the original sRGB set have been removed and replaced with new hues not contained in the original box. Your "new" box contains colors that can't be reproduced by your computer monitor, but which work just fine with a commercial printing press. For example, Adobe RGB has more "crayons" available in the cyan-green portion of the box, compared to sRGB, which is unlikely to be an advantage unless your image's final destination is the cyan, magenta, yellow, and black inks of a printing press.

The other color space, sRGB, is recommended for images that will be output locally on the user's own printer, as this color space matches that of the typical inkjet printer fairly closely. You might prefer sRGB, which is the default for the Sony a6400 and most other cameras, as it is well suited for the range of colors that can be displayed on a computer screen and viewed over the Internet. If you plan to take your image file to a retailer's kiosk for printing, sRGB is your best choice, because those automated output devices are calibrated for the sRGB color space that consumers use.

BEST OF BOTH WORLDS

If you plan to use RAW+JPEG for most of your photos, go ahead and set sRGB as your color space. You'll end up with JPEGs suitable for output on your own printer, but you can still extract an Adobe RGB version from the RAW file at any time. It's like shooting two different color spaces at once— sRGB and Adobe RGB—and getting the best of both worlds.

Of course, choosing the right color space doesn't solve the problems that result from having each device in the image chain manipulating or producing a slightly different set of colors. To that end, you'll need to investigate the wonderful world of *color management*, which uses hardware and software tools to match or *calibrate* all your devices, as closely as possible, so that what you see more closely resembles what you capture, what you see on your computer display, and what ends up on a printed hardcopy. Entire books have been devoted to color management, and most of what you need to know doesn't directly involve your Sony a6400, so I won't detail the nuts and bolts here.

To manage your color, you'll need, at the bare minimum, some sort of calibration system for your computer display, so that your monitor can be adjusted to show a standardized set of colors that is repeatable over time. (What you see on the screen can vary as the monitor ages, or even when the room light changes.) I use the Spyder X Pro monitor color correction system from Datacolor (www.datacolor.com) for my computer's three 27-inch widescreen LCD displays. The unit checks room light levels every five minutes and reminds me to recalibrate every week or two using a small sensor device, which attaches temporarily to the front of the screen and interprets test patches that the software displays during calibration. The rest of the time, the sensor sits in its stand, measuring the room illumination, and adjusting my monitors for higher or lower ambient light levels.

If you're willing to make a serious investment in equipment to help you produce the most accurate color and make prints, you'll want a more advanced system (up to $500) like the various other Spyder products from Datacolor or Colormunki from X-Rite (www.xrite.com).

Lens Compensation

Options: Shading Compensation, Chromatic Aberration, Distortion Compensation: Auto, Off (for each)

Default: Shading/Chromatic Aberration: Auto; Distortion: Off

My preference: Auto for all three

This trio of submenus optimizes lens performance by compensating for optical defects; they're useful because very few lenses in the world are even close to perfect in all aspects. All three items work only with E-mount lenses and not when using A-mount lenses with an adapter accessory.

Shading

One key defect is caused by a phenomenon called *vignetting*, which is a darkening of the four corners of the frame because of a slight amount of fall-off in illumination at those nether regions. This menu option allows you to activate built-in "shading" compensation, which partially (or fully) compensates for this effect. Depending on the f/stop you use, the lens mounted on the camera, and the focal length setting, vignetting can be non-existent, slight, or may be so strong that it appears you've used a too-small hood on your camera. (Indeed, the wrong lens hood can produce a vignette effect of its own.)

Vignetting, even if pronounced, may not be much of a problem for you. I actually *add* vignetting, sometimes, in my image editor when shooting portraits and some other subjects. Slightly dark corners tend to focus attention on a subject in the middle of the frame. On the other hand, vignetting with subjects that are supposed to be evenly illuminated, such as landscapes, is seldom a benefit. Figure 3.9, left, shows an image without shading correction at top, and a corrected image at the bottom. I've exaggerated the vignetting a little to make it more evident on the printed page. Note that this effect is applied to both RAW and JPEG images.

Chromatic Aberration

The second defect involves fringes of color around backlit objects, produced by *chromatic aberration*, which comes in two forms: *longitudinal/axial*, in which all the colors of light don't focus in the same plane, and *lateral/transverse*, in which the colors are shifted in one direction. (See Figure 3.9, top right.) When this feature is enabled, the camera will automatically correct images taken with one of the supported lenses to reduce or eliminate the amount of color fringing seen in the final photograph. (See Figure 3.9, bottom right.)

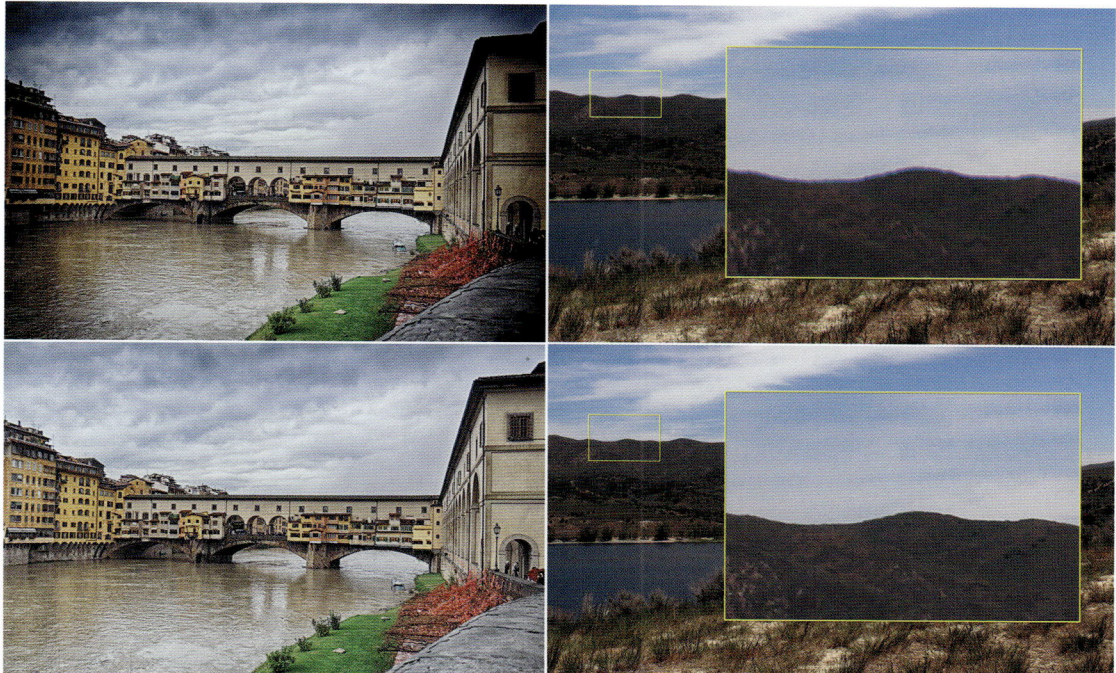

Figure 3.9 Vignetting (top left) is undesirable in a landscape photo, but the camera's shading correction feature can fix dark corners (bottom left). Lateral chromatic aberration, which shows as color fringes (top right), can also be corrected (bottom right).

Distortion

Distortion is the tendency of some lenses to bow outward (most often wide-angle lenses) or curve inward (found in some telephoto lenses). Figure 3.10, left, shows an exaggerated version of the outward-curving variety, called *barrel distortion,* exhibited by many wide-angle lenses—especially in fisheye optics, where the distortion is magically transformed into a feature. This feature works with most E-mount lenses, but not with all.

In Figure 3.10, right, you can see inward bowing, or *pincushion distortion,* as found in many telephoto lenses. Both types can be partially fixed using Photoshop's Lens Correction or Photoshop Elements' Correct Camera Distortion filters. Or, you can apply this in-camera feature to fix mild distortion. You should realize that correcting lens distortion involves warping pixels, mostly at the edges of the frame, providing a little less sharpness in those areas. The image area of your final picture will be slightly smaller than the frame you composed, and, during playback the active focus point is not shown in the review image.

In addition, applying distortion correction involves extra processing, which can reduce the number of consecutive shots possible. Because the correction is applied *after* you take the picture, the effect is not displayed on the screen when shooting in live view.

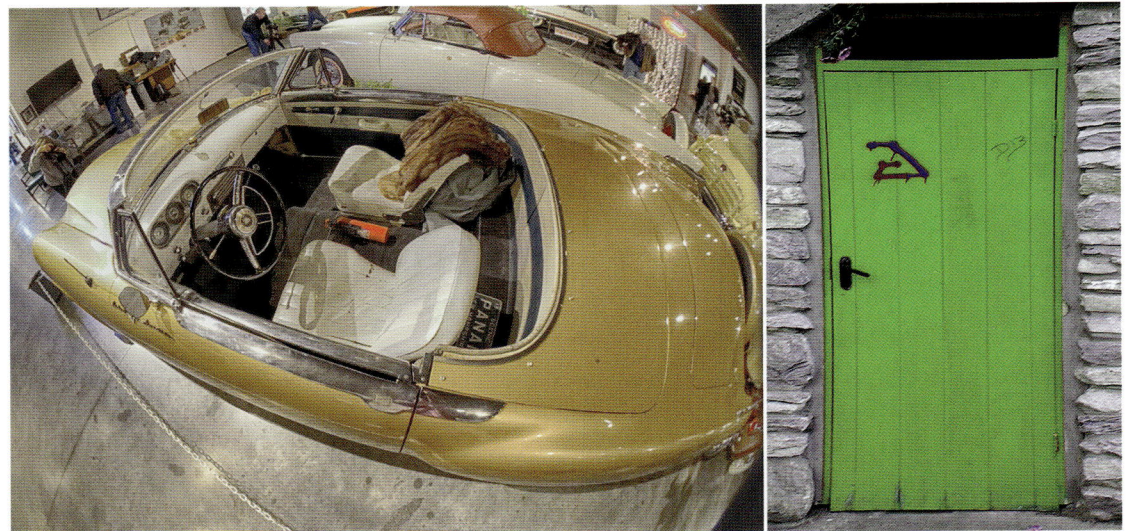

Figure 3.10 Left: Barrel distortion in wide-angle lenses becomes a useful feature with fisheye lenses. Right: Pincushion distortion causes straight lines at the edges of the frame to curve inward.

Auto Mode

Options: Intelligent Auto, Superior Auto

Default: Intelligent Auto

My preference: Superior Auto

This entry, the first on the Camera Settings I-03 page, allows you to specify which of the camera's two fully auto modes (Intelligent Auto and Superior Auto) is activated when the mode dial is moved to the Auto position. (See Figure 3.11.) Most users of a camera as sophisticated as this one won't use either one very often, so Sony has uncluttered the mode dial by allowing you to specify which of the two Auto modes you'd like to activate by default. This entry is grayed out (unavailable) if the mode dial is not set to the Auto position.

If you have the Mode Dial Guide enabled in the Setup 2 menu, when you rotate the mode dial to the Auto position, you can press the center button and rotate the control dial or control wheel to switch between Intelligent Auto and Superior Auto.

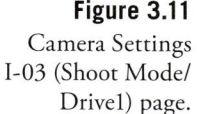

Figure 3.11
Camera Settings
I-03 (Shoot Mode/
Drive1) page.

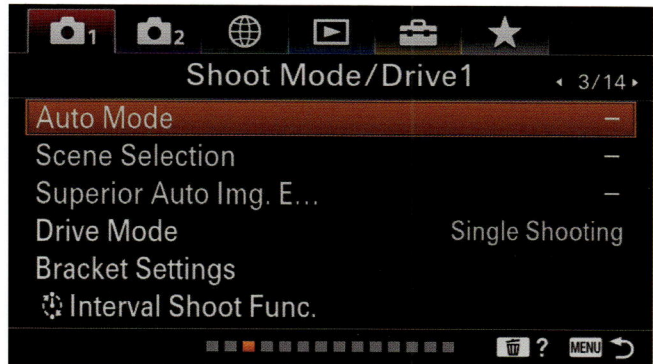

Scene Selection

Options: Select Scene Modes

Default: None

My preference: N/A

This entry is available *only* when the mode dial is set to SCN. It provides an alternate method for choosing among the available scene modes. It would have been brilliant if Sony had made Scene Selection one of the definable actions for a custom key or as a Function Menu option (at least for those who use scene modes a lot), but no such luck. However, it's here if you want to use it.

Superior Auto Image Extract

Options: Auto, Off

Default: Auto

My preference: Auto. I don't use Superior Auto much, but when I do, I use Auto.

Superior Auto is much smarter than Intelligent Auto! As you shoot, the a6400 evaluates a scene and selects a relevant SCN mode. If appropriate, the camera can snap off three consecutive shots when the shutter button is pressed, and then choose one or create a composite that has a higher dynamic range or improved digital noise than you'd get with Intelligent Auto alone. By default, only the final image is saved to the memory card, which makes a lot of sense. But if you want the camera to record all three of the photos it fired, as well as the final photo, choose the Off option. **Note:** Image extract is performed only in Superior Auto mode, and no composite image can be saved if Image Quality is set to RAW or RAW & JPEG. When using Hand-held Twilight, only one image is saved, even if this entry is set to Off. With Auto Object Framing active, two images are always saved, even if you select Auto here.

Drive Mode

Options: Single Shooting; Cont. Shooting (Hi+/Hi/Mid/Low); Self-timer Single (2/5/10 seconds); Self-timer Continuous (2, 5, or 10 seconds/3 or 5 shots); Continuous Bracket (to 3, 5, or 9 images at 0.3/0.7/1.0/2.0/3.0 increments); Single Bracket (3, 5, or 9 images at 0.3/0.7/1.0/2.0/3.0 increments); White Balance Bracket (3 images, Lo/Hi); DRO Bracket (3 images, Lo/Hi)

Default: Single Shooting

My preference: N/A

Just as with the drive (left) button on the back of the camera, there are several choices available through this single menu item. Your choices include:

- **Single Shooting.** Takes one shot each time you press the shutter release button.
- **Continuous Shooting (Hi+, Hi, Mid, Low).** Captures images at a rate of up to 11 frames per second at the Hi+ setting; 8 fps (Hi), 6 fps (Mid), or 3 fps (Lo). The 11 fps setting captures at the maximum possible rate, but the viewfinder or LCD image will "lag," and not show the actual live view image. Use the Hi setting or slower if you want to view what is being captured in real time between frames. **Note:** Focus is locked at the point calculated for the first exposure in a sequence if you're using an f/stop smaller than f/11 (say, f/16 or f/22). That's unlikely to be a problem, because of the greater depth-of-field provided at smaller apertures.

  While the a6400 can otherwise adjust exposure and focus as necessary for each shot, you can lock both at the settings used for the initial frame in a series by changing the AEL w/shutter entry in the Custom Settings menu (explained in Chapter 4) to Auto or Off, and the Focus Mode setting in the Camera Settings I menu to Continuous AF.

> ### Tip
>
> **Note:** Continuous shooting may be slower if you have turned the e-Front Curtain Shutter off, and is not available at all when using Sweep Panorama or Scene Selection (other than Sports Action); when Soft Focus, HDR Painting, Rich-Tone Mono, Miniature, Watercolor, or Illustration Picture Effects are enabled; or when using Auto HDR, Smile Shutter, or the Multi Frame Noise Reduction ISO option.

- **Self-Timer (2 sec./5 sec./10 sec.).** Takes a single picture after two, five, or ten seconds have elapsed. When this choice is highlighted, press the left/right buttons to select among the three durations.
- **Self-Timer Continuous.** The self-timer counts down, and then takes either 3 or 5 images. The left/right buttons switch among the 2/5/10-second and 3/5-image options.

- **Continuous Bracket.** Captures 3, 5, or 9 images in one burst when the shutter release is held down, bracketing them 0.3, 0.7, 1.0, 2.0, or 3.0 stops apart. The left/right buttons are used to select the increment and number of shots. In Manual exposure (when ISO Auto is disabled), or in Aperture Priority, the shutter speed will change. If ISO Auto is set in Manual exposure, the bracketed set will be created by changing the ISO setting. In Shutter Priority, the aperture will change. Use continuous mode when you want all the images in the set to be framed as similarly as possible, say, when you will be using them for manually assembled high dynamic range (HDR) photos.

  Only the last shot in the set is displayed when using Auto Review. With all types of bracketing, the exposure/bracket scale at the bottom of the EVF or LCD monitor (in Display All Info mode) will display indicators showing the number of images shot and the relative amount of under/overexposure. Don't forget that you can dial in exposure compensation, and *that* will affect the amount of over/underexposure applied while bracketing. Continuous bracketing (and Single bracketing) is disabled when using Superior Auto, SCN modes, or Sweep Panorama.

  You can use the built-in flash or an external flash when continuous bracketing is active, and flash output will be adjusted automatically. However, because of the time required for the flash to recycle, you'll need to press the shutter button each time to take subsequent images (effectively switching the camera into Single Bracket mode, described next).

- **Single Bracket.** Captures one bracketed image in a set of 3, 5, or 9 shots each time you press the shutter release, bracketing them 0.3, 0.7, 1.0, 2.0, or 3.0 stops apart. The left/right buttons are used to select the increment and number of shots. In this mode, you can separate each image by an interval of your choice. You might want to use this variation when you want the individual images to be captured at slightly different times, say, to produce a set of images that will be combined in some artistic way.

- **White Balance Bracket.** Shoots three images with adjustments to the color temperature. While you can't specify which direction the color bias is tilted, you can select Lo (the default) for small changes, or Hi, for larger changes using the left/right buttons. Only the last shot taken is displayed during Auto Review.

- **DRO Bracket.** Shoots three images with adjustments to the dynamic range optimization. While you can't specify the amount of optimization, you can select Lo (the default) for small changes, or Hi, for larger changes. Again, only the last shot taken is displayed during Auto Review.

SELF-TIMER WHEN BRACKETING

There are many times when you might want to use the self-timer while bracketing, say, when you are shooting individual images to combine in an image editor to achieve an HDR effect (described in Chapter 7). As self-timer and bracketing are separate Drive mode options, Sony has thrown you a lifeline. See Bracket Settings, described next.

Bracket Settings

Options: Self-timer during bracketing: Off, 2 sec., 5 sec., 10 sec.; Bracket Order: 0-+, -0+

Default: Off, 0-+

My preference: -0+

This item has two entries that let you customize how bracketing is applied.

- **Self-timer during bracketing.** You can choose delays of 2, 5, or 10 seconds before bracketing begins, or disable the self-timer during bracketing. This clever option solves a problem: how to use the self-timer (say, to avoid shaking a camera mounted on a tripod) when bracketing (which resides in the same Drive menu). With continuous bracketing, all exposures will be taken after the self-timer delay; if you're using single bracketing, the delay takes place before each shot in the bracket set is exposed.

- **Bracket order.** The default is metered exposure > underexposure > overexposure. However, if you're shooting photos that will later be manually assembled into an HDR photo, you might find it more convenient to expose in order of progressively more exposure: underexposure > metered exposure > overexposure. The order you choose will also be applied to white balance bracketing.

Interval Shooting Functions

Options: Interval Shooting, Shooting Start Time, Shooting Interval, Number of Shots, AE Tracking Sensitivity, Silent Shooting in Interval, Shoot Interval Priority

Default: Interval Shooting (Off), Shooting Start Time (1 second), Shooting Interval (3 seconds), Number of Shots (30), AE Tracking Sensitivity (Mid), Silent Shooting in Interval (On), Shoot Interval Priority (Off)

My preference: N/A

Interval (or *time-lapse*) shooting has had the distinction of long being one of the most desired features for Sony's E-mount mirrorless cameras. Until recently, you needed an external intervalometer device or a special app to capture individual shots at regular intervals—say, to take progressive photographs of a flower opening. Now, Sony has included this capability in some of its latest models, so your a6400 can now capture a series of shots of the moon marching across the sky, or compile one of those extreme time-lapse picture sets showing something that takes a very, very long time, such as a building under construction.

You probably won't be shooting such construction shots, unless you have a spare a6400 you don't need for a few months (or are willing to go through the rigmarole of figuring out how to set up your camera in precisely the same position using the same lens settings to shoot a series of pictures at intervals). However, other kinds of interval and time-lapse photography are entirely within reach. Best of all, with Sony's free Imaging Edge software, you can turn a series of time-lapse stills into a movie! I'll provide step-by-step instructions for capturing interval stills and time-lapse video in

Chapter 9, and include tips on recommended intervals between shots. You'll also learn more about the seven major settings you have to work with, shown in Figure 3.12:

- **Interval shooting.** Choose On or Off to enable/disable the feature. You'll want to keep this setting at Off until you are ready to begin interval shooting.

- **Shooting start time.** Use this setting to delay the start of image capture, from 0 minutes 0 seconds (begin immediately) to 99 minutes, 59 seconds. Say you're planning on capturing a sunset and know that the best time to begin shooting will be in one hour. Specify 60 minutes and 0 seconds, set up your camera, and the a6400 will begin taking your sequence at the designated time. You're free to do other things in the interim.

- **Shooting interval.** Specify how often an image should be captured. You might need an interval of 3 to 4 seconds to capture the march of fast-moving clouds across the sky, or prefer a more relaxed 10 to 12 seconds to shoot clouds with a slower pace. Intervals can range from 1 to 60 seconds between shots.

- **Number of shots.** This setting determines the total number of exposures in a time-lapse sequence. You can choose from 1 to 9999 shots. A message at the bottom of the screen will display how long it will take to capture the number of shots you specify using the shooting interval you've chosen. If you select the maximum 60-second interval and 9999 shots, your sequence will take almost just shy of one week to capture (166 hours and 36 minutes).

- **Autoexposure Tracking Sensitivity.** When the light levels are changing—say when capturing an entire day's activity, or something that happens fairly quickly, such as a sunset—you can specify whether the a6400 adjusts exposure quickly, or slowly. Select from High, Mid (Medium), or Low sensitivity. Quick changes in exposure can be jarring, especially when combining shots into a time-lapse movie. You may want to experiment to see what works for your particular sequence, but the Mid setting should work for most projects. **Note:** if you *want* to see dramatic light shifts as your scene lightens or darkens, use Manual Exposure and set the shutter speed, ISO, and aperture to give the correct "normal" exposure (say, for mid-day when shooting a day-long series). The dawn/early morning and dusk/night exposures will have different degrees of underexposure—probably for a more dramatic effect.

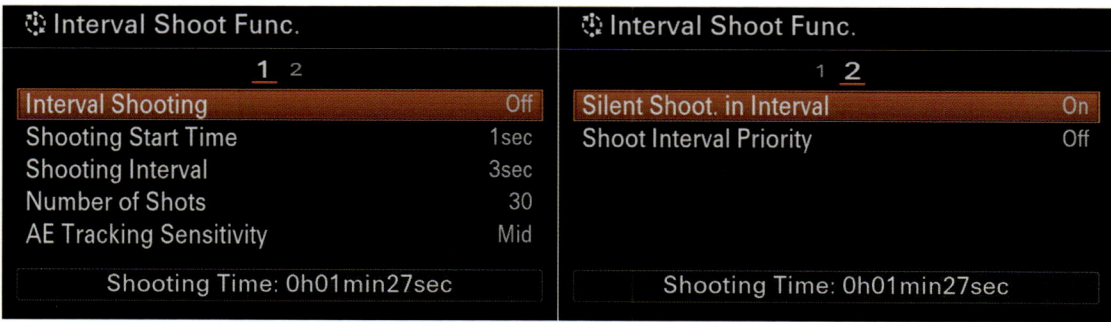

Figure 3.12 Interval Shooting options.

- **Silent Shooting in Interval.** Choose On or Off. If you select On, the a6400 will operate silently, which allows capturing your sequence in "stealth" mode if you need it. Silent shooting also makes the series of shots less intrusive in environments where low noise levels are prized—such as religious ceremonies, concerts, college libraries prior to finals week, or capturing a sleeping baby without interrupting parents' "quiet time."

- **Shoot Interval Priority.** When shooting sequences using Program or Aperture Priority modes, the a6400 will adjust the shutter speed to provide the correct exposure. Unfortunately, when light levels are low, that may result in a shutter speed that is longer than the specified interval. That is, you may want to take a photo every two seconds, but the camera calculates that a four-second exposure is required.

If you select Off for this setting, when the a6400 encounters a conflict, it will go ahead and expose for the correct amount of time, skipping the shot that would have taken place. This is the default behavior and often the best choice. In most cases, there is not enough subject motion between frames to result in a jarring effect. You're more likely to dislike having that conflicting image underexposed, which is what happens when this setting is On. When another interval exposure is due, the a6400 will terminate the previous shot (underexposing it) and begin the next one on schedule. You might use the On option if you feel that just dropping the poorly exposed image from the sequence produces the best series.

Memory Recall 1/2

Options: Select register to store settings

Default: None

My preference: N/A

This is the first entry on the Camera Settings I-04 page. (See Figure 3.13.) The a6400 gives you the option of storing up to three different groups of settings in separate registers *in the camera*, plus four more that are stored *on the current memory card.* You can then make any of those seven different settings active, and recall the adjustments in that setting instantly by rotating the mode dial to the MR position.

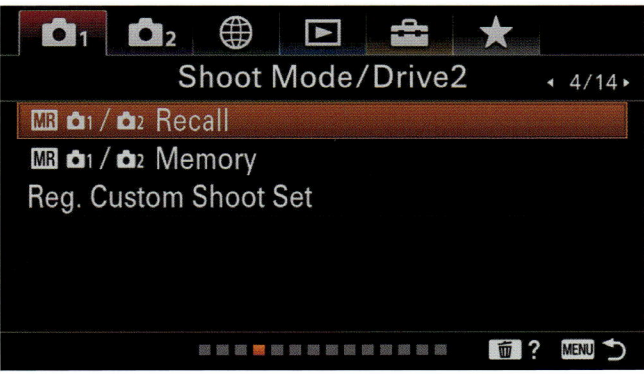

Figure 3.13
Camera Settings I-04 (Shoot Mode/Drive2) page.

Because Sony elected to list the Memory Recall entry *before* the Memory entry, it's easy to get their purpose mixed up. If you have not stored any settings, the Memory Recall entry will be grayed out and unavailable. Just remember this:

- **Memory Recall.** Use this to load settings from a register into your camera's settings "memory." You must have the mode dial set to the MR position to do this. You can then access the settings already stored in the 1, 2, or 3 registers, or replace the values in the current 1, 2, or 3 register with any of four *other* settings (labeled M1, M2, M3, and M4) stored on your memory card. I'll explain how to save those other four sets in the next section.

- **Memory.** This menu entry (which follows this one [and probably should have been named Memory Store]) is used to store sets of settings for later recall. To store the camera's current settings, the mode dial must be in a position *other* than MR. It should be rotated to the shooting mode you want to be stored in the memory register along with the desired f/stop, shutter speed, and camera settings.

I'll explain *recalling* settings here, and show you how to *store* them under the next menu entry, Memory.

This item is a powerful and useful tool. It enables you to save almost all the settings that you use for a particular shooting situation, and then recall them quickly. This function lets you save a trio of distinct sets of camera settings. Each will be a custom-crafted set that you can activate at any time. Simply activate the set that fits your current needs. For example, you might set up Register 1 with the settings you use while shooting volleyball in an indoor arena, Register 2 for use in landscape photography outdoors, and Register 3 for outdoor sports. Whenever you encounter any of those types of scenes, activate the memory register (1, 2, or 3) with the suitable settings for that situation. You can then begin shooting immediately.

Remember that the camera itself has three memory registers (1, 2, and 3), plus four *additional* memory settings, numbered M1, M2, M3, and M4, which are stored on the memory card *currently in the camera*. You can load the M1, M2, M3, or M4 settings into the 1, 2, or 3 positions. If you switch memory cards, you can access four more! Remove your card (or reformat it), and those extra four settings are lost! (Smart move, Sony.)

SETTINGS LIBRARY

You can keep separate memory cards for each type of photography you like to do, and store M1, M2, M3, and M4 settings on each of them. But remember when you reformat the card, those settings are lost. Bonus feature: settings stored on a card can also be recalled on any other a6400 you (or a friend/ colleague) happen to own, so you can share your settings, if you like, by exchanging memory cards.

To recall settings previously stored on your memory card using Memory Recall, just follow these steps:

1. **Rotate the mode dial to the MR positions.** If you've stored and used your memory registers before, the last one you specified will become active.

2. **Access the Memory Recall screen.** A screen like the one shown in Figure 3.14, left, appears when you first rotate the MR position. If you want to change registers during a shooting session, you can navigate to the Memory Recall entry on the Camera Settings II-04 page and press the center button to retrieve it, or, more simply, rotate the mode dial to another position, and then back to MR. The Recall screen will appear automatically.

3. **Evaluate your stored settings.** The currently active register (in this case, Register 3 in Figure 3.14, left) will be highlighted in orange. The screen shows the current settings in that register. You can press the down button to scroll through the list of additional settings that are now stored in that memory slot. If you're satisfied with the current settings, you can press Enter to exit, and begin using those settings.

4. **Change to a different register.** Use the left/right directional buttons to cycle among 1, 2, and 3 (registers stored in your camera) or to continue to M1, M2, M3, or M4 (the registers stored on your current memory card). You can only activate sets of settings that have previously been stored.

5. **Load settings from card (optional).** As I noted, you can also use an alternate group of settings from the M1, M2, M3, or M4 settings stored on your memory card. Press the left/right buttons to activate any of the four; if you have not yet stored settings in a particular memory card set, the message No File will appear. If you have stored settings, they will replace the ones currently shown on your screen.

6. **Confirm.** Press the center button to confirm your choice and exit. Your settings are now active in the camera.

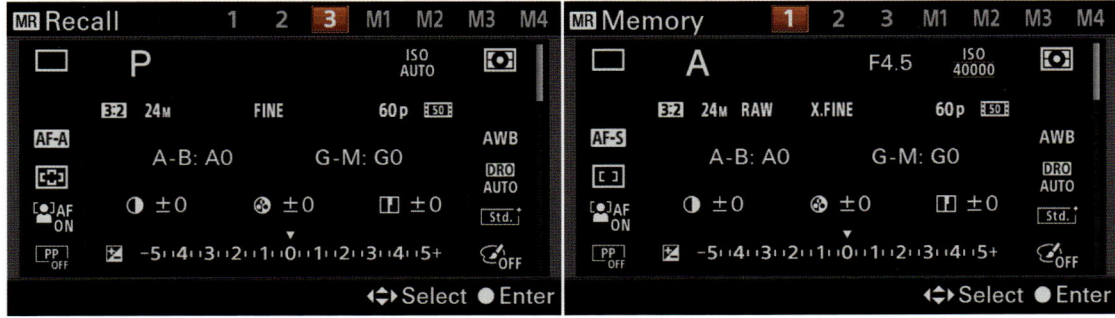

Figure 3.14 Recall settings stored on your memory card (left). Store settings in the 1, 2, or 3 registers, or as M1, M2, M3, or M4 on your memory card (right).

Memory

Options: Store settings

Default: None

My preference: N/A

This entry allows you to store your camera's current settings in registers 1, 2, or 3, or deposit them into the M1, M2, M3, or M4 positions on your memory card.

The power of the Memory feature stems from the fact that so many shooting settings can be saved for instant recall in any memory register. Before you access the Memory item in the menu, with the mode dial in any position *other* than MR, make the desired settings in terms of camera operating mode, drive mode, ISO, white balance, exposure compensation, metering mode, and focus mode. Then, to save your current settings on your memory card in one of the M1, M2, M3, or M4 slots, just follow these steps:

1. **Set up your camera.** Set your camera to the shooting mode, and adjust the camera to use the settings you'd like to store. The register can preserve shooting mode, aperture, shutter speed, and settings from the Camera Settings I menu. If you decided that you wanted to configure your camera for indoor volleyball in the same arena, you might set Fluorescent White Balance, +2/3 exposure compensation, ISO 1600, Continuous AF and Drive mode, Wide Area AF, the Vivid Creative Style, and Large/Fine JPEG.

2. **Navigate to the Memory entry.** Select the Memory entry in the Camera Settings I-04 menu, and press the center button. A screen like the one shown in Figure 3.14, right, appears.

3. **Review settings.** Use the up/down buttons to scroll through the current settings to make sure they are satisfactory. A great deal more information is available than is shown in the figure (note the scroll bar at right). You can press the up/down buttons to view additional screens with detailed listings of your current settings. Exit and change desired settings, then start again at Step 2.

4. **Choose Register.** Press the left/right buttons to select which of the memory locations you'd like to store your current settings in.

   • If you choose 1, 2, or 3, the settings will be loaded into the camera's memory and will be available regardless of which memory card is in the camera.

   • If you choose M1, M2, M3, or M4, the settings will be stored on the memory card and will be available *only* when that memory card resides in the camera.

5. **Proceed or cancel.** Press the center button to confirm and store your settings, or the MENU button to cancel.

6. **Activate register.** To use your stored settings, rotate the mode dial to the MR position, and follow the instructions listed under Memory Recall, above.

Register Custom Shooting Set

Options: Recall Custom Hold 1, 2, or 3

Default: Custom Hold 1

My preference: N/A

This function is an expansion of the Memory feature and available when using P, A, S, or M exposure modes. It allows storing sets of settings for *temporary* recall at the press of a custom key, and lets you choose to store *some* settings and ignore others. You can register three groups of settings but can assign only one at a time to your defined key. The Custom Shooting set is active only while you are holding down the defined key; when you release it the a6400 returns to its previous settings. You might want to use this feature to switch quickly and temporarily from one set of registered settings to another. Perhaps you're shooting landscapes and unexpectedly spy a rare raptor swooping by. If you've registered a set of parameters for "birds in flight" you can press your custom button, capture the bird, then release it and continue with your landscape shooting.

There are three available slots (Recall Custom Hold 1–3) and you can assign each of the three to a different button, giving you three settings available at the press of a defined button. Here's how to use this feature, which is available only when P, A, S, or M modes are active:

1. **Access this setting from the Camera Settings I-04 (Shoot Mode/Drive 2) menu.** The screen shown in Figure 3.15, left, appears.

2. **Choose registration number in which to store your settings.** Select from Custom Hold 1 to Custom Hold 3.

3. **Check current settings.** You can view the current settings of the camera. Only the settings that can be registered are shown. Use the up/down controls to scroll.

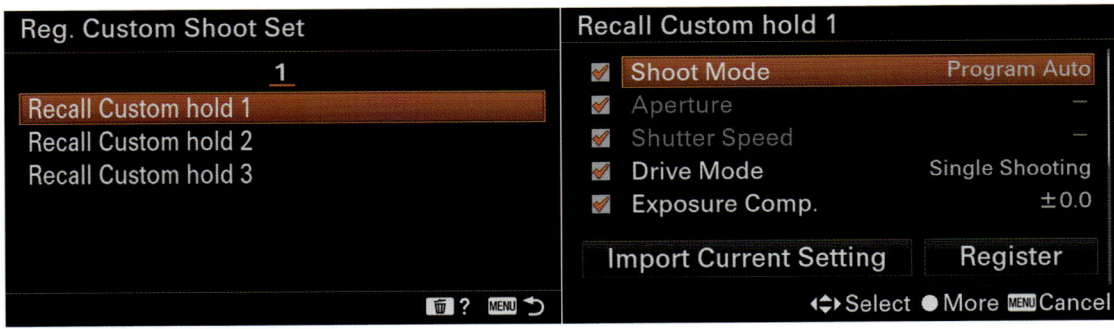

Figure 3.15 Select a Custom Hold register number (left). Register settings (right).

4. **Adjust or disable settings.** There are two columns in the settings display: Enabled/Disabled (represented by a checked/unchecked box) and setting name/and current setting. (See Figure 3.15, right.) The left/right controls switch you from the Enable/Disable column to the Setting Name/Setting column. The available settings that can be stored are shown on the screen. They include exposure, focus settings, and drive modes other than self-timer.

5. **To disable registration of a setting.** Highlight the left column of a setting listing and press the center button to add/remove the check mark.

6. **To change a setting.** Highlight the right column of a setting listing and press the center button. A screen will appear with the available options. For example, for Shoot Mode you can switch from the current mode to Program Auto, Aperture Priority, Shutter Priority, or Manual exposure.

7. **Store settings.** Scroll down to the bottom of the screen and highlight Import Current Setting. Press the center button.

8. **Register additional numbers.** Highlight Register to return to the screen seen in Figure 3.15, left, to register additional groups of settings.

9. **Assign a Custom Key.** To use this feature, you must assign a button to the Recall Custom Hold *x* (1, 2, or 3) behavior. Use the Custom Key entry in the Camera Settings II-08 (Custom Operation 1) menu, which I'll describe in Chapter 4. Note that you can define settings for all three Custom Hold registration numbers and can *define separate buttons* for each one. That means you can instantly (and temporarily) recall three additional sets of memory settings using custom keys, if you can spare that many from other duties.

10. **Use Custom Shooting Set.** Press the defined key to activate the Custom Hold settings assigned to that key, then press the shutter release down all the way to take a picture using those settings. When you release the custom key, your a6400 will return to its previous settings.

Focus Mode

Options: AF-S (Single-shot AF), AF-A (Automatic AF), AF-C (Continuous AF), DMF (Direct Manual Focus), MF (Manual Focus)

Default: AF-S (Single-shot AF)

My preference: Depends on subject matter

This menu item is the first on the Camera Settings I-05 (AF1) page. (See Figure 3.16.) It can be used to set the way in which the camera focuses. I'll discuss focus options in detail in Chapter 8.

■ **Single-shot AF (AF-S).** With this default setting, the camera will set focus and it will keep that focus locked as long as you maintain slight pressure on the shutter release button; even if the subject moves before you take the photo, the focus will stay where it was set and not follow focus on the moving object.

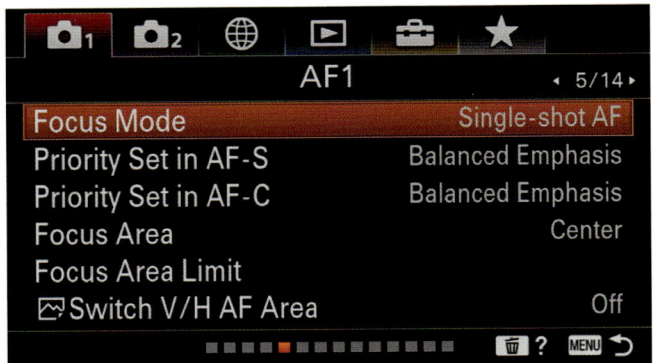

Figure 3.16
The Camera Settings I-05 (AF1) menu.

- **Automatic AF (AF-A).** Begins to focus using AF-S, but will switch to continuous autofocus (AF-C) to follow focus on the main subject if it begins moving. This is a good all-purpose setting when you aren't sure whether your subject will suddenly begin moving around as you shoot.

- **Continuous AF (AF-C).** The camera will continue to adjust the focus if the camera-to-subject distance changes, as when a cyclist approaches your shooting position. The camera will constantly adjust focus to keep the subject sharply rendered. It uses predictive AF to predict the moving subject's position at the time you'll take the next shot and focusing at that distance. This option is useful when you're photographing sports, active children, animals, or other moving subjects, making it possible to get a series of sharply focused shots.

- **Direct Manual Focus (DMF).** Press the shutter button halfway down to let the camera start the focusing process; then, keeping the button pressed halfway, turn the focusing ring to fine-tune the focus manually. You might want to use DMF when you are focusing from a short distance on a small object, and want to make sure the focus point is exactly where you want it.

- **Manual Focus (MF).** If you select Manual focus, you turn the focusing ring on the lens to achieve the sharpest possible focus. With both DMF and Manual focus, the camera will show you an enlarged image to help with the focusing process, if you have the MF Assist option turned on in the Camera Settings I-13 menu.

Priority Set in AF-S/Priority Set in AF-C

Options: AF, Release, Balanced Emphasis
Default: Balanced Emphasis
My preference: Release

These are two separate entries, one for AF-S and one for AF-C autofocus, but functionally they are identical, differing only in the autofocus mode they are applied to. It makes sense to describe them together.

These features let you specify whether the camera *waits* to take the picture until it has achieved sharp focus (when using an autofocus mode, not manual focus mode); whether it takes the picture immediately, even if sharp focus is not guaranteed; or uses a balanced approach somewhere between the two. For most kinds of candid photography, sports, or photojournalism, most of us would rather get the shot rather than lose a fleeting moment, and so Release is often your best choice. If you have a little more time, and the shot won't be affected by a short delay (perhaps half a second, on average), Balanced Emphasis, the default, will do the job. If you're looking for the best sharpness your camera can provide, the AF choice might be your best option. The three choices are as follows:

- **AF.** The shutter is not activated until sharp focus is achieved. This is best for subjects that are not moving rapidly.
  - **AF-S.** When using AF-S, most prefer to set this to AF, because in this focus mode the subject is usually not moving rapidly, and it makes sense to allow a slight extra delay to get the best focus possible. However, I find that with the a6400, when equipped with a lens having a built-in focus motor, in combination with the hybrid AF system, focus is fast enough that I can choose Release instead. If your camera/lens combination is slower to focus, you'll want to stick with the AF setting.
  - **AF-C.** When working in AF-C focus mode, if you select AF, the a6400 will continue to track your subjects' movement, but the camera won't take a picture until focus is locked in. An indicator in the viewing screen will flash green until focus can be achieved. You might miss a few shots, but you will have fewer out-of-focus images. Sports shooters probably won't choose AF priority for AF-C. Instead, they'll select release priority, discussed next.
- **Release.** When this option is selected, the shutter is activated when the release button is pushed down all the way, even if sharp focus has not yet been achieved. As I noted, I prefer this option for AF-C mode, as Continuous Focus focuses and refocuses constantly when autofocus is active, and even though an image may not quite be in sharpest focus, at least I got the shot. Use this option when taking a picture is more important than absolute best focus, such as fast action or photojournalism applications. (You don't want to miss that record-setting home run, or the protestor's pie smashing into the governor's face.) Using this setting doesn't mean that your image won't be sharply focused; it just means that you'll get a picture even if autofocusing isn't *quite* complete. If you've been poised with the shutter release pressed halfway, the camera probably has been tracking the focus of your image.
- **Balanced Emphasis.** In this mode, the shutter is released when the button is pressed, with a slight pause if autofocus has not yet been achieved. It can be selected for both AF-S and AF-C modes, and is probably your best choice if you want a good compromise between speed of activation and sharpest focus. However, you would not want to use this setting if the highest possible continuous shooting rates are important to you.

Focus Area

Options: Wide, Zone, Center, Flexible Spot (Small, Medium, Large), Expand Flexible Spot, Tracking

Default: Wide

My preference: Wide for general use; Tracking: Wide for sports and action

When the camera is set to Autofocus, use this menu option to specify where in the frame the camera will focus when you compose a scene in still photo mode, using the focus area selection you specify. I'll explain these options, the special requirements, and include illustrations of the focusing areas in Chapter 8.

- **Wide.** The camera uses its own electronic intelligence to determine what part of the scene should be in sharpest focus, providing automatic focus point selection. A green frame is displayed around the area that is in focus. Even if you set one of the other options, Wide is automatically selected in certain shooting modes, including both Auto and all SCN modes.

- **Zone.** Select one of nine focus areas (described in Chapter 8), and the camera chooses which section of that zone to use to calculate sharp focus. You can move the focus zone by pressing the defined Focus Settings button (the default is the center button) and then using the four directional buttons to select a zone.

- **Center.** Choose this option if you want the camera to always focus on the subject in the center of the frame. Center the primary subject (like a friend's face in a wide-angle landscape composition); allow the camera to focus on it; maintain slight pressure on the shutter release button to keep focus locked; and re-frame the scene for a more effective, off-center, composition. Take the photo at any time and your friend (who is now off-center) will be in the sharpest focus. Use this option instead of manually selecting a focus point to quickly lock focus on the center of the frame, then press the defined AF lock button to fix the focus at that point so you can recompose the image as you prefer.

- **Flexible Spot.** This mode allows you to move the camera's focus detection point (focus area) around the scene to any one of multiple locations using the directional buttons. When this option is highlighted, use the left/right directional buttons to change the size range of the spot among Small (S), Medium (M), and Large (L). Press the center button to confirm. Thereafter, you can use the directional buttons to move the small, medium, or large spot around within the frame.

  This mode can be useful when the camera is mounted on a tripod and you'll be taking photos of the same scene for a long time, while the light is changing, for example. Move the focus area to cover the most important subject, and it will always focus on that point when you later take a photo.

- **Expand Flexible Spot.** If the camera is unable to lock in focus using the selected focus point, it will also use the eight adjacent points to try to achieve focus.

■ **Tracking.** In this mode, the camera locks focus onto the subject area that is under the selected focus spot when the shutter button is depressed halfway. Then, if the subject moves (or you change the framing in the camera), the camera will continue to refocus *on that subject.* You can select this mode only when the focus mode is set to Continuous AF (AF-C).

This option is especially powerful because you can activate it for any of the focus area options described above. That is, once you've highlighted Tracking on the selection screen, you can then press the left/right directional button and choose Wide, Zone, Center, Flexible Spot, or Expand Flexible Spot. Note that if you are upgrading from a previous a6xxx-series camera, this focus mode was previously called *Lock-On.*

Focus Area Limit

Options: Wide, Zone, Center, Flexible Spot (Small, Medium, Large), Expand Flexible Spot, Tracking

Default: All available

My preference: Deactivate little-used focus area choices.

Experiencing too much of a good thing? This entry allows you to deactivate focus options that you rarely (or never) use, so that they don't appear when you select a focus area using the Focus Area entry (above), or use the Function menu's Focus Area option. Only the choices you enable will be shown; the others will be grayed out.

When you select this entry, the screen shown in Figure 3.17 appears. The check marks above each focus area indicates that that option is available. To disable/enable a particular focus area choice, highlight it using the directional buttons and press the center button to remove/add the check mark. The top row shows the non-tracking options (left to right): Wide, Zone, Center, Flexible Spot (Small), Flexible Spot (Medium), Flexible Spot (Large), and Expand Flexible Spot. The bottom row includes the Tracking counterparts of the exact same choices.

Figure 3.17
Focus Area Limit options.

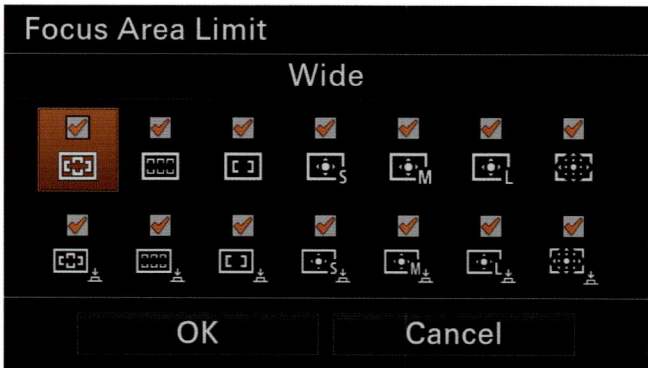

That configuration gives you a great deal of flexibility. You can have one set of focus areas enabled for general use, and choose a different set when using the a6400's Tracking capabilities. In my case, I use the Flexible Spot: (Small) focus area frequently, but disable the Medium and Large options. However, when shooting sports and action, I use Tracking almost exclusively, so I disable *all* the Tracking choices except for Flexible Spot: (Small), (Medium), and (Large). So, all I need to do is press the Fn button, highlight Focus Area, and select Tracking. I can then switch among Small, Medium, or Large by pressing the left/right directional buttons.

But wait, there's more! As you'll learn in Chapter 4, you can assign the Switch Focus Area function to a Custom Key, using that entry in the Camera Settings II-08 menu. After you've enabled/disabled the Focus Area options to your liking, you can cycle among those that remain simply by pressing the assigned function key.

Switch Vertical/Horizontal AF Area (Stills)

Options: Off, AF Point Only, AF Point+AF Area

Default: Off

My preference: Depends on subject

Here you can choose whether the Focus Area mode and the location of the focusing area within the frame adjusts when you change the camera's orientation from horizontal to vertical (see Figure 3.18). It's especially useful when you want to change orientation frequently for the same type of subject matter. For example, when I am photographing family and individual portraits I might shoot one set of images with the camera held horizontally to capture several members of a group, then rotate to use a vertical frame to capture a head-and-shoulders image of an individual. Many sports, such as basketball, involve the same sort of adjustment—a horizontal photo showing two or three players fighting for the ball, followed by a vertically oriented picture of a pair of roundballers going after a rebound off the boards.

Here are some things to consider:

- **You can/must set the Focus Area mode and/or focus point for each orientation individually.** That is, you must choose a Focus Area mode/focus point for horizontal orientation, then shift to each of the two vertical orientations and select a different location for either/both. If you don't specify a new location, the Focus Area and focus point remain where they were.

- **Only three orientations available.** They are horizontal, rotated 90 degrees clockwise with the shutter release on the lower half of the camera, and rotated 90 degrees from horizontal with the shutter release on the upper half of the camera. The horizontal/upside down orientation is the same as the conventional horizontal orientation. When the camera is pointed straight up (toward the sky) or straight down (toward your feet), the a6400 has no idea about how it is otherwise oriented.

Off:

AF point only

AF point + AF area

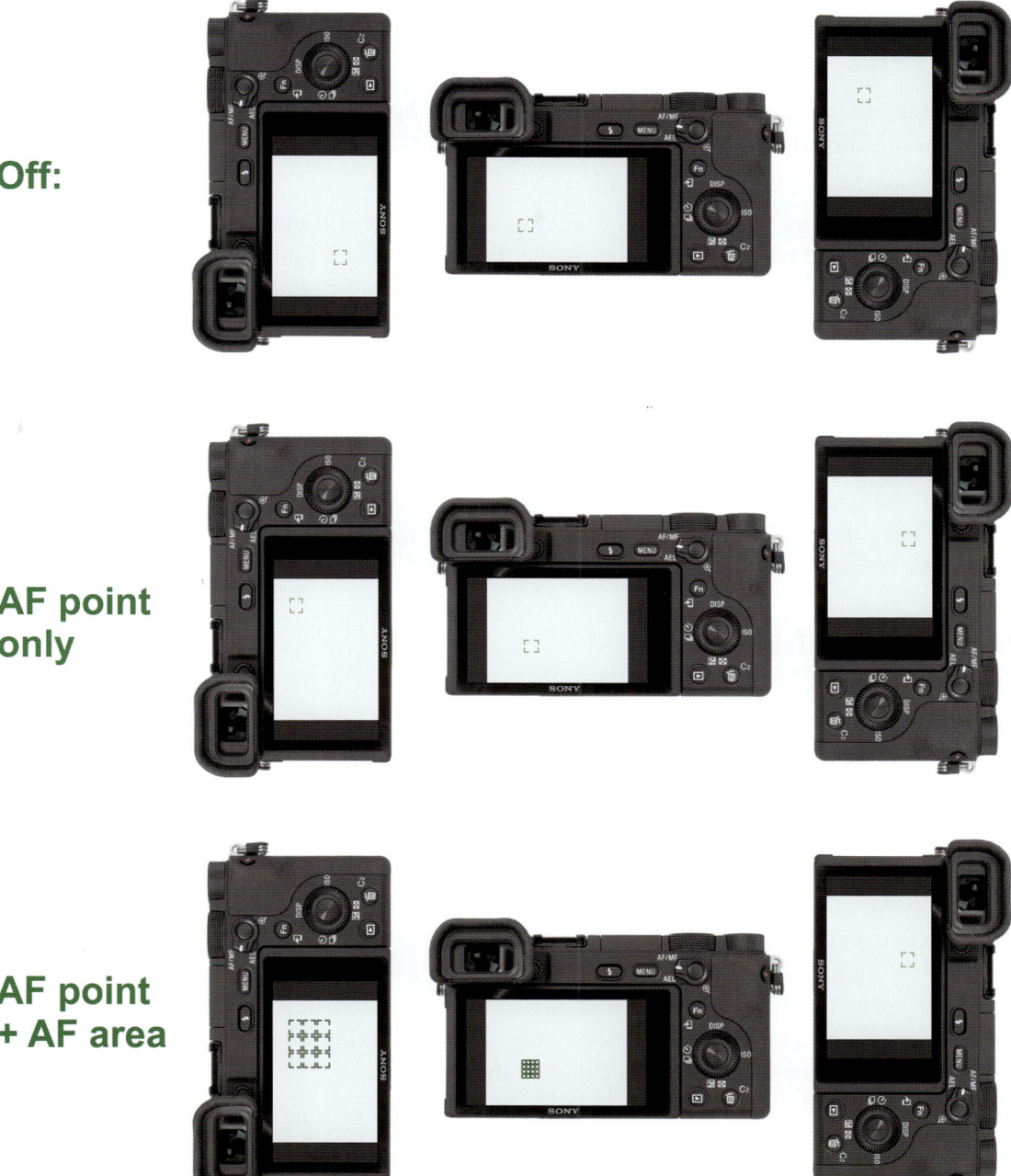

Figure 3.18 When the feature is turned off, the focus points remain in the same relative position as the camera is rotated (Top). When switching is enabled, you can position the focus points in different locations within the frame for each of the three orientations (Center). You can also optionally specify a different Focus Area mode for each presentation (Bottom).

■ **AF Area Mode/Focus Point Switching Disabled.** Changes in orientation are ignored if you are using Intelligent Auto, Movie, or S&Q Motion shooting modes. The feature is also disabled if you press the shutter halfway down (and then change orientations), during autofocus, continuous shooting, self-timer countdown, or Focus Settings adjustments. Using the Focus Magnifier also disables the feature.

You have three options for this feature:

- **Off.** The Focus Area mode and Focus Point (Frame) remain the same regardless of camera orientation. If you've selected a particular Focus Area mode and you've placed the focus at the lower-left area of the frame when shooting horizontally (as seen in Figure 3.18, top center), it will remain in the equivalent position when you rotate the a6400 90 degrees counter-clockwise (Figure 3.18, top left), or 90 degrees clockwise. (See Figure 3.18, top right.)

- **AF Point Only.** The Focus Area mode remains the same while the Focus Point adjusts to the position you have specified for each camera orientation. The center row in Figure 3.18 shows different focus points for each of the three orientations.

- **AF Point+AF Area.** Both the Focus Area mode and Focus Point adjust, so you can use a different Focus Area mode for each orientation. The bottom row shows different AF point locations and AF areas in each orientation.

AF Illuminator (Stills)

Options: Auto, Off

Default: Auto

My preference: Auto

This entry is the first in the Camera Settings I-06 (AF2) menu (see Figure 3.19). The AF illuminator is a light activated when there is insufficient light for the camera's autofocus mechanism to zero in on the subject. This light emanates from the same lamp on the front of the camera that provides the indicator for the self-timer. The extra blast from the AF illuminator provides a bright target for the AF system to help the camera set focus for subjects roughly no farther away than 10 feet. When you're shooting in environments so dark that conventional focusing is difficult, the a6400 will ignore the focus area you've specified and instead focus on whatever the AF assist lamp is able to illuminate. This menu item is a still-photos-only option, as the illuminator does not operate while shooting conventional or Slow & Quick motion movies.

The default setting, Auto, allows the AF illuminator to work any time the camera judges that it is necessary. Turn it off when you would prefer not to use this feature, such as when you don't want to disturb the people around you or call attention to your photographic endeavors. The AF illuminator doesn't work when the camera is set for manual focus or when using AF-C or AF-A while the

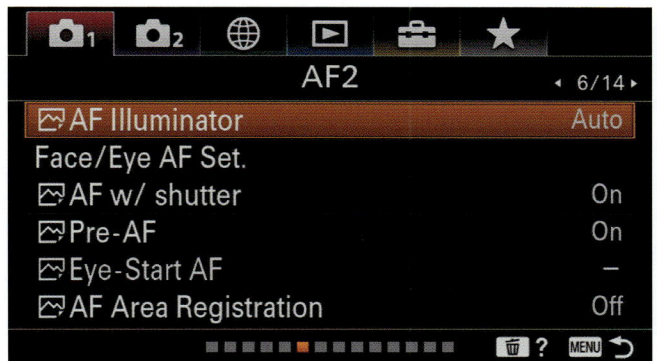

Figure 3.19
The Camera Settings I-06 (AF2) menu.

subject is moving. It is also disabled when using the Focus Magnifier, or one of the EA-LA adapters (which allow using A-mount lenses on the a6400).

Note: Some Sony flash units (currently only the HVL-F45RM and HVL-F60/F60RM include a white LED video light that the a6400 will use as an AF illuminator lamp if the flash is mounted on the camera and powered up.

Face/Eye AF Settings

Options: Face/Eye Priority in AF: On, Off; Subject Detection: Human/Animal; Right/Left Eye Select: Right, Left, Auto; Face Detect Frame Display: On, Off; Animal Eye Display: On, Off

Default: Face/Eye Priority in AF: On; Subject Detection: Human; Right/Left Eye Select: Auto; Face Detect Frame Display: On; Animal Eye Display: On

My preference: I use the defaults; this feature rocks!

When you're photographing people, the a6400 can optionally look for faces and can base its auto-focus decisions on the faces it locates. Even better, you can give certain countenances a higher priority than others by registering them with the camera, so, say, if your significant other is ensconced in the frame, the camera will favor that person as its AF focus (so to speak) over other humans in the frame. Further, the camera can locate human or animal eyes within your frame, and focus on them. Face/Eye detection can't be used with digital zoom, Sweep Panorama, the Focus Magnifier, the Posterization Picture Effect, Landscape/Night Scene/Sunset Scene modes, and 120p/100p movie or 120 fps/100 fps Slow & Quick Motion video. The Eye AF feature is unavailable when capturing all movies and Slow & Quick Motion clips.

Note: For animal eye detection, you must have installed the Firmware 2.0 update that was released in mid-June 2019 (or a later update).

Using this entry, you have the following choices (see Figure 3.20):

■ **Face/Eye Priority in AF.** Choose On and the a6400 can give a higher priority to detected faces. Select Off and AF will proceed without looking for faces. Up to eight faces, if present, may be detected. When autofocus is activated, the camera will attempt to focus on the eyes, if they are located within the active focus area. Note that when using Superior Auto, Face/Eye Priority is locked at On. **Note:** Enabling Face/Eye Priority does *not* mean the camera will automatically focus on those areas. See the sidebar that follows.

The Eye AF portion of Face/Eye Priority AF may not function as expected with subjects which are rapidly moving, have long bangs, closed eyes, or are wearing sunglasses. Shady conditions, backlight, and low-light situations can also hinder eye detection.

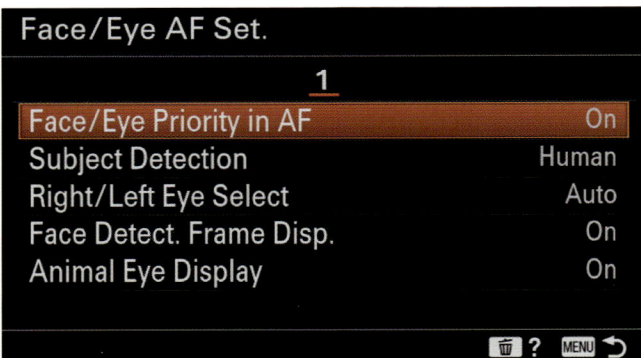

Figure 3.20
Face/Eye AF Settings.

DETECTING VS. FOCUSING

For some unknown reason, Sony has thrown you a curve ball with this feature. Activating Face/Eye Priority in Autofocus means that your a6400 will *detect* faces and eyes, but doesn't guarantee that it will automatically *focus* on them! The difference is so subtle, you may not notice. What actually happens is that when detection is enabled, the camera will prioritize focus on the face/eye it has found *if that face or eye is within the Focus Area you are using.* So, if you're using the Center focus area and your human subject happens to reside outside that area, the camera will helpfully detect a face/eye and display a frame around it, but will focus *only* on whatever is actually within the focus area.

You might not realize this, particularly if the actual subject you have focused on is located near to, but slightly in front of or behind a human. Further, most of our "people" shots have the person in the center of the frame, and, with some focus modes (such as Wide), the focus area is so large that your human may actually be in an appropriate location, anyway. But however, you should be aware of this distinction.

You *can* guarantee, at least, that Eye AF will be used, regardless of your selected Focus Area, by defining Eye AF to a Custom Key, as described next.

- **Subject Detection.** When set to Human, the camera looks for human faces and eyes. If you choose Animal instead, it looks for animal eyes only; apparently creatures' faces are too varied to detect reliably.

- **Right/Left Eye Select.** Chooses whether to detect the left or right eye of the subject. Note that this feature uses the *subject's* eye, which may be on the opposite side from your perspective (that is, your subject's right eye is on the left side of your frame). (See Figure 3.21.)

Figure 3.21
Choose Right Eye, Left Eye, or Auto selection.

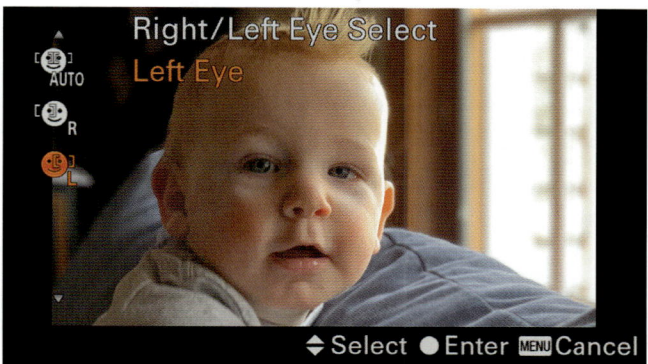

- **Face Detection Frame Display.** The camera automatically shows a small white square around a human eye it is focusing on, and that frame will turn green when the subject is in focus. But you can *also* enable a frame around entire faces with this option. (If you want the frames to display, but disappear after a time, use AF Area Auto Clear, described later in this chapter.)

  Although the eye-focus box is helpful, I find the additional box around the face very useful and leave it on at all times so I know *exactly* what face(s) have been detected. When enabled, a gray selection box appears around detected faces. The box around the face used for autofocus turns white. If there are several faces in the frame and you've registered and prioritized some or all of them, the boxes around the other faces turn reddish-purple. (I'll show you how to register faces later in this chapter.) If you find the boxes distracting, you can turn them off, and face detection, if enabled as described earlier, will still be active.

- **Animal Eye Display.** Again, animal faces are not detected, but you can choose to have the camera place a frame around their eyes when they are found.

Customizing Eye AF

You can customize the eye detection component (Eye AF) of the feature by assigning a custom key to one of these two behaviors, or a different key to each of them. I'll show you how to set up custom keys in Chapter 4.

- **Activate Eye AF with Custom Key.** The Eye AF function can be assigned to a key, and the a6400 will detect and focus on the eye *as long as you are holding down the custom key.* The camera will search for human eyes within the entire frame, regardless of the Focus Area you've selected. Press the shutter release down all the way while holding the key to take the picture. This fixes the potential problem I described in the sidebar above. It also means that if you have a preferred Focus Area setting for a particular shooting session, you don't have to switch to another in order to make Eye AF function properly.

- **Switch Eyes with Custom Key.** If your subjects are always facing you, then setting Right/Left Eye Select to Auto may be your best bet. That's because if you apply the Switch Right/Left Eye behavior to a custom key, should you not like the camera's eye selection, press and hold the defined key to temporarily switch focus to the other eye. Moreover, if you've told the a6400 to always choose the Left (or Right) eye, you can switch to the alternate by pressing the key.

AF with Shutter (Stills)

Options: On/Off

Default: On

My preference: N/A

As you know, a gentle touch on the shutter release button causes the camera to begin focusing when using an autofocus mode. There may be some situations in which you prefer that the camera not re-focus every time you touch the shutter release button, such as when you want to work with *back-button focus*, which I'll explain in detail in Chapter 8.

Let's say you are taking multiple pictures in a laboratory or studio with the subject at the same distance; you have no need to refocus constantly, and there is no need to put an extra burden on the autofocus mechanism and on the battery. But, you don't want to switch to manual focus. Instead, you can set AF w/Shutter to Off. From then on, the camera will never begin to autofocus, or to change the focus when the shutter release is pressed. You can still initiate autofocus by pressing the AF-On button or another key that you've assigned the AF-On function (as I'll describe later under Custom Keys). The AF-On button will start autofocus at any point, independent of the shutter release. Pressing the shutter release still locks *exposure,* unless you've disabled that function, too, using the AEL w/Shutter entry in the Camera Settings I-09 (Exposure 2) entry discussed later in this chapter.

If you happen to be using a Sony A-mount lens on your a6400 with an LA-EA2 or LA-EA4 adapter (described in Chapter 11), you can improve your ability to fine-tune focus using this setting and making a few other adjustments. Just follow these steps:

1. Set AF w/Shutter and Eye-Start AF (discussed shortly) both to Off. The former prevents AF from commencing when the shutter release is pressed halfway, and the latter stops automatic activation of focus when you bring the camera up to your eye.

2. Visit the Custom Key entry in Camera Settings II-08 and assign the AF-On behavior to one key, and Focus Magnifier to another key. I'll show you how to define keys in more detail in Chapter 4.

3. Frame your subject and press your defined AF-On key.

4. Press the defined Focus Magnifier key. The image will enlarge on the display.

5. Rotate the A-mount lens's focus ring to fine-tune focus.

6. Press the shutter release down all the way to take the photo.

Pre-AF (Stills)

Options: Off, On
Default: Off
My preference: N/A

This entry tells the camera to attempt to adjust the focus even before you press the shutter button halfway, giving you a head start that's useful for grab shots. When an image you want to capture appears, you can press the shutter release and take the picture a bit more quickly. However, this pre-focus process uses a lot of juice, depleting your battery more quickly, which is why it is turned off by default. Reserve it for short-term use during quickly unfolding situations where the slight advantage can be useful.

In my tests with the a6400 and various lenses, Pre-AF can be a little slow to respond sometimes, but it does work with all autofocus modes and E-mount optics. If you find Pre-AF to be sluggish, say under low-light conditions, just press the shutter release halfway to commence autofocus manually.

Eye-Start AF (Stills)

Options: On, Off
Default: Off
My preference: Off

The feature is available only when using the EA-LA2 or EA-LA4 adapters and a compatible A-mount lens. These two adapters are the counterparts to the LA1/LA3 (APS-C/full frame) to allow using A-mount lenses on E-mount cameras like the a6400. However, they contain their own semi-translucent mirror phase detect autofocus systems similar to those used in cameras like the

Sony a77 II or a99 II. Both adapters include an autofocus motor built-in, so you can use A-mount lenses that *do not* have built-in motors.

When Eye-Start AF is turned On, the camera will start autofocusing the instant you move the viewfinder to your eye. The display on the LCD vanishes, the camera adjusts autofocus, and, if you're using any Shooting mode other than Manual exposure, it sets the shutter speed and/or aperture so you're ready to take the shot. You don't even need to touch the shutter release button or another button to summon autofocus. Of course, it's not magic. There is a sensor just above the viewfinder window that detects when your face (or anything else) approaches the finder.

This is useful because it increases the odds of capturing a fleeting moment. On the other hand, some people find this feature annoying. When it's On, the camera will begin to autofocus every time a stray hand or other object passes near the viewfinder. Also, if you're wearing the camera around your neck, you may hear a continuous clicking as the camera rubs against your body, triggering the focusing mechanism. When this happens frequently, it will consume a significant amount of battery power.

After experimenting with this feature, you may decide to turn Eye-Start AF off. After you do so, when using the a6400 with the LA2/LA4 adapters, it reverts to its boring old behavior of not initiating focus until you partially depress the shutter button (or another defined button). Naturally, the electronic viewfinder will still activate when your eye (or anything else) is near the sensors (if the FINDER/MONITOR setting, described in Chapter 4, is set to Auto). But you won't get autofocus until you're certain you want AF to start.

AF Area Registration (Stills)

Options: Off, On

Default: Off

My preference: On

This is an absolute killer feature for sports photographers, as it allows you to switch from your current focus point to a pre-registered point—and then back to your original point—just by pressing a custom key. Say you're covering a baseball game and frequently alternate between photographing the batter or some other position and first base, where a lot of action takes place. If you've registered first base (as I'll describe shortly), you're free to focus elsewhere and then, when the batter makes contact and begins running toward first (or the pitcher decides to throw to first to cut off a base runner who's taken a lead), you can press the defined key and the focus point will instantly move back to the registered first base location within the frame.

To use this feature, just follow these steps:

1. **Activate AF Area Registration.** Navigate to this menu entry and choose On, then press the center button to confirm. A message will appear reminding you to register a specific focus area. I'll explain how to do that shortly. Press the center button again to exit to the menu.

2. **Access Custom Keys (Stills).** To relocate the focus point to a registered position, you'll need to define a custom button to do that. Access the Camera Settings II-08 (Custom Operation 1) menu and select the Custom Key (Stills) entry at the top of the list. Press the center button to view the available buttons that can be customized.

3. **Define a custom button.** Select an unused custom button to use and press the center button to view the behavior choices available. Several screens listing available functions can be displayed and each of them correspond to the choices available in the a6400's menu pages. Use the left/right buttons to scroll to the AF2 page for your selected key and choose how you want to enable the switch to the registered autofocus point. The three relevant options are as follows:

   • **Registered AF Area Hold.** Pressing the button switches to the registered location *only* while you hold the button down. When you release the custom key the focus point returns to your previous focus point. This option is useful if you want to be able to switch to the registered area only temporarily.

   • **Registered AF Area Toggle.** Press and release the button to switch to the registered location and press it back to return to your previous focus point. Use this if you think you'll need to take several consecutive images using the registered point. Toggle is the only available option for the left, right, and down keys.

   • **Registered AF Area+AF On.** When the custom key is pressed the focus point switches to the registered area and autofocus is initiated. When you release the custom key, the focus point returns to its previous location. If you've registered first base you can then move the focus point to home plate and continue to capture the batter's efforts. Then, if action unfolds at first base, press the defined button and the a6400 will switch to your registered focus point and focus. You can then continue to hold the key while pressing the shutter release down to take the picture. Release the button and the focus point returns to home plate. (You can avoid the need to hold down the button if you're using back-button focus, which decouples the AF activation feature from the shutter release.) This *sounds* complicated if you don't know how back-button focus works, but I'll explain it in more detail in Chapter 8.

4. **Registered focus frame appears.** When the defined custom key is pressed, the focus frame and points will flash in the viewfinder and on the LCD monitor.

AF Area Registration cannot be used when shooting movies or S&Q video, when using digital zoom, Lock-on AF, while focus is locked, or when you are focusing using the lens's focus ring or the a6400's Touch Focus feature.

Delete Registered AF Area (Stills)

Options: Delete, Cancel

Default: Cancel

My preference: N/A

This is the first entry in the Camera Settings I-07 (AF3) menu. (See Figure 3.22.) Use it to delete a registered focus area. That prevents the camera from shifting to the previously defined area if you accidentally press the defined custom key.

AF Area Auto Clear

Options: Off, On

Default: Off

My preference: Off

This setting controls whether the focus area is shown all the time as you shoot, or whether it disappears a short time after focus is achieved. Choose On if you prefer having an uncluttered screen while you shoot. I prefer to have focus information available at all times, so I leave this setting at its default Off value. When active, it will also hide Face/Eye detection frames.

Display Continuous AF Area

Options: On, Off

Default: On

My preference: On

This item determines whether the previewing display on the monitor or EVF shows the active Wide or Zone focus areas when you're using Continuous AF. It has no effect on their display if you're using Center or Flexible Spot in Continuous AF area modes, or autofocus modes other than AF-C.

Sometimes too much information can be distracting. That's especially true in AF-C mode, because if you've framed a moving subject, the camera can continue to change the active focus areas if your

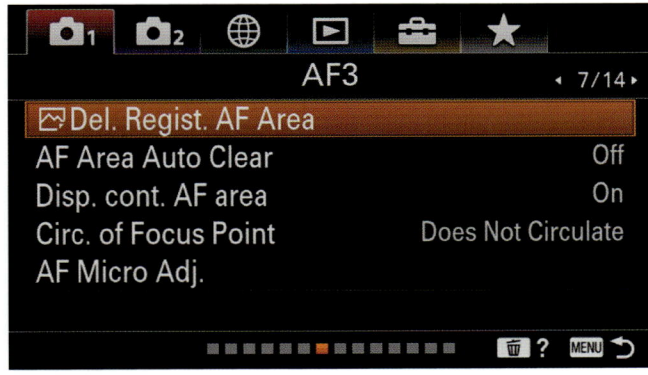

Figure 3.22
Camera Settings I-07 (AF3) menu.

subject is moving. In Wide mode, you may be treated to a dancing array of green rectangles squirming around on your screen as the a6400 focuses and refocuses in anticipation of you eventually pressing the shutter release all the way down and taking a picture. I think that the constantly shifting focus requires less continual feedback about what focus areas are being used, so you may want to switch the feature off. In my case, I don't mind the display, and I tend to leave it on most of the time, even though it consumes a little more battery power.

Circulation of Focus Point

Options: Does Not Circulate, Circulate

Default: Does Not Circulate

My preference: N/A

This setting simply determines whether you can only move the focus point within the image frame, or whether, when it reaches the left, right, top, or bottom edges it wraps around to the opposite side. Unless you played too much Pac-Man in your youth, you will probably prefer Does Not Circulate.

AF Micro Adjustment

Options: AF Adjustment Setting, Amount, Clear

Default: None

My preference: N/A

If you've sprung for the $300 to $400 (in the US) required to purchase the optional LA-EA2 or LA-EA4 mount adapters and are using A-mount lenses on your a6400, you may find that some slight autofocus adjustment is necessary to fine-tune your lens.

This menu item allows choosing a value from –20 (to focus closer to the camera) to +20 (to change the focus point to farther away). You can enable/disable the feature, and clear the value set for each lens. The camera stores the value you dial in for the lens currently mounted on the camera and can log up to 30 different lenses (but each lens must be different; you can't register two copies of the same lens). Once you've "used up" the available slots, you'll need to mount a lesser-used lens and clear the value for that lens to free up a memory slot. This adjustment works reliably only with Sony, Minolta, and Konica-Minolta A-mount lenses. I'll show you how to use this feature in Chapter 12.

A-MOUNT ADAPTERS ONLY

You'll note that no such adjustment is supplied for E-mount lenses. That's because the a6400 calculates focus using *actual data collected at the sensor*—whether operating in contrast detect or phase detect mode. Front- or back-focus issues don't exist. The LA-EA2 and LA-EA4 adapters, on the other hand, use their separate SLT-style AF sensors, and slight alignment issues *can* make a difference. Sony recognizes this and has kindly provided this feature.

Exposure Compensation

Options: From +5 to –5

Default: 0.0

My preference: N/A

This is the first entry on the Camera Settings I-08 (Exposure 1) page (see Figure 3.23). It is one of three ways to specify exposure compensation:

- **This menu entry.** Here you can adjust EV values from +5 to –5 using the directional buttons, or by rotating the control wheel or rear dial.
- **Function menu.** Press the Fn button and navigate to the Exposure Compensation icon (located by default in the top row, fourth from the left). Use the same controls described above.
- **Exposure Compensation (Down) button.** Probably the quickest way is to elect to use the physical button and the control wheel, rear dial, and directional buttons (once the adjustment screen has appeared).

Scroll until you reach the value for the amount of compensation you want to set to make your shots lighter (with positive values) or darker (with negative values). Only values between –3 and +3 will be reflected on the display; higher values will be applied to the taken image, however. When shooting movies, only +2 to –2 values are valid. I'll discuss exposure compensation in more detail in Chapter 9.

Remember that any compensation you set will stay in place until you change it, even if the camera has been powered off in the meantime. It's worth developing a habit of checking your display to see if any positive or negative exposure compensation is still in effect; return to 0.0 before you start shooting. The amount is shown numerically in the EVF, and on a scale in the viewfinder.

Exposure compensation cannot be used when the camera is set to Intelligent/Superior Auto, or when using Scene modes. In Manual exposure mode, the EV settings only apply if ISO has been set to ISO Auto. The EV changes you make with the menus will be in either 1/3 or 1/2 EV increments, depending on the step size you specify in the Exposure Step entry, which I'll explain shortly.

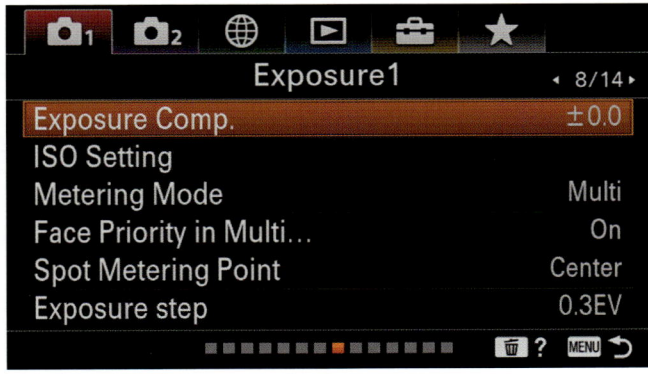

Figure 3.23

The Camera Settings I-08 (Exposure 1) menu.

ISO Setting

Options: ISO Auto, Fixed settings from options from 100 to 102400; Multi Frame Noise Reduction
Default: ISO Auto
My preference: ISO Auto, set to ISO 100 Minimum/ISO 1600 Maximum

This menu item can also be accessed by pressing the right (ISO) button on the control wheel. This entry can be used to specify the ISO (sensor sensitivity) but not when you're using Panorama mode or fully automatic (Intelligent/Superior Auto) and scene modes since the camera always uses ISO Auto. Note too that ISO Auto is not available in M mode; you must set a numerical value. Settings up to 102400 are available when shooting stills, and up to 32000 in Movie mode. (If you've selected a higher sensitivity when you switch to Movie mode, the a6400 will automatically change to 32000.) I'll discuss ISO in more detail in Chapter 7.

The sub-menu that pops up when you select this entry includes three choices: ISO, ISO Range Limit, and ISO Auto Minimum Shutter Speed.

ISO

Your choices in this screen include the following:

■ **Multi Frame NR (Noise Reduction).** The camera takes 4 or 12 shots and first aligns them (because, hand-held, there is probably some camera movement between shots) and sorts out the image pixels that are common to all the shots (and which remain more or less the same in each individual shot) from the random visual noise pixels (which will be different in each shot, because they are *random*). It then creates an image that (in theory) uses only the image pixels, with much less visual noise. The processing takes a few seconds, so you wouldn't want to use it when you plan to take multiple shots within a short period of time.

To activate Multi Frame NR, highlight the entry (which is by default confusingly labeled ISO Auto, rather than Multi Frame Noise Reduction). You can then press the right button to high-light the left option at the bottom of the figure and set either ISO Auto, or select a fixed ISO sensitivity. Then press the right button and choose the amount of multi frame noise reduction to be applied (High or Standard). The camera will take and combine 12 shots if you choose High, and 4 shots if you select Standard.

Multi Frame NR can only be used when Image Quality is set to JPEG, and is unavailable when D-Range Optimizer or Auto HDR are activated. Note: the camera also offers a Hand-held Twilight scene mode, which doesn't let you choose shutter speed, ISO setting, white balance, and other parameters, but produces comparable (or sometimes even better) images. If your image suits the automated settings of the Hand-held Twilight mode, it's certainly faster and requires fewer decisions from you.

■ **ISO Auto.** The true Auto ISO setting is the second entry from the top. You can press the right button and choose a minimum ISO to be used as well as the maximum ISO applied (which prevents the camera from taking a clutch of pictures at, say, ISO 25600, unbeknownst to you). For general shooting, I use ISO 100 and ISO 1600 for my limits and raise the upper end to ISO 3200 or 6400 for indoor subjects (especially sports, which can benefit from faster shutter speeds and/or smaller f/stops). (See Figure 3.24.) **Note:** If you select minimum and maximum ISO here, it will also be applied to Multi Frame Noise Reduction when you choose ISO Auto instead of a fixed sensitivity for that mode.

■ **Fixed ISO settings.** You can Select ISO settings from 100 to 102400, and the camera will take all its shots at that sensitivity. Strictly speaking, ISO 100 is the lowest real sensitivity the camera can produce; that's the "native" sensitivity of the sensor. Use the lowest speeds when you really need say, to use a wider f/stop in very bright conditions, or when you want to use a slower shutter speed to intentionally produce blur of, perhaps, a waterfall. A neutral-density filter attached to your lens can also reduce the amount of light reaching the sensor. The higher sensitivities are lofty enough to meet almost any need, at the expense of additional noise ("grain"), increased contrast, and loss of detail.

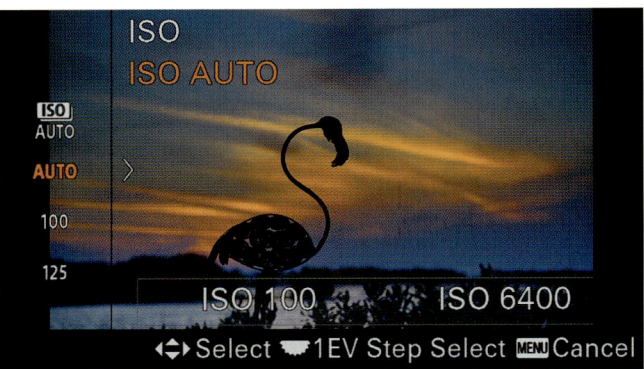

Figure 3.24
Auto ISO allows specifying minimum and maximum ISO sensitivity.

ISO Range Limit

If you want to intentionally restrict the ISO settings that are available (say, to avoid accidentally using settings you find are not usable from a quality standpoint), you can do that here. You can specify the minimum and maximum available ISO settings from 100–102400. The a6400 does let you set the minimum and maximum to the same figure (thus locking you into a single ISO sensitivity), but it is intelligent enough to keep you from setting a maximum that is lower than your minimum.

ISO Auto Minimum Shutter Speed

Use this sub-entry with the a6400 to specify the shutter speed that activates the ISO Auto feature described above. You'll want to use ISO Auto most frequently to avoid having the camera select a blur-inducing slow shutter speed when using P (Program Auto) or A (Aperture Priority) modes. (*You always select the shutter speed yourself in S and M modes.*) Depending on how well you can hand-hold the camera, or your level of trust for the lens and/or in-body image stabilization, you can choose which shutter speed you deem "too slow," and your a6400 will boost the ISO sensitivity as required when ISO Auto is active. You can choose from values that the camera calculates, or supply a specific shutter speed, below which Auto ISO will start to do its stuff.

The camera-calculated minimum speeds are very cool because they are based on the focal length of your lens, giving you faster minimum speeds with telephoto lenses, and longer minimum speeds with wide angles. You can choose general settings or choose specific shutter speeds. The Fast and Faster settings increase the minimum shutter speed by 1 and 2 stops (respectively) from the standard setting for a particular focal length. The Slow and Slower settings lower the minimum shutter speed for that focal length by 1 and 2 stops (respectively).

- **General settings.** Highlight the top entry in the screen, then press the left/right buttons to select one of the following options:
  - **Faster/Fast.** The a6400 will activate ISO Auto at shutter speeds that are faster than the "standard" setting (which is calculated individually based on the focal length or zoom setting of your lens). This is a more conservative setting.
  - **STD (Standard).** The camera detects the current focal length/zoom setting and selects a minimum shutter speed that takes into account the effect the focal length has in magnifying the degree of blur. That is, a 200mm lens calls for higher shutter speeds than, say, a 50mm lens.
  - **Slow/Slower.** This is a more liberal setting that allows slightly slower shutter speeds than specified by STD before ISO Auto kicks in. Use if you have an extraordinarily steady hand.
- **1/4000th–30 seconds.** You can bypass the camera's internal algorithm mumbo-jumbo and scroll down the list to select a shutter speed that you want to use to activate ISO Auto. If you choose 1/4000th second, ISO Auto will effectively be active all the time. Select 30 seconds, and ISO Auto will not activate at all.

Metering Mode

Options: Multi, Center, Spot (Standard, Large), Entire Screen Averaging, Highlight

Default: Multi

My preference: Multi

The metering mode determines how the camera will calculate the exposure for any scene. The camera is set by default to Multi, which is a multi-zone or multi-segment metering approach. No other options are available in Intelligent Auto mode or when you're using digital zoom. You'll find more information on these modes in Chapter 7, where exposure considerations are discussed in detail.

- **Multi.** Evaluates 1,200 individual segments of the scene using advanced algorithms; often, it will be able to ignore a very bright area or a very dark area that would affect the overall exposure. It's also likely to produce a decent (if not ideal) exposure with a light-toned scene such as a snowy landscape, especially on a sunny day. While it's not foolproof, Multi is the most suitable when you must shoot quickly and don't have time for serious exposure considerations. **Note:** When Face Priority in Multi Metering (discussed next) is On, this metering mode will base exposure on faces detected, if any.

- **Center.** Center-weighted metering primarily considers the brightness in a large central area of the scene, while still taking into account the average value of the rest of the frame. This approach ensures that a bright sky that's high in the frame, for example, will not severely affect the exposure. However, if the central area is very light or very dark in tone, your photo is likely to be too dark or too bright (unless you use exposure compensation).

- **Spot.** When using Spot metering, the camera measures only the brightness in a very small central area of the scene; again, if that area is very light or very dark in tone, your exposure will not be satisfactory; it's important to spot meter an area of a medium tone. Use this mode to zero in on a specific area of your image, such as a performer on a darkened stage.

  - **Size of spot.** When Spot is highlighted, press the left/right controls to change from a standard-sized spot to a larger spot.

  - **Position of spot.** By default, the metering spot is placed in the center of the frame. You can optionally link the spot to the current focus point using the Spot Metering Point entry in the Camera Settings I-08 (Exposure 1) menu, discussed shortly.

- **Entire Screen Averaging.** The a6400 calculates exposure based on the average brightness of the entire frame. This setting is useful if the overall scene has similar brightness values throughout; you can recompose slightly, or your subject can move within the frame and the exposure will not change.

■ **Highlight.** In this mode, the camera adjusts the exposure to avoid blowing out the highlights, if at all possible. Use this setting if the highlights of a scene are the most important and you don't care if some shadow detail is lost. You can give Highlight metering some extra muscle by activating D-Range Optimizer or Auto HDR. The a6400 will segment the image into small areas and analyze the difference between the light and dark areas, preserving the highlights but also keeping as much shadow detail as possible.

Face Priority in Multi Metering

Options: On, Off

Default: On

My preference: Off

When you choose On, this setting tells the a6400 to adjust its Multi metering to prioritize exposure for any faces in the scene. Select Off, and the standard 1,200-zone evaluative metering system is used. For most shooting I disable this feature, as Multi metering does a good job of exposing so that faces and other parts of the image are well exposed. I turn it on when I am photographing individuals or groups and their surroundings are extra-bright or dark and I want to make sure the faces receive optimal exposure.

Spot Metering Point

Options: Center, Focus Point Link

Default: Center

My preference: Focus Point Link

If Focus Area is set to Flexible Spot or Expand Flexible Spot, and Spot metering is selected as the Metering Mode, then the Spot metering area can be linked to the focus point, rather than locked in the center. Just choose Focus Point Link here. If Center is selected instead, the focus point is locked in the center of the frame.

Note: Focus Point Link also works when Focus Area is set to Lock-On Flexible Spot or Expand Lock-On Flexible Spot, but the spot metering area is moved to the starting area and does not move once tracking begins. All these AF nuances are explained in Chapter 8.

Exposure Step

Options: 1/3 EV, 1/2 EV

Default: 1/3 EV

My preference: 1/3 EV

This setting specifies the size of the exposure change for both exposure compensation and flash exposure compensation. The 1/3-stop default allows fine-tuning exposure more precisely, while selecting 1/2 EV lets you make larger adjustments more quickly, which is useful when you are trying to capture more dramatic exposure changes. The actual difference between 1/3-stop and 1/2-stop changes is relatively small, so this setting is primarily a convenience feature that's most useful when you plan to, say, use exposure compensation and want to move from 0.0 to plus or minus several whole stops in bigger jumps. I'm never in that much of a hurry, so I opt for the greater precision of the 1/3 EV steps.

Autoexposure Lock with Shutter (Stills)

Options: Auto, On, Off

Default: Auto

My preference: On

This item, the first in the Camera Settings I-09 (Exposure 2) menu (see Figure 3.25), allows the a6400 to lock the exposure (as well as the focus in AF-S mode) when you apply light pressure to the shutter release button. Point the camera at your primary subject and maintain contact with the button while re-framing for a better composition. This technique will ensure that both focus and exposure are optimized for the primary subject. There are three modes to choose from:

- **Auto.** Adjusts focus and then locks in exposure in AF-S mode when you press the shutter release down halfway. In AF-A mode, the camera will do the same thing if the subject is stationary. If the subject is moving (that is, the camera switches to AF-C mode) or you are shooting continuously in burst mode, exposure is *not* locked. However, even if Auto is activated, pressing the AEL lock button overrides this behavior.

- **On.** Exposure is locked when you press the shutter release halfway.

- **Off.** Pressing the shutter release halfway locks only focus. Exposure is not locked when you press the shutter release halfway, and exposure will be adjusted automatically during continuous shooting. Exposure isn't locked until you press the shutter release down all the way to take the photo, or you press the AEL lock button. Use this setting when you prefer to lock exposure manually using the AEL button or when taking the actual picture.

  You might want to choose the Off option to lock focus on one subject in the scene while locking the exposure for an entirely different part of the scene. To use this technique, focus on the most important subject and keep the focus locked by keeping your finger on the shutter release button while you recompose. You can then point the lens at an entirely different area of the scene to read the exposure, and lock in the exposure with pressure on the AEL button. Finally, reframe for the most pleasing composition and take the photo.

  In your image, the primary subject will be in sharpest focus while the exposure will be optimized for the area that you metered. This technique makes the most sense when your primary subject is very light in tone like a snowman or very dark in tone like a black Lab dog. Subjects of that type can lead to exposure errors, so you might want to expose for an area that's a middle tone, such as grass. I'll discuss exposure in detail in Chapter 5; then, the value of this menu option will be more apparent.

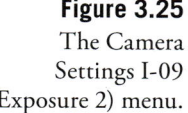

Figure 3.25
The Camera Settings I-09 (Exposure 2) menu.

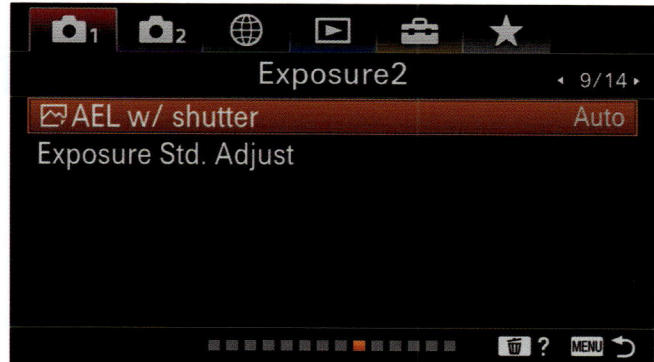

Exposure Standard Adjustment

Options: Adjust Multi, Center, Spot, Entire Screen Averaging, or Highlight metering

Default: None

My preference: None

This setting is a powerful adjustment that allows you to dial in a specific amount of exposure compensation that will be applied to every photo you take using each of the five metering modes. No more can you complain, "My a6400 always underexposes by 1/3 stop!" If that is the case, and the phenomenon is consistent, you can use this menu adjustment to compensate.

Exposure compensation is usually a better idea (does your camera *really* underexpose that consistently?), but this setting does allow you to "recalibrate" your camera yourself. You can fine-tune exposure separately for each of the metering modes. However, you have no indication that fine-tuning has been made, so you'll need to remember what you've done. After all, you someday might discover that your camera is consistently *over*exposing images by 1/3 stop, not realizing that your Exposure Standard Adjustment setting is the culprit.

In practice, it's rare that the a6400 will *consistently* provide the wrong exposure in any of the five metering modes, especially Multi metering, which can alter exposure dramatically based on the camera's internal database of typical scenes. This feature may be most useful for Spot metering, if you always take a reading off the same type of subject, such as a human face or gray card. Should you find that the gray card readings, for example, always differ from what you would prefer, go ahead and fine-tune optimal exposure for Spot metering, and use that to read your gray cards. To use this feature:

1. **Select Exposure Standard Adjustment.** Select this menu entry from the Camera Settings I-09 (Exposure 2) page.

2. **Consider yourself warned.** In the screen that appears, choose OK after carefully reading the warning that Sony insists on showing you every time this option is activated.

3. **Select metering mode to correct.** Choose Multi metering, Center, Spot, Entire Screen Averaging, or Highlight-weighted metering in the screen that follows by highlighting your choice and pressing the center button. You can set the standard adjustment separately for each exposure mode.

4. **Specify amount of correction.** Press the up/down buttons to dial in the exposure compensation you want to apply. You can specify compensation up to + 1 or –1 stops in increments of 1/6 stop, half as large a change as conventional exposure compensation. This is truly *fine-tuning.*

5. **Confirm your change.** Press the center button when finished to return to the previous menu. You can repeat the action to fine-tune the other exposure modes if necessary. When finished, press MENU to exit. **Note:** the values you set will survive using the Reset option of the Setting Reset entry in the Setup 7 menu but will be canceled if you choose Initialize instead.

Flash Mode

Options: Flash Off, Auto Flash, Fill Flash, Slow Sync., Rear Sync.

Default: Depends on shooting mode

My preference: N/A

The first entry in the Camera Settings I-10 (Flash) menu (see Figure 3.26), this item offers options for the several flash modes that are available. Not all the modes can be selected at all times, as shown in Table 3.3, which also tells you whether Flash Exposure Compensation and Red-Eye Reduction (described shortly) are available. I'll describe what these modes do, and the use of flash in detail in Chapter 12.

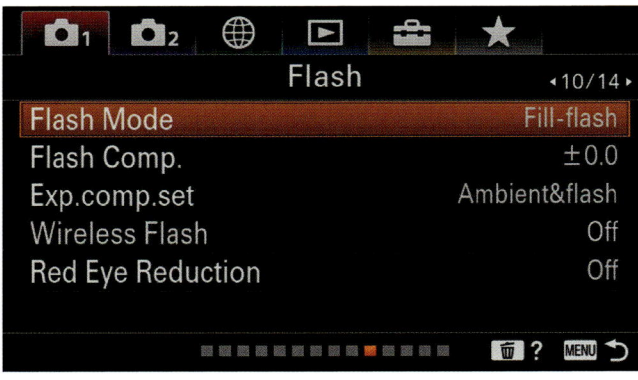

Figure 3.26
Flash Mode is the first entry in the Camera Settings I-10 (Flash) menu.

Table 3.3 Flash Modes

Exposure Mode	Flash Off	Auto Flash	Fill Flash	Slow Sync.	Rear Sync.	Flash Exposure Compensation	Red-Eye Reduction
Intelligent /Superior Auto	●	●	●				●
Program Auto			●	●	●	●	●
Aperture Priority			●	●	●	●	●
Shutter Priority			●	●	●	●	●
Manual Exposure			●	●	●	●	●

Flash Compensation

Options: −3 to +3 in 1/3 or 1/2 EV steps

Default: 0.0

My preference: N/A

This feature controls the flash output. It allows you to dial in plus compensation for a brighter flash effect or minus compensation for a subtler flash effect. If you take a flash photo and it's too dark or too light, access this menu item. Scroll up/down to set a value that will increase flash intensity (plus setting) or reduce the flash output (minus setting) by up to three EV (exposure value) steps. You can select between 1/3 and 1/2 EV increments in the Exposure Step entry described later in this chapter. Flash compensation is not available when using Intelligent/Superior Auto, Sweep Panorama, or Scene Selection. It is a "sticky" setting so be sure to set it back to zero after you finish shooting. I'll discuss this and many other flash-related topics in detail in Chapter 13.

Exposure Compensation Settings

Options: Ambient & Flash, Ambient Only

Default: Ambient & Flash

My preference: Ambient & Flash

When this item is at the default setting, any exposure compensation value that you set will apply to both the ambient light exposure and to the flash exposure when using flash. You'd want to stick to this option in flash photography when you find that both the available-light exposure and the flash exposure produce an image that's too dark or too light. Setting plus or minus exposure compensation will affect both. However, in another situation when using flash, you might want to control only the brightness of the light exposure and not the flash exposure.

The Ambient Only option allows you to control only the brightness of the background such as a city skyline behind a friend when you're taking flash photos at night in a scene of this type. Setting exposure compensation will now allow you to get a brighter or a darker background (at a + and – setting, respectively) without affecting the brightness of your primary subject who will be exposed by the light from the flash. (Any exposure compensation you set will have no effect on the flash intensity.)

Wireless Flash

Options: Off, On
Default: Off
My preference: N/A

Sony is still playing catch-up in the electronic flash arena, having supported only optically triggered wireless flash until recently, but now offers radio-controlled wireless flash using the Sony AF-WRC1M/FA-WRR1 wireless radio commander/receiver combination or radio-compatible external flash units like the Sony HVL-45RM and HVL-F60RM. This entry allows you to enable/disable both optical and radio wireless modes. I'll explain these and other flash options in Chapter 12.

Red Eye Reduction

Options: On, Off
Default: Off
My preference: Off

When flash is used in a dark location, red-eye is common in pictures of people, and especially of animals. Unfortunately, your camera is unable, on its own, to totally *eliminate* the red-eye effects that occur when an electronic flash bounces off the retinas of your subject's eyes and into the camera lens. The effect is worst under low-light conditions (exactly when you might be using a flash) as the pupils expand to allow more light to reach the retinas. The best you can hope for with this option is to *reduce* or minimize the red-eye effect. After all, the feature is called red-eye *reduction,* not red-eye *elimination.*

It's fairly easy to remove red-eye effects in an image editor (some image importing programs will do it for you automatically as the pictures are transferred from your camera or memory card to your computer). But, it's better not to have glowing red eyes in your photos in the first place.

To use this feature, you first have to attach an external flash to the multi interface shoe. When Red Eye Reduction is turned on through this menu item, the flash issues a few brief bursts prior to taking the photo, theoretically causing your subjects' pupils to contract, reducing the red-eye syndrome. It works best if your subject is looking toward the flash. Like any such system, its success ratio is not great.

White Balance

Options: Auto WB, Daylight, Shade, Cloudy, Incandescent, Fluorescent (4 options), Flash, Underwater Auto, C.Temp/Filter, Custom 1–3, Custom Setup
Default: Auto WB (AWB)
My preference: AWB

This is the first entry in the Camera Settings I-11 (Color/WB/Image Processing) menu. (See Figure 3.27.) The various light sources that can illuminate a scene have light that's of different colors. A household lamp using an old-type (not daylight balanced) bulb, for example, produces light that's quite amber in color. Sunlight around noon is close to white but it's quite red at sunrise and sunset; on cloudy days, the light has a bluish bias. The light from fluorescents can vary widely, depending on the type of tube or bulb you're using. Some lamps, including sodium vapor and mercury vapor, produce light of unusual colors.

The Auto White Balance feature works well, particularly outdoors and under artificial lighting that's daylight balanced. Even under lamps that produce light with a slight color cast such as green or blue, you should often get a pleasing overall color balance. One advantage of using AWB is that you don't have to worry about changing it for your next shooting session; there's no risk of having the camera set for, say, incandescent light, when you're shooting outdoors on a sunny day.

The a6400 also lets you choose a specific white balance option—often called a preset—that's appropriate for various typical lighting conditions, because the AWB feature does not always succeed in providing an accurate or the most pleasing overall color balance.

Figure 3.27
The Camera Settings I-11 (Color/WB/Image Processing1) menu.

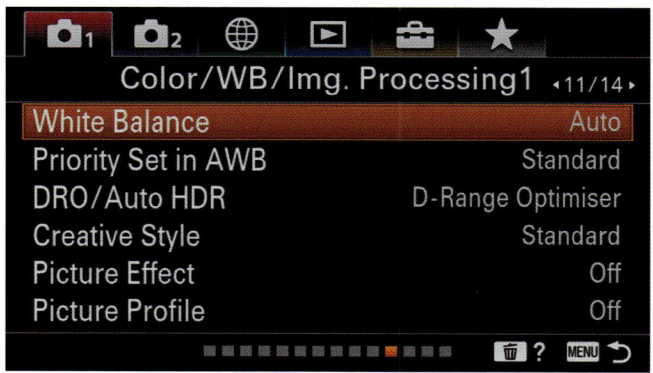

Your choices include:

- **Daylight.** Sets white balance for average daylight.
- **Shade.** Compensates for the slightly bluer tones encountered in open shade conditions.
- **Cloudy.** Adjusts for the colder tones of a cloudy day.
- **Incandescent.** Indoor illumination is typically much warmer than daylight, so this setting compensates for the excessive red bias.
- **Fluorescent (four types).** You can choose from Warm White, Cool White, Day White, and Daylight fluorescent lighting.
- **Flash.** Suitable for shooting with the a6400's built-in flash or an attached and powered-up external electronic flash unit.
- **Underwater Auto.** Although you may find a vendor offering an underwater housing for your a6400, it's more likely that your "underwater" shooting will involve photographing fish and other sea life through the glass of an aquarium of the commercial variety. This setting partially tames the blue-green tones you can encounter in such environments (see Figure 3.28, top), producing a warmer tone that some (but not all) may prefer (see Figure 3.28, bottom).
- **C.Temp/Filter/Custom/Custom Setup.** These advanced features provide even better results once you've learned how to fine-tune color balance settings, which I'll explain in Chapter 9.

When any of the presets are selected, you can press the right button to produce a screen that allows you to adjust the color along the amber (yellow)/blue axis, the green/magenta axis, or both, to fine-tune color rendition even more precisely. The screen shown in Figure 3.29 will appear, and you can use the up/down and left/right controls to move the origin point in the chart shown at lower right to any bias you want. The amount of your amber/blue and/or green/magenta bias are shown numerically to the left of the chart. You'll find more information about White Balance in Chapter 9.

My recommendation: If you shoot in RAW capture, though, you don't have to be quite as concerned about white balance, because you can easily adjust it in your software after the fact. Here again, as with ISO and exposure compensation, the white balance item is not available in Intelligent Auto mode; the camera defaults to Auto White Balance.

Priority Setting in AWB

Options: Standard, Ambience, White
Default: Standard
My preference: Standard

You can finally exercise some control over Auto White Balance. This setting allows you to fine-tune how AWB works, producing "automatic" color balance that may more closely suit your personal taste than the default balance the a6400 is initially set for.

Figure 3.28
The Underwater Auto setting can reduce the blue cast of typical subsurface photos.

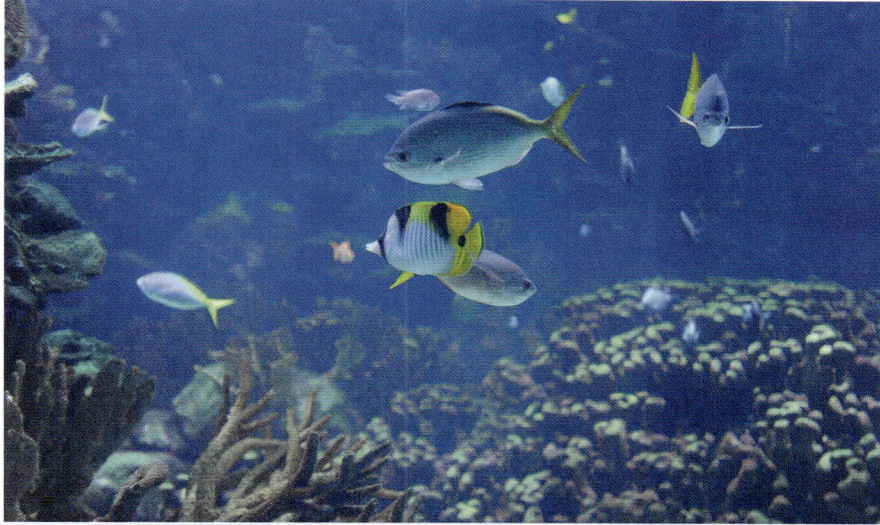

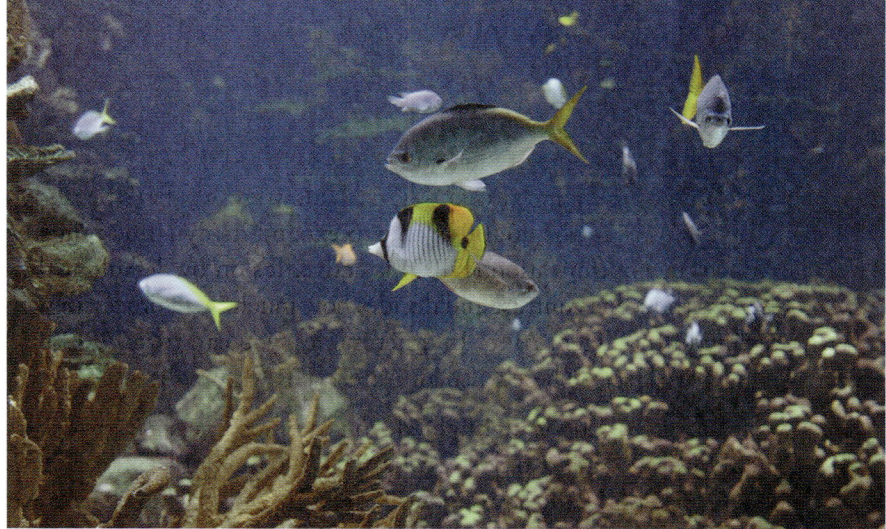

Figure 3.29
Fine-tune the color bias of your images using this screen.

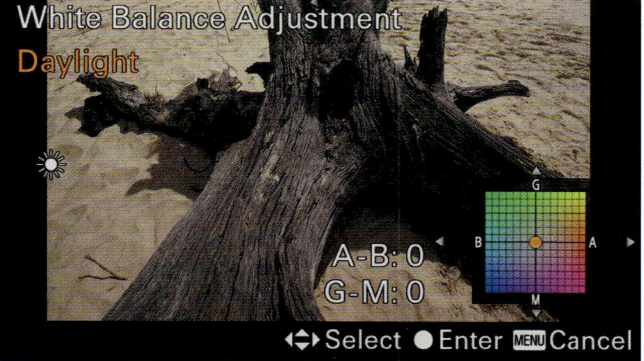

You have three choices:

- **Standard.** The camera makes its own adjustments for white balance, based on its interpretation of the colors it sees in your scenes. The a6400 does a pretty good job of telling daylight from incandescent illumination and responding accordingly, and a fair job with other forms of illumination. This will work for you most of the time, although you'll want to use one of the presets or other white balance customizing features described above when appropriate.

- **Ambience.** Detects the light source and, if a naturally warm source is identified, will bias the color to keep warmer tones. Your interior photos, fireside chats, and similar scenes can keep their rosy colors. An indicator on your shooting settings screens will indicate that Ambience (or White) bias is being used.

- **White.** The reverse of Ambience, this setting tries to preserve whites in scenes with warm color temperatures.

DRO/Auto HDR

Options: DRO Off; DRO Auto (Auto or Levels 1–5); Auto HDR (Auto or 1–6 EV intervals)
Default: DRO Auto
My preference: DRO Off

The brightness/darkness range of many images is so broad that the sensor has difficulty capturing detail in both bright highlight areas and dark shadow areas. That's because a sensor has a limited dynamic range. However, the a6400 is able to expand its dynamic range using extra processing when dynamic range optimization (DRO) is active. It's on by default at the Auto level where the camera evaluates the scene contrast and decides how much extra processing to apply; this is the only available setting in Intelligent Auto. In other modes, you can turn DRO off, or set it manually to one of five intensity levels. There's also an Auto HDR feature discussed in a moment.

When the DRO Auto option is highlighted, you can press the left/right controls to set the DRO to a specific level of processing, from 1 (weakest) to 5 (strongest). You'll find that DRO can lighten shadow areas; it may darken bright highlight areas too, but not to the same extent. By level 3, the photos you take will exhibit much lighter shadow areas for an obviously wide dynamic range; DRO Auto will never provide such an intense increase in shadow detail.

In addition, you'll find the Auto HDR (High Dynamic Range) feature, available only in the P, A, S, or M shooting modes (Program, Aperture Priority, Shutter Priority, and Manual). If you select this option instead of DRO, the camera will take three photos, each at a different exposure level, and it will combine them into one HDR photo with lighter shadow areas and darker highlight areas than in a conventional shot. You can control the intensity of this feature. After scrolling to Auto HDR, press the left/right controls to choose an exposure increment between shots, from 1.0 to 6.0 EV. The one you select will specify the difference in exposure among the three photos it will shoot: 1 EV (minor exposure difference) for a slight HDR effect to 6 EV (a huge exposure difference) for a dramatic high dynamic range effect. If you don't choose a level, the camera selects an HDR level for you. I'll provide tips and examples of DRO and HDR in Chapter 7.

Notes: DRO and Auto HDR are both automatically set to Off when using Picture Effects or Picture Profiles. Auto HDR cannot be used at all with Intelligent Auto or any scene mode; DRO is disabled when using Sunset, Night Scene, or Night Portrait scene modes. In other scene modes, DRO is set to Auto.

Creative Style

Options: Standard, Vivid, Neutral, Portrait, Landscape, Black & White; adjustable versions of these, plus Clear, Deep, Light, Sunset, Night, Autumn, and Sepia

Default: Standard

My preference: Standard

This option gives you six basic Creative Styles with fixed combinations of contrast, saturation, and sharpness. Each of these basic styles display a prefix number on the screen: 1: Standard, 2: Vivid, 3: Neutral, 4: Portrait, 5: Landscape, 6: B&W. Each of the basic styles *also* appears a second time (without the number prefix) and with the addition of Clear, Deep, Light, Night, Autumn, Sepia, and Sunset. You can adjust the contrast, saturation, and sharpness of each style using the left/right controls to choose an attribute, and the up/down controls to adjust that attribute. You can apply Creative Styles when you are using any shooting mode except Intelligent Auto.

Sony has made Creative Styles a little confusing by providing both a numbered listing of the six basic styles, plus a second, unnumbered list that includes the basic styles and seven more. But there is method to this madness. You can adjust *all 13* styles to suit your preferences. Effectively, that means you can have *two* Standard/Vivid/Neutral/Portrait/Landscape/B&W styles, both the basic, numbered version and the non-numbered variation. I discuss the use of Creative Styles in Chapter 9.

Picture Effect

Options: Off, Toy Camera, Pop Color, Posterization, Retro Photo, Soft High-key, Partial Color, High Contrast Monochrome, Soft Focus, HDR Painting, Rich-Tone Monochrome, Miniature, Watercolor, Illustration

Default: Off

My preference: Off

This camera feature allows you to create JPEG photos with special effects provided by the camera's processor in JPEG capture mode (but not in RAW or RAW & JPEG) when the camera is in P, A, S, or M mode. It's not available for use when shooting movies. Scroll through the options in this item and watch the change in the preview image display that reflects the effect that each option can provide if you activate it; if you find one that looks interesting, press the center button or touch the shutter release button to confirm your choice and return to shooting mode.

When some effects are highlighted, left/right triangles will appear next to their label, indicating you can press the left/right keys to select an option available for that effect. Not all provide this extra benefit.

- **Toy Camera.** Produces images like you might get with a Diana or Holga "plastic" camera, with vignetted corners, image blurring, and bright, saturated colors. It's at Normal by default, but when you press the left/right buttons you can select Normal, Cool, Warm, Green, or Magenta.
- **Pop Color.** This setting adds a lot of saturation to the colors, making them especially vivid and rich looking. When used with subjects that have a lot of bright colors, the effect can be dramatic. Duller subjects gain a more "normal" appearance; try using this setting on an overcast day to see what I mean.
- **Posterization.** This option produces a vivid, high-contrast image that emphasizes the primary colors (as shown in Figure 3.30, upper left) or in black-and-white, with a reduced number of tones, creating a poster effect. The default rendition is Color, but a monochrome option also appears if you press the left/right keys.
- **Retro Photo.** Adds a faded photo look to the image, with sepia overtones.

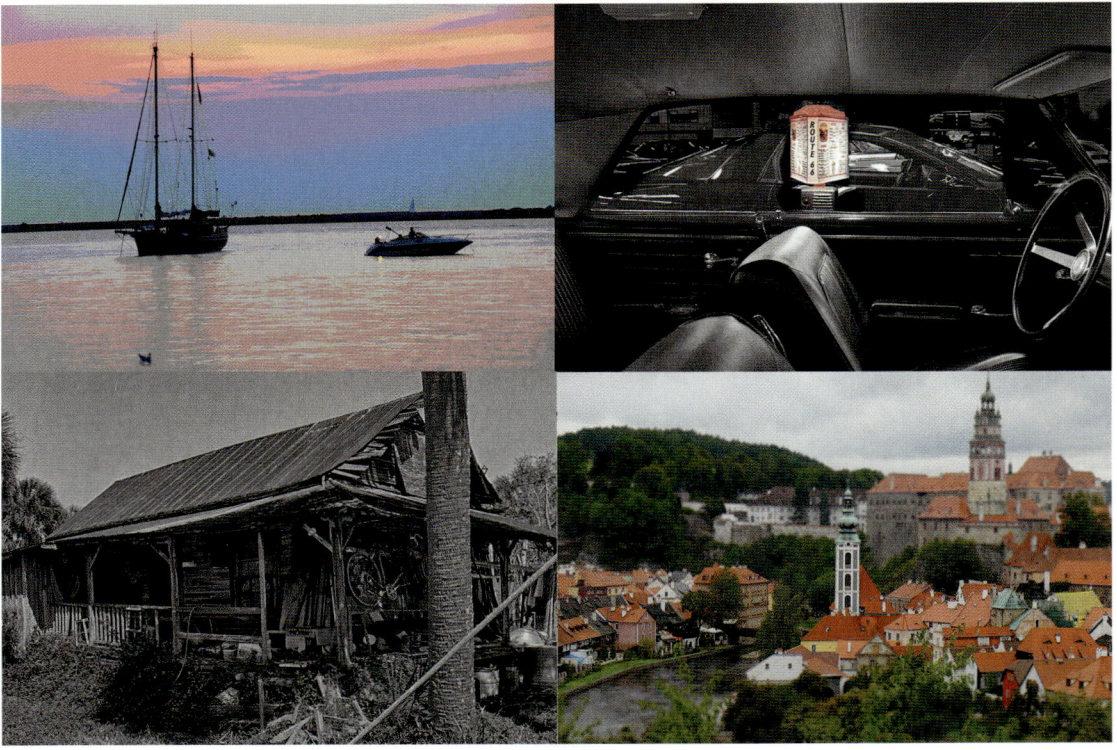

Figure 3.30 Posterization (top left), Partial Color (top right), Rich-Tone Monochrome (lower left), Miniature (lower right).

- **Soft High-key.** Produces bright images.

- **Partial Color.** Attempts to retain the selected color of an image, while converting other hues to black-and-white. (See Figure 3.30, upper right.) It's at Red by default, indicating that photos will retain red tones, but you can also choose Blue, Green, or Yellow.

- **High Contrast Monochrome.** Converts the image to black-and-white and boosts the contrast to give a stark look to the image.

- **Soft Focus.** Creates a soft, blurry effect. It's at Mid by default (for a medium intensity); press the left/right buttons to specify Lo or Hi intensity.

- **HDR Painting.** Produces a painted look by taking three pictures consecutively and then using HDR techniques to enhance color and details. It's at Mid by default (for a medium intensity); press the left/right buttons to specify Lo or Hi intensity. The camera will quickly shoot three photos, at varying exposures, and combine them into one. (This is most suitable for static subjects; do not move the camera until all three shots have been fired.)

- **Rich-tone Monochrome.** Uses the same concept as the one above HDR Painting but creates a long-gradation black-and-white image (by darkening bright areas but keeping dark tones rich) from three consecutive exposures. (See Figure 3.30, lower left.)

- **Miniature.** You select the area to be rendered in sharp focus using the Option button. The effect is similar to the tilt-shift look used to photograph craft models. (See Figure 3.30, lower right.) Press the left/right keys to position the blurry area to the left, right, top, bottom, or middle of the image; watch the preview display while scrolling among them to get a feel for the effect that each one can provide.

- **Watercolor.** Creates a look with blurring and runny colors, as if the image were painted using watercolors.

- **Illustration.** Emphasizes the edges of an image to show the outlines more dramatically. The left/right buttons can be used to adjust the effect from Low, to Mid, or High levels.

Picture Profile

Options: Picture Profiles PP1–PP10, Off

Default: Off

My preference: Off

Picture Profiles are a great tool for advanced movie shooters. You can customize the picture quality, including color and gradation of your movies by defining the parameters included in each of ten different Picture Profiles. To make these adjustments, connect the camera to a TV or monitor using the HDMI port, and use the picture on the screen as a guide while making your changes. After connecting the camera to your HDTV/monitor, navigate to this menu entry and select which Picture Profile you want to modify. Press the right button to access the index screen, then press the up/down buttons to select the parameter to be changed. Then make your adjustments and press the center button to confirm.

Even a short course in how each of the parameters affects video images, and a discussion of how to select the best settings would require a chapter or two of technical discussion and is thus beyond the scope of this book. I'm going to provide a quick listing of each type of setting for a reminder; your Sony manual provides more information about each of these. The ten Picture Profile presets already have default values:

- **PP1:** Example setting using [Movie] gamma
- **PP2:** Example setting using [Still] gamma
- **PP3:** Example setting of natural color tone using the [ITU709] gamma
- **PP4:** Example setting of a color tone faithful to the [ITU709] standard
- **PP5:** Example setting using [Cine1] gamma
- **PP6:** Example setting using [Cine2] gamma
- **PP7:** Example setting using [S-Log2] gamma
- **PP8:** Example setting using [S-Log3] gamma with the Picture Profile's Color Mode set to [S-Gamut3.Cine]
- **PP9:** Example setting using [S-Log3] gamma with the Picture Profile's Color Mode set to [S-Gamut3]
- **PP10:** Example setting for HDR Movies using [HLG2] gamma

The list that follows is not for the faint-of-heart. As I noted, you can find entire books and motion-picture school classes on color grading and adjusting these parameters:

- **Black Level.** Sets the black level (–15 to +15). Black level is the level of brightness at which no light is emitted from a screen, resulting in a pure black screen. Adjustment of this parameter ensures that blacks are seen as black, and not a dark shade of gray.
- **Gamma.** Selects a gamma curve, a formula that corrects for the nonlinear relationship between the brightness (*luminance*) captured by a sensor and the brightness of the image as it's displayed on a monitor. In other words, correction is needed to make what you see on a screen more closely resemble what the camera captured in real life. You can choose from 14 different gamma curves.
- **Black Gamma.** Corrects gamma in low-intensity areas, using Range and Level controls.
- **Knee.** Sets "knee point" and slope for video signal compression to prevent overexposure by limiting signals in high-intensity areas of the subject to the dynamic range of your camera. In short, a higher knee level produces more detail in the highlights; a lower knee level produces fewer details in the highlights. Your adjustments include:
  - **Mode.** In Auto mode, the knee point and slope are set automatically; in Manual mode, they are set manually.
  - **Auto Set.** Even when the Mode is set to Auto, you can still choose maximum point for the knee point, from 90 to 100 percent, and Sensitivity, from High, Medium, or Low.
  - **Manual Set.** When Mode is set to manual, you specify a knee point (75 to 105 percent), and Slope from gentle (–5) to steep (+5).

- **Color Mode.** Sets type and level of colors, from among Movie, Still, Cinema, Pro, ITU-709 Matrix, Black & White, and S-Gamut, S-Gamut3.Cine, S-Gamut3, BT-2020, and 709.

- **Saturation.** Sets the color saturation, from –32 to +32 values.

- **Color Phase.** Sets the color phase (–7 to +7).

- **Color Depth.** Sets the color depth for each color phase.

- **Detail.** Sets parameters including Level, and Detail adjustments including Mode, Vertical/Horizontal Balance, B/W Balance, Limit, Crispning (sic), and Hi-Light Detail.

- **Copy.** Copies the settings of the picture profile to another picture profile number.

- **Reset.** Resets the picture profile to the default setting. You cannot reset all picture profile settings at once.

Soft Skin Effect (Stills)

Options: Off/On (Lo, Mid, Hi)

Default: Off

My preference: Off

This item, the first in the Camera Settings I-12 menu, can be used to instruct the camera's processor to minimize blemishes and wrinkles in the detected face, which usually helps produce a more flattering picture. (See Figure 3.31.) I find it more suitable for photos of women than of men. If you choose On, press the left/right buttons and select the low, middle, or high intensity for skin softening. This effect does not work when shooting movies or in any continuous shooting mode, including bracketing and continuous self-timer, nor when using the Sports Action scene mode, Sweep Panorama, or RAW capture mode.

Figure 3.31

The Camera Settings I-12 (Color/WB/Image Processing2) menu.

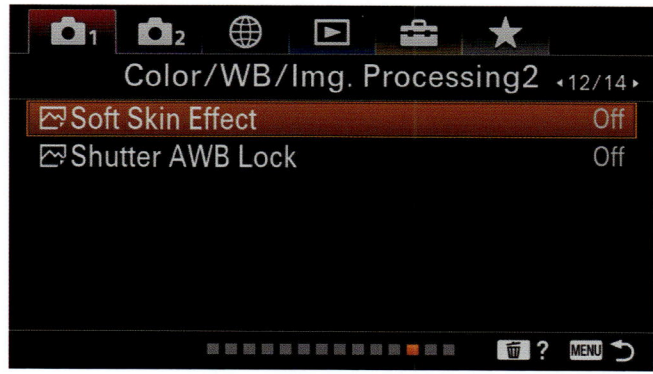

Shutter AWB Lock (Stills)

Options: Shutter Halfway Down, Continuous Shooting, Off

Default: Off

My preference: Off

As described earlier, your a6400 actually has *two* Auto White Balance controls—the standard AWB setting and Underwater Auto. Each selects the appropriate white balance for their respective conditions. However, neither auto white balance option is perfect; you may find that white balance adjustments may occur as you hold the shutter release down halfway, or during continuous shooting. If color consistency between individual shots is important, you can tell the camera to *lock* color balance temporarily. There are two ways of doing that:

- **Shutter Halfway Down.** If you choose this setting, the camera will always lock the white balance at its current setting whenever AWB or Underwater Auto are active and the shutter release is half-pressed. If the Drive mode is Continuous, when you press the shutter release down all the way and hold it down, the white balance is locked for the entire sequence.

- **Continuous Shooting.** White balance is locked *only* during continuous shooting. Either Auto WB setting may continue to make adjustments when the shutter release is half-pressed.

- **Off.** White balance may change during a half-press or continuous shooting when either of the two Auto white balance presets are enabled. (The non-auto fixed presets, of course, do not change until you adjust them.)

Focus Magnifier

Options: Activate

Default: Off

My preference: N/A

This is the first entry in the Camera Settings I-13 (Focus Assist) menu. (See Figure 3.32.) If you like to focus manually, this is a very useful aid, one of several that Sony generously offers to enhance the chore of achieving sharp focus. (The others include Manual Focus Assist and Peaking Level.) Here's how to tell the three aids apart:

- **Focus Magnifier.** Enlarges the viewfinder/LCD image to 5.9X or 11.7X so you can view the subject you are trying to bring into focus more easily. It operates when using any Focus Mode other than AF-C, which means you can use it with AF-A or AF-S in addition to Manual Focus (MF) or Direct Manual Focus. (You need to activate the autofocus capability using the AF in Focus Magnification entry discussed shortly.)

  You must summon the Focus Magnifier *manually*, either by accessing this menu entry or by pressing a custom key that you define to activate it. **Note:** as you'll learn in Chapter 8, with Direct Manual Focus, the camera autofocuses automatically when the shutter release is pressed halfway; you can then fine-tune focus manually.

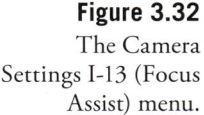

Figure 3.32
The Camera Settings I-13 (Focus Assist) menu.

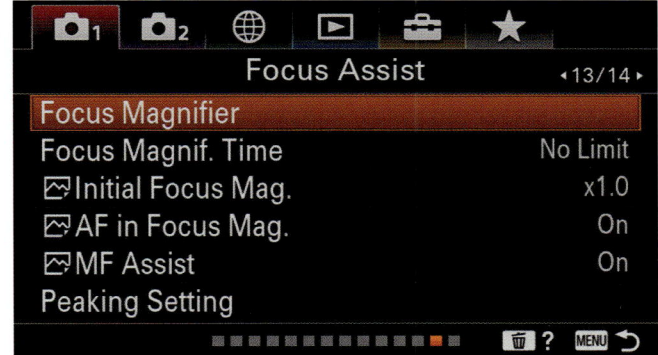

■ **Manual Focus Assist.** This feature, discussed shortly, *automatically* provides a magnification of 5.9X (or 11.7X) if you press the center button when you rotate the lens focus ring while in Manual Focus *or* Direct Manual Focus mode. In that sense, it is easier to use than the Focus Magnifier, because no special menu entry or defined button is needed to activate it. However, it cannot be used with AF-S or AF-C focus modes. If you only want to use magnification *sometimes*, and for autofocus as well as manual focus, you're better off with the focus magnifier.

■ **Peaking Level.** This option, also described later in this chapter, operates in Manual Focus or Direct Manual Focus modes. Peaking outlines out-of-focus areas with your choice of red, yellow, or white highlighting. If you zoom in using the focus magnifier or manual focus assist, the colored highlighting is retained. This option is especially useful when attempting to manually focus in dark or dim conditions.

To use the Focus Magnifier, just follow these steps:

1. **Summon Focus Magnifier.** If you're not using AF-C as your focus mode, press the defined key for Focus Magnifier, or use this menu entry to activate it. The viewfinder/LCD monitor image is first presented with 1.0X magnification (that is, none). Press the center button and the image is enlarged to 5.9X, and a navigation window appears at lower left showing an orange rectangle that represents the current location of the blown-up section. (See Figure 3.33.)

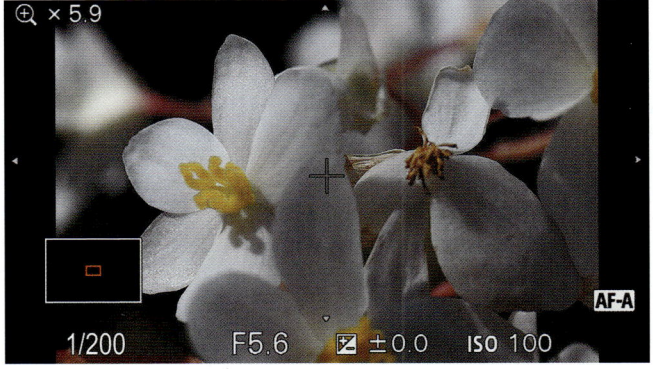

Figure 3.33
The focus magnifier makes manual focusing easier.

2. **Adjust the magnified area.** A quartet of triangles surrounds the image, indicating that you can move the enlarged window around with the frame. Use the left/right/up/down keys to move the enlarged area. Note that you can also rotate the control wheel to move the window from side to side, and the control dial to move the window vertically. This is *much* slower, and not recommended.

3. **Center the magnifier.** You can press the Trash button to center the magnified section back in the center of the frame.

4. **Zoom in/out.** Pressing the center button enlarges the image from 1X to 5.9X and 11.7X. An additional press exits the magnifier.

5. **Focus.** Use one of these options:

   - **Manual focus mode.** Rotate the lens's focus ring to achieve sharp focus. A scale along the bottom of the screen shows the approximate focus distance.

   - **Direct Manual focus mode.** Press the shutter release halfway to autofocus on the enlarged image, and then (optionally) rotate the focus ring to fine-tune.

   - **AF-S or AF-C mode.** Press the shutter button halfway to autofocus on the enlarged image. Remember you must set AF in Focus Magnification to On to use this technique. If Off is specified instead, pressing a half-press cancels magnification.

To use the focus magnifier most easily, you'll want to avoid a visit to this menu entry each time you want to activate it. It's easy to fix that by assigning focus magnifier to a custom key. Visit the Custom Settings II-08 menu, select Custom Key (Shooting), highlight the Custom Button 2 entry (or Custom Button 1, if you prefer), and choose Focus Magnifier as its definition. You can assign the focus magnifier to a different button instead, but the Custom 2 button at lower right on the back panel makes the most sense. Once you've learned the functions of your camera, you won't need the default In Camera Guide function in shooting mode, anyway. And, even if you've redefined the button to summon the focus magnifier, it still functions as a Trash button in playback mode, so you've lost virtually nothing.

TOUCH FUNCTIONS

If you've activated the a6400's touch functions in the Setup 3 menu (explained in Chapter 6), you can use the touch screen to summon the Focus Magnifier and drag its viewing window around within the frame when you're using Direct Manual Focus (only).

Focus Magnification Time

Options: 2 sec., 5 sec., No Limit

Default: 2 sec.

My preference: 5 sec.

This entry can be used to specify the length of time that the Focus Magnifier will magnify the image during manual focusing. If you find that it takes you longer than two seconds to manually focus using MF Assist, you can change the time to five seconds, or to No Limit; the latter will cause the image to remain magnified until you tap the shutter release button (you don't need to actually take a picture), press the center button/multi-selector button again to return to full frame, or double tap the LCD monitor if you have enabled Touch Operation.

Initial Focus Magnification (Stills)

Options: 1.0X, 5.9X

Default: 1.0X

My preference: 5.9X

You can specify the initial magnification presented when the Focus Magnifier is invoked. The default is 1.0X (no magnification), which is fine if your first step is frequently to move the magnification window around in the frame before zooming in. At 1.0X, you see the entire frame and can position the window anywhere you like. I prefer to skip that step and jump right in at 5.9X, which usually positions the window close enough that I can go ahead and move it within the frame if I want. The 5.9X magnification is automatically used in Manual focus mode if you have enabled Touch Operation and double tap the LCD monitor to zoom in.

AF in Focus Magnification (Stills)

Options: On, Off

Default: Off

My preference: Off when not shooting macro/close-up images

As I mentioned earlier, the Focus Magnifier works just fine in AF-S and AF-A autofocus modes. You can use it to view an enlarged image to confirm that correct focus has been achieved automatically, or to fine-tune focus when working with Direct Manual Focus (DMF) mode.

Once you've enabled the AF focus magnification option, activate the Focus Magnifier as described earlier and adjust the enlarged area using the directional controls and the navigation box. Avoid positioning the enlarged area at the edges of the frame, as the camera may be unable to focus at those positions. When you're ready, press the shutter release halfway. In any AF mode or DMF, the a6400 will focus on the center of the enlarged area. If you're using DMF, you can fine-tune focus with the lens's focus ring. Then press the shutter release down all the way to take the photo.

Autofocus using focus magnification cannot be used when shooting movies; when the Focus mode is set to AF-C; when using AF-A and continuous shooting; or a shooting mode other than P, A, S, or M. The feature is also disabled when using one of the EA-LA mount adapters. Certain autofocus features are disabled when using the focus magnifier, including Eye-AF, Center Lock-on AF, Eye-Start AF, Pre-AF, and Face Priority in AF.

Manual Focus Assist (Stills)

Options: On, Off

Default: On

My preference: On

Forget about the need to activate the Focus Magnifier manually. Set this entry to On and any time you are using manual focus or manual focus in the DMF mode, the a6400 will automatically enlarge the screen so you can better judge by eye whether the important part of your subject is in sharp focus. As you begin to focus manually by rotating the focus ring on the lens, the image on the LCD will appear at 5.9X its normal size (press the center button to zoom in to 11.7X). This version of the Focus Magnifier is available only for still photography. You can then scroll around the image using the directional controls. As with the manually activated Focus Magnifier, this feature makes it easier to check whether the most important subject area is in the sharpest focus. When you stop turning the focus ring, the image on the LCD display will revert back to normal (non-magnified) so you can see the entire area that the camera will record. You can turn this feature Off however, if you find that you don't need it, and adjust the magnifier time-out using Focus Magnifier Time, the entry described previously.

Peaking Setting

Options: Peaking Display (On, Off); Peaking Level (High, Mid, Low); Peaking Color (Red, Yellow, White)

Default: Off, Mid, White

My preference: On, High, Red

This is a useful manual focusing aid (available only when focusing in Manual and Direct Manual modes) that's difficult to describe and to illustrate. You're going to have to try this feature for yourself to see exactly what it does. *Focus peaking* is a technique that outlines the area in sharpest focus with a color that can be red, white, or yellow. The colored area shows you at a glance what will be very sharp if you take the photo at that moment. If you're not satisfied, simply change the focused distance (with manual focus). As the focus gets closer to ideal for a specific part of the image, the color outline develops around hard edges that are in focus. You can choose how much peaking is applied (High, Medium, and Low), select a specific accent color (Red, Yellow, or White), or turn the feature off.

Figure 3.34
You can choose any
of three colors for
peaking color (for
manual focus), but
only if you have acti-
vated the Peaking
Level item. For these
blossoms, red was a
better choice than
white or yellow.

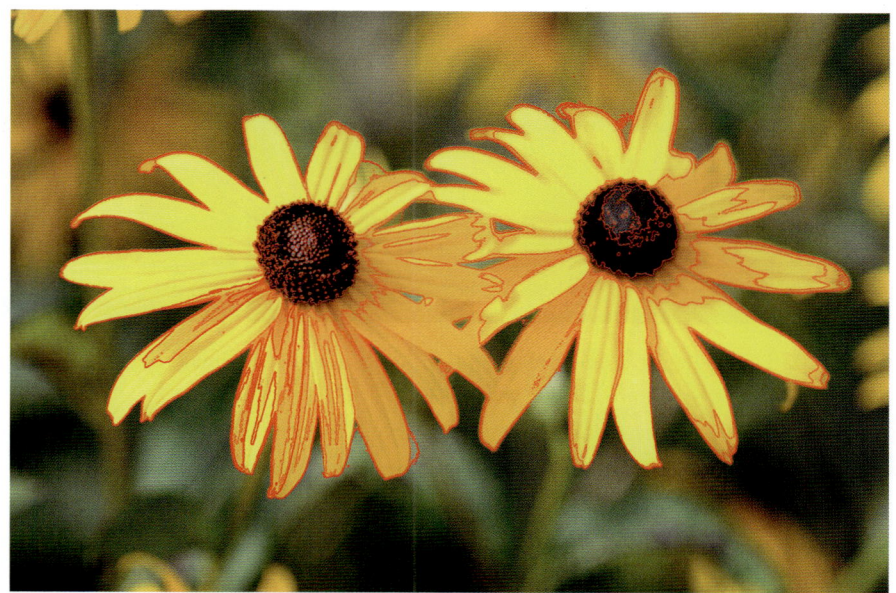

Peaking Color allows you to specify which color is used to indicate peaking when you use manual focus. White is the default value, but if that color doesn't provide enough contrast with a similarly hued subject, you can switch to a more contrasting color, such as red or yellow. (See Figure 3.34.)

Face Registration

Options: New Registration, Order Exchanging, Delete, Delete All

Default: None

My preference: N/A

This menu entry, the first in the Camera Settings I-14 (Shooting Assist) menu, is used to log into your camera's Face Detection memory the visages of those you photograph often. (See Figure 3.35.) When you access it, the screen shown in Figure 3.36 (left) appears.

Figure 3.35
The Camera
Settings I-14
(Shooting Assist)
menu.

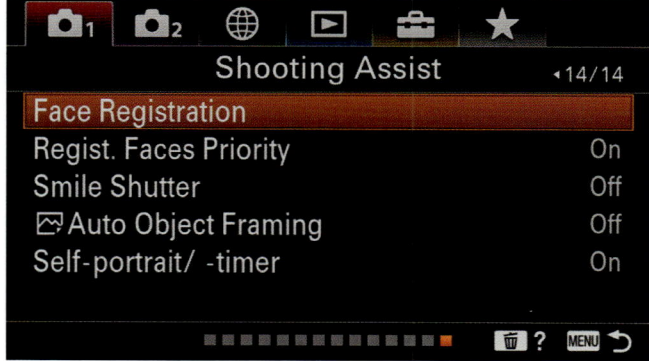

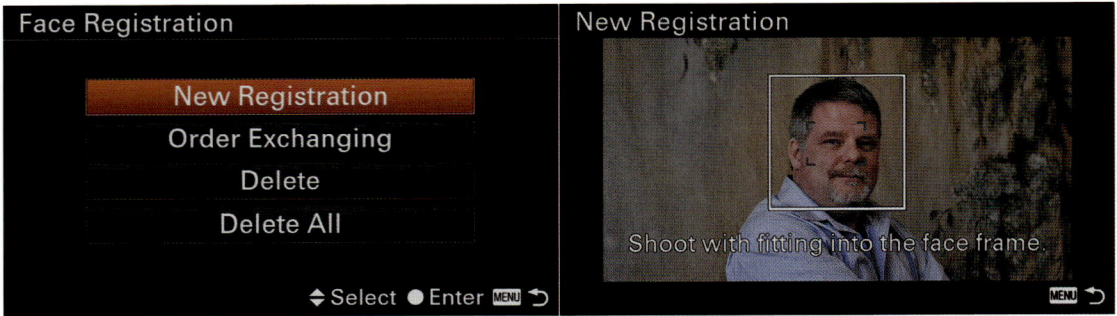

Figure 3.36 Face Registration has four options (left). Capture an image of the face you want to register (right).

New Registration allows you to log up to eight different faces. Line up your victim (subject) against a brightly lit background to allow easier detection of the face. A white box appears that you can use to frame the face. (See Figure 3.36, right.) Press the shutter button. A confirmation message appears (or a Shoot Again warning suggests you try another time, usually because you need to frame the face better). When Register Face? appears, choose Enter or Cancel, and press the MENU button to confirm.

The Order Exchanging option allows you to review and change the priority in which the faces appear, from 1 to 8. (See Figure 3.37.) The a6400 will use your priority setting to determine which face to focus on if several registered faces are detected in a scene. For example, place close family members high on your list, and relegate that annoying brother-in-law to last place. You can also select a specific face and delete it from the registry (say, you broke up with your significant other!) or delete *all* faces from the registry (your SO got custody of the camera). Face data remains in the camera when you delete individual faces but is totally erased when you select Delete All.

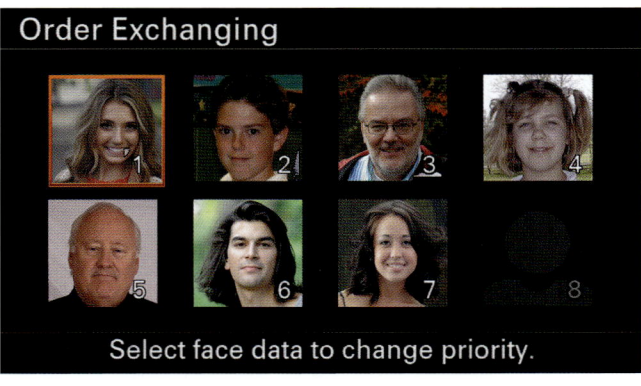

Figure 3.37
You can change the order—and therefore the priority—assigned to each face.

Registered Faces Priority

Options: On, Off
Default: On
My preference: Off

This entry simply tells the a6400 whether it should give a higher priority to registered faces during the autofocus process. Switch this on if you would prefer that faces you've registered (such as family members or friends) are given a higher priority than strangers or people you hold in less esteem.

Smile Shutter

Options: Off, On (Normal Smile, Slight Smile, Big Smile)
Default: Off
My preference: Off

Your camera can detect faces and zero in its focusing prowess on them. You can also tell the camera to use face detection to identify a face and look for a smile; it takes a photo each time it sees a smile (actually, just an array of pearly white teeth). This is an interesting high-tech feature, because the subject's smile acts as a sort of remote control.

Activate this feature, and press the left/right buttons to specify Normal Smile (the default), Big Smile, and Slight Smile. Set Big Smile, for example, and the camera won't take a photo when the detected face smiles only slightly; it will wait for a serious toothy grin. You will need to experiment to find out which level to use. The sensitivity of this feature depends on factors such as whether the subject shows his or her teeth when smiling, whether the eyes are covered by sunglasses, and others. I suggest leaving it at Normal Smile, changing it only if that does not work as you had expected.

There is no limit to the number of smiles and images you can take with this feature; you, or whoever is in front of the camera, can keep smiling repeatedly, and the camera will keep taking more pictures until it runs out of memory storage or battery power. Of course, the main purpose of this feature is not to act as a remote control; it's really intended to make sure your subject is smiling before the photo is taken. Whenever Smile Shutter triggers the shutter release, it also flashes the red light of the AF Illuminator as a signal to the person that a picture is being taken.

The normal caveats about which faces can be detected (no bangs, hats, sunglasses) apply, up to eight faces may be detected, and the feature works best with open mouths. It's disabled when shooting movies (including slow/quick motion video), using Sweep Panorama, the Focus Magnifier, Picture Effects, or in Landscape, Night Scene, Sunset, Hand-held Twilight, or Anti-Motion Blur scene modes. If Touch Tracking is turned on, you can tap a face on the LCD screen, and Smile Shutter will monitor that face, looking for a smile.

Auto Object Framing (Stills)

Options: Off, Auto

Default: Auto

My preference: Off

When this feature is active, the a6400 analyzes three types of images: close-up shots, images taken using Lock-On AF (discussed in Chapter 8), and images containing faces (only when Face Detection is activated). When it's On and the camera detects a close-up subject, tracked object, or face, it takes the photo as you composed it but also makes another image and saves that to the memory card as well. This second photo is made after cropping the photo you had composed into one that the camera thinks is a more pleasing composition. If you have Setting Effect On specified in the Live View Display entry of the Camera Settings II-07 menu, a white frame appears to show the cropped area before it is stored. The camera's processor uses the Rule of Thirds compositional technique when making its cropping decision so the eyes will not be in the center of the image area, for example.

Since cropping makes the image smaller, the processor adds pixels to ensure that the photo will be full size. It uses Sony's By Pixel Super Resolution Technology for the "up sampling;" this technology maintains very good image quality. Sure, Auto Portrait Framing is a feature intended to attract novices and inveterate snap shooters, but I find it useful at parties when taking quick shots of friends; in most cases, the photo with automatic cropping is preferable to the original (sloppily composed) shot. Of course, both photos are available on the memory card so you can use either of them.

Self-Portrait/-Timer

Options: On, Off

Default: Off

My preference: Off

This entry simplifies taking selfies by automatically triggering the self-timer when you press the shutter release. There's no need to change the Drive mode; just choose On and flip the LCD monitor 180 degrees upward. Press the shutter release down all the way, or tap the subject on the monitor. The self-timer will activate and take a picture after three seconds. If you need a longer delay, leave this setting at Off and use the conventional self-timer mode in the Drive settings.

4

Camera Settings II Menu

Additional shooting options are available from the Sony a6400's Camera Settings II menu. These settings are adjustments that you generally don't make during a particular shooting session but need to tweak more often than those in the Setup menu, which is described in Chapter 6. This menu has some very cool features, including the ability to assign many different behaviors to a variety of buttons and controls on your camera or lens. Sony has moved many menu items for the a6400 when compared to its predecessor a6300 and a6000 cameras, grouping some (but not all) related settings together more logically.

Camera Settings II Menu Entries

Figure 4.1 shows the first screen of the Camera Settings II menu. As you can see, at most only a half-dozen items are displayed at one time. The items found in this menu include:

Camera Settings II Menu

Movie (Pages 01–03)

- Exposure Mode (Movies)
- Exposure Mode (S&Q)
- File Format (Movies)
- Record Setting (Movies)
- S&Q Settings (S&Q)
- Proxy Recording
- AF Drive Speed (Movies)
- AF Track Sensitivity (Movies)
- Auto Slow Shutter (Movies)
- Initial Focus Magnification (Movies)
- Audio Recording
- Audio Recording Level
- Audio Level Display
- Wind Noise Reduction
- Marker Display (Movies)
- Marker Settings (Movies)
- Movie with Shutter

Shutter/SteadyShot (Page 04)

- Silent Shooting (Stills)
- e-Front Curtain Shutter
- Release without Lens
- Release without Card

- SteadyShot
- Zoom
- Zoom Setting
- Zoom Ring Rotate

Display/Auto Review (Pages 06-07)

- DISP Button
- FINDER/MONITOR
- Finder Frame Rate (Stills)
- Zebra Setting

- Grid Line
- Exposure Settings Guide
- Live View Display
- Auto Review

Custom Operation (Pages 08-09)

- Custom Key Settings (Stills)
- Custom Key Settings (Movies)
- Custom Key Settings (Playback)
- Function Menu Settings
- My Dial Settings
- Dial/Wheel Setup

- Av/Tv Rotate
- Dial/Wheel EV Compensation
- Function of Touch Operations
- MOVIE Button
- Dial/Wheel Lock
- Audio Signals

Exposure Mode (Movies)

Options: Program Auto, Aperture Priority, Shutter Priority, Manual Exposure

Default: Program Auto

My preference: Program Auto works well for me when shooting movies

This setting is the first on the Camera Settings II-01 (Movie 1) menu. It is available only when the mode dial is in the Movie position and allows you to specify which exposure mode is used (from among P, S, A, and M options) when shooting movies; the mode you select can be different from the one set for still photography or S&Q modes.

Exposure Mode (S&Q)

Options: Program Auto, Aperture Priority, Shutter Priority, Manual Exposure

Default: Program Auto

My preference: Program Auto

This setting is identical to the previous entry, except that it applies only to S&Q (Slow-motion and Quick-motion) capture and is grayed out if the mode dial is not set to the S&Q position. As before, the mode you select here can be different from the one set for still photography or movie shooting modes.

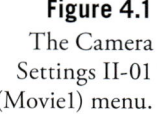

Figure 4.1
The Camera
Settings II-01
(Movie1) menu.

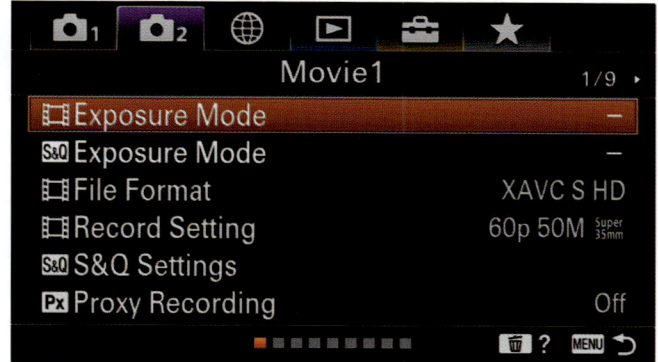

File Format (Movies)

Options: XAVC S 4K, XAVC S HD, AVCHD

Default: XAVC S HD

My preference: AVCHD

The a6400 offers full HD (high-definition) video recording in the AVCHD format. Advanced video shooters can also choose from the XAVC S 4K or XAVC S HD formats, which support faster recording speeds for improved quality, as I'll explain in Chapter 10.

By default, movies are recorded in XAVC S HD, but this menu item allows you to switch to XAVC S 4K or AVCHD. In any case, you'll need a fast memory card of at least 64GB capacity to support the higher frame rates possible with these pro formats. The XAVC S 4K format is especially demanding because of its ultra-high 3840 × 2160–pixel resolution (roughly four times that of full HD).

AVCHD clips are limited to roughly 2GB in size; when your movie file reaches that limit, the a6400 will continue recording using a new file that it creates automatically. If you're using an external recorder, video monitor, or other device using the a6400's HDMI connection, the real-time image is *not* displayed on the camera's LCD monitor as you shoot.

Record Setting (Movies)

Options: Varies

Default: XAVC S: 60p 50M

My preference: XAVC S: 60p 50M

This item allows you to choose from various options if you are using XAVC S 4K, XAVC S, or AVCHD. Your choices are shown in the left-hand column of Table 4.1. Note that the frame rates apply to countries using the NTSC system, such as the US, Japan, and some other countries. For countries that use the PAL system, 25, 50, and 100 frame rates replace 30, 60, and 120 fps respectively. All the terminology and concepts will make more sense when you read Chapters 10 and 11, which provide more of an education on many aspects of movie making.

Table 4.1 Camera Settings II Menus

Format	Record Setting	Bit Rate	Resolution
XAVC S 4K	30p 100M/25p 100M	100 Mb/sec	3840 × 2160
	30p 60M/25p 60M	60 Mb/sec	3840 × 2160
	24p 100M	100 Mb/sec	3840 × 2160
	24p 60M	60 Mb/sec	3840 × 2160
XAVC S	60p 50M/50p 50M	50 Mb/sec	1920 × 1080
	60p 25M/50p 25M	25 Mb/sec	1920 × 1080
	30p 50M/25p 50M	50 Mb/sec	1920 × 1080
	30p 16M/25p 16M	16 Mb/sec	1920 × 1080
	24p 50M/50p 50M	50 Mb/sec	1920 × 1080
	120p 100M/100p 50M	100 Mb/sec	1920 × 1080
	120p 60M/100p 60M	60 Mb/sec	1920 × 1080
AVCHD	60i 24M/50i 24M (FX)	24 Mb/sec	1920 × 1080 interlaced
	60i 17M/50i 17M (FH)	17 Mb/sec	1920 × 1080 interlaced

Note: Sony adds a *Super 35mm* label to the a6400's movie formats (other than high-speed 120p/100p video). That simply means the video is captured using an APS-C-sized sensor. It really has meaning only with cameras having a full-frame sensor; those models, such as the a7R III and a7 III, have the option of recording video using the full sensor width *or* using the APS-C format's "cropped" sensor.

S&Q Settings (S&Q)

Options: Record Setting: 60p, 30p, 24p (NTSC); Frame Rate: 120, 60, 30, 15, 8, 4, 2, 1 frames per second

Default: 30p, 120 fps

My preference: N/A

This is a great feature if you want to shoot some slow-motion movies as a special effect, analyze the dynamics of a particular motion, or speed up a sequence to provide a humorous herky-jerky appearance. Sony's implementation of high/slow frame rate photography, which it now calls slow-motion/ quick-motion, allows you to capture a *silent* (no sound) slow-motion video at up to 120 frames-per-second rate (100 fps for PAL). It will play back 4X or 5X slower, depending on whether you select 30p/25p or 24p as your Record Setting option within this menu entry. You can also record at slower speeds (down to 1 frames per second) for speeded-up, Charlie Chaplinesque footage.

Here are your options, and how it works:

- **Record setting.** This parameter is labeled a bit misleadingly. It determines the *playback* speed of your video clip and, therefore, how much of a slow-motion/fast-motion effect you will see when viewing the movie. Your choices are 60p, 30p, or 24p when using the NTSC television system. Think of this setting as a *factor,* which, when dividing the Frame Rate, determines the motion effect you get. All will become clear in a moment.

- **Frame rate.** Here you select the number of frames per second captured in S&Q mode. You can select 120, 60, 30, 15, 8, 4, 2, and 1 frames per second. (Scroll down to find the last two options.) When the frames per second is divided by the record setting, you will arrive at the slow-motion effect or speed factor. I'll show you some typical results next.

Slow-Motion

When you capture video at any frame rate and then play it back at a *slower* frame rate, the result is slow-motion. For example, if you choose 120 fps for the Frame Rate, a 10-second video will include 1,200 individual frames (120 fps × 10). If you've chosen 30 fps for your Record Setting, those frames will require 40 seconds to play back (1,200 frames divided by 30). The playback time is increased 4X. Other playback times involve different amounts of slow-motion: 24 fps gives you 5X playback. (When shooting at 120 fps, the 60 fps Record Setting is not available.) Table 4.2 shows the amount of slow motion you get with each combination of frame rates from 30 to 120, and playback settings of 60, 30, and 24 frames per second.

Quick Motion

Frame rates *slower* than 30 fps gives you speeded-up quick-motion instead of slow-motion. For example, with a Frame Rate of 4 frames per second you'll capture just 40 frames in 10 seconds. When viewed at a Record Setting of, say, 24 fps, that 10-second clip will be compressed into only 1.7 seconds of viewing time. Obviously, because of the speed-up factor, you'll get the maximum effect when you shoot longer sequences that can be displayed very, very quickly. Look over Table 4.2, and the explanation that follows to calculate your own slow/quick-motion effects.

To calculate the *slow-motion* effects you can look forward to, multiply any of the figures labeled "slow-motion" by the number of seconds captured in your original clip. For example, if you shot a two-minute, 120 fps sequence and played it back at 30p (4X slow-motion), you'd need 8 minutes to watch the whole thing. Going the other way, a two-minute clip captured at 4 fps and played back at 30p, would zip by in four seconds of frantic action.

Obviously, in real life you probably won't be shooting slow-motion video for two whole minutes (a golf swing or sports action sequence can be captured in a few seconds), and will be shooting quick-motion, time-lapse-like clips (such as a blooming flower or the march of the stars across the night sky) for longer periods so you'll have time to enjoy what you see. As you work with this cool feature,

Table 4.2 Slow-Motion/Quick-Motion Effects			
Capture Frame Rates	60p Playback	30p Playback	24p Playback
120 fps	Not possible	4X slow-motion	5X slow-motion
60 fps	1X standard speed	2X slow-motion	2.5X slow-motion
30 fps	2X quick-motion	1X standard speed	1.25X quick-motion
15 fps	4X quick-motion	2X quick-motion	1.6X quick-motion
8 fps	7.5X quick-motion	3.75X quick-motion	3X quick-motion
4 fps	15X quick-motion	7.5X quick-motion	6X quick-motion
2 fps	30X quick-motion	15X quick-motion	12X quick-motion
1 fps	60X quick-motion	30X quick-motion	24X quick-motion

you may have to experiment to see which combination of frame rate capture speeds and the three possible playback speeds work best for you in a given situation. Also, keep in mind that many video-editing programs can handle clips captured at various frame rates and output them at a different rate for playback.

All movies are recorded in XAVC S HD format, and, as noted earlier, are silent. When shooting slow-motion video, TC Run and TC Output (under TC/UB Settings, described later), and 4K Output Selection are disabled. And, obviously, fast frame rates require shorter shutter speeds, so be ready to boost your ISO settings if necessary to cope.

Proxy Recording

Options: On, Off

Default: Off

My preference: Off

If you like, you can record a compact, low–bit rate version of your XAVC S movies simultaneously while capturing your main movie. Although lower in quality, these "proxy" recordings are suitable for emailing, display on a smartphone or tablet, or uploading online.

While capturing your full HD (1920 × 1080) video, the a6400 also saves a standard HD (1280 × 720) version at a paltry 9 Mb/second, using the same frame rate (that is, 60/50p, 30/25p, or 24p) selected for the main video. You must use the XAVC S HD record setting with a frame rate other than 120/100p. A "Px" label appears over a main movie's icon during image review to indicate that a proxy movie was recorded at the same time (the proxy itself cannot be displayed or edited in-camera). Any time you delete the main movie from your memory card the proxy is erased, too.

AF Drive Speed (Movies)

Options: Fast, Normal, Slow

Default: Normal

My preference: Normal for most scenes, Fast for sports and action

This entry is the first in the Camera Settings II-02 (Movie 2) menu. (See Figure 4.2.) It is a movies-only setting for the a6400 that is used to adjust how quickly the camera focuses while capturing video. It's used in conjunction with AF Track Sensitivity (Movies), described next. Unlike stills, when focus changes while shooting movies it is apparent in the clip and can be undesirable. Your three options are as follows:

- **Fast.** The camera focuses as quickly as possible, but with slightly less precision. This setting is good for sports, action, photojournalism, and street photography, and any situation where it's important to keep the main subjects in focus as they move around. In such situations, the automatic focus adjustments add to the feeling of following the action; any delay in refocusing would be disconcerting.

- **Normal.** The AF responds smoothly to subject movement by refocusing gradually. With scenes that are not filled with constant action, this mode may be the least noticeable to the viewer.

- **Slow.** Focusing is much less speedy and is a good choice if your subjects are moving at a constant rate of speed and direction. This setting will allow the a6400 to smoothly follow focus. Choose Slow to be on the safe side, in such situations, particularly when using older lenses that are themselves somewhat pokey in achieving focus.

Figure 4.2
The Camera Settings II-02 (Movie2) menu.

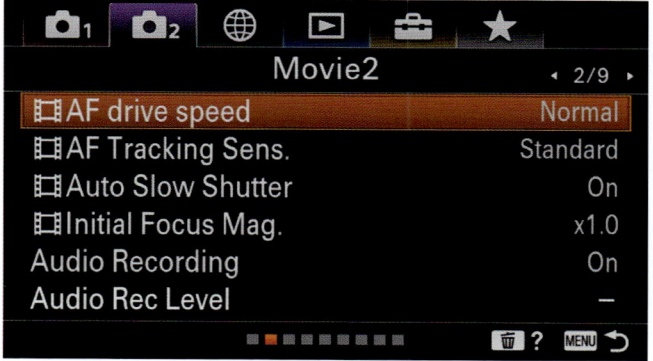

AF Track Sensitivity (Movies)

Options: Responsive or Standard

Default: Standard

My preference: Standard

This entry works hand in hand with the AF Drive Speed entry above. It is another movies-only setting and determines how quickly the camera unlocks focus from the subject it is currently tracking and focuses instead on another subject that intervenes. For example, if you're shooting a football game as a running back is breaking through the line and a referee bolts along the sideline in front of you. With this feature set to High, the camera will very quickly switch to the ref, and then should return its attention to the running back—but often, not quickly enough. A better choice would be to use Normal, so that the camera briefly ignores the referee, who is likely to have moved on in a second or two. Focus tracking will remain on your running back. Your options include:

- **Responsive.** The camera quickly responds to new subjects that cross the frame. This is the best setting to use for fast-moving subjects, such as sports or frenetic children, *as long as you don't expect intervening subjects.* The camera will smoothly follow your subjects, especially if AF Drive Speed has been set to Fast, too.

- **Standard.** Response to movement is a bit slower, so that the camera doesn't constantly refocus as subjects move about the frame. This is the default and should be used when there is only moderate movement, and especially if the movement is across the width or height of the frame (rather than coming toward you or away from you), and when you're using a small f/stop, because the increased depth-of-field will eliminate the need for most refocusing.

Auto Slow Shutter (Movies)

Options: On, Off

Default: On

My preference: Off

When shooting movies in very dark locations, the best way to ensure that the video clips are bright is to use a slow shutter speed. When this menu item is On, the camera can automatically switch to a slower shutter speed than its default. This is a useful feature, since it works in any camera operating mode; there's no need to use S mode and set a slow shutter speed yourself in dark locations. I like to leave it off, because when I am capturing video with a slow shutter speed, I want to make sure I have the camera mounted on a tripod, and the need to activate this feature manually is a reminder to me that I need to do so.

Initial Focus Magnification (Movies)

Options: 1.0X, 4.0X

Default: 1.0X

My preference: 4.0X

This is the Movie counterpart of the Stills setting in the Camera Settings I-13 menu. You can specify the initial magnification presented when the Focus Magnifier is invoked. The default is 1.0X (no magnification), which is fine if your first step is frequently to move the magnification window around in the frame before zooming in. At 1.0X, you see the entire frame and can position the window anywhere you like. I prefer to skip that step and jump right in at 4.0X (not 5.9X, as with still magnification), which usually positions the window close enough that I can go ahead and move it within the frame if I want.

Audio Recording

Options: On, Off

Default: On

My preference: On

Use this item to turn off sound recording when you're shooting videos, if desired. In most cases you'll want to leave the setting On, to capture as much information as possible; the audio track can be deleted later, if desired, with software. However, there could be occasions when it's useful to disable sound recording for movies, for example, if you know ahead of time that you will be dubbing in other sound, or if you have no need for sound, such as when panning over a vista of the Grand Canyon. At any rate, this option is there if you want to use it.

Audio Rec Level

Options: On, Off

Default: On

My preference: On

You can adjust the recording level of the camera's built-in or external microphones using this entry, which also enables/disables the audio level overlay on the screen while movies are captured. To use this feature, just follow these steps:

1. Rotate the mode dial to the Movie position.
2. Navigate to the Camera Settings II-02 menu, highlight Audio Rec Level, and press the center button.
3. The screen shown in Figure 4.3 appears. Rotate the front or rear dials or control wheel or use the left/right controls to adjust the volume level up or down.

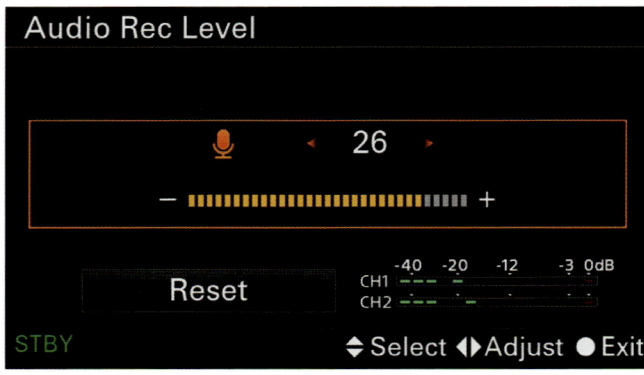

Figure 4.3
Set Audio level.

4. Press the center button to confirm and exit the screen.

5. Alternatively, you can use the up/down buttons to highlight Reset to return the recording level to the default value. Then press MENU to exit.

6. If Audio Recording and Audio Level Display are set to On, an overlay appears at the lower left of the EVF or LCD monitor showing the current audio levels for the left/right channels (Ch1/Ch2).

Audio Level Display

Options: On, Off

Default: On

My preference: N/A

This entry, the first in the Camera Settings II-03 (Movie 3) menu, enables/disables display of audio level indicator bars, so you can monitor sound recording levels visually. (See Figure 4.4.) The volume bars do not appear when Audio Recording is set to Off, or the DISP setting is set to No Disp. Info., or you are recording slow-motion or quick-motion video. When in movie standby mode, the bars will display so you adjust the sound level before starting to capture.

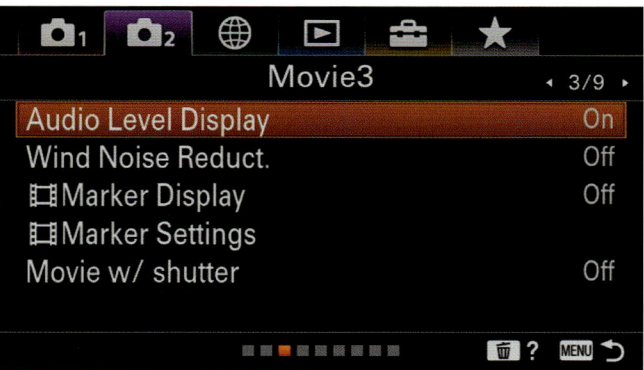

Figure 4.4
The Camera Settings II-03 (Movie3) menu.

Wind Noise Reduction

Options: On, Off

Default: Off

My preference: Off

Designed to muffle the howling sound produced by a loud wind passing over the built-in microphones, this item (when On) is for use when recording video. It's off by default because Wind Noise Reduction (provided by the camera's processor) does degrade sound quality, especially bass tones, and the recording volume is reduced. I recommend setting it to On only when shooting in a location with loud wind noises.

Marker Display (Movies)

Options: On, Off

Default: Off

My preference: N/A

When shooting video that will end up being displayed in other than HDTV's 16:9 ratio, it's useful to know exactly where the boundaries of other types of frames are, so the image can be composed to keep important subject matter contained within those boundaries. This setting lets you turn the display of any of four different types of markers on or off, as described in the Marker Settings entry that follows.

Marker Settings (Movies)

Options: Center, Aspect Ratio, Safety Zone, Guideframe

Default: Center

My preference: N/A

This entry allows you to choose which markers are displayed during video capture. You can select any or all of the following, if you like, although using more than one or two markers is likely to be confusing. Your choices (shown in Figure 4.5) are as follows:

- **Center—On/Off.** Determines whether the center marker is shown in the middle of the shooting screen. The default value is Off.
- **Aspect Ratio—Off/4:3/13:9/14:9/15:9/1.66:1/1.85:1/2.35:1.** This activates a marker showing your preferred aspect ratio. The default is Off.
- **Safety Zone—Off/80%/90%.** Sets the safety zone display that represents the standard range that can be received by a household standard-definition television.
- **Guideframe—On/Off.** Enables/disables a guideframe that can be used to verify whether a subject is parallel or perpendicular.

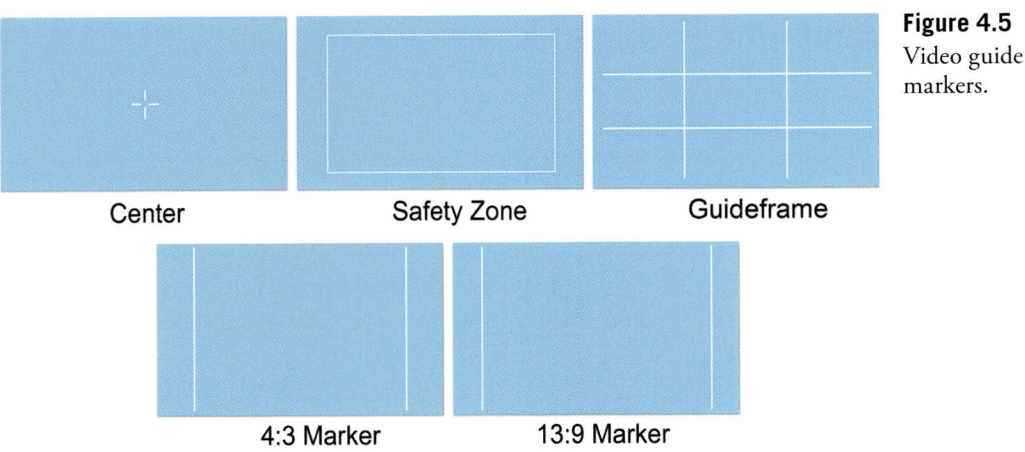

Figure 4.5
Video guide markers.

Center   Safety Zone   Guideframe

4:3 Marker   13:9 Marker

Movie with Shutter

Options: On, Off
Default: Off
My preference: Off

Your a6400 gives you the option of using the shutter release to start and stop shooting movies as an alternate to the Movie button located to the right of the viewfinder. Select On, and either button can be used; choose Off, and only the movie button will activate/stop movie capture. It's usually easier to find the shutter release, which is larger and located on top of the camera, when your eye is up to the viewfinder. It's easy to press the AF-ON or even AEL button by mistake. If your current session will be confined to video capture, you'll probably decide that using the shutter button will be more convenient.

I like this option when I am capturing movies hand-held. If the a6400 is mounted on a tripod and I am generally framing, composing, or focusing using the LCD monitor, I'll usually use either the Movie button or a remote release like the Sony RMT-DSLR2 to stop/start video capture. (The latter helps avoid camera motion from "stabbing" the Movie button with a finger.)

Silent Shooting (Stills)

Options: On, Off
Default: Off
My preference: Off

This is the first entry in the Camera Settings II-04 (Shutter/Steady Shot) menu. (See Figure 4.6.) Because the a6400 model has an electronic front curtain shutter (described next), you can take still photographs without the audible clunk that the physical shutter makes. Silent Shooting is available only in P, S, A, or M shooting modes.

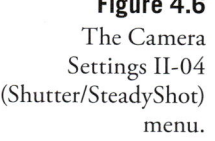

Figure 4.6
The Camera
Settings II-04
(Shutter/SteadyShot)
menu.

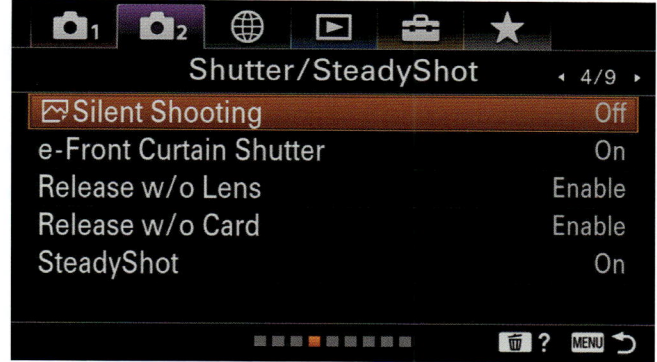

However, the most important limitation of silent shooting is that you can't use electronic flash when in this mode. There's a whole list of other functions that are not available in quiet mode. You can't use it when making Bulb exposures, using Auto HDR, Picture Effect, or Picture Profile settings, nor when using Long Exposure noise reduction. It's also disabled if you have the electron front-curtain shutter enabled. Bracket shooting is not available when shooting RAW or RAW & JPEG formats when you've specified Uncompressed for your JPEG format.

You can turn the silent shutter feature on or off using this menu entry. Note that even with silent shutter activated, the camera will not be totally silent. The opening and closing of the aperture as the f/stop changes may make a faint noise, and the focusing motor and zoom motor (in power zoom lenses) may also be heard. However, I've spooked a few colleagues when they saw me take a picture and could not hear the familiar shutter click.

The "rolling shutter" in silent shooting mode (the camera records the a6400's 4,000 lines in a full-resolution image, one line after another) may produce distortion with moving subjects, because as a subject crosses the frame, the portion at the top of the frame will be in a different position from the part of the subject at the bottom of the frame. This "Jell-o" effect may be most noticeable when shooting uncompressed RAW images. To reduce the distortion, change the RAW file type to Compressed, and use continuous shooting. You'll get the best results, however, capturing in JPEG mode.

e-Front Curtain Shutter

Options: On, Off
Default: On
My preference: N/A

This feature reduces the lag time between when you press the shutter, and when the picture is actually taken. It can also reduce a certain type of blurring due to slight camera motion when the physical shutter "clunks" open. When set to On, the electronic front shutter curtain is used by the camera at the start of the exposure, rather than the mechanical shutter. (The physical rear shutter curtain is still used to conclude the exposure.)

Although e-front curtain shutter usually works very well, when you are using an unusually wide aperture, such as the Sony/Zeiss T* FE 55mm f/1.8 ZA lens, for example, and a very fast shutter speed, areas of the photo may exhibit a secondary (ghost) image and bokeh (the out-of-focus portion of the image) may be affected. When that happens, set this menu item to Off and the camera will use only its mechanical shutter mechanism, and the problem will not occur. Sony also recommends turning the e-curtain Off when you are using a lens made by another manufacturer, as exposure may be uneven or incorrect.

The problems pop up because the e-curtain is, in effect, *too* fast. It reduces the shutter lag to the point that the iris may not have sufficient time to close completely before the exposure begins. So, the f/stop used at the beginning of the exposure can be different from the one used for the rest of the exposure (after the iris closes down to the correct aperture completely). The overall exposure will thus be incorrect, regardless of shutter speed. In addition, at higher shutter speeds, *exposure grading* can occur. At those higher speeds, the "slit" (the gap between the front and rear curtains) is increasingly small as the shutter speed becomes faster, and parts of the image exposed initially will receive more exposure than those exposed later.

Exposure grading is worse with lenses that need a longer time to close their irises, and so is more likely with non-Sony lenses, older Sony lenses, and Sony/Minolta/third-party A-mount lenses used with one of the LA-EA adapters. The irises of those lenses aren't designed to respond at the speeds demanded by an electronic front curtain shutter. In addition, even theoretically compatible lenses may have slower iris response due to dust/grit infiltration. You'll want to use newer, good condition E-mount lenses, or adapted lenses that are manually stopped down to the "taking" aperture prior to exposure.

Release w/o Lens

Options: Disable, Enable
Default: Enable
My preference: Enable

By default, the a6400 will refuse to try to take a photo when a lens is not mounted on the camera; this is a logical setting, especially for distracted folks who fail to notice that they have a lens-less camera body hanging around their necks. If you chose Enable, however, the camera will open its shutter when you depress the shutter release button when no lens is mounted. This option will be useful if you attach the camera to some accessory such as a telescope or a third-party optic that's not recognized as a lens. I prefer to select Enable, because I frequently use oddball third-party and "foreign" lenses on my camera, such as my favorite Lensbaby distortion lens or a fisheye lens designed with a different camera mount. In such cases, I have to calculate exposure manually, because, without any aperture information supplied to the camera by the lens, the a6400 has no way of determining the correct settings even in Aperture Priority mode.

Release w/o Card

Options: Disable, Enable
Default: Enable
My preference: Disable

The ability to trip the shutter without having a memory card installed is not especially useful, unless you want to hand your camera to someone for demonstration purposes and do not want to give them the capability of actually taking a picture. This happens frequently at trade shows, where vendors want you to try out their equipment, but would prefer you not leave the premises with any evidence/image samples, especially if the memory card in question belongs to the vendor rather than you.

On the contrary, it's more likely that you'd prefer to have your own camera inoperable if you've forgotten to insert a memory card. It's easy to miss the orange No Card warning that flashes when the non-picture is taken. Disabling release when a card is absent can help you avoid losing a card (you removed it to load some pictures onto someone else's computer) or having to sheepishly ask the bride and groom if they would be willing to re-stage their wedding.

SteadyShot

Options: On, Off
Default: On
My preference: On

The a6400 has the ability to use optical image stabilization (Optical SteadyShot or OSS) built into certain lenses. If for some reason you want to disable SteadyShot, you can use this menu entry. Some lenses, like the Sony FE 24-105 f/4 G OSS have an Optical Steady Shot On/Off Switch. If so, this menu setting is not available.

SteadyShot is on by default to help counteract image blur that is caused by camera shake, but you should turn it off when the camera is mounted on a tripod, as the additional anti-shake feature is not needed, and slight movements of the tripod can sometimes "confuse" the system. In other situations, however, I recommend leaving SteadyShot turned on at all times.

Zoom

Options: None
Default: None
My preference: N/A

This is the first entry in the Camera Settings II-05 (Zoom) menu. (See Figure 4.7.) This setting *activates* the Smart, ClearImage, and Digital Zoom feature, enabling you to zoom in and out using your lens's physical zooming controls or the left/right directional buttons. The setting itself has no options (you'll make those in the Zoom Settings entry that follows this one) and you must use it

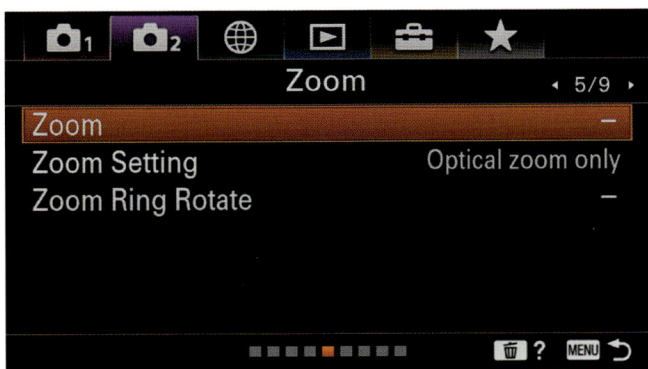

Figure 4.7
The Camera Settings II-05 (Zoom) menu.

each time you want to zoom. I recommend assigning the Zoom function to a Custom Key, as described later in this chapter.

This type of ersatz zooming is useful once you understand what it does and how it works, but Sony has done its best to make the feature as confusing as possible. Part of the confusion comes from the fact that you have a total of *five* different ways to zoom while you're taking still photographs or movies. This list will sort out the options for you:

- **Optical zoom with zoom ring.** Zoom lenses always have a ring around their barrel that can be rotated back and forth to zoom in or out on your subject. The sole exception is lenses that have a power zoom lever that takes the place of the zoom ring.

- **Optical Power Zoom.** Certain E-mount lenses include a PZ (power zoom) designation in their name. These include the Sony E PZ 16-50mm f/3.5-5.6 OSS lens, Sony E PZ 18-200mm f/3.5-6.3 OSS lens, and Sony E PZ 18-105mm f/4 G OSS lens. They all have a zooming motor built in that can be activated by sliding a switch on the lens barrel itself. Alternatively, you can zoom these lenses using a camera's zoom switch (if you own a model that has one).

- **Smart Zoom.** This is one of three zoom options that take you beyond the true optical zoom range of your lens into the realm of digitized zooming, which produces a zoom *effect* by taking the pixels in the center of the original image and filling the frame with them. Smart Zoom doesn't process pixels; it just crops out of the center of the frame, producing a maximum of 2.0x "zoom."

- **ClearImage Zoom.** When using this option, some quality is lost, as this kind of zooming doesn't produce any actual additional information; it just *interpolates* the pixels captured optically to simulate a zoomed-in perspective. Pixels are created to fill the frame at the resolution of the given Image Size setting (Large, Medium, or Small). ClearImage Zoom has many options, and I'll explain them later in this chapter. When a zoom scale is shown in the viewfinder or on the LCD monitor, a C label appears whenever you leave optical zooming behind and enter the ClearImage realm. When ClearImage Zoom is used alone, you'll typical achieve 1X to 4X magnifications *over and above* whatever optical zoom setting you've used.

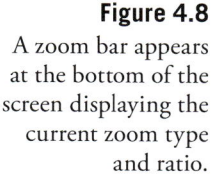

Figure 4.8
A zoom bar appears at the bottom of the screen displaying the current zoom type and ratio.

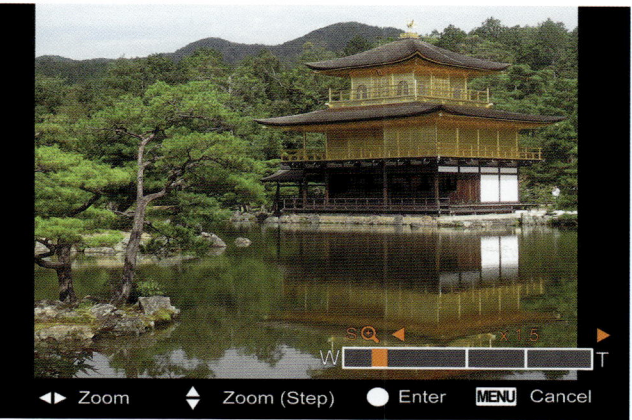

- **Digital Zoom.** This option gives you even higher magnifications than ClearImage Zoom, with an additional decrease in image quality. When a zoom scale is shown in the viewfinder or on the LCD monitor a D label appears when you are using digital zoom. I'll explain the options later in the chapter. When Digital Zoom is active, it takes up where ClearImage Zoom leaves off.

Zoom Setting

Options: Optical Zoom Only, ClearImage Zoom, Digital Zoom

Default: Optical Zoom Only

My preference: Optical Zoom Only

The a6400 has three different types of selectable zoom settings: Optical Zoom, ClearImage Zoom, and Digital Zoom, and you can choose any *one* of them here. A fourth type, Smart Zoom, need not be specified; it is invoked automatically when Image Size is set to Medium or Small, and you are using either ClearImage Zoom and Digital Zoom. As I noted earlier, Smart Zoom does not digitally manipulate pixels; it simply fills the frame with pixels cropped out of the center of the image.

My preference is to stick with optical zoom only. I own lots of great lenses, and I don't hesitate to switch to one of them when I need some extra reach. Neither ClearImage nor Digital Zoom give me the image quality I am looking for. However, if you don't own a lens with enough telephoto magnification and/or don't need the best quality for some applications, the two electronic zoom modes are available.

Of course, you can always shoot without the electronic zoom features and crop to the effective magnification you want in your image editor. ClearImage Zoom and Digital Zoom are not available when using Sweep Panorama, Smile Shutter, or when Image Quality is set to RAW or RAW & JPEG. When working with those ersatz zooms, the metering mode is locked at Multi, and Focus Area setting is disabled (the focus area frame in the zoomed image is shown by a dotted line). Descriptions of each type of zoom follow.

Using Optical Zoom Only

This is what you get when you select Optical Zoom Only. Simply turn the zoom ring on the lens (or use the power zoom button on a lens equipped with one, such as the 16-50mm kit lens). Your zooming is limited to the focal length range(s) provided by the lens mounted on your camera. With the 16-50mm kit lens, you'll get only the field of view offered by the lens, and nothing more. If you have a fixed focal length lens mounted, you get no zooming at all.

This mode provides the best image quality, because the full 24 megapixels of the a6400's sensor are used (when Large Image Size is selected in the Camera Settings I-01 menu) to record the photo. The magnification range is determined by the lens itself. For example, the 16-50mm kit lens allows a roughly 1X to 3X zoom range.

You should always use the optical zoom to magnify your image first, before resorting to one of the "fake" zoom options, because optical zoom produces the least amount of image degradation. Indeed, with a good-quality zoom lens, you may notice little, if any, loss in sharpness as you zoom in and out. Note that if you have selected Optical Zoom Only and set Image Size to Medium or Small, the Smart Zoom version (described next) is available. Table 4.3 shows the zoom magnifications you can expect.

Using Smart Zoom

You can't "choose" Smart Zoom from the Zoom Settings menu. It is activated when you use either ClearImage Zoom or Digital Zoom, and have Image Size set to Medium or Small. Like the other two digital options, Smart Zoom varies its magnification effect depending on the Image Size you select in the Camera Settings I-01 menu. It produces a zoom *effect* by taking the pixels in the center of the original image and filling the frame with them.

As Smart Zoom is available only when you have set the camera to M (medium) or S (small) image size. It provides a limited amount of zooming, but, technically, requires no quality-reducing interpolation. As I noted, the camera simply produces each "zoomed" image by cropping the photo to the zoomed size. The resolution of your final image corresponds to the resolution of the Medium or Small image size, as explained in Chapter 2. When using Smart Zoom, an S label appears in the viewfinder or LCD monitor zoom scale to indicate that the feature is in effect.

Table 4.3 Zoom Ratios

Image Size	Smart Zoom	Clear Image Zoom	Digital Zoom
Large	—	1.0x–2.0x	2.1x–4.0x
Medium	1.0x–1.4x	1.5x–2.8x	2.9x–5.7x
Small	1.0x–2.0x	2.1x–4.0x	4.1x–8.0x

Using ClearImage Zoom

This digital zoom mode also varies its magnification effect depending on the Image Size you select in the Camera Settings I-01 menu, and shown in Table 4.3, above:

Large Image Size. When ClearImage Zoom is activated, rotate the zoom ring on any E-mount zoom lens you have mounted, or use the power zoom switch on lenses that have them (such as the 16-50mm kit lens). The a6400 will use image processing to magnify the image, if required. A scale on the LCD is divided into two parts. The left-hand portion shows the amount of optical zoom applied using the actual zooming characteristics of a zoom lens; the focal length (say, 16-50mm) appears under the scale. When the indicator crosses the center portion of the scale, the focal length readout freezes at the maximum focal length of the lens (say, 50mm), and ClearImage Zoom kicks in, and the magnifying glass icon has a "C" next to it to show that additional magnification is being applied using image processing.

Medium/Small Image Size. However, if you choose Medium or Small Image Size, the zooming begins as before with the left-hand portion of the scale showing the optical zoom range. Once the indicator crosses the marker, the camera will first simply crop the image (without any processing) from 1X to 1.4X (Medium) or 1.1X to 2.0X (Small), in Smart Zoom mode. The magnifying glass shows an "S" label. If you continue zooming, then image processing will be used to provide additional zooming from 1.5X to 2.8X (Medium) or 2.1X to 4.0X (Small). The magnifying glass icon will then display a "C" to show the processing mode being used.

Clear Image Zoom provides a *simulated* zoom effect that operates even if you don't have a zoom lens! However, you could simply shoot Large JPEGs and later crop them with image-editing software in your computer to make the subject larger in the frame. This automated feature is useful if you do not own a sufficiently long telephoto lens, since it's possible to make a subject larger in the frame.

Using Digital Zoom

With this variation, the camera gives you even higher magnifications, up to 4X in Large JPEG photos creating more impressive simulated zooming effects to fill the frame with a distant subject. However, the higher the level of digital zoom that you use the greater the loss of image quality will be. That's because the camera crops the photo to simulate the use of a longer lens, discarding millions of pixels; the processor then uses interpolation (adding pixels) to restore the image to its original full size. That works well with Clear Image Zoom but above 2X magnification, the camera's processor can no longer use the most sophisticated technology (which Sony calls Bi-pixel Super Resolution) so the image quality suffers; it gets worse at each higher magnification level.

That's why I recommend leaving the Digital Zoom item at Off and using only Clear Image Zoom unless you absolutely must have greater magnification of a distant subject. If you often need telephoto focal lengths, you might want to save up and add such a lens to your arsenal, perhaps Sony's new 55-210mm f/4.5-6.3 OSS E-mount zoom, with built-in SteadyShot stabilizer. (In the US, you can buy this lens for about $350.)

Large Image Size. When Large is selected, Clear Image Zoom magnification, a high-quality image processing algorithm, will be used from 1.0X to 2X, while from 2.1X to 4X, the reduced image quality process, Digital Zoom, will be activated.

Medium Image Size. Select Medium resolution, and the highest quality Smart Zoom trimming will be applied from 1.0X to 1.4X, and Clear Image Zoom from 1.5X to 2.8X, and Digital Zoom from 2.9X to 5.7X.

Small Image Size. Select Small and Smart Zoom will be applied from 1.0X to 2.0X, and Clear Image Zoom will be applied from 2.1X to 4.0X, and Digital Zoom from 4.1X to 8.0X.

Zoom Ring Rotate

Options: Left/Right (Wide-Tele), Right/Left (Wide-Tele)

Default: Left (W), Right (T)

My preference: N/A

This setting controls whether power zooming (with PZ-designated lenses that have a power zoom feature) proceeds from wide-angle to telephoto settings when the zoom control is pressed from left to right, or in the reverse direction, from right to left. The setting is compatible only with power zoom lenses that support this feature.

DISP Button

Options (Monitor): Graphic Display, Display All Info., No Disp. Info., Histogram, Level, For Viewfinder, Monitor Off

Options (Viewfinder): Graphic Display, Display All Info., No Disp. Info., Histogram, Level

My preference: Activate all but Graphic Display

This is the first entry in the Camera Settings II-06 (Display/Auto Review 1) menu. (See Figure 4.9.) Use this item to specify which of the available display options will—and will not—be available in Shooting mode when you use the LCD or viewfinder and press the DISP button to cycle through

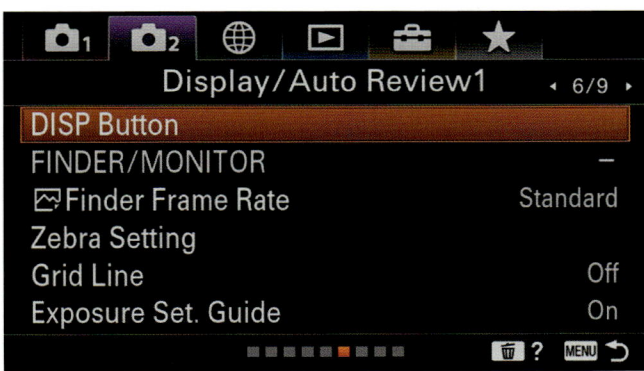

Figure 4.9

The Camera Settings II-06 (Display/Auto Review 1) menu.

the various displays. Choose from Monitor or Viewfinder and mark or unmark the screens you want to enable or disable. The Monitor selection includes a For Viewfinder option that displays a text/ graphic display of your current settings on the back-panel LCD.

You can use this menu item to deselect one or more of the display options, so it/they will never appear on the LCD when you press the DISP button. To make that change, scroll to an option and press the center button to remove the check mark beside it. Naturally, at least one display option must remain selected. If you de-select all of them, the camera will warn you about this and it will not return to Shooting mode until you add a check mark to one of the options. If you turn the camera off while none are selected, the camera will interpret this as a Cancel command and return to your most recent display settings.

The Monitor setup screen is shown at left in Figure 4.10. The same screens shown are also available for the electronic viewfinder (Figure 4.10, right), except For The Viewfinder and Monitor Off. The viewfinder versions of the display screens have some slight differences; for example, at the bottom of the viewfinder version is an analog exposure indicator. You can select a different set of displays for the viewfinder and monitor. That is, you can choose to view the Graphic Display only in the EVF and Display All Info only on the LCD monitor. Here's a recap of the available display options for the monitor.

■ **Graphic Display.** When selected, this display shows basic shooting information, plus a graphic display of shutter speed and aperture (except when Sweep Panorama is the mode in use). If you learn how to interpret it, you'll note that it indicates that a fast shutter speed will freeze motion, that a small aperture (large f/number) will provide a great range of acceptably sharp focus, and other information of this type. (See Figure 4.11.)

■ **Display All Info.** The default screen when you first turn the camera on, this option displays data about current settings for a complete overview of recording information. (See Figure 4.12.) Not all the information in the figure may be displayed at one time, and there are additional icons not shown because they occupy the same space on the screen as another indicator.

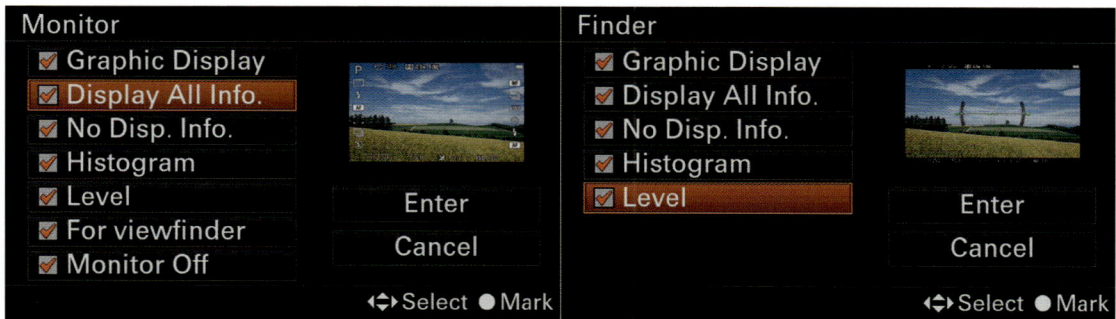

Figure 4.10 Select which display screens are shown on the LCD monitor (left) or viewfinder (right).

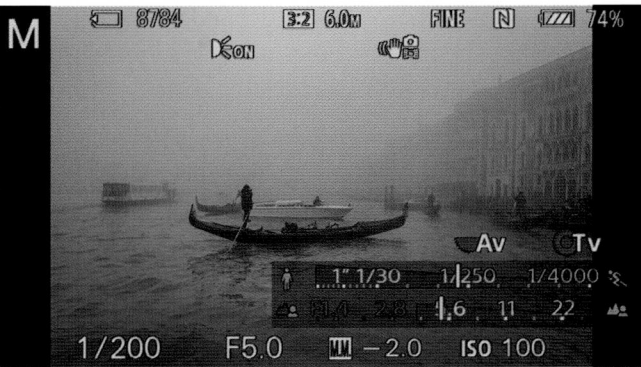

Figure 4.11
Graphic Display.

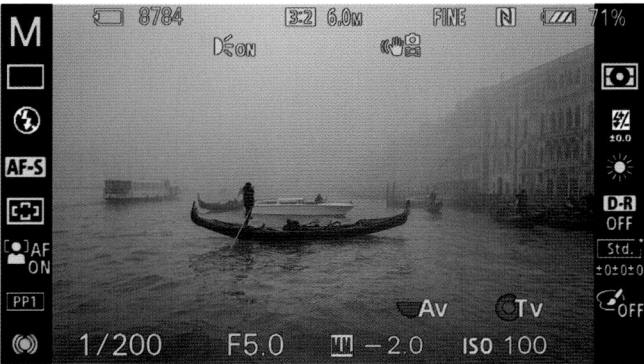

Figure 4.12
Display All
Information.

- **No Disp. Info.** Despite its name, this display option provides the basic shooting information as to settings, in a conventional size.

- **Histogram.** Activate this option if you want to be able to view a live luminance histogram to assist you in evaluating the exposure before taking a photo, a feature to be discussed in Chapter 9. The basic shooting data will appear in addition to the histogram. (See Figure 4.13.)

- **Level.** This display shows how much the camera is rotated around the lens axis (horizontal tilt) as well as how far it is tilted forward and backward. When the camera is not perfectly level, orange indicators show the amount of forward/backward and horizontal tilt. (See Figure 4.14.) When the camera is level in both directions, the indicators turn green. (See Figure 4.15.)

- **For Viewfinder.** This display can be shown only on the LCD monitor. When visible, you can press the Fn button to produce the Quick Navi screen, which I explained in Chapter 2. (See Figure 4.16.)

- **Monitor Off.** When this option is selected, pressing the DISP button eventually takes you to a blank monitor screen, which you might need to use when a brightly lit LCD is distracting or intrusive.

Figure 4.13
Histogram.

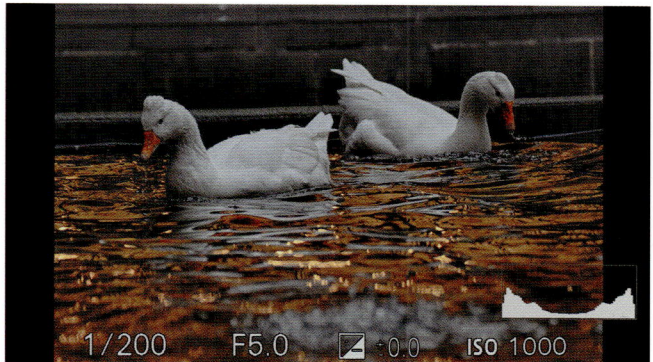

Figure 4.14
Level showing
degree of tilt.

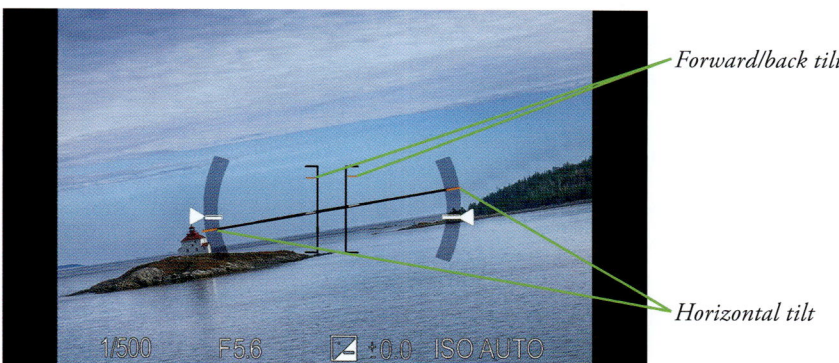

Forward/back tilt

Horizontal tilt

Figure 4.15
Camera leveled.

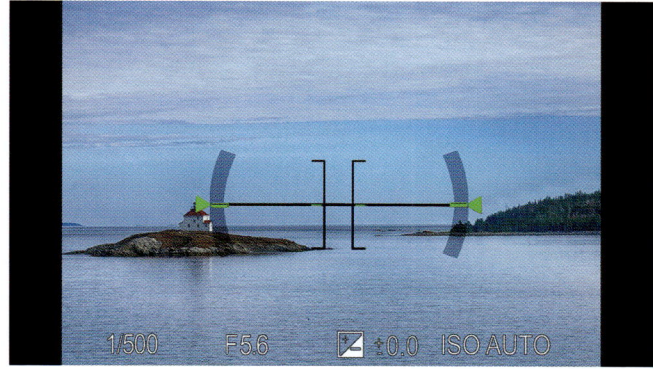

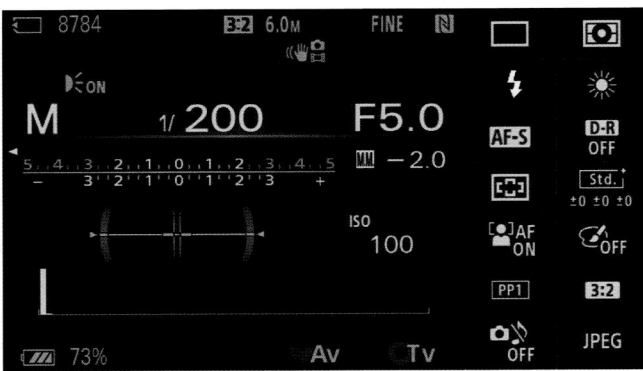

Figure 4.16

For Viewfinder display.

FINDER/MONITOR

Options: Auto, Viewfinder, Monitor

Default: Auto

My preference: N/A

This also uses the eye sensor located above the viewfinder window, but it controls only whether the camera turns off the LCD and switches the view to the viewfinder when your eye comes near the EVF. With the default setting of Auto, the screen goes blank and the viewfinder activates when your eye (or any other object) approaches the Eye-Start sensor. Helpfully, the eye sensor is *disabled* when you tilt the LCD monitor away from the camera body, presumably because in that mode you'll be working exclusively with the LCD and do not want the a6400 to switch to viewfinder mode if your hand (or any other object) passes in front of the sensor.

Switch to the Viewfinder or Monitor options and the eye sensor no longer initiates a switch from one display to the other. The display is then *always* sent to the viewing device you selected, and the other one is turned off. You might want to use the Monitor option if you are doing work involving critical focusing using the LCD, and as you examine the screen closely, your face will frequently be close to the back of the camera where the Eye-Start sensor might detect it. Or, perhaps, you are shooting at a concert or other venue where the bright LCD can be distracting to others. Choose Viewfinder, and the shooting preview, menus, photos displayed for review during playback, and so forth will be shown only in the EVF.

Of course, if you disable automatic switching between the two, you'll still want to have the option of activating the viewfinder or monitor displays manually. To do that, you'll need to assign the FINDER/MONITOR switching function to a key. I'll show you how to do that later in this chapter, when I describe the Custom Key option in the Camera Settings II-08 (Custom Operation 1) menu.

Finder Frame Rate (Stills)

Options: 50/60 fps, 100/120 fps

Default: 50/60 fps

My preference: 60 fps

While the a6400's high-resolution electronic viewfinder provides a gorgeous image at 60 frames per second (the default in the USA), its image can be made even smoother looking by upping the refresh rate to 120 fps. (Countries using the PAL system use 50/100 fps instead.) The higher frame rate can reduce "smearing" and other visual effects, which you might prefer when shooting sports and other fast-moving still subjects. However, the smoothness comes at a price: the 100/120 fps EVF rendition is provided at a lower resolution. In addition, the slower, default frame rate is always used during playback, movie shooting, and when viewing content on another device through an HDMI connection.

Zebra Setting

Options: On, Off, IRE 70, 75, 80, 85, 90, 95, 100, 100+

Default: Off, Zebra Level: 70

My preference: 80

This feature warns you when highlight levels in your image are brighter than a setting you specify in this menu option. It's somewhat comparable to the flashing "blinkies" that digital cameras have long used during image review to tell us, after the fact, which highlight areas of the image we just took are blown out.

Zebra patterns are a much more useful tool, because you are given an alert *before* you take the picture and can specify exactly how bright *too bright* is. The Zebra feature has been a staple of professional video shooting for a long time, as you might guess from the moniker assigned to the unit used to specify brightness: IRE, a measure of video signal level, which stands for *Institute of Radio Engineers.*

When you want to use Zebra pattern warnings, access this menu entry and specify an IRE value from 70 to 100, and 100+. Once you've been notified, you can adjust your exposure settings to reduce the brightness of the highlights, as I'll describe in Chapter 7.

So, exactly how bright *is* too bright? A value of 100 IRE indicates pure white, so any Zebra pattern visible when using this setting (or 100+) indicates that your image is extremely overexposed. Any details in the highlights are gone and cannot be retrieved. Settings from 70 to 90 can be used to make sure facial tones are not overexposed. Generally, Caucasian skin falls in the 80 IRE range, with darker skin tones registering as low as 70, and very fair skin or lighter areas of your subject edging closer to 90 IRE. Once you've decided the approximate range of tones that you want to make sure do *not* blow out, you can set the camera's Zebra pattern sensitivity appropriately and receive the flashing striped warning on the LCD of your camera. (See Figure 4.17.) The pattern does not appear in output to a device through the HDMI port, nor in your final image, of course—it's just an aid to keep you from blowing it, so to speak.

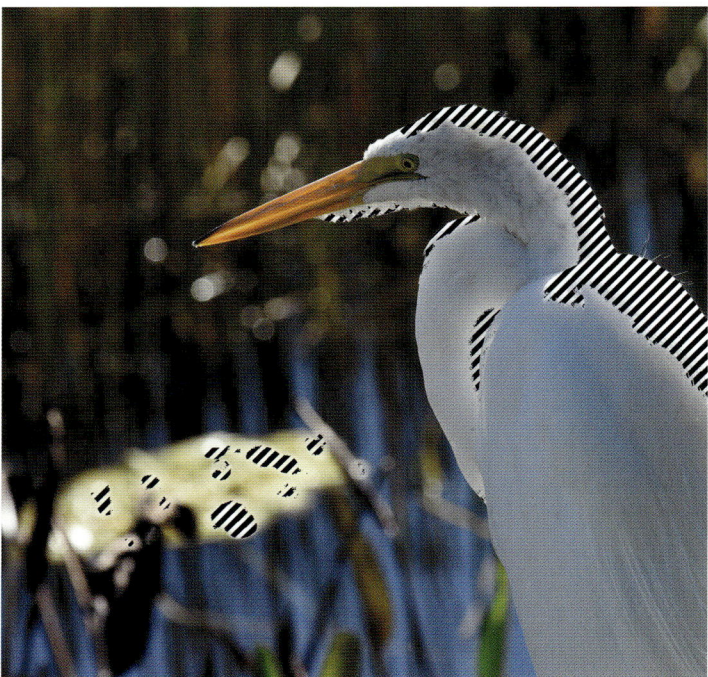

Figure 4.17
The flashing stripes show an area is overexposed.

Grid Line

Options: Rule of Thirds Grid, Square Grid, Diag.+Square Grid, Off
Default: Off
My preference: Off

This feature allows you to activate one of three optional grids, so it's superimposed on the LCD or EVF display. The grid pattern can help you with composition while you are shooting architecture or similar subjects. I sometimes use the Rule of Thirds grid to help with composition, but you might want to activate another option when composing images of scenes that include diagonal, horizontal, and perpendicular lines. (See Figure 4.18.)

Figure 4.18
Grid lines can help you align your images on the LCD or EVF.

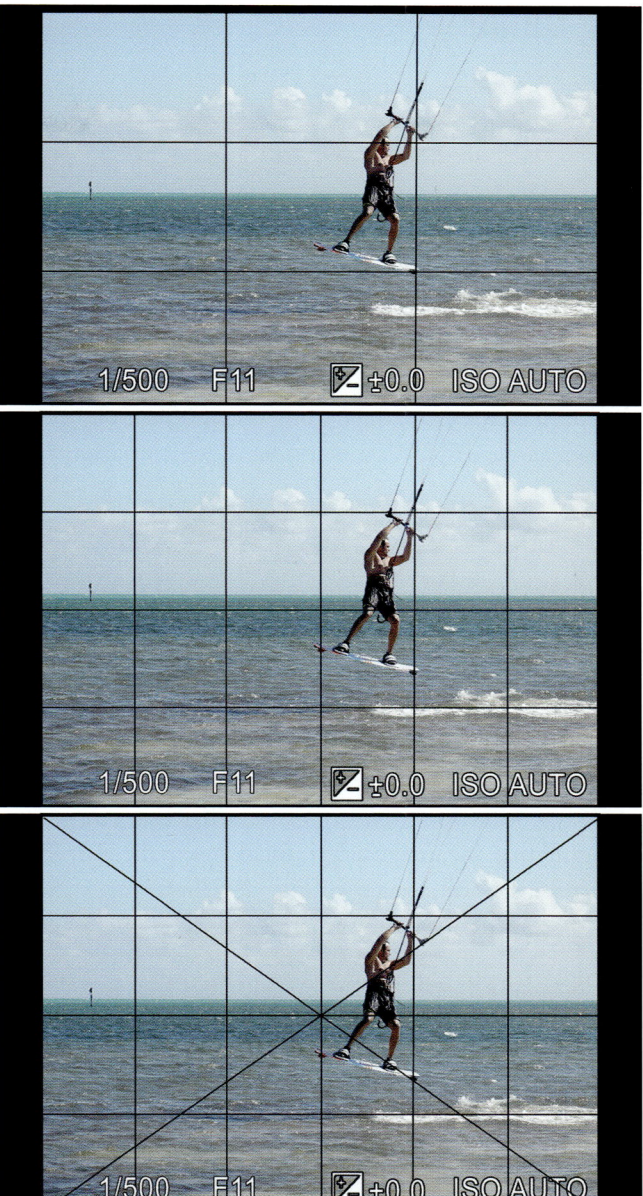

Exposure Setting Guide

Options: On, Off

Default: Off

My preference: N/A

This feature is of most use to those with poor eyesight, but a convenience for all. All it does is show a scrolling scale on the LCD or viewfinder with an enlarged rendition of the current shutter speed or aperture highlighted in orange. It more or less duplicates the display of both that already appears on the bottom line of the screen, but in a larger font and with the next/previous setting flanking the current value. In Aperture Priority, the scale shows f/stops. In Shutter Priority, you see shutter speeds. In Program mode, both are visible. When using Manual exposure, a single scrolling line appears showing shutter speed *or* aperture, depending on whether you rotate the rear or front dials. I like to leave it switched on, as the display is a reminder of which parameter I'm fooling with at the moment.

Live View Display

Options: Setting Effect ON, Setting Effect OFF

Default: Setting Effect ON

My preference: Setting Effect ON, unless using flash in manual mode

This is the first entry in the Camera Settings II-09 (Display/Auto Review 2) menu. (See Figure 4.19.) In one sense, as a mirrorless camera, the a6400 is always in a "live view" mode, showing you what the sensor sees. However, what you see is not necessarily what you get, as the sensor image can be processed (often by brightening the image electronically to make it easier to view under low-light conditions). So, in the mirrorless world, the term "live view" now means how the camera represents the actual image that will be captured by the camera.

When this option is set to ON, your exposure settings, any Picture Effects you may have chosen, and other adjustments that change the image are applied in live view. Choose OFF, and those parameters will not be applied. That's because there are times when you don't want to see the effects

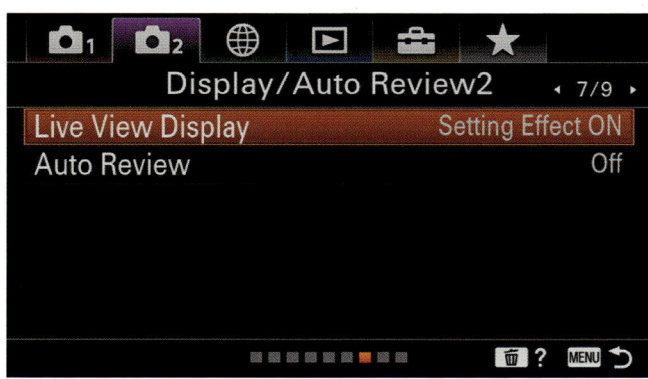

Figure 4.19
The Camera Settings II-07 menu.

of the settings you've made on the screen/EVF. For example, when you are using flash in manual mode, the camera has no way of knowing exactly how much light will be illuminating your scene. That f/16 aperture may be ideal for a shot exposed by your studio strobes, but the a6400 will, when Setting Effect is set to ON, show you a preview based on the ambient light, rather than the flash. The result? Your viewfinder or LCD monitor image is very, very dim. You'll want to select Setting Effect OFF so the camera will boost the electronic image to viewable levels.

When Setting Effects are active, the live view display in the EVF or the LCD reflects the *exact* effects of any camera features that you're using to modify the view, including exposure compensation and white balance. In that mode, this allows for an accurate evaluation of what the photo will look like and enables you to determine whether the current settings will provide the effects you want.

The ON option can be especially helpful when you're using any of the Picture Effects, because you can preview the exact rendition that the selected effect and its overrides will provide. It's also very useful when you're setting some exposure compensation, as you can visually determine how much lighter or darker each adjustment makes the image. And when you're trying to achieve correct color balance, it's useful to be able to preview the effect of your white balance setting.

If you'd like to preview the image without the effect of settings visible, you can set this feature to OFF. Naturally, the display will no longer accurately depict what your photo will look like when it's taken. So, for most users, ON is the most suitable option. Unfortunately, this setting has caused more than a few minutes of head-scratching among new users who switch to Manual exposure mode and find themselves with a completely black (or utterly white) screen. The black screen, especially, may fool you into thinking your camera has malfunctioned.

Setting Effect OFF cannot be set when using Intelligent Auto, any scene mode, or shooting conventional or S&Q movies.

Auto Review

Options: Off, 2 sec., 5 sec., 10 sec.

Default: Off

My preference: N/A

When this item is set to 2, 5, or 10 seconds, the camera can display an image on the LCD or viewfinder for your review immediately after the photo is taken. When you shoot a continuous or bracketed series of images, only the last picture that's been recorded will be shown, and if you're using a shooting mode that performs processing on an image, there may be a slight delay before the image appears. During this display, you can press the Zoom In button to get a closer look at your image, delete a disappointing shot by pressing the Delete button, or cancel picture review by tapping the shutter release button or performing another function. (You'll never be prevented from taking another picture because you were reviewing images.) This option can be used to specify whether the review image appears for 2, 5, or 10 seconds, or not at all.

Depending on how you're working, you might want a brief display, or you might prefer to have time for a more leisurely examination (when you're carefully checking compositions). Other times, you might not want to have the review image displayed at all, such as when you're taking photos in a darkened theater or concert venue, and the constant flashing of images might be distracting to others. Turning off picture review or keeping the duration short also saves battery power. You can always review the last picture you took at any time by pressing the Playback button.

Custom Key (Stills)

Options: More than 90 different definitions for Custom Buttons 1 and 2, Center Button; Left/ Right/Down Buttons; AF-MF/AEL Button; Focus Hold Button (on lens)

Default: Various

My preference: N/A

This is the first entry on the Camera Settings II-08 (Custom Operation 1) menu. (See Figure 4.20.) It allows customization of as many as 8 buttons of the camera, the control wheel, and one additional button, Focus Hold, found on some lenses. Indeed, the following is a list of the only buttons on the camera that you *cannot* redefine to perform some other function:

- **Shutter release.** It is always used to take a picture and will initiate autofocus (although you can assign AF-ON and other AF functions to a different key).

- **Up directional button.** It is used to change your information display in shooting and Playback modes, and as a directional button in menus.

- **Playback button.** Activates picture review.

- **Fn (Function) button.** (Almost) always summons the Function menu, and in Playback mode sends the current image to a smart device.

- **Movie button.** Starts/stops movies. However, you can specify whether you want the button to commence video capture always, or only when the mode dial is set to the Movie position.

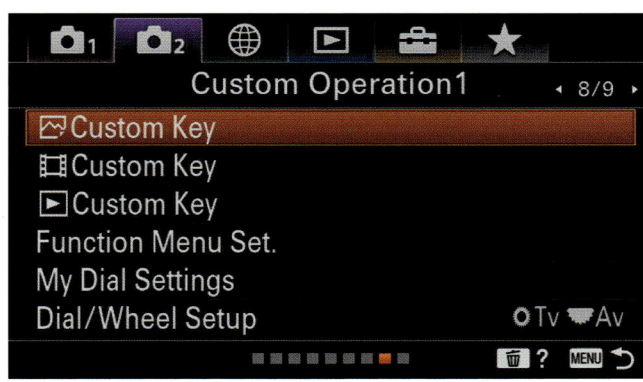

Figure 4.20
The Camera Settings II-08 (Custom Operation1) menu.

Your custom key definitions override any default definitions for those buttons when in Shooting mode; they retain their original functions in Playback mode (unless you redefine them, as I'll describe shortly). Because button definition is such a personal choice, I steer away from recommending particular definitions for each of the buttons, even though certain functions can be accessed *only* by assigning them to a custom key setting. Our fingers and agility vary, so, while buttons like the AEL (Autoexposure Lock) button are traditionally used for something like back-button focus, you may prefer to assign that function to a different key.

When assigning definitions to keys, keep in mind that certain behaviors can be used *only* when you have made them available using a custom key definition. For example, if you want to use the Bright Monitoring feature, which temporarily turns the Live View Setting Effect to Off to increase the brightness level of the screen in dark locations, you must assign it to a key. Fortunately, for most features, the Fn menu is faster and more easily configured, because you can change which functions appear there if the original 12 don't suit your needs. I'll show you how to do that later in this chapter.

Each of the customizable buttons (except the down button) have a default behavior assigned for shooting mode, listed below. In Movie mode, these buttons have the exact same behavior, unless you choose a different option. In Playback mode, only the Fn button and C1 buttons can be redefined.

- Custom 1: Focus Mode
- Custom 2: White Balance
- AF/MF (switch in AF/MF position): Switches between AF and MF while held down
- AEL (switch in AEL position): Locks exposure while held down
- Control Wheel Center button: Eye AF
- Left button: Drive Mode
- Right button: ISO
- Down button: Exposure Compensation
- Up button: DISP. (Not customizable)
- Focus Hold (on lens): Focus Hold

Basic Functions

When you access the Custom Key entry, you'll work with one of four screens, like the one shown in Figure 4.21. Each screen shows a set of buttons that can be redefined, with an accompanying graphic as you highlight each. Press the center button to view a list of possible definitions for that key. The functions available for the Custom buttons 1 and 2, AF/MF, AEL, center, and Focus Hold buttons are listed below. In all cases, choosing Not Set deactivates that button. Note that not all functions are available for each of these Custom Keys. For example, the Custom 2 button doesn't have the Switch Focus Area option, and the center button lacks both Focus Area and In-Camera Guide choices, but adds the Standard behavior, which leaves the button at its standard behavior as an OK/Enter button.

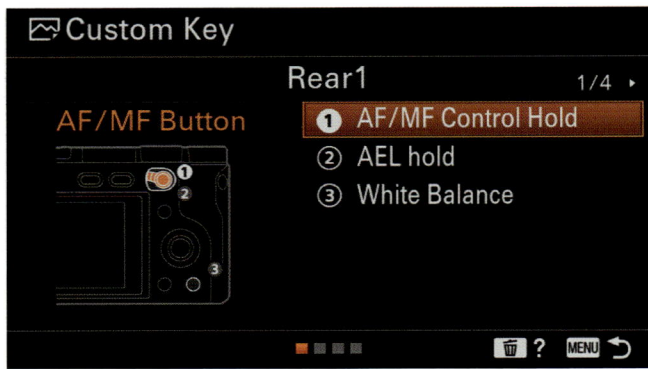

Figure 4.21
Choose which button to define from a set of four screens.

The remaining Custom Keys each have a select number of the following:

Quality/Image Size
- File Format
- JPEG Quality
- JPEG Image Size
- Aspect Ratio

Shoot Mode/Drive
- Drive Mode
- Self-timer During Bracket
- Interval Shooting
- Memory Recall
- Recall Custom Hold 1
- Recall Custom Hold 2
- Recall Custom Hold 3

Autofocus Mode
- Focus Mode
- AF/MF Control Hold
- AF/MF Ctrl Toggle
- Focus Standard
- Focus Area
- Switch Focus Area
- Register AF Area Hold
- Register AF Area Toggle
- Register AF Area+AF-ON
- Tracking On
- Face Priority in AF
- Eye AF
- Switch Right/Left Eye
- AF On
- Focus Hold

Exposure
- Exposure Comp
- ISO
- ISO Auto Min SS
- Metering Mode
- Face Priority in Multi Metering
- AEL Hold
- AEL Toggle
- AEL Spot Hold
- AEL Spot Toggle

Flash
- Flash Mode
- Flash Compensation
- Wireless Flash
- FEL Lock Hold
- FEL Lock Toggle
- FEL Lock/AEL Hold
- FEL Lock/AEL Toggle

Color/White Balance/Image Processing
- White Balance
- Priority Set in AWB
- AWB Lock Hold
- AWB Lock Toggle
- DRO/Auto HDR
- Creative Style
- Picture Effect
- Picture Profile
- Soft Skin Effect

Focus Assist
- Focus Magnifier
- Peaking Display Selection
- Peaking Level
- Peaking Color

Shooting Assist
- Smile Shutter
- Auto Object Framing
- In-Camera Guide

Movie
- Movie
- S&Q Frame Rate
- Audio Rec Level
- Audio Level Display
- Marker Display Settings

Shutter/SteadyShot
- Silent Shooting
- SteadyShot

Zoom
- Zoom

Display/Auto Review
- Aperture Preview
- Shot Result Preview
- Finder/Monitor Selection
- Finder Frame Rate
- Zebra Display Select
- Zebra Level
- Grid Line
- Live View Display Selection
- Bright Monitoring

Custom Operation
- My Dial 1 During Hold
- My Dial 2 During Hold
- My Dial 3 During Hold
- My Dial 1→2→3
- Toggle My Dial 1
- Toggle My Dial 2
- Toggle My Dial 3
- Audio Signals

Network

- Sent to Smartphone

Playback

- Playback

Setup

- Monitor Brightness
- Gamma Display Assist
- Touch Operation Select
- TC/UB Display Switch
- Not Set

HOLD THAT THOUGHT

You'll note that some behaviors toggle or cycle through functions; each time you press the Custom Key, the a6400 switches from one function to its alternate (such as MF to AF), or cycles among the available choices (such as Focus Areas). Others require that the button be held down to activate the function; when you release the button, the setting returns to its previous value.

For example, you have several options for assigning the very useful autoexposure lock (AEL) functions to one of the definable keys.

- **AEL Hold.** Exposure is locked while the button is held down.
- **AEL Toggle.** The AEL button can be pressed and released, and the exposure remains locked until the button is pressed again.
- **Center Point AEL Hold.** Exposure is locked on the center point of the frame while the button is held down.
- **Center Point AEL Toggle.** Toggles exposure lock on/off using the center point of the frame.

Other Useful Key Definitions

Here are some other possible custom key definitions you might find useful:

- **FINDER/MONITOR switch.** If you turn off automatic switching between FINDER and MONITOR, you'll want to have a button that will quickly toggle between the two.
- **Eye AF.** It's handy to have a button that activates the a6400's impressive Eye-AF feature.
- **More pairs.** Several custom buttons can be assigned pairs of related functions. For example, if you've set one to change ISO sensitivity, the other button can be used to specify ISO Auto Minimum Shutter Speed. Image Size/Quality is another good pair for button combinations.
- **Freed-up keys.** Once you assign ISO to another control, that leaves the right button, formerly used to set ISO, free for a new definition. You could assign it to Metering Mode or another function.

■ **Temporary Dial/Wheel settings.** You can assign functions to the control wheel and/or control dial and recall them instantly by using a Custom Key. You have three different definitions that can be registered. I'll show you how to do that using the My Dial Settings entry later in this chapter.

Custom Key (Movies)

Options: Definitions for Custom Button 1, Center Button; Left/Right/Down Buttons; AF-MF/AEL Button; Focus Hold Button (on lens)

Default: Follow Custom (Stills)

My preference: N/A

You can assign *different* functions to each of the customizable controls when shooting movies, assuming you have such a need and an excellent memory. The default definition for those controls is Follow Custom (Stills), which uses whichever behaviors you have assigned using the Custom Key (Stills) entry.

Custom Key (Playback)

Options: Definitions for Custom Button 1, plus Fn/Send to Smartphone button

Default: Varies

My preference: N/A

Only a limited number of controls and functions are available using this entry. The Custom 1 button can be assigned behaviors during Playback, most of them options from the Playback menu itself. The C1 button follows the setting made for Stills/Movie mode (unless you choose another behavior). The Fn button, which by default sends the displayed image to your smartphone, can also be defined to perform other functions, such as FINDER/MONITOR, various Playback, and Touch settings.

Function Menu Settings

Options: 36 different Function menu settings

Default: Top row: Drive Mode, Focus Mode, Focus Area, Exposure Compensation, ISO, Metering mode; Bottom row: Flash Mode, Flash Compensation, White Balance, Creative Style, Prioritize Record Media, Shoot Mode

My preference: N/A

When you press the Fn button when in Shooting or Movie modes, a screen like the one shown in Figure 4.22, left, pops up, with six settings each in two rows arrayed along the bottom. The default options are illustrated. This entry allows you to change the function of any of the 12 positions in the Function menu, so you can display only those you use most, and arrange them in the order that best suits you. There are 47 different functions available, including Not Set. Browse through the list below and decide which 12 you want to display on the Function menu.

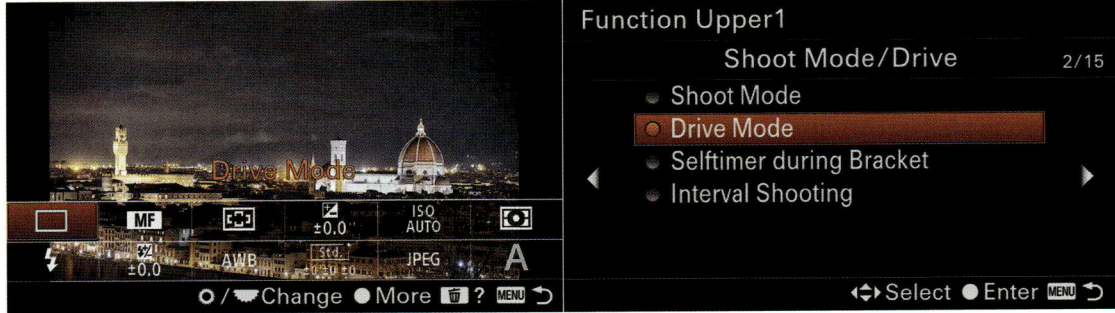

Figure 4.22 Function menu default settings (left). Function menu settings (right).

When you access Function Menu Set, your current Function menu appears. Highlight the position you want to change and press OK. A screen like the one shown in Figure 4.22, right, appears. There are 15 screens in all, each listing possible definitions you can assign to that position. You can then select from among these options, all explained in detail elsewhere in this book, and press OK to select and confirm. Your options include:

- File Format
- JPEG Quality
- JPEG Image Size
- Aspect Ratio
- Shoot Mode
- Drive Mode
- Self-timer During Bracket
- Interval Shooting
- Focus Mode
- Focus Area
- Left/Right Eye Select
- Exposure Compensation
- ISO
- ISO Auto Minimum Shutter Speed
- Metering Mode

- Face Priority in Multi Metering
- Flash Mode
- Flash Compensation
- Wireless Flash
- White Balance
- Priority Set in AWB
- DRO/Auto HDR
- Creative Style
- Picture Effect
- Picture Profile
- Soft Skin Effect
- Peaking Display
- Peaking Level
- Peaking Color
- Smile Shutter

- Auto Object Framing
- S&Q Frame Rate
- Audio Recording Level
- Audio Level Display
- Marker Display
- Silent Shooting
- SteadyShot
- Finder Frame Rate
- Zebra Display
- Zebra Level
- Grid Line
- Live View Display
- Audio Signals
- Gamma Display Assist
- Touch Operation
- Not Set

Note that you can select Not Set to leave a position blank if you want to unclutter your screen, or even duplicate an entry in multiple positions, accidentally or on purpose. Don't underestimate the power of this function. You can, in effect, create your own pop-up Function menu using any of nearly four *dozen* different functions.

My Dial Settings Setup

Options: Three separate definitions each for control wheel and control dial

Default: Not Set

My preference: N/A

This is an extremely versatile feature, which allows you to temporarily assign a different behavior to the control wheel and/or control dial, and still return them to their default functions easily. Most of the time in shooting mode, you'll want to use the wheel/dial to control shutter speed or aperture. But a quick spin of the dial/wheel can be convenient for making other settings, such as ISO or white balance adjustments. You can assign that alternate function to one of those controls, and then recall it by pressing a Custom Key that you've defined (as described above).

When you access this entry, a screen similar to the one shown in Figure 4.23 appears. The two bottom rows represent the control wheel and control dial, and the right three columns show the current values for the three definitions for each, called My Dial 1, My Dial 2, or My Dial 3. Before you have added any definitions, each of the current settings will be Not Set, represented by double-dashes like the one highlighted in orange at right in the figure.

Figure 4.23
My Dial Settings.

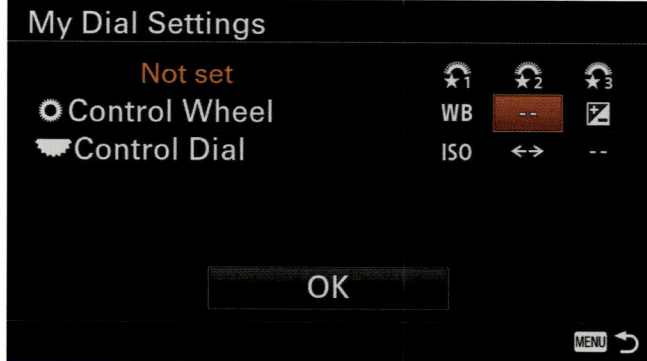

Note: Each of the three My Dial settings applies to both the control wheel and control dial, but you do not have to define a function to both. For example, you could use My Dial 1 to assign a particular function to the control wheel, but leave the control dial at Not Set (which means it would retain its default behavior).

To assign a definition, just follow these steps:

1. **Access My Dial Setup.** The settings screen appears.
2. **Choose your control and My Dial register.** Use the directional buttons to highlight My Dial 1, My Dial 2, or My Dial 3, either in the control wheel row or the control dial row.

3. **Press the center button.** A set of screens will appear with five pages that encompass 11 possible functions that can be assigned.

- Move AF Point Left/ Right
- Move AF Point Up/ Down
- Aperture

- Shutter Speed
- Exposure Compensation
- ISO
- White Balance
- Color Temperature

- Creative Style
- Picture effect
- Audio Recording Level
- Not Set

4. **Press the center button to confirm.** You can then repeat steps 2 and 3 to define additional My Dial registers.

5. **Highlight OK.** Press OK to exit.

6. **Assign My Dial 1, 2, or 3 to a Custom Key.** Use the Custom Key (Stills) entry described earlier to assign the temporary behavior to the button you will use to switch to the alternate function. You have three different modes for activating the feature:

- **My Dial 1 (or 2, or 3) During Hold.** When you press the assigned Custom Key, the alternate function for the specified My Dial register is active. As soon as you release it, the wheel/ dial resumes its default function.

- **My Dial 1→2→3.** When you press and hold the Custom Key, rotating that control switches among each of the registers in turn, and then wraps around to the first. Think of this as a meta-control: instead of activating a particular My Dial register and its settings, it allows you to quickly cycle among all three of them, each with their own set of settings. I suspect only those who truly need a larger number of alternate actions for the control wheel and control dial will really need this (and I don't envy them the learning curve required to remember which My Dial settings contain which customized functions).

- **Toggle My Dial 1 (or 2, or 3).** The specified My Dial register is activated when the Custom Key is pressed, and deactivated when the Custom Key is pressed again. Use this if you need to turn on particular features for a period of time, and then return to the controls' default operation with a second key press.

Dial/Wheel Setup

Options: Reverse functions

Default: Control Dial: Aperture; Control Wheel: Shutter Speed

My preference: N/A

By default, in Manual exposure mode the control dial controls the f/stop, and the control wheel adjusts the shutter speed. This entry allows you to reverse those functions for Manual exposure only if you prefer. (Either the control dial or control wheel can be used to adjust shutter speed [in Shutter Priority mode] and aperture [in Aperture Priority mode]). You may have a special reason for wanting to reverse the dial/wheel directions, but you're better off leaving it alone.

Av/Tv Rotate

Options: Normal, Reverse functions

Default: Normal

My preference: N/A

This entry, the first in the Camera Settings II-09 menu (see Figure 4.24), lets you specify the direction of rotation of the control dial and control wheel when using them to adjust the aperture or shutter speed. When the default Normal is in effect, clockwise rotation produces a smaller f/stop or faster shutter speed; counterclockwise rotation sets a larger f/stop or slower shutter speed. Choose Reverse, and clockwise rotation sets a larger f/stop or slower shutter speed, while counterclockwise produces a smaller f/stop or faster shutter speed. This is a personal preference setting.

Dial/Wheel Ev Comp

Options: Off, Wheel, Dial

Default: Off

My preference: Off

If you like, you can use the control wheel or control dial to set exposure compensation. When you do that, the other control retains its original function. That is, if you choose the control wheel to set EV, then the control dial can still be used to adjust shutter speed in Shutter Priority mode, and the control dial to select aperture in Aperture Priority mode. Select the control dial for EV instead, and the control wheel retains its shutter speed or aperture function, respectively.

Figure 4.24
Camera Settings
II-09 (Custom
Operation2) menu.

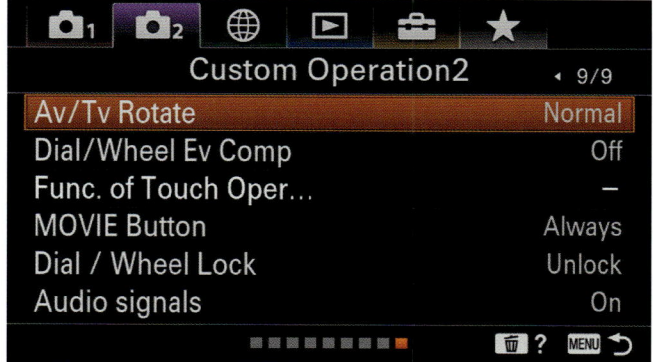

Function of Touch Operations

Options: Touch Shutter, Touch Focus, Touch Tracking

Default: Touch Focus

My preference: Touch Tracking

As I noted in Chapter 2, the a6400's touch screen can operate in three different modes: Touch Shutter, Touch Focus, and Touch Tracking. You can have only one mode active at a time, but their functions overlap enough that one of the three will likely do the job for you. This entry allows you to activate the mode you prefer. To recap:

- **Touch Shutter.** Tap the screen to specify the focus point. The camera will then immediately take a picture. While Touch Shutter is enabled, you can activate it or deactivate it by tapping the icon at the upper-right corner of the screen (and shown earlier in Figure 2.6). You can tell Touch Shutter is enabled when the orange bar appears to the left of the Touch icon.

  This mode is most useful when you're composing your image using the LCD monitor. Just tap to take a single picture, or keep touching the screen when Drive Mode is set to Continuous Shooting to capture a burst. This mode is unavailable when using the viewfinder, or Movie, S&Q Motion, Sweep Panorama, Smile Shutter, or Manual Focus modes; when using Digital or Clear Image Zoom; and when Focus Area is set to Digital or Clear Image Zoom.

- **Touch Focus.** Tap the LCD screen and select a focus point or zone anywhere that the a6400 is able to achieve autofocus (that is, most of the frame other than the edges).

  - **Tap the LCD screen.** The camera will focus at that point. Or slide your finger around the screen to move the focus area around within the frame. You can do this whether composing on the LCD monitor or looking through the viewfinder.

  - **Double tap the LCD screen.** In Manual Focus mode, a double-tap on the LCD activates the focus magnifier.

  In autofocus mode, the a6400 will focus when you press the shutter release down halfway. You can deactivate touch focus by pressing the center button, or by tapping the "cancel focus" icon (a pointing finger with an X next to it) that appears at upper right on the screen. A quick tap may not register; this function requires a firm press.

  This mode is not available for autofocus activation when Focus Area is set to Flexible Spot or Expand Flexible Spot, but you can still move the focus frame around. In Movie mode, Spot Focus can be used with the LCD only. Touch Focus is not available when using Sweep Panorama, Digital Zoom, or with A-mount lenses when using the LA-EA2 or LA-EA4 adapters.

■ **Touch Tracking.** In this mode, you can specify a subject that will be tracked by tapping the LCD monitor. Tracking will start and continue until you press the center button or tap the Cancel Tracking icon in the upper-right corner of the LCD monitor. The camera will focus on the tracked subject when you press the shutter release down halfway. Note that this feature is not available with Hand-held Twilight and Anti-Motion Blur Scene modes; when using Sweep Panorama or Manual Focus modes; with Smart, Clear Image, or Digital zoom features; and when using the LA-EA2 or LA-EA4 lens adapters. It is also disabled in Movie mode when Record Setting is set to 120p/100p.

MOVIE Button

Options: Always, Movie Mode Only
Default: Always
My preference: Always

Movie recording can be started in any operating mode by pressing the Movie record button. This feature is on by default, but if you find that you occasionally press the button inadvertently, you might want to choose the Off option. After you do so, pressing the button will have no effect; when you want to record a movie, you'll need to rotate the mode dial to the Movie position. I usually prefer Always, because I find that impromptu video-capture situations are more frequent than accidental movie start-ups.

Dial/Wheel Lock

Options: Unlock, Lock
Default: Unlock
My preference: Unlock

If you want to avoid accidentally changing settings by inadvertently using the control dial or control wheel, you can implement this locking option. Choose Lock and the controls are frozen whenever the Fn button is pressed and held down. A "Locked" indicator appears on the screen. If the default Unlock option is selected, pressing the Fn button has no effect on the controls. I sometimes use this when using Manual exposure in a situation where the lighting does not change drastically, and I want to avoid accidentally changing my aperture or shutter speed settings.

Audio Signals

Options: On, Off

Default: On

My preference: Off

Enables and disables the beeping/chirping sounds the camera makes when various operations happen, such as achieving autofocus or the self-timer countdown. Most of the time I don't require the feedback and, on the contrary, want to blend in without calling attention to myself, so I disable the noises. The self-timer countdown is especially noticeable, even in environments with a moderate amount of noise. Couple this setting with Silent Shooting and you can often take pictures virtually unnoticed.

5

Network and Playback Menus

Your a6400 is equipped with a built-in wireless communication system that includes a whole collection of impressive abbreviations, acronyms, and buzzwords—and functions to match! Wi-Fi, NFC, and Bluetooth have arrived, so you can easily and quickly transfer files from your camera to a smartphone or computer, upload to Facebook, control your camera remotely, and perform other tasks. This chapter provides an introduction to connecting your camera to other devices using the Network menu. Then, we'll move on to the Playback menu to discuss some of the options available when reviewing images.

Network Menu

The section explains the basic functions on the Network menu, in order, although you probably won't be *using* them in this order. For example, you should make Wi-Fi Settings or assign a name to a device in the Network 2 menu *before* you use the functions in the Network 1 menu. (See Figure 5.1.) I'll summarize all the entries first, and then later cover the major options in logical/functional order rather than the order they appear in the menus. Detailed networking/information technology topics and software operation discussions are beyond the scope of this book, which is primarily a *photography* tome, not a software tutorial, so some sections may provide just an overview. Consult the PlayMemories Home and Imaging Edge/Imaging Edge Mobile help files for detailed descriptions of how to transfer, post-process, and organize your stills and videos. Because the Network menu entries are *functions,* the settings all relate to your own camera/device configuration, so I won't provide any **My Preference** notes for them.

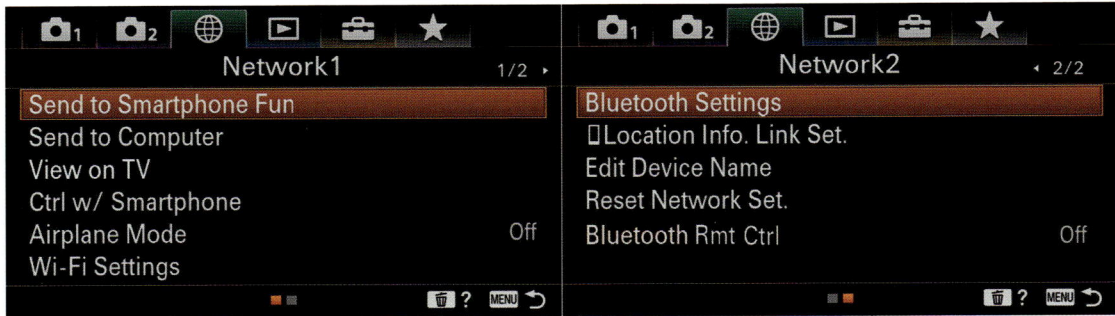

Figure 5.1 The Network 1 and 2 menus.

The Network menu contains the following entries:

- Send to Smartphone Function
- Send to Computer
- View on TV
- Control with Smartphone
- Airplane Mode
- Wi-Fi Settings

- Bluetooth Settings
- Location Info Link Settings
- Edit Device Name
- Reset Network Settings
- Bluetooth Remote Control

Send to Smartphone Function

Options: Send to Smartphone (Select on This Device, Select on Smartphone); Sending Target (Proxy Only, Original Only, Proxy & Original)

Using the Imaging Edge Mobile app (which replaces the PlayMemories Mobile app you may have used with your previous Sony camera) on your smart device, you can transfer still photographs, XAVC X video, and slow- or quick-motion movies from your camera's memory card. This entry lets you specify whether the files to be transferred are selected on the camera or on the smart device, and whether you transfer the original file only, or, in the case of videos, a proxy (lower-quality, faster transfer) movie only, or both the original and proxy. (See Chapter 4 for a description of proxy recordings in the Camera Settings II-01 menu.)

The Imaging Edge Mobile app allows you to choose the Image Copy Size for stills, original, 2MB, or VGA, so you can speed up transfer, if necessary, by selecting a smaller file size. RAW files are converted to JPEG before transmission. 4K video, XAVC S movies recorded at 120/100p, and AVCHD movies cannot be transferred at all. Only the proxy movies can be sent. Be aware that your smart device may not be able to play back some files; even if they transfer fine, your phone or tablet may not be able to display them. That's a limitation of the destination device, not your a6400. You may need to find a third-party gallery app for your Android or iOS device that can handle a wider variety of files.

Note that when the Fn button's Playback behavior is set to its default value, pressing it while a still image or movie is displayed summons the Send to Smartphone function, bypassing this menu. If you don't transmit to your smart device often, you can safely redefine the Fn button to another behavior for Playback, as this menu entry is always available.

Send to Computer

Options: None

You can transfer images stored on your memory card to a computer through a wireless access point or broadband router connection using the PlayMemories Home application *on your computer.* PlayMemories Home is the Windows/Mac counterpart to the Imaging Edge Mobile (previously PlayMemories Mobile) app on your smart device. Don't confuse the two! Proxy movies cannot be transferred using this facility.

SOFTWARE SHUFFLE

Sony is constantly updating its free software, which may cause some confusion, especially since it has done a little renaming of some key applications as they are upgraded. Here's a quick summary:

- **Imaging Edge.** This is the suite of three applications that runs on Mac and Windows computers. The trio includes Viewer (for browsing, filtering images by rating, and creating time-lapse movies); Edit (used to crop/straighten images, adjust their brightness and color, and convert RAW files into JPEG or TIFF formats); and Remote (for taking photos with a camera tethered by USB cable to your computer). Note that Remote has an additional function of creating higher resolution images by combining four shots using Pixel Shift Multi shooting, currently available only on Sony's full-frame E-mount cameras.

- **PlayMemories Home.** This older software (which I think will eventually be folded into the Imaging Edge suite), allows you to manage and perform simple edits on your PC or Mac. You can organize your images/videos by the date, camera/lens, or other attributes, plus search and share them (including uploads to the PlayMemories Online cloud).

- **Imaging Edge Mobile.** This is a replacement for PlayMemories Mobile; indeed, if you already have the previous app on your device, it will be automatically replaced the next time you perform an update. Its functions include Remote Shooting (to preview, change settings, and take photos with your smart device) and Transfer Images/Movies (you can select files to transfer from the smart device or the a6400).

View on TV

Options: Connect to TV; Slideshow settings

You don't need to hard-wire your network-enabled smart TV to the a6400 to transfer still images. This entry allows you to set up displays and slide shows wirelessly, selecting images, the display interval, playback size, and any special effects. Movies cannot be transferred using this facility. Operations controlled from the TV vary by model, so you'll need to consult your DLNA-compatible smart TV's manual to make the best use of this feature.

Control with Smartphone

Options: Control with Smartphone (On, Off); Smartphone Connection (Display QR Code); Always Connected (On, Off)

You can control your camera using your smart device and a Wi-Fi connection. This entry turns the feature on or off, displays a QR code to quickly link the camera and device, and specifies whether, once activated, the camera remains connected to the smartphone at all times (draining your battery significantly) or maintains the link only when you connect manually.

Airplane Mode

Options: On, Off

Choosing On disables wireless functions; Off enables them. Use this to save power, or when required (as when boarding an airplane).

Wi-Fi Settings

Options: WPS Push, Access Point Settings, Display MAC Address, SSID/PW Reset

This entry includes features for connecting the a6400 to a Wi-Fi access point, either semi-automatically using WPS Push or by manually registering by entering the SSID name of the access point and entering security information. You can also view the device's MAC Address. Each device on a network has a unique Media Access Control number. You generally have no need to know this, unless you want to block a device from your network and use the MAC address to identify the unwanted device.

SSID/PW Reset deletes the current SSID and password. You might want to do this for security reasons (say, you load/give/sell your a6400 to someone else) or need to start over in registering your camera with a network. Reset Network Settings removes all network settings from the camera. I'll describe the key components of the Wi-Fi Settings screen later in the chapter.

Bluetooth Settings

Options: Bluetooth Function (On, Off); Pairing; Display Device Address

Your a6400 can access the GPS information available from your smartphone and embed that data in your image files using low-energy Bluetooth connectivity. Use this, and you no longer have to wonder where you took a photo; the GPS data can be displayed by many applications, including Lightroom's Map tab. This entry allows you to turn off Bluetooth sharing, pairing your phone with your camera, and displaying the device's address. Keep in mind that when you initialize your camera, as described in Chapter 6, pairing settings are canceled as well.

Location Information Link Setting

Options: Location Info Link, Auto Time Correction, Auto Area Adjustment

This entry allows the a6400 to access the location information from your smartphone, after you've enabled Bluetooth connectivity in the previous entry. One of the cool features is to use the Auto Time Correction option to allow your smartphone's (very) accurate time information to be used to set the time and date used by your camera. It's the "let's synchronize our watches" version for the 21st century. You can also activate Auto Area Adjustment, so the camera "knows" where it is and uses the correct time zone. Turn this on if you want to embed in your image files the local time when you took a picture; turn it off if you'd prefer the time reflect your "back home" norm.

Edit Device Name

Options: Change Device Name

By default, the label applied to your camera is ILCE-6400. You can change it to something else, if, say, you own three or four a6400's and want to differentiate between them—or simply want to personalize your camera's "name."

Reset Network Settings

Options: Reset and Reboot

Changes all network settings to their factory defaults and reboots your a6400.

Bluetooth Remote Control

Options: On/Off

The Sony RMT-P1BT remote control operates by Bluetooth LE (low-energy) radio signals, and became compatible with the a6400 beginning with the June 2019 Version 2.0 firmware upgrade. This remote, at a little less than $80, is not as inexpensive as infrared remote controls, drains much less juice from your camera, has a range of about 16 feet, and isn't dazzled by bright sunlight (which can give IR remotes fits). It can start/stop movie recording, too.

Making a Connection

For this section, I'm basing my descriptions in this chapter on the assumption that you are *not* an IT specialist, and don't need (or want) to compare the advantages of WEP versus WPA security, and would rather not set IP addresses yourself. Alternatively, I will assume that if you *are* an IT specialist and find these topics compelling, you already know most of what you need and would rather not hear it from me, again. As Thoreau once said, "Simplify, simplify!" (but without explaining the redundant "Simplify").

If you want to connect using your smartphone or tablet, the first thing you should do is venture over to your smart device's app store and download the Imaging Edge Mobile app, which I described earlier in this chapter. (If you already have the older PlayMemories Mobile app, it will be upgraded to the newer version during your next update.) Then follow the instructions that follow for connecting through NFC or Wi-Fi. The a6400 has an additional option for linking your smartphone to the camera through Bluetooth so GPS information can be embedded in your photographs.

Using NFC One-Touch

If you have an Android device, connecting with NFC is your simplest option. NFC stands for *Near Field Communication*, a wireless access method found in Android-based smartphones and tablets. It's not available with iOS devices, although Apple Pay uses it to send your money hither and yon. Once you've installed the PlayMemories Mobile app on your device, linking the a6400 and the device is as simple as tapping the area on your phone containing its transceiver with the camera's transceiver (located under the "N" mark on the right side of the hand grip). Just follow these steps:

1. Turn on NFC on your smart device. Cancel any sleep or lock-screen functions so the device will not disconnect before you are finished shooting.

2. Access the Control w/Smartphone entry in the camera's Network 1 menu and make sure the feature is On.

3. Power up the a6400. The NFC "N" mark will display on the camera's screen, indicating that NFC is available.

4. Tap the matching NFC mark on the camera with your device for several seconds. If either the camera or phone are in a third-party case, you may need to remove the case to make the connection.

5. Once connected, the Imaging Edge Mobile application on the phone should launch automatically.

6. You can now preview the a6400's image on your smartphone, take pictures using it as a remote control, and transfer your shots from the camera to your device.

7. To transfer images, choose Send to Smartphone Functions from the Network 1 menu, select Send to Smartphone, and select images. Use NFC to connect the camera to the phone if not already linked.

Connecting Using QR Code

Both iOS and NFC connections can also be made using a QR code. Just follow these steps:

1. Choose Control w/Smartphone from the Network 1 menu and choose the Smartphone Connection choice from the screen that appears. (See Figure 5.2, left.) The device is represented by a smartphone icon.

2. A QR code will appear on the camera's LCD. (See Figure 5.2, right.)

3. In Imaging Edge Mobile, select Scan NFC/QR Code of the Camera from the screen seen at left in Figure 5.3.

4. Choose Scan QR Code of the Camera from the screen that appears next. (See Figure 5.3, center.)

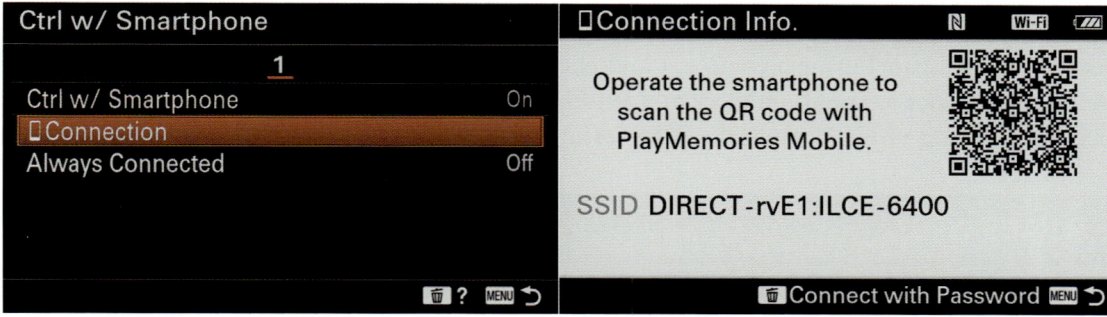

Figure 5.2 Choose Smartphone Connection (left) and a QR code will appear on the a6400's LCD monitor.

Figure 5.3
Select Scan NFC/
QR Code of the
Camera (left), start
the scan (center),
and point the
device's camera at
the QR code on the
a6400's LCD
(right).

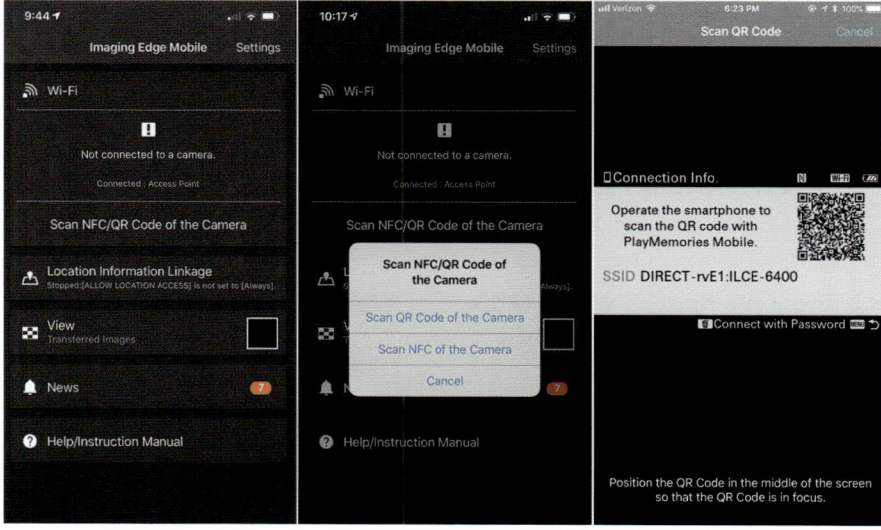

5. A window will appear with a crosshair in its center. Position the crosshair on the QR code to connect. (See Figure 5.3, right.)

6. The smart device will connect with the a6400 and display a screen asking if you want to Join the connection. Choose OK to complete the link. Some operating systems may ask you to install a Profile on your phone or tablet the first time you connect to a Sony camera, and you may be asked to confirm the SSID (shown at right in Figure 5.3) and a password.

Using WPS Push

Wi-Fi Protected Setup works only when you're in range of a network provided by a wireless router that is equipped with a WPS button. Not all are. Examine your router and look for a button labeled WPS, or with a ⓕ symbol. Or, find the owner's manual for your router or use a Google search (try "*routername* manual PDF") to locate the WPS button, if one is available. Some routers that support WPS provide it with software instead of a physical button; in that case, you'll need to access the router's control panel using a computer and click the button on the WPS page. The WPS Push tactic is great, but it would not work at a Wi-Fi hotspot in a supermarket, for instance, since the network owner is unlikely to use the WPS feature for hundreds of customers.

WHAT'S WPS?

The abbreviation WPS indicates Wi-Fi Protected Setup. This is a security standard that makes it easier and quicker to connect a device, including your a6400, to a wireless home network. It eliminates the need to key in the password. Because it's possible for an aggressive hacker to recover the WPS PIN number, some experts suggest turning the router's WPS feature off when you're not actually using it; this may not be possible with all router models but check the owner's manual for the one you own.

Just follow these steps:

1. **Access Network 1 menu and choose Wi-Fi Settings.** If your router provides WPS, scroll to the WPS Push item in the camera's Wi-Fi settings menu (the top entry at left in Figure 5.4) and press the center button.

2. **Press the router's WPS button.** A screen will appear advising you to press the router's WPS button within 2 minutes. When you press the button (or use the software) to do so, the camera should be able to establish connectivity.

3. **Confirm registration.** Once the connection is established, a screen reporting "Registered. SSID *network name*" appears. Press the center button to confirm.

Registering Manually

You can also select an access point manually when within range of a wireless network; you'll need to know the network password, if one is in place, to do so. Just follow these steps:

1. **Access the Network 1's Wi-Fi Settings entry.** Scroll to Access Point Set, seen just below WPS Push at left in Figure 5.4. Press the center button. A Wi-Fi Standby screen will appear confirming that the camera is searching for available access points.

2. **Wait for the camera to find your network.** The a6400 will find the nearby access points (networks) in less than a minute. (See Figure 5.4, right.) If there is more than one network or available access point, all of those found will be shown. If your smartphone has a hotspot feature and it's turned on, that "network" may appear as well.

    When several networks are displayed, some may belong to nearby businesses or your neighbors, and you can ignore them (their signal strength is probably weaker than your own network in any case, even if your neighbor's network is not protected by a password). In my case, my wireless router resides in my office; in other, more distant rooms is a wired access point, and, on the second floor, a wireless repeater. Scroll to the one you intend to use and press the center button to confirm.

3. **Input the password (if necessary).** The next screen that appears may have a field for entering your network password, if your router/access point is set up to require one. If not, proceed to Step 4. Otherwise, press the center button and enter the password. When finished, highlight OK and press the center button.

4. **IP Address Setting.** The next screen will appear, showing the IP Address Setting as Auto and Priority Connection as Off. These defaults should work perfectly. Select OK and press the center button. A screen will appear showing the camera trying to connect to the network.

    If the Auto IP Address Setting option does not work, and you have some networking expertise, change from Auto to Manual, and a screen appears that allows you to enter the IP address, Subnet Mark, and Default Gateway. You can safely leave the Priority Connection parameter set to Off. Fortunately, you probably won't have to resort to these additional steps.

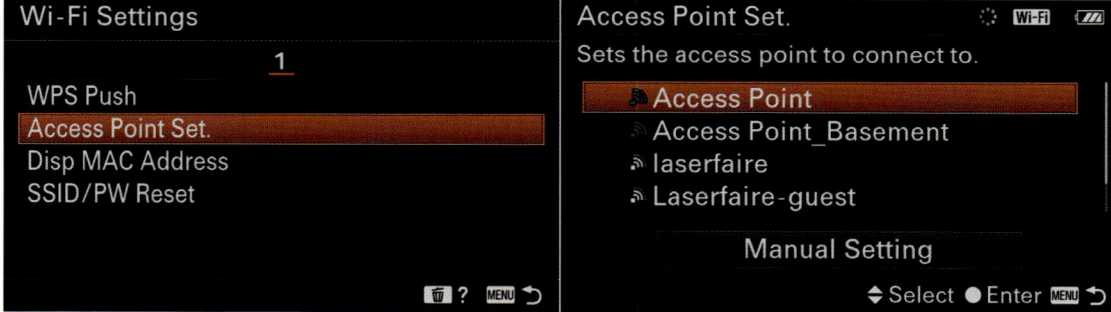

Figure 5.4 Access Point Settings can be used to select an access point/hotspot. (Left.) The camera displays the available networks that are within range. (Right.)

5. **Confirm connectivity.** After the Wi-Fi connectivity has been made, a screen will appear confirming that your network has been registered. An orange dot will appear next to the connected network. If you get a screen with a note stating *cannot authenticate*, or that the *input value is invalid*, you'll need to start again at step 1; make sure you have the correct password for the network and be extra careful when keying it in. Remember that when a capital letter is required, you must use the shift feature (an arrow pointing upward) on the virtual keyboard.

6. **Try it again later.** After you have established Wi-Fi connectivity, you can revert to using the a6400 as usual; a touch of the shutter release button returns it to shooting mode. The camera will retain the connection to the network until you turn it off or it goes into power-saving sleep mode; Wi-Fi is then temporarily disconnected. When you're ready to use Wi-Fi again, activate the a6400 while in range of the same network, scroll to Access Point Settings in the Wireless menu, and press the center button. The camera will quickly find your network to re-establish Wi-Fi connectivity.

If you're connecting to a public Wi-Fi hotspot, the steps should be the same, but you'll most likely find a screen that requires you to agree to the hotspot's terms and conditions. Some hotspots may not require you to enter a password.

Selecting an Access Point Manually

If the desired access point (network) is not displayed on the screen as described in Step 2 above, you may need to enter it yourself. Just follow these steps:

1. **Choose Manual Setting.** Scroll down to Manual Setting (see Figure 5.5, left) and press the center button.

2. **Select Manual Registration.** Press the center button to begin the manual registration process. The screen shown at right in Figure 5.5 appears.

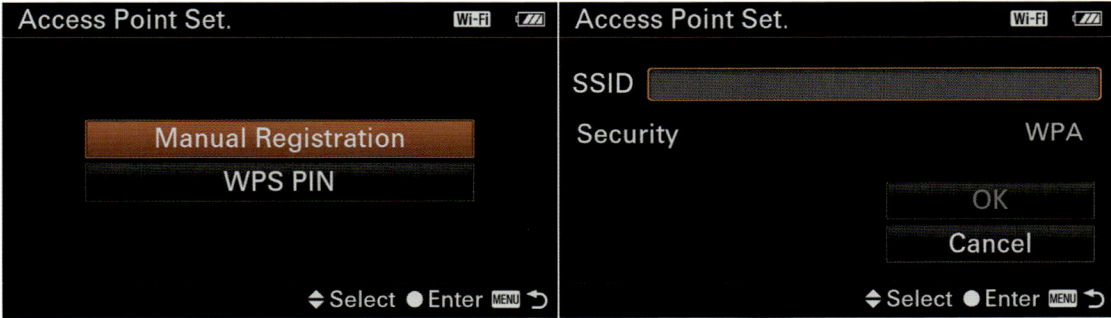

Figure 5.5 Manual registration (left) requires you to complete extra steps, including the SSID (right).

3. **Enter SSID.** On the Manual Registration screen, there's a field for entering the SSID name of the access point (network) you plan to use. Press the center button when this field is visible, and the virtual keyboard appears. Enter the data. When you're finished press the center button.

4. **Change Security (if necessary).** Again, if you have some networking expertise, you'll know if the security setting on your router is WPA (Wi-Fi Protected Access, the default), WEP (Wired Equivalent Privacy, an older, easily "hacked" protection scheme), or None (effectively, no security). If you want to change the Security setting, highlight that field and press the center button. Select your choice and press the MENU button to return.

5. **Enter password.** The next screen will ask for your password, which you can enter using the virtual keyboard.

6. **Enter WPS PIN (if necessary).** If your WPS connection requires a PIN, you can enter it.

Take care not to lose the network connection by inadvertently using the Initialize or the Reset Network Settings item of the Wireless menu. If you do so, the camera will eliminate all your network settings and you'll need to repeat the steps in this section.

Connecting with Bluetooth

The good news is that Sony has finally brought simple Bluetooth LE connections to its camera line, allowing you to share GPS data from your phone with the a6400. You can use devices with Android 5.0 versions or later compatible with Bluetooth 4.0 and later; and Apple devices including iPhone 4s (and later) or iPad (3rd generation and later). The camera will embed the data in the EXIF image information, making it available for mapping and other applications that can access it.

I love Bluetooth—my smartphone is linked to my vehicle's hands-free calling feature, the soundbar on my smart TV, and the remote control I use to snap photos with my iPhone's camera. My Fitbit tells my health app how well I slept the night before using a Bluetooth connection, and my wireless headphones allow me to listen to music or take calls without removing the phone from my pocket. When I play "music," (I've been told it's debateable) my bass guitar "talks" to my amp from 16 feet away, with no cable required.

The bad news—and it isn't really bad—is that you need to temporarily forget your traditional way of connecting to a new Bluetooth device. Do not try to pair your a6400 with your smart device using your smart device's Settings screen. If you accidentally do so, you'll need to use your phone's Bluetooth Forget Device command and start over. Your a6400 connects to your phone or tablet using the Imaging Edge Mobile app and can't link up any other way. Make sure your Bluetooth Remote Control setting, described earlier, is set to Off. While your camera can be paired with as many as 15 different devices, it can share location information with only one smartphone and can't connect to two devices simultaneously.

Then, just follow these steps (and remember that when you use the Setup menu's Initialize command, your Bluetooth connects are removed, too):

1. Select Bluetooth Settings from the Network 2 menu. The screen shown at left in Figure 5.6 appears.

2. Highlight Pairing and press the center button. The screen shown at right in Figure 5.6 pops up.

3. Launch the Imaging Edge App. Choose Location Image Linkage to produce the screen shown at left in Figure 5.7.

4. Select OK and the screen shown at right in the figure appears. It displays any cameras you've already linked (in my case a Sony a7R III), and currently non-paired cameras, including my a6400. Highlight the a6400's label (it appears as ILCE-6400) and choose OK to begin pairing.

5. Imaging Edge and your camera will link up.

6. The matching Location Information Linkage menu entry in the camera's menu system, which I described earlier in this chapter, allows your a6400 to automatically set itself to the correct time, and determine your current geographical area. You'll never have to adjust your Date/Time and Area Setting entries in the Setup 5 menu as long as you keep your phone linked to the camera.

7. If you encounter difficulties, make sure your phone/tablet's Bluetooth is enabled, Airplane Mode on the camera is Off, and the camera is not connected to other devices. Choose Reset Network Settings in the Network 2 menu and try pairing again.

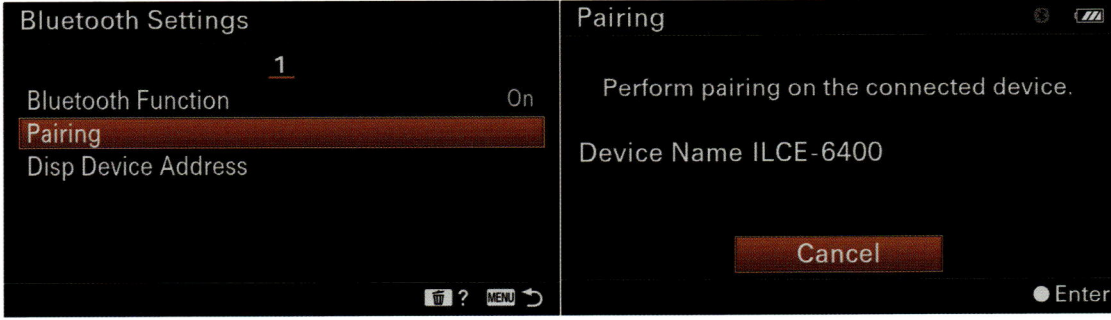

Figure 5.6 Select pairing (left) and the camera will display the screen shown at right.

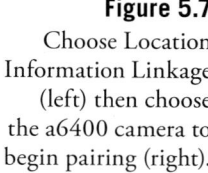

Figure 5.7

Choose Location Information Linkage (left) then choose the a6400 camera to begin pairing (right).

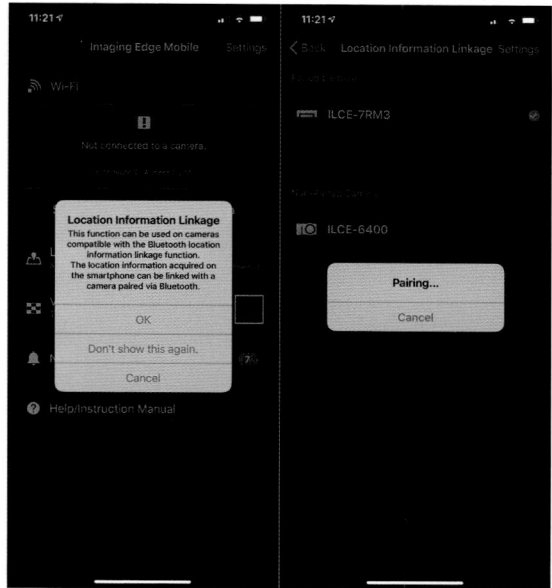

Viewing Images on a TV

As with any current digital camera, it's possible to view JPEG photos and video clips on an HDTV when you connect the a6400 to the TV using an HDMI cable. This is an extra-cost accessory. Buy the Type D cable with a micro HDMI connector at one end (for plugging into the camera) and a conventional HDMI plug (to connect to the TV's HDMI port) at the other. An inexpensive cable is fine; there's no need to pay more for one of the premium brands unless you need a cable that's longer than about 6 feet. Make the cable connection and you can now display photos and movies on the oversized screen.

After the Wi-Fi connection has been made with a Digital Living Network Alliance/DLNA-compatible (network-enabled or Wi-Fi Direct–enabled) HDTV, you can use this menu item, on the second screen of Wireless options. Use it to display photos on the HDTV without cable connection after Wi-Fi connectivity has been confirmed. The benefit of Wi-Fi Direct is that you do not need to register your access point on the camera before doing so; in other words, the TV need not be connected to the network if you are using Wi-Fi Direct. Movie clips cannot be transferred to a TV for display over Wi-Fi; to show those, connect the camera to the HDTV using an optional Type D HDMI cable.

Use the menu options to instruct the camera as to which device (TV) it should send to, which photos to display (all or only those in a specific folder), and whether the display time should be long or short if using the slide show feature. Press the center button if you do want to use the slide show feature. At any time, you can move to another image for the display by scrolling to the left or right.

It's also possible to transfer JPEG photos, but not videos, to an HDTV without cable connection. If you have a networked TV (or a network-friendly game machine such as PlayStation or Xbox), you can view the images in your camera on that display without using the HDMI cable.

Of course, the HDTV must be DLNA (Digital Living Network Alliance) compliant and it must first be connected to your home network via Wi-Fi as per the instructions that came with the device. The a6400 must also be communicating with your network via Wi-Fi, of course. (Use the steps provided earlier.)

Tip

There is an exception to the DLNA rule. Some HDTVs are Wi-Fi Direct enabled; if yours is, then it need not be connected to your network. Mine is not, so I have not been able to try this feature.

There are simply too many types of Wi-Fi-enabled HDTVs to provide full specifics on exactly how you'll transfer JPEGs to the device. Sony's published documents specifically recommend their Bravia HDTV, as you might expect, but you can use any DLNA- (or Wi-Fi Direct–) enabled TV. A Bravia HDTV does provide a few extra display features that are possible only when using a Sony camera.

In any event, start by accessing the View on TV item in the camera's Network menu and press the center button. The camera will confirm the Wi-Fi connection to your network and it will search for a compatible TV. Be sure to consult your TV's instructions for setting the media display component to receive information from the camera. When connectivity with the TV has been confirmed, you can begin the sharing process using connection controls like those described earlier in this chapter.

Remote Control

Shooting photos remotely with your a6400 is the next best thing to shooting tethered using Lightroom. All you need is your camera and your smartphone. You can also shoot remotely using the new, free Imaging Edge software, which you can download from your country's Sony website. For casual remote-control shooting, whether you want to exercise some creative options (to get unusual viewpoints), you are stalking wildlife, or are a double-naught spy, your smartphone and camera will do the job.

Once you've connected your camera to the smartphone, the screen shown at left in Figure 5.8 appears. There are a limited number of settings you can make from the smartphone, but you can always use the controls *on the camera itself* to make additional adjustments. You're stuck with the exposure mode (such as P, A, S, or M) already set on the a6400. But you can change White Balance, switch from single to continuous shooting, select an f/stop or shutter speed if using Aperture Priority or Shutter Priority (respectively), or select both f/stop and shutter speed when using Manual

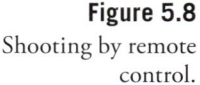

Figure 5.8
Shooting by remote
control.

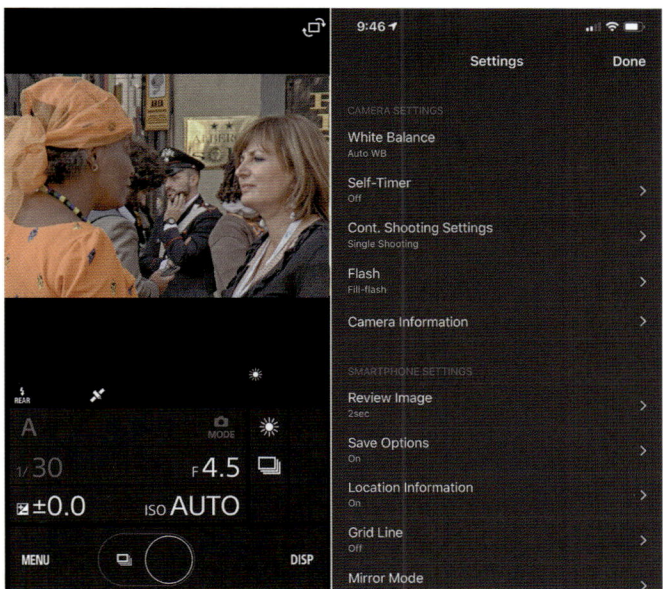

exposure. Adjust ISO, make exposure compensation settings, activate the self timer, and use a menu like the one shown at right in the figure. Note the GPS indicator at center left (it looks like a satellite) indicating that location information from your linked smartphone is being recorded. Tap the "shutter button" icon at bottom center and take a picture. If you have specified Always Connected under the Control with Smartphone entry in the Network 1 menu, you'll always be ready to go when the camera and smartphone are in proximity.

Playback Menu

This menu controls functions for deleting, protecting, displaying, and printing images. **Tip:** While you can access the Playback menu at any time using the Menu system, you can bring it up on your screen more quickly just by pressing the Playback button first, then the MENU button, which causes the *most recent* Playback menu page you've accessed to appear. Note that most of the entries in the Playback menus are *functions,* not *settings,* and so have no useful "default" values.

- Protect
- Rotate
- Delete
- Rating
- Rating Set (Custom Key)
- Specify Printing
- Photo Capture

- Enlarge Image
- Enlarge Initial Magnification
- Enlarge Initial Position
- Continuous Playback for Interval
- Playback Speed for Interval

- Slide Show
- View Mode
- Image Index
- Display as Group
- Display Rotation
- Image Jump Setting

Protect

Options: Multiple Images, All with (Current View Mode), Cancel All Images

This is the first entry in the Playback menu. (See Figure 5.9.) You might want to protect certain images or movie clips on your memory card from accidental erasure, either by you or by others who may use your camera from time to time. This menu item enables you to tag one or more images or movies for protection, so a delete command will not delete it. Protected files are marked with a key symbol. (Formatting a memory card deletes everything, including protected content.) This menu item also enables you to cancel the protection from all tagged photos or movies. If all you want to do is protect/unprotect the image currently on the screen, just press the center button during playback.

To use this feature, make sure to specify whether you want to do so for stills or movies; use the View Mode item in the Playback 3 menu (described later) to designate the desired view mode. There, you can select from Date View, Folder View (Still), AVCHD View, XAVC S HD View, or XAVC S 4K View to see only items matching that parameter.

Then, access the Protect menu item, choose Multiple Images, and press the center button. An image (or thumbnail of a movie) will appear; scroll among the photos or videos using the control wheel to reach the photo you want to tag for protection; press the center button to tag it with an orange check mark at the bottom-left corner of the image. (If it's already tagged, pressing the button will remove the tag, eliminating the protection you had previously provided.)

After you have marked all the items you want to protect, press the MENU button to confirm your choice. A screen will appear asking you to confirm that you want to protect the marked images; press the center button to do so. Later, if you want, you can go back and select the Cancel All Images option to unprotect all the tagged photos or movies.

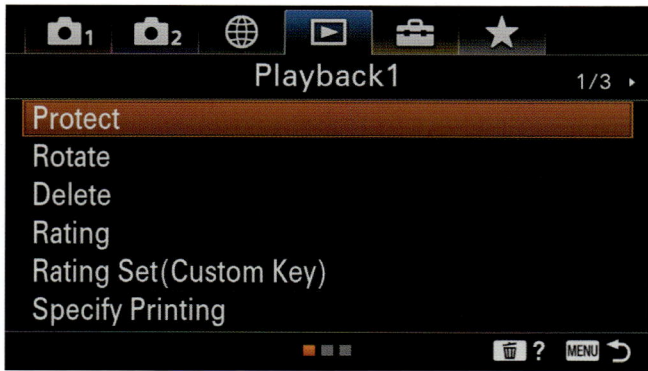

Figure 5.9
Playback 1 menu.

Rotate

Options: None

When you select this menu item, you are immediately presented with a new screen showing the current or most recently reviewed image along with an indication that the center button can be used to rotate the image. (This feature does not work with movies.) Scroll left/right to reach the image you want to rotate. Successive presses of the center button will now rotate the image 90 degrees at a time. The camera (and some software, such as Imaging Edge) will remember whatever rotation setting you apply here. You can use this function to rotate an image that was taken with the camera held vertically, when you have set Display Rotation to Manual. Press the MENU button to exit.

Delete

Options: Multiple Img., All with (Current View Mode)

Sometimes we take pictures or video clips that we know should never see the light of day. Maybe you were looking into the lens and accidentally tripped the shutter. Perhaps you really goofed up your settings. You want to erase that photo *now,* before it does permanent damage to your reputation as a good photographer. Unless you have turned Auto Review off in the Camera Settings II-7 (Display/Auto Review 2) menu, you can delete a photo immediately after you take it by pressing the Trash key (Delete button). Also, you can use that method to delete any individual image that's being displayed on the screen in Playback mode.

However, sometimes you need to wait for an idle moment to erase all pictures that are obviously not "keepers." I sometimes do this during halftime when shooting sports, to eliminate a series of continuous shots I know were a waste of storage space. This menu item makes it easy to remove selected photos or video clips (Multiple Images), or to erase all the photos or video clips taken, sorted by your currently active view mode (such as folder or date). (Change the type of view using the View Mode option, described later.) Note that there is no delete method that will remove images tagged as Protected.

To remove one or more images (or movie files), select the Delete menu item, and use the up/down directional buttons, front dial, rear dial, or the control wheel to choose the Multiple Images option. Press the center button, and the most recent image *using your currently active view* (Date View, Folder View [Still], Folder View [MP4], or AVCHD View) will be displayed on the LCD.

Scroll left/right through your images and press the center button when you reach the image you want to tag for deletion; an orange check mark appears next to the image. You can press the DISP button to see more information about a particular image. You can also press the AEL/Thumbnail button to view thumbnails of multiple images and select them in that mode.

The number of images marked for deletion is incremented in the indicator at the lower-left corner of the LCD, next to a trash can icon. When you're satisfied (or have expressed your dissatisfaction with the really bad images), press the MENU button, and you will be asked if you're sure you want to proceed. To confirm your decision, press the center button. The images (or video clips) you had tagged will now be deleted. If you want to delete *everything* on the memory card, it's quicker to do so by using the Format item in the Setup menu, as discussed later in this chapter.

Rating

Options: One to five stars, Off

This setting lets you apply a quality rating to still images (but not movies) you've shot. You can also use the rating system to represent some other criteria. Simply select this menu item (or define a custom key as a dedicated Rating button, as described next). You can use this entry to give images one, two, three, four, or five stars, or turn the rating off. The Image Jump function (described later in this chapter) can display only images that have been given a specific rating, or any rating at all. Suppose you were photographing a track meet with multiple events. You could apply a one-star rating to jumping events, two stars to relays, three stars to throwing events, four stars to hurdles, and five stars to dashes. Then, using the Image Jump feature, you could review only images of one type. I personally find this type of use more helpful than simply critiquing my own work.

With a little imagination, you can apply the rating system to all sorts of categories. At a wedding, you could classify pictures of the bride, the groom, guests, attendants, and parents of the couple. If you were shooting school portraits, one rating could apply to first grade, another to second grade, and so on. Given a little thought, this feature has many more applications than you might think. Ratings can be used to specify images for a slide show, too, or to select images in Digital Photo Professional.

To use the Ratings menu entry, follow these steps:

1. Choose the Rating menu item.
2. The most recently viewed image appears.
3. Press the center button, and an icon appears, flanked by left/right triangles. (See Figure 5.10, left.)
4. Use the left/right controls to scroll among Off, and the individual star settings available. (You can specify which ratings can be applied, as I'll describe shortly.)
5. Press MENU to confirm and exit.
6. The star rating (if any) that you've applied will henceforth be overlaid on the image each time you review it.

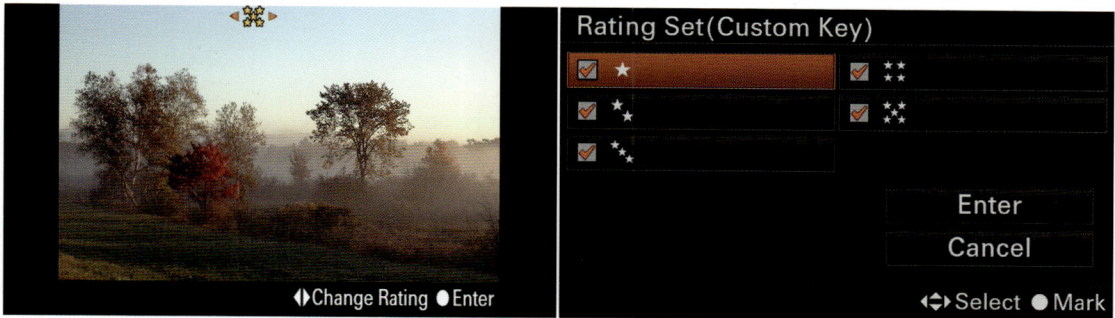

Figure 5.10 You can apply one to five stars or turn ratings off (left). If you rarely use a particular star value, you can deactivate it when using a Custom Key.

Rating Set (Custom Key)

Options: Activate any (or all) star ratings

This is a clever option that allows you to specify *which* star ratings can be applied when rating images using a defined Custom Key for the Rating function. For example, if you're rating by quality and don't deign to mark your really bad images, you can disable the * or ** star values. Thereafter, you'll only need to consider ***, ****, or ***** ratings.

For this to work, you must apply the Rating behavior to a custom key of your choice, as I described in Chapter 4. After that, you can visit this menu entry, shown in Figure 5.10, right, and highlight individual star values. Press the center button to mark/unmark them, then highlight Enter and press the center button again to confirm and exit. When rating an image using the Custom Key, just press the key multiple times. The ratings change to the next available value each time you press the key. (This should be your default way of applying ratings!)

Specify Printing

Options: Multiple Images, Cancel All, Print Setting

Most digital cameras are compatible with the DPOF (Digital Print Order Format) protocol, which enables you to tag JPEG images on the memory card (but not RAW files or movies) for printing with a DPOF-compliant printer; you can also specify whether you want the date imprinted as well. Afterward, you can transport your memory card to a retailer's digital photo lab or do-it-yourself kiosk or use your own DPOF-compatible printer to print out the tagged images in the quantities you've specified.

Choose multiple images using the View Mode filters described earlier to select to view either by Date or by Folder. Press the center button to mark an image for printing with an orange check mark next to the image, and the MENU button to confirm when you're finished. The Print Setting entry lets you choose to superimpose the date onto the print. The date will be added during printing by the output device, which controls its location on the final print.

Photo Capture

Options: Capture video frame

This menu entry, the first in the Playback 2 menu, can be accessed only when you're playing back a video clip. (See Figure 5.11.) You can use it to extract a still frame from a movie you've captured. Just follow these steps:

1. **Select the movie.** In Playback mode, navigate to the movie you want to clip from.

2. **Press MENU.** Choose Photo Capture from the Playback 2 menu. The first frame of the video will appear, along with a display offering playback controls.

3. **Play video.** Press the center button to start playback of the video at normal speed.

4. **Pause.** Press the center button again to pause playback when you reach the approximate location containing the desired frame.

5. **Select frame.** Use one of the following controls to navigate to the exact frame you want to extract:

   • **Up button.** Plays back slowly so you can monitor the action easily.

   • **Forward/Reverse.** Press the left/right buttons to move to next frame/previous frame.

   • **Down button.** Saves the currently displayed frame to your memory card.

Enlarge Image

Options: Zoom In, Zoom Out

Whenever you are playing back still images (not movies), you can use this menu entry to magnify the image. (You can also double-tap the touch screen to zoom in.) The a6400 will try to zoom in on the point used to focus the image, if possible, and will zoom into the center of the frame if not. Press the Magnify/AF/MF button to zoom in. The MENU button exits. Use the control wheel to

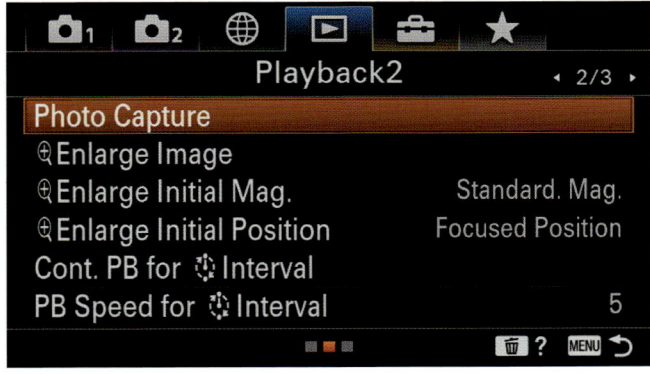

Figure 5.11
Playback 2 menu.

zoom in and out, and you can scroll around inside the enlarged image using the control wheel's direction controls. Rotate the front or rear dials to view the next or previous image (respectively) at the same magnification. Press MENU or the center button to exit. The initial magnification of the image is set using the entry that follows.

Enlarge Initial Magnification

Options: Standard Magnification, Previous Magnification
Default: Standard Magnification

Here you can choose the initial magnification used by the Enlarge Image entry. Use Standard Magnification to always see any image you magnify at the same zoom level. This is a good choice if you magnify from time to time to closely examine an image and may want to zoom in or out to view more or less of your subject matter. When you select Previous Magnification, the enlargement resumes at the most recent level used. For example, if you are checking focus of your images as you shoot and zooming in tightly, it's convenient to return to the same zoom level for each successive image.

Enlarge Initial Position

Options: Focused Position, Center
Default: Focused Position

By default, whenever you magnify an image during playback, the a6400 centers the enlargement around the area in the frame where focus was achieved. That's often the best choice, because when evaluating an image during playback, focus is the parameter most often checked. However, I prefer the enlargement positioned in the center of the frame, so I can move the magnifying window around anywhere I like. That setting potentially minimizes the amount of "travel" if the previous area I examined is located some distance in the frame from my new area of interest.

Continuous Playback for Interval

Options: Plays back interval shots

Use this setting to play back a sequence of images you captured using the Interval feature described in Chapter 9, or when shooting with the Continuous drive mode. Select the image or image group you want to view, and then press the center button to display the images. Press the center button again to pause during playback, or to resume playback. Change the playback speed by rotating the control dial or control wheel while you are watching. You can also adjust playback speed using the menu entry described next. If you want to create a movie from the sequence, use the Imaging Edge software, as outlined in Chapter 9.

Playback Speed for Interval

Options: Playback speeds from 1 (Slow) to 9 (Fast)

Default: 5

While you can adjust the speed of playback for interval sequences while viewing the clip (as described above), you can also set a value to be used automatically. You can still speed up or slow down while watching your sequence. The camera accomplishes playback speed by skipping frames, depending on the speed requested. The faster playback goes, the jerkier the motion will appear.

Slide Show

Menu Options: Repeat (On/Off), Interval: 1 second, 3 seconds, 5 seconds, 10 seconds, 30 seconds

Use this menu option, the first in the Playback 3 menu (see Figure 5.12) when you want to display all the still images on your memory card in a continuous show. You can display still images in a continuous series, with each one displayed for the amount of time that you set. Choose the Repeat option to make the show repeat in a continuous loop. After making your settings, press the center button and the slide show will begin. You can scroll left or right to go back to a previous image or go forward to the next image immediately, but that will stop the slide show. The show cannot be paused, but you can exit by pressing the MENU button.

View Mode

Options: Date View, Folder View (Still), AVCHD View, XAVC S HD View, XAVC S 4K View

Adjusts the way the camera displays image/movie files, which is useful for reviewing only certain types of files, or for deleting only particular types, as described above. You can elect to display files by Date View, Folder View (still photos only), AVCHD View (just AVCHD movies), or XAVCS clips in both HD (high-definition) and 4K modes.

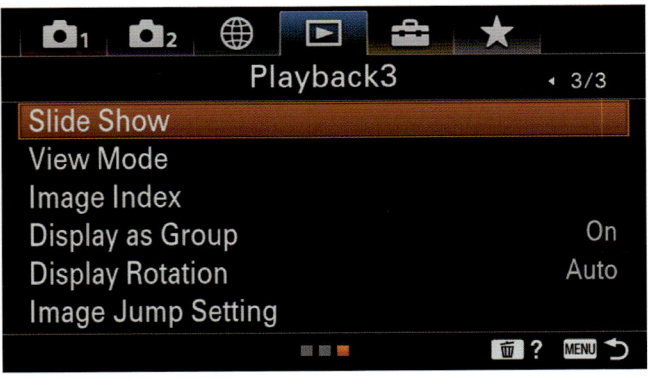

Figure 5.12
Playback 3 menu.

Image Index

Options: 9, 25

You can view an index screen of your images on the camera's LCD by pressing the down directional button (Index button) while in Playback mode. By default, that screen shows up to 9 thumbnails of photos or movies; you can change that value to 25 using this menu item. Remember to use the View Mode menu item first, to identify the folder that the index display should access; by default, it will show thumbnails of still photos, but you might want to view thumbnails of your movie clips instead. When viewing an index, highlight the bar at the left side of the screen and use the control wheel's directional controls to move quickly among available thumbnails. Press the center button to switch to View Mode quickly.

Display as Group

Options: On, Off

Default: On

If you shoot sports, you'll love this feature. The a6400 is smart enough to know that when you shoot a burst of images in continuous shooting mode it would be helpful to group them all together. That makes it easy to evaluate the first shot in a particular set of images captured sequentially, without having to wade through all of them. When set to On, the camera groups images in a burst together, and overlays a "stack" icon on the group, so you'll know you are viewing/evaluating only the first image in that burst. The View Mode must be set to Date View to use this feature. Set this option to Off and you'll be shown every picture you captured, one by one, during image review.

Display Rotation

Options: Auto, Manual, Off

Default: Auto

You can use this function to determine whether a vertical image is rotated automatically during picture review. If you want to rotate the image more, use the Rotate entry, described earlier.

■ **Auto.** The image will be shown in the orientation indicated by information in the image, no matter how the camera itself is rotated during picture review. For example, a vertical image will be shown in the correct orientation, as shown at top in Figure 5.13 when the camera is held horizontally. It will be shown smaller in size to fit the long dimension of the image into the short dimension of the screen. Rotate the camera 90 degrees, and the a6400 will automatically rotate the photo so it's *still* shown in the correct orientation, but it will now fill the LCD screen, as you can see in Figure 5.13 bottom.

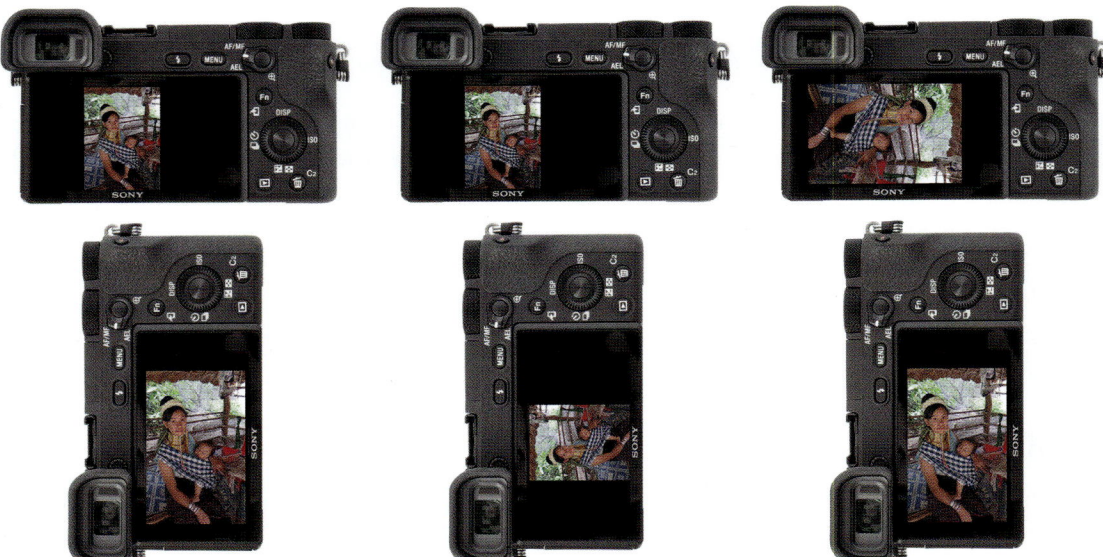

Figure 5.13 Display Rotation Auto.

Figure 5.14 Display Rotation Manual.

Figure 5.15 Display Rotation Off.

- **Manual.** With this setting, the image is always displayed on the LCD in the same orientation it was taken. That is, a vertically oriented photo will be displayed in a smaller size, just as it is when using Auto, as shown at top in Figure 5.14. However, when you rotate the camera during picture review, the a6400 does *not* automatically rotate the image at the same time, so it will be shown with an incorrect orientation (see Figure 5.14 bottom).

- **Off.** With this setting, both vertical and horizontal images are displayed to fill the screen as much as possible with the image. Vertical shots are larger, as shown at top in Figure 5.15, but the camera must be rotated to view them in the correct orientation (see Figure 5.15, bottom).

Image Jump Setting

Options: Select Dial/Wheel; Image Jump Method (One by One, Protect Only, Rating Only [All], Rating Only [1–5 stars, or Without Rating Only])

Default: Select Dial/Wheel: Dial; Image Jump Method: One by One

You can select which control to use when scrolling among images during playback, either the Control Dial or Control Wheel. The default method, One by One, is usually most convenient, but it would have been nice if Sony had provided options other vendors use that allow jumping ahead by 10 or 100 images. This feature is much better than nothing, as you can elect to jump only between Protected images, images that have been rated, or images with particular star ratings. That allows you to "mark" images that you want to evaluate later, using either the protection attribute or a star rating.

6

Setup Menu and My Menu

Even more options are available from the Sony a6400's Setup menu, which allows you to further tailor the camera's behavior; view, print, and protect images; and adjust important camera settings, such as monitor brightness or audio volume. With the My Menu tabs, you can create custom menu listings of your most frequently accessed entries for immediate recall.

Setup Menu

Use the lengthy Setup menu to adjust infrequently changed settings, such as language, date/time, and power-saving options. The first six items in the Setup 1 menu are shown in Figure 6.1.

Figure 6.1
The Setup 1 menu.

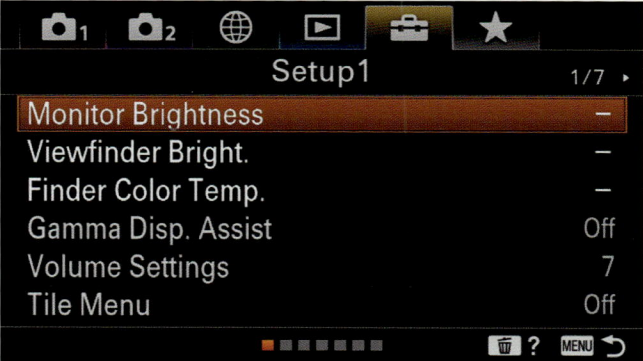

The Setup menu options include:

- Monitor Brightness
- Viewfinder Brightness
- Finder Color Temp.
- Gamma Display Assist
- Volume Settings
- Tile Menu
- Mode Dial Guide
- Delete Confirm
- Display Quality
- Power Save Start Time
- Auto Power OFF Temperature
- NTSC/PAL Selector
- Cleaning Mode

- Touch Operation
- Touch Panel/Pad
- Touch Pad Settings
- Demo Mode
- TC/UB Settings
- IR Remote Ctrl
- HDMI Settings
- 4K Output Selection (Movies)
- USB Connection
- USB LUN Setting
- USB Power Supply
- PC Remote Settings
- Language

- Date/Time Setup
- Area Setting
- Copyright Info
- Format
- File Number
- Set File Name
- Select REC Folder
- New Folder
- Folder Name
- Recover Image Database
- Display Media Information
- Version
- Setting Reset

Monitor Brightness

Options: Manual, Sunny Weather

Default: Manual

My preference: Manual

When you access this menu item, two controls appear. The first is a Brightness Setup bar (shown just above the grayscale/color patches in Figure 6.2). It's set to Manual adjustment by default, but press the center button and you can change it to Sunny Weather for a brighter display. You might

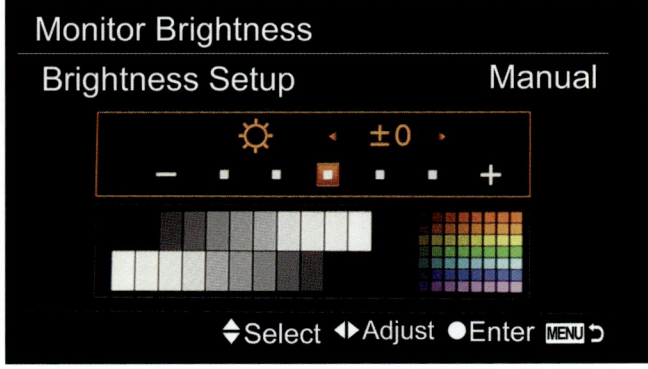

Figure 6.2
Adjust monitor brightness.

resort to this setting if you're shooting outdoors in bright sun and find it hard to view the LCD even when shading it with your hand.

If you set it to Sunny Weather, the LCD brightness will automatically increase, making the display easier to view in very bright light. This makes the display unusually bright so use it only when it's really necessary. Remember too that it will consume a lot more battery power, so have a spare battery available.

The grayscale steps and color patches can be used as you manually adjust the screen brightness using the left/right directional buttons. Scroll to the right to make the LCD display brighter or scroll to the left to make the LCD display darker, in a range of plus and minus 2 (arbitrary) increments. As you change the brightness, keep an eye on the grayscale and color chart in order to visualize the effect your setting will have on various tones and hues. The zero setting is the default and it provides the most accurate display in terms of exposure, but you might want to dim it when the bright display is distracting while shooting in a dark theater, perhaps. A minus setting also reduces battery consumption but makes your photos appear to be underexposed (too dark).

Some find the default value too dim and prefer to boost the brightness of the monitor. I prefer to choose Manual but then to leave the display at the zero setting. This ensures the most accurate view of scene brightness on the LCD for the best evaluation of exposure while previewing the scene before taking a photo.

Viewfinder Brightness

Options: Auto, Manual
Default: Auto
My preference: Manual

In Manual mode, this entry operates exactly the same as the Monitor Brightness option just described. A notice will appear on the LCD monitor advising you to look through the viewfinder and make your adjustments. The default setting is Auto. Again, some find the default setting a little on the dim side and prefer to boost the brightness a bit.

Finder Color Temperature

Options: +2 to −2
Default: 0
My preference: N/A

While looking through the viewfinder, press the left/right buttons to adjust the color balance of the finder to make it appear warmer (using the left button) or colder/bluer (using the right button), according to your preference. Our eyes can adjust to differences in color when viewing, but if you find that what you see is often what you get, you may want to use this adjustment.

Gamma Display Assist

Options: Off, Auto, S-Log2→709 (800%), S-Log3→709 (800%), HLG (BT.2020), HLG (709)

Default: Off

My preference: N/A

As you'll learn in Chapter 10, the a6400 is capable of recording movies using Picture Profiles (which were introduced in Chapter 3). These profiles can use gamma correction to extend the dynamic range (range of tones from black to white) recorded during video capture. Movies captured using S-Log gamma profiles appear to be very low in contrast until processed using software on your computer. As a result, reviewing these clips in the camera can be difficult. This menu entry allows selecting options that will adjust the display of extended dynamic range clips so they appear *in the camera* with a more normal look. You'll still need to process the video in your video-editing software.

You can turn Gamma Display Assist off, allow the camera to select an appropriate adjustment automatically, or manually set the assist feature to use the particular gamma you are working with.

Volume Settings

Options: 0–15

Default: 2

My preference: N/A

This menu item affects only the audio volume of movies that are being played back in the camera. It's grayed out unless you have selected movies, as opposed to stills, with the Still/Movie Select menu item. When you select Volume Settings, the camera displays a scale of loudness from 0 to 15; scroll up/down to the value you want to set and it will remain in effect until changed.

You might want to use this menu item to pre-set a volume level that you generally prefer. However, you can also adjust the volume whenever you're displaying a movie clip, to set it to just the right level. To do so, press the down directional button and use the up/down directional buttons to raise or lower the volume.

Tile Menu

Options: On, Off

Default: Off

My preference: Off

The Tile menu is a holdover from the first Sony APS-C E-mount cameras, and features icons representing the six main menu tabs. While it might be marginally useful when you first begin working with your a6400, it's really an unnecessary intermediate step. Turn it Off and when you press the MENU button, you'll be whisked to the conventional menu system, where you can quickly navigate to the tab you want.

Mode Dial Guide

Options: On, Off
Default: On
My preference: Off

This is the first entry on the second page of the Setup menu. (See Figure 6.3.) The On setting activates an on-screen description of the current shooting mode as you rotate the mode dial. You might want to enable this extra help when you first begin using your a6400, and turn it off after you're comfortable with the various mode dial settings.

Delete Confirm

Options: Delete First, Cancel First
Default: Cancel First
My preference: Delete First

Determines which choice is highlighted when you press the trash button to delete an image. The default Cancel First is the safer option, as you must deliberately select Delete and then press the center button to actually remove an image. Delete First is faster; press the trash button, then the center button, and the unwanted image is gone. You'd have to scroll down to Cancel if you happened to have changed your mind or pressed the trash button by mistake.

Display Quality

Options: High, Standard
Default: Standard
My preference: Standard

This setting allows you to slightly increase the quality of the display, using a different scaling algorithm when showing the full sensor view in shooting mode, and when playing back images for review. The effect is noticeable, but minimal, and the High setting uses extra power, so I generally prefer the default Standard setting.

Figure 6.3
The Setup 2 menu.

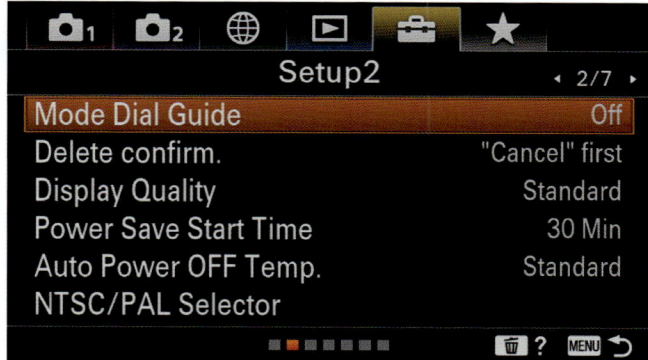

Power Save Start Time

Options: 30 minutes, 5 minutes, 2 minutes, 1 minute, 10 seconds

Default: 1 minute

My preference: 5 minutes

This item lets you specify the exact amount of time that should pass before the camera goes to "sleep" when not being used. The default of 1 minute is a short time, useful to minimize battery consumption. You can select a much longer time before the camera will power down, or a much shorter time. Because I always carry at least three batteries with me, power saving is not as crucial, so I use a 5-minute delay. To awaken your camera from its slumber, just tap the shutter release.

Auto Power Off Temperature

Options: Standard, High

Default: Standard

My preference: Standard

Your camera may overheat if operated continuously (as when shooting movies) for periods of time, and continued use after that point can result in damage. The a6400 can turn itself off when its internal temperature gets too high, which is particularly useful if the camera is mounted on a tripod so that your hands don't feel the increasing warmth. Shooting 4K video, for example, can generate a lot of heat and deplete your battery rather quickly. This option allows you to stretch the safe operating time by switching from the default Standard mode to High (which allows operation when the camera is hotter than normal). Sony recommends not holding the camera in your hands when you've activated the High setting.

NTSC/PAL Selector

Options: NTSC, PAL

Default: Depends on the country where the camera is sold

My preference: N/A

This allows you to switch the camera between the two major television video systems, NTSC (used in the North and South America, Korea, Japan, and some other Pacific countries), and PAL, which is used in Europe, the Middle East, and elsewhere. To switch from one video system to another, you must be using a memory card that was formatted while the camera was using that video system. Otherwise, you'll be prompted to reformat the card or use a different card. Your camera will be set up at the factory to default to the video system used in your country. If you switch to the alternate system, the start-up screen will display a message "Running on NTSC" or "Running on PAL" to make sure you're aware of the change. Note that a few countries in South America (Brazil, Argentina, Paraguay, and Uruguay) use a modified PAL system, while others, including Bulgaria, France, Greece, Guiana, Iran, Iraq, Monaco, Russia, and Ukraine use a third system, called SECAM.

Cleaning Mode

Options: None
Default: N/A
My preference: N/A

This is the first item on the third page of the Setup menu (see Figure 6.4). Use this entry when you want to use the a6400's automatic image sensor cleaning feature. I like to use this mode a couple extra times with the camera pointing downward and the lens removed so that, theoretically, any artifacts on the sensor will shake loose and exit the camera.

Touch Operation

Options: On, Off
Default: On
My preference: On

This is the entry you use to enable or disable the a6400's touch screen. I showed you how to set it up in Chapter 2. The first step in using touch controls is to activate that capability using this menu entry. It's On by default, but if you've disabled it, you must return to this option to reactivate the touch features.

In its wisdom, Sony has spread the touch menu entries across two different menu tabs. Here in the Setup 3 menu you can activate/deactivate touch operation, and make additional touch settings in the two entries that follow this one. However, the a6400's touch features have three different modes, all mutually exclusive (that is, you can only have one active at a time). To choose the touch mode, you'll need to visit the Function of Touch Operations entry in the Camera Settings II-09 menu, described in Chapter 4.

Figure 6.4
The Setup 3 menu.

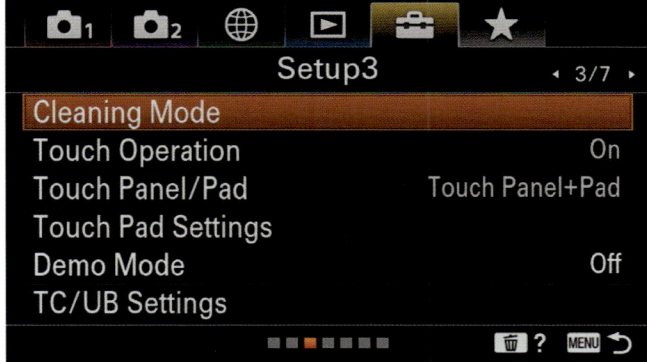

To recap, the three available functions are as follows:

- **Touch shutter.** As you compose your images using the LCD monitor, you can tap the screen to specify the focus point. The camera will then immediately take a picture.

- **Touch focus.** You can tap the LCD screen to select a focus point or zone anywhere that the a6400 is able to achieve autofocus (that is, most of the frame other than the edges). Tap the screen and/or slide your finger around when using either the LCD or viewfinder. The camera will focus at that point. In manual focus mode, double-tap the LCD to activate the focus magnifier.

- **Touch tracking.** You can specify a subject that will be tracked by tapping the LCD monitor. Tracking will start and continue until you press the Center button or tap the Cancel Tracking icon in the upper-right corner of the LCD monitor. The camera will focus on the tracked subject when you press the shutter release down halfway.

Touch Panel/Pad

Options: Touch Panel+Pad, Touch Panel Only, Touch Pad Only

Default: Touch Panel+Pad

My preference: Touch Panel+Pad

The LCD monitor can function in one of two modes—or you can activate both modes at the same time. You can find a description of how to use the Touch Panel and Touch Pad configurations in Chapter 2; I won't repeat that information here.

- **Touch Panel+Pad.** The a6400 switches between the two individual modes (described next); when you are composing your image on the LCD monitor, the screen functions as a Touch Panel. If you bring the camera up to your eye, the screen switches to Touch Pad mode.

- **Touch Panel Only.** When you're using the LCD monitor to compose, you can touch the LCD monitor screen to specify the focus area.

- **Touch Pad Only.** When you're using the electronic viewfinder to compose, you can touch the LCD monitor screen to specify the focus area. You don't have to tap the exact area if you have elected Relative Positioning in the Touch Pad Settings entry (next).

Touch Pad Settings

Options: Operation in Vertical Orientation: On, Off; Touch Position Mode: Absolute Position, Relative Position; Operation Area: Whole screen, Right/Left half of screen, Upper/Lower Right/ Left corners.

Default: Operation in Vertical Orientation: On; Touch Position Mode: Absolute Position; Operation Area: Whole screen

My preference: N/A

Additional settings that relate only to the touch pad configuration can be selected from this menu entry:

- **Operation in Vertical Orientation.** Here you can specify whether touch controls are available when the camera is oriented in the vertical position (On), or only when the camera is held in horizontal orientation (Off).

- **Touch Position Mode.** Choose Absolute Position, to allow you to quickly move the focusing frame to a distant position on the LCD. This setting automatically changes the Operation Area (described next) to encompass the full screen. Use Relative Position to move the focus point relative to the location on the LCD.

- **Operation Area.** By default, the entire touch pad is sensitive when using the EVF. However, if your *ocular dominance* favors your left eye (i.e., you're "left-eyed"), you may be more comfortable choosing an active area on the left side of the screen that avoids contact with your nose. The "relative" orientation remains the same, but is limited to that reduced area. However, if you selected Absolute Position for the Touch Position above, the entire screen is used, regardless of your setting here.

Demo Mode

Options: On, Off
Default: Off
My preference: N/A

This is a semi-cool feature that allows your camera to be used as a demonstration tool, say, when giving lectures or showing off at a trade show. When activated, if the camera is idle for about one minute it will begin showing a protected AVCHD movie that you have previously created, which is not impressive on the camera's built-in LCD, but can have a lot more impact if the a6400 is connected to a large-screen HDTV through the HDMI port. Just follow these steps:

1. Use the File Format entry in the Camera Settings II-01 menu and select AVCHD as the movie format, as explained in Chapter 3. Demo mode works only with AVCHD files.

2. Shoot the clip that you want to use as your demonstration, in AVCHD format.

3. In the Playback 3 menu, access the View Mode and select AVCHD View so that only AVCHD videos will appear.

4. In the Playback 1 menu, choose Protect and select the demo clip, which should be the movie file with the oldest recorded date and time.

5. Connect the a6400 to the optional AC adapter. Because Demo mode uses a lot of juice, it operates only when the external power source is connected.

6. Demo mode will no longer be grayed out in the Setup 3 menu. Select it and choose On.

7. After about one minute of idling, the demo clip will begin playing. Note that, because the AC adapter is connected, your automatic power-saving setting is ignored, and that Demo mode will not operate if no movie file is stored on your memory card.

TC/UB Settings

Options: TC/UB Display Settings, TC Preset, UB Preset, TC Format, TC Run, TC Make

Default: Various

My preference: N/A

The Time Code (TC) and User Bit (UB) settings are information that can be embedded and used to sync clips and sound when editing movies. I'll describe this advanced feature in a little more detail in Chapter 10, but pro movie-making techniques are largely beyond the scope of this book. When you're ready to use time codes and user bits effectively, a full-length book devoted to cinematography will have what you need.

IR Remote Control

Options: On, Off

Default: Off

My preference: N/A

This is the first entry in the Setup 4 menu. (See Figure 6.5.) The a6400 can be operated at distances of about 20 feet (indoors) or 6 feet (outdoors in full sunlight) using infrared signals using the Sony RMT-DSLR1 and its replacement, the RMT-DSLR2 Wireless Remote Commander controls. It can also be triggered with an array of third-party remotes, and smartphones with an infrared transmitter and accompanying remote control app.

Constantly "looking" for the IR signal using the sensor on the front of the camera can sap battery power (because the a6400 does not go into power save mode), so it's wise to turn the remote control feature on only when it's actually needed. Choose On, and you can take pictures using the Shutter, 2 Sec., Start/Stop buttons on the RMT-DSLR1/2 controls, plus the Movie button found on the RMT-DSLR2 control. The RMT-DSLR1 model cannot be used to shoot movies; the RMT-DSLR2 remote can be used to activate movie shooting as long as the Movie button on the camera is not set to Movie Mode Only in the Custom Settings II-09 menu.

Figure 6.5
The Setup 4 menu.

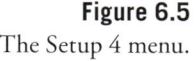

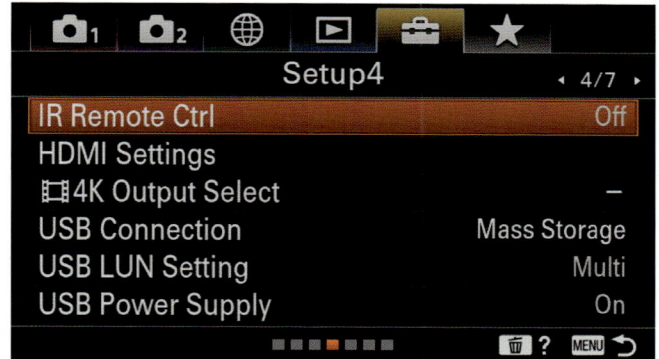

For best performance, make sure a lens hood or other object doesn't interfere with the IR signal reaching the a6400's IR sensor on the front of the camera. If the camera is set for an autofocus mode, it will attempt to focus when you press the Shutter or 2 Sec. buttons. If it cannot focus, the picture won't be taken.

Note: The IR remote control cannot be used while the Bluetooth Remote Control setting in the Network 2 menu is set to On. Compatibility with the Sony RMT-P1BT Bluetooth remote control was added with the Version 2.0 firmware for the a6400 in June 2019.

HDMI Settings

Options: HDMI Resolution, 24/60p Output, HDMI Info. Display, TC Output, REC Control, CTRL for HDMI

Default: HDMI Resolution: Auto; 24/60p Output: 60p; HDMI Info. Display: On; TC Output: Off; CTRL for HDMI: On

My preference: N/A

You can view the display output of your camera on a high-definition television (HDTV) when you connect it to the a6400 if you make the investment in an HDMI cable (which Sony does not supply); get the Type C with a mini-HDMI connector on the camera end. (Still photos can also be displayed using Wi-Fi, without cable connection, as discussed earlier.) When connecting HDMI-to-HDMI, the camera automatically makes the correct settings. If you're lucky enough to own a TV that supports the Sony Bravia synchronization protocol, you can operate the camera using that TV's remote control when this item is On. Just press the Link Menu button on the remote, and then use the device's controls to delete images, display an image index of photos in the camera, display a slide show, protect/unprotect images in the camera, specify printing options, and play back single images on the TV screen.

Your options are:

- **HDMI Resolution (Auto, 2160/1080p, 1080p, 1080i).** The camera can adjust its output for display on a high-definition television when at the Auto setting. This usually works well with any HDTV. If you have trouble getting the image to display correctly, you can set the resolution manually here to 2160/1080p (for 4K and Full HD), 1080p, or 1080i.

- **24p/60p Output.** You can select either 60p or 24p output to the HDMI port when connected to a 1080 60i–compatible television and Record Setting (described in Chapter 4) has been set to 24p 24M (FX), 24p 17M (FH), or 24p 50M. If a different setting was used, this setting is ignored, and the output conforms to the HDMI Resolution setting above instead.

- **HDMI Info. Display.** Choose On or Off. Choose On if you want the shooting information to display when the camera is connected to an HDTV television/monitor using an HDMI cable. Select Off if you don't want to show the shooting information on the display. You might want to suppress the shooting information when you're showing your images as a slide show.

- **TC Output.** Choose on or off to enable/disable including time code in the HDMI output signal. Use On if you are outputting to professional video equipment and want to include the time code information. Note that the time code is *data* and will not actually appear on the screen. If this setting is on and you are sending the signal to a television or some other device, the image may not appear properly. Change this setting to off when outputting to devices not equipped to handle TC information.

- **REC Control.** This setting is available only when TC Output is set to on. Choose on or off. The setting allows you to start and stop REC Control–compatible external video recorders connected to the camera. A REC or STBY icon will be displayed on the camera's screen as appropriate.

- **CTRL for HDMI.** This option can be useful when you have connected the camera to a non-Sony HDTV and find that the TV's remote control produces unintended results with the camera. If that happens, try turning this option Off, and see if the problem is resolved. If you later connect the camera to a Sony Bravia sync-compliant HDTV, set this menu item back to On.

4K Output Selection (Movies)

Options: Memory Card+HDMI, HDMI Only (30p), HDMI Only (24p), HDMI Only (25p)

Default: N/A

My preference: N/A

When your a6400 is connected to an external video recorder or playback device and set to Movie mode, you can use this setting to specify how 4K movies are recorded and output. Note that when using one of these choices, the camera's movie counter does not appear on the screen. Face/Eye Priority in AF, Face Priority in Multi Metering, and Tracking are disabled.

Your choices are as follows:

- **Memory Card+HDMI.** A 4K movie in 30p is saved on the camera's internal memory card *and* output to the external device. Use this if you want two copies of your video, including one on the memory card. **Reminder:** Use a fast memory card for these huge files!

- **HDMI Only (30p).** A 4K movie in 30p is output only to the external device, and not recorded on your memory card. HDMI Info. Display is disabled.

- **HDMI Only (24p).** A 4K movie in 24p is output only to the external device. HDMI Info. Display is disabled.

- **HDMI Only (25p).** If the NTSC/PAL Selector described earlier is set to PAL, you can use this option to shoot a 4K movie in 25p, and output only to the external device. HDMI Info. Display is disabled.

USB Connection

Options: Auto, Mass Storage, MTP, PC Remote

Default: Auto

My preference: N/A

This entry allows you to select the type of USB connection protocol between your camera and computer.

- **Auto.** Connects your a6400 to your computer or other device automatically, choosing either Mass Storage or MTP connection as appropriate.

- **Mass Storage.** In this mode, your camera appears to the computer as just another storage device, like a disk drive. You can drag and drop files between them.

- **MTP.** This mode, short for Media Transfer Protocol, is a newer version of the PTP (Picture Transfer Protocol) that was standard in earlier cameras. It allows better two-way communication between the camera and the computer and is useful for both image transfer and printing with PictBridge-compatible printers.

- **PC Remote.** This setting is used with Sony's Remote Camera Control software to adjust shooting functions and take pictures from a linked computer.

USB LUN Setting

Options: Multi, Single

Default: Multi

My preference: N/A

This setting specifies how the a6400 selects a Logical Unit Number when connecting to a computer through the USB port. Normally, you'd use Multi, which allows the camera to adjust the LUN as necessary, and is compatible with the PlayMemories Home software. Use Single to lock in a LUN if you have trouble making a connection between your camera and a particular computer. PlayMemories Home software will usually not work when this setting is active. But don't worry, Single is rarely necessary.

USB Power Supply

Options: On, Off

Default: On

My preference: On

When set to On, the camera receives charging power from a connected computer or other device through the micro USB cable link. Use this setting if you want to charge the a6400's battery when connected to a computer or other device. Set to Off, and power is not supplied. You'd want to use this to avoid draining power from the computer host. Although I most frequently connect my camera to a desktop computer, if I am using a laptop, I set this to Off, as I have plenty of NP-FW50 batteries, and recharging the laptop is sometimes inconvenient.

PC Remote Settings

Options: Still Image Save Destination: PC Only, PC+Camera; RAW+JPEG PC Save Image: RAW & JPEG, JPEG Only, RAW Only

Default: Still Image Save Destination: PC+Camera; RAW+JPEG PC Save Image: RAW & JPEG

My preference: I use the default settings.

This is the first entry on the Setup 5 menu. (See Figure 6.6.) A smartphone connection isn't your only remote operation option. Link your camera to a laptop or desktop PC and you can use the free Imaging Edge software to take pictures with your camera remotely. This entry allows you to specify where the images you take are stored; you can elect to have them saved on your computer only (and not on the a6400's memory card), or on both. You can also specify whether JPEG only, RAW only, or both are transferred to your computer.

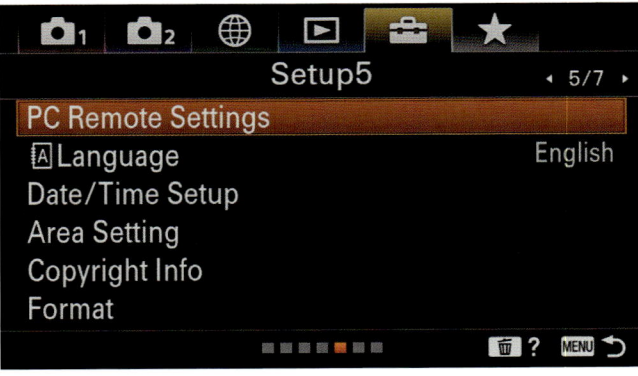

Figure 6.6
The Setup 5 menu.

Why you might want to make these choices will become apparent when you look at the options in more detail:

■ **Still Image Save Destination.** This sub-menu tells the a6400 where to store the images it captures. You must choose your preferred option ahead of time; you cannot change destinations while shooting.

• **PC Only.** No files (JPEG or RAW) will be saved to the camera's internal memory card. You might want to do that when taking large numbers of images, as eschewing card storage effectively prevents filling up the memory card. You can capture as many images as you like, or, at least, as many as will fit onto your computer's disk drive.

• **PC+Camera.** The chief advantage of this mode is that it automatically provides you with backup, making it the best choice for everyday usage, and especially when capturing important photos. When you've finished shooting you'll have one copy on your computer (ready for image editing, emailing, or other workflow), and a backup copy on your memory card. You will be limited by the capacity of the card, but given that most cards will store thousands of images, that doesn't present much of a problem. Note that when your card is full, write protected, defective, or otherwise unavailable, you won't be able to take photos at all, even if Release Without Card in the Camera Settings II-04 menu is set to Enable.

■ **RAW+JPEG Save Image.** This setting specifies *which* image file type is transferred to your computer. You can select JPEG Only, RAW Only, or RAW & JPEG. It affects *only* the image type transferred—not which image file types are captured. That is, if you elect to transfer JPEG Only images to your computer, your File Format in the Camera Settings I-01 menu must be set to either JPEG or RAW & JPEG.

The advantage of choosing to transfer only one file type to your computer is chiefly in transfer speed. You can store both RAW and JPEG versions on your memory card (If PC+Camera is selected above), but transfer *only* the JPEG file to your computer, at a much greater speed. This can be an advantage for tethered shooting, as the computer will not display the image just shot until the image has been completely transferred.

On the other hand, if security is a main concern, you can elect to transfer only the RAW file, which, of course is the most "important" version of your image, since it has more information available for eventual editing. Transferring only the RAW file is slightly faster than shuttling both RAW and JPEG versions to the computer. I tend not to use this option as much.

Language

Options: English, French, Spanish, Italian, Japanese, Chinese languages

Default: Language of country where camera is sold

My preference: N/A

If you accidentally set a language you cannot read and find yourself with incomprehensible menus, don't panic. Just find the Setup menu, the one with the red toolbox for its icon, and select the first entry in the Setup 5 menu, the line that has a symbol that looks like an alphabet block "A" to the left of the item's heading. No matter which language has been selected, you can recognize this menu item by the "A." Scroll to it, press the center button to select this item, and scroll up/down among the options until you see a language you can read.

Date/Time Setup

Options: Daylight Saving, Date/Time, Date Format

Default: None

My preference: N/A

Use this option to specify the date and time that will be embedded in the image file along with exposure information and other data. Having the date set accurately also is important for selecting movies for viewing by date. Use the left/right directional buttons to navigate through the choices of Daylight Savings Time On/Off; year, month, day, hour, minute, and date format. You can't directly change the AM/PM setting; you need to scroll the hours past midnight or noon to change that setting. Use the up/down directional buttons or rotate the control wheel to change each value as needed.

Area Setting

Options: World time zones

Default: None

My preference: N/A

When you select this option, you are presented with a world map on the LCD. Use the left/right directional buttons to scroll until you have highlighted the time zone that you are in. Once the camera is set up with the correct date and time in your home time zone, you can use this setting to change your time zone during a trip, so you will record the local time with your images without disrupting your original date and time settings. Just scroll back to your normal time zone once you return home.

Copyright Info

Options: Write Copyright Info, Set Photographer, Set Copyright, Display Copyright Info

Default: Off

My preference: Add all information

Your choices include:

- **Write Copyright Info.** Turn On to embed copyright information in your image file; Off to disable this feature. If you choose On, a copyright symbol will appear on the shooting screen to indicate that copyright data is being written to the image file.

- **Set Photographer.** Enter the name of the photographer. Highlight this and press the center button to move to the next screen, where a blank line appears. Highlight that and press the center button, and the text entry screen appears. It functions much like the multi-tap cell phone keypads in the pre-smartphone era: highlight a button and press the center button multiple times to enter a particular character. For example, if you highlight the "abc" button, pressing once inserts an a, twice a b, and three times a c. When finished, highlight OK and press the center button to return to the initial screen, where you can highlight OK again and press the center button a last time to confirm.

- **Set Copyright.** Define your copyright terms, such as *Cpr. 2020 David D. Busch*. Strictly speaking, "Cpr." should be used rather than a lowercase c between two parentheses. Text is entered as described above.

- **Disp. Copyright Info.** Displays whatever copyright information you've specified.

Format

Options: OK, Cancel

Default: None

My preference: N/A

As you'd guess, you'll use Format to re-format your memory card while it's in your a6400. To proceed with this process, choose the Format menu item and select "OK" and press the center button to confirm, or Cancel to chicken out.

Use the Format command to erase everything on your memory card and to set up a fresh file system ready for use. This procedure removes all data that was on the memory card, and reinitializes the card's file system by defining anew the areas of the card available for image storage, locking out defective areas, and creating a new folder in which to deposit your images. It's usually a good idea to reformat your memory card in the camera (not in your camera's card reader using your computer's operating system) before each use. Formatting is generally much quicker than deleting images one by one. Before formatting the card, however, make sure that you have saved all your images and videos to another device; formatting will delete everything, including images that were protected.

File Number

Options: Series, Reset
Default: Series
My preference: N/A

This is the first entry on the Setup 6 menu. (See Figure 6.7.) The default for the File Number item is Series, indicating that the a6400 will automatically apply a file number to each picture and video clip that you make, using consecutive numbering; this will continue over a long period of time, spanning many different memory cards, and even if you reformat a card. Numbers are applied from 0001 to 9999; when you reach the limit, the camera starts back at 0001. The camera keeps track of the last number used in its internal memory. So, you could take pictures numbered as high as 100–0240 on one card, remove the card and insert another, and the next picture will be numbered 100–0241 on the new card. Reformat either card, take a picture, and the next image will be numbered 100–0242. Use the Series option when you want all the photos you take to have consecutive numbers (at least, until your camera exceeds 9999 shots taken).

If you want to restart numbering back at 0001 frequently, use the Reset option. In that case, the file number will be reset to 0001 *each* time you format a memory card or delete all the images in a folder, insert a different memory card, or change the folder name format (as described in the next menu entry). I do not recommend this since you will soon have several images with exactly the same file number.

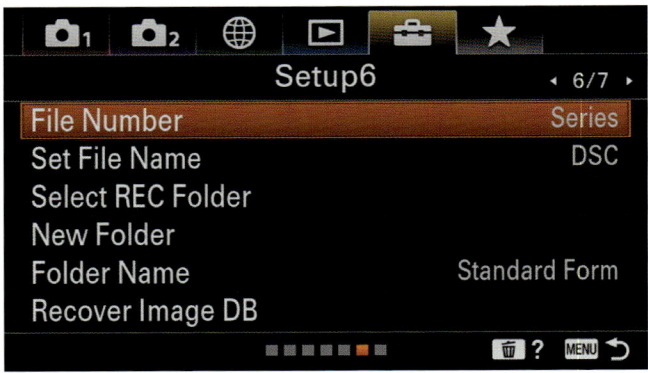

Figure 6.7
The Setup 6 menu.

Set File Name

Options: Choose three-letter prefix

Default: DSC

My preference: a64

This entry allows you to specify the first three characters in the file name applied to your images. The a6400, like other cameras in the Sony product line, automatically applies a name like _ DSC0001.jpg or DSC_0001.nef to your image files as they are created. You can use this menu option to change the names applied to your photos, but only within certain strict limitations. In practice, you can change only three of the eight characters, the *DSC* portion of the file name. The other five are mandated either by the Design Rule for Camera File System (DCF) specification that all digital camera makers adhere to or to industry conventions.

DCF limits file names created by conforming digital cameras to a maximum of eight characters, plus a three-character extension (such as .jpg, .nef, or .wav in the case of audio files) that represents the format of the file. The eight-plus-three (usually called 8.3) length limitation dates back to an evil and frustrating computer operating system that we older photographers would like to forget (its initials are D.O.S.), but which, unhappily, lives on as the wraith of a file naming convention.

Of the eight available characters, four are used to represent, in a general sense, the type of camera used to create the image. By convention, one of those characters is an underline, placed in the first position (as in _DSCxxxx.xxx) when the image uses the Adobe RGB color space, and in the fourth position (as in DSC_xxxx.xxx) for sRGB and RAW files. That leaves just three characters for the manufacturer (and you) to use. The remaining four characters are used for numbers from 0000 to 9999, which is why your a6400 "rolls over" to DSC_0000 again when the 9999 number limitation is reached.

Because the default DSC characters don't tell you much, don't hesitate to change them to something else. I use a64 for my a6400. You can change the three characters to anything else that suits your purposes, including your initials (DDB_ or JFK_, for example), or even customize for particular shooting sessions (EUR_, GER_, FRA_, and JAP_ when taking vacation trips). You can also use the file name flexibility to partially overcome the 9999 numbering limitation. You could, for example, use the template 641_ to represent the first 10,000 pictures you take with your a6400, and then 642_ for the next 10,000, and 643_ for the 10,000 after that.

That's assuming that you don't rename your image files in your computer. In a way, file naming verges on a moot consideration, because, they apply *only* to the images as they exist in your camera. After (or during) transfer to your computer, you can change the names to anything you want, completely disregarding the 8.3 limitations (although it's a good idea to retain the default extensions). If you shot an image file named DSC_4832.jpg in your camera, you could change it to Paris_EiffelTower_32.jpg later on.

Select REC Folder

Options: Folder
Default: None
My preference: N/A

This entry allows you to select which folder, among all those on your current memory card, to use for your images. I like to create several folders (using the New Folder entry, described next), and can switch among them, say, to keep all images of a particular type in one folder, and other images in a different folder on the memory card.

New Folder

Options: N/A
Default: None
My preference: N/A

This item will enable you to create a brand-new folder. Press the center button, and a message like "10100905 folder created" or "102MSDCF folder created" appears on the LCD. The alphanumeric format will be determined by the Folder Name option you've selected (and described next), either Standard Form or Date Form.

Although your a6400 will create new folders automatically as needed, you can create a new folder at any time, and switch among available folders already created on your memory card. (Of course, a memory card must be installed in the camera.) This is an easy way to segregate photos by folder. For example, if you're on vacation, you can change the Folder Name convention to Date Form (described next). Then, each day, create a new folder (with that date as its name), and then deposit that day's photos and video clips into it. A highlighted bar appears; press the up/down buttons to select the folder you want to use, and press the center button.

I use this feature frequently when I am traveling. I use 128GB or 256GB memory cards, and can often fit an entire trip's images on a single card. Each evening I copy the folder with that day's date to my laptop and to an external hard disk attached to the laptop, giving me two backup copies to supplement the original images that reside on my memory card.

Folder Name

Options: Standard Form, Date Form
Default: Standard Form
My preference: Standard Form

If you have viewed one of your memory card's contents on a computer, you noticed that the top-level folder on the card is always named DCIM. Inside it, there's another folder created by your camera. Different cameras use different folder names, and they can co-exist on the same card. For example, if your memory card is removed from your Sony camera and used in, say, a camera from another vendor that also accepts Secure Digital cards, the other camera will create a new folder using a different folder name within the DCIM directory.

By default, the camera creates its folders using a three-number prefix (starting with 100), followed by MSDCF. As each folder fills up with 999 images, a new folder with a prefix that's one higher (say, 101) is used. So, with the "Standard Form," the folders on your memory card will be named 100MSDCF, 101MSDCF, and so forth.

You can select Date Form instead, and the Alpha will use a *xxxymmdd* format, such as 10040904, where the 100 is the folder number, 4 is the last digit of the year (2014), 09 is the month, and 04 is the day of that month. If you want the folder names to be date-oriented, rather than generic, use the Date Form option instead of Standard Form. This entry allows you to switch back and forth between them, both for folder creation (using the New Folder entry described above) and REC folder preference (also described above).

Tip

Whoa! Sony has thrown you a curveball in this folder-switching business. Note that if you are using Date Form naming, you can *create* folders using the date convention, but you can't switch among them—but only when Date Form is active. If you *do* want to switch among folders named using the date convention, you can do it. But you have to switch from Date Form back to Standard Form. *Then* you can change to any of the available folders (of either naming format). So, if you're on that vacation, you can select Date Form, and then choose New Folder each day of your trip, if you like. But if, for some reason, you want to put some additional pictures in a different folder (say, you're revisiting a city and want the new shots to go in the same folder as those taken a few days earlier), you'll need to change to Standard Form, switch folders, and then resume shooting. Sony probably did this to preserve the "integrity" of the date/folder system, but it can be annoying.

Recover Image Database

Options: OK, Cancel

Default: None

My preference: N/A

The Recover Image DB function is provided in case errors crop up in the camera's database that records information about your movies. According to Sony, this situation may develop if you have processed or edited movies on a computer and then re-saved them to the memory card that's in your camera. You will also encounter this message when using an SD card you have formatted and used in another brand of camera. Highlight this menu option and press the center button, and the camera will prompt you, "Check Image Database File?" Press the center button to confirm, or the MENU button to cancel.

Display Media Information

Options: None

Default: None

My preference: N/A

This is the first entry on the Setup 7 menu. (See Figure 6.8.) It gives you a report of how many still images and how much movie time can be recorded on the memory card that's in the camera, given the current shooting settings. This can be useful, but that information is already displayed on the screen when the camera is being used to shoot still photos (unless you have cycled to a display with less information), and the information about minutes remaining for movie recording is displayed on the screen as soon as you press the Record button. But, if you want confirmation of this information, this menu option is available.

Version

Options: None

Default: N/A

My preference: N/A

Select this option to display the version number of the firmware (internal operating software) installed in your camera. From time to time, Sony updates the original firmware with a newer version that adds or enhances features or corrects operational bugs. For example, the Version 2.0 software, introduced not that many months after the a6400 itself, added features like animal eye detection and support for a Bluetooth remote. When a new version is released, it will be accompanied by instructions, which generally involve downloading the update to your computer and then connecting your camera to the computer with the USB cable to apply the update. It's a good idea to check occasionally at the Sony website, www.esupport.sony.com, to see if a new version of the camera's firmware is available for download. (You can also go to that site to download updates to the software that came with the camera, and to get general support information.)

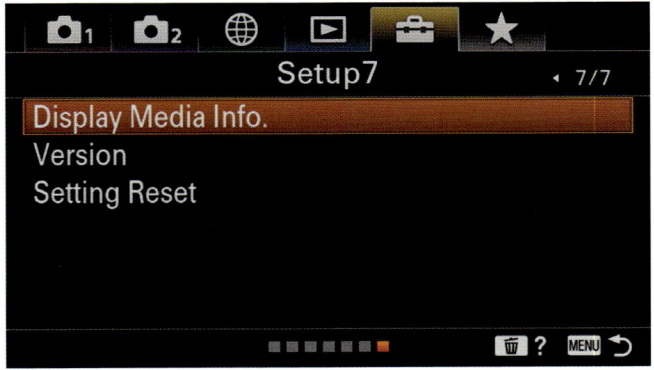

Figure 6.8
The Setup 7 menu.

Setting Reset

Options: Camera Settings Reset, Initialize

Default: N/A

My preference: N/A

If you've made a lot of changes to your camera's settings, you may want to return the features to their defaults, so you can start over without manually going back through the menus and restoring everything. This menu item lets you do that. Your choices are as follows:

- **Camera Settings Reset.** Resets the main parameters in the Camera Settings I and II menus to their default values. Your Fn settings remain.

- **Initialize.** Resets *all* Camera Settings I and II adjustments to their default settings, including the time/date and downloaded applications, but *not* including any AF Micro Adjustments or Wi-Fi settings you may have entered.

My Menu

Options: Add Item, Sort Item, Delete Item, Delete Page, Delete All

Default: None

My preference: N/A

The My Menu feature lets you create your own customized menu containing the entries you use most often, which can save you a lot of time wading through the a6400's many pages of menu tabs and entries. Of course, since you can create up to five My Menu screens, each with as many as five menu items, you can find you've created your own maze of entries—but, at least, it is your *maze*. Virtually any menu entry from the other main menu tabs (except for the Playback menu) can be added to your personalized menu. The My Menu system can be handy and quick to access (if one of your My Menu pages was the one you used last, it will pop up first when you press the MENU button). But you might have used a different menu, so it would have been helpful to be able to assign My Menu to a custom key. Pay attention, Sony!

The first time you access My Menu, no custom pages will exist, so you'll see a screen similar to the one in the screen shown at left in Figure 6.9, except all the entries except Add Item will be grayed out. Press the center button, and you'll be shown a screen with a list of menu entries (see Figure 6.9, right). Use the left/right controls to scroll among available menu pages, and up/down controls to highlight a particular entry you want to add. Press the center button and you'll be given the opportunity to choose which page to add it to, numbered from 1 through 5. (See Figure 6.10, left.)

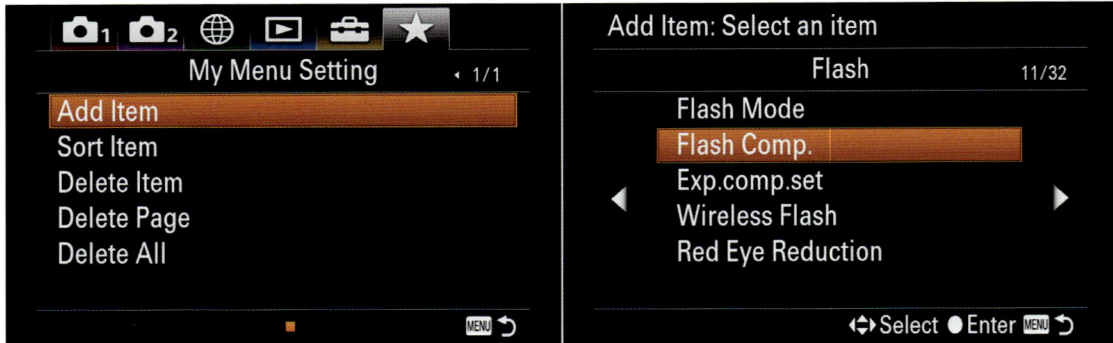

Figure 6.9 Select Add Item (left) and then choose the command to be added (right).

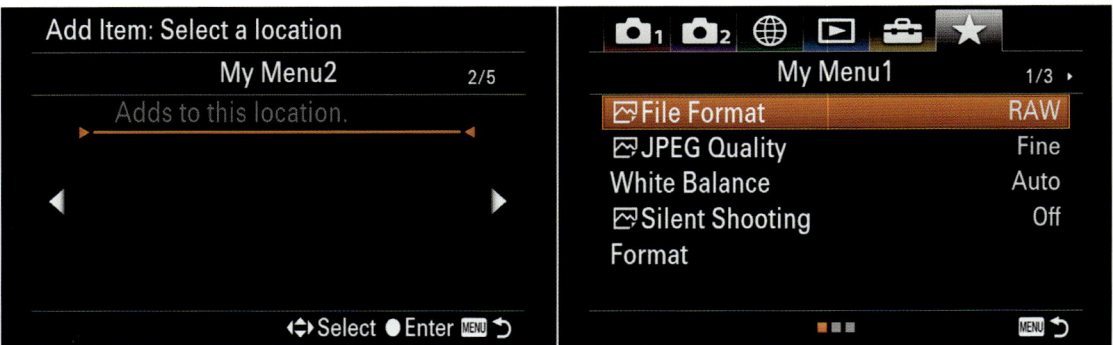

Figure 6.10 Choose the page number the new command will be added to (left). A typical My Menu page will have one or more entries (right).

You don't need to fill up one page before starting another one. Conceivably, you could have five My Menu pages, each with a single entry. After you've created a new My Menu page, the command function page (Add, Sort, etc.) moves to the end of the line, eventually becoming Page 6 when the other five My Menu pages have been created. Each newborn My Menu page will look something like Figure 6.10 (right), but with your personal entries included. The additional options available include:

- **Sort.** Highlight a My Menu item and press the center button. You can then use the up/down controls to move it within its current menu, or the left right controls to transport it to a different My Menu page.

- **Delete Item/Delete Page/Delete All.** Highlight an entry or page and press the center button to remove that item or page from My Menu. Delete All will remove all your My Menu items so you can start from scratch.

7

Nailing the Optimum Exposure

Left to its own devices, your a6400 can do an excellent job of providing the proper exposure for most scenes. But even a camera as smart as the a6400 frequently can benefit from intelligent input. For example, when you shoot with the main light source behind the subject, you end up with *back-lighting*, which can result in an overexposed background and/or an underexposed subject. The Sony a6400 recognizes backlit situations nicely, and, in most cases, can properly base exposure on the main subject using the default Multi metering mode, producing a decent photo.

But, as a creative photographer, there will be many instances where you would rather *not* have automatic correction for backlighting. What if you *want* to underexpose the subject, to produce a silhouette effect? The a6400 does a poor job of exposing intentional silhouettes and will end up producing unwanted detail in what should have been inky black areas of your image. Fortunately, the camera has metering modes and other exposure options that allow you to produce the image you are looking for. If you're looking for an extensive exposure range, features like the a6400's built-in DRO and Auto HDR features can fine-tune your exposure as you take photos, preserving detail in the highlights and shadows as required. Your Sony a6400 also has the capability of *fine-tuning* exposure separately for each of the metering modes, so you can consistently add or subtract a little exposure to suit your creative tastes.

In the next few pages, I'm going to give you a grounding in exposure concepts, either as an introduction or as a refresher course, depending on your current level of expertise. When you finish this chapter, you'll understand most of what you need to know to take well-exposed photographs creatively in a broad range of situations.

Getting a Handle on Exposure

This section explains the fundamental concepts that go into creating an exposure. If you already know about the role of f/stops, shutter speeds, and sensor sensitivity in determining an exposure, you might want to skip to the next section, which explains how the a6400 calculates exposure.

You're probably well aware of the traditional "exposure triangle" of aperture (quantity of light, light passed by the lens), shutter speed (the amount of time the shutter is open), and the ISO sensitivity of the sensor—all working *proportionately* and *reciprocally* to produce an exposure. The trio is itself affected by the amount of illumination that is available to work with. So, if you double the amount of light, increase the aperture by one stop, make the shutter speed twice as long, or boost the ISO setting 2X, with any one of those changes you'll get exactly twice as much exposure. Similarly, you can *increase* any of these factors while *decreasing* one of the others by a similar amount to keep the same exposure.

Working with any of the three controls involves trade-offs. Larger f/stops provide less depth-of-field, while smaller f/stops increase depth-of-field (and potentially at the same time can *decrease* sharpness through a phenomenon called *diffraction*). Shorter shutter speeds do a better job of reducing the effects of any camera/subject motion, while longer shutter speeds make that motion blur more likely. Higher ISO settings increase the amount of visual noise and artifacts in your image, while lower ISO settings reduce the effects of noise. (See Figure 7.1.)

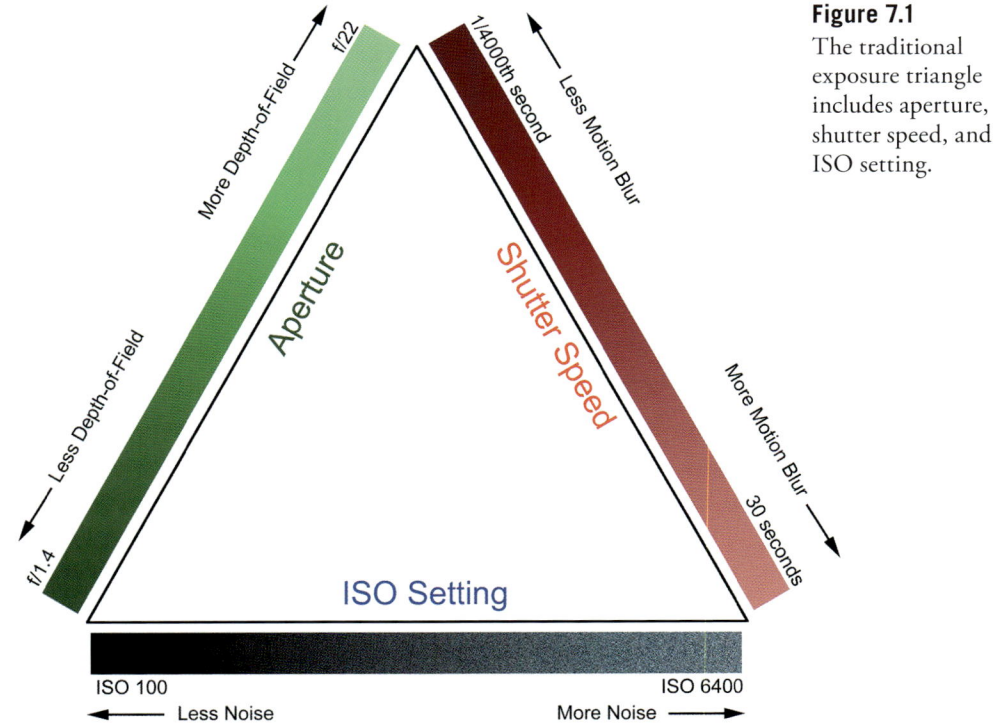

Figure 7.1

The traditional exposure triangle includes aperture, shutter speed, and ISO setting.

Exposure determines the look, feel, and tone of an image, in more ways than one. Incorrect exposure can impair even the best-composed image by cloaking important tones in darkness, or by washing them out so they become featureless to the eye. On the other hand, correct exposure brings out the detail in the areas you want to picture, and provides the range of tones and colors you need to create the desired image. However, getting the perfect exposure can be tricky, because digital sensors can't capture all the tones we are able to see. If the range of tones in an image is extensive, embracing both inky black shadows and bright highlights, the sensor may not be able to capture them all. Sometimes, we must settle for an exposure that renders most of those tones—but not all—in a way that best suits the photo we want to produce. You'll often need to make choices about which details are important, and which are not, so that you can grab the tones that truly matter in your image. That's part of the creativity you bring to bear in realizing your photographic vision.

For example, look at two bracketed exposures presented in Figure 7.2. For the image at top left, the highlights (chiefly the clouds at upper left and the top-left edge of the skyscraper) are well exposed, but everything else in the shot is seriously underexposed. The version at the top right, taken an instant later with the tripod-mounted camera, shows detail in the shadow areas of the buildings, but the highlights are completely washed out. The camera's sensor simply can't capture detail in both dark areas and bright areas in a single shot. With digital camera sensors, it's tricky to capture detail in both highlights and shadows in a single image, because the number of tones, the *dynamic range* of the sensor, is limited.

The solution is to resort to a technique called High Dynamic Range (HDR) photography. It's included as a built-in feature of the camera (through the DRO/HDR Photography entry in the Camera Settings I-11 menu). However, I elected to produce the image shown at the bottom of the figure by merging the two original shots using a Photoshop/Photoshop Elements feature called Merge to HDR. There are also specialized software tools like Photomatix (about $100 from www.hdrsoft.com), HDR Efex Pro as part of the Nik Collection ($99) from DxO Optics (www.nikcollection.dxo.com), or Aurora HDR ($39.95 from www.aurorahdr.com).

I'll explain more about HDR photography, and how to explore it with your a6400, later in this chapter. For now, though, I'm going to concentrate on showing you how to get the best exposures possible without resorting to such tools, using only the features of your camera.

To understand exposure, you need to appreciate the aspects of light that combine to produce an image. Start with a light source—the sun, a household lamp, or the glow from a campfire—and trace its path to your camera, through the lens, and finally to the sensor that captures the illumination.

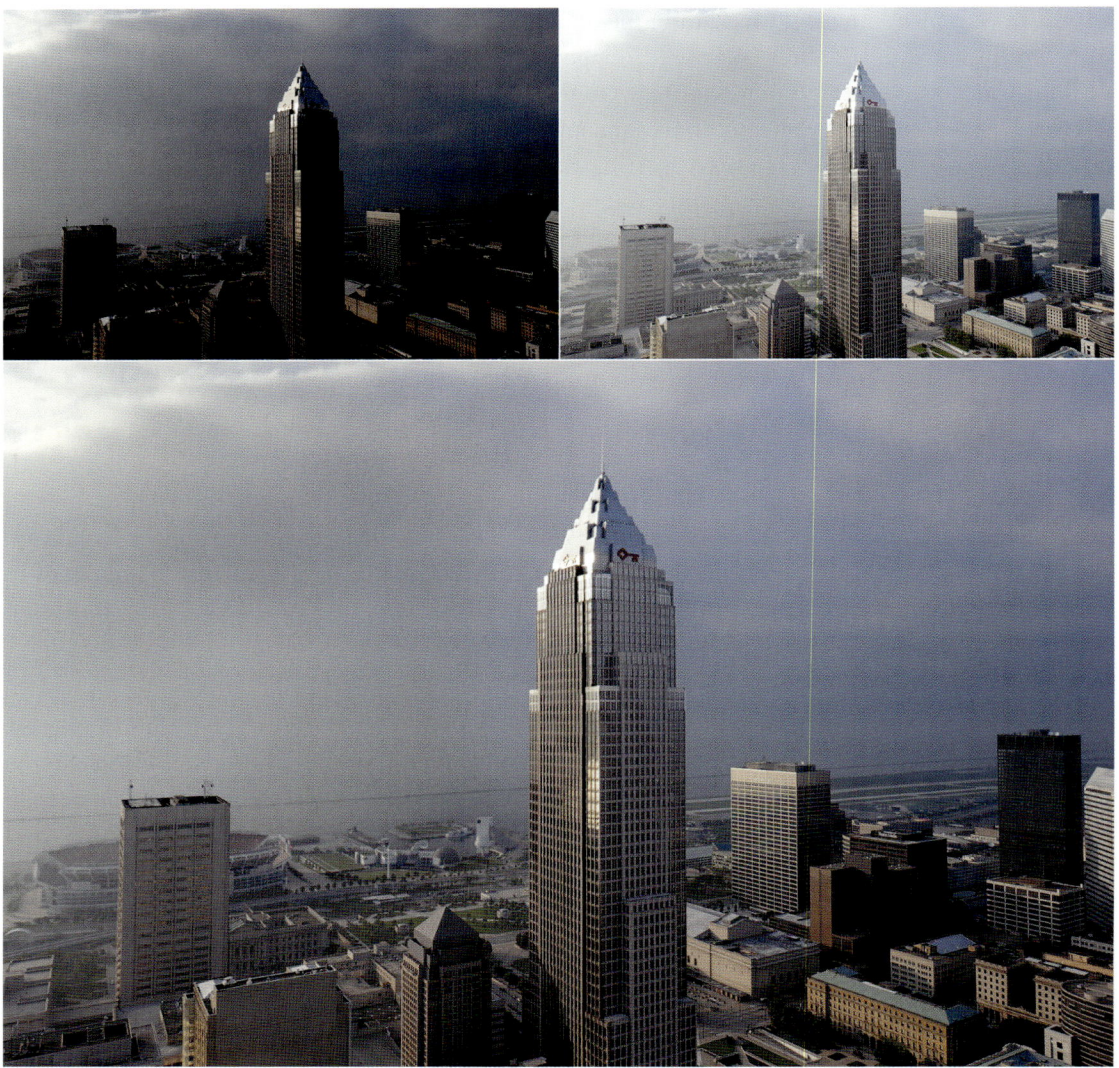

Figure 7.2 At top left, exposure for the highlights loses shadow detail. At top right, exposure for the highlights washes out the background. Bottom, combining the two exposures produces the best compromise.

Here's a brief review of the things within our control that affect exposure, listed in "chronological" order (that is, as the light moves from the subject to the sensor):

- **Light at its source.** Our eyes and our cameras—film or digital—are most sensitive to that portion of the electromagnetic spectrum we call visible light. That light has several important aspects that are relevant to photography, such as color and harshness (which is determined primarily by the apparent size of the light source as it illuminates a subject). But, in terms of exposure, the important attribute of a light source is its intensity. We may have direct control over intensity, which might be the case with an interior light that can be brightened or dimmed. Or, we might have only indirect control over intensity, as with sunlight, which can be made to appear dimmer by introducing translucent light-absorbing or reflective materials in its path.

- **Light's duration.** We tend to think of most light sources as continuous. But, as you'll learn in Chapter 12, the duration of light can change quickly enough to modify the exposure, as when the main illumination in a photograph comes from an intermittent source, such as an electronic flash.

- **Light reflected, transmitted, or emitted.** Once light is produced by its source, either continuously or in a brief burst, we are able to see and photograph objects by the light that is reflected from our subjects toward the camera lens; transmitted (say, from translucent objects that are lit from behind); or emitted (by a candle or television screen). When more or less light reaches the lens from the subject, we need to adjust the exposure. This part of the equation is under our control to the extent we can increase the amount of light falling on or passing through the subject (by adding extra light sources or using reflectors), or by pumping up the light that's emitted (by increasing the brightness of the glowing object).

- **Light passed by the lens.** Not all the illumination that reaches the front of the lens makes it all the way through. Filters can remove some of the light before it enters the lens. Inside the lens barrel is a variable-sized diaphragm that dilates and contracts to produce an aperture that controls the amount of light that enters the lens. You, or the Alpha's autoexposure system, can vary the size of the aperture to control the amount of light that will reach the sensor. The relative size of the aperture is called the f/stop. (See Figure 7.3, which is a graphic representation of the relative size of the lens opening, not an actual photo of the aperture of a lens.)

- **Light passing through the shutter.** Once light passes through the lens, the amount of time the sensor receives it is determined by the camera's shutter; this mechanism can remain open for as long as 30 seconds (or even longer if you use the camera's Bulb setting) or as briefly as 1/4000th second.

- **Light captured by the sensor.** Not all the light falling onto the sensor is captured. If the number of photons reaching a particular photosite doesn't pass a set threshold, no information is recorded. Similarly, if too much light illuminates a pixel in the sensor, then the excess isn't recorded or, worse, spills over to contaminate adjacent pixels. We can modify the minimum and maximum number of pixels that contribute to image detail by adjusting the ISO setting. At higher ISO levels, the incoming light is amplified to boost the effective sensitivity of the sensor.

F/STOPS AND SHUTTER SPEEDS

Especially if you're new to advanced cameras, it's worth quickly reviewing some essential concepts. For example, the lens aperture, or f/stop, is a ratio, much like a fraction, which is why f/2 is larger than f/4, just as 1/2 is larger than 1/4. However, f/2 is actually *four times* as large as f/4. (Think back to high school geometry where we learned that to double the area of a circle, you multiply its diameter by the square root of two: 1.4.)

The full f/stops available with an f/2 lens are f/2, f/2.8, f/4, f/5.6, f/8, f/11, f/16, and f/22. Each higher number indicates an aperture that's half the size of the previous number. Hence, it admits half as much light as the one before. Figure 7.3 shows a simplified representation. (Of course, you can also set intermediate apertures with the a6400, such as f/6.3 and f/7.1, which are the 1/3-stop increments between f/5.6 and f/8.)

Shutter speeds are actual fractions (of a second), so that 1/60, 1/125, 1/250, 1/500, 1/1000, and so forth represent 1/60th, 1/125th, 1/250th, 1/500th, and 1/1000th second. Each higher number indicates a shutter speed that's half as long as the one before. (And yes, intermediate shutter speeds can also be used, such as 1/640th or 1/800th second.) To avoid confusion, Sony uses quotation marks to signify long exposures: 0.8", 2", 2.5", 4", and so forth; these examples represent 0.8-second, 2-second, 2.5-second and 4-second exposures, respectively.

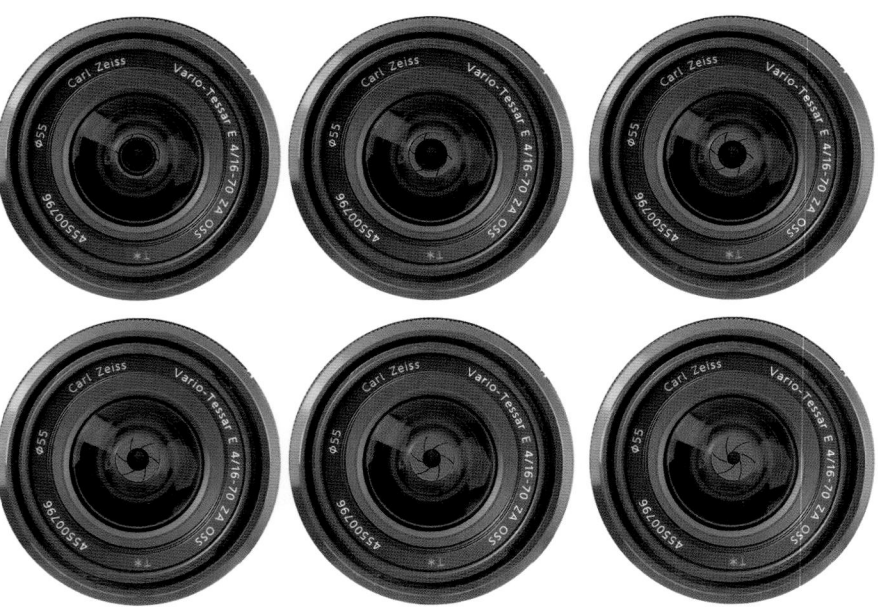

Figure 7.3
Top row (left to right): f/4, f/5.6, f/8; bottom row: f/11, f/16, f/22.

These factors all work proportionately and reciprocally to produce an exposure. That is, if you double the amount of light, increase the aperture size by one stop, make the shutter speed twice as long, or double the ISO, you'll get twice as much exposure. Similarly, you can reduce any of these and reduce the exposure when that is preferable.

As we'll see however, changing any of those aspects in P, A, or S mode does not change the actual exposure; that's because the camera also makes changes when you do so, in order to maintain the same exposure. That's why Sony provides other methods for modifying the exposure in those modes.

Equivalent Exposure

One of the most important aspects in this discussion is the concept of "equivalent exposure." This term means that exactly the same amount of light will reach the sensor at various combinations of aperture and shutter speed. Whether we use a small aperture (large f/number) with a long shutter speed or a wide aperture (small f/number) with a fast shutter speed, the amount of light reaching the sensor can be exactly the same. Table 7.1 shows equivalent exposure settings using various shutter speeds and f/stops; in other words, any of the combination of settings listed will produce exactly the same exposure.

When you set the camera to P mode, it sets both the aperture and the shutter speed that should provide a correct exposure, based on guidance from the light metering system. In P mode, you cannot change the aperture or the shutter speed individually, but you can shift among various aperture/shutter speed combinations by rotating the control wheel, providing what is called *program shift*. (If you use program shift, an asterisk will appear next to the P on your display screens to let you know you've made an adjustment.) If you change the ISO, the camera will set a different combination automatically. As the concept of equivalent exposure indicates, the image brightness will be exactly the same in every photo you shoot with the various combinations because they all provide the same exposure.

Table 7.1 Equivalent Exposures

Shutter speed	f/stop	Shutter speed	f/stop
1/30th second	f/22	1/500th second	f/5.6
1/60th second	f/16	1/1000th second	f/4
1/125th second	f/11	1/2000th second	f/2.8
1/250th second	f/8	1/4000th second	f/2

F/STOPS VERSUS STOPS

In photography parlance, *f/stop* always means the aperture or lens opening. However, for lack of a current commonly used word for one exposure increment, the term *stop* is often used. In the past, EV (Exposure Value) served this purpose, and was used as a measure of the total sensitivity range of a device such as a light meter, but exposure value and its abbreviation have since been inextricably intertwined with its use in describing exposure compensation. In this book, when I say "stop" by itself (no *f/*), I mean one whole unit of exposure, and am not necessarily referring to an actual f/stop or lens aperture. So, adjusting the exposure by "one stop" can mean changing to the next shutter speed increment (say, from 1/125th second to 1/200th second) or the next aperture (such as f/4 to f/5.6). Similarly, 1/3-stop or 1/2-stop increments can mean either shutter speed or aperture changes, depending on the context. Be forewarned.

In Aperture Priority (A) and Shutter Priority (S) modes, you can change the aperture or the shutter speed, respectively. The camera will then change the other factor to maintain the same exposure. I'll cover all of the operating modes and the important aspects of exposure with each mode in this chapter.

How the a6400 Calculates Exposure

Although it can make some good guesses based on how the brightness levels vary within a scene, your a6400 has no way of knowing for sure what it's pointed at. So, it must make some assumptions and calculate the correct exposure based on its internal rules. One parameter is that the brightness of all—or part—of a scene will average down to a so-called middle-gray tone. The conventional wisdom is that this tone is roughly 18 percent gray. Unfortunately, while the traditional 18 percent value is a middle gray in terms of what the eye sees, the a6400 is calibrated for a slightly darker tone. This section explains how your a6400 decides on an exposure in one of its semi-automatic (non-manual) modes.

Your camera calculates exposure by measuring the light that passes through the lens and reaches the sensor, based on the assumption that each area being measured reflects about the same amount of light as a neutral gray card that reflects a "middle" gray of about 12 to 18 percent reflectance. (The photographic "gray cards" you buy at a camera store have an 18 percent gray tone; your camera is calibrated to interpret a somewhat darker 12 percent gray. I'll explain more about this later.) That "average" 12 to 18 percent gray assumption is necessary, because different subjects reflect different amounts of light. In a photo containing, say, a white cat and a dark gray cat, the white cat might reflect five times as much light as the gray cat. An exposure based on the white cat will cause the gray cat to appear to be black, while an exposure based only on the gray cat will make the white cat washed out.

This is more easily understood if you look at some photos of subjects that are dark (they reflect little light), those that have predominantly middle tones, and subjects that are highly reflective. I'm not going to use actual cats but, rather will include a more human figure in the frame (which is more common, unless you're a cat photographer), accompanied by a card with a trio of gray reference patches. The next figure shows what you would end up with if you exposed a set of photographs using a different gray patch for each.

Correctly Exposed

The image shown in Figure 7.4, left, represents how a photograph might appear if you inserted the patches shown at bottom left into the scene, and then calculated exposure by measuring the light reflecting from the middle gray patch, which, for the sake of illustration, we'll assume reflects approximately 12 to 18 percent of the light that strikes it. The exposure meter in the camera sees an object that it thinks is a middle gray (the middle patch), calculates an exposure based on that, and the patch in the center of the strip is rendered at its proper tonal value. Best of all, because the resulting exposure is correct, the black patch at left and white patch at right are rendered properly as well.

When you're shooting pictures with your a6400 camera, and the meter happens to base its exposure on a subject that averages that "ideal" middle gray, then you'll end up with similar (accurate) results. The camera's exposure algorithms are concocted to ensure this kind of result as often as possible, barring any unusual subjects (that is, those that are backlit, or have uneven illumination). The camera has five different metering modes (described in an upcoming section), each of which is equipped to handle certain types of unusual subjects, as I'll outline.

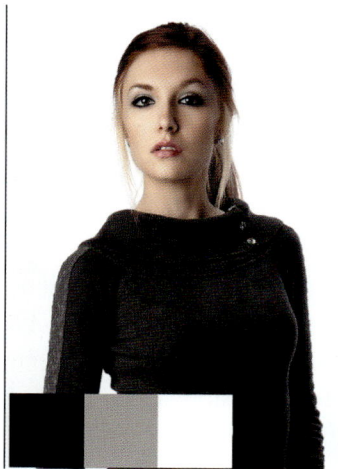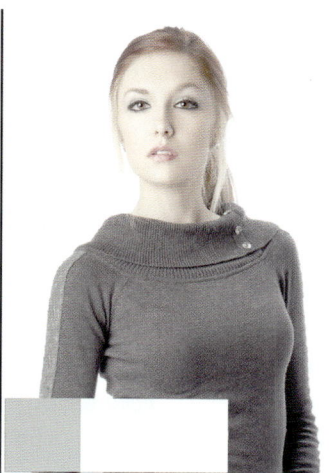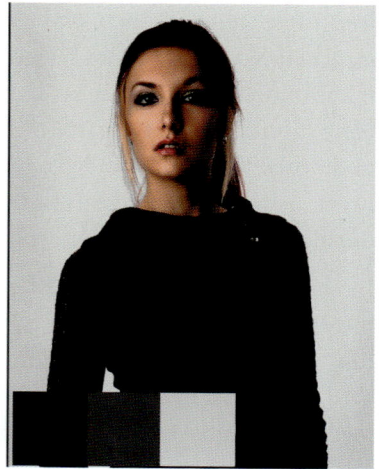

Figure 7.4 Exposure based on the middle-gray tone in the center of the card is accurate (left). Metering the black square, the black patch looks gray, the gray patch appears to be a light gray, and the white square is seriously overexposed (center). With exposure calculated from the white patch, the photo is underexposed (right).

Overexposed

Figure 7.4, center, shows what would happen if the exposure were calculated based on metering the leftmost, black patch, which is roughly the same tonal value of the darkest areas of the subject's hair. The light meter sees less light reflecting from the black square than it would see from a gray middle-tone subject, and so figures, "Aha! I need to add exposure to brighten this subject up to a middle gray!" That lightens the "black" patch, so it now appears to be gray.

But now the patch in the middle that was *originally* middle gray is overexposed and becomes light gray. And the white square at right is now seriously overexposed and loses detail in the highlights, which have become a featureless white. Our human subject is similarly overexposed. You should always be *aware* when overexposure occurs but note that it's not *always* a bad thing. Some slight overexposures add a dreamy look to an image; once you know how the rules are derived, you'll know how and when to break them.

Underexposed

The third possibility in this simplified scenario is that the light meter might measure the illumination bouncing off the white patch and try to render *that* tone as a middle gray. A lot of light is reflected by the white square, so the exposure is *reduced*, bringing that patch closer to a middle gray tone. The patches that were originally gray and black are now rendered too dark. Clearly, measuring the gray card—or a substitute that reflects about the same amount of light—is the only way to ensure that the exposure is precisely correct. (See Figure 7.4, right.)

As you can see, the ideal way to measure exposure is to meter from a subject that reflects 12 to 18 percent of the light that reaches it. If you want the most precise exposure calculations, the solution is to use a stand-in, such as the evenly illuminated gray card I mentioned earlier. But, because the standard Kodak gray card reflects 18 percent of the light that reaches it and, as I said, your camera is calibrated for a somewhat lighter 12 percent tone, you would need to add about one-half stop *more* exposure than the value metered from the card. Of course, in most situations, it's not necessary to do this. Your camera's light meter will do a good job of calculating the right exposure, especially if you use the exposure tips in the next section. But, I felt that explaining exactly what is going on during exposure calculation would help you understand how your camera's metering system works.

In some very bright scenes (like a snowy landscape or a lava field), you won't have a mid-tone to meter. Another substitute for a gray card is the palm of a human hand (the backside of the hand is too variable). But a human palm, regardless of ethnic group, is even brighter than a standard gray card, so instead of one-half stop more exposure, you need to add one additional stop. That is, if your meter reading is 1/500th of a second at f/11, use 1/500th second at f/8 or 1/200th second at f/11 instead. (Both exposures are equivalent.)

Or, you might want to resort to using an evenly illuminated gray card I just mentioned. Small versions are available that can be tucked in a camera bag. Place it in your frame near your main subject, facing the camera, and with the exact same even illumination falling on it that is falling on your subject. Then, use the Spot metering function (described in the next section later) to calculate exposure.

But, the standard Kodak gray card reflects 18 percent of the light while, as I noted, your camera is calibrated for a somewhat darker 12 percent tone. If you insisted on getting a perfect exposure, you would need to add about one-half stop more exposure than the value provided by taking the light meter reading from the card. Of course, in most situations, it's not necessary to do this. Your camera's light meter will do a good job of calculating the right exposure, especially if you use the exposure tips in the next section. But, I felt that explaining exactly what is going on during exposure calculation would help you understand how your camera's metering system works.

In serious photography, you'll want to choose the *metering mode* (the pattern that determines how brightness is evaluated) and the *exposure mode* (determines how the appropriate shutter speed and aperture is set). I'll describe both aspects in later sections.

ORIGIN OF THE 18 PERCENT "MYTH"

Why are so many photographers under the impression that camera light meters are calibrated to the 18 percent "standard," rather than the true value, which may be 12 to 14 percent, depending on the vendor? You'll find this misinformation in an alarming number of places. I've seen the 18 percent "myth" taught in camera classes; I've found it in books, and even been given this wrong information from the technical staff of camera vendors. (They should know better—the same vendors' engineers who design and calibrate the cameras have the right figure.)

The most common explanation is that during a revision of Kodak's instructions for its gray cards in 1977, the advice to open up an extra half stop was omitted, and a whole generation of shooters grew up thinking that a measurement off a gray card could be used as-is. Kodak restored the proviso in 1997 during the next update of the instructions but by then it was too late

EXTERNAL METERS CAN BE CALIBRATED

The light meters built into your camera are calibrated at the factory. But if you use a hand-held incident or reflective light meter, you *can* calibrate it, using the instructions supplied with your meter. Because a hand-held meter *can* be calibrated to the 18 percent gray standard (or any other value you choose), my rant about the myth of the 18 percent gray card doesn't apply.

The Importance of ISO

Another essential concept when discussing exposure, ISO control allows you to change the sensitivity of the camera's imaging sensor. Sometimes photographers forget about this option, because the common practice is to set the ISO once for a particular shooting session (say, at ISO 100 or 200 for bright sunlight outdoors, or ISO 800 or 1600 when shooting indoors) and then forget about it. Or some shooters simply leave the camera set to ISO Auto. That enables the camera to change the ISO it deems necessary, setting a low ISO in bright conditions or a higher ISO in a darker location. That's fine, but sometimes you'll want to set a specific ISO yourself, in the range of ISO 100 to ISO 51200. Indeed, when shooting movies, only ISO settings from ISO 100 to ISO 25600 can be set.

TIP

When shooting in the Program (P), Aperture Priority (A), and Shutter Priority (S) modes, all discussed soon, changing the ISO does not change the exposure. If you switch from using ISO 100 to ISO 1600 in A mode for example, the camera will simply set a different shutter speed. If you change the ISO in S mode, the camera will set a different aperture, and in P mode, it will set a different aperture and/or shutter speed. In all of these examples, the camera will maintain the same exposure. If you want to make a brighter or a darker photo in P, A, or S mode, you would need to set + or − exposure compensation, as discussed later.

However, when you use the Manual (M) mode, changing the ISO also changes the exposure, as discussed shortly.

The camera provides the best possible image quality in the ISO 100 to 400 range. We use higher ISO levels such as ISO 1600 in low light and ISO 6400 in a very dark location because it allows us to shoot at a faster shutter speed. That's often useful for minimizing the risk of blurring caused by camera shake, which can occur even with optical image stabilization (OSS) built into many lenses. And, of course, you must also contend with movement of the subject, which no amount of image stabilization will fix.

Although you can set a desired ISO level yourself, the a6400 also offers an ISO Auto option. When enabled, the camera will select an ISO that should be suitable for the conditions: a low ISO on a sunny day and a high ISO in a dark location. In Intelligent Auto, Superior Auto, Scene Selection, or Sweep Panorama modes, ISO Auto is the only available option. The camera will set an ISO no higher than 3200, except in the Anti Motion Blur and Hand-held Twilight scene modes where it can set ISO to 6400.

Over the past few years, there has been something of a competition among the manufacturers of digital cameras to achieve the highest ISO ratings. The highest announced ISO numbers have been rising annually, from 1600 to 3200, 6400, 102400, and far beyond.

Choosing a Metering Mode

The Sony a6400 has five different schemes for evaluating the light received by its exposure sensors. The quickest way to choose among them is to assign Metering Mode to a key using the Custom Key settings in the Camera Settings II-08 menu, as described in Chapter 4. Then, you can press the defined key and to produce the Metering Mode screen; then scroll up/down among the options. Without a custom key, the default method for choosing a metering mode is to use the Camera Settings I-08 (Exposure 1 menu), the Function menu, or the Quick Navi menu. (See Figure 7.5.)

Figure 7.5
Choose one of five metering modes.

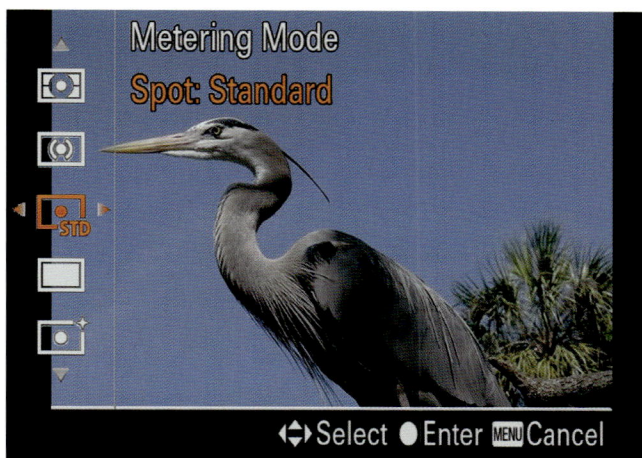

Multi Metering

In this "intelligent" (multi-segment) metering mode, the a6400 measures the illumination falling on all the pixels in the sensor, but slices up the frame into 1,200 different zones, as shown at left in Figure 7.6. The camera evaluates the measurements to make an educated guess about what kind of picture you're taking, based on examination of exposure data derived from thousands of different real-world photos. For example, if the top section of a picture is much lighter than the bottom portions, the algorithm can assume that the scene is a landscape photo with lots of sky. However, if there is a lighter area in the center of the frame, and the camera detects skin tones, the a6400 will assume that you're shooting a portrait and not a landscape photo and expose for the human subject.

The Multi system can recognize individual elements in a very bright scene, and it can automatically increase the exposure to reduce the risk of a dark photo. This will be useful when your subject is a snow-covered landscape or a close-up of a bride in white. Granted, you may occasionally need to use a bit of exposure compensation, but often, the exposure will be close to accurate even without it. (In my experience, the Multi system is most successful with light-toned scenes on bright days. When shooting in dark, overcast conditions, it's more likely to underexpose a scene of that type.)

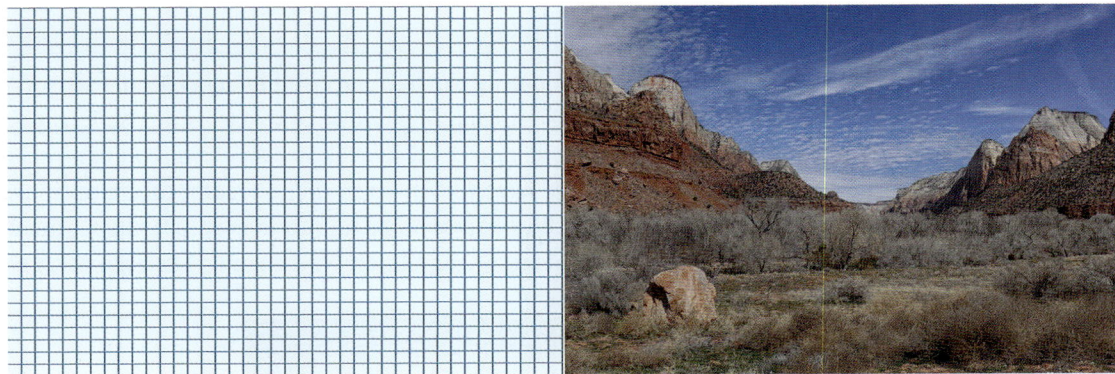

Figure 7.6 Multi metering uses 1,200 zones and is suitable for complex scenes like this one.

As I mentioned, multi-segment metering is especially suitable for people. If you activate Face Priority in Multi Metering in the Camera Settings II-06 (AF 2) menu's Face/Eye AF Settings entry, the a6400 will use any detected faces to calculate exposure. The sensor has enough resolution to allow detecting eyes, noses, and mouths, and thus confirm to its satisfaction that humans are in the photo (and contain detail that should be preserved, possibly at the expense of other areas, such as sky or background). If human faces are also located within the current autofocus area, the a6400 will consistently try to preserve detail in those faces. You can disable face detection if you're shooting landscapes.

The Multi metering mode is best for most general subjects, because it can intelligently analyze a scene and make an excellent guess of what kind of subject you're shooting a great deal of the time. The camera can tell the difference between low-contrast and high-contrast subjects by looking at the range of differences in brightness across the scene. Because the a6400 has a fairly good idea about what kind of subject matter you are shooting, it can underexpose slightly when appropriate to preserve highlight detail when image contrast is high. (It's often possible to pull detail out of shadows that are too dark using an image editor, but once highlights are converted to white pixels, they are gone forever.) A typical scene suitable for Multi metering is shown at right in Figure 7.6.

Center-weighted Metering

Center-weighted metering was the only available option with cameras some decades ago. In this mode you get conventional metering without any "intelligent" scene evaluation. The light meter considers brightness in the entire frame but places the greatest emphasis on a large area in the center of the frame, as shown at left in Figure 7.7, on the theory that, for most pictures, the main subject will not be located far off-center.

Of course, Center metering is most effective when the subject in the central area is a mid-tone. Even then, if your main subject is surrounded by large, extremely bright or very dark areas, the exposure might not be exactly right. (You might need to use exposure compensation, a feature discussed

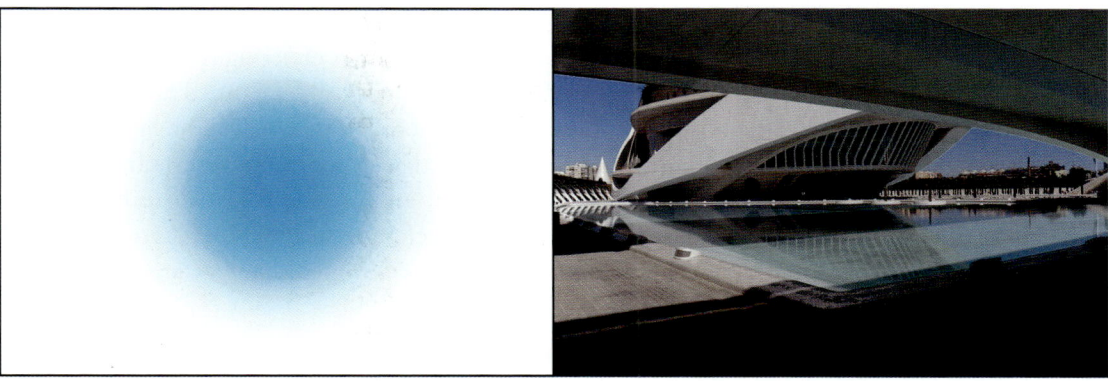

Figure 7.7 Center metering calculates exposure based on the full frame but emphasizes the center area.

shortly.) However, this scheme works well in many situations if you don't want to use one of the other modes, for scenes like the one shown in at right in Figure 7.7. This mode can be useful for close-ups of subjects like flowers, or for portraits.

Spot Metering

Spot metering mode confines the reading to a very small area in the center of the image, as shown at left in Figure 7.8. When Spot is highlighted, you can press the left/right controls to choose from a standard-size spot, or a larger one. By default, the spot is located in the center of the frame, unless you use the Spot Metering Point entry of the Camera Settings I-08 (Exposure 1) menu to link it to the current focus area. However, when you use the Flexible Spot or Expand Flexible Spot focus area options, the spot metering will *always* be at the area where the camera sets focus. So, you have the option of linking the exposure spot to the focus area *all* the time, or only when using the two Flexible Spot settings.

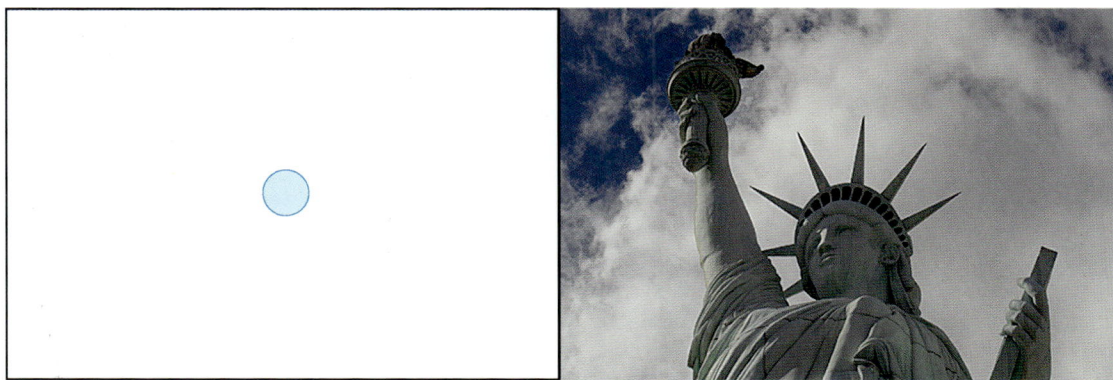

Figure 7.8 Spot metering calculates exposure based on a spot that's only a small percentage of the image area, such as the face of the Statue of Liberty.

The Spot meter does not apply any "intelligent" scene evaluation. Because the camera considers only a small target area, and completely ignores its surroundings, Spot metering is most useful when the subject is a small mid-tone area. For example, the "target" might be a tanned face, a medium red blossom, or a gray rock in a wide-angle photo; each of these is a mid-tone. The Spot metering technique is simple if you want to Spot meter a small area that's dead center in the frame. If the "target" is off-center, you would need to point the lens at it and use the AE Lock technique discussed later in this chapter. (Lock exposure on your target before re-framing for a better composition so the exposure does not change.) For Figure 7.8, right, Spot metering was used to base the exposure on the Statue of Liberty's face.

If you Spot meter a light-toned area or a dark-toned area, you will get underexposure or overexposure, respectively; you would need to use an override for more accurate results. On the other hand, you can Spot meter a small mid-tone subject surrounded by a sky with big white clouds or by an indigo blue wall and get a good exposure. (The light meter ignores the subject's surroundings, so they do not affect the exposure.) That would not be possible with Center-weighted metering, which considers brightness in a much larger area.

Entire Screen Averaging

This option tells the a6400 to simply measure all the illumination in the frame and calculate exposure based on the average value. (See Figure 7.9, left.) That may not lead to the optimal exposure for an image (if some large very bright or very dark areas are present), but it does have one advantage: because only the average reflectance is used, the exposure will not change as your subjects move around in the frame. The woman's hands shown at right in Figure 7.9 darted back and forth as she worked, but the exposure remained constant for several successive images.

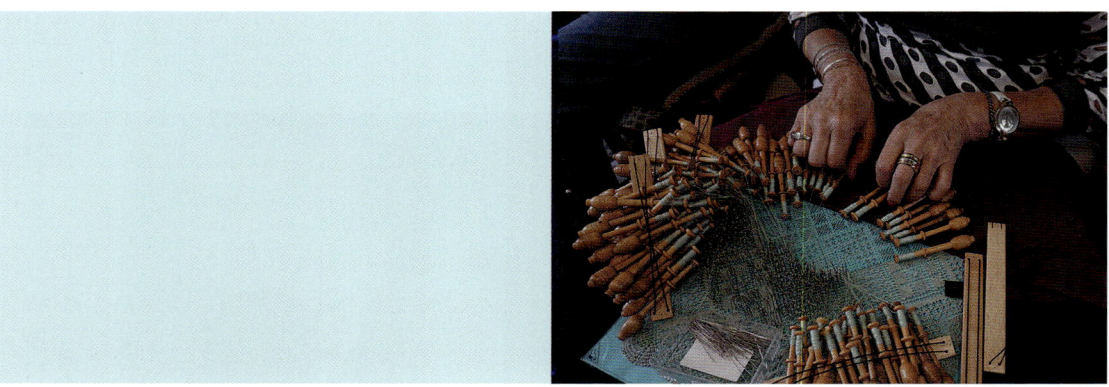

Figure 7.9 When using Entire Screen Averaging, the exposure will not change if a subject, such as this artisan's fast-moving hands, moves within the frame.

Highlight-weighted Metering

This choice pays special attention to the highlights of an image. Figure 7.10, left, doesn't really show the active metering area, but it is a graphical representation of what areas are most important in the photo at right in Figure 7.10. If your subject is surrounded by very dark areas, this metering method will help avoid overexposure.

Highlight metering is *not* a spot metering mode, despite its icon, which is the same as the Spot icon, with an asterisk added. With this mode, the camera's Exmor processor seeks out highlight areas of your image and bases exposure on a setting that will keep those highlights from being overexposed. Less emphasis ("weight") is given to non-highlight areas.

So, if you're shooting spotlit performers on-stage at a concert or play, the a6400 can calculate the correct exposure using the performers, and ignoring, for the most part, the dark surroundings. You'd have your choice of measuring exposure in Spot mode, as described in the previous section, placing the metering spot on the performer's face or shirt, or, you could select Highlight-weighted metering and allow the camera to identify the performer when figuring exposure. Your results might be similar with either, depending on how well you "placed" the Spot area and how cleverly the a6400 sorts out your subject from the background. I tend to use Spot mode when the area I want to meter is clearly defined, and Highlight-weighted when there is a range of highlights.

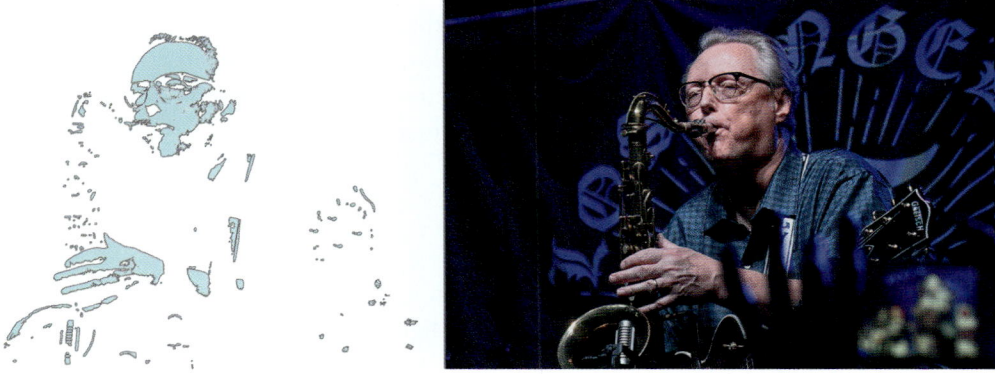

Figure 7.10 Highlight-weighted metering will help avoid overexposure of subjects surrounded by dark areas.

LOCKING EXPOSURE

An important tool when using any metering method is the ability to *lock* exposure once you've set shutter speed, aperture, and ISO to your satisfaction, allowing you to reframe your image before taking a picture. While the a6400 has a dedicated AE-L button, there is an abundance of alternatives. One option is the shutter release button itself, or your choice of the Custom buttons which can be defined using the Custom Keys feature described in Chapter 4. Your defined control can be set to function when held down, as a toggle, or some other configuration.

INSTANT SWITCHING

If you frequently use one metering method, but occasionally like to switch to another method on the fly, you can redefine one of the a6400's custom keys to change to your alternate mode at the press of a button, using the Custom Keys feature I explained in Chapter 4.

The really cool thing is that you can define one button for, say, Center-weighted metering, another one for Spot metering, and then set the main metering mode switch to Matrix, and thus be able to switch among those three on a whim. I've done this as a way to compare the exposure settings of the three metering methods while composing a single image in the viewfinder. I've also found the capability useful when I'm, say, working with Multi metering and want to zero in on an area of the frame temporarily using Spot metering.

Choosing an Exposure Mode

After you set a desired metering mode, you have several methods for choosing the appropriate shutter speed and aperture, semi-automatically or manually. Just press the center button and spin the mode dial to the exposure mode that you want to use. If the Mode Dial Guide is activated in the Setup 2 menu (as described in Chapter 6), you'll see a display that briefly explains what the selected mode does. Your choice of which is best for a given shooting situation will depend on aspects like your need for extensive or shallow depth-of-field (the range of acceptably sharp focus in a photo) or the desire to freeze action or to allow motion blur. The semi-automatic Aperture Priority and Shutter Priority modes discussed in the next section emphasize one aspect of image capture or another, but the following sections introduce you to all four of the modes that photographers often call "creative."

Aperture Priority (A) Mode

When using the A mode, you specify the lens opening (aperture or f/stop) with the front or control wheel. After you do so, the camera (guided by its light meter) will set a suitable shutter speed considering the aperture and the ISO in use. If you change the aperture, from f/5.6 to f/11 for example, the camera will automatically set a longer shutter speed to maintain the same exposure, using guidance from the built-in light meter. (I discussed the concept of equivalent exposure earlier and provided the equivalent exposure chart.)

Aperture Priority is especially useful when you want to use a particular lens opening to achieve a desired effect. Perhaps you'd like to use the smallest aperture (such as f/22) to maximize depth-of-field (DOF), to keep the entire subject sharp in a close-up picture. Or, you might want to use a large aperture (small f/number like f/4) to throw everything except your main subject out of focus, as in Figure 7.11. Maybe you'd just like to "lock in" a particular f/stop, such as f/8, because it allows your lens to provide the best optical quality. Or, you might prefer to use f/2.8 with a lens that has a maximum aperture of f/1.4, because you want the best compromise between shutter speed and optical quality.

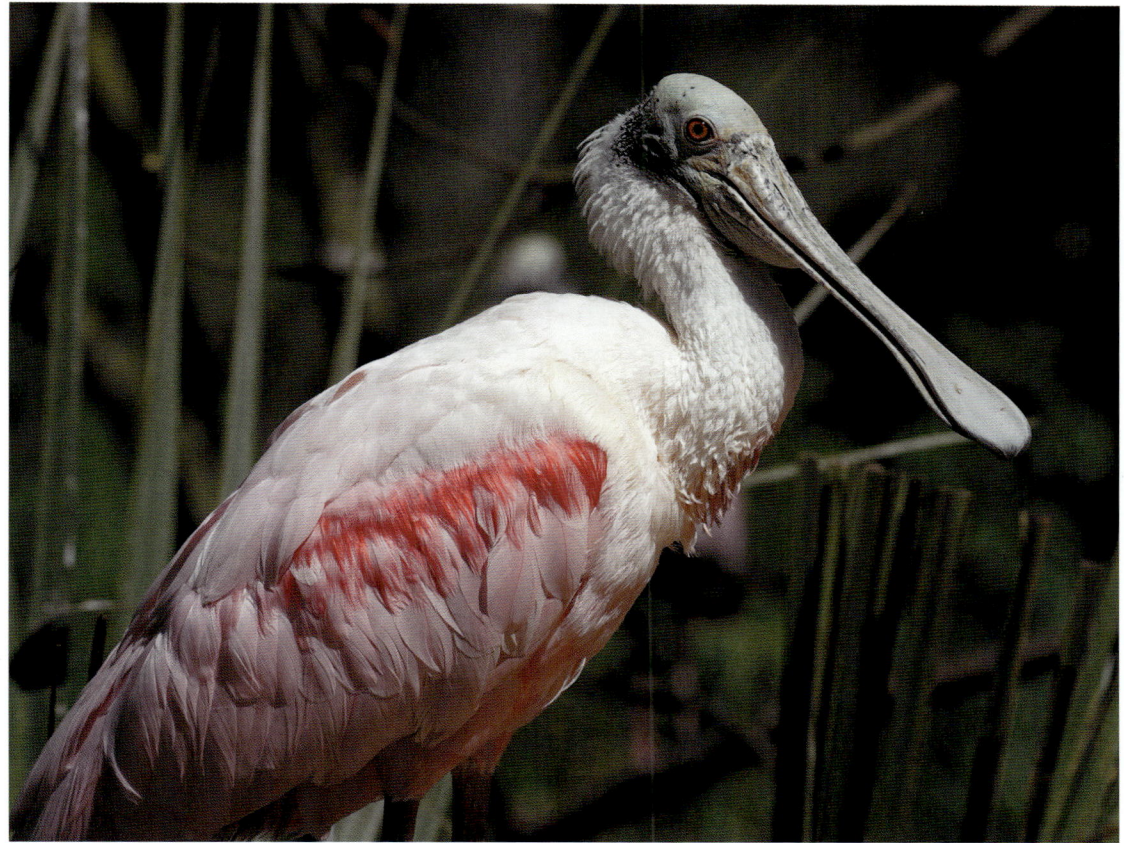

Figure 7.11 Use Aperture Priority mode to "lock in" a wide aperture (denoted by a large f/stop) when you want to blur the background.

Aperture Priority can even be used to specify a *range* of shutter speeds you want to use under varying lighting conditions, which seems almost contradictory. But think about it. You're shooting a soccer game outdoors with a telephoto and want a relatively fast shutter speed, but you don't care if the speed changes a little should the sun duck behind a cloud. Set your camera's shooting mode to A, and adjust the aperture using the control dial or control wheel until a shutter speed of, say, 1/1000th second is selected at the ISO level that you're using. (In bright sunlight at ISO 400, that aperture is likely to be around f/11.) Then, go ahead and shoot, knowing that your a6400 will maintain that f/11 aperture (for sufficient DOF as the soccer players move about the field), but will drop down to 1/800th or 1/500th second if necessary should a light cloud cover part of the sun.

When the camera cannot provide a good exposure at the aperture you have set, the +/– symbol and the shutter speed numeral will blink in the LCD monitor display. The blinking warns that the camera is unable to find an appropriate shutter speed at the aperture you have set, considering the ISO level in use, and over- or underexposure will occur. That's the major pitfall of using Aperture

Priority: you might select an f/stop that is too small or too large to allow an optimal exposure with the available shutter speeds.

Here are a couple of examples where you might encounter a problem. Let's say you set an aperture of f/2.8 while using ISO 400 on an extremely bright day (perhaps at the beach or in snow); in this situation, even your camera's fastest shutter speed might not be able to cut down the amount of light reaching the sensor to provide the right exposure. (The solution here is to set a lower ISO or a smaller aperture, or both, until the blinking stops.) Or, let's say you have set f/16 in a dark arena while using ISO 100; the camera cannot find a shutter speed long enough to provide a correct exposure so your photo will be underexposed. (In low light, the solution is to set a higher ISO or a wider aperture, or both, until the blinking stops.) Aperture Priority is best used by those with a bit of experience in choosing settings. Many seasoned photographers leave their camera set on Aperture Priority all the time.

When to use Aperture Priority:

- **General landscape photography.** The a6400 is a great camera for landscape photography, of course, because its high resolution allows making huge, gorgeous prints, as well as smaller prints that are filled with eye-popping detail. Aperture Priority is a good tool for ensuring that your landscape is sharp from foreground to infinity, if you select an f/stop that provides maximum depth-of-field.

  If you use A mode and select an aperture like f/11 or f/16, it's your responsibility to make sure the shutter speed selected is fast enough to avoid losing detail to camera shake, or that the a6400 is mounted on a tripod. One thing that new landscape photographers fail to account for is the movement of distant leaves and tree branches. When seeking the ultimate in sharpness, go ahead and use Aperture Priority, but boost ISO sensitivity a bit, if necessary, to provide a sufficiently fast shutter speed, whether shooting hand-held or with a tripod.

- **Specific landscape situations.** Aperture Priority is also useful when you have no objection to using a long shutter speed, or, particularly, *want* the a6400 to select one. Waterfalls are a perfect example. You can use A mode, set your camera to ISO 100, use a small f/stop, and let the camera select a longer shutter speed that will allow the water to blur as it flows. Indeed, you might need to use a neutral-density filter to get a sufficiently long shutter speed. But Aperture Priority mode is a good start.

- **Portrait photography.** Portraits are the most common applications of selective focus. A medium-large aperture (say, f/5.6 or f/8) with a longer lens/zoom setting (in the 85mm-135mm range) will allow the background behind your portrait subject to blur. A *very* large aperture (I frequently shoot wide open with my 85mm f/1.8 lens) lets you apply selective focus to your subject's *face*. With a three-quarters view of your subject, as long as her eyes are sharp, it's okay if the far ear or her hair is out of focus.

- **When you want to ensure optimal sharpness.** All lenses have an aperture or two at which they perform best, providing the level of sharpness you expect. That's usually about two stops down from wide open, and thus will vary depending on the maximum aperture of the lens. My 85mm f/1.8 is good wide open, but it's even sharper at f/2.8 or f/4; I shoot my 70-200mm f/4 wide open at concerts, but, if I can use f/5.6 instead, I'll get better results. A relatively slow lens with, say, an f/5.6 maximum aperture at the telephoto end, really needs to be set at f/11 if I crank it out to its maximum focal length. Aperture Priority allows me to use each lens at its very best f/stop.

- **Close-up/Macro photography.** Depth-of-field is typically very shallow when shooting macro photos, and you'll want to choose your f/stop carefully. Perhaps you might want to use a wider stop to emphasize your subject. Or, you might need the smallest aperture you can get away with to maximize depth-of-field. Aperture Priority mode comes in very useful when shooting close-up pictures. Because macro work is frequently done with the camera mounted on a tripod, and your close-up subjects, if not living creatures, may not be moving much, a longer shutter speed isn't a problem. Aperture Priority can be your preferred choice.

Shutter Priority (S) Mode

Shutter Priority is the inverse of Aperture Priority. You set the shutter speed you'd like, using the control dial or control wheel, and the camera sets an appropriate f/stop considering the ISO that's in use. When you change the shutter speed, the camera will change the aperture to maintain the same (equivalent) exposure using guidance from the built-in light meter. Shutter Priority mode gives you some control over how much action-freezing capability your digital camera brings to bear in a particular situation. In other cases, you might want to use a slow shutter speed to add some blur to a sports photo that would be mundane if the action were completely frozen (see Figure 7.12).

Take care when using a slow shutter speed such as 1/8th second, because you'll potentially get blurring from camera shake unless you're using a tripod or other firm support. Of course, this applies to any mode, but in most modes the camera displays a blinking camera shake warning icon when the shutter speed is long. That does not appear in S mode however, perhaps because Sony assumes that users of Shutter Priority are aware of the potential problem caused by camera shake. The SteadyShot stabilizer in OSS-designated lenses is useful but cannot work miracles.

As in Aperture Priority, you can encounter a problem in Shutter Priority mode; this happens when you select a shutter speed that's too long or too short for correct exposure under certain conditions. I've shot outdoor soccer games on sunny fall evenings and used Shutter Priority mode to lock in a 1/1000th second shutter speed, only to find that my camera refused to produce the correct exposure when the sun dipped behind some trees and there was no longer enough light to shoot at that speed, even with the lens wide open.

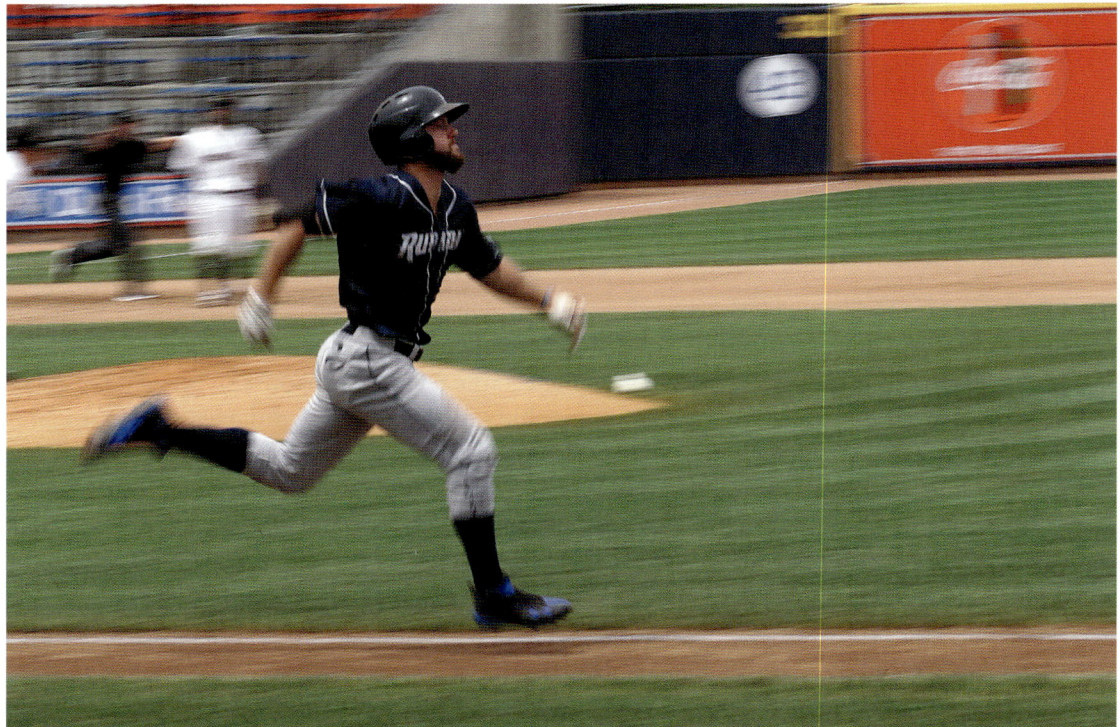

Figure 7.12 Set a slow shutter speed when you want to introduce blur into an action shot, as with this panned image of a base runner.

In cases where you have set an inappropriate shutter speed, the aperture numeral and the +/− symbol will blink on the LCD. When might this happen? Let's say you set 1/15th second shutter speed while using ISO 400 on that extremely bright day; in this situation, even the smallest aperture available with your lens might not be able to cut down the amount of light reaching the sensor to provide a correct exposure. (The solution here is to set a lower ISO or a faster shutter speed, or both, until the blinking stops.) Or, let's say you have set 1/250th second in the arena while using ISO 100; your lens does not offer an aperture that's wide enough to enable the camera to provide a good exposure so you'll get the blinking and your photo will be underexposed. (In low light, the solution is to set a higher ISO or a longer shutter speed, or both, until the blinking stops.)

When to use Shutter Priority:

- **To reduce blur from subject motion.** Set the shutter speed of the a6400 to a higher value to reduce the amount of blur from subjects that are moving. The exact speed will vary depending on how fast your subject is moving and how much blur is acceptable. You might want to freeze a basketball player in mid-dunk with a 1/1000th second shutter speed or use 1/200th second to allow the spinning wheels of a motocross racer to blur a tiny bit to add the feeling of motion.

- **To add blur from subject motion.** There are times when you want a subject to blur, say, when shooting waterfalls with the camera set for a one- or two-second exposure in Shutter Priority mode.

- **To add blur from camera motion when *you* are moving.** Say you're panning to follow a base runner. You might want to use Shutter Priority mode and set the a6400 for 1/60th second, so that the background will blur as you pan. The shutter speed will be fast enough to provide a sharp image of the athlete, as shown in Figure 7.12.

- **To reduce blur from camera motion when *you* are moving.** In other situations, the camera may be in motion, say, because you're shooting from a moving train or auto, and you want to minimize the amount of blur caused by the motion of the camera. Shutter Priority is a good choice here, too.

- **Landscape photography hand-held.** If you can't use a tripod for your landscape shots, you'll still probably want the sharpest image possible. Shutter Priority can allow you to specify a shutter speed that's fast enough to reduce or eliminate the effects of camera shake. Just make sure that your ISO setting is high enough that the a6400 will select an aperture with sufficient depth-of-field, too.

- **Concerts, stage performances.** I shoot a lot of concerts with my 70-200mm f/4 lens, and have discovered that, when vibration reduction is taken into account, a shutter speed of 1/180th second is fast enough to eliminate camera shake that can result from hand-holding the camera with this lens, and also to avoid blur from the movement of all but the most energetic performers. I use Shutter Priority and set the ISO so the camera will select an aperture in the f/4-5.6 range.

Program Auto (P) Mode

The Program mode uses the camera's built-in smarts to set an aperture/shutter speed combination, based on information provided by the light meter. If you're using Multi metering, the combination will often provide a good exposure. Rotate the control dial or control wheel and you can switch to other aperture/shutter speed combinations, all providing the same (equivalent) exposure. The P on the screen changes to P*. You can't use Program Shift when working with flash. To reverse Program Shift, change to another exposure mode (you can immediately switch back to P mode) or turn the camera off.

In the unlikely event that the correct exposure cannot be achieved with the wide range of shutter speeds and apertures available, the shutter speed and aperture will both blink. (The solution is to set a lower ISO in bright light and a higher ISO in dark locations until the blinking stops.) The P mode is the one to use when you want to rely on the camera to make reasonable basic settings of shutter speed and aperture, but you want to retain the ability to adjust many of the camera's settings yourself. All overrides and important functions are available, including ISO, white balance, metering mode, exposure compensation, and others.

When to use Program mode:

- **When you're in a hurry to get a grab shot.** The a6400 will do a pretty good job of calculating an appropriate exposure for you, without any input from you.

- **When you hand your camera to a novice.** Set the a6400 to P, hand the camera to your friend, relative, or *trustworthy* stranger you meet in front of the Eiffel Tower, point to the shutter release button and viewfinder, and say, "Look through here, and press this button."

- **When no special shutter speed or aperture settings are needed.** If your subject doesn't require special anti- or pro-blur techniques, and depth-of-field or selective focus aren't important, use P as a general-purpose setting. You can still make adjustments to increase/decrease depth-of-field or add/reduce motion blur with a minimum of fuss.

Making Exposure Value Changes

Sometimes you'll want a brighter or darker photo (more or less exposure) than you got when relying on the camera's metering system. Perhaps you want to underexpose to create a silhouette effect, or overexpose to produce a high-key (very light) effect. It's easy to do so by using the a6400's exposure compensation features, available only in P, S, A, M, Panorama, and Movie modes. There are several ways to set exposure compensation:

- **Exposure Compensation button.** Pressing the down directional button to summon the Exposure Comp. screen is the fastest method for adding/subtracting exposure. Then rotate the control wheel or use the left/right directional buttons to provide plus or minus five stops of exposure in one-third stop increments.

  In Manual exposure mode, exposure compensation can be dialed in *only* when ISO Auto is activated, as the camera will leave your shutter speed and aperture settings undisturbed and add or subtract exposure by changing ISO sensitivity instead.

- **Exposure Compensation menu.** If you want additional exposure compensation, venture to the Camera Settings 4 menu, where the Exposure Comp. entry will let you set plus or minus five stops of exposure using the front or control wheels. This option is not available if you've made a setting with the exposure compensation dial; its menu entry will be grayed out.

- **Function menu.** Unless you've redefined your Function menu to remove it, exposure compensation can also be applied by pressing the Fn button. Its default position is at the far right of the top row of functions. The Function menu entry also lets you choose up to five stops of compensation.

In my experience, adding exposure compensation is the option that's most often necessary. I'll often set +2/3 when using Multi metering if the camera underexposed my first photo of a light-toned scene. With Center-weighted or Spot metering, +1.3 or an even higher level of plus compensation is almost always necessary with a light-toned subject. Since the camera provides a live preview of the scene (when Setting Effect is turned on), it's easy to predict when the photo you'll take is likely to be obviously over- or underexposed. When the histogram display is on, you can make a more accurate prediction about the exposure; I'll discuss this feature shortly. Of course, you can also use plus compensation when you want to intentionally overexpose a scene for a creative effect.

You won't often need to use minus compensation. This feature is most likely to be useful when metering a dark-toned subject, such as close-ups of black animals or dark blue buildings, for example. Since these dark-toned subjects lead the camera to overexpose, set –2/3 or –1 compensation (when using Multi metering) for a more accurate exposure. (The amount of minus compensation that you need to set may be quite different when using the other two metering modes.) Minus compensation can also be useful for intentionally underexposing a scene for a creative effect, such as a silhouette of a sailboat or a group of friends on a beach.

Any exposure compensation you set will remain active for all photos you take afterward. The camera provides a reminder as to what value is currently set in some display modes. Turning the a6400 off and then back on does not set compensation back to zero; when you no longer need to use it, be sure to do so yourself. If you inadvertently leave it set for +1 or –1, for example, your photos taken under other circumstances will be over- or underexposed.

Manual Exposure (M) Mode

Part of being an experienced photographer comes from knowing when to rely on your a6400's automation (including Intelligent Auto, Superior Auto, P mode, and SCN mode settings), when to go semi-automatic (with Shutter Priority or Aperture Priority), and when to set exposure manually (using M). Some photographers actually prefer to set their exposure manually. This is quite convenient since the camera is happy to provide an indication of when your settings will produce over- or underexposure, based on its metering system's judgment. It can even indicate how far off the "correct" (recommended) exposure your photo will be at the settings you have made.

I often hear comments from novices first learning serious photography claiming that they must use Manual mode in order to take over control from the camera. While a back-to-basics approach does force you to learn photographic principles, it's not always necessary. For example, you can control all important aspects when using semi-automatic A or S mode as discussed in the previous sections. This allows you to control depth-of-field (the range of acceptable sharpness) or the rendition of motion (as blurred or as frozen). You can set a desired ISO level; that will not change the exposure. You would use exposure compensation when you want a brighter or a darker photo.

Manual mode provides an alternative that allows you to control the aperture and the shutter speed and the exposure simultaneously. For example, when I shot the Manchegan *molino de viento* in Figure 7.13, I was not getting exactly the desired effect with A or S mode while experimenting with various levels of exposure compensation. So, I switched to M mode, set ISO 100, and then set an aperture/shutter speed that might provide the intended exposure. After taking a test shot, I changed the aperture slightly and the next photo provided the exposure for the interpretation of the scene that I wanted.

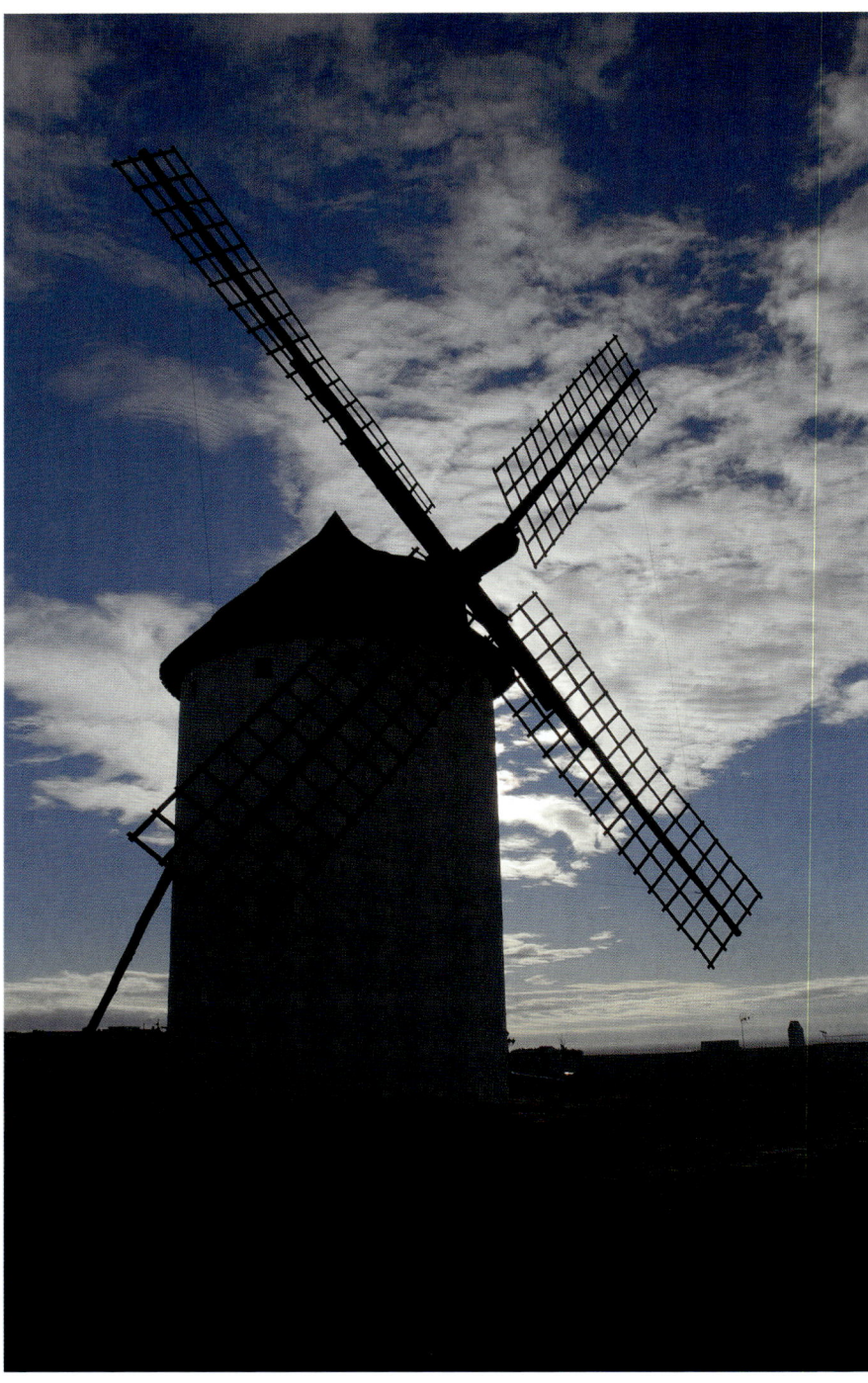

Figure 7.13
Manual mode allowed setting the exact exposure for this silhouette shot, by metering the windmill, then underexposing.

Manual mode is also useful when working in a studio environment using multiple flash units. The additional flash units are triggered by slave devices (gadgets that set off the flash when they sense the light from another flash, or, perhaps from a radio or infrared remote control). In some cases, M mode is the only suitable choice. Your camera's exposure meter doesn't compensate for the extra illumination, and can't interpret the flash exposure at all, so you need to set the aperture and shutter speed manually.

The Basic M Mode Technique

Depending on your proclivities, you might not need to use M mode very often, but it's still worth understanding how it works. Here are your considerations:

- Rotate the mode dial to M.
- Use the control dial to adjust aperture and the control wheel to adjust shutter speed (unless you've swapped their functions, as described in Chapter 6). The setting that is currently active will be highlighted in orange.
- If you have Exposure Set Guide in the Camera Settings II-06 menu set to On, enlarged labels showing the changing shutter speed or aperture will be displayed near the bottom of the screen, unless you choose the Graphic display mode with the DISP button. In that case, scales will show the current shutter speed and aperture at the same time.
- Any change you make to either factor affects the exposure, of course, so if you have Live View Display in the Custom Settings 2 menu set to Setting Effect ON, you'll see the display getting darker or brighter as you change settings.
- If the display you're viewing includes the histogram graph, that will provide an even better indication of the exposure you'll get as you set different apertures or shutter speeds. I'll explain histograms later in this chapter.
- A guide at the bottom of the monitor or viewfinder indicates exposure. To use the suggested exposure, adjust the shutter speed or f/stop until the MM guide reads ±0.0.

Long Exposures

You can specify exposures as long as 30 seconds when using P, A, or S modes. In Manual exposure mode, you can select B (for bulb exposure), located *after* the 30-second option. Bulb cannot be selected when using Auto HDR, Continuous Shooting, Speed Priority Continuous, or Multi Frame Noise Reduction.

In Bulb mode, you can press and hold the shutter release button, and the shutter will remain open as long as the button is depressed. Standing there with your finger on the trigger, so to speak, can produce vibration, so I prefer to use a wired release with a locking button, such as the Sony RM-VPR1 ($50).

Adjusting Exposure with ISO Control in M Mode

As mentioned in the previous section, changing the ISO level is another method of changing the exposure in M mode, whether you adjust it yourself manually, or activate Auto ISO and let the camera do it for you when you add or subtract exposure compensation.

Most photographers control the aperture and/or shutter speed exclusively to adjust exposure, sometimes forgetting about the option to adjust ISO. The common practice is to set the ISO once for a particular shooting session (say, at ISO 100 outdoors on a bright day or ISO 1600 when shooting indoors). There is also a tendency to use the lowest ISO level possible because of a concern that high ISO levels produce images with obvious digital noise (such as a grainy effect). However, changing the ISO is a valid way of adjusting exposure in M mode, particularly with the a6400.

Indeed, I find myself using ISO adjustment as a convenient alternate way of adding or subtracting EV (exposure values) when shooting in Manual mode, and as a quick way of choosing equivalent exposures when in automatic or semi-automatic modes. For example, I've selected a manual exposure with both f/stop and shutter speed suitable for my image using, say, ISO 400. I can change the exposure in full-stop increments by pressing the ISO button (right directional button), and spinning the control dial or control wheel one click at a time. (The control dial adjusts ISO in larger increments than the control wheel; choose the latter when making finer adjustments.) The difference in image quality/noise is not much different at ISO 200 or ISO 800 than at ISO 400 and this exposure control method allows me to shoot at my preferred f/stop and shutter speed while retaining control of the exposure.

Or, perhaps, I am using Shutter Priority mode and the metered exposure at ISO 400 is 1/500th second at f/11. If I decide on the spur of the moment I'd rather use 1/500th second at f/8, I can press the ISO button and quickly switch to ISO 200. Of course, it's a good idea to monitor your ISO changes, so you don't end up at ISO 6400 or above accidentally; a setting like that will result in more digital noise (graininess) in your image than you would like. In M mode, you can use Auto ISO, as discussed in the section that follows. Higher ISO levels are necessary only when shooting in a very dark location where a fast shutter speed is important; this might happen during a sports event in a dark arena, for example.

Using ISO Auto

ISO Auto is a powerful feature, available in P, S, A, M, and Movie modes. In your camera's Fn and Camera Settings I-08 ISO menus, it's designated as Auto; the setting labeled ISO Auto is actually Multi Frame Noise Reduction, and it's easy to get the two confused. ISO Auto provides two major benefits. First, if the shutter speed and aperture settings in use won't provide a proper exposure, ISO Auto can adjust the ISO setting to compensate. Second, you can use ISO Auto to "lock in" a particular shutter speed or aperture (or both, in Manual mode), and use ISO sensitivity to compensate for changing or low-light conditions.

In the first case, suppose you were shooting a moving subject in Aperture Priority mode and your selected f/stop would result in a shutter speed of 1/8th second at ISO 400. All the image stabilization in the world can't protect you from blur caused by *subject* movement. If you were using ISO Auto with the a6400 and had specified a minimum shutter speed of 1/30th second in the Camera Settings I-08 menu (as described in Chapter 3), the camera's exposure system would automatically increase ISO from 400 to 1600. Most of us would prefer a slight increase in noise from the ISO boost than a blurry photograph.

With the a6400, the minimum (slowest) shutter speed allowed before ISO Auto kicks in can be specified in the Camera Settings I-08 menu. The setting has no effect when you're using Shutter Priority, as the shutter speed you choose is already locked in. But in Program and Aperture Priority modes, you can choose that minimum. If you were shooting action and wanted to ensure that P and A modes would try to use a shutter speed of 1/250th second or faster, you could select that speed as the minimum speed before ISO Auto would increase sensitivity. If you were shooting subjects with little movement, you might select 1/8th second and count on the camera and/or lens's image stabilization to give you sharp results. For most general applications, a minimum of 1/30th second should work well.

We're not done yet. ISO Auto also allows you to choose a *minimum* and *maximum* ISO speed to be used. If you want to avoid noise, you could set the Minimum ISO to 100 and the Maximum to 800, and still gain the benefits of using ISO Auto. If you wouldn't mind seeing a little noise, you could set the Maximum somewhat higher. Coupled with Minimum Shutter speed, ISO Auto gives you quite a bit of flexibility in controlling the range of shutter speeds and apertures used.

Don't forget that in Manual Exposure mode you can use ISO Auto in a special way. As you might expect, in Manual Exposure mode, the shutter speed and aperture are selected by you and fixed at those settings until you change them. However, if ISO Auto is active, you can add or subtract exposure compensation, as described earlier, by pressing the down directional button to access the exposure compensation screen, or by using the menu, or Function menu.

Exposure Bracketing

While exposure compensation lets you adjust exposure, sometimes you'll want to quickly shoot a series of photos at various exposures in a single burst. Doing so increases the odds of getting one photo that will be exactly right for your needs, and is particularly useful when assembling high dynamic range (HDR) composite images manually. This technique is called bracketing.

Bracketing is a method for shooting several consecutive exposures using different settings, as a way of improving the odds that one will be exactly right. Alternatively, bracketing can be used to create a series of photos with slightly different exposures (or white balances) in anticipation that one of the exposures will be "better" from a creative standpoint. For example, bracketing can supply you with a normal exposure of a backlit subject, one that's "underexposed," producing a silhouette effect, and a third that's "overexposed" to create still another look.

Years ago, before high-tech cameras became the norm, it was common to bracket exposures when shooting color slide film especially, by taking three (or more) photos at different exposures in Manual mode. Eventually, exposure compensation became a common feature as cameras gained semi-automatic modes; it was then possible to bracket exposures by setting a different compensation level for each shot in a series, such as 0, –1, and +1 or 0, –1/3, and +2/3.

Today, cameras like the a6400 give you a lot of options for automatically bracketing exposures. When Bracket is active, you can take a series of consecutive photos: one at the metered ("correct") exposure, and others with more or less exposure. Figure 7.14 shows an image with the metered exposure (center), flanked by exposures of 2/3 stop more (left), and 2/3 stop less (right).

Bracketing cannot be performed when using Auto mode, any SCN mode, Sweep Panorama mode, or when using the Smile Shutter or Auto HDR features. If flash is used, you must take the photos one at a time, manually, rather than in a continuous burst. Exposure bracketing can be used with both RAW and JPG capture. When it's set, the camera will fire the shots in a sequence if you keep the shutter release button depressed; you can also decide to shoot the photos one at a time.

Bracketing is activated using the Drive Mode settings, which can be found in the Camera Settings I-03 menu, Function menu, and summoned by pressing the left directional button or some other button you've defined as the Drive button. Four different bracketing modes can be selected: continuous bracket, single bracket, white balance bracket, and DRO (dynamic range optimizer) bracket. With the Bracket Settings entry (which immediately follows Drive Mode in the Camera Settings I-03 menu), you can activate Self-Timer During Bracketing for exposure bracketing, and change the order in which the bracketed images are captured.

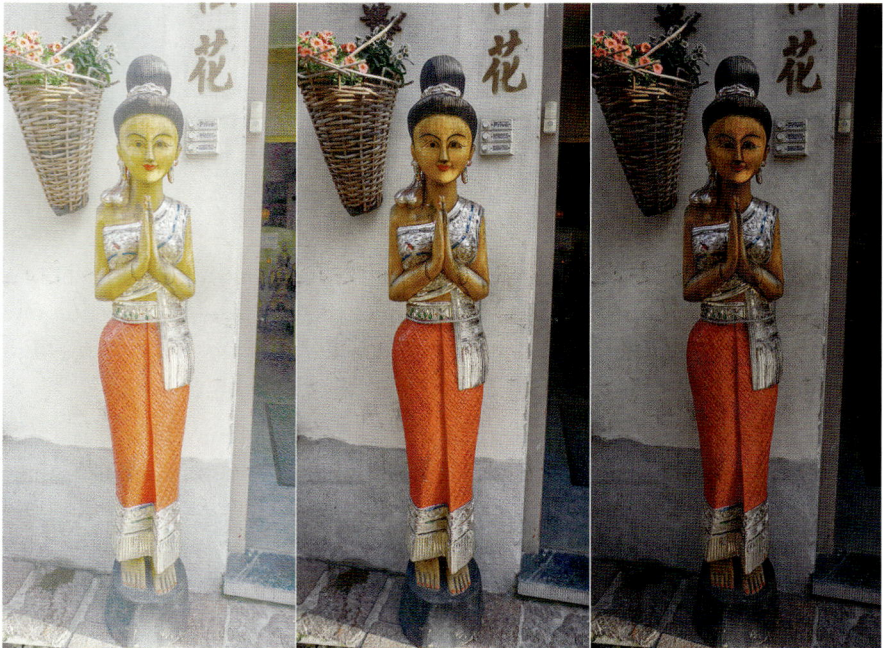

Figure 7.14
Metered exposure (center) accompanied by bracketed exposures of 2/3 stop more (left) and 2/3 stop less (right).

Continuous Bracketing

This mode captures three, five, or nine images in one burst when the shutter release is held down, bracketing them 0.3, 0.7, or 1.0 stops apart. Increments of 2.0 or 3.0 stops are also available, but only 3 or 5 images can be taken. These larger increments are especially useful when capturing images you'll combine later in your image editor to produce a high dynamic range (HDR) image. Use continuous bracketing when you want all the images in the set to be framed as similarly as possible, say, when you will be using them for manually assembled high dynamic range (HDR) photos.

When you highlight Cont. Bracket. in the Drive menu, the left/right buttons are used to select the increment between shots and the number of shots. In Manual Exposure (when ISO Auto is disabled), or in Aperture Priority, the shutter speed will change. If ISO Auto is set in Manual exposure, the bracketed set will be created by changing the ISO setting. In Shutter Priority, the aperture will change. You can use flash when continuous bracketing is active, but, because of the time required for the flash to recycle, you'll need to press the shutter button each time to take subsequent images (effectively switching the camera into Single Bracket mode, described next). Continuous Bracketing (and Single Bracketing) is disabled when using Intelligent Auto.

Only the last shot in the set is displayed when using Auto Review. With all types of bracketing, the exposure/bracket scale at the bottom of the EVF or LCD monitor (in Display All Info mode) will display indicators showing the number of images shot and the relative amount of under- or overexposure.

Don't forget that you can dial in exposure compensation, and *that* will affect the amount of over-/ underexposure applied while bracketing, too. You can bracket your exposures based on something other than the base (metered) exposure value. Set any desired exposure compensation, either a plus or a minus value. Then set the Bracketing level you want to use. The camera will bracket exposures as over, under, and equal to the *compensated* value.

Single Bracketing

This mode captures one bracketed image in a set of 3, 5, or 9 shots each time you press the shutter release, bracketing them 0.3, 0.7, 1.0 stops apart. Only 3 and 5 shots are available with the 2.0 or 3.0 EV increments. The left/right buttons are used to select the increment and number of shots. In this mode, you can separate each image by an interval of your choice. You might want to use this variation when you want the individual images to be captured at slightly different times, say, to produce a set of images that will be combined in some artistic way.

HDR ISN'T HARD

The 1.0 to 3.0 EV options are the ones you might try first when bracketing if you plan to perform High Dynamic Range magic later in Photoshop (with Merge to HDR), Elements (with Photomerge), or with another image editor that provides an HDR feature. That will allow you to combine images with different exposures into one photo with an amazing amount of detail in both highlights and shadows. To get the best results, mount your camera on a tripod, shoot in RAW format, and use BRK C3.0EV to get three shots with 3 EV of difference in exposure. Of course, with this camera, you also have the option of using the Auto HDR feature as well; this can provide very good results in the camera without the need to use any special HDR software.

White Balance Bracketing

In this mode, the camera shoots three images, each with a different adjustment to the color temperature. While you can't specify which direction the color bias is tilted, you can select Lo (the default) for small changes, or Hi, for larger changes using the left/right buttons. Only the last shot taken is displayed during Auto Review.

DRO Bracketing

This mode takes three images, with Lo (the default) or High adjustments to the dynamic range optimization. Use the left/right buttons to specify the degree of adjustment. Again, only the last shot taken is displayed during Auto Review.

Dealing with Digital Noise

Visual noise is that random grainy look with colorful speckles that some like to use as a visual effect, but most consider to be objectionable. That's because it robs your image of detail even as it adds that "interesting" texture. Noise is caused by two different phenomena: high ISO levels and long exposures. The a6400 offers a menu item to minimize high ISO noise and long exposure noise. In Chapter 3, I discussed the Camera Settings I-02 menu item that you can use to modify the noise reduction processing; you might want to review the sections about High ISO NR and Long Exposure NR as a refresher.

High ISO Noise

Digital noise commonly appears when you set an ISO above ISO 1600 with the a6400. High ISO noise appears as a result of the amplification needed to increase the effective sensitivity of the sensor. While higher ISOs do pull details out of dark areas, they also amplify non-signal information randomly, creating noise.

High ISO Noise Reduction is very useful, although at default, it also tends to make images slightly softer as blurring the noise pattern also blurs some intricate details. The higher the ISO, the more aggressive the processing will be, depending on whether you've specified Normal or Low. The Low level for NR provides images that are more grainy but with better resolution of fine detail. Even if you've chosen Off, the camera still applies some noise reduction.

High ISO NR is grayed out when the camera is set to shoot only RAW-format photos. The camera does not use this feature on RAW-format photos since noise reduction—at the optimum level for any photo—can be applied in the software you'll use to modify and convert the RAW file to JPEG or TIFF. (If you shoot in RAW & JPEG, the JPEG images, but not the RAW files, will be affected by this camera feature.) I'll discuss Noise Reduction with software in the next section.

Figure 7.15 shows two pictures that I shot at ISO 6400. For the first, I used the default (Normal) High ISO NR, and for the second shot, I set the NR to Off. (I've exaggerated the differences between the two slightly so the grainy/less grainy images are more evident on the printed page. The halftone screen applied to printed photos tends to mask these differences.)

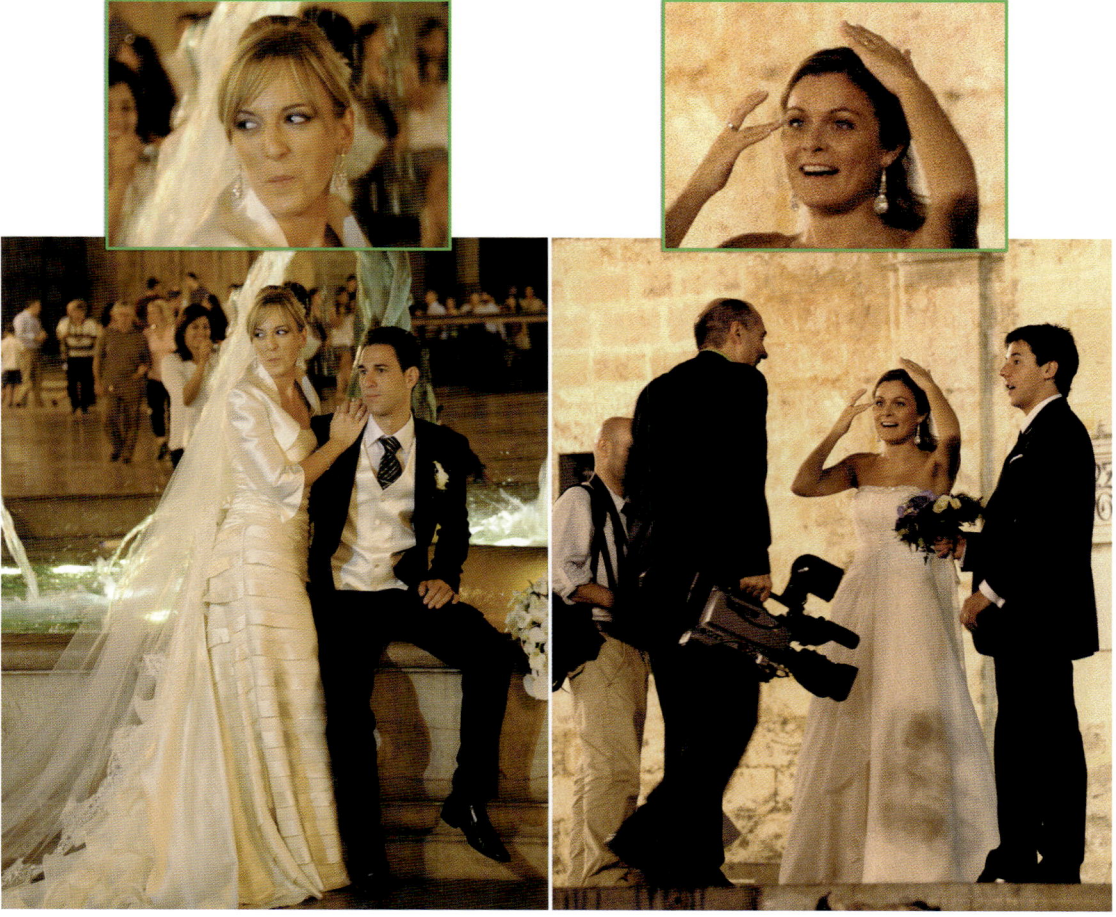

Figure 7.15 The Normal level for High ISO NR (left) produces a smoother (less grainy) image than one made with High ISO NR turned off (right).

Long Exposure Noise

A similar digital noise phenomenon occurs during long time exposures, which allow more photons to reach the sensor, increasing your ability to capture a picture under low-light conditions. However, the longer exposures also increase the likelihood that some pixels will register as random, "phantom," photons, often because the longer an imager collects photos during an exposure, the hotter it becomes, and that heat can be mistaken by the sensor as actual photons. The camera tries to minimize this type of noise automatically; there is no separate control you can adjust to add more or less noise reduction for long exposures.

CMOS imagers like the one in the a6400 contain millions of individual amplifiers and A/D (analog to digital) converters, all working in unison though the BIONZ X digital image processor chip. Because these circuits don't necessarily all process in precisely the same way all the time, they can introduce something called fixed-pattern noise into the image data.

Long exposure noise reduction is used with JPEG exposures longer than one full second. (This feature is not used on RAW photos and in continuous shooting, bracketing, Panorama mode, Sports Action, and Hand-held Twilight scene modes.) When it's active, long exposure noise reduction processing removes random pixels from your photo, but some of the image-making pixels are unavoidably vanquished at the same time.

It's possible that you prefer the version made without NR, and you can achieve that simply by shooting RAW. Indeed, noise reduction can be applied with most image-editing programs. You might get even better results with an industrial-strength product like Nik Dfine, part of the Nik collection (now owned by DxO), or Topaz DNoise or Enhance (www.topazlabs.com). You can apply noise reduction to RAW photos with Sony's Image Data Converter or any other versatile converter software. Some products are optimized for NR with unusually sophisticated processing, such as Photo Ninja (www.picturecode.com) and DXO Optics Pro's version 9 or higher (www.dxo.com).

Multi Frame Noise Reduction

Tucked away in the ISO menu, and assigned the label ISO Auto, is the Multi Frame Noise Reduction feature. (As I've said before, you should not confuse MFNR with the true Auto ISO setting that resides just below it in the same menu screen.) When you select this feature, you can specify the NR Effect, choosing from Normal or High. In Normal mode, the a6400 takes four images, retains the pixels that are more or less the same in each image (and which make up your picture), while ignoring the randomly placed noise pixels that differ between frames. Select High, and a total of 12 images are captured, and processed in much the same way, producing a final image with even less noise (although the processing takes longer). MFNR is a good choice when you must use a high ISO setting, want an image with less noise, and are willing (or able) to accept the delay the processing produces. The Maximum and Minimum allowable ISO settings you specify for Auto ISO are also applied to Multi Frame Noise Reduction.

SPECIAL MODES FOR FINE HIGH ISO QUALITY

As I'll discuss in the section on scene modes, the a6400 offers two modes for use in low light at high ISO for superior image quality. When you use Hand-held Twilight and Anti Motion Blur, the camera shoots a series of photos and composites them into one after discarding most of the digital noise. These are automatic modes so they're not ideal for all types of serious photography but they, along with Multi Shot NR, certainly provide the "cleanest" images possible at high ISO with your camera.

Using Dynamic Range Optimizer and HDR

Dynamic Range Optimizer (DRO) and Auto HDR (discussed next) are features you can select from the Camera Settings I-11 menu or the Function menu, as explained in Chapter 3. When enabled, the camera will examine your images as they are exposed, and, if the shadows appear to have detail even though they are too dark, will attempt to process the image so the shadows are lighter, with additional detail, without overexposing detailed highlights. The processed image is always saved as a JPEG, so if you are shooting RAW you won't notice a difference.

High dynamic range (HDR) photography, especially, is quite the rage these days, and entire books have been written on the subject. It's not really a new technique—film photographers have been combining multiple exposures for ages to produce a single image of, say, an interior room while maintaining detail in the scene visible through the windows.

Suppose you wanted to photograph a dimly lit room that had a bright window showing an outdoors scene. Proper exposure for the room might be on the order of 1/60th second at f/2.8 at ISO 200, while the outdoors scene probably would require f/11 at 1/400th second. That's almost a 7 EV step difference (approximately 7 f/stops) and well beyond the dynamic range of any digital camera, including the Sony a6400. (An additional problem, of course, is the mixed illumination: daylight outdoors and probably tungsten or fluorescent lamps indoors. Pro photographers sometimes gel the windows with corrective film so that inside/outside illumination matches.) That's a lot of work!

Until camera sensors gain much higher dynamic ranges (which may not be as far into the distant future as we think), special tricks like DRO and HDR photography will remain basic tools. With the Sony cameras, you can use DRO to expand the dynamic range of a single image, create in-camera HDR using multiple exposures, or shoot HDR the old-fashioned way—with separate bracketed exposures that are later combined in a tool like Photomatix or Adobe's Merge to HDR image-editing feature. I'm going to show you how to use all of them.

Here is an overview of how the DRO and Auto HDR features work:

■ **DRO Off.** No optimization. You're on your own; the camera will not apply extra processing even to your JPEG photos. Of course, if you are shooting RAW (or RAW & JPEG) photos, you can apply DRO effects to your photo when converting it with the downloadable Image Data Converter SR software. (Other programs have different tools for lightening shadow areas and/or darkening highlight areas.) Use Off when shooting subjects of normal contrast, or when you want to capture an image just as you see it, without modification by the camera.

■ **DRO.** Press the left/right buttons after scrolling to DRO Auto and you can then set a specific intensity level for the Dynamic Range Optimizer, from Level 1 through Level 5.

If you do not want to set a specific level, simply scroll to DRO Auto and allow the camera to decide on the amount of increased dynamic range. With the Auto setting, the camera dives into your image, looking at various small areas to examine the contrast of highlights and shadows, making modifications to each section to produce the best combination of brightness and tones with detail. In my experience, Auto provides a mid level of DRO that's worth leaving on at all times.

■ **HDR Auto.** In this mode, the a6400 creates a high dynamic range photo. It starts by taking three JPEG photos, each at a different exposure; the three are then composited into one by the processor using the best-exposed areas from each photo. The final image will have a high dynamic range effect, with great detail in shadow areas and increased detail in bright areas. You can specify how dramatic the effect should be.

After scrolling to HDR Auto, press the left/right buttons and set an HDR Level, from 1.0 EV to 6.0 EV. (One EV equals one stop of exposure.) The higher the level you set, the greater the exposure difference will be among the three photos the camera will shoot to produce one with High Dynamic Range. There's no "best" setting; it depends on your personal preference. At a very high EV level, the effect will be dramatic, but the photo may not appear to be "natural" looking. See the section that follows for more on HDR photography.

Tip

The primary method for DRO processing is lightening the dark tones and mid tones of an image. The higher the level of DRO you set, the more significantly the processor will lighten those areas; that causes digital noise to be more and more noticeable, especially in photos made at ISO 800 and at higher ISO levels. This is one reason why you would not always want to set Level 4 or 5 for DRO, particularly when using a high ISO setting. The other reason is that very high DRO produces a somewhat unnatural-looking effect with all shadow areas lighter than "normal." Auto and Levels 1 to 3 retain the most natural-looking effect.

When you activate DRO, you have your choice of specifying the aggressiveness of the processing (from Level 1 through Level 5), in which case it will *always* be applied at the level you specify. Or, you can set the feature to Auto and let the camera decide the ideal amount of optimization (or even when to apply it at all). Auto is usually your best choice, because the camera is pretty smart about choosing which images to process, and which to leave alone. Indeed, the camera's programming usually does a better job than a similar feature available in the Image Data Converter SR software you may have installed on your computer.

Figure 7.16 shows an image with DRO turned off, and using Level 1, Level 3, and Level 5 optimization. (The differences between, say, Level 1 and 2, or 2 and 3 are subtle and wouldn't show up well on the printed page [see the shadow at the top of each image], so I skipped the even-numbered levels.) The printed page also doesn't show that DRO tends to increase the amount of noise in an image as it works more aggressively; it's usually a good idea to avoid using the feature at high ISO levels where noise tends to be a real problem under any conditions.

The innovative DRO tool helps adjust the relative brightness range of your JPEG images as they are taken. The DRO has no effect on RAW images. (To apply dynamic range effects to RAW files, use the downloadable Image Data Converter SR or another RAW converter.) As you'd guess, DRO processing is available only when you are shooting in the Program, Aperture Priority, Shutter Priority, or Manual exposure mode. The DRO feature cannot be activated when one of the Picture Effects is used. In Auto and SCN modes, the camera decides whether DRO will be activated, providing you with no control over this feature.

The DRO feature has been around for a while on Sony models and the a6400 offers a broad range of options when you access it. You get three basic options: Off, DRO, and HDR Auto; several sub-settings are available for the last two. You'll get the most dramatic enhancement with Auto HDR, much lighter shadow areas, and slightly darker highlight areas. This feature is entirely different than Dynamic Range Optimizer as discussed in a moment but is accessed from the DRO menu item.

Once you have selected either DRO or Auto HDR, you can select further options by pressing the right directional button on the control wheel and then choosing level or EV increment (respectively).

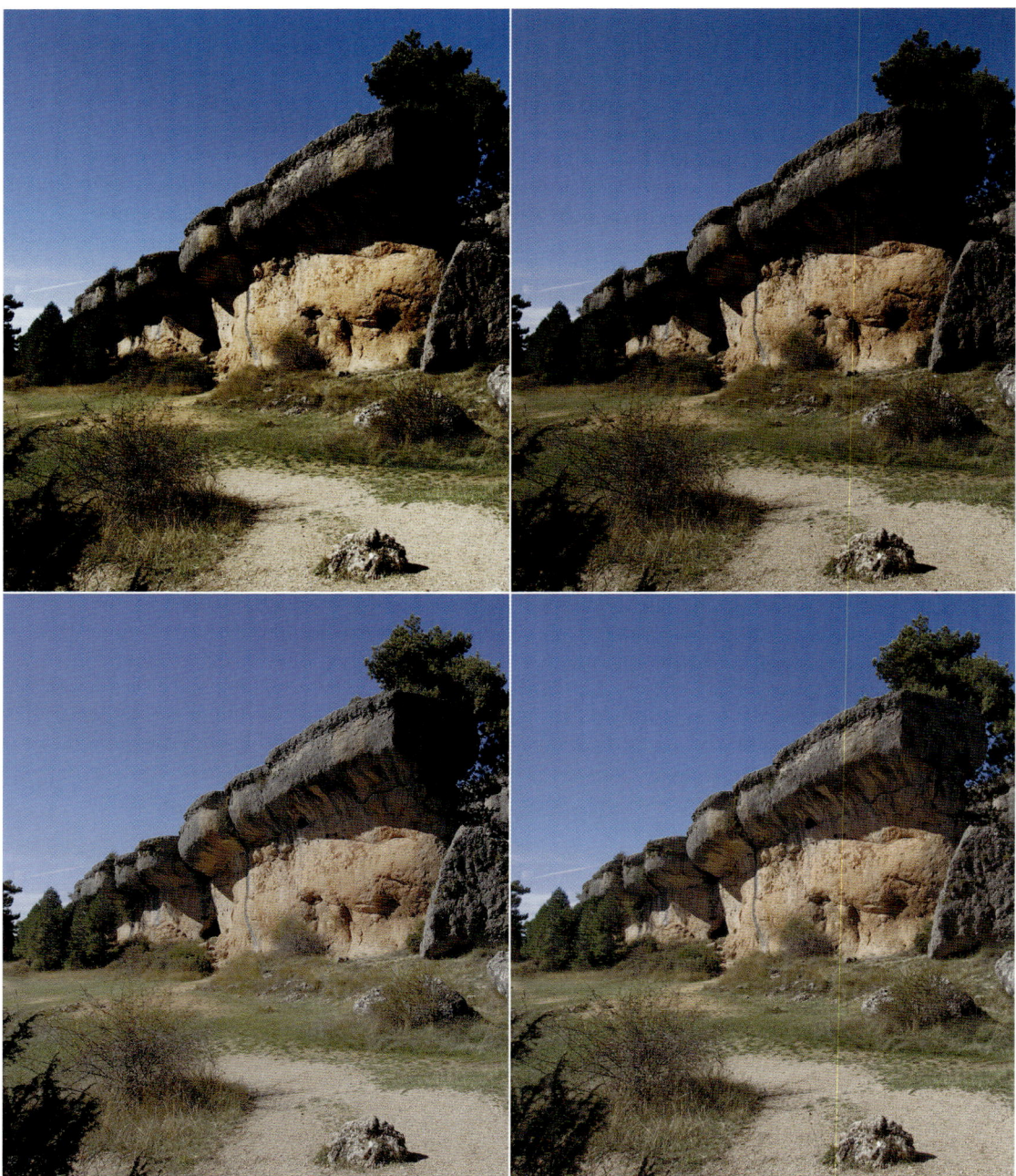

Figure 7.16 DRO Off (upper left); Level 1 (upper right); Level 3 (lower left); and Level 5 (lower right).

Auto HDR

The camera's in-camera Auto HDR feature is simple and surprisingly effective in creating high dynamic range images. It's also remarkably easy to use. It can be dialed in using the DRO/Auto HDR entries found in the Camera Settings menu, Function menu, and any key you might define with that function.

Although Auto HDR combines only three images to create a single HDR photograph, in some ways it's as good as the manual HDR method I'll describe in the section after this one. For example, it allows you to specify an exposure differential of six stops/EV between the three shots, whereas the camera shooting bracketed exposures is limited to no more than three EV between shots.

Figure 7.17 illustrates how the three shots that the camera's Auto HDR feature merges might look. There is a two-stop differential between each of the images, from the overexposed image at top, the intermediate exposure in the middle, and the underexposed image at the bottom. The in-camera HDR processing is able to combine the three to derive an image similar to the one shown in Figure 7.18, which has a much fuller range of tones.

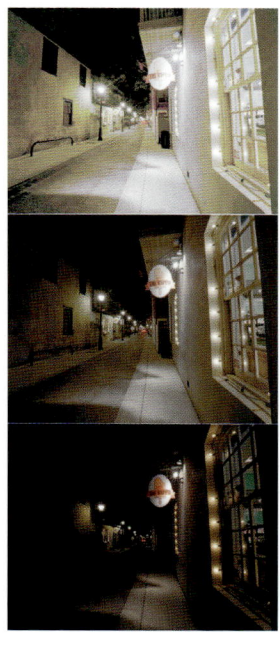

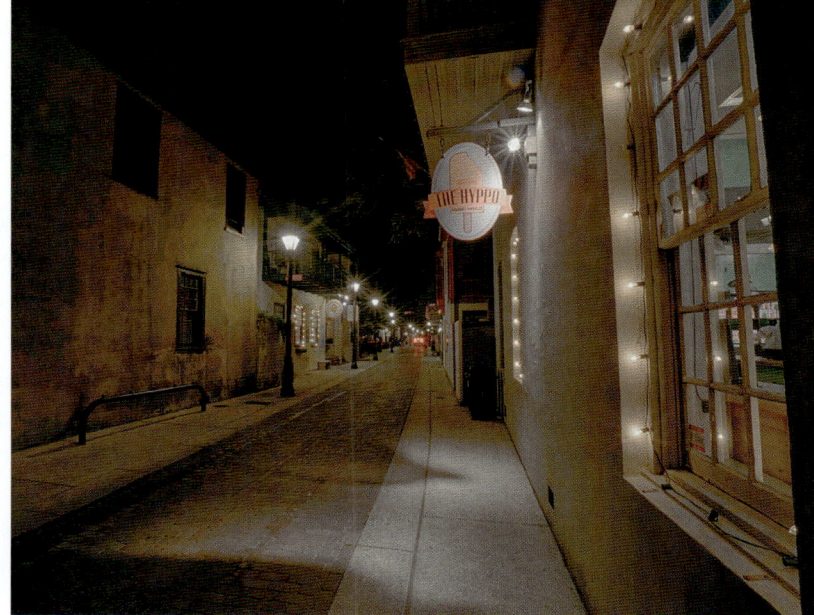

Figure 7.17 The three images can be automatically combined…

Figure 7.18 …to produce this merged high dynamic range (HDR) image.

To use the camera's HDR feature, select it in the Camera Settings I-11 menu's DRO/Auto HDR entry, or from the Fn menu. You can manually specify an increment from 1 EV to 6 EV, or choose Auto and allow the camera to select the appropriate differential. When you press the shutter release, the camera will take all three shots consecutively, align the images (because, if the camera is hand-held, there is likely to be a small amount of movement between shots), and then save one JPEG image to your memory card. The feature does not work if you have selected RAW or RAW+JPEG formats.

When using the in-camera HDR Auto feature, whether you use the options or not, be sure to mount the camera on a tripod or other solid support to ensure that the three photos (views of the scene) that are taken are identical. For the same reason, your subject should be static; it should not be moving even slightly. If the a6400 detects obvious camera shake, it will provide an HDR! indicator in the LCD or EVF display. Until you set the camera on some firm support, you will not be able to proceed.

The HDR Auto feature, like DRO processing, is not available when shooting RAW or RAW & JPEG images. You'll find that in flash photography, the in-camera HDR feature does not produce much of a benefit even if used at a high level. Note too that in scenes with low contrast (flat lighting, without dark shadows and bright highlights), the camera will not take the shots to create an HDR image. It will provide an HDR! indicator in the LCD or EVF display and you will not be able to proceed. Unless the light changes soon, you might as well disable this feature.

Bracketing and Merge to HDR

If your credo is "If you want something done right, do it yourself," you can also shoot HDR manually, without resorting to the camera's HDR mode. Instead, you can shoot individual images either by manually bracketing or using the camera's auto bracketing modes, described earlier in this chapter.

Although my goal in this book is to show you how to take great photos *in the camera* rather than how to fix your errors in Photoshop, the Merge to HDR Pro feature in Adobe's flagship image editor (and a variation also found in Photoshop Elements) is too cool to ignore. The ability to have a bracketed set of exposures that are identical except for exposure is key to getting good results with this Photoshop feature, which allows you to produce images with a full, rich dynamic range that includes a level of detail in the highlights and shadows that is almost impossible to achieve with digital cameras.

When you're using Merge to HDR Pro, you'd take several pictures, some exposed for the shadows, some for the middle tones, and some for the highlights. The exact number of images to combine is up to you. Four to seven is a good number. Then, you'd use the Merge to HDR Pro command to combine all of the images into one HDR image that integrates the well-exposed sections of each version. Here's how.

The images should be as identical as possible, except for exposure. So, it's a good idea to mount the camera on a tripod, use a remote release, and take all the exposures in one burst. Just follow these steps:

1. **Set up the camera.** Mount the camera on a tripod.

2. **Set the camera to shoot a bracketed burst of five to nine images with an increment of at least 2 EV.**

   The description of how to do this is found earlier in this chapter. As I noted there, you can set the camera to shoot up to nine exposures, each one increment apart, and use all nine for your HDR merger.

TIP

If you want to use more than nine exposures, you can skip the camera's auto bracketing feature and switch to Manual exposure and take as many exposures as you want, at any increment you desire. In Manual mode, make sure Auto ISO is off, and you adjust exposures *only* by changing the shutter speed. You should be very careful when you make the adjustment to avoid jostling the camera.

3. **Choose an f/stop.** Set the camera for Aperture Priority and select an aperture that will provide a correct exposure at your initial settings for the series of manually bracketed shots. *And then leave this adjustment alone!* You don't want the aperture to change for your series, as that would change the depth-of-field and, potentially, the image size of some elements. You want the camera to adjust exposure *only* using the shutter speed.

4. **Choose manual focus.** You don't want the focus to change between shots, so set the camera to manual focus, and carefully focus your shot.

5. **Choose RAW exposures.** Set the camera to take RAW files, which will give you the widest range of tones in your images. (This is an advantage of manually creating HDR files; the camera's Auto HDR feature can't be used when RAW or RAW+JPEG is active.)

6. **Take your bracketed set.** Press the button on the remote (or carefully press the shutter release or use the self-timer) and take the set of bracketed exposures.

7. **Continue with the Merge to HDR Pro steps listed next.** You can also use a different program, such as Photomatix or Nik software, if you know how to use it.

DETERMINING THE BEST EXPOSURE DIFFERENTIAL

How do you choose the number of EV/stops to separate your exposures? You can use histograms, described at the end of this chapter, to determine the correct bracketing range. Take a test shot and examine the histogram. Reduce the exposure until dark tones are clipped off at the left of the resulting histogram. Then, increase the exposure until the lighter tones are clipped off at the right of the histogram. The number of stops between the two is the range that should be covered using your bracketed exposures.

The next steps show you how to combine the separate exposures into one merged high dynamic range image. Figure 7.19 shows the results you can get from a three-shot bracketed sequence.

1. **Copy your images to your computer.** If you use an application to transfer the files to your computer, make sure it does not make any adjustments to brightness, contrast, or exposure. You want the real raw information for Merge to HDR Pro to work with.

2. **Activate Merge to HDR Pro.** Choose File > Automate > Merge to HDR Pro.

3. **Select the photos to be merged.** Use the Browse feature to locate and select your photos to be merged. You'll note a check box that can be used to automatically align the images if they were not taken with the camera mounted on a rock-steady support. This will adjust for any slight movement of the camera that might have occurred when you changed exposure settings.

4. **Choose parameters (optional).** The first time you use Merge to HDR Pro, you can let the program work with its default parameters. Once you've played with the feature a few times, you can read the Adobe Help files and learn more about the options than I can present in this non-software-oriented camera guide.

5. **Click OK.** The merger begins.

6. **Save.** Once HDR merge has done its thing, save the file to your computer.

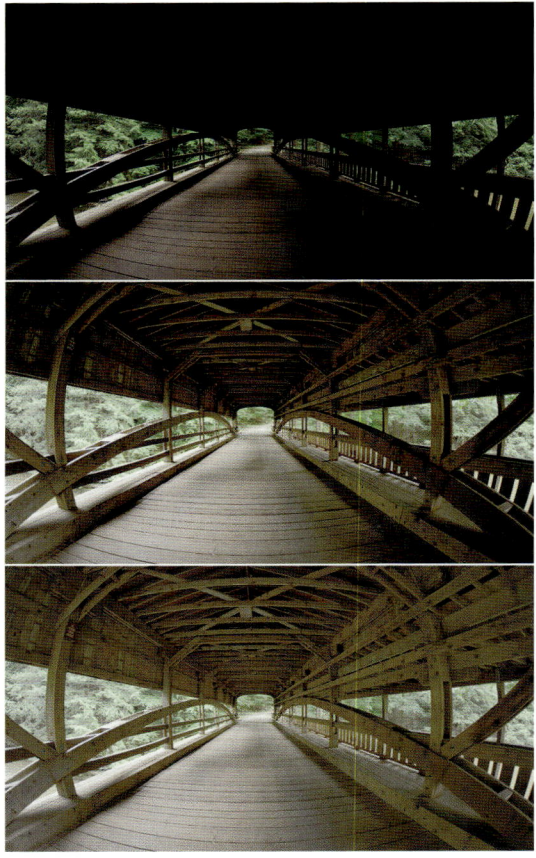

Figure 7.19 Three bracketed photos should look like this.

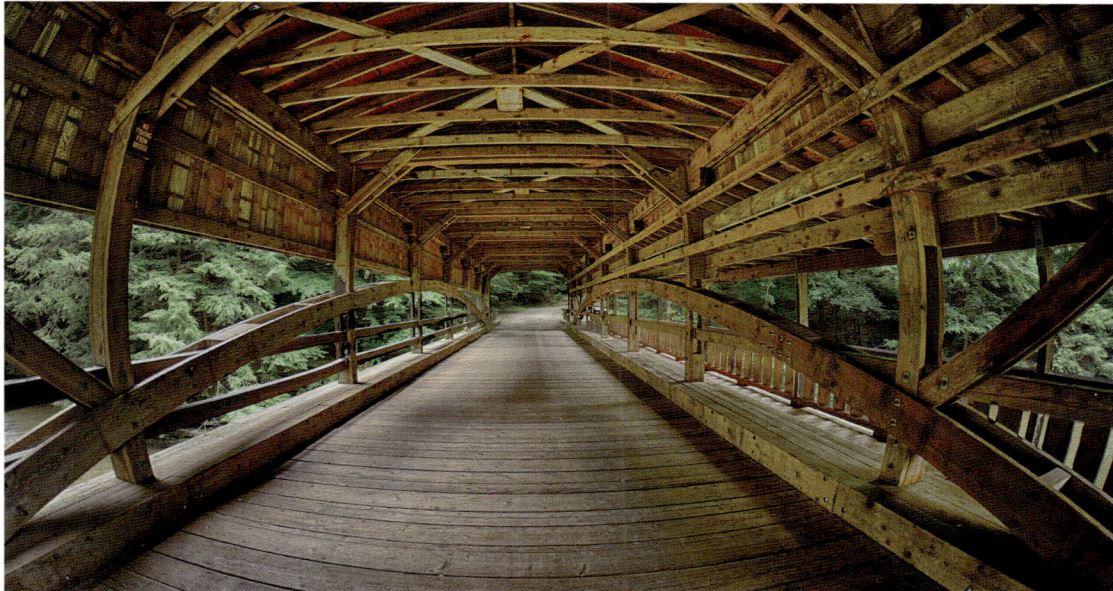

Figure 7.20 You'll end up with an extended dynamic range photo like this one.

If you do everything correctly, you'll end up with a photo something like the one shown in Figure 7.20.

What if you don't have the opportunity, inclination, or skills to create several images at different exposures, as described? If you shoot in RAW format, you can still use Merge to HDR, working with a *single* original image file. What you do is import the image into Photoshop several times, using Adobe Camera Raw to create multiple copies of the file at different exposure levels.

For example, you'd create one copy that's too dark, so the shadows lose detail, but the highlights are preserved. Create another copy with the shadows intact and allow the highlights to wash out. Then, you can use Merge to HDR to combine the two and end up with a finished image that has the extended dynamic range you're looking for. (This concludes the image-editing portion of the chapter. We now return you to our alternate sponsor: photography.)

Exposure Evaluation with Histograms

While you may be able to improve poorly exposed photos in your image-editing software or with DRO or HDR techniques, it's definitely preferable to get the exposure close to correct in the camera. This will minimize the modifications you'll need to make in post-processing, which can be very time-consuming and will degrade image quality, especially with JPEGs. A RAW photo can tolerate more significant changes with less adverse effects, but for optimum quality, it's still important to have an exposure that's close to correct.

Instead, you can use a histogram, which is a chart displayed on the camera's screen that shows the number of tones that have been captured at each brightness level. Two types of histograms are available, a "live" histogram that appears at the lower-right corner of the screen in Shooting mode, and a larger, more detailed version that appears in Histogram mode during playback. The live version can help you make exposure decisions as you shoot, whereas the playback version is useful in determining corrections to be made before you take your next shot. I'll explain both versions, but first it's useful to understand exactly what you're seeing when you view a histogram.

The Live Histogram

The camera's live histogram offers the most reliable method for judging the exposure as you shoot (although the Zebra feature described in Chapter 4 can be used to isolate specific problems involving blown highlights). A pair of live histograms are also available for display for both the viewfinder and monitor; activate both with the DISP Button (Monitor/Finder) item in the Camera Settings II-6 menu, as discussed in Chapter 4. After activating, press the DISP button a few times to reach the display that includes the histogram, which will be shown at lower right in the viewfinder and LCD monitor screens.

In Shooting mode, you'll get a luminance (brightness) histogram that shows the distribution of tones and brightness levels across the image given the current Camera Settings I settings, including exposure compensation, Dynamic Range Optimizer (DRO) level in use, or the aperture, shutter speed, and ISO that you have set if using Manual mode. This live histogram (displayed before taking a photo) is useful for judging whether the exposure is likely to be satisfactory or whether you should use a camera feature to modify the exposure. When the histogram looks better, take the photo. I'll show you how to evaluate histograms later in this chapter.

The Playback Histograms

You can view histograms in Playback mode, too; press the DISP button until the display shown in Figure 7.21 appears. The top graph, called the luminance or brightness histogram, is conventional, showing the distribution of tones across the image. Each of the other three histograms is in a specific color: red, green, and blue. That indicates the color channel you're viewing in that histogram: red, green, or blue. These additional graphs allow you to see the distribution of tones in the three individual channels. It takes a lot of expertise to interpret those extra histograms and, frankly, the conventional luminance histogram is the only one that many photographers use.

As a bonus in Playback mode, another feature is available when the histograms are visible: any areas of the displayed image that are excessively bright, or excessively dark, will blink. This feature, often called "blinkies," warns that you may need to change your settings to avoid loss of detail in highlight areas (such as a white wedding gown) or in shadow areas (such as a black animal's fur). The camera also includes the Zebra feature to indicate overexposure, as discussed in Chapter 4. You can use the histogram information along with the flashing blinkie and Zebra alerts to guide you in modifying the exposure, and/or setting the DRO feature (discussed earlier), before taking the photo again.

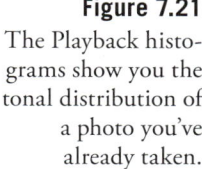

Figure 7.21
The Playback histograms show you the tonal distribution of a photo you've already taken.

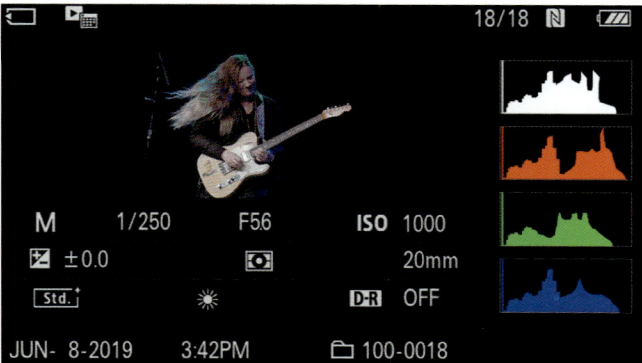

Tonal Range

Histograms help you adjust the tonal range of an image, the span of dark to light tones, from a complete absence of brightness (black) to the brightest possible tone (white), and all the middle tones in between. Because all values for tones fall into a continuous spectrum between black and white, it's easiest to think of a photo's tonality in terms of a black-and-white or grayscale image, even though you're capturing those tones in three separate color layers of red, green, and blue.

Because your images are digital, the tonal "spectrum" isn't really continuous: it's divided into discrete steps that represent the different tones that can be captured. Figure 7.22 may help you understand this concept. The gray steps shown range from 100 percent gray (black) at the left, to 0 percent gray (white) at the right, with 20 gray steps in all (plus white).

Along the bottom of the chart are the digital values from 0 to 255 recorded by your sensor for an image with 8 bits per channel. (8 bits of red, 8 bits of green, and 8 bits of blue equal a 24-bit, full-color image.) Any black captured would be represented by a value of 0, the brightest white by 255, and the midtones would be clustered around the 128 marker. The actual scale may be "finer" and record say, 0 to 4,094 for an image captured when the a6400 is capturing RAW images with 14 bits per channel.

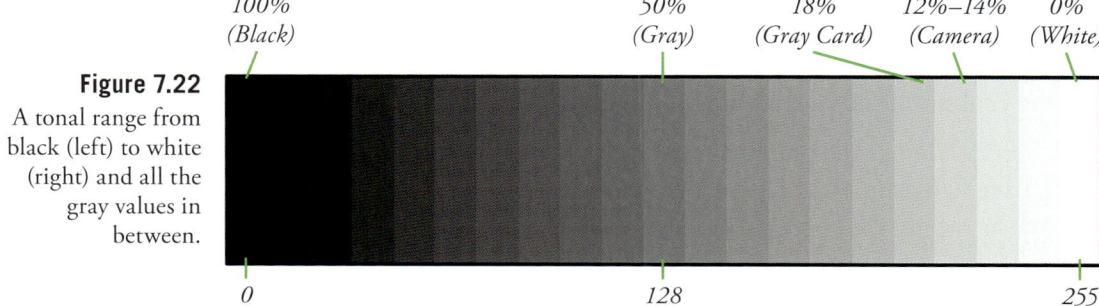

Figure 7.22
A tonal range from black (left) to white (right) and all the gray values in between.

Grayscale images (which we call black-and-white photos) are easy to understand. Or, at least, that's what we think. When we look at a black-and-white image, we think we're seeing a continuous range of tones from black to white, and all the grays in between. But, that's not exactly true. The blackest black in any photo isn't a true black, because *some* light is always reflected from the surface of the print, and if viewed on a screen, the deepest black is only as dark as the least-reflective area a computer monitor can produce. The whitest white isn't a true white, either, because even the lightest areas of a print absorb some light (only a mirror reflects close to all the light that strikes it), and, when viewing on a computer monitor, the whites are limited by the brightness of the display's LCD or LED picture elements. Lacking darker blacks and brighter, whiter whites, that continuous set of tones doesn't cover the full grayscale tonal range.

The full scale of tones becomes useful when you have an image that has large expanses of shades that change gradually from one level to the next, such as areas of sky, water, or walls. Think of a picture taken of a group of campers around a campfire. Since the light from the fire is striking them directly in the face, there aren't many shadows on the campers' faces. All the tones that make up the *features* of the people around the fire are compressed into one end of the brightness spectrum—the lighter end.

Yet, there's more to this scene than faces. Behind the campers are trees, rocks, and perhaps a few animals that have emerged from the shadows to see what is going on. These are illuminated by the softer light that bounces off the surrounding surfaces. If your eyes become accustomed to the reduced illumination, you'll find that there is a wealth of detail in these shadow images.

This campfire scene would be a nightmare to reproduce faithfully under any circumstances. If you are an experienced photographer, you are probably already wincing at what is called a *high-contrast* lighting situation. Some photos may be high in contrast when there are fewer tones and they are all bunched up at limited points in the scale. In a low-contrast image, there are more tones, but they are spread out so widely that the image looks flat. Your digital camera can show you the relationship between these tones using a *histogram.*

Histogram Basics

Your a6400's histograms are a simplified display of the numbers of pixels at each of 256 brightness levels, producing an interesting mountain range effect. Although separate charts may be provided for brightness and the red, green, and blue channels, when you first start using histograms, you'll want to concentrate on the brightness histogram.

Each vertical line in the graph represents the number of pixels in the image for each brightness value, from 0 (black) on the left to 255 (white) on the right. The vertical axis measures that number of pixels at each level.

Although histograms are most often used to fine-tune exposure, you can glean other information from them, such as the relative contrast of the image. Figure 7.23, top, is a simplified rendition of a histogram of an image having normal contrast. In such an image, most of the pixels are spread

Figure 7.23
Top: This image has fairly normal contrast, even though there is a peak of light tones at the right side representing the sky. Center: This low-contrast image has all the tones squished into one section of the grayscale. Bottom: A high-contrast image produces a histogram in which the tones are spread out.

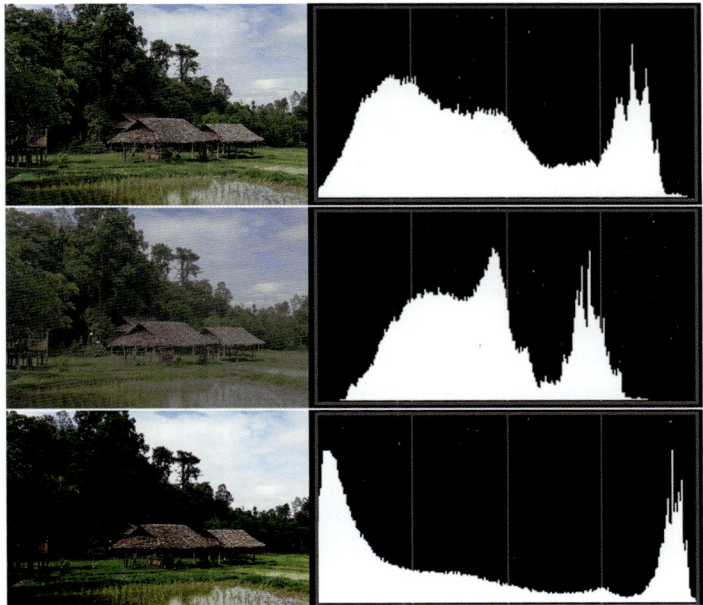

across the image, with a healthy distribution of tones throughout the midtone section of the graph. That large peak at the right side of the graph represents all those light tones in the sky. A normal-contrast image you shoot may have less sky area, and less of a peak at the right side, but notice that very few pixels hug the right edge of the histogram, indicating that the lightest tones are not being clipped because they are off the chart.

With a lower-contrast image, like the one shown in Figure 7.23, center, the basic shape of the previous histogram will remain recognizable, but gradually will be compressed together to cover a smaller area of the gray spectrum. The squished shape of the histogram is caused by all the grays in the original image being represented by a limited number of gray tones in a smaller range of the scale.

Instead of the darkest tones of the image reaching into the black end of the spectrum and the whitest tones extending to the lightest end, the blackest areas of the scene are now represented by a light gray, and the whites by a somewhat lighter gray. The overall contrast of the image is reduced. Because all the darker tones are actually a middle gray or lighter, the scene in this version of the photo appears lighter as well.

Going in the other direction, increasing the contrast of an image produces a histogram like the one shown in Figure 7.23, bottom. In this case, the tonal range is now spread over the entire width of the chart, but, except for the bright sky, there is not much variation in the middle tones; the mountain "peaks" are not very high. When you stretch the grayscale in both directions like this, the darkest tones become darker (that may not be possible), and the lightest tones become lighter (ditto). In fact, shades that might have been gray before can change to black or white as they are moved toward either end of the scale.

The effect of increasing contrast may be to move some tones off either end of the scale altogether, while spreading the remaining grays over a smaller number of locations on the spectrum. That's exactly the case in the example shown. The number of possible tones is smaller and the image appears harsher.

Understanding Histograms

The important thing to remember when working with the histogram display in your a6400 is that changing the exposure does *not* change the contrast of an image. The curves illustrated in the previous three examples remain exactly the same shape when you increase or decrease exposure. I repeat: The proportional distribution of grays shown in the histogram doesn't change when exposure changes; it is neither stretched nor compressed. However, the tones as a whole are moved toward one end of the scale or the other, depending on whether you're increasing or decreasing exposure. You'll be able to see that in some illustrations that follow.

So, as you reduce exposure, tones gradually move to the black end (and off the scale), while the reverse is true when you increase exposure. The contrast within the image is changed only to the extent that some of the tones can no longer be represented when they are moved off the scale.

To change the *contrast* of an image, you must do one of four things:

- **Change the a6400's contrast setting** using the menu system. You'll find these adjustments in your camera's Creative Styles feature, as discussed in Chapter 9.

- **Use your camera's shadow-tone "booster."** As previously discussed, D-Range Optimizer can also adjust contrast.

- **Alter the contrast of the scene itself,** for example, by using a fill light or reflectors to add illumination to shadows that are too dark.

- **Attempt to adjust contrast in post-processing** using your image editor or RAW file converter. You may use features such as Levels or Curves (in Photoshop, Photoshop Elements, and many other image editors), or work with HDR software to cherry-pick the best values in shadows and highlights from multiple images.

Of the four of these, the third—changing the contrast of the scene—is the most desirable, because attempting to fix contrast by fiddling with the tonal values is unlikely to be a perfect remedy. However, adding a little contrast can be successful because you can discard some tones to make the image more contrasty. However, the opposite is much more difficult. An overly contrasty image rarely can be fixed, because you can't add information that isn't there in the first place.

What you *can* do is adjust the exposure so that the tones *that are already present in the scene* are captured correctly. Figure 7.24, top, shows the histogram for an image that is badly underexposed. You can guess from the shape of the histogram that many of the dark tones to the left of the graph have been clipped off. There's plenty of room on the right side for additional pixels to reside without having them become overexposed. So, you can increase the exposure (either by changing the f/stop

Figure 7.24

Top: A histogram of an underexposed image may look like this. Center: Adding exposure will produce a histogram like this one. Bottom: A histogram of an overexposed image will show clipping at the right side.

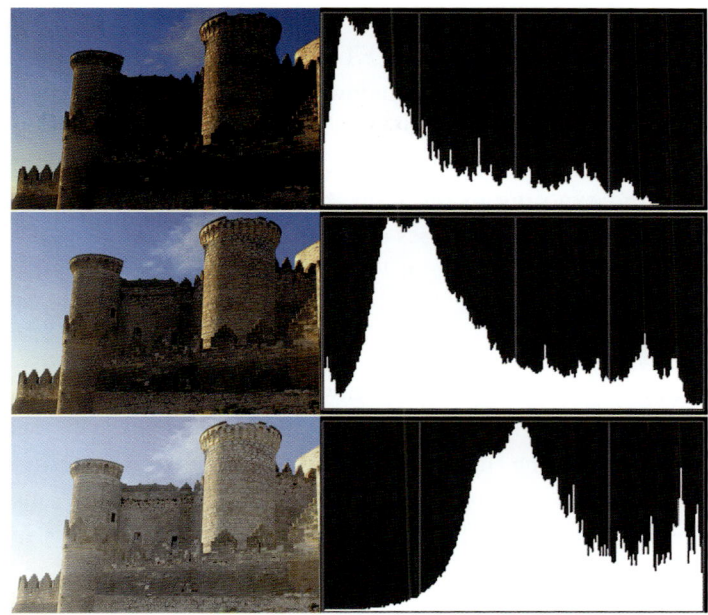

or shutter speed, or by adding an EV value) to produce the corrected histogram shown in Figure 7.24, center.

Conversely, if your histogram looks like the one shown in Figure 7.24, bottom, with bright tones pushed off the right edge of the chart, you have an overexposed image, and you can correct it by reducing exposure. In addition to the histogram, the a6400 has its Highlights and Zebra options, which, when activated, shows areas that are overexposed with flashing tones (often called "blinkies"). Depending on the importance of this "clipped" detail, you can adjust exposure or leave it alone. For example, if all the dark-coded areas in the review are in a background that you care little about, you can forget about them and not change the exposure, but if such areas appear in facial details of your subject, you may want to make some adjustments.

In working with histograms, your goal should be to have all the tones in an image spread out between the edges, with none clipped off at the left and right sides. Underexposing (to preserve highlights) should be done only as a last resort, because retrieving the underexposed shadows in your image editor will frequently increase the noise, even if you're working with RAW files. A better course of action is to expose for the highlights, but, when the subject matter makes it practical, fill in the shadows with additional light, using reflectors, fill flash, or other techniques rather than allowing them to be seriously underexposed.

A traditional technique for optimizing exposure is called "expose to the right," (ETTR) which involves adding exposure to push the histogram's curve toward the right side *but not far enough to clip off highlights*. The rationale for this method is that extra shadow detail will be produced with a minimum increase in noise, especially in the shadow areas. It's said that half of a digital sensor's response lies in the brightest areas of an image, and so require the least amount of amplification (which is one way to increase digital noise). ETTR can work, as long as you're able to capture a satisfactory amount of information in the shadows.

Exposing to the Right

It's easier to understand exposing to the right if you mentally divide the histogram into fifths (unfortunately, the a6400's histogram uses quarters instead). And, for the sake of simplicity and smaller numbers, assume you're shooting in 14-bit RAW. Any 14-bit image can record a maximum of 16,383 different tones per channel. However, each fifth of the histogram does *not* encompass 3,277 tones (one-fifth of 16,383).

Instead, the right-most fifth, the highlights, shown in Figure 7.25, accounts for fully *half*, or 50 percent of the tones; the next fifth accounts for 1/4 (25 percent); and so on, with 1/8th, 1/16th, and 1/32nd assigned to the remaining fifths. These "fifths" are fuzzy rather than hard boundaries. But note that in the left-most area, approximately only 512 different tones are captured. When processing your RAW file, there are only 512 tones to recover in the shadows, which is why boosting/amplifying them increases noise. (The effect is most noticeable in the red and blue channels; your sensor's Bayer array has twice as many green-sensitive pixels as red or blue.)

Instead, you want to add exposure—as long as you don't push highlights off the right edge of the histogram—to brighten the shadows. Because there are 8,192 tones available in the highlights, even if the RAW image *looks* overexposed, it's possible to use your RAW converter's Exposure slider (such as the one found in Adobe Camera Raw) to bring back detail captured in that surplus of tones in the highlights. This procedure is the exact opposite of what was recommended for film of the transparency variety—it was fairly easy to retrieve detail from shadows by pumping more light through them when processing the image, while even small amounts of extra exposure blew out highlights. You'll often find that the range of tones in your image is so great that there is no way

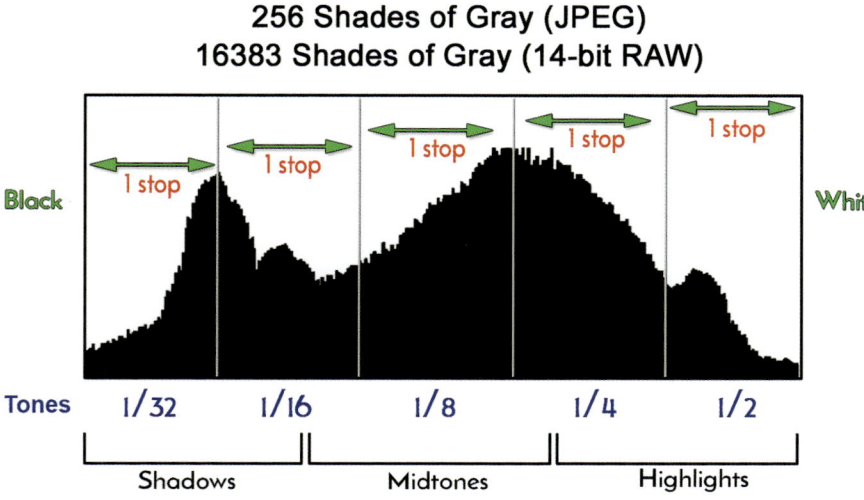

Figure 7.25

Tones are not evenly allocated throughout a histogram.

to keep your histogram from spilling over into the left and right edges, costing you both highlight and shadow detail. Exposing to the right may not work in such situations. A second school of thought recommends *reducing* exposure to bring back the highlights, or "exposing to the left." You would then attempt to recover shadow detail in an image editor, using tools like Adobe Camera Raw's Exposure slider. But remember, above all, that this procedure will also boost noise in the shadows, and so the technique should be used with caution. In most cases, exposing to the right is your best bet.

Dealing with Channels

The more you work with histograms, the more useful they become. One of the first things that histogram veterans notice is that it's possible to overexpose one channel even if the overall exposure appears to be correct. For example, flower photographers soon discover that it's really, really difficult to get a good picture of a red rose. The exposure looks okay—but there's no detail in the rose's petals. The image's histogram will show you why: typically, you'll find a peak at the right edge that indicates that highlight information has been lost. In fact, the green channel is often blown, too, and so the green parts of the flower also lack detail. Only the blue channel's histogram may be entirely contained within the boundaries of the chart, and, on first glance, the white luminance histogram at top of the column of graphs may appear to be fairly normal. (See Figure 7.26.)

Any of the primary channels—red, green, or blue—can blow out all by themselves, although bright reds seem to be the most common problem area. More difficult to diagnose are overexposed tones in one of the "in-between" hues on the color wheel. Overexposed yellows (which are very common) will be shown by blowouts in *both* the red and green channels. Too-bright cyans will manifest as excessive blue and green highlights, while overexposure in the red and blue channels reduces detail in magenta colors. As you gain experience, you'll be able to see exactly how anomalies in the RGB channels translate into poor highlights and murky shadows.

Figure 7.26
Tones are not evenly allocated throughout a histogram.

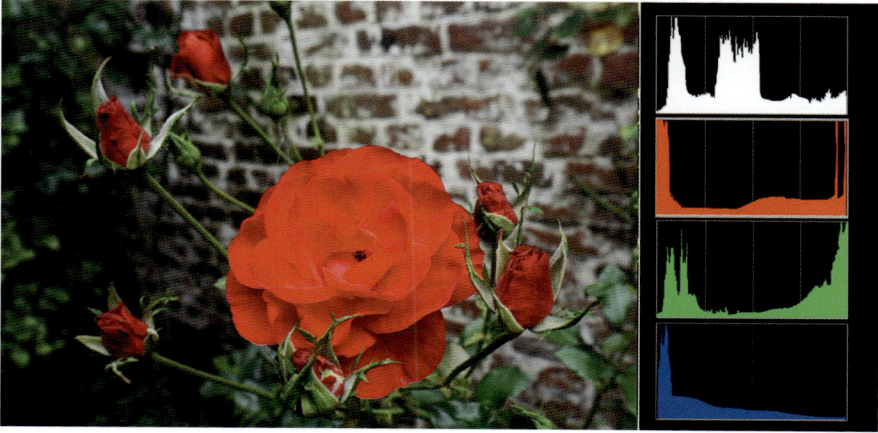

The only way to correct for color channel blowouts is to reduce exposure. As I mentioned earlier, you might want to consider filling in the shadows with additional light to keep them from becoming too dark when you decrease exposure. In practice, you'll want to monitor the red channel most closely, followed by the blue channel, and slightly decrease exposure to see if that helps. Because of the way our eyes perceive color, we are more sensitive to variations in green, so green channel blowouts are less of a problem, unless your main subject is heavily colored in that hue. If you plan on photographing a frog hopping around on your front lawn, you'll want to be extra careful to preserve detail in the green channel, using bracketing or other exposure techniques outlined in this chapter.

Automatic and Specialized Shooting Modes

After the long discussion of exposure control and other issues, let's get back to the remaining shooting modes. When you set the Intelligent Auto or the Superior Auto mode, the camera will use its programmed intelligence to try to identify the type of scene and set itself accordingly. These "auto-pilot" modes are useful when you suddenly encounter a picture-taking opportunity and don't have time to decide exactly what settings you might want to make in a semi-automatic or manual mode. Instead, you can spin the mode dial to one of the Auto modes, or, if you have a little more time, to the most appropriate scene mode, and fire away, knowing that you have a fighting chance of getting a usable or very good photo.

The a6400 also offers more specialized modes, for use in particular situations: Sweep Panorama and two special scene modes that provide surprisingly fine quality at high ISO levels—Hand-held Twilight and Anti Motion Blur.

Auto and Scene Modes

The two Auto modes and the scene modes are especially helpful when you're just learning to use your a6400, because they let you get used to composing and shooting, and obtaining excellent results, without having to struggle with unfamiliar controls to adjust things like shutter speed, aperture, ISO, and white balance. Once you've learned how to make those settings, you'll probably prefer to use P, A, S, and M modes since they provide more control over shooting options.

The fully automatic modes may give you few options for overrides, or none at all. For example, the AF mode, AF area, ISO, white balance, Dynamic Range Optimizer, and metering mode are all set for you. In most modes, you can select the drive setting and the flash mode, though not all settings for those options are available. You cannot adjust exposure compensation or Creative Styles in any of these modes.

Here are some essential points to note about the Intelligent Auto, Superior Auto, and SCN modes:

- **Intelligent Auto.** This is the setting to use when you hand your camera to a total stranger and ask him or her to take your picture. All the photographer has to do is press the shutter release button. Every other crucial decision is made by the camera's electronics, and many settings, such as ISO, white balance, metering mode, exposure compensation, and focus settings are not available to you for adjustment. However, you still are able to set the drive mode to Continuous shooting, add the self-timer (but not to Bracketing), and you can set the flash mode for any attached flash to Auto Flash, Fill Flash, or Flash Off. If the camera detects a subject suitable for a scene mode, it will switch to that mode and display its choice in the upper-left corner of the screen.

- **Superior Auto.** This mode is exactly like Intelligent Auto, but provides an extra benefit. In scenes that include extremely bright areas as well as shadow areas, the camera can activate its Auto HDR (high dynamic range) feature to provide more shadow detail. And in dark locations, when an extremely high ISO will be used, the camera can activate a special mode that fires several shots and composites them into one after discarding the digital noise data.

- **Portrait.** The first of the scene modes that you'll encounter, this mode tends to use wide apertures (large f/numbers) and faster shutter speeds. This is intended to provide shallow depth-of-field to blur the background while minimizing the risk of blurry photos caused by camera shake or subject movement. It's also optimized to provide "soft" skin tones. The drive mode cannot be set to Continuous shooting, but you can do the following: set the self-timer to take three shots; use the Remote Commander; set AF, MF, or DMF in the Function submenu; and set the flash mode for an attached flash to Auto Flash, Fill Flash, or Flash Off.

- **Sports Action.** In this mode, the Alpha favors fast shutter speeds to freeze action and it switches to Continuous drive mode to let you take a quick sequence of pictures with one press of the shutter release button. Continuous Autofocus is activated to continually refocus as a subject approaches the camera or moves away from your shooting position. You can find more information on autofocus options in Chapter 8.

- **Macro.** This mode is similar to the Portrait setting, favoring wider apertures to isolate your close-up subjects, and fast shutter speeds to eliminate the camera shake that's accentuated at close focusing distances. However, if your camera is mounted on a tripod or if you're using a lens with SteadyShot, you might want to use Aperture Priority mode instead. That will allow you to specify a smaller aperture (larger f/number) for additional depth-of-field to keep an entire three-dimensional subject within the range of acceptably sharp focus.

- **Landscape.** The Alpha tries to use smaller apertures for more depth-of-field to try to render the entire scene sharply; it also boosts saturation slightly for richer colors. You have some control over flash and can use the self-timer; most other settings are not available in this mode.

- **Sunset.** Increases saturation to emphasize the red tones of a sunrise or sunset. You can use the Fill Flash or Flash Off settings, but most other adjustments are unavailable to you.

- **Night Scene.** This is another mode for low-light photography. Similar to Night Portrait, but the flash is forced off. Use a tripod if at all possible or set the camera on a solid object, because the shutter speed will be long in low light. Most settings are not available, other than the Self-timer and Remote Commander.

- **Hand-held Twilight.** This is one of the two special modes designed for use in low light when hand-holding the a6400. The camera will set a high ISO (sensitivity) level to enable it to use a fast shutter speed to minimize the risk of blurring caused by camera shake. (In extremely dark conditions; however, the shutter speed may still be quite long.) When you press the shutter release button, the camera takes six shots in a quick series. The processor then composites them into one after discarding most of the digital noise data for a "cleaner" image than you'd get in a conventional high ISO photo. You'll get one image that's of surprisingly fine quality. Flash is never fired in this mode and you have access to virtually no camera options.

- **Night Portrait.** This mode is intended for taking people pictures in dark locations with flash using a long shutter speed. The Flash mode is set to Slow Sync. A nearby subject will be illuminated by flash while a distant background (such as a city skyline) will be exposed by the available light during the long exposure. Because the shutter speed will be long, it's necessary to use a tripod or set the camera on something solid like the roof of a car. If using an OSS-designated lens with a SteadyShot stabilizer, make sure it's on, unless the camera is mounted on a tripod; in that case, turn the stabilizer off using the SteadyShot item in the Setup menu. You can use the Self-timer or the Remote Commander in Night Portrait mode.

- **Anti Motion Blur.** Similar to Hand-held Twilight, this mode is also designed for use in dark locations, but it's more effective at reducing blurring that might be caused by a subject's motion or by a shaky camera. That's because the camera will set an even faster shutter speed that may require it to set a higher ISO level. (Of course, in an extremely dark location, the shutter speed may still be a bit long.) Again, the camera fires a series of six shots and composites them into one with minimal digital noise.

Sweep Panorama Mode

I showed you some panorama techniques in Chapter 3, but here's a recap. A conventional panorama mode has been available for several years with many other cameras, especially those with a built-in lens. That allows you to shoot a series of photos, with framing guided by an on-screen display to make sure they overlap correctly, and you can then "stitch" them together in special software to make a single, very wide, panoramic image. Some cameras can even do this for you with in-camera processing but most (though not all) require you to use a tripod. Your Sony camera offers the most convenient type of panorama mode; it's automatic (but allows you to use some overrides) and it can produce very good results without a tripod. Of course, it's easier to keep the camera perfectly level while shooting the series when using a tripod, but that's not always practical. Here are a few tips to consider:

- **Choose a direction.** You can select one of four directions for your panorama: right, left, up, or down. Select any of these options in the Camera Settings 1 menu, using the Panorama Direction item. It's only available when the camera is set to Sweep Panorama mode. The default setting, right, is probably the most natural for many people; it requires you to pan the camera from the left to the right across a wide vista. Occasionally, you might want to use one of the other options. The up or down motion is the one you'll need to make a panoramic photo of very tall subjects, such as skyscrapers and nearby mountains.

- **Change settings while in Panorama mode.** When you select this Shooting mode, the camera presents you with a large arrow and urgent-sounding instructions to press the shutter button and move the camera in the direction of the arrow. Don't let the camera intimidate you with this demand; what it is neglecting to tell you is that you can take all the time you want, and that you are free to change certain settings before you shoot.

  Press the MENU button and you can set the focus mode, white balance, and metering mode. Other useful functions include exposure compensation; Image Size in the Image Size menu, which lets you set either the Standard or the Wide panorama option; and the Creative Style modes in the Brightness/Color menu. Once you have those settings fine-tuned to your satisfaction, *then* go ahead and press the shutter release button.

- **Smooth and steady does it.** While keeping the shutter release button depressed, immediately start moving the camera smoothly and steadily in an arc; pivot your feet or the camera on a tripod head and keep going until the shutter stops clicking. The on-screen guide that appears during the exposure will help you keep the speed and direction of movement right. If you moved the camera at a speed that was too fast or too slow, you'll get an error message and the camera will prompt you to start over.

- **Beware of moving objects.** The Sweep Panorama mode is intended for stationary subjects, such as mountain ranges, city skylines, or expansive gardens. There's nothing to stop you from shooting a scene that contains moving cars, people, or other objects, but be aware of problems that can arise in that situation. Because you're taking multiple overlapping shots that are then stitched into a single image, the camera may capture the same car or person two or more times in slightly different positions; this can result in a truncated or otherwise distorted picture of that particular subject. Press the Playback button to view your just completed panorama; press the center button to view a moving playback of the image.

8

Mastering Autofocus Options

Yes, I waxed ecstatic over the real-time tracking autofocus features of the a6400 in the introduction of this book. It's not easy to overestimate the importance of this particular breakthrough, which gives this modestly priced camera an advantage over other vendors' cameras with much higher price tags. The a6400 has the ability to lock in on subjects, track their motion, switch to face detection/tracking, then progress to even more precise eye detection—and then back-track to the other methods as movement continues through the frame. That's particularly impressive because, when mirrorless digital cameras were introduced, autofocus was something they weren't particularly good at.

Indeed, the mirrors found in traditional SLRs had two distinct advantages: they allowed previewing an image through an optical viewfinder, and made it possible to direct some of the incoming illumination to a separate electronic autofocus system. At the moment of exposure, focus was locked, and the mirror flipped up out of the way, allowing the light to pass through the camera body to the film or digital sensor. Autofocus was fast, and reasonably accurate.

Of course, the mirror system had its own set of drawbacks. Moving mirrors are noisy and bulky, and increase the distance between the lens mounting flange and the film or sensor, resulting in larger cameras. Mirror-based viewing systems also mean that autofocus can't take place during exposure, which is particularly problematic when capturing video. Those mirrors were, at best, a kluge introduced to allow previewing an image through the same lens used to take the picture; early cameras had no mirrors, nor did the first 35mm cameras (dating from the first Leica prototypes of 1913). Compact models with mirrors for previewing images didn't start to make in-roads until just before World War II, and mirrorless cameras from Leica and others were prized for their light weight, smaller size, and quietness for another 30 to 35 years.

We eventually became so accustomed to the limitations of single-lens reflex models with mirrors that the first digital mirrorless cameras seemed very limited, especially when it came to autofocus. The first few generations of mirrorless cameras from Sony and other vendors had to use a slower AF method, based on what the sensor sees. But that was then, and this is now. Sony has combined the slow, but inherently very accurate method of autofocus, called *contrast detection,* with a much speedier *phase detection* system to produce a single "4D" (Sony's terminology) *hybrid* AF system that combines speed with accuracy and exceptional tracking capabilities.

However, there is still one logistical problem to overcome: the camera doesn't really know, for certain, *what* subject *you* want to be in sharp focus. It may select an object and lock in focus with lightning speed. (Sony claims 0.02-second response in some cases.) However, the focus plane isn't guaranteed to be your intended center of interest in your photograph. Or, the camera may lock focus too soon, or too late. This chapter will help you understand the options available with your Sony a6400 so you can help the camera understand what you want to focus on, when, and maybe even why.

Getting into Focus

Learning to use the a6400 autofocus system is easy, but you do need to fully understand how the system works to get the most benefit from it. Once you're comfortable with autofocus, you'll know when it's appropriate to use the manual focus option, too. The important thing to remember is that focus isn't absolute. For example, some things that appear to be in sharp focus at a given viewing size and distance might not be in focus at a larger size and/or closer distance. That family portrait hanging over the mantle may look fine when you're seated on the sofa, but it appears less sharp when examined from two feet away.

In addition, the goal of optimum focus isn't always to make things look sharp. For some types of subjects, not all of an image needs to be sharp. Controlling exactly what is sharp and what is not is part of your creative palette. Use of depth-of-field characteristics to throw part of an image out of focus while other parts are sharply focused is one of the most valuable tools available to a photographer. But selective focus works only when the desired areas of an image are in focus properly. For the digital camera photographer, correct focus can be one of the trickiest parts of the technical and creative process.

As I said in the introduction to this chapter, there are two major focusing methods used by modern digital cameras: *phase detection,* used by all digital cameras with mirrors, including the fixed-mirror Sony models like the a77 II; and *contrast detection,* which was the primary focusing method employed by all mirrorless models until very recently.

Contrast Detection

Contrast detection relies on examining the image formed on the sensor, and how it works is illustrated, if over-simplified, in Figure 8.1. At top in the figure, the transitions between the edges of the vertical wood grain grooves are soft and blurred because of the low contrast between them. The traditional contrast detection autofocus system looks only for contrast between edges, and those edges can run in any direction. At the bottom of the figure, the image has been brought into sharp

Figure 8.1

Using the contrast detection method of autofocus, a camera can evaluate the increase in contrast in the edges of subjects, starting with a blurry image (top) and producing a sharp, contrasty image (bottom).

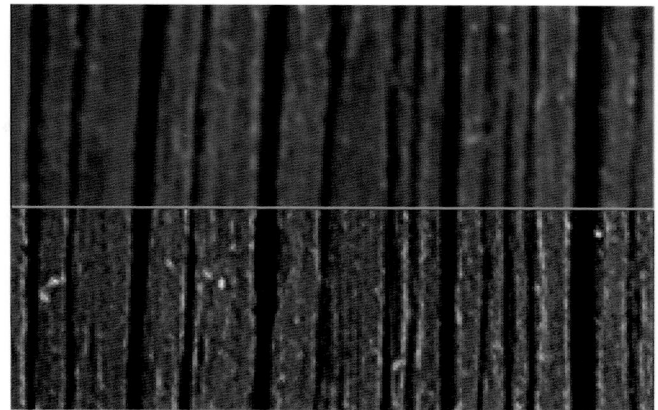

focus, and the edges have much more contrast; the transitions are sharp and clear. Although this example is a bit exaggerated so you can see the results on the printed page, it's easy to understand that when maximum contrast in a subject is achieved using contrast detection, it can be deemed to be in sharp focus.

Contrast detection works best with static subjects, because it is inherently slower and not well-suited for tracking moving objects. Contrast detection works less well in dim light, because its accuracy depends on its ability to detect variations in brightness and contrast. You'll find that contrast detection works better with faster lenses, too, because larger lens openings admit more light that can be used by the sensor to measure contrast.

Phase Detection

Phase detection is an alternative focusing method used in many advanced cameras including digital SLRs and current Sony Alpha SLT models, like the a77 II and a68. Phase detection is built right into the sensor of your a6400, and it is also used in a different way when you use A-mount (rather than E-mount) lenses attached to the optional LA-EA2 or LA-EA4 A-mount lens adapters. Both adapters have their own built-in phase detection autofocus systems that bypass and replace the hybrid AF technology built into your camera.

However, most importantly, phase detection is an integral part of the a6400's advanced sensor-based hybrid AF system, which combines slower contrast detection with faster phase detection to give us, potentially, the best of both worlds.

With phase detection, each autofocus sampling area (either a separate sensor with dSLRs and SLT models or pixels embedded in the sensor in the case of cameras like the a6400) is divided into two halves. The two halves are compared, much like (actually, exactly like) a two-window rangefinder used in surveying, weaponry, and non-SLR cameras such as the venerable Leica M film models. The contrast between the two images changes as focus is moved in or out, until sharp focus is achieved when the images are "in phase," or lined up. Figure 8.2 can help you visualize how this works.

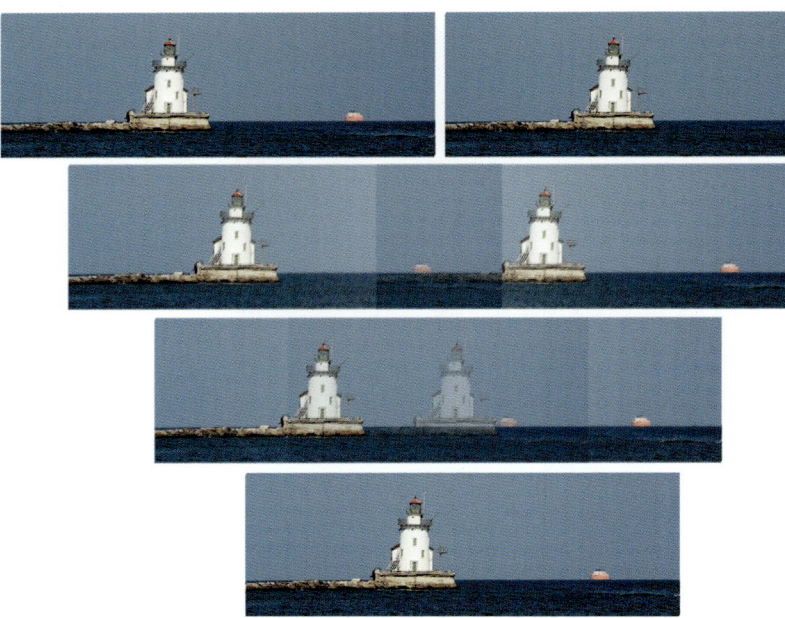

Figure 8.2

Phase detection "lines up" portions of your image using rangefinder-like comparison to achieve focus.

Figure 8.3 is another way of visualizing phase detection. (This is a greatly simplified view just for illustration purposes.) In Figure 8.3 (left), a typical horizontally oriented focus sensor is looking at a series of parallel vertical lines in a weathered piece of wood. The lines are broken into two halves by the sensor's rangefinder prism, and you can see that they don't line up exactly; the image is slightly out of focus. The rangefinder approach of phase detection tells the camera exactly how much out of focus the image is, and in which direction (focus is too near, or too far), thanks to the amount and direction of the displacement of the split image.

The camera can snap the image into sharp focus and line up the vertical lines, as shown in Figure 8.3, right, in much the same way that rangefinder cameras align two parts of an image to achieve sharp focus. Even better, because it knows the amount of focus travel needed, the camera is able to adjust the speed of the lens's AF motor to move the lens elements slowly or quickly, depending on how much focus adjustment is needed.

As with any rangefinder-like function, accuracy is better when the "base length" between the two images is larger, so the two split images have greater separation. (Think back to your high school trigonometry; you could calculate a distance more accurately when the separation between the two points where the angles were measured was greater.) For that reason, phase detection autofocus is more accurate with larger (wider) lens openings than with smaller lens openings, and, with the Sony a6400, does not work at all when the f/stop is f/13 or smaller. Obviously, the "opposite" edges of the lens opening are farther apart with a lens having an f/2.8 maximum aperture than with one that has a smaller, f/5.6 maximum f/stop, and the base line is much longer. The camera is able to perform these comparisons and then move the lens elements directly to the point of correct focus very quickly, in milliseconds.

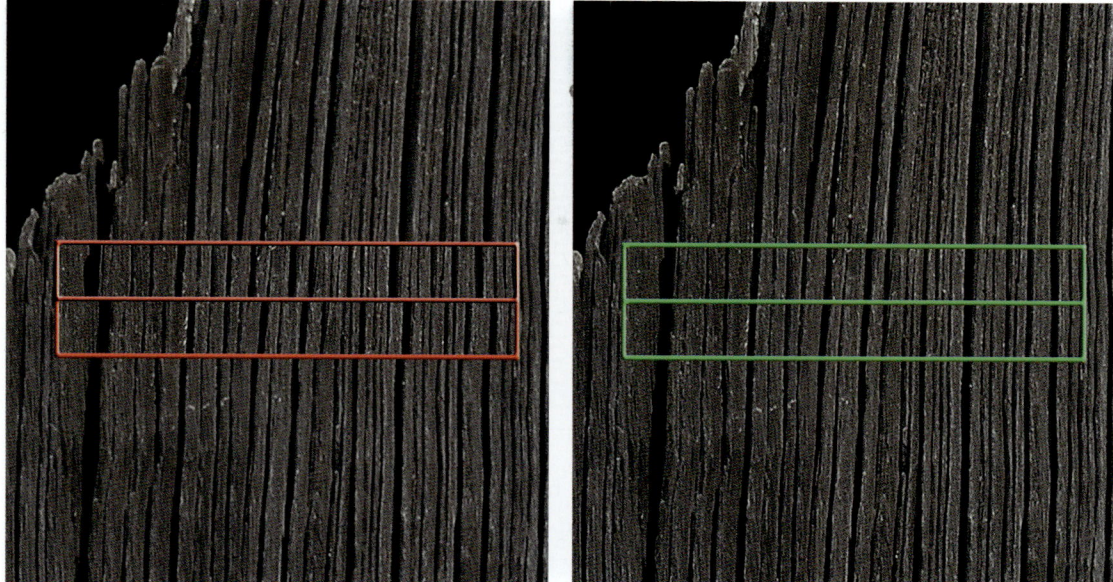

Figure 8.3 When an image is out of focus, the split lines don't align precisely (left); using phase detection, a camera can align the features of the image and achieve sharp focus quickly (right).

Because of the speed advantages of phase detection, makers of mirrorless cameras have been adding on-chip phase detect points to their sensors. Sony, because it designs and makes its own sensors, has been able to do a stellar job with this. The a6400 has a whopping 425 phase detect pixels embedded in its sensor.

Comparing the Two Hybrid Components

Sony a6400 autofocus uses both phase detection autofocus (PDAF) and contrast detection autofocus (CDAF) to provide a combination of fast and accurate AF. Figure 8.4 shows the layout of the autofocus points and zones used by the a6400.

- **Phase detection points.** The green squares in the figure represent the approximate location of 425 phase detect points embedded in the a6400's sensor (a matrix measuring 25 × 17). These pixels cover almost all of the frame. That can be important for sports photographers, who may have subjects in all parts of the image. As I write this, Sony has not released figures detailing the percentage of the frame covered by PDAF, but my quick-and-dirty calculations estimate that fully 81 percent of the frame can be used for phase detect AF. That's outstanding.

- **Contrast detection zone.** The shaded red area represents the sensor area that contains the 169 separate contrast detection zones (they are not individual pixels). While the CDAF area is smaller than the PDAF coverage, approximately 73 percent of the frame is accounted for, concentrated in the center area.

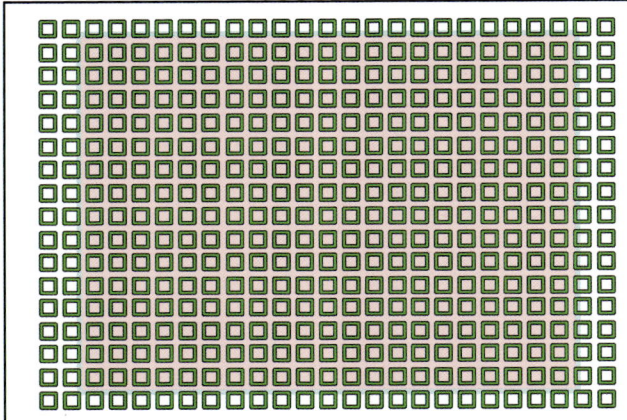

Figure 8.4

Autofocus zones for phase detection (green boxes) and contrast detection (red shaded area).

The hybrid autofocus system of the a6400 uses both types of AF. The camera begins by rapidly focusing using PDAF, because the rangefinder approach always tells the camera whether to move focus closer or farther, and by approximately how much. No hunting is required, which is often the case with contrast detection, which needs to tweak the focus point until it settles on the sharpest position.

Once the PDAF has done its stuff, contrast detection kicks in, using its finicky but more accurate focusing capabilities to fine-tune focus. So, you end up with speedy initial focus (PDAF) and slightly slower final adjustments (CDAF), providing a perfect hybrid compromise. That's why Sony didn't switch to phase detection completely. Here's a quick rundown of the advantages of a hybrid system:

- **Contrast detection works with more image types.** Contrast detection doesn't require subject matter to have lines that are at angles to the PDAF points to work optimally, as phase detection does. Any subject that has edges running in any direction can be used to achieve sharp focus.

- **Contrast detection can focus on larger areas of the scene.** Whereas phase detection focus can be achieved *only* at the points that fall on one of the special autofocus sensor pixels, with contrast detection much larger portions of the image can be used as focus zones. Focus is achieved with the actual sensor image, so focus point selection is simply a matter of choosing which part of the sensor image to use. (This point is highlighted by the fact, discussed below, that in Flexible Spot mode, you can move the Autofocus Area to many parts of the sensor, whereas with a phase detection system, you can move the Autofocus Area only to the specific locations where the special autofocus sensors used for phase detection are located.)

- **Contrast detection can be more accurate with some types of scenes.** Phase detection can fall prey to the vagaries of uncooperative subject matter: if suitable lines aren't available, the system may achieve less than optimal focus. In addition, accuracy decreases as the maximum aperture baseline used for calculations becomes smaller. Although AF is always conducted with the lens wide open, a lens with a maximum aperture of f/5.6 will focus with less accuracy than one with an f/1.4 maximum aperture. Contrast detection focus is more clear-cut. In most cases, the camera is able to determine clearly when sharp focus has been achieved.

■ **Phase detection "knows" which direction to focus.** The split image seen by phase detection sensors reveal instantly whether focus is too close or too far. As I mentioned earlier, there is no need to "hunt" for the focus point, as the AF system can immediately adjust in the proper direction. That boosts focus speed considerably.

■ **Phase detection "knows" how far out of focus a subject is.** The separation between the two halves of the image let the AF system know whether the subject is grossly out of focus, or whether only a slight adjustment is needed. That means faster autofocus, too.

■ **Phase detection isn't as dependent on scene brightness.** As long as the split images are illuminated well enough for the AF system to make an evaluation, greater or lesser amounts of light don't have as much of an effect on speed and accuracy. Remember, the reason phase detect systems operate less well at smaller f/stops is because the baseline diameter of the aperture is smaller.

■ **Sony's 4D high-density tracking can follow moving subjects.** The a6400's phase detection system can achieve focus quickly (even when shooting continuously at 11 frames per second), whether your subject is moving horizontally or vertically (what Sony calls *area*), toward you, or away from you (*depth* in Sony-speak). To those three dimensions, the system adds the fourth dimension of time (which the company labels as *steadfast*), so focus can be maintained as it changes position. The 4D AF also deploys *high-density* tracking to zero in on moving subjects, using focus areas that are smaller than the 425 phase detect sensor areas shown in Figure 8.5.

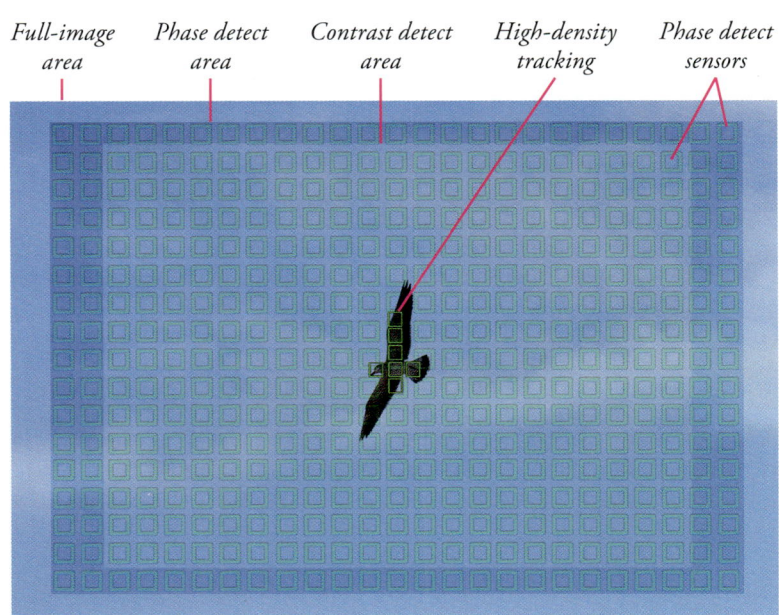

Full-image area   Phase detect area   Contrast detect area   High-density tracking   Phase detect sensors

Figure 8.5
Within the image frame are phase detect areas consisting of 425 pixels embedded in the sensor, 169 contrast detect zones, and high-density tracking areas that can follow your subject as it moves.

TRICKY BITS

There are a few restrictions you need to keep in mind when using the a6400's hybrid AF system.

- **Larger than f/13.** Sony advises that focal plane phase detection AF is disabled whenever an aperture of f/13 or smaller is used; the a6400 will rely *only* on slower contrast detection in that case.

- **Compatible lenses.** Not all lenses are compatible with the phase detection component. Older lenses, and lenses that need to be updated using firmware, don't support phase detection, which in turn blocks use of the Automatic AF, AF Track Duration, and AF Drive Speed features explained in Chapter 3. A-mount lenses used with the LA-EA2 or LA-EA4 adapters do not support focal plane phase detection, although most can be used with the phase detection built into the adapter itself.

Focus Modes and Options

Now that you understand the fundamental principles of how the a6400 achieves focus, let's discuss the practical application of these principles to your everyday picture-taking activities, by setting the various modes and options available for the autofocus system. We'll also discuss the use of manual focus, and when that method might be preferable to autofocus.

As you've come to appreciate by now, the a6400 offers many options for your photography. Focus is no exception. Of course, as with other aspects of this camera, you can set the shooting mode to either Auto option or a scene mode such as Sports Action, and the camera will do just fine in most situations, using its default settings for autofocus. But, if you want more creative control, the choices are there for you to make.

So, no matter what shooting mode you're using, your first choice is whether to use autofocus or manual focus. Yes, there's also a Direct Manual Focus (DMF) option, discussed in Chapter 3, but that still provides autofocus, with the option of *fine-tuning* focus manually before taking the shot. Manual focus presents you with great flexibility along with the challenge of keeping the image in focus under what may be difficult conditions, such as rapid motion of the subject, darkness of the scene, and the like. Later in this chapter, I'll cover manual focus as well as DMF. For now, I'll assume you're going to rely on the camera's conventional AF mode.

FOCUS MODES/FOCUS AREA MODES

Your camera has a lot of modes! To keep the various focus options straight, remember that *focus modes* determine *when* the camera focuses: once, continuously using autofocus, or manually. *Focus area modes* determine *where* in the frame the a6400 collects the information used to achieve autofocus.

The Sony a6400 has three basic AF modes: AF-S (Single-shot autofocus) and AF-C (Continuous autofocus), as well as Automatic AF (AF-A), which switches between the two other modes as required. Once you have decided on which of these to use, you also need to tell the camera how to select the area used to measure AF. In other words, after you tell the camera *how* to autofocus, you also have to tell it *where* to direct its focusing attention. I'll explain both *AF modes* and *AF area modes* in more detail later in this chapter.

MANUAL FOCUS

When you select manual focus (MF) in the Focus Mode entry in the Camera Settings 1-05 menu, using the Function menu, or by switching using a defined button, the a6400 lets you set the focus yourself by turning the focus ring on the lens. There are some advantages and disadvantages to this approach. While your batteries will last slightly longer in manual focus mode, it will take you longer to focus the camera for each photo. And unlike older 35mm film SLRs, digital cameras' electronic viewfinders and LCDs are not designed for optimum manual focus. I recommend trying the various AF options first, and switching to manual focus only if AF is not working for you, or you want to carefully select the plane of focus when working with selective focus, close-up photography, or other focus-critical work. And then be sure to take advantage of the focus peaking feature and the automatic frame enlargement (MF Assist), which can make it easier to determine when the focus is precisely on the most important subject element. And remember, if you use the DMF mode, you can fine-tune the focus after the AF system has finished its work. Those who have the 16-50mm kit lens should note that the zoom ring becomes the focus ring when you depress the shutter halfway.

Focus Pocus

Back in the pre-AF days, manual focusing was problematic because our eyes and brains have poor memory for correct focus, which is why your eye doctor must shift back and forth between sets of lenses and ask, "Does that look sharper or was it sharper before?" in determining your correct prescription. Similarly, manual focusing involves jogging the focus ring back and forth as you go from almost in focus, to sharp focus, to almost focused again. The little clockwise and counterclockwise arcs decrease in size until you've zeroed in on the point of correct focus. What you're looking for is the image with the most contrast between the edges of elements in the image.

The a6400 can assess sharpness quickly, and it's also able to remember the progression perfectly, making the entire process fast and precise. Unfortunately, even this high-tech system doesn't really know with any certainty *which* object should be in sharpest focus. Is it the closest object? The subject in the center of the frame? Something lurking *behind* the closest subject? A person standing over at the side of the picture? Many of the techniques for using autofocus effectively involve telling the camera exactly what it should be focusing on.

Adding Circles of Confusion

But there are other factors in play, as well. You know that increased depth-of-field brings more of your subject into focus. But more depth-of-field also makes autofocusing (or manual focusing) more difficult because the contrast is lower between objects at different distances. So, autofocus with a 300mm lens (or zoom setting) may be easier than at a 16mm focal length (or zoom setting) because the longer lens has less apparent depth-of-field. By the same token, a lens with a maximum aperture of f/1.8 will be easier to autofocus (or manually focus) than one of the same focal length with an f/4 maximum aperture, because the f/4 lens has more depth-of-field and a dimmer view. It's also important to note that lenses with a maximum aperture smaller than f/5.6 would give your Sony Alpha's autofocus system fits, because the smaller opening (aperture) would allow less light to enter or to reach the autofocus sensor.

To make things even more complicated, many subjects aren't polite enough to remain still. They move around in the frame, so that even if the camera's lens is sharply focused on your main subject, the subject may change position and require refocusing. An intervening subject may pop into the frame and pass between you and the subject you meant to photograph. You (or the camera) have to decide whether to focus on this new subject, or to remain focused on the original subject. Finally, there are some kinds of subjects that are difficult to bring into sharp focus because they lack enough contrast to allow the camera's AF system (or our eyes) to lock in. Blank walls, a clear blue sky, or other low-contrast subject matter may make focusing difficult even with the hybrid AF system.

If you find all these focus factors confusing, you're on the right track. Focus is, in fact, measured using something called a *circle of confusion*. An ideal image consists of zillions of tiny little points, which, like all points, theoretically have no height or width. There is perfect contrast between the point and its surroundings. You can think of each point as a pinpoint of light in a darkened room. When a given point is out of focus, its edges decrease in contrast and it changes from a perfect point to a tiny disc with blurry edges (remember, blur is the lack of contrast between boundaries in an image). (See Figure 8.6.)

If this blurry disc—the circle of confusion—is small enough, our eyes still perceives it as a point. It's only when the disc grows large enough that we can see it as a blur rather than as a sharp point that a given point is viewed as being out of focus. You can see, then, that enlarging an image, either by displaying it larger on your computer monitor or by making a large print, also magnifies the size of each circle of confusion. Moving closer to the image does the same thing. So, parts of an image

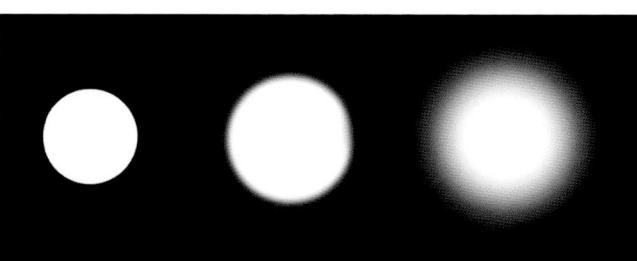

Figure 8.6
When a pinpoint of light (left) goes out of focus, its blurry edges form a circle of confusion (center and right).

that may look perfectly sharp in a 5 × 7–inch print viewed at arm's length, might appear blurry when blown up to 11 × 14 inches and examined at the same distance. Take a few steps back, however, and the image may look sharp again.

To a lesser extent, the viewer also affects the apparent size of these circles of confusion. Some people see details better at a given distance and may perceive smaller circles of confusion than someone standing next to them. For the most part, however, such differences are small. Truly blurry images will look blurry to just about everyone under the same conditions.

Technically, there is just one plane within your picture area, parallel to the back of the camera (actually the sensor) that is in sharp focus. That's the plane in which the points of the image are rendered as precise points. At every other plane in front of or behind the focus plane, the points show up as discs that range from slightly blurry to extremely blurry. In practice, the discs in many of these planes will still be so small that we see them as points, and that's where we get depth-of-field: the range of planes that includes discs that we perceive as points rather than blurred splotches. The size of this range increases as the aperture is reduced in size and is allocated roughly one-third in front of the plane of sharpest focus, and two-thirds behind it. (See Figure 8.7.)

Figure 8.7
The focused plane (the head and thorax of the butterfly) is sharp, but the area in front of and behind it are blurred because the depth-of-field (the range of acceptably sharp focus) is shallow in this image.

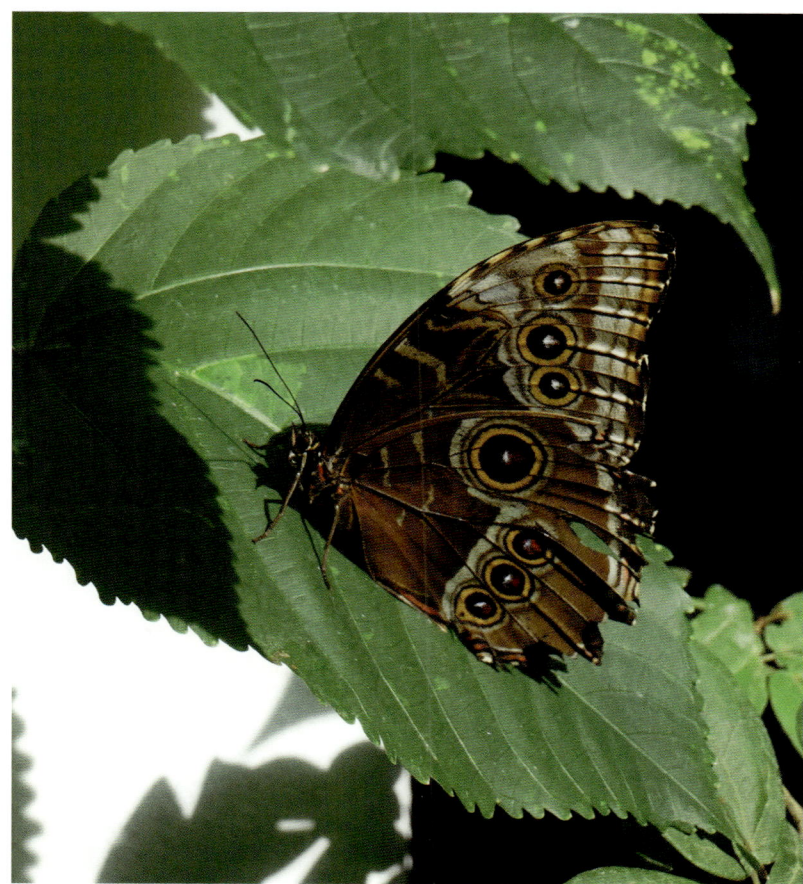

Your Focus Mode Options

Manual focus can come in handy, as I'll explain later in this chapter, but autofocus is likely to be your choice in the great majority of shooting situations. Choosing the right AF mode and the way in which focus points are selected is your key to success. Using the wrong mode for a particular type of photography can lead to a series of pictures that are all sharply focused—on the wrong subject.

But autofocus isn't some mindless beast out there snapping your pictures in and out of focus with no feedback from you. There are several settings you can modify to regain a fair amount of control. Your first decision should be which of the autofocus modes to select: Single-shot (AF-S), Continuous AF (AF-C), or Automatic AF (AF-A). DMF first uses autofocus, and then allows you to fine-tune focus manually. I like to keep the C1 button defined as the Focus Mode button, so I can press it and switch quickly among modes. Alternatively, you can press the MENU button, go to the Camera Settings I-05 menu, and navigate to the line for Focus Mode. Press the center button, then highlight your autofocus mode choice from the submenu, and press the center button again. You can also set autofocus mode by pressing the Fn button and using the Function menu.

FOCUS INDICATOR

At the lower-left corner of your screen, you'll find a green focus confirmation indicator that's active while focusing is underway. It consists of a round green disk that may have rounded brackets at either side. If the *disk glows steadily*, the image is in focus. Only the *disk appears* when using AF-S; in AF-C mode, the *disk is surrounded by the brackets* and indicates that the focus plane may change if the subject moves. If the *brackets are flashing and no disk appears*, focusing is in progress; if the *disk is flashing*, focusing has failed. (See Figure 8.8.)

Figure 8.8
The focus indicator icon shows focus status.

Steady:
Image
in focus
(AF-S)

Flashing:
Focus has
failed

Image in focus,
but focus may
change
(AF-C)

Focus in
progress

Single-Shot AF (AF-S) Mode

With Single-Shot AF (AF-S), the camera will lock in focus when you press the shutter release (or defined AF start button) and will not adjust focus if your subject moves or you change the distance between you and your subject, as long as you hold down the button.

In AF-S mode, focus is locked. By keeping the button depressed halfway, you'll find you can reframe the image by moving the camera to aim at another angle; the focus (and exposure) will not change. Maintain pressure on the shutter release button and focus remains locked even if you recompose, or if the subject begins running toward the camera, for example.

> **Tip**
>
> In this chapter, I'm assuming that you're using P, A, S, or M mode where you have full control over the camera features. This is important because the camera will use *only* AF-S in either Intelligent Auto or Superior Auto modes, in any scene mode *except* Sports Action, in Sweep Panorama, and whenever the Smile Shutter feature is active. And it will set Continuous AF (AF-C) only in Movie mode, regardless of what focus mode you've selected for still images.

When sharp focus is achieved in AF-S mode, the solid green focus indicator appears in the lower-left corner of the screen and you'll hear a little beep, if sound is enabled. One or more green focus confirmation frames will also appear to indicate the area(s) of the scene that will be in sharpest focus.

For non-action photography, AF-S is usually your best choice, as it minimizes out-of-focus pictures (at the expense of spontaneity). Because of the small delay while the camera zeroes in on correct focus, you might experience slightly more shutter lag. This mode uses less battery power than Continuous AF.

If you have set the a6400 for Pre-AF in the Camera Settings I-06 menu, you may notice something that seems strange: the camera's autofocus mechanism will begin seeking focus even before you touch the shutter release button. In this mode, no matter which AF method is selected, the camera will continually alter its focus as it is aimed at various subjects, *until* you press the shutter release button halfway. At that point, the camera locks focus, in Single-shot AF mode.

Continuous AF (AF-C) Mode

When Continuous AF is active, focus is constantly readjusted as your subject (or you) moves. The difference between Single-shot AF and Continuous AF comes at the point the shutter release button (or defined focus start button) is pressed halfway. (See the discussion of *back-button focus* later in this chapter.)

Switch to this mode when photographing sports, young kids at play, and other fast-moving subjects. In this mode, the camera can lock focus on a subject if it is not moving toward the camera or away from your shooting position; when it does, you'll see a green circle surrounded by brackets. (There will be no beep.) But if the camera-to-subject distance begins changing, the camera instantly begins to adjust focus to keep it in sharp focus, making this the more suitable AF mode with moving subjects.

Focus or Release Priority?

The current focus plane is fixed and cannot be changed at a certain point in the picture-taking process. With AF-S mode, that point is when you press the shutter release halfway. As long as you keep your finger on the button, the camera will not refocus until you press down all the way, or take your finger off the release. In AF-C mode, the camera will focus, but will continue to refocus as long as the shutter release is held down halfway. Focus is *not* locked until you press down all the way to take a picture.

In either mode, when you simply press the shutter release down all the way, focus activation, locking, and picture taking take place one after the other—but still happen in the order I just described. That's where focus/release priority come into play. When the shutter release is pressed down all the way in a continuous motion, do you want the camera to wait until sharp focus is achieved—even if that means missing the exact instant you wanted to capture? Or do you want to have the a6400 go ahead and take the picture anyway, even if there is a possibility that the image isn't perfectly focused? I explained the priority options in Chapter 3, but here's a recap to using the Priority Set in AF-S/AF-C entries in the Camera Settings I-05 menu:

- **AF Priority.** The shutter is not activated until sharp focus is achieved. You can choose the AF Priority option for both AF-S and AF-C modes individually. Use AF Priority for subjects that are not moving rapidly. The a6400's AF system is fast enough that the slight delay should be negligible. However, if you're using an A-mount lens that does not have a built-in AF motor with the EA-LA adapter, you can experience a significant delay. Sports shooters and others who depend on capturing the decisive moment and can countenance no delay at all generally use Release Priority, discussed next.

- **Release Priority.** When this option is selected, the shutter is activated when the release button is pushed down all the way in both AF-S and AF-C modes, even if sharp focus has not yet been achieved. I prefer this option for AF-C mode, as Continuous Focus focuses and refocuses constantly when autofocus is active, and even though an image may not quite be in sharpest focus, at least I am able to get my shot. Using Release Priority does *not* mean that your image won't be sharply focused; it just means that you'll get a picture even if autofocusing isn't *quite* complete. If you've been poised with the shutter release pressed halfway, the camera probably has been tracking the focus of your image. And keep in mind that the a6400's AF system is *very* speedy.

- **Balanced Emphasis.** In this mode, the shutter is released when the button is pressed, with a slight pause if autofocus has not yet been achieved. It can be selected for both AF-S and AF-C modes, and is probably your best choice if you want a good compromise between speed of activation and sharpest focus. However, you would not want to use this setting if the highest possible continuous shooting rates are important to you.

Automatic AF (AF-A) Mode

The camera begins using AF-S, and switches to AF-C if the subject begins moving. Use this mode when you're not certain that your subject will begin moving, and you'd like to take advantage of AF-S, as described earlier, until the subject does move. You might use AF-A to photograph a sleeping pet, which, if awakened by the activity, might respond with sudden movement.

Direct Manual Focus (DMF)

The camera focuses automatically, then "releases" the focusing ring on lenses that have separate zoom and focus rings (some, like the 16-50mm kit lens, combine both functions) so you can fine-tune focus manually. I use this a lot when shooting close-ups of subjects that may move, such as small animals. The a6400 autofocuses, and then I can adjust the focus precisely. If my subject moves, I can just refocus and adjust again.

Manual Focus (MF)

Focusing is up to you in MF mode, but you have aids like focus peaking and MF assist to help you. I'll cover manual focus in more detail later in this chapter.

Autofocus Magnified

A very cool way to improve your AF accuracy is to use autofocus in conjunction with the Focus Magnifier that you probably work with most often when manually focusing. Just follow these steps:

1. **Turn on AF in Focus Magnifier** in the Camera Settings I-13 menu (as described in Chapter 3).
2. **Define a key,** such as the C1 button, as the activating button for Focus Magnifier. (Or access the feature directly from the Camera Settings I-13 menu.)
3. **Activate Focus Magnifier.** An orange box will appear on the screen. Use the directional buttons to position the orange box over the area you want to bring into focus.
4. **Press the center button.** The Focus Magnifier will enlarge the image contained within the orange box.
5. **Activate AF.** Press the shutter release halfway to activate autofocus (or use another key you may have defined to perform that function, say, if you're using back-button focus as described later in this chapter).
6. **AF focus commences.** The a6400 will use the current AF settings to focus on the area you've selected with the orange box.

Setting the AF Area

So far, you have allowed the camera to choose which part of the scene will be in the sharpest focus using its focus detection points called *AF areas* by Sony. However, you can also specify a single focus detection point that will be active. Use the Function menu, or press the MENU button, navigate to the Focus Area item in the Camera Settings I-05 menu, press the center button, and select one of the options. Press the center button again to confirm.

Here is how the AF Area options work:

■ **Wide.** The camera chooses the appropriate focus area(s) in order to set focus on a certain subject in the scene. There are no focus brackets visible on the screen until you press the shutter release button halfway to lock focus. You can move the brackets within the frame with the directional buttons.

You'll see several pairs of brackets when several parts of the scene are at the same distance from the camera. When most of the elements of a scene are at roughly the same distance, the camera displays a single, large green focus bracket around the entire edge of the screen. If Face Detection

VANISHING BRACKETS

When the Focus Area mode is Wide, Zone, or DMF, the a6400 may show the currently active focus area(s) using one or more large brackets (seen in the version at upper left in Figure 8.9), or the high-density focus points (shown at lower center). If all areas of the screen are considered, a green frame appears around the potential focus area (Figure 8.9, upper right).

You can set Display Continuous AF Area in the Camera Settings I-07 menu if you want to see the focus area displayed as you use AF-C. Indeed, if you're working with AF-C, you'll see the high-density points "dance" as the a6400 continually refocuses as your subject or camera moves.

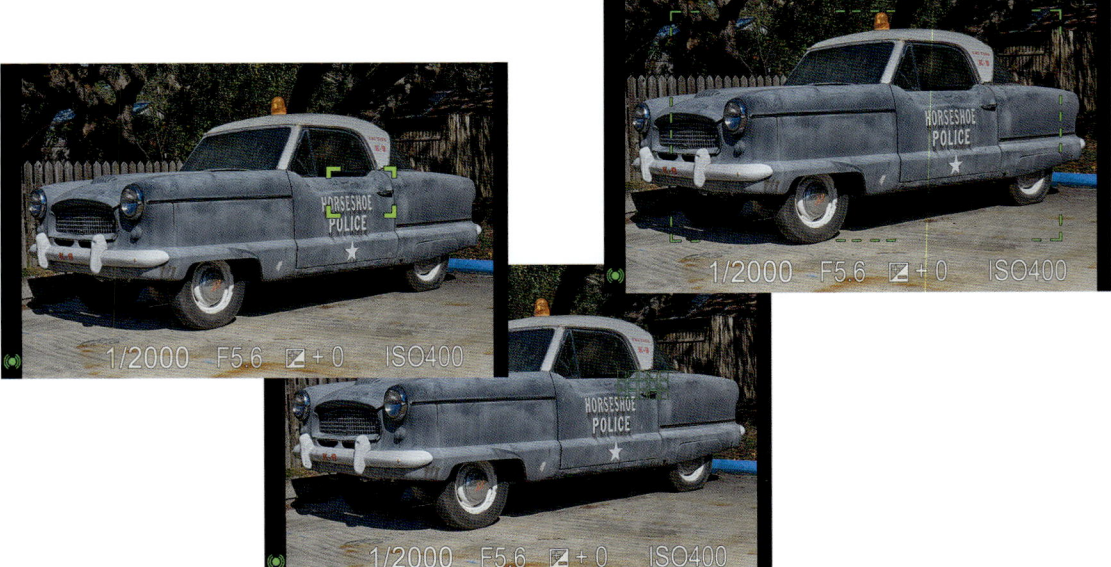

Figure 8.9 With Wide AF Area, the camera either displays a large green bracket indicating that most of the scene is at the same distance to the camera (left), or it displays one or more smaller brackets to indicate the specific area(s) of the scene that will be in sharpest focus (lower center). If the camera decides that all areas of the frame should be considered, a bracket around the entire focusing area is shown (upper right).

is active, the AF system will prioritize faces when making its decision as to where it should set focus. Even if you set one of the other options, Wide is automatically selected in certain shooting modes, including both Auto and all SCN modes. Use this mode to give the camera complete control over where to focus.

■ **Zone.** A 3 × 3 array of up to nine focus areas is shown on the screen in white. You can move the focus zone by pressing the directional buttons to shift the array to one of nine overlapping areas—three at the top of the frame, three at the bottom of the frame, and three in the middle. Select one of those nine focus areas, and the camera chooses which sections within that zone to use to calculate sharp focus. When you activate focus (usually by pressing the shutter release halfway down), the zones will be highlighted in green as focus is achieved, or the high-density focus points will illuminate in green. Use this mode when you know your subject is going to reside in a largish area of the frame, and want to allow the a6400 to select the exact focus zone. (See Figure 8.10.) As with the Wide Area option, the camera may switch from a larger area to a smaller area depending on the subject, and the zone can be relocated with the directional buttons.

■ **Center.** Activate this AF area and the camera will use only a single focus detection point in the center of the frame to set focus. Initially, a pair of black focus brackets appears on the screen. Touch the shutter release button and the camera sets and locks focus on the subject in the center of the image area; the brackets then turn green to confirm the area that will be in the sharpest focus in your image. (See Figure 8.11.) Choose this option if you want the camera to always focus on the subject in the center of the frame. Center the primary subject (like a friend's face in a wide-angle landscape composition), allow the camera to focus on it, maintain slight pressure on the shutter release button to keep focus locked, and re-frame the scene for a more effective, off-center, composition. Take the photo at any time and your friend (who is now off-center) will be in the sharpest focus.

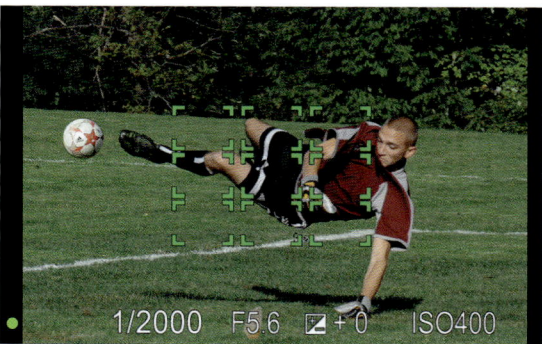

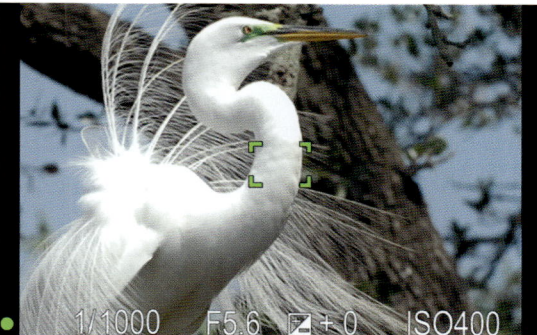

Figure 8.10 In Zone mode, an array of nine areas appears, and you can move the zone to nine different locations on the screen. The camera selects one or more focus zones within that array.

Figure 8.11 In the Center AF Area mode, the camera displays the focus brackets in the center of the screen; the brackets turn green after focus has been set.

■ **Flexible Spot.** This mode enables you to move the camera's focus detection point (focus area) around the scene to any one of multiple locations, using the directional buttons. When opting for Flexible Spot, you can use the left/right buttons to choose Small, Medium, or Large spots. This mode can be useful when the camera is mounted on a tripod and you'll be taking photos of the same scene for a long time, while the light is changing, for example. Move the focus area to cover the most important subject, and it will always focus on that point when you later take a photo. When you initially select this AF Area mode, a small pair of focus brackets appears in the center of the screen along with four triangles pointing toward the four sides of the screen. (See Figure 8.12.) The triangles merely indicate that the AF area can be moved in any direction.

Use the directional controls to move the brackets around the screen, which allows great versatility in the placement of the active focus detection point. Move the brackets until they cover the most important subject area and touch the shutter release button. The brackets will turn green and the camera will beep to confirm that focus has been set on the intended area.

■ **Expand Flexible Spot.** If the camera is unable to lock in focus using the selected focus point, it will also use the eight adjacent points to try to achieve focus.

■ **Tracking AF.** In this mode, the camera locks focus onto the subject area that is under the selected focus spot when the shutter button is depressed halfway. Then, if the subject moves (or you change the framing in the camera), the camera will continue to refocus *on that subject*. You can select this mode only when the focus mode is set to Continuous AF (AF-C).

This option is especially powerful, because you can activate it for any of the five focus area options described above. That is, once you've highlighted Tracking AF on the selection screen, you can then press the left-right directional button and choose Wide, Zone, Center, Flexible Spot, or Expand Flexible Spot. The camera will lock on a subject, using one of those five area modes to follow it. Tracking makes good use of the touch screen: it's easy to tap the subject you want to track on the LCD, and the camera will continue to follow it as it moves. You'll find more about Tracking AF in the following section.

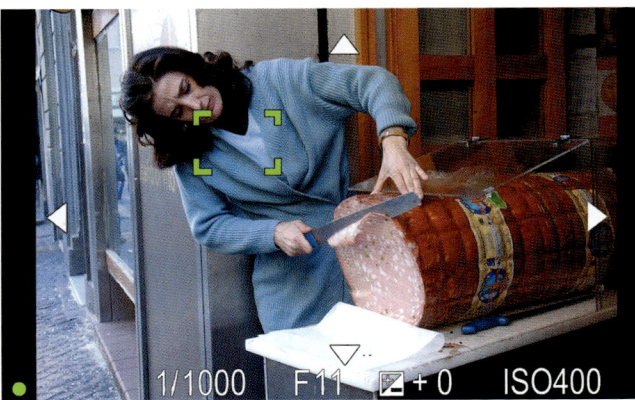

Figure 8.12
When the Flexible Spot AF Area mode is initially selected, the active focus detection point is delineated with brackets that turn green when focus is confirmed and locked; the arrows indicate that you can move the brackets in any of the four directions.

Just as you're limited in the use of the AF mode in certain operating modes, there's a limitation with AF Area as well. For example, Flexible Spot is not available for selection in automatic modes: in either Auto mode or any SCN mode, the camera will always use Multi as the AF Area mode.

Tracking Subjects, Faces, and Eyes

Tracking may not work if the subject is moving too quickly, is too small or too large to be isolated effectively, has only reduced contrast against its background, or if the ambient light is too dark or changes dramatically while you're tracking.

Tracking AF is not limited to following and focusing on faces or eyes, of course; it can track any moving subject. In general, you can turn it on and forget it. It does, however, only work in still photography mode; you can't use it when shooting movies. One thing to keep in mind is that it's sometimes difficult to track subjects other than humans; if your chosen subject happens to be near a face (say, an active pet, when you have the Animal subject option turned off), the a6400's AF system will sometimes jump to the face/eyes, and begin tracking it, instead. The desired subject needn't be physically near the face; proximity in two-dimensions is sufficient to fool the AF system. Perhaps you want to photograph a close-up of a bride's hand wearing her new wedding ring, with the groom smiling in the background. If the groom's face is "close" enough to the ring in the frame, instead of a sharp photo of the bride's hand and a smiling groom (who you wanted to be out of focus for creative effect), you end up with a sharp husband and blurry wedding ring.

To use Tracking AF, just follow these steps:

1. **Choose AF-C.** Tracking works only when you are using continuous autofocus because, well, it refocuses continually.

2. **Activate Tracking AF.** Use the Function menu and choose Focus Area. Scroll down past the Expand Flexible Spot entry and highlight Tracking AF.

3. **Choose Focus Area.** Using Tracking AF does *not* mean you lose access to the AF area modes. With Tracking AF highlighted, use the left/right controls to select Wide, Zone, Center, Flexible Spot, or Expand Flexible Spot. That will give you both Tracking AF *and* the area mode you prefer. If you switch from AF-C to AF-S, you lose the lock on capabilities, and the camera just reverts to whatever focus area mode you select here.

4. **Start tracking.** When you activate focus by pressing the shutter release halfway, the camera will use your selected focus area option to lock in focus, as always. (See Figure 8.13, left.) However, once focus has been locked, the camera will *track* your subject as it roams around the screen. You'll see the green focus area box moving as your subject moves (or you reframe the image with the camera). (See Figure 8.13, right.) If a face is detected, a tracking rectangle around the face will be shown. (You'll learn more about face detection in an upcoming section.)

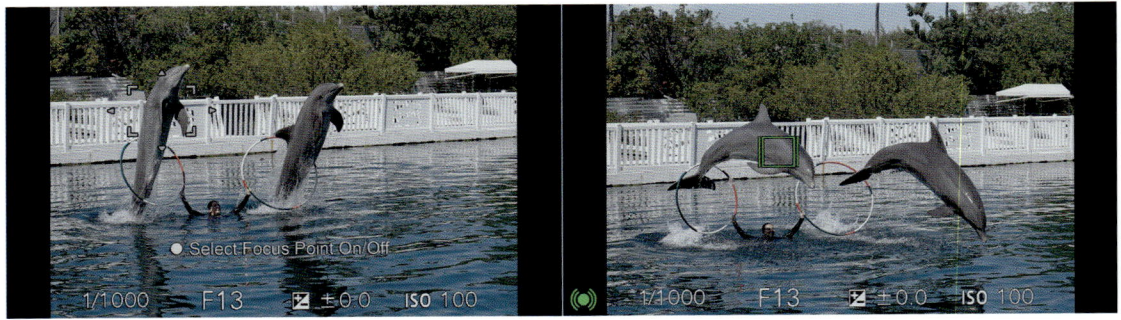

Figure 8.13 Left: Decide on the object the camera should track, center it, and press OK to instruct the a6400 as to your preferred target. Right: When Tracking is active, the camera maintains focus on your preferred target, tracking it as it moves around the scene.

Face Detection and Eye AF

As hinted already, the a6400 has a couple more tricks up its sleeve for setting the AF area. By default, Face/Eye Priority in the Face/Eye AF Settings entry of the Camera Settings I-06 menu is on, enabling the camera to attempt to identify any human faces in the scene, *and give them priority*. Note that if you want to autofocus on *some other subject* in the frame that does not include a face or eye, you should turn Face/Eye Priority off.

If the camera finds one or more faces, the camera will surround each one (up to eight in all) with a white frame on the screen. (Later, I'll discuss a feature that allows you to specify favorite faces that the camera should prioritize.) If it judges that autofocus is possible for one or more faces, it will turn the frames around those faces orange. When you press the shutter button halfway down to lock autofocus, the frames will turn green, confirming that they are in focus. The camera will also attempt to adjust exposure (including flash, if activated) as appropriate for the scene. When the a6400 detects a face, it overrides the AF Area mode you've selected, and locks onto that face (unless you've remembered to turn Face/Eye Priority off).

Face Detection is not just for autofocus; if you've turned on Face Priority in Multi Metering, the camera will also base its *exposure* on detected faces when the Metering Mode is set to Multi. I often prefer to exercise my own control as to exactly where the camera should focus, but when shooting any scene in which people are the most important (and, to a lesser extent, when capturing photos of animals), the Face/Eye Detection facility can be a useful feature. It's also an ideal choice if you need to hand the camera to someone to photograph you and your family or friends at an outing in the park.

Tracking and Faces

Face/Eye tracking when using Continuous AF is far more useful than using AF-C alone. Even without face or eye detection the camera *can* change focus as a person approaches the camera, but it's not the best feature for that purpose with a fast-action subject. With face/eye detection/tracking active, once the camera knows what your preferred human or animal subject is, it can maintain focus as it moves around the image area, as a person might do while mingling with a large group of friends at a party, or an animal going through its paces when performing a trick or chasing a ball.

Whenever a face is your target, the camera can continue tracking that person even if the face is not visible; it will then make the body the target for tracking. If you also activate the camera's Smile Shutter feature (in the Camera Settings I-14 menu) in addition to Face Detection, the camera will not only track the targeted face, but it will take a photo if your subject smiles.

Face/Eye Detection Settings

I described all five of the available Face/Eye Detection settings in detail in Chapter 3 and will not repeat that information here. However, to recap:

- **Face/Eye Priority in AF.** Choose On to give a higher priority to detected faces. Select Off and AF will proceed without looking for faces. Enabling Face/Eye Priority does *not* mean the camera will automatically focus on those areas. The face/eye must reside in your current focus area.

- **Subject Detection.** When set to Human, the camera looks for human faces and eyes. If you choose Animal instead, it looks for animal eyes only.

- **Right/Left Eye Select.** Chooses whether to detect the left or right eye of the subject.

- **Face Detection Frame Display.** The camera automatically shows a small white square around a human eye it is focusing on, and that frame will turn green when the subject is in focus. You can *also* enable a frame around entire faces.

- **Animal Eye Display.** Animal faces are not detected, but you can choose to have the camera place a frame around their eyes when they are found.

Using Manual Focus

As I noted earlier, manual focus is not as straightforward as with an older manual focus 35mm SLR equipped with a focusing screen optimized for this purpose and a readily visible focusing aid. But Sony's designers have done a good job of letting you exercise your initiative in the focusing realm, with features that make it easy to determine whether you have achieved precise focus. It's worth becoming familiar with the techniques for those occasions when it makes sense to take control in this area.

Here are the basic steps for quick and convenient setting of focus:

- **Select Manual Focus.** After you do so (in the Focus Mode entry in the Camera Settings I-05 menu), the letters MF will appear in the LCD display when you're viewing the default display that includes a lot of data. (You can change display modes by pressing the DISP button.)

- **Aim at your subject and turn the focusing ring on the lens.** As soon as you start turning the focusing ring, the image on the LCD is enlarged (magnified) to help you assess whether the center of interest of your composition is in focus. (That is, unless you turned off this feature, called MF Assist, through the Camera Settings I-13 menu.) Use the up/down/left/right directional controls to move around the magnified image area until you're viewing the most important subject element, such as a person's eyes. Turn the focusing ring until that appears to be in the sharpest possible focus.

  The enlargement lasts two seconds before the display returns to normal; you can increase that with the MF Assist Time menu item. In situations where you want to use manual focus without enlargement of the preview image, you can turn this feature off in the Custom Settings menu, using the MF Assist item.

- **If you have difficulty focusing, zoom in if possible and focus at the longest available focal length.** If you're using a zoom lens, you may find it easier to see the exact effect of slight changes in focus while zoomed in. Even if you plan to take a wide-angle photo, zoom to telephoto and rotate the ring to set precise focus on the most important subject element. When you zoom back out to take the picture, the center of interest will still be in sharp focus.

- **Use Peaking of a suitable color.** Focus peaking provides a colored overlay around edges that are sharply focused; this makes it easier to determine when your subject is precisely focused. The overlay is white, but you can change that to another color when necessary. The alternate hue may be needed to provide a strong contrast between the peaking highlights and the color of your subject. Access the Peaking Color item of the Camera Settings I-13 menu to adjust the color. To make the overlay even more visible, select High in the Peaking Level item; you can also turn peaking Off with this item, if desired.

- **Consider using the DMF option.** Your third option is DMF, or Direct Manual Focus. Activate it and the camera will autofocus with Single-shot AF and lock focus when you press the shutter release button halfway. As soon as focus is confirmed, you can turn the focusing ring to make fine-tuning adjustments, as long as you maintain slight pressure on the shutter release button. The MF Assist magnification will be activated immediately.

  This method gives you the benefit of autofocus but gives you the chance to change the exact point of focus, to a person's eyes instead of the tip of the nose, for example. This option is useful in particularly critical focusing situations, when the precise focus is essential, as in extremely close focusing on a three-dimensional subject. Because depth-of-field is very shallow in such work, you'll definitely want to focus on the most important subject element, such as the pistil or stamen inside a large blossom. This will ensure that it will be the sharpest part of the image.

Back-Button Focus

Once you've been using your camera for a while, you'll invariably encounter the terms *back focus* and *back-button focus*, and wonder if they are good things or bad things. Actually, they are *two different things,* and are often confused with each other. *Back focus* is a bad thing, and occurs when a particular lens consistently autofocuses on a plane that's *behind* your desired subject. Fortunately, that's a malady only cameras with outboard AF sensors have, so you shouldn't experience back or front focus unless you're using an EA-LA2 or EA-LA4 A-mount adapter.

Back-button focus, on the other hand, is a tool you can use to separate two functions that are commonly locked together—exposure and autofocus—so that you can lock in exposure while allowing focus to be attained at a later point, or vice versa. It's a *good* thing, although using back-button focus effectively may require you to unlearn some habits and acquire new ways of coordinating the action of your fingers.

As you have learned, the default behavior of your camera is to set both exposure and focus (when AF is active) when you press the shutter release down halfway. When using AF-S mode, that's that: both exposure and focus are locked and will not change until you release the shutter button, or press it all the way down to take a picture and then release it for the next shot. In AF-C mode, exposure is locked and focus is set when you press the shutter release halfway, but the a6400 will continue to refocus if your subject moves for as long as you hold down the shutter button halfway. Focus isn't locked until you press the button down all the way to take the picture. In AF-A mode, the camera will start out in AF-S mode, but switch to AF-C if your subject begins moving.

What back-button focus does is *decouple* or separate the two actions. You can retain the exposure lock feature when the shutter is pressed halfway, but assign autofocus *start* and/or autofocus *lock* to a different button. So, in practice, you can press the shutter button halfway, locking exposure, and reframe the image if you like (perhaps you're photographing a backlit subject and want to lock in exposure on the foreground, and then reframe to include a very bright background as well).

But, in this same scenario, you *don't* want autofocus locked at the same time. Indeed, you may not want to start AF until you're good and ready, say, at a sports venue as you wait for a ballplayer to streak into view in your viewfinder. With back-button focus, you can lock exposure on the spot where you expect the athlete to be, and activate AF at the moment your subject appears. The a6400 gives you a great deal of flexibility, both in the choice of which button to use for AF, and the behavior of that button. You can *start* autofocus, *lock* autofocus at a button press, or *lock it while holding the button*. That's where the learning of new habits and mind-finger coordination comes in. You need to learn which back-button focus techniques work for you, and when to use them.

Back-button focus lets you avoid the need to switch from AF-S to AF-C when your subject begins moving unexpectedly. Nor do you need to use AF-A and *hope* the camera switches when appropriate. You retain complete control. It's great for sports photography when you want to activate autofocus precisely based on the action in front of you. It also works for static shots. You can press and release your designated focus button, and then take a series of shots using the same focus point. Focus will not change until you once again press your defined back button.

Want to focus on a spot that doesn't reside under one of the a6400's focus areas? Use back-button focus to zero in focus on that location, then reframe. Focus will not change. Don't want to miss an important shot at a wedding or a photojournalism assignment? If you're set to *focus priority*, your camera may delay taking a picture until the focus is optimum; in *release priority* there may still be a slight delay. With back-button focus you can focus first, and wait until the decisive moment to press the shutter release and take your picture. The a6400 will respond immediately and not bother with focusing at all.

Activating Back-Button Focus

To enable back-button focus, just follow these steps:

1. **Select an AF-ON button.** In the Camera Settings II-08 menu, select Custom Key Settings.
2. **Redefine a button of your choice.** I recommend defining the AEL button as AF On. It's on the first page of the available Custom Keys. You can use a different button, even one that's not on the back panel, but activation may not be as intuitive. And, who's ever heard of Top-Button Focus, anyway?
3. **Redefine AF/MF button.** In the entry immediately above the AEL Button choice on the first page of the Custom Key Settings submenu, select AF/MF Button, and set it to AF/MF Toggle (the default is AF/MF Hold, meaning you have to hold down the button to switch between autofocus and manual focus).
4. **Turn off shutter button AF activation.** In the Camera Settings I-06 menu, set AF w/Shutter to Off. When you want to disable back-button focus (temporarily or permanently), change it back to On. The other two settings in Steps 2 and 3 can be left as-is.

That's all there is to it. Henceforth, pressing the shutter release will *not* activate autofocus. Autoexposure metering will still be initiated by pressing the button halfway, as long as the AEL w/Shutter entry in the Camera Settings I-09 menu is set to Auto or On (and *not* Off), and pressing it all the way takes a picture. You can start AF by pressing the AEL button (the switch has to be in the AEL position, rather than AF/MF; with the switch in the AF/MF position, the button will toggle between autofocus and manual focus).

Useful Menu Items for AF

I discussed how to set all the autofocus options, which are scattered among the Camera Settings I and Camera Settings II menus, plus how to define Custom Keys to activate certain features in Chapters 3 and 4. I'm not going to repeat the instructions for each menu item here. If you need a recap, here is a list of the a6400 autofocus features that you should keep in mind.

■ **AF Illuminator (Camera Settings I-06).** This menu item is set at Auto by default, indicating that the illuminator on the front of the camera will provide a burst of light in a dark location when using in AF-S mode. That provides a bright target for the autofocus system. Turn this feature off when you feel the red burst might be intrusive.

■ **Face Registration/Registered Faces Priority (Camera Settings I-14).** Mentioned briefly earlier in this chapter, this menu item is quite versatile, and was described in Chapter 3. You can register up to eight faces that should get priority in terms of autofocus and then specify the order of priority from the most important faces to the least important.

To register a face, point the camera at the person's face, make sure it's within the large square on the screen, and press the shutter release button. Do so for several faces. When you're taking a photo of a scene that contains more than one registered face, the camera will prioritize faces based on which were the first to be registered in the process you used.

Take advantage of the Order Exchanging option of this menu item so the faces you consider the most important are prioritized. When you access it, the camera displays the registered faces with a number on each; the lower the number the higher the priority. You can now change the priority in which the faces will be recognized, from 1 (say your youngest child) to 8 (perhaps your cousin twice removed). You can also use the Delete or the Delete All options to delete one or more faces from the registry, such as your ex and former in-laws.

■ **Smile Shutter (Camera Settings I-14).** If you activate this feature, the face detection system will try to find smiling faces. In fact, it will not take a photo until it finds at least one. Press the Option button (the down directional key) and you get three options: Normal Smile, Big Smile, Small Smile. Set the one you want and the camera will watch for a smile of that magnitude; it will cover the relevant face(s) with an orange frame which will turn green after focus is set. And as mentioned earlier, when the camera will be tracking a face using the Tracking AF feature while Smile Shutter is on, it will prioritize this face while doing so.

Feature Finder

Here's a summary of autofocus considerations that were discussed elsewhere in this book, primarily here and in Chapter 3 (Camera Settings I entries) and Chapter 4 (Camera Settings II entries) under the explanations of the various autofocus settings. I'll recap the most important aspects here, as a quick guide to help you locate the longer discussions, and as a way to locate the menu items themselves quickly. Table 8.1 provides some guidelines for particular types of subjects. Remember that some of these are also available in the Function menu.

- **Focus Mode (Camera Settings I-05).** Choose focus modes from AF-S, AF-C, DMF, and MF.
- **Priority Set AF-S/AF-C (Camera Settings I-05).** Select whether focus is *release priority* (take picture immediately, even if sharp focus not achieved) or *focus priority* (don't take picture until sharp focus locked in). You can also choose *balanced emphasis* as a compromise between the two. There are separate entries for AF-S and AF-C.
- **Focus Area (Camera Settings I-05).** Select the number and location of autofocus points used, from Wide, Zone, Center, Flexible Spot, Expand Flexible Spot, and Tracking.
- **Focus Area Limit (Camera Settings I-05).** Choose which focus area modes are available.
- **Switch Vertical/Horizontal AF Area (Camera Settings I-05).** Allows you to define different AF points and AF area modes for different camera orientations.
- **AF Illuminator (Camera Settings I-06).** Enables/disables use of the AF illuminator as an autofocus aid.
- **Face/Eye AF Settings (Camera Settings I-06).** Allows turning Face/Eye Detection priority on/off, specifying Human or Animal subjects, selecting right or left eyes, turning face frames on/off, and displaying a frame around animal eyes.
- **AF w/Shutter (Camera Settings I-06).** Choose On to start AF when the shutter is pressed halfway, or Off to decouple AF start from shutter release.
- **Pre-AF (Stills) (Camera Settings I-06).** Enables/disables AF start when camera is brought up to the eye.
- **Eye-Start AF (Camera Settings I-06).** AF begins when the a6400 viewfinder window is brought up to your eye. Available only when using an A-mount lens with a LA-EA2 or LA-EA4 adapter.
- **AF Area Registration (Camera Settings I-06).** Allows you to define a particular focusing position within the frame to move the focus frame at the press of a defined Custom Key.
- **Delete Registered AF Area (Camera Settings I-07).** Removes a pre-defined registered AF area that you no longer want to use.
- **AF Area Auto Clear (Custom Settings I-07).** Removes on-screen AF indicators after a period of time.
- **Display Continuous AF area (Camera Settings I-07).** Enables/disables display of AF areas during continuous autofocus.

- **Circulation of Focus Point (Camera Settings I-07).** Enables/disables wrap-around of focus point/frame as you move them toward the edges of the frame.

- **AF Micro Adjustment (Camera Settings I-07).** Fine-tune autofocus for specific A-mount lenses when used with EA-LA2 or EA-LA4 adapters. I will explain this process in Chapter 11.

- **Focus Magnifier Time (Camera Settings I-13).** Controls how long the focus magnifier is active.

- **Initial Focus Magnification (Camera Settings I-13).** Amount of magnification used when focus magnifier is invoked.

- **Autofocus in Focus Magnifier (Camera Settings I-13).** Allows using focus magnifier during autofocus.

- **Manual Focus Assist (Camera Settings I-13).** Turns manual focus magnifier on or off.

- **Peaking Settings (Camera Settings I-13).** These two settings specify the color outline of manually focused sharp areas, and the intensity of the effect.

- **AF Drive Speed (Movies) (Camera Settings II-02).** Choose between slow and accurate AF, or fast and slightly less accurate in video mode.

- **AF Tracking Sensitivity (Movie) (Camera Settings II-02).** Adjust how long the camera waits to refocus on intervening objects when shooting movies.

Table 8.1 Focus Guidelines

Subject	Focus Mode	Focus Area	Priority Setup	Face/Eye Detection
Portraits	AF-S	Flexible Spot	AF	On
Street photography	AF-C	Wide	Balanced Emphasis	On
General sports action	AF-C	Tracking AF: Expand Flexible Spot: Medium	Release	Off
Birds in Flight	AF-C	Tracking AF: Expand Flexible Spot: Medium	Balanced Emphasis	Off
Football, soccer, basketball	AF-C	Tracking AF: Expand Flexible Spot: Small	Release	Off
Kids, Pets	AF-C	Zone	Balanced Eemphasis	On
Track events, auto racing	AF-C	Wide	Release	Off
Landscapes	AF-S	Wide	AF	Off
Concerts, performances	AF-S	Flexible Spot	AF	On

9

Advanced Shooting

Of the primary foundations of great photography, only one of them—the ability to capture a compelling image with a pleasing composition—takes a lifetime (or longer) to master. The art of *making* a photograph, rather than just *taking* a photograph, requires an aesthetic eye that sees the right angle for the shot, as well as a sense of what should be included or excluded in the frame; a knowledge of what has been done in the medium before (and where photography can be taken in the future); and a willingness to explore new areas. The more you pursue photography, the more you will learn about visualization and composition. When all is said and done, this is what photography is all about.

The other basics of photography—equally essential—involve more technical aspects: the ability to use your camera's features to produce an image with good tonal and color values; to achieve sharpness (where required) or unsharpness (when you're using selective focus); and to master appropriate white/color balance. It's practical to learn these technical skills in a time frame that's much less than a lifetime, although most of us find there is always room for improvement. You'll find the basic information you need to become proficient in each of these technical areas in this book.

The final and most rewarding stage comes when you begin exploring advanced techniques that enable you to get stunning shots that will have your family, friends, and colleagues asking you, "How did you *do* that?" These more advanced techniques deserve an entire book of their own, but there is plenty of room in this chapter to introduce you to some clever things you can do with your a6400.

Exploring Ultra-Fast Exposures

Fast shutter speeds (such as 1/1000th second) can stop action because they capture only a tiny slice of time: a high-jumper frozen in mid-air, perhaps. The Sony a6400 has a top shutter speed of 1/4000th second for ambient light exposures. Electronic flash can also freeze motion by virtue of its extremely short duration—as brief as 1/50000th second or less. When you're using flash, the short duration of the actual burst of light can freeze a moving subject; that can also give you an ultra-quick glimpse of a moving subject when the scene is illuminated only by flash.

The a6400 is fully capable of immobilizing all but the very fastest movement if you use a shutter speed of 1/4000th second (without flash). Some cameras have speeds up to 1/8000th second or higher, but those are generally overkill when it comes to stopping action; I can rarely find a situation where even 1/4000th second is required to freeze high-speed motion. For example, each of the images shown in Figure 9.1 required a shutter speed of just 1/2000th second to freeze the action.

Virtually all sports action can be captured at 1/2000th second or a slower shutter speed, and for many sports a slower shutter speed is actually preferable—for example, to allow the wheels of a racing automobile or motorcycle, or the propeller on a classic aircraft, to blur realistically.

There may be a few situations where a shutter speed faster than 1/4000th second is required. If you wanted to use an aperture of f/1.8 at ISO 100 outdoors in bright sunlight, say, to throw a background out of focus with the shallow depth-of-field available at f/1.8, a shutter speed of 1/4000th second would more than do the job. You'd need a faster shutter speed only if you set a higher ISO, and you probably wouldn't do that if your goal were to use the widest aperture possible. Under *less*

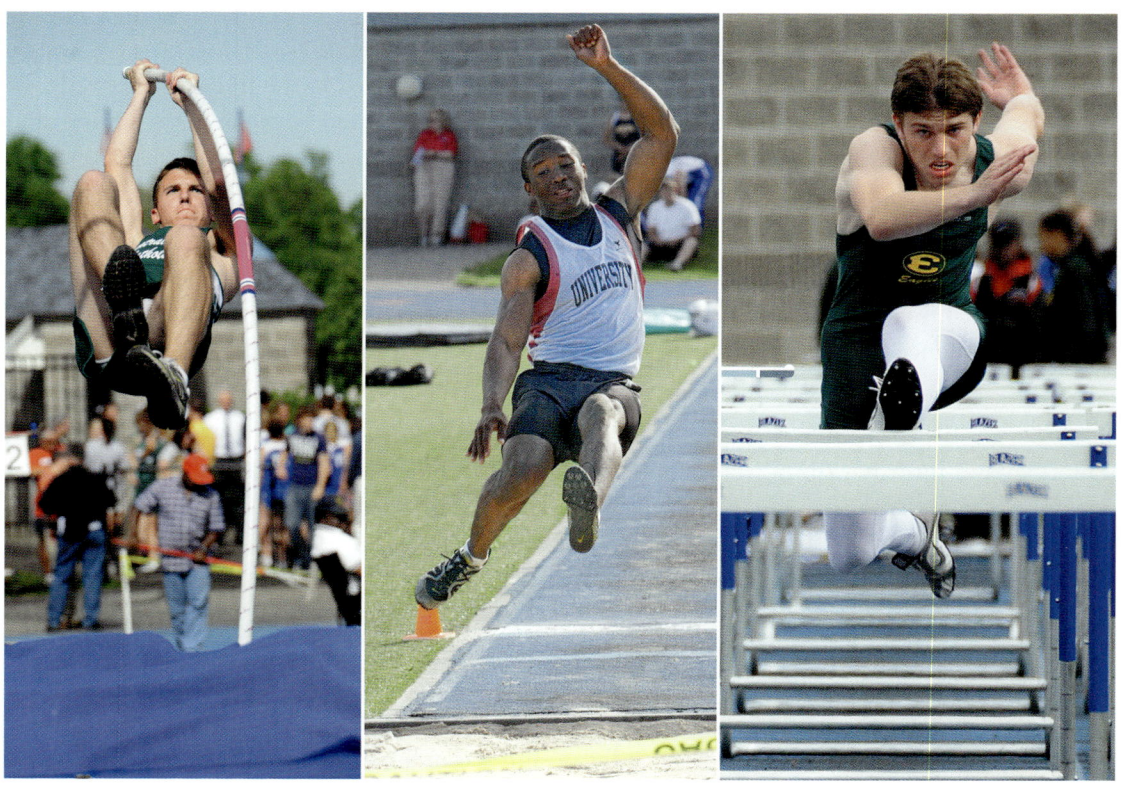

Figure 9.1 A shutter speed of 1/2000th second will freeze most action.

than full sunlight, I doubt you'd even need to use a shutter speed of 1/4000th second in any situations you're likely to encounter.

Electronic flash works well for freezing the motion of a nearby subject when flash is the only source of illumination. Since the subject is illuminated for only a split second, you get the effect that would be provided by a very fast shutter speed and also the high level of light needed for an exposure. This feature can be useful for stopping the motion of a nearby subject.

Of course, as you'll see in Chapter 12, the tiny slices of time extracted by the millisecond duration of an electronic flash exact a penalty. To use flash, the a6400 employs a shutter speed no faster than 1/160th second, which is the fastest shutter speed—called sync speed—in flash photography with your a6400.

You can have a lot of fun exploring the kinds of pictures you can take using very brief exposure times, whether you decide to take advantage of the action-stopping shutter speeds (between 1/1000th and 1/4000th second) or the brief burst of light from flash that can freeze the motion of a nearby subject. Here are a few ideas to get you started:

- **Take revealing images.** Fast shutter speeds can help you reveal the real subject behind the façade, by freezing constant motion to capture an enlightening moment in time. Legendary fashion/portrait photographer Philippe Halsman used leaping photos of famous people, such as the Duke and Duchess of Windsor, Richard Nixon, and Salvador Dali, to illuminate their real selves. Halsman said, *"When you ask a person to jump, his attention is mostly directed toward the act of jumping and the mask falls so that the real person appears."* Try some high-speed portraits of people you know in motion to see how they appear when concentrating on something other than the portrait.

- **Create unreal images.** High-speed photography can also produce photographs that show your subjects in ways that are quite unreal. A helicopter in mid-air with its rotors frozen or a motocross cyclist leaping over a ramp, but with all motion stopped so that the rider and machine look as if they were frozen in mid-air, makes for an unusual picture. (See the frozen rotors at top in Figure 9.2.) When we're accustomed to seeing subjects in motion, seeing them stopped in time can verge on the surreal.

- **Capture unseen perspectives.** Some things are *never* seen in real life, except when viewed in a stop-action photograph. MIT professor Dr. Harold Edgerton's famous balloon burst photographs were only a starting point for the inventor of the electronic flash unit. Freeze a hummingbird in flight for a view of wings that never seem to stop. Or, capture the splashes as liquid falls into a bowl, as shown in Figure 9.3. No electronic flash was required for this image (and wouldn't have illuminated the water in the bowl as evenly). Instead, a clutch of high-intensity lamps bounced off a green card and an ISO setting of 1600 allowed the camera to capture this image at 1/2000th second.

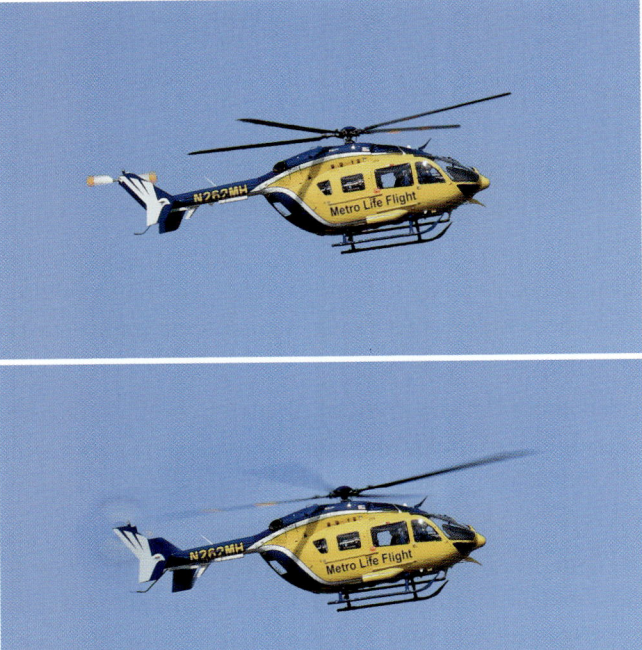

Figure 9.2
Freezing a helicopter's rotors with a fast shutter speed makes for an image that doesn't look natural (top); a little blur helps convey a feeling of motion (bottom).

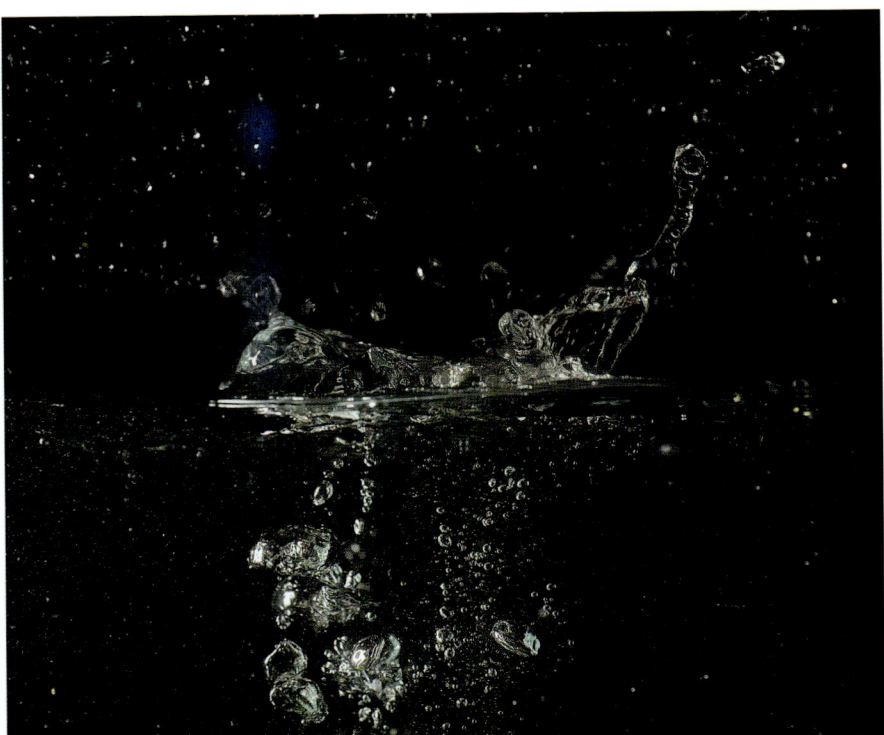

Figure 9.3
A large amount of artificial illumination and an ISO 1600 setting made it possible to capture this shot at 1/2000th second without use of electronic flash.

Long Exposures

Longer exposures are a doorway into another world, showing us how even familiar scenes can look much different when photographed over periods measured in seconds. At night, long exposures produce streaks of light from moving, illuminated subjects like automobiles or amusement park rides. Or, you can move the camera or zoom the lens to get interesting streaks from non-moving light sources, such as the Ferris wheel lights shown in Figure 9.4. Extra-long exposures of seemingly pitch-dark subjects can reveal interesting views using light levels barely bright enough to see by. At any time of day, including daytime (in which case you'll often need the help of neutral-density filters to make the long exposure practical), long exposures can cause moving objects to vanish entirely, because they don't remain stationary long enough to register in a photograph.

Because the a6400 produces such good images at longer timed exposures, and there are so many creative things you can do with long-exposure techniques, you'll want to do some experimenting. Get yourself a tripod or another firm support and take some test shots with long exposure noise reduction both enabled and disabled in the Camera Settings menu (to see whether you prefer low noise or high detail) and get started.

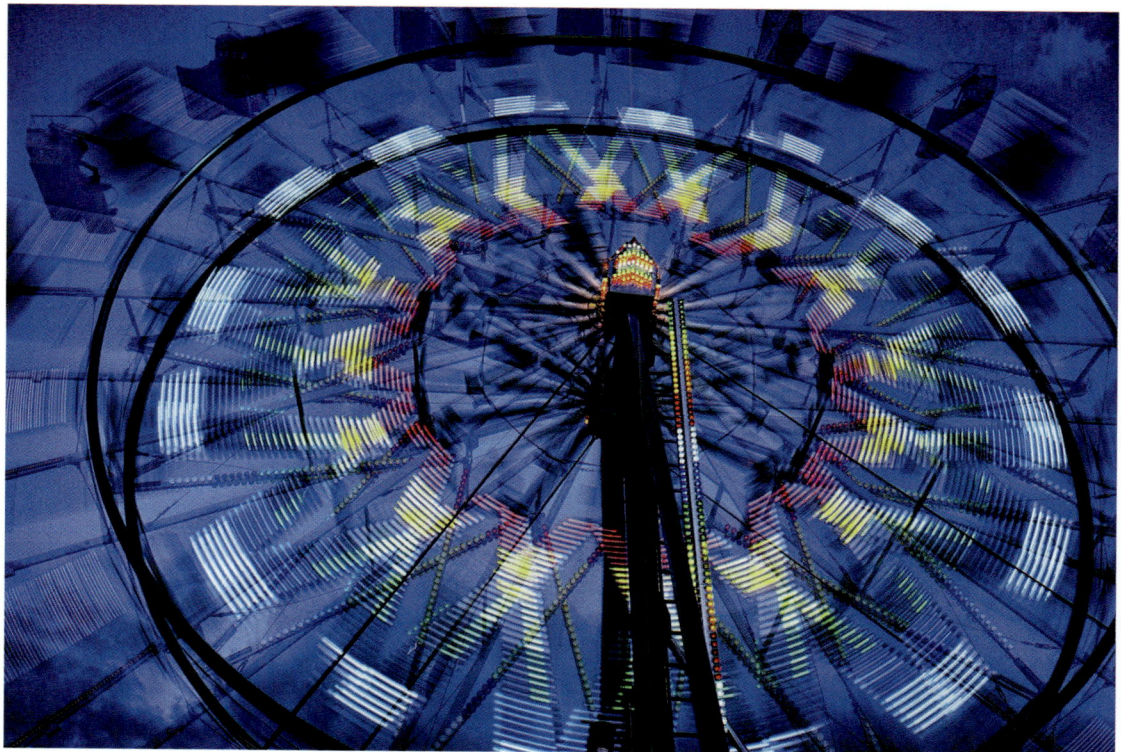

Figure 9.4 Zooming during a long exposure can produce interesting streaks of light.

Here are some things to try:

- **Make people invisible.** One very cool thing about long exposures is that objects that move rapidly enough won't register at all in a photograph, while the subjects that remain stationary are portrayed in the normal way. That makes it easy to produce people-free landscape photos and architectural photos at night, or even in full daylight if you use one or more dark neutral-density filters to allow an exposure of at least a few seconds. At ISO 100 and f/16, for example, a pair of 8X (three-stop) neutral-density filters will allow you to make an exposure of nearly two seconds on a sunny day. Overcast days and/or even more neutral-density filtration would work even better if daylight people vanishing is your goal. They'll have to be walking *very* briskly and across the field of view (rather than directly toward the camera) for this to work. At night, it's much easier to achieve this effect with the 20- to 30-second exposures that are possible in low light without any filter.

- **Create streaks.** If you aren't shooting for total invisibility, long exposures with the camera on a tripod can produce some interesting streaky effects. Even a single 8X ND filter will let you shoot at f/22 and 1/6th second in daylight. Indoors, you can achieve interesting streaks with slow shutter speeds, as shown in Figure 9.5. I shot the ballet dancers using a 1/2-second exposure, triggering the shot at the beginning of a movement.

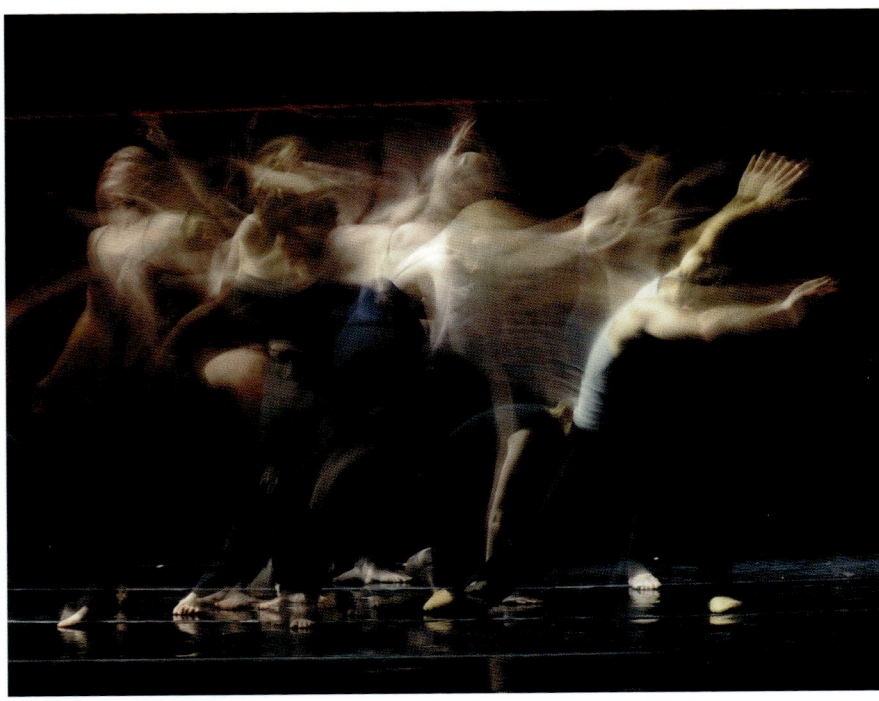

Figure 9.5
The shutter opened as the dancers began their movement from a standing position, and finished about one-half second later when they had bent over and paused.

Tip

Neutral-density filters are gray (non-colored) filters that reduce the amount of light passing through the lens, without adding any color or effect of their own.

- **Produce light trails.** At night, car headlights, taillights, and other moving sources of illumination can generate interesting light trails. Your camera doesn't even need to be mounted on a tripod; hand-holding the camera for longer exposures adds movement and patterns to your trails. If you're shooting fireworks, a longer exposure—with the camera on a tripod—may allow you to combine several bursts into one picture, as shown in Figure 9.6.

- **Blur waterfalls, etc.** You'll find that waterfalls and other sources of moving liquid produce a special type of long-exposure blur, because the water merges into a fantasy-like veil that looks different at different exposure times, and with different waterfalls. Cascades with turbulent flow produce a rougher look at a given longer exposure than falls that flow smoothly. Although blurred waterfalls and rapids have become almost a cliché, there are still plenty of variations for a creative photographer to explore. Figure 9.7 illustrates some waves breaking over rocks on a Mediterranean shoreline.

Figure 9.6
I caught the fireworks after a baseball game from a half-mile away, using a four-second exposure to capture several bursts in one shot.

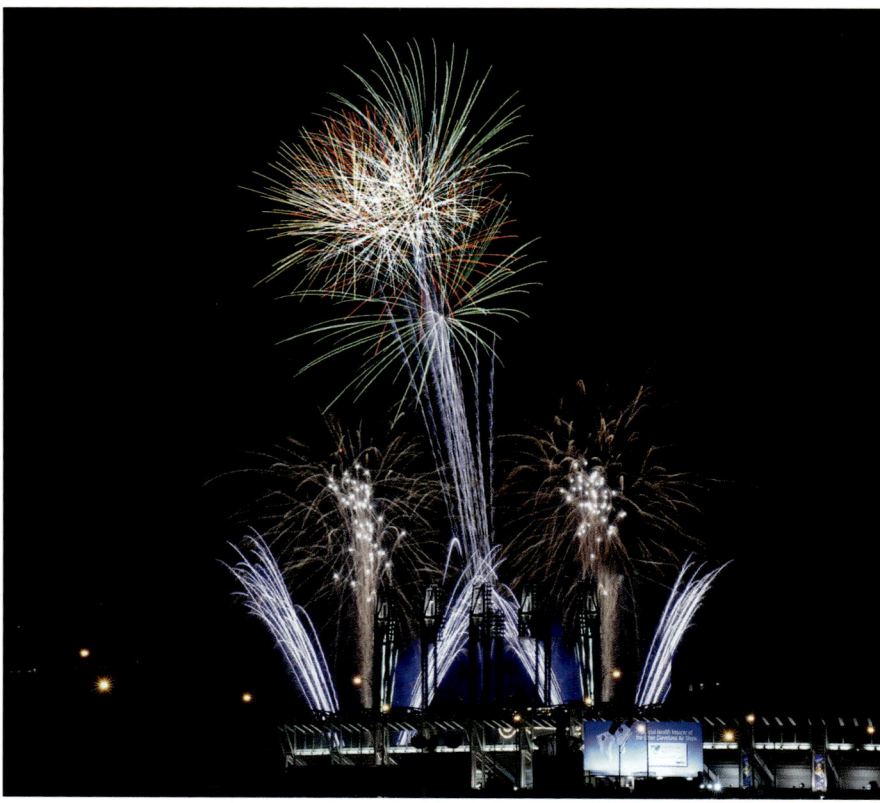

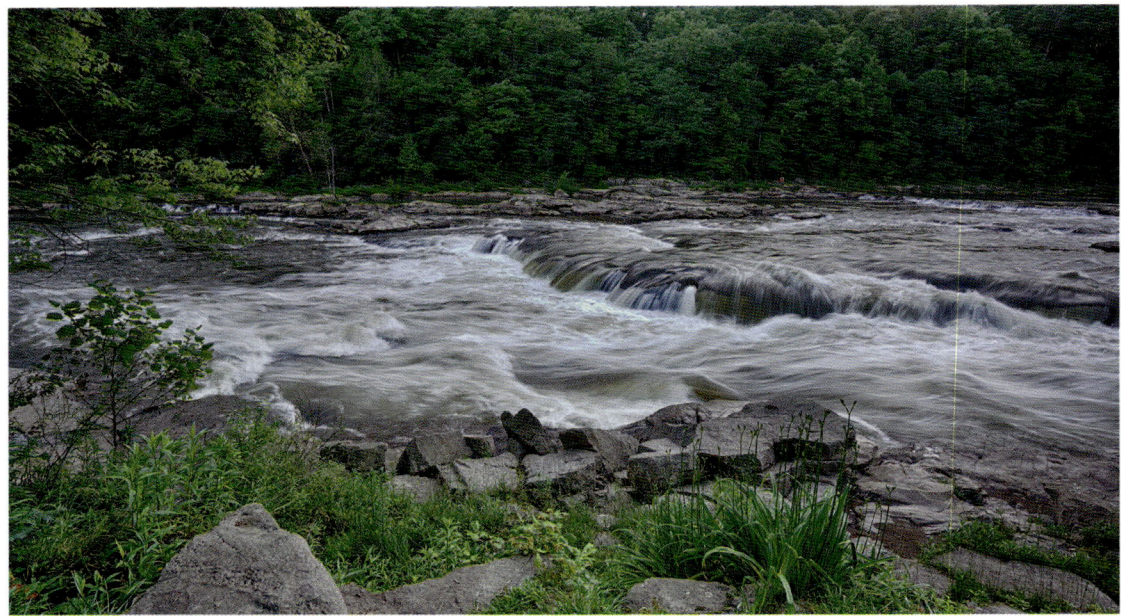

Figure 9.7 A long exposure can produce an impression of motion in a still photo.

- **Show total darkness in new ways.** Even on the darkest, moonless nights, there is enough starlight or glow from distant illumination sources to see by, and, if you use a long exposure, there is enough light to take a picture, too. I was visiting a Great Lakes park hours after sunset, but found that a several-second exposure revealed the skyline scene shown in Figure 9.8, even though in real life, there was barely enough light to make out the boats in the distance. Although the photo appears as if it were taken at twilight or sunset, in fact the shot was made at 10 p.m.

Continuous Shooting

The a6400's continuous shooting mode is one of the most outstanding features of the camera. Frame rates of up to 11 fps—with autofocus—are indispensable for the sports photographer, and useful for anyone photographing an event in which, even if you have lightning-fast reflexes, a decisive moment may occur a fraction of a second after you've completed an exposure. At an air show I covered earlier this year, I took more than 1,000 images in a couple hours. I was able to cram hundreds of Large/Fine JPEGs on a single memory card. That's a lot of shooting. Given an average burst of about eight frames per sequence at the camera's highest frame (nobody really takes 15 to 20 shots or more of one pass, even with a slow-moving biplane as shown in Figure 9.9), I was able to capture more than 100 different sequences like the one shown before I needed to swap cards. For some types of action (such as football), even longer bursts come in handy, because running and passing plays

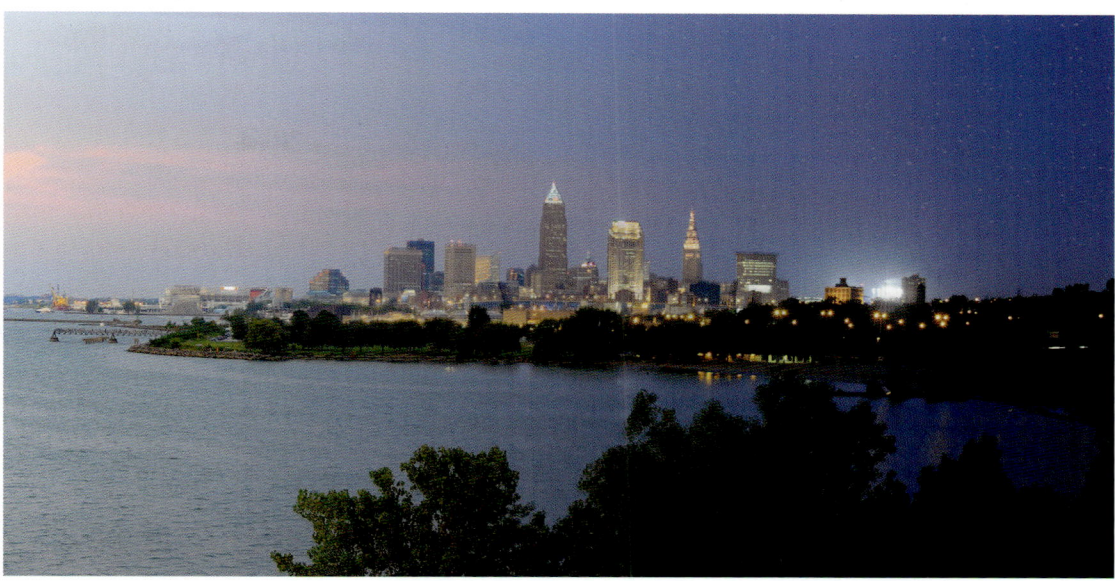

Figure 9.8 A long exposure transformed this night scene into a picture apparently taken at dusk.

Figure 9.9
Air shows make a
perfect subject for
continuous bursts.

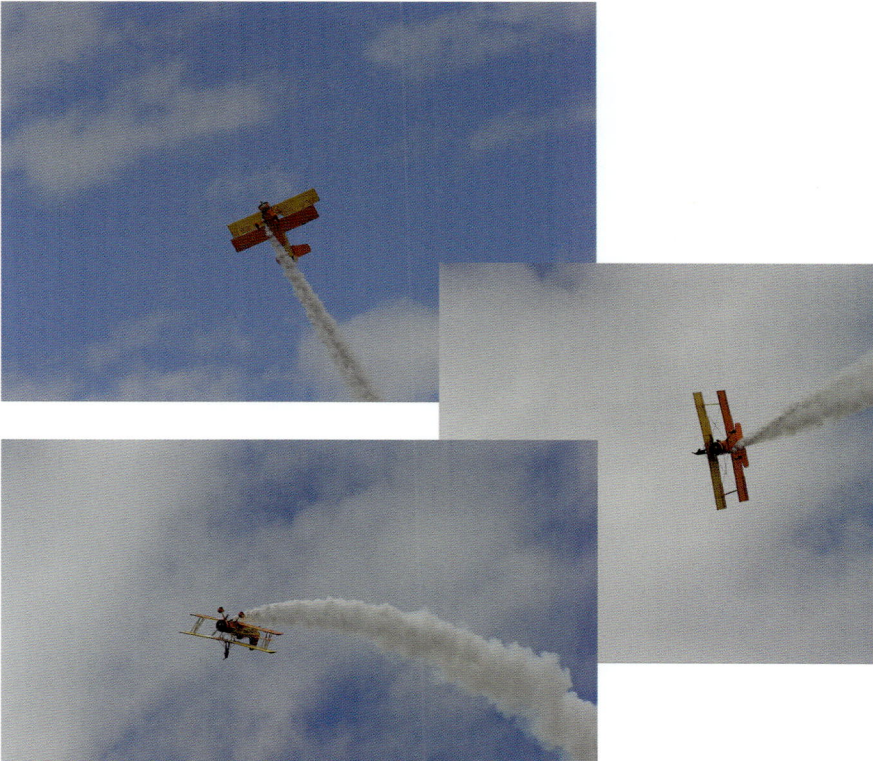

often last 5 to 10 seconds; there's also a change in character as the action switches from the quarterback dropping back to pass or hand off the ball, then to the receiver or running back trying to gain as much yardage as possible. (See Figure 9.10.)

To use the a6400's continuous advance mode, press the drive button (left directional button), access the Function menu, or go to the Drive Mode entry in the Camera Settings I-03 menu. Then navigate to the Cont. Shooting option. Press the left/right buttons to select Hi+ (11 fps), Hi (8 fps), Med (6 fps), or Lo (3 fps). To get the maximum frame rates, set the e-Front Curtain Shutter option in the Camera Settings II-04 menu to On.

If you set the AF mode (in the Function submenu) to AF-C, Continuous autofocus (with phase detection AF) will be available in all continuous drive modes, but only as long as the subject is covered by the active focus detection point(s). This feature is useful when a moving subject is approaching the camera or moving away from it; the a6400 will continuously adjust to focus on the subject as the distance changes, so the entire set of photos should be sharply focused.

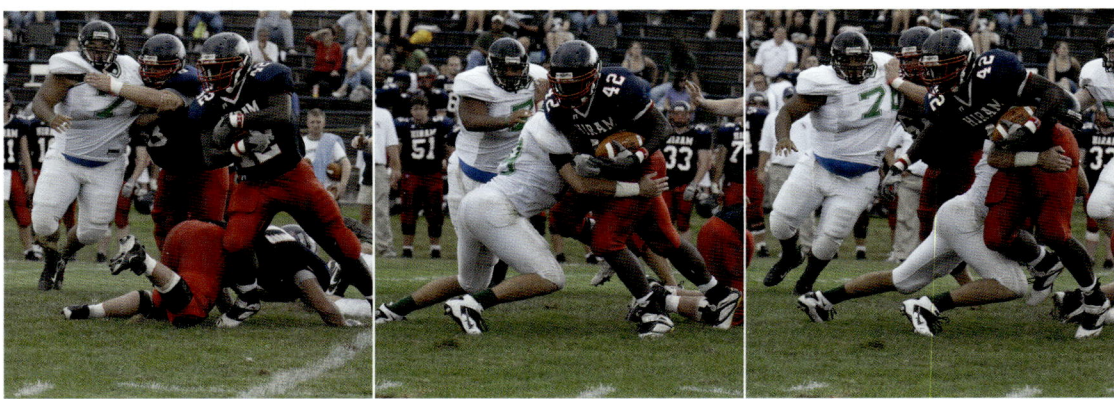

Figure 9.10 Continuous shooting allows you to capture an entire sequence of exciting moments as they unfold.

SOUNDS OF SILENCE

One thing I can guarantee any time you are firing off 11 frames per second is that bystanders will make comments about the rapid-fire machine-gun noises emanating from your a6400. Your first impulse may be to consider using the camera's cool "Silent Shooting" mode found in the Camera Settings II-04 menu. It is a truly silent shooting mode. The trade-off? You can't shoot with Hi+, Hi, or Med continuous drive modes. In fact, you can only use the "Continuous Shooting: Lo" mode so don't expect to be able to shoot with high FPS in the silent mode. Additionally, the following functions are not available for you to use in tandem with "Silent Mode": Flash shooting, Auto HDR, Picture Effect, Picture Profile, Long Exposure NR, e-Front Curtain Shutter, S. Auto Img. Extract, Bulb shooting, or Multi Frame NR. That being said, it is great when you don't want to scare off an animal or insect, or you wish to be a little more incognito.

TIP

Set Focus Mode to Continuous AF (AF-C) and AEL w/Shutter to Off or Auto, and the same exposure and focus setting will be retained for an entire burst. The a6400 will not attempt to refocus or adjust exposure between frames. You'd find this useful for sequences that will be shown as individual shots, and which should have a similar appearance.

When using the Hi+ setting to shoot at 11 fps, you may notice a little lag on your viewing screen, as the a6400 is displaying the most recent shot you took rather than the real-time sensor image. A slower frame rate, such as Hi (at 8 fps) allows, the camera to show the real-time image on the EVF or LCD monitor without the annoying lag.

Continuous shooting is not available if you're using Sweep Panorama; if you select a scene mode other than Sports Action; when DRO/Auto HDR is set to Auto HDR; when Smile Shutter is enabled; or when Picture Effect is set to Soft Focus, HDR Painting, Rich-tone Mono, Miniature, Watercolor, or Illustration. Continuous shooting is also disabled when ISO is set to Multi Frame NR, or if your battery level is low.

Once you have decided on a continuous shooting mode and speed, press the center button to confirm your choice. Then, while you hold down the shutter button, the a6400 will fire continuously until it reaches the limit of its capacity to absorb images in its memory buffer, given the image size and quality you have selected and other factors, such as the speed of your memory card and the environment you are shooting in. You can expect to capture up to 11 frames in one burst when shooting RAW, and as many as 44 frames of JPEG images.

The reason the cameras cannot let you shoot hundreds of photos in a single burst is that continuous images are first shuttled into the a6400's internal memory buffer, then doled out to the memory card as quickly as the card can write the data. Technically, the camera takes the data received from the digital image processor and converts it to the output format you've selected—either JPEG or RAW or both—and deposits it in the buffer ready to store on the card.

The internal "smart" buffer can suck up photos much more quickly than the memory card and, indeed, some memory cards are significantly faster or slower than others. When the buffer begins to fill, the framing speed slows significantly; eventually the buffer fills and then you can't take any more continuous shots until the a6400 has dumped some of them to the card, making more room in the buffer. (If you often need to shoot long bursts, be sure to use a fast memory card, rated at least as Class 10 with 30 to 95MB/s or faster writing speeds, since it can write images more quickly than a slower card, freeing up buffer space faster; this allows for shooting a longer series of photos.)

So, if you're in a situation in which continuous shooting is an issue, you may need to make some quick judgments. If you're taking photos at a breaking news event where it's crucial to keep the camera firing no matter what and quality of the images is not a huge issue, your best bet may be to set the image size to Small and the quality to Standard. On the other hand, if you're taking candid shots at a family gathering and want to capture a variety of fleeting expressions on people's faces, you may opt for taking Large size shots at the Fine quality setting, knowing that the drive speed may slow occasionally; if using a fast card however, I doubt you'll find that to be a problem unless you want to shoot several dozen photos in a burst (unlikely). A good thing to bear in mind at all times is that the speeds given for the four Continuous shooting options are *maximums* that can be reached; you may find the speed slower when the camera has difficulty maintaining focus on an erratically moving subject (in AF-C mode) and it will definitely be slower when you're not using a fast shutter speed.

Customizing White Balance

Back when we were shooting with 35mm cameras, color films were standardized, or balanced, for a particular "color" of light. Most were balanced for daylight, but you could also buy "tungsten" balanced film for shooting under incandescent lamps that produced light of an amber color. This type of film had a bluish color balance, intended to moderate the effect produced by light that was amber. Nothing of this type is necessary with digital cameras like the Sony a6400 because you can set any white balance option that will be suitable considering the color of the light.

This is important because various light sources produce illumination of different "colors," although sometimes we are not aware of the difference. Indoor illumination tends to be somewhat amber when using light bulbs that are not daylight balanced, while noonday light outdoors is close to white, and the light early and late in the day is somewhat red/yellow.

White balance is measured using a scale called color temperature. Color temperatures were assigned by heating a theoretical "black body radiator" and recording the spectrum of light it emitted at a given temperature in degrees Kelvin. So, daylight at noon has a color temperature in the 5,500K to 6,000K degree range. Indoor illumination is around 3,400K degrees. Hotter temperatures produce bluer images (think blue-white hot) while cooler temperatures produce redder images (think of a dull-red glowing ember). Because of human nature, though, bluer images are actually called "cool" (think wintry day) and redder images are called "warm" (think ruddy sunset), even though their color temperatures are reversed.

Take a photo indoors under warm illumination with a digital camera sensor balanced for cooler daylight and the image will appear much too red/yellow. An image exposed outdoors with the white balance set for incandescent (tungsten) illumination will seem much too blue. These color casts may be too strong to remove in an image editor from JPEG files. Of course, if you shoot RAW photos, you can later change the WB setting to the desired value in RAW converter software; this is a completely "non-destructive" process so full image quality will be maintained.

Mismatched white balance settings are easier to achieve accidentally than you might think, even for experienced photographers. I'd just arrived at a concert after shooting some photos indoors with electronic flash and had manually set WB for Flash. Then, as the concert began, I resumed shooting using the incandescent stage lighting—which looked white to the eye—and ended up with a few shots like Figure 9.11 (left). Eventually, I caught the error during picture review, and changed my white balance. Another time, I was shooting outdoors, but had the camera white balance still set for incandescent illumination, resulting in the excessively blue image shown in Figure 9.11 (right).

The Auto White Balance (AWB) setting, available from the White Balance item of the Camera Settings I-11 menu, examines your scene and chooses an appropriate value based on its perception of the color of the illumination and even the colors in the scene. However, the process is not fool-proof (with any camera). Under bright lighting conditions, it may evaluate the colors in the image and still assume the light source is daylight and balance the picture accordingly, even though, in fact, you may be shooting under extremely bright incandescent illumination. In dimmer light, the camera's electronics may assume that the illumination is tungsten, and if there are lots of reddish colors present, set color balance for that type of lighting. With mercury vapor or sodium lamps, correct white balance may be virtually impossible to achieve with any of the so-called presets. In those cases, you should use flash instead, or Custom WB with JPEGs, or shoot in RAW format and make your corrections after importing the file into your image editor with a RAW converter.

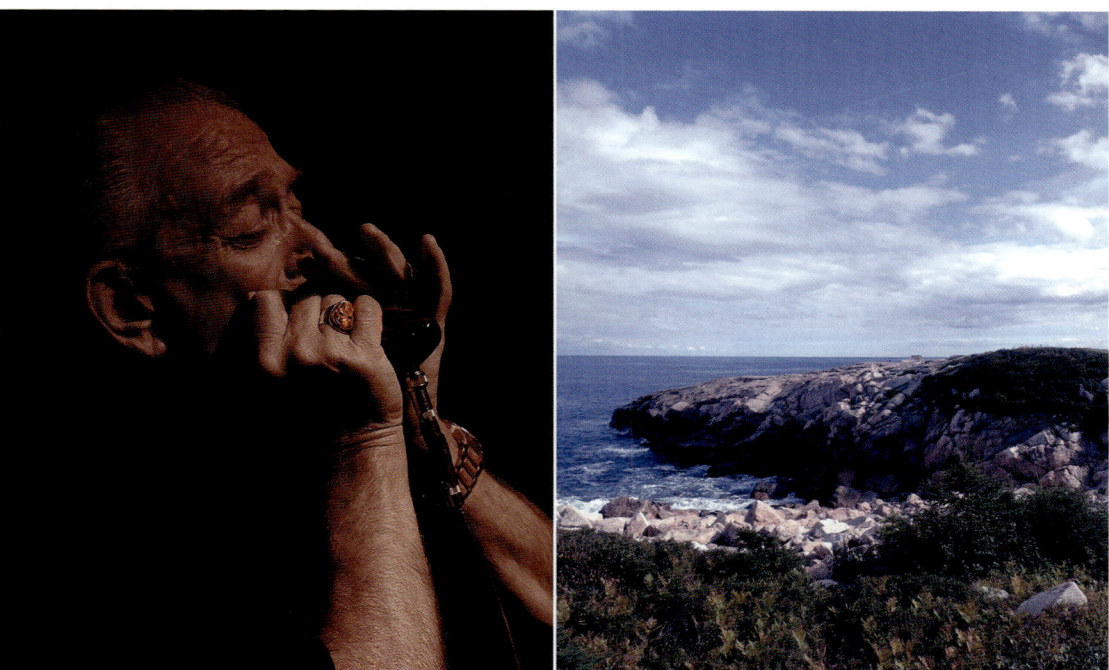

Figure 9.11 An image exposed indoors with the WB set for daylight or electronic flash will appear too reddish (left). An image exposed in daylight with the WB set for incandescent (tungsten) illumination will appear too blue (right).

The a6400 provides many WB options, often called presets by photographers, each intended for use in specific lighting conditions. You can choose from Daylight, Shade, Cloudy, Incandescent (often called Tungsten by photographers), four types of Fluorescent (Warm White, Cool White, Day White, and Daylight), Flash, and Underwater Auto. However, the a6400 also offers a method for setting a desired color temperature/filter as well as a custom WB feature.

The Daylight preset provides WB at 5,200K, while the Shade preset uses 7,000K to give you a warming effect that's useful in the bluish light of a deeply shaded area. The chief difference between direct sun and an area in shade, or even incandescent light sources, is nothing more than the proportions of red and blue light. The spectrum of colors used by the a6400 is continuous, but it is biased toward one end or the other.

However, some types of fluorescent lights produce illumination that has a severe deficit in certain colors, such as only particular shades of red. If you looked at the spectrum or rainbow of colors encompassed by such a light source, it would have black bands in it, representing particular wavelengths of light that are absent. You can't compensate for this deficiency by adding all tones of red. That's why the fluorescent setting of your Sony may provide less than satisfactory results with some kinds of fluorescent bulbs. If you take many photographs under a particular kind of non-compatible fluorescent light, you might want to investigate specialized filters intended for use under various types of fluorescent light, available from camera stores, or develop skills in white balance adjustment using an image editor or RAW converter software program. However, you do get four presets for fluorescent WB with the a6400 and one of these should provide close to accurate white balance with the common types of lights.

It's when you find that AWB and the various presets simply cannot produce pleasing white balance in a certain lighting conditions that you'll need the other options (discussed shortly): use the white balance adjustment feature, set a specific color temperature, or calibrate the WB system to set a custom white balance.

Fine-Tuning Preset White Balance

After you scroll to any of the WB options (AWB, Daylight, Shade, etc.), pressing the right directional button reveals the White Balance Adjustment screen, with a grid, shown in Figure 9.12. This feature enables you to fine-tune the white balance by biasing it toward certain colors. Use any of the four directional keys to move the orange dot (cursor) from the center of the grid: upward to bias the WB toward green (G), downward toward magenta (M), right toward amber (A), or left toward blue (B). You can move the cursor seven increments (although Sony doesn't reveal exactly what those increments are) in any of the four directions.

Naturally, you can also move the orange dot to any point within the grid: toward amber/magenta, for example. While biasing the WB, examine the scene in the LCD or viewfinder preview display; stop making adjustments when the white balance looks fine. The camera will visually change to match your new setting if you've set Live View Display in the Camera Settings II-07 menu to

Figure 9.12

Use this feature when you want to fine-tune white balance when using AWB or any of the presets.

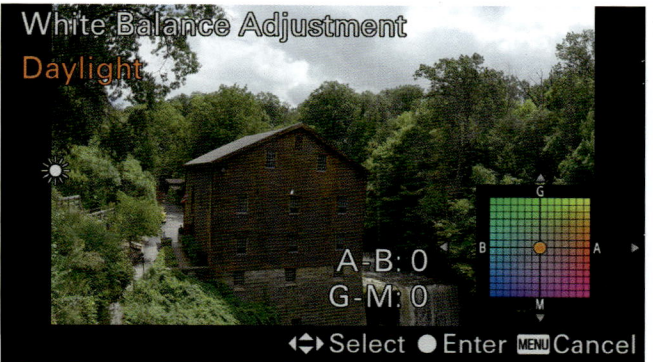

Setting Effect On. Tap the shutter release to escape from the WB settings adjustments. Let's look at the options in more detail:

- **Cooler or warmer.** Pressing the left/right directional buttons changes the white balance to cooler (left) or warmer (right) along the Blue/Amber scale. There are seven increments, and the value you "dial in" will be shown in the upper-left corner of the screen as an A-B value (yes, the labels are *reversed* from the actual scale at the right side of the screen). The red dot will move along the scale to show the value you've selected. Typically, blue/amber adjustments are what we think of as "color temperature" changes, or, "cooler" and "warmer." These correspond to the way in which daylight illumination changes: warm at sunrise and sunset, very cool in the shade (because most of the illumination comes from reflections of the blue sky), and very cool at high noon. Indoor light sources can also be cooler or warmer, depending on the kind of light they emit.

- **Green/magenta bias.** Press the up/down buttons to change the color balance along the green (upward) or magenta (downward) directions. Seven increments are provided here, too, and shown as vertical movement in the color balance matrix at the right of the screen. Color changes of this type tend to reflect special characteristics of the light source; certain fluorescent lights have a "green" cast, for example.

- **Either or both.** Because the blue/amber and green/magenta adjustments can be made independently, you're free to choose just one of them, or both if your fine-tuning requires it.

- **Never mind.** If you want to cancel all fine-tuning and shift back to neutral, just press the down directional button. The red dot in the color chart will be restored to the center position.

Setting White Balance by Color Temperature

If you want to set a specific white balance based on color temperature, choose C. Temp/Filter in the White Balance menu and press the right button. You'll see an adjustment screen similar to the one shown in Figure 9.12, but with a scrolling list of color temperatures displayed along the right edge of the screen.

Here's how to use this feature.

- **Change color temperature.** Rotate the control wheel on the camera back to select a specific color temperature in 100K increments, from 2,500K (a level that makes your image much bluer, to compensate for amber illumination) to 9,900K (a level that makes images much redder to correct for light that is extremely blue in color). The live preview changes as you scroll to give you an indication as to the white balance you can expect at any K level. If you have a color temperature meter accessory, or reliable tips that guide you in making the optimal setting, this WB feature will be particularly useful. Even if you don't have that accessory or useful information, you may want to experiment with this setting using the live preview, especially if you are trying to achieve creative effects with color casts along the spectrum from blue to red.

- **Fine-tune the color temperature.** In addition to color temperature, you can change the blue/amber or green magenta bias, exactly as described earlier; move the cursor in any direction with the directional keys. If you change your mind, press the MENU button to cancel the bias adjustments you've made.

  This feature corresponds to the use of CC (Color Compensation) filters that were used to compensate for various types of lighting when shooting film. When you use C. Temp/Filter, the color filter value you set takes effect in conjunction with the color temperature you set. In other words, both of these settings work together to give you very precise control over the degree of color correction you are using.

Setting a Custom White Balance

If you often shoot in locations that are illuminated by artificial light of unusual colors, the best bet is to set a custom white balance. This calls for teaching (calibrating) the WB system to render white as white under a specific type of illumination. When white is accurately rendered, other colors will look accurate as well. You can use this feature under more common types of lighting too; it's very useful under tungsten lamps, for example, when the Incandescent WB option does not adequately correct for the amber color of the light. Custom WB is the most accurate way of getting the right color balance, short of having a special meter that gives you a precise reading of color temperature. It's easy to do with the a6400. Just follow these steps:

1. Navigate to White Balance in the Camera Settings I-11 menu.

2. Use the directional buttons or the control wheel to scroll up/down through the list of white balance options until the Custom Setup (not the Custom entry, which is located just above it) option is highlighted. Press the center button. The LCD will display a message telling you to press the shutter button to capture the white balance data. (Custom is used to *choose* the custom WB setting you have saved; Custom Setup *creates* that setting.)

3. Point the camera at a white object (such as a sheet of white paper) large enough to fill the small circle that's displayed in the center of the frame. Your target must be in the same light as the subject you plan to photograph, not in some entirely different part of the scene where the illumination is different.

4. Press the shutter release button. The target (such as the sheet of white paper) that you had aimed at, as well as the custom white balance data, appears on the LCD or EVF screen. (The image is not recorded to the memory card.)

5. Press the center button to return to the live view on the LCD.

The a6400 will retain the custom setting you just captured until you repeat the process to replace the setting with a new one. At any time in the future, you can activate this custom WB setting; that would make sense anytime you'll be shooting in the same type of lighting that was present when you calibrated the system. To do so, scroll to the Custom (not Custom Setup) option in the White Balance menu and press the center button to confirm your choice.

Interval Shooting

I introduced you to interval shooting in Chapter 3, where I listed all the options and settings in the Camera Settings I-03 menu's Interval Shooting Function entry. As I noted there, with previous Sony cameras, this very popular feature has previously required a special app or external device to trigger successive shots over a specific period of time. Today, interval shooting is built right into your a6400's capabilities (and has been added to some other Sony models via a firmware upgrade).

This section will help you get the most from this capability, and provide some ideas for setting up and capturing your own sequences. There is a lot more to interval shooting than you might think. Here are a few to get you started:

- **Time-lapse nature movies.** Although interval shooting captures a series of *still* images, which you can view one at a time, it's easy to combine a set of consecutive exposures to create a time-lapse movie. This technique is often used to good effect in nature films, such as Walt Disney's pioneering *The Living Desert*. I'll show you how to create a time-lapse movie later in this chapter.

- **Star trails.** You don't need interval shooting to capture images of the heavens—a long exposure will suffice. However, still photos of the sky longer than a certain length produce blurry images (even if the camera is mounted on a tripod), due to the rotation of the Earth and the apparent "movement" of the stars. You can, however, use interval photography to capture a series of sharp star images over a period of time and combine them into a sweeping star trail image. I'll show you how to do that later in this chapter, as well.

- **Sunsets.** I shoot plenty of sunset photos, particularly in Florida during the winter, and find that images taken at different times as the sun sinks below the horizon often look dramatically different. Interval shooting is particularly useful for capturing the elusive "green flash," a phenomenon in which the sun changes color (usually green, but other colors are possible) for one or two seconds. If you take one photo every second or two for a long enough period, you have a better chance of capturing the green flash—if it happens at all. (It doesn't always appear.)

The green flash is caused by the separation of the light into different colors as it is refracted through the thickest section of atmosphere (much like the way a prism or raindrops creates a rainbow). The shorter wavelengths of blue, indigo, and violet are scattered by the atmosphere, while the longer red, orange, and yellow colors are absorbed, making the "middle" color, green, most visible for a few seconds. (I *knew* that the mnemonic ROY G. BIV would come in handy after elementary school!)

- **Capture the decisive moment.** You know deer and other wild-life wander into your backyard to munch on the delectables in your garden during the daytime. It would almost be worth the loss of lettuce to capture a few images of them—but you don't have four or five hours to waste waiting for them to show up. (I know erecting a "Deer Crossing" sign doesn't work; it appears the animals either can't read, or ignore them.) Instead, set up your camera (indoors, and shoot through a window if you wish), take a series of photos, and then review them to find your prize photo.

- **Documentation.** Use your imagination, and you'll discover dozens of ways to document things using sequences of photos take at intervals. Wondering how hard your friends worked at helping you re-roof your garage? You can capture an entire workday with shots taken every ten minutes or so to create a hilarious series showing who spent the most time hammering, and who took the most frequent beer breaks (and ended up hammered). How often do you toss and turn at night? A dim nightlight can provide enough illumination to capture images at intervals and see if you slept like a log, or rolled like one.

- **Self-portraits.** You can use your self-timer to take a self-portrait or two—but what if you wanted to shoot 30 or 40 shots of you mugging for the camera or assuming different poses? Choose an interval of 10 seconds or more, and you can take as many consecutive photos of yourself—or someone else—without the need to press the shutter button each time.

Interval Shooting Checklist

Interval photography is not a technique where you can get your best shots by winging it. The shooting process can be—and usually is—lengthy, so you don't want to spend two hours driving to a location, then 10 minutes or 10 hours capturing a sequence to discover poor planning has ruined your final results. This section provides some tips for preparing for your interval or time-lapse shooting session.

- **Know your subject.** If you plan to shoot a sunset, make sure you know exactly *when* the sun will set, so you can arrive early enough to set up your equipment and adjust your camera. You can Google the necessary information, but an app for Android and iOS devices called The Photographer's Ephemeris can tell you exactly when a celestial even will occur, and even provide you with a map that will help you calculate your best location. If, say, you want to shoot the sun setting behind a lighthouse, the app will tell you the precise spot to stand, and when. If you're capturing the ebb and flow of tides, you'll need to know the time of high and/or low tides at a specific location. Don't forget to scout the location ahead of time, too.

■ **Use a sturdy tripod.** If you don't have a sturdy tripod, take along an empty sack (I use the lightweight mesh bags that oranges come in), fill it with rocks when you arrive at your location, and hang it from the center column of your tripod to add ground-hugging weight. Successful interval photography calls for a camera that doesn't move between shots so the successive images show what has changed between intervals. That's not to say that some interesting photos can't be taken by panning and/or moving the camera between intervals. You want to avoid *unwanted* movement, and save intentional movement for experimental photography.

■ **Have a fully charged battery or another power source.** Interval photography drains the a6400's batteries at an alarming pace. For long sequences, you'll want to use a charged battery or external power. Turn off picture review to reduce power consumption.

■ **Make sure the camera is protected** from the elements, accidents, and theft.

■ **Consider Disabling Long Exposure Noise Reduction.** As you'll recall from Chapter 3, when Long Exposure NR is enabled, the a6400 takes an additional dark "comparison" frame using the same exposure time so sensor noise can be removed. If you're taking a 20-second exposure at intervals of less than 40 seconds, you do *not* want the camera to follow the original shot with an additional 20-second dark frame. That's true whenever the total time required for the original/dark frame exposures is longer than your interval. You'll have to accept a little noise to maintain your shooting rate. Of course, if you are taking a 20-second exposure once a minute, there's no problem and Long Exposure NR can be left on.

■ **Focus manually.** There aren't many common interval-shooting situations in which I'd want to have focus change from shot to shot. Perhaps you're expecting a herd of deer to cavort through your garden and would like the camera to attempt to focus on the nearest beast. Most of the time, however, consistent manual focus is best. Choose whether you want to focus on the foreground, middle range, or background, and set your focus point there. If you're capturing photos of, say, a flower opening, use the Focus Magnifier to help you choose the precise plane of focus. Depth-of-field can be used creatively with small apertures (to increase the range of sharpness) or large f/stops (to allow selective focus).

■ **Manual exposure—or not?** If you set exposure manually, each picture you take will use the same ISO, f/stop, and shutter speed setting. If the light remains even during the sequence, that can be a good thing. If the light changes (say, throughout a day), that can be bad, or distracting, or, in some cases, add a certain desirable look. Your a6400's Interval Photography setting for Autoexposure Tracking Sensitivity can be used to fine-tune exposure. If autoexposure is active, you can specify a fast response to changes (High), or opt for slower adjustments using the Medium or Low sensitivity settings.

Know that quick changes in exposure can be distracting, especially when combining shots into a time-lapse movie. If you *want* to see dramatic light shifts as your scene lightens or darkens, use Manual Exposure and set the shutter speed, ISO, and aperture to give the correct "normal" exposure.

- **Choose an interval.** The time *between* each shot can be important. If you wait too long, you may miss an important event; choose a very brief interval, and you can end up with too many photos that are almost identical and lacking in the time-lapse effect. The interval is especially important if you intend to combine your shots into a time-lapse movie. With, say, slow-moving clouds, one shot every 10 seconds may produce a majestic march across the sky; fast-moving clouds can require taking one picture every three to five seconds. Sunsets work best with 30-second intervals; I get good results using 60-second gaps between shots when shooting the stars.

  To add Charlie Chaplin–like movement to pedestrians, one shot every second or two does the job. (Fun fact: The cameras used for Chaplin's comedies were hand-cranked at frame rates of around 14 to 16 frames per second; when projected at the eventual standard of 24 fps, the motion was speeded up. To compensate, Chaplin later had some frames duplicated in printing to simulate the 24 fps rate—while the motion was less frenetic, it became jerkier in the process.)

- **Choose number of shots to capture.** For practical reasons, you need to know how long it will take to capture your sequence. When you've chosen an interval and number of shots, the a6400 displays the total elapsed time, but common sense will tell you that if you are shooting one frame every 10 seconds (six per minute), if you want to capture 60 minutes' worth of action, you'll need to take 360 shots. Conversely, if you plan to convert your images into a movie, you'll know that at, say, 30 frames per second, your 360 images will provide a movie only 12 seconds in length! Obviously, for time-lapse movies, you'll probably be capturing a lot more than 360 images; the a6400 allows as many as 9999 frames—about 5.5 minutes' worth at 30 fps.

- **Choose your start time.** Use this setting to delay the start of image capture, from 0 minutes, 0 seconds (begin immediately) to 99 minutes, 59 seconds. While you may want to begin shooting immediately, you should still set a short delay (say 20 seconds) as a start time so the camera can settle down in its tripod perch. If you want to begin capturing an event, say, a sunset, in 10 minutes, you can specify that much of a delay, and spend the intervening time setting up other cameras, performing other tasks, or chatting with your companions about how great your photos are going to be.

A REMINDER

The interval cannot be shorter than the shutter speed; for example, you cannot set one second as the interval if the images will be taken at two seconds or longer.

Settings Recap

I detailed all seven major settings for the Interval Shooting Functions entry of the Camera Settings I-04 menu in Chapter 3. Here's a quick recap:

- **Interval shooting.** Choose On or Off to enable/disable the feature. You'll want to keep this setting at Off until you are ready to begin interval shooting.

- **Shooting start time.** Use this setting to delay the start of image capture, from 0 minutes, 0 seconds (begin immediately) to 99 minutes, 59 seconds.

- **Shooting interval.** Specify how often an image should be captured.

- **Number of shots.** This setting determines the total number of exposures in a time-lapse sequence. You can choose from 1 to 9999 shots. A message at the bottom of the screen will display how long it will take to capture the number of shots you specify using the shooting interval you've chosen.

- **Autoexposure Tracking Sensitivity.** Select from High, Mid (Medium), or Low sensitivity.

- **Silent Shooting in Interval.** Choose On or Off. If you select On, the a6400 will operate silently, which allows capturing your sequence in "stealth" mode if you need it.

- **Shoot Interval Priority.** When shooting sequences using Program or Aperture Priority modes, the a6400 will adjust the shutter speed to provide the correct exposure. That may result in a shutter speed that is longer than the specified interval. Choose Off for this setting and the a6400 will go ahead and expose for the correct amount of time, skipping the shot that would have taken place.

Choose On, and when another interval exposure is due, the a6400 will terminate the previous shot (underexposing it) and begin the next one on schedule. You might use the On option if you feel that just dropping the poorly exposed image from the sequence produces the best series. You may be able to avoid the underexposure by activating Auto ISO Sensitivity, and selecting a minimum shutter speed that is shorter than the interval time. In that case, the camera will increase the ISO setting (if necessary) to produce the correct exposure using the automatically selected shutter speed. The chief drawback is that increasing the ISO automatically may also increase the amount of noise in your image. Significant changes in graininess may detract from your sequence or time-lapse movie.

Viewing Your Interval Sequences

You can view your sequences as if they were a time-lapse movie in the camera. You can also create an actual time-lapse movie from your photos; I'll describe that in the section following this one. To view your sequence as a movie in the camera, just follow these steps:

1. **Choose speed.** In the Playback 2 menu, select Playback Speed for Interval and choose a speed from 1 (slow) to 9 (fast).

   - **At the slowest speed,** the a6400 will display each frame you took one after the other, so you'll see every image captured. The apparent speed of motion will be determined by length of the interval between each frame, and, to a certain extent, the size of the image file. That is, motion captured with larger intervals will appear to be moving faster, so sequences shot at 10-second intervals will seem "slower" than those taken at 20-second intervals. In addition you may need to take into account how many images can fit into the camera's buffer as they are displayed. Images captured in Large JPEG Extra Fine format may take longer to display than those captured in Small JPEG Standard format. In most cases, the difference in speed will be much less than the difference caused by the interval.

   - **At faster speeds,** the a6400 "skips" frames, playing back every second, third, fourth, etc. image, producing faster apparent motion, but also resulting in a jerkier appearance. In effect, faster playback speeds decrease the interval between shots.

2. **Select Continuous Playback.** Navigate to the Continuous Playback for Interval entry in the Playback 2 menu. Scroll to the sequence of images you captured, and press the center button. The camera will display the images in order quickly, at the speed you've specified.

Time-Lapse Movies

It's easy to convert your sequence of images into a time-lapse movie. All you need is the Viewer module from the free Imaging Edge software suite. It can quickly convert your individual frames into a Full HD (1920 × 1080) or Ultra HD (3840 × 2160) MP4 video clip. Just follow these steps.

1. **Deposit sequence in a folder.** Copy all the frames you want to use to a new folder on your computer. You'll find it easier to select them if they are located in their own folder. Your images can be RAW or JPEG files.

2. **Launch Viewer.** The left-hand panel displays your computer's directory tree. Select the drive and folder that contain your files.

3. **Sort files.** In the Viewer's Tools menu, choose Sort > Sort by Date and Time Taken.

4. **Select All.** Press Control-A (Command-A on a Mac) to select all the files in the folder. Note that you must have at least 15 images to create a time-lapse movie.

5. **Commence processing.** In the Tools menu, choose Create Time Lapse Movie (see Figure 9.13, left).

6. **Select options.** The screen shown at right in Figure 9.13 appears. There are four adjustments you can make.

- **Output method.** In general, you can leave the Apply Each RAW File's own settings to each RAW file marked. The app will use the parameters you specified in the camera for white balance, etc. If, for some reason, the RAW settings differ among your files, you can apply the parameters for an image you select (say, the first one in a sequence) and apply them to all subsequent frames.

- **Save Format.** Here you can choose a color space and/or compression level for your video. I recommend going with the defaults. If you needed an extra-high-quality movie, you could change to Compression Level 1.

- **Save To.** Select a folder to save your video to, and specify a file name. You can use the original file name or select various combinations of Date Taken, Date and Time Taken, and a 5-digit number generated by the program.

- **Trimming.** Here you can specify the aspect ratio of your movie. For greatest compatibility with other video you may want to add or intercut, choose the 16:9 ratio standard for HD/UHD movies. You can also select 4:3, 3:2, or 1:1 aspect ratios, or tell the program to use whatever proportions the a6400 was set to when the stills were captured.

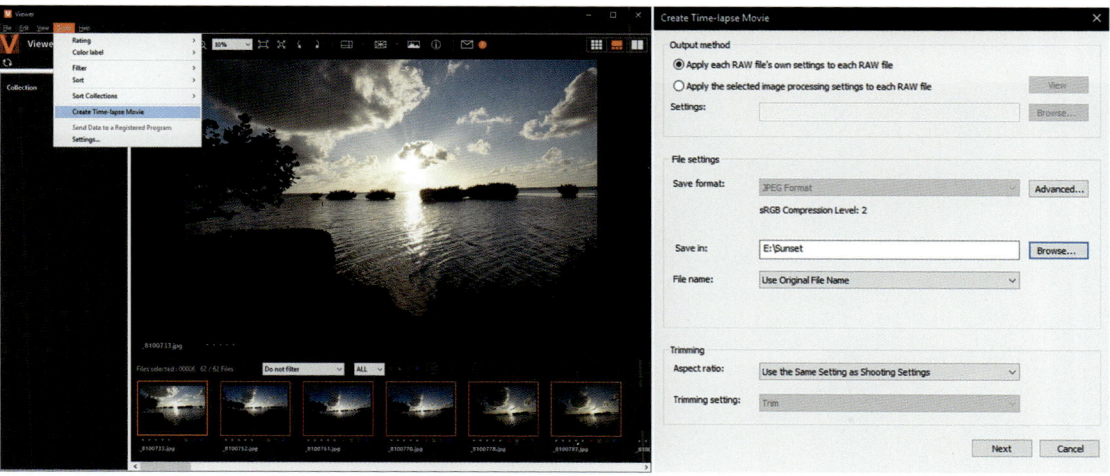

Figure 9.13 Select images and start process (left). Select options (right).

7. **Click Next.** If you're working with JPEG still photos instead of RAW images, the program will suddenly come to the conclusion that no further processing (adjusting white balance and so forth) is required, and tell you "Some of the selected images will not be processed because they do not have to be developed or are in unsupported formats." Ignore this message if Sony's programmers haven't corrected this bug in your current release of the Imaging Edge software. The program will tell you which files it skipped (basically, all your JPEG images), and invite you to click Next once again to proceed.

8. **Edit settings.** The Edit screen, shown at left in Figure 9.14, appears. It has several options that you can reveal from drop-down lists.

    • **Time Lapse Setting.** This panel is shown at far left in Figure 9.14. You can adjust playback speed from 1X to 16X, and view the total time recorded, although with the most recent copy of Viewer that I used, the speed didn't seem to vary as described. Look for a fix in a future update of the software.

    • **Music.** Allows you to select music tracks on your computer, and to download additional music from Sony's website (Figure 9.14, center right).

    • **Music Settings.** Here you can balance the volume of the music you added with the soundtrack already recorded on your video. That allows you to have the music predominate, fade in, fade out, and/or loop continuously during playback. (Figure 9.14, far right.)

9. **Save your work or produce a movie.** You can stop working at this point and return to this point by clicking Save Project. It's a good idea to do this, just in case your final video needs to be tweaked and redone. When you're ready to produce your time-lapse clip, click Next.

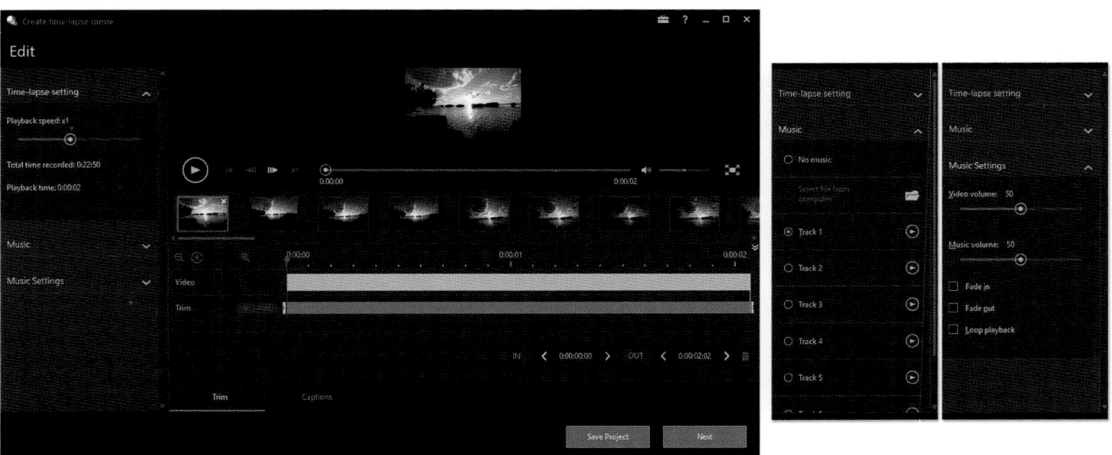

Figure 9.14 Edit time-lapse settings (left); add music (center right); select music settings (far right).

10. **Specify file name, folder, and format.** When the Save screen shown in Figure 9.15 appears, you can type in a new filename for your movie, specify a different directory to save your file in, or choose one of three movie formats:

   - **4K.** This choice produces a 2160p/30 fps MP4 video clip in XAVC S format. (You can read about various video formats and parameters in Chapter 10.) You'll need a 4K-compatible display to view this UHD movie.

   - **Good for Viewing on a TV or Computer.** This is usually your best choice, as it delivers a 1080p/30 fps MP4 file in AVC format, viewable on any HDTV or modern-day computer screen that can handle Full HD.

   - **Smaller Size for Easier Uploading.** Choose this to create a Standard HD 720p/30 fps MP4 clip in AVC format. This creates a much smaller file that can be transferred over the Internet, and uploaded to YouTube more easily.

11. **Click Save.** The program will create your video clip and store it in the specified folder. The process may take some time, but a progress bar (seen at center in Figure 9.15) will keep you updated.

Figure 9.15
Choose file name, folder, and movie format.

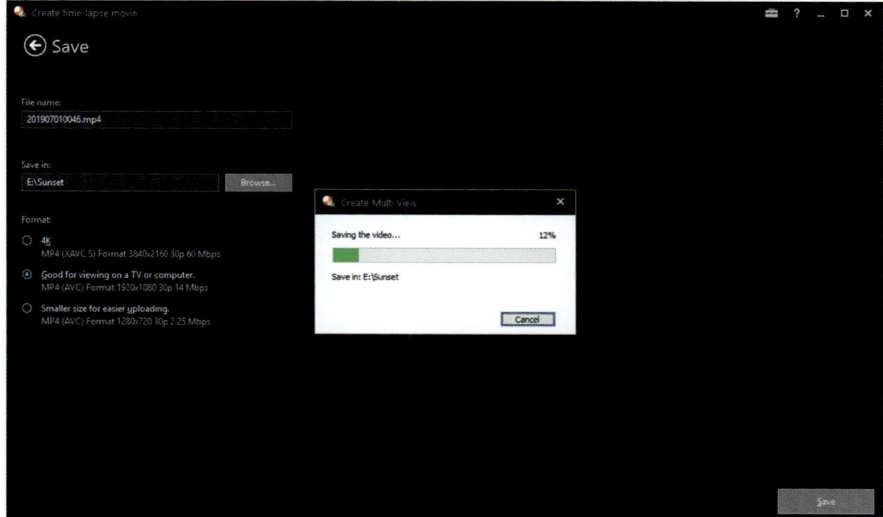

Star Trails

Star trails are another great application for interval shooting. As I noted earlier, you can shoot the night sky using long exposures with your a6400 mounted on a tripod. However, because of the rotation of the Earth, longer exposures will record the apparent motion of the celestial objects through the sky, producing a light trail. If you use a very, very long exposure, the light trail will record as continuous streaks, centered around the Polaris (the North Star) in the northern hemisphere and Sigma Octantis (which is, unfortunately, too dim to be easily seen with the naked eye) in the southern hemisphere.

Such long exposures can result in excessive noise and sensor overheating, so it's more common for photographers to take a series of individual exposures and combine them to produce a single star trail image. If you want your stars to appear as reasonably sharp points, you'll need to keep the exposure short enough that their movement in the sky isn't apparent. Fortunately, there's a simple formula you can use to calculate that exposure time, the "500 Rule." Divide 500 by the focal length of your lens to determine the longest exposure (in seconds) before stars start to produce a blurred trail. For example, with a 50mm lens, the longest exposure would be 10 seconds (500 divided by 50). Capturing the complete canopy of stars generally requires a wider viewing perspective. With the a6400's kit lens, the 16mm setting would be best, and allow exposures as long as roughly 30 seconds.

For Figure 9.16, I set my camera to ISO 200, and used a basic exposure of 30 seconds at f/5.6. I selected an interval of 32 seconds and 170 total exposures, which totals about 90 minutes. Noise reduction was OFF! Then, I followed these steps, using Photoshop:

1. **Transfer files to a folder.** Select a folder on your computer, and copy all your files to that location.
2. **In Photoshop:** Choose Files > Scripts > Load Files into Stack.
3. **Browse to folder.** Click the Browse button and navigate to the folder where your images are stored.
4. **Click OK.** Photoshop will create a file with one layer for each of your captured images.
5. **Select All layers.** Then click Layer Blending Options from the Layers palette, and choose Lighten.
6. **Flatten image.** You'll want to flatten your image (the multi-layer file will be huge!) You'll end up with an impressive star trail image.

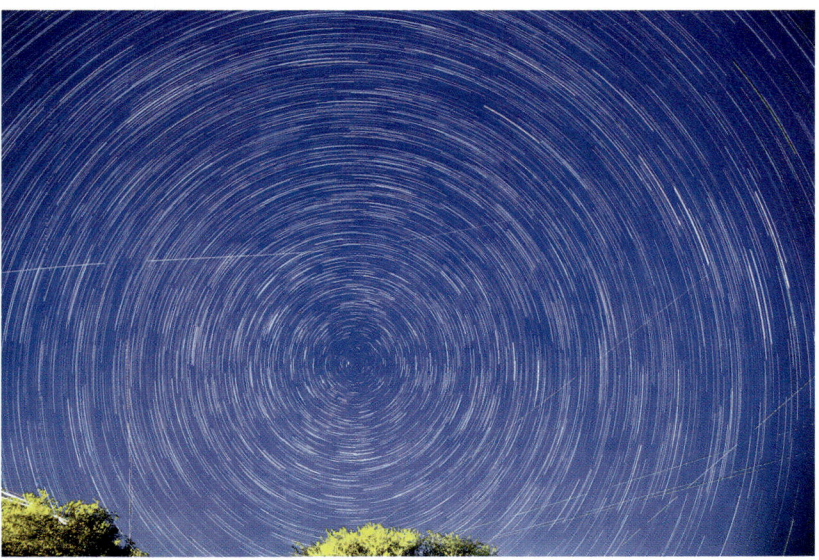

Figure 9.16
Capturing a star trail.

10

Movie Making

As we've seen during our exploration of its features so far, the a6400 is superbly equipped for taking still photographs of very high quality in a wide variety of shooting environments. But this camera's superior level of performance is not limited to stills. It's highly capable in the movie-making arena as well. It can shoot Full HD (high-definition) and 4K (ultra-high-definition) clips. Sony has also provided options for controlling all important aspects of a video sequence.

So, even though you may have bought your camera primarily for shooting stationary scenes, you acquired a device that's also great for recording high-quality video. Whether you're looking to record informal clips of the family on vacation, the latest viral video for YouTube, or a set of scenes that will be painstakingly crafted into a cinematic masterpiece using editing software, the a6400 will perform admirably.

The a6400 can shoot HD video at 1920 × 1080 resolution using Sony's AVCHD encoding, plus MP4 video, which allows both 1920 × 1080 full HD and 1280 × 720 standard HD. They also can capture HD video in the newer XAVC S format, including superior 4K video *internally* using XAVC S 4K.

The camera also uses something called *Picture Profiles* to tailor color, saturation, sharpness, and some video-centric attributes. You can visualize Picture Profiles as Creative Styles for video. This chapter will show you the fundamentals of shooting video and provide an introduction to your camera's more advanced features, including the XAVC S format in HD and 4K resolutions.

This chapter deals with conventional video; S&Q (slow- and quick-motion video) settings were explained in Chapter 4.

Some Fundamentals

Recording a video with the a6400 is extraordinarily easy to accomplish—just press the black button with the red dot at the upper right of the camera's back to start. Sony has tucked the default Movie button off to the side to minimize the chance that you'll start recording a movie accidentally. That's because video can be captured in *any* exposure mode; rotating the mode dial to the Movie position isn't always necessary. (If you start recording movies in Sweep Panorama mode, however, the camera will actually use P mode and the video won't be a panorama.) After you press the button, the camera will confirm that it's recording with a red REC and numerals showing the elapsed time in the EVF and LCD monitor. Press the activation button again when you want to stop recording. (You can also define a different button to activate/deactivate video, such as the C1 key, using the Custom Keys options described in Chapter 4.)

Before you start, though, there are some settings to prepare the camera to record the scene the way you want it to. Setting up the camera for recording video can be a bit tricky, because it's not immediately obvious, either from the camera's menus or from Sony's manuals, which settings apply to video recording and which do not. I will unravel that mystery for you, and throw in a few other tips to help improve your movies.

I'll show you how to optimize your settings before you start shooting video, but here are some considerations to be aware of as you get started. Many of these points will be covered in more detail later in this chapter:

- **Use the right card.** Because movie capture, is, basically, full-time "continuous" shooting, you'll need to use a memory card with sufficient capacity and a fast enough write speed to handle the streams of video you'll be shooting.

  - **For AVCH format.** Sony recommends using an SD, SDHC, or SDXC memory card with Class 4 or UHS Speed Class U1, or faster. You can also use Sony Memory Sticks of the Pro Duo II, PRO-HG, or Micro II variety. With slow cards, your recording may stop after a minute or two until the card is able to offload the captured video from your camera. In practice, virtually all memory cards sold today are Class 10, but you may still have some older cards in your kit.

  - **For XAVC S format.** Sony recommends SDXC memory cards 64GB or larger, and Speed Class 10 or UHS U1 or faster write speeds. If you elect to use the 30p or 24p options with 100M bit transfer rates, you *must* have a UHS-1 U3–compatible memory card inserted. (I'll explain more about bit transfer rates later in this chapter.)

- **Avoid extraneous noise.** Try not to make too much noise when changing camera controls or when using a conventional zoom lens's mechanical zooming ring. The sound made by a mechanical zoom ring rotating will be picked up and it will be audible when you play a movie. (Lenses with power zoom are virtually silent, however.) And don't make comments that you will not want to hear on the audio track.

- **Minimize zooming.** While it's great to be able to use the zoom for filling the frame with a distant subject (especially the power zoom on lenses equipped with that feature), think twice before zooming. As well, remember that any more than the occasional minor zoom will be very distracting to friends who watch your videos. And digital zoom will definitely degrade video quality. Don't use the digital zoom if quality is more important than recording a specific subject such as a famous movie star far from a distance.

- **Use a fully charged battery.** A fresh battery will allow about one hour of filming at normal (non-Winter) temperatures, but that can be shorter if there are many focus adjustments. Individual clips can be no longer than 29 minutes, 59 seconds, however.

- **Keep it cool.** Video quality can suffer terribly when the imaging sensor gets hot so keep the camera in a cool place. When shooting on hot days especially, the sensor can get hot more quickly than usual; when there's a risk of overheating, the camera will stop recording and it will shut down about five seconds later. Give it time to cool down before using it again. And remember that when you record a couple of very long clips in a series, the sensor will start to get warm; it's better to wait a few minutes to let it cool before starting to record another clip. This limitation generally won't affect serious movie makers, who tend to shoot a series of short scenes that are assembled into a finished movie with an editor. But if you plan to set up your camera and shoot your kid's school pageant non-stop for an hour, you're out of luck.

- **Activate dual recording (optional).** If you are shooting an XAVC S or AVCHD movie, you can elect to record an MP4 simultaneously, giving you a standard high-definition (1280 × 720) MPEG video that can be viewed immediately without needing to process with a video-editing program. Use the Proxy Recording option in the Camera Settings II-01 menu to activate this capability. You'll definitely want to use a larger memory card when working with this option.

- **Preview the movie's aspect ratio for stills.** There's an item in the Image Size menu for Aspect Ratio and it's at 3:2 by default, but you can change that to 16:9. *The setting in this item won't affect your video recording.* Setting the 16:9 option will merely cause the camera to display a correctly formatted preview of the scene when you are shooting stills, before you start movie recording, in the format that will be used for the video clip. This gives you a better feel for what will be included in the frame after you press the record button.

Choosing a File Format

Visit the File Format entry in the Camera Settings II-01 menu (as discussed in Chapter 4) and select the file format for your movies. The a6400 offers full HD (high-definition) video recording in the AVCHD format. Advanced video shooters can also choose from the XAVC S 4K or XAVC S HD formats, which support faster recording speeds for improved quality, as I'll explain in Chapter 10.

By default, movies are recorded in XAVC S HD, but this menu item allows you to switch to XAVC S 4K AVCHD. In any case, you'll need a fast memory card of at least 64GB capacity to support the higher frame rates possible with these pro formats. The XAVC S 4K format is especially demanding because of its ultra-high 3840 × 2160–pixel resolution (roughly four times that of full HD).

AVCHD clips are limited to roughly 2GB in size; when your movie file reaches that limit, the a6400 will continue recording using a new file that it creates automatically. If you're using an external recorder, video monitor, or other device using the a6400's HDMI connection, the real-time image is *not* displayed on the camera's LCD monitor as you shoot.

So your first choice will be should you be shooting standard/full high-definition movies, or ultra-high-definition (4K) video? If your memory card (which must be a 64GB or larger SDXC card to use the fastest bit rates) or external recorder, like the Atomos Shogun, can handle the data rates, 4K is alluring, even if your movies will never be viewed in anything other than 1080p format. All that extra detail is hard to resist.

Video gurus who have studied the Sony cameras have concluded that the a6400's 4K video provides the most detailed movies with the best dynamic range and noise characteristics. Each pixel in the Super 35 image area is captured directly, producing more information than is required for even a 4K video frame, and then downscaled.

In the discussions that follow, you'll see reference to a "Super 35" format that is applied to many of the full HD formats. In practice, Super 35 is simply the area captured by an APS-C-format camera like the a6400, but cropped to the 16:9 proportions of SD/HD/UHD video, effectively 6000 × 3376 pixels. Sony says that when capturing 4K video at 24p/25p, each pixel is read directly from the full width of the sensor and then downscaled to the selected video resolution. (At 30p, a tighter crop is used.) The alternative is a process called *pixel binning,* which averages the data from several adjacent pixels, producing a lower-quality image. Directly capturing pixels produces an improved image, which should have reduced moiré effects, sharper detail with less noise, and a reduction of "rolling shutter" problems (described next).

Choosing a Record Setting

Once you've selected the File Format from among XAVC S 4K, XAVC S HD, AVCHD, or MP4, you can use the next entry in the Camera Settings II-01 menu to select your Record Setting. This entry allows you to choose the size, frame rate, and image quality for your movies, and the available options differ, depending on the file format you've specified. Tables 10.1 to 10.3 later in this section spell out your choices. Each of the tables lists the frame rates, whether progressive scanning or interlacing is used, and the bit transfer rate of the video information from the sensor to the memory card (or external video recorder).

How Video Is Captured

In truth, both videos and stills are captured in much the same way, but the technology used for the sensor can cause problems that are most evident when shooting movies. To understand why, it's necessary to understand the difference between a *rolling shutter* and a *global shutter,* and how *interlacing* differs from *progressive scan.*

An image (still or video) captured by the sensor consists of rows and columns of pixels. With the a6400, there are 4,000 different rows, each row consisting of 6,000 individual pixels. A "rolling" shutter captures each row one after the other, so that, effectively, the pixels in the top row are captured at a different moment in time than those in the bottom row. This gap is very brief, and typically isn't noticeable in still photographs. But with video this difference can manifest itself as anomalies such as wobble (or Jell-O effect when the camera is moving or vibrating), skew (which is a diagonal bending of an image due to wobble), smear (produced when part of the image, such as an automobile tire, is rotating), and other defects.

A "global" shutter, on the other hand, captures the entire image in one instant, eliminating these problems. Although your a6400 does have a rolling shutter, the high speed of its sensor (aided by the improved on-sensor copper wiring of this all-new 24M sensor) almost eliminates the rolling shutter effects.

That leads us to progressive scanning versus interlacing. Line-by-line scanning during capture and playback can be done in one of two ways. With *interlaced scanning*, odd-numbered lines (lines 1, 3, 5, 7, and so forth) are captured with one pass, and then the even-numbered lines (2, 4, 6, 8, and so forth) are grabbed. With the 1080/60i format, roughly 60 pairs of odd/even line scans, or 60 *fields* are captured each second. (The actual number is 59.94 fields per second.) Interlaced scanning was developed for and works best with analog display systems such as older television sets. It was originally created as a way to reduce the amount of bandwidth required to transmit television pictures over the air. Modern LCD, LED, and plasma-based HDTV displays must de-interlace a 1080i image to display it. (See Figure 10.1.)

Figure 10.1

The inset shows how lines of the image alternate between odd and even in an interlaced video capture.

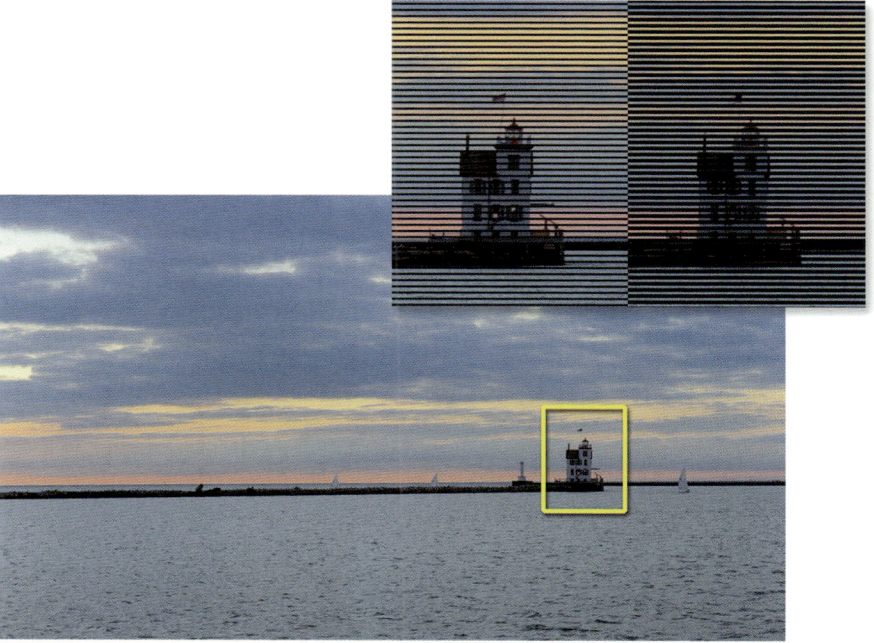

Newer devices work better with a second method, called *progressive scanning* or *sequential scanning*. Instead of two interlaced fields, the entire image is scanned as consecutive lines (lines 1, 2, 3, 4, and so forth). This happens at a rate of 30 frames per second (not fields), or, more precisely, 29.97 frames per second. (All these numbers apply to the NTSC television system used in the United States, Canada, Japan, and some other countries; other places use systems like PAL, where the nominal scanning figures are 50/25 rather than 60/30.)

One problem with interlaced scanning appears when capturing video of moving subjects. Half of the image (one set of interlaced lines) will change to keep up with the movement of the subject while the other interlaced half retains the "old" image as it waits to be refreshed. Flicker or *interline twitter* results. That makes your progressive scan (p) options a better choice for action photography. Interlaced video frame rates are indicated with an (i) designation; for example, within the AVCHD choices, 60i 24M (FX) indicates interlaced video, while 60p 28M (PS) represents progressive scan video. (I'll explain the 24M/28M part in the next section.)

Computer-editing software like Final Cut Pro can handle either type, and convert between them (although AVCHD, XAVC S 4K, and XAVC S HD may not be compatible with the other software you own). The choice between 24 fps and 60 fps (NTSC), or 25 fps and 50 fps (PAL) is determined by what you plan to do with your video. The short explanation is that, for technical reasons I won't go into here, shooting at 24 fps (or 25 fps) gives your movie more of the so-called "cinematic" look that film would produce, excellent for showing fine detail. However, if your clip has moving subjects, or you pan the camera, 24 fps (or 25 fps) can produce a jerky effect called "judder." The 60 fps (or 50 fps) option produces a home-video look that some feel is less desirable, but which is smoother and less jittery when displayed on an electronic monitor. I suggest you try both and use the frame rate that best suits your tastes and video-editing software.

Frame Rates

Even intermediate movie shooters can be confused by the choice between 24/25 frames per second and 50/60 fields per second. The difference lies in the two "worlds" of motion images—film and video. The standard frame rate for motion picture film is 24 fps, while the video rate, at least in the United States, Japan, and other places using the NTSC standard is 30/60 fps. That's actually 60 interlaced *fields* per second; that's where we get the 60i (60 fps *interlaced* specification). With interlaced video, the capture device grabs odd-numbered lines in one scan, even-numbered video lines in another scan, and they are combined to produce the final image we view. *Progressive* scan images (as in 60p) grab all the video lines of an image in order. In countries where NTSC is not used, instead of 30/60 fps, you'll find 25/50 fps.

ABOUT 120/100p

You'll note that when shooting XAVC S HD, you can select 120p (at 100 Mbs transfer rates; NTSC only) or 120/100p (at 60 Mbs transfer rate; both NTSC and PAL). These high frame rates—amounting to 120 and 100 frames per second—produce video that can be converted to play back at conventional speeds, either 30/25 fps (four times slower than recorded) or 24 fps (five times slower than recorded; NTSC only).

Bit Rates

Bit rates represent the speed of transfer from your camera to your memory card or external video recorder. The higher the bit rate, the more demands made on your media in storing that data quick enough to keep pace with the video capture. Higher average bit rates range from 6 Mbps (megabits per second) for 1280 × 720 (720p) MP4 movies, to as much as 28 Mbps maximum for AVCHD, 60p full-HD clips. When using XAVC formats, the demands are even higher: 50 Mbps with XAVC S HD and 60 to 100 Mbps with XAVC S 4K. Tables 10.1 to 10.3 show the frame rates, bit rates, and resolution of the various recording settings for video. Note that frame rates of 30/25, 60/50, and 120/100 represent NTSC/PAL systems, respectively.

Table 10.1 XAVC S 4K

Record Setting	Resolution	Bit Rate
30p/25p 100M	3840 × 2160	Approx. 100 Mbps
30p/25p 60M	3840 × 2160	Approx. 60 Mbps
24p 100M (NTSC) Super 35mm	3840 × 2160	Approx. 100 Mbps
24p 60M (NTSC) Super 35mm	3840 × 2160	Approx. 60 Mbps

Table 10.2 XAVC S HD

Record Setting	Resolution	Bit Rate
60p/50p 50M Super 35mm	1920 × 1080	Approx. 50 Mbps
30p/25p 50M Super 35mm	1920 × 1080	Approx. 50 Mbps
24p 50M (NTSC) Super 35mm	1920 × 1080	Approx. 50 Mbps
120p 100 M (NTSC)	1280 × 720	Approx. 100 Mbps
120p/100p 60M	1280 × 720	Approx. 60 Mbps

Table 10.3 AVCHD		
Record Setting	**Resolution**	**Bit Rate**
60i/50i 24M (FX) Super 35mm	1920 × 1080	Approx. 24 Mbps
60i/50i 17M (FH) Super 35mm	1920 × 1080	Approx. 17 Mbps
60p/50p 28M (PS) Super 35mm	1920 × 1080	Approx. 28 Mbps
24p/25p 24M (FX) Super 35mm	1920 × 1080	Approx. 24 Mbps
24p/25p 17M (FH) Super 35mm	1920 × 1080	Approx. 17 Mbps

Choosing Metering/Exposure Modes

You can use Multi, Center, or Spot metering when shooting movies. I recommend sticking with Multi metering, unless you have a special reason for, say, Spot metering, as I explained in Chapter 7.

Next, you'll want to select exposure mode, from among Program, Aperture Priority, Shutter Priority, or Manual. Rotate the mode dial to the Movie position, and specify which of these modes is used for movies with the Exposure Mode setting in the Camera Settings II-01 menu. The mode you select will be used when the mode dial is in the Movie position. If the Mode Dial Guide is set to On in the Setup 2 menu, you can press the center button and change to the exposure mode of your choice after rotating the mode dial to the Movie position. Of course, using the Movie position on the mode dial isn't mandatory, as you can use any exposure mode for movie recording. That mode will over-ride the Exposure Mode setting you might have made for movie shooting.

- **Program mode.** The P mode works well for movies, allowing the camera to set the aperture/ shutter speed. Program shift (to other aperture/shutter speed combinations) can be used before you start recording, but it will not be available during actual recording.

- **Aperture Priority.** You might prefer to use Aperture Priority (A) mode for full control over the specific aperture; in that case, you can preset a desired aperture and you can also change it anytime while recording. However, remember that your shutter speed may change in Aperture Priority mode, and when shooting movies, it is often desirable to use a specific shutter speed (as I'll explain in an upcoming section).

- **Shutter Priority.** Switch to S mode if you want control over the shutter speed; this is a more advanced technique in Movie mode. You can preset a shutter speed and you can change it while recording. Again, be careful as to your settings to avoid a very dark or overly bright video, especially if you have set a specific ISO level. The live view display before and during recording will help to guide you. I recommend Shutter Priority highly, especially for beginners.

- **Manual Exposure.** Manual exposure may be best when you want to maintain tight control over shutter speed and aperture, say, to maintain exposure as lighting conditions change, or to keep the same depth-of-field in a scene under changing conditions.

Selecting Shutter Speeds

Both Manual Exposure and Shutter Priority modes allow you to explicitly choose a shutter speed. You might think that setting your camera to a faster shutter speed will help give you sharper video frames. But the choice of a shutter speed for movie making is a bit more complicated than that. As you might guess, it's almost always best to leave the shutter speed at 1/30th or 1/60th second, and allow the overall exposure to be adjusted by varying the aperture and/or ISO sensitivity.

Remember that. Effectively, you're better off working in Shutter Priority mode, so that the aperture or ISO settings are your only way of adjusting the exposure. A "slow" 1/30th or 1/60th second shutter speed doesn't mean your movies will have the same amount of blur that a typical still photograph will have using those shutter speeds.

We don't normally stare at a video frame for longer than 1/30th or 1/24th second, so while the shakiness of the *camera* can be disruptive (and often corrected by your camera lens's Optical Steady Shot [OSS]), if there is a bit of blur in our *subject's* from movement, we tend not to notice. Each frame flashes by in the blink of an eye, so to speak, so a shutter speed of 1/30th or 1/60th second works a lot better in video than it does when shooting stills. Even shots with lots of movement, such as the frame shown in Figure 10.2, are often sufficiently sharp at 1/60th second.

Indeed, higher shutter speeds actually introduce problems of their own. If you shoot a video frame using a shutter speed of 1/250th second, the actual moment in time that's captured represents only about 12 percent of the 1/30th second of elapsed time in that frame. Yet, when played back, that

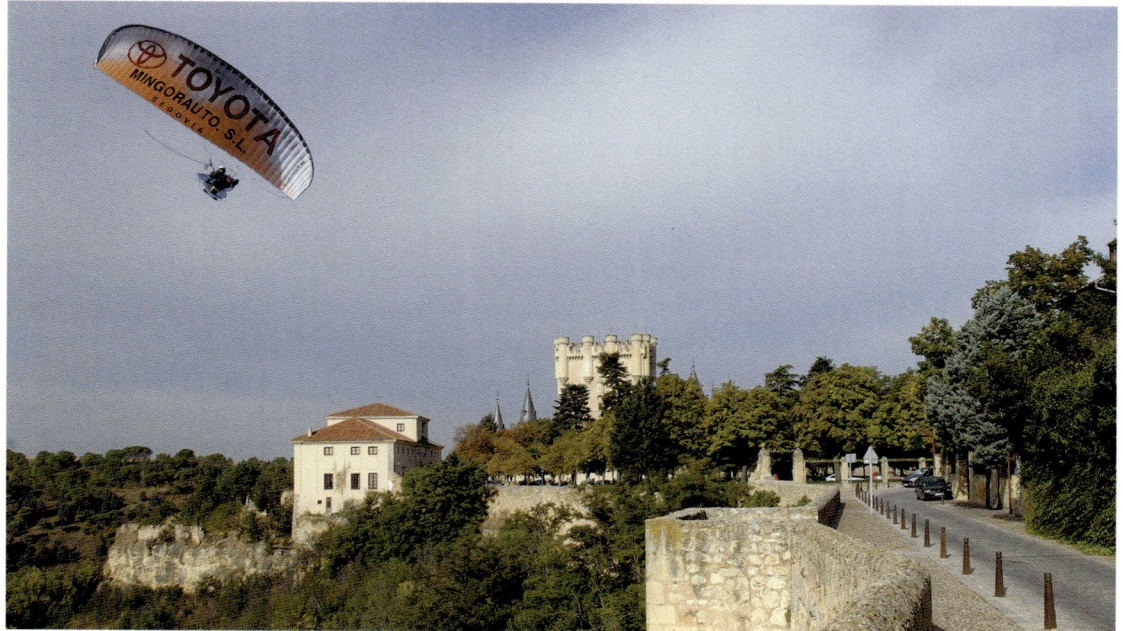

Figure 10.2 Movement adds interest to a video clip.

frame occupies the full 1/30th of a second, with 88 percent of that time filled by stretching the original image to fill it. The result is often a choppy/jumpy image, and one that may appear to be *too* sharp.

The reason for that is more social imprinting than scientific: we've all grown up accustomed to seeing the look of Hollywood productions that, by convention, were shot using a shutter speed that's half the reciprocal of the frame rate (that is, 1/48th second for a 24 fps movie). Movie cameras use a rotary shutter (achieving that 1/48th second exposure by using a 180-degree shutter "angle"), but the effect on our visual expectations is the same. For the most "film-like" appearance, use 24 fps and 1/60th second shutter speed.

Faster shutter speeds do have some specialized uses for motion analysis, especially where individual frames are studied. The rest of the time, 1/30th or 1/60th of a second will suffice. If the reason you needed a higher shutter speed was to obtain the correct exposure, use a slower ISO setting, or a neutral-density filter to cut down on the amount of light passing through the lens. A good rule of thumb is to use 1/60th second or slower when shooting at 24 fps; 1/60th second or slower at 30 fps; and 1/125th second or slower at 60 fps.

Monitoring and Adjusting Exposure

As you work, you'll discover that the a6400's Zebra feature (in the Camera Settings II-06 menu, as explained in Chapter 4) can be a marvelous aid in monitoring your exposure. If you are using Shutter Priority, as I recommended, you'll have the shutter speed fixed and, based on what you see in the viewfinder or LCD monitor and Zebra display feedback, adjust the aperture or ISO sensitivity to get the exposure you want. As I explained in Chapter 4, you can adjust the Zebra feature's threshold setting, perhaps specifying 95% so that you're alerted only when the brightest highlights start to clip (making the stripes less distracting), or use 85% so you'll know when human skin starts to be overexposed. Zebra display may not work for you when using S-Log2/S-Log3 gamma settings (described later in this chapter), as those very low contrast renditions don't lend themselves to that kind of monitoring.

Should you need to adjust exposure from what the camera recommends, exposure compensation works quite well while filming. Although the autoexposure system does a good job (especially with Multi metering) to vary the aperture when the ambient lighting changes, you can certainly dial in exposure compensation when you need to do so or want to do so for a certain effect. You could even use this function as a limited kind of "fade to black" in the camera, though you probably won't be able to fade quite all the way to black.

If the preview display (when Live View Display is set to Setting Effect On in the Camera Settings II-07 menu) suggests that your movie will be dark (underexposed) and if it does not get brighter after you set plus EV compensation, there's another problem: the camera cannot provide a good exposure for the movie at the ISO that you have set (as discussed earlier). Switch to a higher ISO level until the brightness is as desired or switch to ISO Auto to enable the camera to set a higher ISO level to prevent the "underexposure."

You can also "lock" exposure to keep the same exposure settings as lighting changes or you reframe your scene. Occasionally, you may find that you start having an exposure problem during recording; this might happen when pointing the lens toward a light-tone area that causes the camera to begin underexposing. While plus compensation will allow you to increase brightness, it's preferable to use the defined AE Lock button (either the physical AEL button or one you specify using Custom Keys in the Setup menu) to maintain a pleasing exposure during the entire video clip.

Why would you need this feature? Let's say you're filming entertainers against grass and foliage, but you're moving the camera and will soon be filming a second group against a white sky. As soon as you do so, the backlighting will cause the video to get darker. Don't let that happen. Before pointing the lens toward the backlit area, press AEL and keep it depressed. This will prevent the exposure from changing as you point the lens toward the backlit part of the scene. This is preferable to waiting until an underexposure problem starts and then setting plus exposure compensation that suddenly makes the video brighter.

Choosing an Autofocus Mode

As I said in Chapter 8, you'll generally want sharp focus in your image—somewhere—but exactly where and how focus is achieved can be an important part of your creative process. On the one hand, while shooting certain types of scenes—particularly action scenes—you'll want the camera to automatically retain focus on your main subjects, and keep them tightly in focus. Other times, you'll want to use selective focus to emphasize a subject and de-emphasize the background, or "pull" focus to dramatically change the focus (so to speak) of the scene, say, refocusing to cause a blurry subject to suddenly come into sharp relief.

As with still photography, you have both manual focus and autofocus tools at your disposal, which allow you to specify *when* to focus and what to focus on. An important step before shooting is to ensure autofocus is turned on through the Focus Mode entry of the Camera Settings I-05 or Function menus. Only Continuous AF (AF-C) and Manual Focus (MF) can be used when shooting movies. Here are some points to consider.

- **AF-C or MF.** If the mode dial is in the Movie position, only AF-C and MF are available.

- **Presto change-o.** If the mode dial is *not* in the Movie position, and you have selected a Focus Mode other than AF-C or MF, when you begin shooting movies, the a6400 will automatically switch to AF-C.

- **Lock focus.** As video is captured, the a6400's Continuous autofocus will refocus as you move the camera, or subjects in the frame change location. To lock focus, press the shutter release halfway, or use a key you've assigned that function. When you release the button, the camera will refocus. Ordinarily, it does an excellent job of not refocusing constantly, and changes focus only when the a6400 detects camera or subject movement.

■ **Manual focus.** If you prefer manual focus, you'll need to set it before commencing video capture. I find that manual focus is fine for situations such as a stage play where the actors will usually be at roughly the same distance to your position during the entire performance, and for more professional productions where precise focus is a must, or when changing focus during a shot (*focus pulling*) is used creatively. In other cases, however, you'll probably want to rely on the camera's effective full-time continuous autofocus ability while recording a video clip.

■ **Focus area modes.** You can use all focus area modes, as described in Chapter 8, except for Tracking AF. Try Flexible Spot AF. As in still image making, you can use the Flexible Spot AF Area (also discussed in Chapter 8) while recording a video clip. This feature is most suitable for a static scene you'll record with the camera on a tripod, where an important small subject is off-center and will remain in the same location.

By placing the AF Area exactly on that part of the scene, you'll be sure that the focus will remain on the most important part of the scene during the entire recording. (In truth, you could use manual focus for the same purpose.) If you decide to try this, compose the scene as desired before pressing the record button. Set the AF Area to Flexible Spot in the Camera Settings menu. When you press the center button (or designated Focus Standard button), locator brackets will appear on the screen, indicating the current location of the active focus detection point. Move the bracket with the directional buttons so they cover the primary subject and press OK (the center button) to confirm. You can now begin recording the video, confident that the focus will always be on your primary subject (assuming it does not move while you're recording).

■ **AF Drive Speed/Tracking Sensitivity.** As I explained in Chapter 4, you can specify how quickly the a6400 focuses in movie mode, and the responsiveness of the autofocus system to moving subjects. Because video captures your subject in continuous sequences, changes in focus during a shot are visible when the clip is played back, so the speed and response of the AF system is an important aspect to consider. Fast focusing and response works well with most subjects, but may induce vertigo when the camera constantly adjusts focus on fast, herky-jerky motion.

Using Frame Guides

Frame guides are a useful way of visualizing the area that will be captured within a larger visible display. In ancient times, interchangeable-lens rangefinder film cameras that used an optical viewfinder would have bright frame outlines appear, often automatically when a particular lens was mounted on the camera, and sometimes through the use of an attachment that fit over the built-in viewfinder. In the digital age, frame guides have been popular with digital cameras that use an optical viewfinder, providing a masked-off display to preview the actual image area that will be captured in crop or video modes. Cameras with electronic displays like the a6400 don't necessarily need frame guides, because the capture area can be enlarged and masked off electronically to show only the actual image area.

Even so, frame guides are a popular tool for videographers, because they allow viewing the area outside the actual frame that will be captured (the "look-around area") so you can monitor moving subjects before they enter the frame. In professional productions, it's useful to look at the region outside the captured frame to detect when boom microphones, careless crew members, or other objects threaten to intrude on the frame.

The a6400 cameras offers a variety of frame guides that can be turned on or off in the Camera Settings II-03 menu, including grid lines, aspect ratios, frame center markings, and "safety" areas. These markers appear *only* on the EVF or LCD monitor, and not in the captured video itself (see Figure 10.3 for example placement).

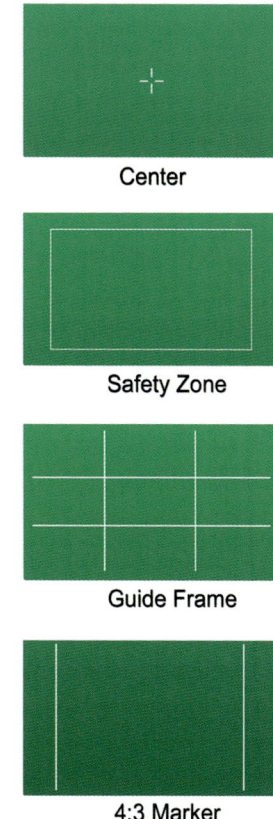

Center

Safety Zone

Guide Frame

4:3 Marker

- **Marker Display.** This Camera Settings II-03 menu entry works in conjunction with the Marker Settings option (described next), and simply turns settings on or off.

- **Marker Settings.** This menu entry allows you to specify Center, Aspect Ratio, Safety Zone, or Guide Frame. Each can be specified individually, and turned on or off independently, so you can display any, all, or none.

  - **Center.** This crosshair can be used to determine whether your subject is placed in the exact center of the screen.

  - **Aspect Ratio.** Use these guides to frame your image so the important subject matter is contained within a desired aspect ratio, or to frame the image for later cropping to that aspect ratio. You can select from 4:3, 13:9, 14:9, 15:9, 1.66:1, 1.85:1, or 2.35:1. (Two of these are shown at bottom in Figure 10.3.) These conform to various movie formats in common use. (*Star Wars*, for example, was filmed in CinemaScope, with a 2.35:1 aspect ratio.)

  - **Safety Zone.** It's common to shoot movies knowing in advance that they will be cropped down eventually for display in a slightly different format. The director simply makes sure that the important parts of the frame are included in the "safety zone" that will never be cropped out. For example, you wouldn't want to put two characters who are talking to each other at opposite ends of the entire frame, but would instead locate them in the safety zone so both would be visible. Your camera's safety zone display can be set for 80 percent or 90 percent of the frame to represent the area that will always be shown when the movie is viewed on a standard HDTV.

  - **Guideframe.** This grid is used to help you determine whether horizontal and vertical lines are skewed, and can also be used as a Rule of Thirds guide for composition.

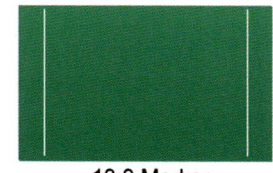

13:9 Marker

Figure 10.3 Video guide markers.

Time Codes and User Bits

The Time Code (TC) and User Bit (UB) settings are information that can be embedded and used to sync clips and sound when editing movies. Advanced video shooters find SMPTE (Society of Motion Picture and Television Engineers)-compatible time codes embedded in the video files to be an invaluable reference during editing. To oversimplify a bit, the time system provides precise *hour:minute:second:frame* markers that allow identifying and synchronizing frames and audio. The time code system includes a provision for "dropping" frames to ensure that the fractional frame rate of captured video (remember that a 24 fps setting actually yields 23.976 frames per second, while 30 fps capture gives you 29.97 actual "frames" per second) can be matched up with actual time spans.

Using time codes and user bits is a college-level film school class on its own, but I'm going to provide a quick overview to get your started. If you're at the stage where you're using time codes, you don't need this primer, anyway. However, the a6400's TC/UB Settings entry in the Setup 3 menu includes the following options:

■ **TC Preset.** Sets the time code. If you'll be shooting 60i/50i, you can choose time codes from 00:00:00:00 (hours, minutes, seconds, frame) to 23:59:59:29 or 23:59:59:24, respectively. With 24p, you can set multiples of four from 0 to 23 frames. If you own the RMT-VP1K remote commander, the time code can be reset to zero using a button on the controller.

■ **UB Preset.** Sets the user bit, which is a marker you can insert in your video, say to designate a scene or take. There are four digits in each user bit (for example, 01:02:03:04), and the digits are each hexadecimal in nature, so you could create a code like C0 FF EE if you were feeling facetious.

■ **TC Format.** Sets the recording method for the time code. You can choose from DF (drop frame) or NDF (non-drop-frame) formats. Drop frames are a way of compensating for the discrepancy between the nominal number of frames per second and the actual number (for example, 30 fps yields 29.97 actual frames per second, and 60 fps gives you 59.95 frames per second). In drop-frame format, the camera will skip some time code numbers at intervals to eliminate the discrepancy. The first two frame numbers are removed every minute except for every tenth minute (think of it as a leap year). You may notice a difference of several seconds per hour when using the non-drop-frame option.

■ **TC Run.** Sets the count-up format for the time code. You can choose Rec Run, in which the time code counts up only when you are actually capturing video, or Free Run (also known as Time of Day), which allows the time code to run up even between shooting clips. The latter is useful when you want to synchronize clips between multiple cameras that are shooting the same event. When using Free Run, even if the cameras record at different times, you'll be able to match the video that was captured at the exact same moment during editing.

- **TC Make.** Sets the recording format for the time code on the recording medium. Choose Preset to record a new time code, or Regenerate to read the previous time code setting and record the new time code consecutively. When Regenerate is selected, the time code advances no matter what TC Run setting has been selected.

- **UB Time Rec.** Sets whether or not to record the time as a user bit.

Picture Profiles

If you've been taking photos for a while, you're probably familiar with all the fixes and tweaks you can do with your still images within image editors like Photoshop. It's relatively easy to adjust color tones, contrast, sharpness, and other parameters prior to displaying or printing your photo. Movies are a little trickier, because any given video typically consists of *thousands* of individual photos, captured at 24 frames per second (or faster), with the possibility that each and every frame within a particular sequence might need fixes or creative adjustments.

Shooting video does not preclude doing post-processing during editing. Indeed, many videographers deliberately shoot relatively low-contrast video in order to capture the largest dynamic range possible, and then fine-tune the rendition later using their editing software. Picture Profiles let you do that—and also allow you to adjust your camera so that the video you capture is *pre-fine-tuned* in order to reduce or eliminate the amount of post-processing you do later.

The a6400 cameras are furnished with nine "canned" picture profiles, which you can think of as Creative Styles for movies. The parameters included in these profiles can be further adjusted by you to better suit the "look" you are striving for in your videos. You can connect your camera to a TV or monitor using the HDMI Out connector and an HDMI cable, view the image produced by the camera on the larger screen, and then make adjustments to the picture profile. I described the process in how-to form briefly in Chapter 3.

Needless to say, creating and using Picture Profiles is a highly technical aspect of video making, at least in terms of the amount of knowledge you need to have to correctly judge what changing one of the parameters will do to your video. I hope to get you started with a quick description of what those parameters do, so you'll have a starting point when you start to explore them.

Gamma, Gamma Ding Dong

The Picture Profile presets in the Camera Settings menu already have their own default values, each adjusted for a particular type of shooting, using various gamma and color tone settings. You can use these as-is, or make your own adjustments.

What's gamma? Thanks to our evolutionary heritage, humans don't see differences in tones in a linear manner. An absolutely smooth progression of pixels from absolute black to pure white (with 0 representing black and 256 representing white) would not look like a continuous gradient to our eyes. We'd be unable to detect differences in shadows and highlights that have the same change in tonal values as midtones. So, everything from computer monitors to printers use a correction factor (gamma) to cancel out the differences in the way we see tones.

This correction takes the form of a curve, called a *gamma curve.* If you remember your geometry, the x and y axes on a graph are used to define the shape of a curve, and in the case of gamma curves, the values use logarithmic units (ack!) to define the slope. That's where the terms S-Log2, S-Log3, and other mind-numbing jargon comes from. The whole shebang is needed to reconcile the ability of sensors to capture, video systems to display, and printers to output a range of tones in a linear way with the actual tones we perceive non-linearly. Gamma correction and gamma compression are used to help make sure that what we get is what we see. While gamma correction between computer platforms (that is, between Macs and PCs) may be different, the actual gamma values defined by video standards like NTSC and PAL are fixed and well-known. Picture Profiles allow you to configure your camera to capture video using a desired amount of gamma and color tone correction.

The nine predefined Picture Profiles in the a6400, originally listed in Chapter 3, are as follows:

- **PP1:** Example setting using [Movie] gamma
- **PP2:** Example setting using [Still] gamma
- **PP3:** Example setting of natural color tone using the [ITU709] gamma
- **PP4:** Example setting of a color tone faithful to the [ITU709] standard
- **PP5:** Example setting using [Cine1] gamma
- **PP6:** Example setting using [Cine2] gamma
- **PP7:** Example setting using [S-Log2] gamma
- **PP8:** Example setting using [S-Log3] gamma with S-Gamut3 Cine specified under Color Mode
- **PP9:** Example setting using [S-Log3] gamma with S-Gamut3 specified under Color Mode

And here are the parameters you can adjust:

- **Black Level.** Sets the black level (–15 to +15). Black level is the level of brightness at which no light is emitted from a screen, resulting in a pure black screen. Adjustment of this parameter ensures that blacks are seen as black, and not a dark shade of gray.

■ **Gamma.** Selects a gamma curve to adjust the relationship between the brightness (*luminance*) captured by a sensor and the brightness of the image as it's displayed on a monitor. As I've noted, this correction is needed to make what you see on a screen more closely resemble what the camera captured in real life. You can choose from nine different gamma curves:

- **Movie:** This is a standard gamma curve suitable for video.

- **Still:** A default gamma curve for still photography.

- **Cine 1:** Reduces contrast in dark areas, and emphasizes gradations in the highlights.

- **Cine 2:** Similar to Cine1, but optimized for image editing using the full video signal.

- **Cine 3:** Produces increased contrast in highlights and shadows.

- **Cine 4:** Similar to Cine 3, but with more contrast in the shadows. Compared to the default Movie gamma, there is reduced contrast in the shadows and higher contrast in highlights.

- **ITU709 (800%):** Offers a greater dynamic range, but less than S-Log2 or S-Log3.

- **S-Log2:** Produces a much lower contrast image that can be processed by a video editor (such as Final Cut Pro) to create a very high dynamic range video clip. (Sony claims up to 13 stops of dynamic range.) Use the Gamma Display Assist option in the Setup 1 menu of your camera to make the unprocessed clip easier to evaluate during playback in your camera.

- **S-Log3:** Produces an even lower contrast (flatter) image than S-Log2. Video using this gamma can be graded using software to gain an additional 1.5 stops of dynamic range over S-Log2. You'll want to use the Gamma Display Assist setting when viewing such clips on your a6400's viewfinder or LCD monitor.

■ **Black Gamma.** Provides special correction for gamma in low-intensity areas, using Range and Level controls. This adjustment will make the video look more/less contrasty. Negative values make the darker parts of the image darker, but can lead to clipped blacks.

■ **Knee.** Sets "knee point," which is the brightness level (*luma* in tech-talk) at which knee compression starts. It also allows adjusting the knee slope, or the *amount* of knee compression used. That prevents overexposure ("blown highlights") by limiting signals in high-intensity areas of the subject to the dynamic range of your camera. In short, a higher knee level produces more detail in the highlights; a lower knee level produces fewer details in the highlights. Too much compression may prevent exposure from reaching 100 percent. It includes Mode, Auto Set, and Manual Set options so you can set knee point and slope yourself, or allow the a6400 to automatically select the settings for you.

■ **Color Mode.** Sets type and level of colors, from among Movie, Still, Cinema, Pro, ITU-709 Matrix, Black & White, and S-Gamut.

■ **Saturation.** Sets the color saturation, from −32 to +32 values. This can be useful for reducing color in dark scenes that you want to appear low key, and help reduce noise levels in dark scenes.

- **Color Phase.** Sets the color phase (–7 to +7).
- **Color Depth.** Sets the color depth for each color phase.
- **Detail.** Sets parameters including Level, and Detail adjustments including Mode, Vertical/Horizontal Balance, B/W Balance, Limit, Crispning (sic), and Hi-Light Detail.
- **Copy.** Copies the settings of the picture profile to another picture profile number.
- **Reset.** Resets the picture profile to the default setting. You cannot reset all picture profile settings at once.

S-Log2/S-Log3

S-Log2 and S-Log3 are log gamma curves that are used when the video will be processed after shooting, and captures a much larger range of tones (as many as 14.5 stops!) than standard gamma curves. Indeed, the tones captured using S-Log2/S-Log3 can't be displayed in all their glory on a standard TV or monitor, which are generally adjusted for the broadcast television BT-709 standard. Instead, the unprocessed video will look darker and lower in contrast because all those tonal values have been squeezed into the BT-709 (also called REC-709) range.

Video signals normally encompass brightness levels from 0 percent to 109 percent (you read that right: modern video cameras can record detail in highlights that are actually brighter than was possible when the video age began; the old scale was retained, reminiscent of Nigel Tufnel's 11 setting on his amp). However, even the 109 percent provides too much of a limitation; cameras can capture detail in highlights that are even brighter than *that*. So, a log gamma curve like S-Log2 or S-Log3 is used to *compress* all that image detail to fit into the space allowed for conventional video signals. Post-processing in a video editor allows working with all that information and produces a finished video that contains the filmmaker's selection of tonal values in a form that can be displayed comfortably. The full dynamic range can be used to produce the finished movie. You might find that useful when exposing for highlights while avoiding blowing out the sky, or for capturing detail in shadows without losing mid tones and highlights.

The Picture Profile 7 (PP7) is already set up for S-Log2, while PP8 and PP9 use the more drastic S-Log3 gamma. They should be your choice if you want to work with that long curve. I've oversimplified things a bit, because there are many other great things you can do with S-Log2/S-Log3, such as overexposing or "pushing" your video to reduce noise (but at the risk of losing some detail in brighter skin tones), and then output (called "grading") to produce an optimized final image. As you get started using these gamma curves, you'll discover the amazing improvement they can make under certain lighting conditions, particularly on bright but overcast outdoor shoots.

DON'T FORGET GAMMA ASSIST

I noted in Chapter 6 that movies captured using S-Log gamma profiles appear to be very low in contrast until processed using software on your computer. As a result, reviewing these clips *in the camera* can be difficult. If you want to review your video with the a6400, don't forget to apply the Display Gamma Assist entry in the Setup 1 menu. It allows selecting options that will adjust the display of extended dynamic range clips so they appear *in the camera* with a more normal look. You'll still need to process the video in your video-editing software. As explained in Chapter 6, you can turn Gamma Display Assist off, allow the camera to select an appropriate adjustment automatically, or manually set the assist feature to use the particular gamma you are working with.

Shooting in 4K

In practice, shooting 4K is not much different than shooting full HD or standard HD. The only changes you might make involve your realization that as long as you are capturing higher quality video you might as well upgrade your technique (and, perhaps, your auxiliary equipment).

While 4K video still seems new and exotic, given the usual pace of technology, it's very likely that your next HDTV will have 4K capabilities (if your current set does not), and cable/satellite/streaming systems as well as Blu-Ray discs will all make the leap sooner than any of us expect. I've already made a switch to 4K video with my "big" camera—a Sony a7R III—and am in the process of doing the same with my a6400.

Shooting in 4K is still in its infancy: few of us own 4K high-definition televisions that allow playing back 4K content at its full resolution. However, the number of 4K-capable TVs is growing all the time, and there are some definite benefits to shooting ultra-high resolution now, even before the ability to take advantage of the format is widespread. Simply speaking, if you shoot 4K and then convert it to conventional full HD, your video will generally be much higher in quality than if you originated in 1920 × 1080 resolution. All you need is editing software like Adobe Premiere Pro, Final Cut Pro, or Corel Video Studio that can work with and edit your 4K clips.

The key thing to know is that your a6400 can record 4K video internally, export 4K video to an external recorder or to *both* simultaneously. If you want to record *only* to the memory card, you don't need to do anything special other than select XAVCS 4K under the File Format entry and your desired frame/bit rate under Record Setting (both in the Camera Settings II menu).

If you prefer to output your 4K video to the HDMI port (say, to a video recorder), or the HDMI port *and* the memory card, you need to visit the 4K Output Selection entry in the Setup 4 menu. Set the mode dial to Movie and attach your camera to the external device using a micro HDMI cable.

You will probably want to use an external microphone, either plugged into the a6400's microphone jack or connected through the multi interface shoe on top of the camera. A move to professional microphones using the XLR interface might also seem prudent. I'll have more on audio later in this chapter.

Once you've ventured down the upgrade road, if you will be shooting a great amount of pro-level video, you'll probably consider an external video recorder such as the Atomos Shogun Inferno ($1,200), Shogun Flame ($995), or new Shogun Ninja V ($695), all-in-one monitors/recorders that give you a way to capture the a6400's "clean" uncompressed video output, with a 7-inch calibrated touch screen external monitor. Although these products dwarf your a6400 in size, such a rig can provide everything you need to shoot video worthy of feature-film presentation. (Keep in mind that several off-beat theatrical flicks were shot entirely using GoPro action cams mounted to the faces of a team of stuntmen.)

TIP

If you read my Chapter 4 advice on redefining the available options in the Function menu, consider using Function Menu Set in the Camera Settings II-8 menu if you intend to shoot a lot of video. Among those you might consider substituting are Zebra settings, Audio levels, and Color balance/temperature settings (remember it's more difficult to adjust color in video than in individual still photos). Or, you might want to add Picture Profiles, Wind Noise Reduction, or the Movie setting (which allows you to switch among P, A, S, or M movie exposure modes). Marker Display or TC/UB settings are other entries you might want to add to your Function menu.

As I noted in Chapter 6, the 4K Output Selection entry in the Setup 4 menu allows you to specify exactly where and how your 4K video is captured. To recap, you have four choices:

- **Memory Card+HDMI.** A 4K movie in 30p is saved on the camera's internal SDXC memory card *and* output to the external recorder. This option gives you two copies, including one you can review right in the camera, and a second on your external recorder.

- **HDMI Only (30p).** A 4K movie in 30p is output only to the external device, and not recorded on your memory card. HDMI Info. Display is disabled.

- **HDMI Only (24p).** A 4K movie in 24p is output only to the external device. HDMI Info. Display is disabled.

- **HDMI Only (25p).** If the NTSC/PAL Selector described earlier is set to PAL, you can use this option to shoot a 4K movie in 25p, and output only to the external device. HDMI Info. Display is disabled.

Tips for Movie Making

I'm going to close out this introductory movie chapter with a general discussion of movie-making concepts that you need to understand as you move toward more polished video production.

Here are some basic tips:

■ **Keep things stable and on the level.** Camera shake's enough of a problem with still photography, but it becomes even more of a nuisance when you're shooting video. While the a6400's image stabilization found in lenses with the OSS designation can help minimize this, it can't work miracles. Placing your camera on a tripod will work much better than trying to hand-hold it while shooting. One bit of really good news is that compared to pro dSLRs, the a6400 can work very effectively on a lighter tripod, due to the camera's light weight. On windy days however, the extra mass of a heavy tripod is still valuable.

■ **Use a shooting script.** A shooting script is nothing more than a coordinated plan that covers both audio and video and provides order and structure for your video. A detailed script will cover what types of shots you're going after, what dialogue you're going to use, audio effects, transitions, and graphics.

■ **Plan with storyboards.** A storyboard is a series of panels providing visuals of what each scene should look like. While the ones produced by Hollywood are generally of very high quality, there's nothing that says drawing skills are important for this step. Stick figures work just fine if that's the best you can do. The storyboard just helps you visualize locations, placement of actors/actresses, props, and furniture, and also helps everyone involved get an idea of what you're trying to show. It also helps show how you want to frame or compose a shot. You can even shoot a series of still photos and transform them into a "storyboard" if you want, such as in Figure 10.4.

Today's audience is used to fast-paced, short-scene storytelling. In order to produce interesting video for such viewers, it's important to view video storytelling as a kind of shorthand code for the more leisurely efforts print media offers. Audio and video should always be advancing the story. While it's okay to let the camera linger from time to time, it should only be for a compelling reason and only briefly.

It only takes a second or two for an establishing shot to impart the necessary information. For example, many of the scenes for a video documenting a model being photographed in a rock 'n' roll music setting might be close-ups and talking heads, but an establishing shot showing the studio where the video was captured helps set the scene.

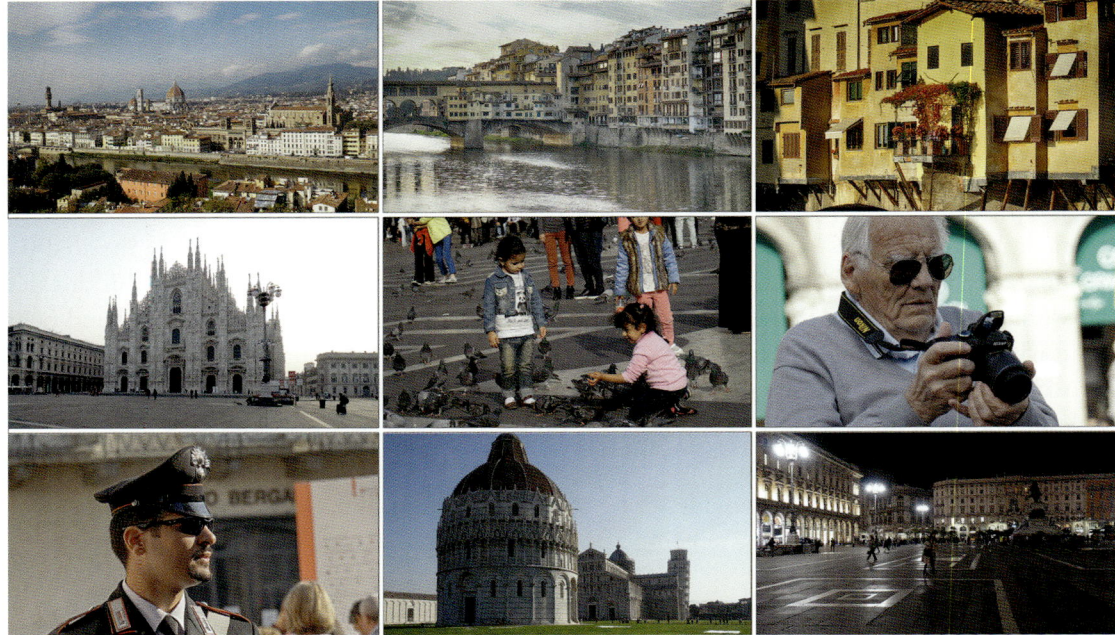

Figure 10.4 A storyboard is a series of simple sketches or photos to help visualize a segment of video.

- **Provide variety.** Provide variety too. Change camera angles and perspectives often and never leave a static scene on the screen for a long period of time. (You can record a static scene for a reasonably long period and then edit in other shots that cut away and back to the longer scene with close-ups that show each person talking.)

- **When editing, keep transitions basic!** I can't stress this one enough. Watch a television program or movie. The action "jumps" from one scene or person to the next. Fancy transitions that involve exotic "wipes," dissolves, or cross fades take too long for the average viewer and make your video ponderous.

Composition

In movie shooting, several factors restrict your composition, and impose requirements you just don't always have in still photography (although other rules of good composition do apply). Here are some of the key differences to keep in mind when composing movie frames:

- **Horizontal compositions only.** Some subjects, such as basketball players and tall buildings, just lend themselves to vertical compositions. But movies are generally shot and shown in horizontal format only. (Unless you're capturing a clip with your smartphone; I see many vertically oriented YouTube videos.) So if you're shooting a conventional video and interviewing a local basketball star, you can end up with a worst-case situation like the one shown in Figure 10.5. If you want to show how tall your subject is, it's often impractical to move back far enough to show him full-length. You really can't capture a vertical composition. Tricks like getting down on the floor and shooting up at your subject can exaggerate the perspective, but aren't a perfect solution.

- **Wasted space at the sides.** Moving in to frame the basketball player as outlined by the yellow box in Figure 10.5 means that you're still forced to leave a lot of empty space on either side. (Of course, you can fill that space with other people and/or interesting stuff, but that defeats your intent of concentrating on your main subject.) So when faced with some types of subjects in a horizontal frame, you can be creative, or move in *really* tight. For example, if I was willing to give up the "height" aspect of my composition, I could have framed the shot as shown by the green box in the figure, and wasted less of the image area at either side.

- **Seamless (or seamed) transitions.** Unless you're telling a picture story with a photo essay, still pictures often stand alone. But with movies, each of your compositions must relate to the shot that preceded it, and the one that follows. It can be jarring to jump from a long shot to a tight close-up unless the director—you—is very creative. Another common error is the "jump cut" in which successive shots vary only slightly in camera angle, making it appear that the main subject has "jumped" from one place to another. (Although everyone from French New Wave director Jean-Luc Goddard to Guy Ritchie—Madonna's ex—have used jump cuts effectively in their films.) The rule of thumb is to vary the camera angle by at least 30 degrees between shots to make it appear to be seamless. Unless you prefer that your images flaunt convention and appear to be "seamy."

Figure 10.5
Movie shooting requires you to fit all your subjects into a horizontally oriented frame.

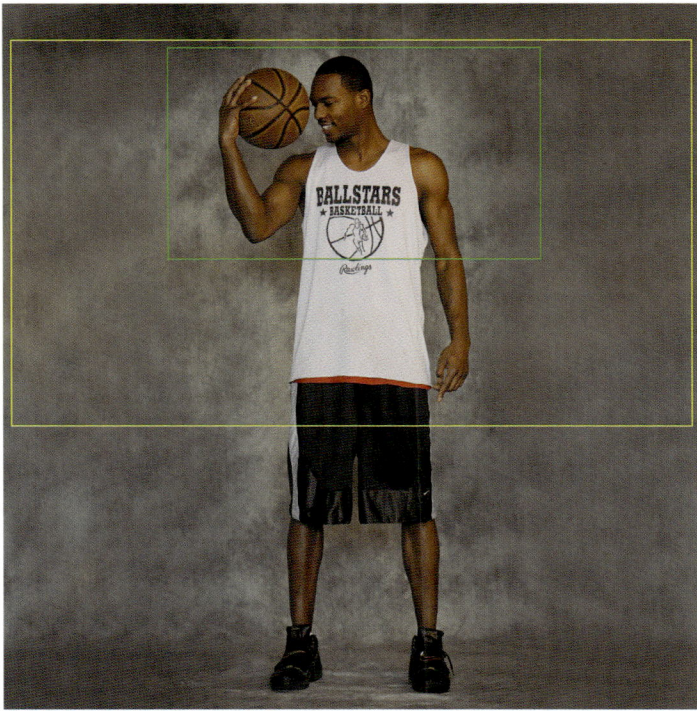

■ **The time dimension.** Unlike still photography, with motion pictures there's a lot more emphasis on using a series of images to build on each other to tell a story. Static shots where the camera is mounted on a tripod and everything is shot from the same distance are a recipe for dull videos. Watch a television program sometime and notice how often camera shots change distances and directions. Viewers are used to this variety and have come to expect it. Professional video productions are often done with multiple cameras shooting from different angles and positions. But many professional productions are shot with just one camera and careful planning, and you can do just fine with your a6400 camera.

Here's a look at the different types of commonly used compositional tools:

■ **Establishing shot.** Much like it sounds, this type of composition, as shown at top left in Figure 10.6, establishes the scene and tells the viewer where the action is taking place. Let's say you're shooting a video of your offspring's move to college; the establishing shot could be a wide shot of the campus with a sign welcoming you to the school in the foreground. Another example would be for a child's birthday party; the establishing shot could be the front of the house decorated with birthday signs and streamers or a shot of the dining room table decked out with party favors and a candle-covered birthday cake. In this case, I wanted to show the studio where the video was shot.

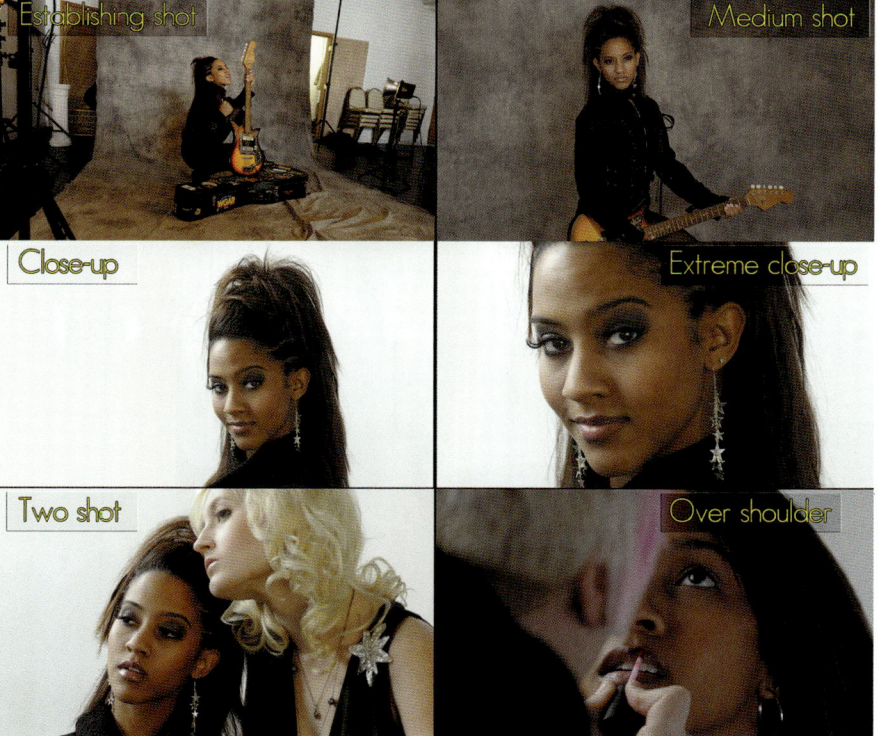

Figure 10.6

Mix up your shots using these compositional options.

- **Medium shot.** This shot is composed from about waist to head room (some space above the subject's head). It's useful for providing variety from a series of close-ups and also makes for a useful first look at a speaker. (See Figure 10.6, top right.)

- **Close-up.** The close-up, usually described as "from shirt pocket to head room," provides a good composition for someone talking directly to the camera. Although it's common to have your talking head centered in the shot, that's not a requirement. In the middle-left image in Figure 10.6 the subject was offset to the right. This would allow other images, especially graphics or titles, to be superimposed in the frame in a "real" (professional) production. But the compositional technique can be used with a6400 videos, too, even if special effects are not going to be added.

- **Extreme close-up.** When I went through broadcast training, this shot was described as the "big talking face" shot and we were actively discouraged from employing it. Styles and tastes change over the years and now the big talking face is much more commonly used (maybe people are better looking these days?) and so this view may be appropriate. Just remember, the a6400 is capable of shooting in high-definition video and you may be playing the video on a high-def TV; be careful that you use this composition on a face that can stand up to high definition. (See middle right, Figure 10.6.)

- **"Two" shot.** A two shot shows a pair of subjects in one frame. They can be side by side or one subject in the foreground and one in the background. This does not have to be a head-to-ground composition. Subjects can be standing or seated. A "three shot" is the same principle except that three people are in the frame. (See Figure 10.6, lower left.)

- **Over-the-shoulder shot.** Long a composition of interview programs, the "over-the-shoulder shot" uses the rear of one person's head and shoulder to serve as a frame for the other person. This puts the viewer's perspective as that of the person facing away from the camera. (See Figure 10.6, lower right.)

Lighting for Video

Much like in still photography, how you handle light pretty much can make or break your videography. Lighting for video can be more complicated than lighting for still photography, since both subject and camera movement are often part of the process.

Lighting for video presents several concerns. First off, you want enough illumination to create a useable video. Beyond that, you want to use light to help tell your story or increase drama. Let's take a better look at both.

Illumination

You can significantly improve the quality of your video by increasing the light falling in the scene. This is true indoors or out, by the way. While it may seem like sunlight is more than enough, it depends on how much contrast you're dealing with. If your subject is in shadow (which can help him from squinting) or wearing a ball cap, a video light can help make him look a lot better.

Lighting choices for amateur videographers are a lot better these days than they were a decade or two ago. An inexpensive incandescent video light, which will easily fit in a camera bag, can be found for $15 or $20. You can even get a good-quality LED video light for as little as $40 (see Figure 10.7). Work lights sold at many home improvement stores can also serve as video lights since you can set the camera's white balance to correct for any color casts. You'll need to mount these lights on a tripod or other support, or, perhaps, to a bracket that fastens to the tripod socket on the bottom of the camera.

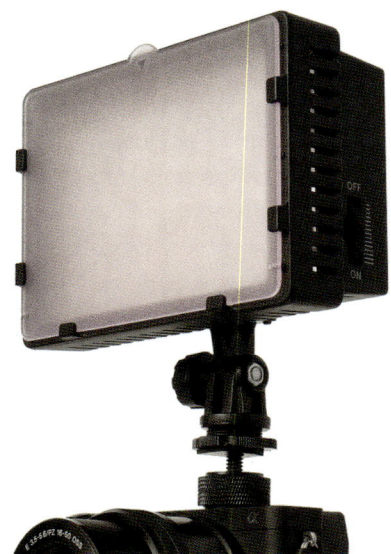

Much of the challenge depends upon whether you're just trying to add some fill light on your subject versus trying to boost the light on an entire scene. A small video light will do just fine for the former. It won't handle the latter. Fortunately, the versatility of the a6400 comes in quite handy here. Since the camera shoots video in Auto ISO mode, it can compensate for lower lighting levels and still produce a decent image. For best results though, better lighting is necessary.

Figure 10.7 This LED video light cost just $40.

Creative Lighting

While ramping up the light intensity will produce better technical quality in your video, it won't necessarily improve the artistic quality of it. Whether we're outdoors or indoors, we're used to seeing light come from above. Videographers need to consider how they position their lights to provide even illumination while up high enough to angle shadows down low and out of sight of the camera.

When considering lighting for video, there are several factors. One is the quality of the light. It can either be hard (direct) light or soft (diffused) light. Hard light is good for showing detail, but it can also be very harsh and unforgiving. "Softening" the light, but diffusing it somehow, can reduce the intensity of the light but make for a kinder, gentler light as well.

While mixing light sources isn't always a good idea, one approach is to combine window light with supplemental lighting. Position your subject with the window to one side and bring in either a supplemental light or a reflector to the other side for reasonably even lighting.

Lighting Styles

Some lighting styles are more heavily used than others. Some forms are used for special effects, while others are designed to be invisible. At its most basic, lighting just illuminates the scene, but when used properly it can also create drama.

Let's look at some types of lighting styles:

- **Three-point lighting.** This is a basic lighting setup for one person. A main light illuminates the strong side of a person's face, while a fill light lights up the other side. A third light is then positioned above and behind the subject to light the back of the head and shoulders. (See Figure 10.8, left.)

- **Flat lighting.** Use this type of lighting to provide illumination and nothing more. It calls for a variety of lights and diffusers set to raise the light level in a space enough for good video reproduction, but not to create a particular mood or emphasize a particular scene or individual. With flat lighting, you're trying to create even lighting levels throughout the video space and minimize any shadows. Generally, the lights are placed up high and angled downward (or possibly pointed straight up to bounce off of a white ceiling). (See Figure 10.8, right.)

- **"Ghoul lighting."** This is the style of lighting used for old horror movies. The idea is to position the light down low, pointed upward. It's such an unnatural style of lighting that it makes its targets seem weird and ghoulish.

- **Outdoor lighting.** While shooting outdoors may seem easier because the sun provides more light, it also presents its own problems. As a general rule of thumb, keep the sun behind you when you're shooting video outdoors, except when shooting faces (anything from a medium shot and closer) since the viewer won't want to see a squinting subject. When shooting another human this way, put the sun behind your subject and use a video light to balance light levels between the foreground and background. If the sun is simply too bright, position the subject in the shade and use the video light for your main illumination. Using reflectors (white board panels or aluminum foil–covered cardboard panels are cheap options) can also help balance light effectively.

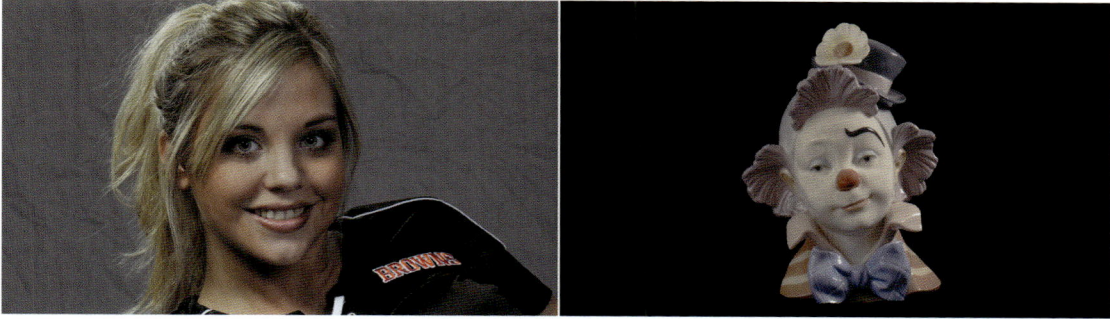

Figure 10.8 Three-point lighting (left) and flat lighting (right).

Audio

When it comes to making a successful video, audio quality is one of those things that separates the professionals from the amateurs. We're used to watching top-quality productions on television and in the movies, yet the average person has no idea how much effort goes in to producing what seems to be "natural" sound. Much of the sound you hear in such productions is actually recorded on carefully controlled sound stages and "sweetened" with a variety of sound effects and other recordings of "natural" sound.

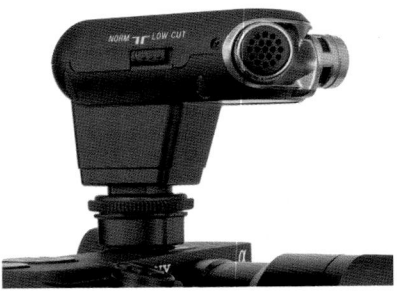

Figure 10.9 An external microphone improves audio quality.

Your a6400 has a pair of stereo microphones on its front surface, able to capture Dolby Digital Audio. There is no way to plug in an external microphone with the unadorned camera. You must use an adapter plugged into the multi interface shoe, or a microphone designed specifically for Sony cameras, such as the (roughly $110) Sony ECM-XYSTM1 mic shown in Figure 10.9. If you stick with the built-in microphones, you must be extra careful to optimize the sound captured by those fixed sound-grabbers. You will find an Audio Recording entry in the Camera Settings II-02 menu (it just turns sound on or off), as well as a Wind Noise Reduction on/off switch. But that's as far as your camera adjustments go.

Tips for Better Audio

Since recording high-quality audio is such a challenge, it's a good idea to do everything possible to maximize recording quality:

- **Turn off any sound makers you can.** Little things like fans and air handling units aren't obvious to the human ear, but will be picked up by the microphone. Turn off any machinery or devices that you can plus make sure cell phones are set to silent mode. Also, do what you can to minimize sounds such as wind, radio, television, or people talking in the background.

- **Make sure to record some "natural" sound.** If you're shooting video at an event of some kind, make sure you get some background sound that you can add to your audio as desired in postproduction.

- **Consider recording audio separately.** Lip-syncing is probably beyond most of the people you're going to be shooting, but there's nothing that says you can't record narration separately and add it later. It's relatively easy if you learn how to use simple software video-editing programs like iMovie (for the Macintosh) or Windows Movie Maker (for Windows PCs). Any time the speaker is off-camera, you can work with separately recorded narration rather than recording the speaker on-camera. This can produce much cleaner sound.

WIND NOISE REDUCTION

The a6400 does offer a low-cut filter feature that can further reduce wind noise; it's accessed with the Wind Noise Reduction item of the Camera Settings II-03 menu, discussed in Chapter 3. However, this processing feature also affects other sounds, making the wind screen far more useful.

Lens Craft

I'll cover the use of lenses with the a6400 in more detail in Chapter 11, but a discussion of lens selection when shooting movies may be useful at this point. In the video world, not all lenses are created equal. The two most important considerations are depth-of-field, or the beneficial lack thereof, and zooming. I'll address each of these separately.

Depth-of-Field and Video

Have you wondered why professional videographers have gone nuts over still cameras that can also shoot video? The producers of *Saturday Night Live* could afford to have Alex Buono, their director of photography, use the niftiest, most-expensive high-resolution video cameras to shoot the opening sequences of the program. Instead, Buono opted for a pair of digital SLR cameras. One thing that makes digital still cameras so attractive for video is that they have relatively large sensors. That provides two benefits compared to cameras with a smaller sensor. In addition to improved low-light performance, the large chip allows for unusually shallow depth-of-field (a limited range of acceptable sharpness) for blurring the background; this effect is difficult or impossible to match with most professional video cameras since they use smaller sensors.

As you'll learn in Chapter 11, a larger sensor calls for the use of longer focal lengths to produce the same field of view, so, in effect, a larger sensor allows for making images with reduced depth-of-field. And *that's* what makes cameras like the a6400 attractive from a creative standpoint. Shallow depth-of-field makes it easier to blur a cluttered background to keep the viewers' eyes riveted on the primary subject. Your camera, with its larger sensor, has a distinct advantage over consumer camcorders in this regard, and even does a much better job than some small-sensor professional video cameras.

Zooming and Video

When shooting still photos, a zoom is a zoom is a zoom. The key considerations for a zoom lens used only for still photography are the maximum aperture available at each focal length ("How *fast* is this lens?"), the zoom range ("How far can I zoom in or out?"), and its sharpness at any given f/stop ("Do I lose sharpness when I shoot wide open?").

When recording video, the priorities may change, and there are two additional parameters to consider. The first two I listed, lens speed and zoom range, have roughly the same importance in both still and video photography. Zoom range gains a bit of importance in videography, because you can always/usually move closer to shoot a still photograph, but when you're zooming during a shot most of us don't have that option (or the funds to buy/rent a dolly to smoothly move the camera during capture). But, oddly enough, overall sharpness may have slightly less importance under certain conditions when shooting video. That's because the image changes in some way many times per second (30/60 times per second), so any given frame doesn't hang around long enough for our eyes to pick out every single detail. You want a sharp image, of course, but your standards don't need to be quite as high when shooting video.

Here are your primary considerations:

- **Zoom lens maximum aperture.** The "speed" of the lens matters in several ways. A zoom with a relatively wide maximum aperture (small f/number) lets you shoot in lower light levels with fewer exposure problems. A wide aperture like f/1.8 also enables you to minimize depth-of-field for selective focus. Keep in mind that with most zooms, the maximum aperture gets smaller as you zoom to longer focal lengths. A variable-aperture f/3.5 to 5.6 lens like the power zoom kit lens, offers a fairly wide f/3.5 maximum aperture at its shortest focal length but only f/5.6 worth of light-capturing ability at the long end. Zooms with a wide and constant (not variable) maximum aperture such as f/2.8 are available, but they are larger, heavier, and more expensive.

- **Power zoom.** An ideal movie zoom should have a power zoom feature, and that's available with Sony lenses with the PZ designation. PZ lenses offer smooth, silent zooming that's ideal for video shooting. Mechanical zooming with other lenses during capture can produce jerky images, even with vibration reduction turned on.

- **Zoom range.** Use of zoom during actual capture should not be an everyday thing, unless you're shooting a kung-fu movie. However, there are effective uses for a zoom shot, particularly if it's a "long" one from wide angle to telephoto. The Sony 18-200mm zoom, which has a relatively quiet autofocus motor and built-in stabilizer, can be used in this way, with mechanical zooming, of course. Most of the time, you'll use the zoom range to adjust the perspective of the camera *between* shots, and a longer zoom range can mean less trotting back and forth to adjust the field of view. Zoom range also comes into play when you're working with selective focus (longer focal lengths produce shallower depth-of-field), or want to expand or compress the apparent distance between foreground and background subjects. A longer range gives you more flexibility.

- **Linearity.** Interchangeable lenses may have some drawbacks, as many photographers who have been using the video features of their digital SLRs have discovered. That's because lenses with mechanical zooming are rarely linear unless they were specifically designed for shooting movies. Rotating the zoom ring manually at a constant speed doesn't always produce a smooth zoom. There may be "jumps" as the elements of the lens shift around during the zoom. Keep that in mind if you plan to zoom during a shot, and are using a non-linear lens. In practice, those include virtually all the lenses at your disposal, aside from power zoom lenses, a special E-mount cine lens, or a cine lens in an entirely different mount that you can use with your a6400 with an optional third-party adapter.

11

Working with Lenses

Although the a6400's E-mount lens system is fairly new, introduced in 2010, the number of lenses that operate with full autoexposure and autofocus features is large and growing rapidly. In addition to E-mount lenses intended for your a6400's APS-C sensor, additional full-frame FE lenses for the Alpha a7 series are available from Sony, Zeiss, and other vendors. These FE lenses can also be used with the a6400.

If you're willing to use an adapter, there are at least 100 or more different lenses in Sony/Minolta A-mount or Canon EF-mount—often available at bargain prices—that can be used on your a6400 or Sony a7-series full-frame camera (if you have one), with autofocus and autoexposure. And the number of lenses that can be used with *manual* focus and Aperture Priority autoexposure using adapters for Nikon, Yashica, Contex, Contarex, Alpha, and other types of lenses is mind-boggling. Indeed, Pulitzer Prize–winning photographer (and Sony guru) Brian Smith has called the Sony product line the "universal mount" cameras.

Figure 11.1
A full-range of E-mount lenses, including this Sony FE 70-200mm F4 G OSS, work well on the a6400.

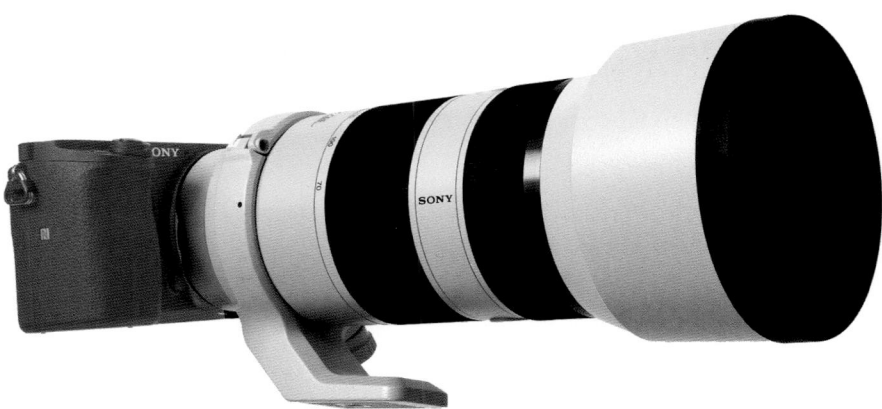

This chapter will help you wend your way through the confusing world of lenses for the a6400. Before we get into the actual lenses themselves, it may be useful to explore some aspects that affect how you choose and use optics.

Don't Forget the Crop Factor

From time to time you've heard the term *crop factor*, and you've probably also heard the term *lens multiplier* or *focal length multiplication factor*. While some of these terms are misleading and inaccurate, they're used to describe the same phenomenon: the fact that cameras like the Sony a6400— and all other digital interchangeable-lens cameras using a sensor smaller than the "full-frame" 24mm × 36mm format—provide a field of view (or scene coverage) that's smaller than you get with a camera employing the larger sensor. The a6400 (as well as numerous other cameras of several brands) uses a sensor that's 15.6mm × 23.5mm in size.

In practical terms, let's say you're using a 35mm lens on a full-frame Sony a7 III-series camera; you get a field of view of 63 degrees. But if you use that same 35mm focal length lens on an a6400, the field of view is only 44 degrees because the smaller sensor records only a part of the image that the lens projects. Knowledgeable photographers often discuss this effect as the *crop factor*, and you'll often find a reference in lens reviews to a *focal length equivalent;* that's 1.5X with the sensor size used by a camera like the a6400. In other words, a 35mm lens used on the a6400 is equivalent to a 52.5mm focal length on a full-frame camera like the a7 III. The most accurate expression to describe this concept might be something like *field of view equivalency factor*.

Figure 11.2 quite clearly shows the phenomenon at work. The green rectangle, marked 1X, shows the field of view you might expect with a 24mm lens mounted on a full-frame digital model like the a7R III. It provides a very wide-angle perspective, roughly 84 degrees (measured diagonally by

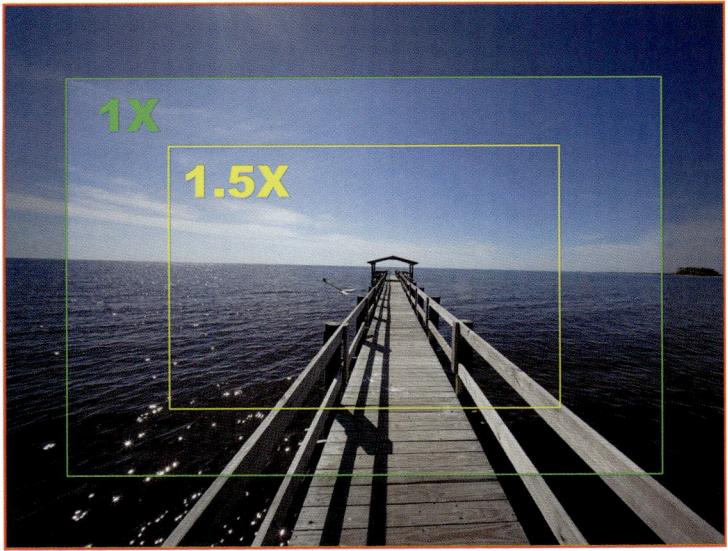

Figure 11.2

This image illustrates the field of view provided by a full-frame camera like the Sony a7R III (1X) with a 24mm lens, as well as the field of view you'd get when using a camera with a smaller sensor (1.5X crop) like the a6400.

convention). The yellow rectangle marked 1.5X shows the field of view you'd get with that 24mm lens installed on a camera like the a6400 that uses a 15.6mm × 23.5mm (APS-C—Advanced Photo System) sensor. It's easy to see from the illustration that the APS-C rendition is narrower—roughly 61 degrees diagonally—and, compared to the full-frame version, *cropped*.

That 24mm lens on your a6400 has the same field of view as a 36mm lens would on the a7R III. While you can calculate the relative field of view by dividing the focal length of the lens by .667, we humans tend to perform multiplication operations in our heads more easily than division, so such field of view comparisons are usually calculated using the reciprocal of .667—1.5—so we can multiply instead (24 / .667 = 36; 24 × 1.5 = 36). That's the origin of the misleading term *multiplication factor*. The sensor image is trimmed or cropped—not multiplied.

Tip

Frankly, all of this is useful only if you were previously using a 35mm SLR and frames of 24mm × 36mm film or have used or may use a full-frame dSLR like the a7 III series. In that case, you might find it helpful to use the crop factor "multiplier" to translate a lens's real focal length into the full-frame equivalent, even though nothing is actually being multiplied. If you have always owned a digital camera with a smaller sensor, you already have a good feel as to the field of view that you get at a focal length such as 24mm, 35mm, or 50mm. It's highly unlikely that you would think in terms that require you to do any calculations.

In any event, I strongly prefer *crop factor* to *focal length multiplier*, because nothing is being multiplied (as I said above). When working with telephoto lenses, a 100mm lens doesn't "become" a 150mm lens; the depth-of-field and lens aperture remain the same. (I'll explain more about these later in this chapter.) Only the field of view is cropped. Of course, the term *crop factor* has a drawback: it implies that a 24mm × 36mm frame is "full" and anything else is "less than full."

I get e-mails all the time from medium-format photographers who own cameras like the Hasselblad H6D-50c, which has a 43.8 × 32.9mm sensor that's 67 percent larger than "full-frame." By their logical reckoning, the 24mm × 36mm sensors found in full-frame cameras like the Sony a7R III are "cropped." Take a look at the outer, darkened area within the red rectangle in Figure 11.2. That represents the whopping 104-degree field of view you'd get with a Hasselblad HCD 24mm f/4.8 ($6,295; body an extra $14,495 if you're compiling a holiday gift list).

Choosing a Lens

The a6400 is most frequently purchased with a lens, often the retractable 16-50mm f/3.5-5.6 Power Zoom model with OSS, Sony's Optical SteadyShot Stabilizer discussed in previous chapters. (See Figure 11.3.) A zoom is useful but you might prefer the 16mm f/2.8 pancake lens because its minimal size/weight provide great portability that's ideal while hiking or touring for days while on vacation. Or, if you want a do-everything, walk-around lens, you might want the 18-200mm f/3.5-6.3 OSS zoom. If you already own some lenses for an Alpha SLT A-mount camera, you might want to just purchase one of the E-mount adapters discussed later and use the lenses you already have.

In this section, I'll discuss the Sony E-mount lenses, the starter models, as well as the wide-angle lenses. Here are your choices in these categories:

- **Sony 16-50mm power zoom OSS f/3.5-5.6 (SELP-1650).** If you did not buy the a6400 in a kit, you might still want to consider this lens with power zooming that's ideal for anyone who often shoots movies, as discussed in Chapter 10. It's quite compact when not in use since the internal barrel retracts when the camera is turned off and it's a fine performer overall. ($300.) You may see this lens disparaged in user groups as being less than tack sharp, but many of the photos in my books of European destinations were taken with this lens. I like it a lot.

- **Sony 18-55mm OSS f/3.5-5.6 (SEL-1855).** If you do not own the power zoom lens because you don't often shoot video, consider this model with conventional (mechanical) zooming and the same maximum apertures. It may be hard to find new; Sony lists it at $299 on its US website, but you can find excellent used examples for less than half that at keh.com and other resellers. It's sharp, small in size, and fast enough at shorter focal lengths for most available-light shooting. Granted, it is a stop and a half slower at the telephoto end; this is typical with lenses of this type.

- **Sony 16mm f/2.8 (SEL-16F28).** This flat, pancake-style wide-angle lens ($250) is also sharp and downright tiny, with dimensions of 0.89 × 2.44 inches. The f/2.8 maximum aperture is much wider than you'll get with most affordable zooms and makes this lens more suitable for available-light shooting. Granted, it does not zoom, but it's my favorite super-compact optic.

The 16mm lens accepts two add-on accessories that mount on the front, with the VCL-ECF2 fisheye conversion lens ($180) shown in Figure 11.4. It gives you a fisheye view for interesting landscapes, interiors, and other subjects. Given that fisheye lenses are typically used infrequently by most shooters, the relatively low cost of this accessory offsets the less than tack-sharp results you can expect. Mount the five-ounce VCL-ECU2 wide-angle converter ($160) instead, to transform this 16mm lens into a super-wide 12mm (18mm equivalent) lens. I've gotten great results from mine, although it works best when the host lens is stopped down at least one or two apertures from wide open.

Note: the VCL-ECF2 and VCL-ECU2 replace earlier versions with similar specifications; however, the new versions can now be used with both this Sony 16mm f/2.8 lens, and the 20mm f/2.8 lens described next.

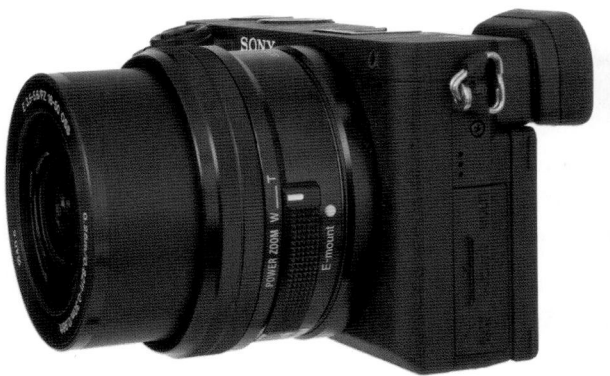

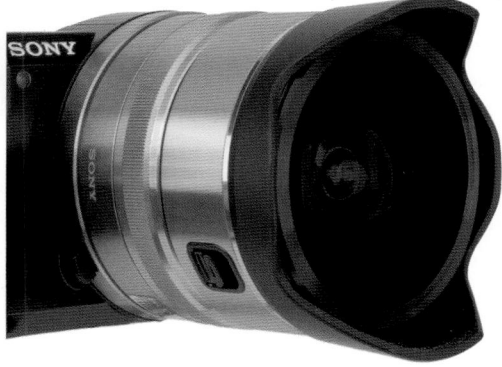

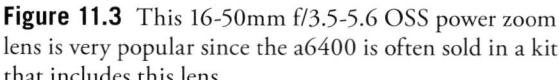

Figure 11.3 This 16-50mm f/3.5-5.6 OSS power zoom lens is very popular since the a6400 is often sold in a kit that includes this lens.

Figure 11.4 The 16mm "pancake" lens is unusually compact, even when equipped with the fisheye attachment shown.

- **Sony 20mm f/2.8 (SEL-20F28).** Also very compact and featuring the same maximum aperture, this ($350) lens accepts the same add-on converters as the 16mm f/2.8 lens, and provides very fine image quality.

- **Sony 35mm f/1.8 OSS (SEL-35F18).** Because of the 1.5X crop factor discussed earlier, this 52.5mm equivalent lens might be considered to be the "normal" lens in the system (that is, comparable to the very popular 50mm f/1.8 lens in a dSLR system). The very wide maximum aperture and OSS stabilizer make it ideal for low-light photography. Move very close to the subject, use f/1.8, and you can blur the background with shallow depth-of-field. The lens is pricey ($450) because it's equipped with a superior optical formula to control aberrations and a high-speed linear focusing motor that's almost silent, a definite benefit when shooting video.

- **Sony 50mm f/1.8 OSS (SEL-50F18).** This more affordable ($300) model, also with a very wide maximum aperture, is a short telephoto on the a6400 and would be useful for street photography from moderate distances, and for portraits. The f/1.8 aperture is useful for blurring a background in a situation where you're shooting a head-and-shoulders portrait. Since this is a fast lens with OSS stabilizer that compensates for camera shake at slower shutter speeds, it's another fine choice for available-light photography.

- **Sony 10-18mm f/4 OSS (SEL-1018).** If you're really into wide-angle and ultra-wide-angle photography, this lens is an ideal choice ($850). At the 10mm end (a 15mm equivalent) an image can encompass more than our two eyes can see without scanning. We often shoot at small apertures in wide-angle image making, but this lens is adequately fast for low-light photography indoors when using f/4 and the OSS stabilizer. You should be pleased with the image quality provided by this ultra-wide zoom because it features an impressive optical formula with super extra-low dispersion glass and three aspherical elements to minimize optical distortions (discussed later in this chapter).

The lenses in the E-mount system range from the sublime to the meticulous, and can prove useful for various kinds of photography. Next, let's take a look at zooms that extend beyond 100mm and the macro lens. I'll be covering the high-grade Carl Zeiss ZA series later. If you're keeping score, Sony does make APS-C lenses (that is, non-full-frame optics) in E-mount intended for video shooting, such as the 18-110mm f/4 G OSS PZ lens (SELP18-110G). That particular lens costs $3,500 and is not really appropriate even for well-heeled a6400 owners who shoot video, so I won't be describing it further in this chapter. Otherwise, here are your additional E-mount options in the Sony designated APS-C lineup:

- **Sony 18-105mm f/4 G PZ OSS (SELP-18105G).** This lens and the 10-18mm zoom described above, were the only two lenses I took with me on my most recent trip to Europe. Featuring a relatively wide maximum aperture of f/4 at all focal lengths, this power zoom lens's G designation indicates superior optical elements for fine image quality. It's made with two ED and three aspherical elements for controlling optical aberrations (inherent lens flaws) for across-the-frame sharpness at most apertures, including f/4. It's a bit pricey ($600) but offers good value. As the power zoom designation indicates, this is another of the Sony lenses with power zooming. (See Figure 11.5.)

- **Sony 18-135 f/3.5-5.6 OSS (SEL18135).** You can't argue with success, and this lens is one of the most popular in the "walk-around lens" category in the Sony lineup. It's sharp and has a linear AF motor that operates smoothly for video. I value it highly for its extra telephoto reach and affordable $600 retail price. However, I prefer the 18-105mm f/4 despite its more modest zoom range.

- **Sony (PZ) OSS 18-200mm f/3.5-6.3 (SELP-18200/SEL-18200LE).** Sony has offered three versions of this lens, with the most recent (the SELP-18200), having a power zoom and the PZ label appended to its product name. It's priced at $1,200. The non-power-zoom version (SEL-18200LE) has an MSRP of $899. You may also find a few of the original (SEL-18200) at $850 or less. All of them dwarf the a6400, and their maximum aperture is very small at the longest telephoto setting, but they have a great zoom range that makes them suitable for a6400 owners who really prefer to carry only a single lens. They all range in price from roughly $850 to

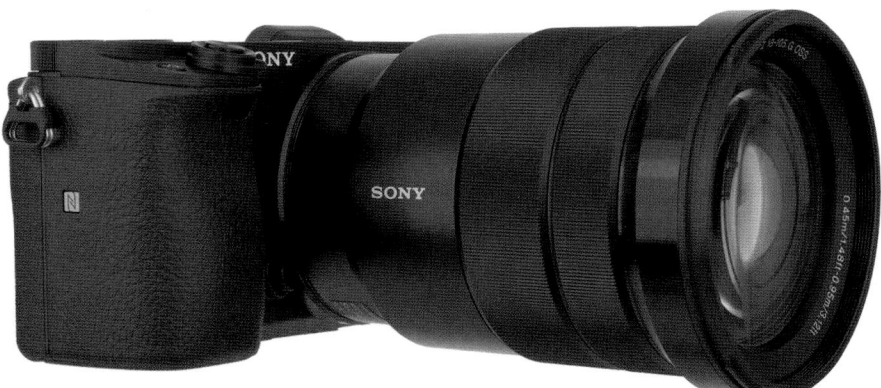

Figure 11.5
The Sony 18-105mm f/4 G PZ OSS lens.

$1,200, so they are not cheap, but they provide great focal length versatility. The built-in OSS stabilization reduces the risk of blur caused by camera shake, a definite asset in a telephoto lens that's quite slow (with small maximum apertures especially at long focal lengths). At the maximum 200mm focal length, you should be able to get sharp photos when hand-holding the camera/lens at a shutter speed of 1/60th second.

The power zoom version targets a6400 owners who shoot video often and will really appreciate the ability to zoom quietly and extremely smoothly.

■ **Sony 55-210mm f/4.5-6.3 OSS (SEL-55210).** This is an affordable ($350) OSS lens with enough telephoto reach for some wildlife photography and for shooting amateur sports events. Of course, the maximum apertures are a bit small, especially at long focal lengths. As well, you will get the best image quality at f/8. You will need to use a higher ISO on dark days to be able to shoot at shutter speeds fast enough to "freeze" the motion of your subjects at f/6.3 and especially if you decide to use f/8. At this writing, Sony doesn't have a fast medium-to-long telephoto in E-mount.

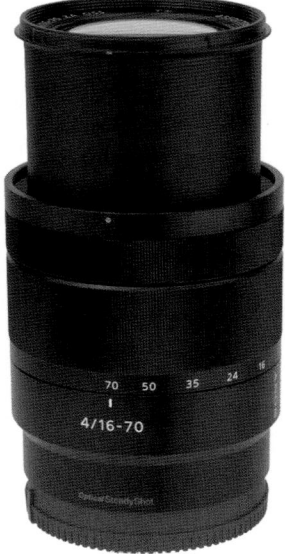

■ **Sony 30mm f/3.5 Macro (SEL-30M35).** This is the current macro lens in the line. You'll find that it features a minimum working distance of about one inch; move in extremely close to the subject and you can make images with 1X magnification (a 1:1 reproduction ratio). That might be a problem with a nature subject like a bee, but it's certainly practical with coins, stamps, and jewelry, for example. The maximum aperture of f/3.5 is small, but in macro, we usually use a small aperture such as f/16 for adequate depth-of-field to sharply render an entire three-dimensional subject. This lens is compact, lightweight, and affordable ($280). Of course, because I own both A-mount and E-mount Sony cameras, and an A-mount-to-E-mount adapter, I ended up purchasing the A-mount version of this lens. For close-up work, having the smallest, lightest lens and the fastest autofocusing isn't essential, and I saved money by not buying both.

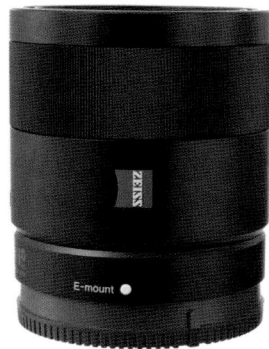

■ **Carl Zeiss Vario-Tessar T* 16-70mm f/4 ZA OSS (SEL-1670Z).** A mid-range APS-C zoom with a relatively wide maximum aperture of f/4 at all focal lengths, this zoom incorporates four aspherical elements for superior image quality and Sony's OSS stabilizer ($1000). It's shown in Figure 11.6, top, zoomed to the maximum focal length, and retracted (bottom). This is one lens that gets significantly longer as you zoom, making it much less compact at the telephoto settings. I already owned the 16-50mm kit lens, so I purchased my a6400 in a bundle with this optic. While it lacks the power zoom feature, I like the longer reach.

Figure 11.6 The Carl Zeiss 16-70mm f/4 lens extended (top) and retracted to its widest zoom setting (bottom).

■ **Carl Zeiss Sonar T* 24mm f/1.8 ZA OSS (SEL-24F18Z).** This moderately wide-angle (36mm equivalent) APS-C lens with OSS stabilizer and a maximum aperture of f/1.8 is perfect for low-light street photography. I also find it useful indoors for nearby sports action (you might also like it for basketball when shooting at the baseline) and for shooting interiors where an ultra-wide view is not crucial (think larger venues, cathedrals, and museums where flash is prohibited). Frankly, this lens could easily be the star of your stable with superb image quality and freedom from distortion thanks to the use of ED glass and aspherical elements.

A linear stepping motor provides fast, low-noise autofocus that's ideal when shooting video. Sure, it's pricey ($900), and not exactly compact at 2 3/8 × 2 1/2 inches and nearly 8 ounces, but if you need f/1.8 and its angle of view, nothing else will do the job. This lens can be hard to find since it's often back-ordered. I have owned mine for over a year now and have gotten excellent results with this superb lens.

The Sony "Trinity"

If your needs aren't met by Sony's current APS-C E-Mount lineup, or if you either plan to add a Sony full-frame camera to your stable in the future or already are using one, you'll want to consider a few of the superb full-frame lenses the company offers, all of which have the FE designation to differentiate them from their E-mount APS-C siblings.

Indeed, serious photographers, whether shooting the a6400 or a full-frame model like the a7 III series, consider the lenses that make up the E-mount "trinity" to be must-have optics in terms of image quality and flexibility, regardless of price (each of them costs in excess of $1,000). Originally, the Sony trinity consisted of three lenses, with 16-35mm, 24-70mm, and 70-200mm focal lengths, all with constant f/4 maximum apertures. (That is, the maximum aperture does not change as you zoom; it remains f/4 as you zoom from the widest to longest position.) In 2016, however, Sony introduced new, more expensive lenses that are even better optically, have more rugged builds, and each boast f/2.8 maximum apertures. Two of them—the Sony 24-70mm f/2.8 G Master and 70-200 f/2.8 G Master, supplement two of the original trinity. A third, an 85mm f/1.4 G Master is a medium telephoto that's especially suitable for portraiture. The company has continued to add more G Master optics, many of them with price tags in the thousands of dollars, so we won't be spending a lot of time considering those options. The original three can be seen in Figure 11.7.

■ **Sony FE 16-35mm f/4 ZA OSS (SEL-1635Z).** This is the lens you need for your architectural, landscape, and indoor photography in tight quarters. It covers an almost perfect range of focal lengths, from a wide 16mm to a 35mm "normal lens" field of view. One wonderful thing about this optic is that it has *curved* aperture blades, producing smooth circular defocused highlights for great *bokeh*. At around $1,350, it's a bit of a stretch for the a6400, but if you shoot a lot of wide-angle images at least it's more affordable than the f/2.8 G Master version, priced at about $2,200.

Figure 11.7
Sony's three key FE
lenses, left to right:
16-35mm f/4,
24-70mm f/4, and
70-200mm f/4.

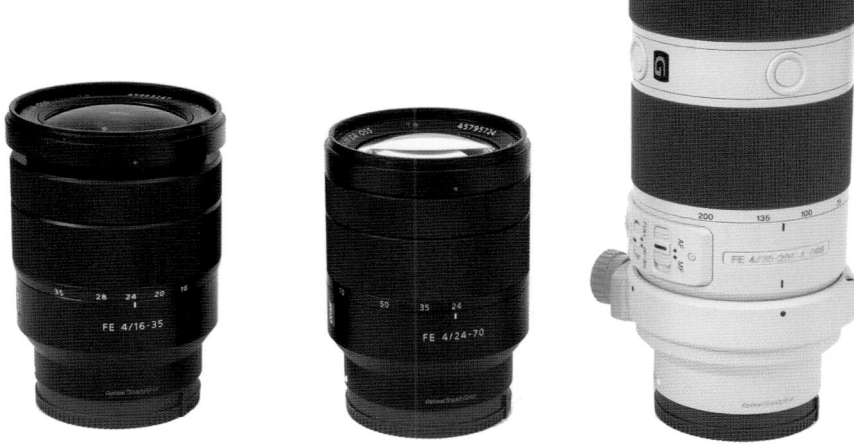

- **Sony Vario-Tessar T* FE 24-70mm f/4 ZA OSS (SEL-2470Z).** This lens includes my personal least-used focal length range. I tend to see my subjects either with a wide-angle view, often with an apparent perspective distortion aspect, or with a telephoto/selective focus approach. Another Zeiss-branded product, it is useful as a walk-around lens for travel photography, full-length and three-quarters portraits, and indoor sports like basketball and volleyball. Unfortunately, it won't be the sharpest optical knife in your toolkit, despite the Zeiss label. I find it perfectly acceptable when stopped down two or three stops from maximum aperture, but for $900, I expected more.

  You might explore the $450 Sony FE 28-70mm f/3.5-5.6 OSS SEL-28700 kit lens. It's abominably slow (f/5.6) at the 70mm zoom position, but you might find that saving $500 while filling out your trinity alleviates the pain. If you have very deep pockets, the SEL-2470 GM 24-70mm f/2.8 G Master lens is priced at about $2,200.

- **Sony FE 70-200mm f/4 G OSS (SEL-70200G).** This is one of my favorite lenses, although it's very expensive at around $1,400. I'm able to justify it for my a6400, because I use it as a primary lens on my Sony a7R III full-frame camera as well. Indeed, I often choose which camera I am going to use based on the type of work and the effective focal length of this lens. If I am shooting portraits, fashion, and concerts, I often go with the a7R III, because the 70-200mm focal lengths and fast f/4 maximum aperture are perfect for subjects that can benefit from the a7R's 36-megapixel resolution. On the other hand, for sports and wildlife photography, I am more likely to combine my a6400 and this lens. The camera's 24M resolution doesn't cost me much detail, but the effective 105-300mm equivalent focal length works very well for those subjects.

  The Sony SEL-70200GM f/2.8 version is a bit heftier (in effect nullifying the lightweight benefits of the a6400 itself) and is *much* more expensive, at $2,500.

Other E-Mount Lenses

Because Sony's full-frame and APS-C mirrorless cameras complement each other so well, I've discovered that many photographers (including me) purchase both. In that case, the decision to spring for extra money to buy full-frame lenses becomes even easier. The next sections will list my choices of other full-frame lenses from Sony, Zeiss, and other vendors. They include walk-around lenses, some fast primes for photojournalism and other available-light applications, and even a stellar macro.

Sony FE Lenses

These are some of my favorite full-frame lenses suitable for both the Sony a6400 and full-frame mirrorless models. Again, I'm not going to delve into the ultra-expensive lens category, where lenses like the FE 200-600mm f/5.6-6.3 and 400mm f/2.8 G Master reside. Instead, I'm going to stick with cheap-o lenses priced at less than $5,000. (Hah!)

- **Sony FE 55mm/1.8 Sonnar T* ZA (SEL-55F18Z).** So, why get excited about a "normal" lens with an f/1.8 maximum aperture and a $1000 price tag? After all, both Nikon and Canon offer full-frame 50mm f/1.8 prime lenses for $200 or less. In this case, your ten Benjamins buys you one of the sharpest lenses ever made, with exquisite resolution at every f/stop—including wide open. Given that perspective, this lens is actually a bargain. You'll love using it for head-and-shoulders or 3/4 length portraits using selective focus at f/1.8. It's said to rival super-costly lenses, like the 55mm f/1.4 Zeiss Otus, which has a $4,000 price tag. Sony has introduced a less expensive ($250) Sony FE 50mm f/1.8 FE (SEL-50F18F) lens. Unless you definitely plan to upgrade to full frame in the future, the APS-C 50mm f/1.8 optic is roughly the same price and should have better image quality.

- **Sony FE 24-240mm f/3.5-6.3 OSS (SEL-2440).** On first glance, a 10X zoom lens stretching from a semi-wide-angle 24mm field of view to the super telephoto realm at 240mm (36mm to 360mm equivalent on the a6400) sounds very tempting. With a second look, this optic's $1,000 price adds to the appeal. The reality check comes only when you realize that mating this hefty (1.72 pound), somewhat slow lens (f/6.3 at maximum zoom) to the compact a6400 counters the best reason for toting around a tiny mirrorless camera. If you truly want to walk around with only a single lens and can justify the bulk, this optic does fit the bill. It would also be an efficient choice for photography that might call for extreme wide-angle views and telephoto reach in rapid succession. Given its modest price tag, you can expect this lens will be a jack-of-all-trades and master of none. I'd rather carry a medium-sized camera bag and fill it with the trio of lenses described in the previous section, even at a cost premium of $3,000.

- **Sony FE 28-135mm f/4 G PZ OSS (SELP-28135G).** The specs alone might lead you to believe this is a faster, heavier (5 pounds) walk-around lens with a more restricted zoom range. You'd be wrong. This $2,500 monster is especially designed for pro-level 4K video productions, and if heavy-duty movie making isn't on your agenda, you probably don't want or need this lens. Video shooters, though, will delight in its near-silent precision-variable 8-speed power zoom, and responsive manual control rings for zoom (with direction reversal for smooth zooms), focus pulling, and aperture.

■ **Sony FE 28mm f/2.0 (SEL-28F20).** Here's a lens that comes with its own bag of tricks. It's a compact prime lens with a fast f/2.0 aperture, so you can shoot in low light and even gain a modicum of selective focus with its (relatively) shallow depth-of-field wide open. Despite its $450 price, it boasts an advanced optical design with ED (extra-low dispersion) glass elements that improve contrast and reduce troublesome chromatic and spherical aberrations. (You'll find descriptions of lens aberrations later in this chapter.) If that's not enough, you can attach either of two adapter optics to the front. There is a 21mm wide-angle version (SEL-075UWC, $250), which converts it to a 21mm f/2.8 wide angle that focuses down to eight inches, and a 16mm fisheye attachment (SEL-057FEC, $300) that I personally find more interesting and fun. But then, I own eight different fisheye lenses, so I'm susceptible.

■ **Sony Distagon T* FE 35mm f/1.4 ZA (SEL-35F14Z).** This Zeiss lens is a photojournalist's dream, with a wide-angle focal length that lets you get up close and personal with your subject, and a fast f/1.4 aperture suitable for low light and selective focus. The Zeiss T* (T-star) coating suppresses contrast loss from internal reflections among the lens elements. It's great for video, too, as the aperture ring can be de-clicked with a switch. The only drawback is the price: $1,600, which is a lot to pay for a lens that doesn't give you a range of different focal lengths to work with. However, the shooters this lens is designed for will confirm that it's worth it.

■ **Sony Sonnar T* FE 35mm f/2.8 ZA (SEL-35F28Z).** This tiny lens is a perfect match for the compact camera. At a mere eight ounces and measuring 2.42 × 1.44 inches, it makes a great walk-around lens for stealthy photographers. The image quality is great, but you'd expect that from a Zeiss lens that, at $800, is not bargain-basement cheap.

■ **Sony FE 90mm f/2.8 Macro G OSS (SEL-90M28G).** I expect that Sony will make additional macro lenses available for the E-mount cameras, but until then this $1,100 lens is an excellent choice. Its 90mm focal length gives you a decent amount of distance between the camera and your close-up subject, even at its minimum focusing distance of 11 inches. With internal focusing such that only the internal elements move, the lens doesn't get longer as you focus, avoiding a common problem. You can add a set of auto extension tubes to get even closer. I use Fotodiox Pro 10mm and 16mm tubes. Those tubes are primarily plastic and not especially rugged, but are serviceable for light-duty use.

■ **Sony FE 70-300mm f/4.5-5.6 G OSS (SEL-70300G).** This lens's $1,200 price tag becomes more palatable when you realize that it gives a6400 owners the equivalent of a 105mm-450mm telephoto lens. I plan to purchase one when they become available, as I can use it on my a7R II and a6400.

Zeiss Touit Lenses

While the Zeiss FE lenses produced and sold by Sony all feature autofocus, Zeiss also independently sells its own optics, including this Touit trio of fast prime lenses designed specifically for Sony APS-C cameras like the a6400. They are priced more affordably than the full-frame lenses, but still have excellent optical quality, rugged builds, and excellent autofocus/autoexposure features. If you've been meaning to get a round Touit, these were your options at the time this book was written:

- **Zeiss Touit 12mm f/2.8 lens.** With a full-frame equivalent focal length of 18mm, this compact lens verges on ultra-wide-angle territory. It's fast f/2.8 maximum aperture makes it a good choice for indoor architectural photography. It has a list price of $999, but has been selling with rebates and instant savings at many retailers for as little as $699.

- **Zeiss Touit 32mm f/1.8 lens.** If you think Zeiss is nice, then you'll find this lens and its f/1.8 maximum aperture ideal for street photography, photojournalism, indoor sports, and other subjects photographed under low lighting conditions. At $720, it costs less than half of the Sony Zeiss 35mm f/1.4 full-frame lens.

- **Zeiss Touit 50mm f/2.8M lens.** For about $1,000, you can own this superb macro lens, which offers a 1:1 magnification ratio and a minimum focus distance of 6 inches. Combined with third-party extension tubes from Fotodiox, Vello, and other vendors, you can get even closer.

Zeiss Loxia Lenses

Wandering back into full-frame lens territory, the Zeiss Loxia lenses are among the best you can buy for Sony E-mount cameras, with, so far, five lenses available, all manual focus. Not including autofocus helps keep the price down on these otherwise premium-quality super-sharp lenses. Of course "low price" is a relative term, as these optics all cost between $1,000 and $1,500. If you choose one of these, keep in mind that your a6400 has a wealth of manual-focus-friendly features, including focus peaking and focus magnification, all described elsewhere in this book. You can get all five in a special kit, a de-click tool kit, case, and other accessories for about $6,000.

- **Zeiss Loxia 50mm f/2 Planar T* lens.** If you've been involved with photography for any length of time, you'll recognize the Zeiss Planar name, first applied to a symmetrical lens design as far back as 1896. This fast manual focus lens does a good job of correcting for chromatic aberration and distortion, and is one of the best lenses you can buy for roughly $950. Like all the Loxia lenses, the manual aperture ring can be de-clicked, using a supplied tool, for use when constantly varying apertures are desired when shooting video.

- **Zeiss Loxia 35mm f/2 Biogon T* lens.** Another name out of the past, Biogon lenses have historically been some of the best wide-angle optics you can buy, and this fast 35mm f/2 lens has been optimized for use with digital cameras (that is, illumination emerges from the back of the lens at a less steep angle, as explained in Chapter 2). Your $1,300 buys you a well-corrected lens suitable for street photography, architecture, landscapes, and other subjects.

- **Zeiss Loxia 21mm f/2.8 T* lens.** This lens was introduced in December 2015, for $1,500. It's an extra-compact lens using the famed Distagon design, which overcomes some of the drawbacks of many wide angles to provide consistent sharpness from edge to edge, with little light falloff and excellent correction for chromatic aberrations.

- **Zeiss Loxia 85mm f/2.4 T* lens.** This $1,300 lens is weather-sealed and the manual aperture can be "de-clicked" to afford silent operation when shooting video.

- **Zeiss Loxia 25mm f/2.4 T* lens.** Another weather-sealed, de-clickable lens, it has two low-dispersion and one aspherical element for excellent image quality, and is priced at $1,400.

Zeiss Batis Lenses

Here we have reasonably priced full-frame autofocus lenses from Zeiss. If you're looking for a futuristic touch, they each feature an illuminated OLED (organic LED) display that dynamically shows focus distance and depth-of-field. In the good old days, prime (non-zoom) lenses had etched or painted color-coded depth-of-field markers on the lens barrel, but those largely disappeared when zoom lenses became dominant. Now depth-of-field can be displayed on your lens in a more useful form. As I write this, the five available Batis lenses are as follows:

- **Zeiss Batis 85mm f/1.8 lens.** This is a $1,200 medium-telephoto autofocus lens that's ideal for portraits, and a primo choice for low-light photography and selective focus. It was the first Zeiss lens introduced that had optical image stabilization (the equivalent of Sony's trademarked OSS).

- **Zeiss Batis 25mm f/2.0 lens.** There's a bit of overlap in potential use between this autofocus lens and Sony's own 28mm f/2.0 optic. This one is more expensive at $1,300, sharper, and isn't compatible with Sony's wide-angle/fisheye adapters.

- **Zeiss Batis 18mm f/2.8 lens.** This has the widest field of view in the Batis line, with a list price of about $1,400, boasting the same weather-resistant build and OLED readouts.

- **Zeiss Batis 40mm f/2 CF lens.** Priced a little less than $1,200, the CF in the product name stands for Close Focusing. It has a minimum focusing distance of 9.4 inches, and a maximum magnification of 1:3.3.

- **Zeiss Batis 135mm f/2.8 lens.** This has the longest telephoto (so far) in the Batis line, with a list price of about $1,700, with an optical image stabilization, floating elements, and the rugged weather-resistant build and OLED readouts found in the other Batis optics.

Other Third-Party Lenses

It's fairly easy for third parties to adapt their existing full-frame lenses to fit your camera. There are some interesting lenses available. I've purchased a bunch of them, including a 28mm f/1.4 Kamlan lens I bought from their Kickstarter campaign. Several companies are developing fast 50-58mm f/0.95 to f/1.1 lenses that look interesting for low-light photography and applications in which a wide aperture is desirable to produce extremely shallow depth-of-field. Third-party lenses often produce quirky or interesting bokeh effects in their out-of-focus highlights.

Here's a sampling of some of the other lenses to consider:

■ **7Artisans.** This newish company has introduced a flurry of almost a dozen E-mount manual lenses priced at a few hundred dollars (or less), including a 7.5mm f/2.8 fisheye, 35mm f/1.2 wide-angle, and other interesting fast lenses, mostly in the wide-angle-to-short tele (12mm-55mm range).

■ **Mitakon/Zhongyi.** This company makes an ultra-fast 85mm f/1.2 manual focus lens ($800), and hyperfast 50mm f/0.95 and 35mm f/0.95 lenses ($800 and $600, respectively) in Sony E-mount, with the two latter optics having the distinction of being the world's fastest full-frame E-mount lens. They also offer a 24mm f/1.7 for a bargain $350.

■ **Voigtlander.** Probably the oldest name in camera gear, dating back to its founding in Vienna in 1756 (well before the invention of photography itself), this company produces some interesting lenses, including 10mm and 12mm f/5.6 Heliar and a 15mm f/4.5 Heliar. I own the 10mm lens, and it is one of my all-time favorites—although it has to be used on my a7R III to take full advantage of its incredible field of view. On a full-frame camera, it's the widest rectilinear (non-fisheye) lens available, with a breathtaking 130-degree field of view. With the a6400's cropped sensor, though, it's a more mundane manual focus non-zoom lens with a 109-degree field of view, and a slow f/5.6 maximum aperture. The Sony 10-18mm zoom is probably a better bet—unless, like a growing number of us, you also own a Sony full-frame E mount camera and can use it on both.

■ **Venus Optics Laowa 12mm f/2.8 Zero-D Len.** Another full-frame lens that may be of interest to discerning a6400 owners is this super-low-distortion manual focus wide angle. It's not a fisheye—it's a rectilinear lens with two aspherical elements and three extra-low dispersion (ED) elements for impressive optical quality. Available since early 2017, it focuses down to seven inches, making some interesting distorted perspective shots possible.

■ **Samyang/Rokinon.** This company's manual focus 12mm f/2.8 fisheye resides in my fisheye collection, and I often alternate its use with my 15mm f/2.8 Sigma fisheye. I use them in manual focus mode with adapters, but Samyang/Rokinon also sells lenses in E-mount (sometimes under the Bower brand name). They include a 14mm f/2.8, 24mm f/1.4, 35mm f/1.4, 50mm f/1.4, 85mm f/1.4, 135mm f/2, and a 100mm f/2.8 macro lens that produce 1:1 (life-size) magnification at a minimum focusing distance of 12 inches. The company has introduced its first *autofocus* lenses, and Sony fans are the beneficiaries. The 14mm f/2.8 ED AS IF UMC and 50mm f/1.4 AS IF UMC are full-frame (FE-style) lenses, but work just as well on the a6400.

Because of the popularity of the camera line, third-party vendors have rushed to produce lenses for these models. Because the a6400's "flange-to-sensor" distance is relatively short, there's room to use various types of adapters between camera and lens and still allow focusing all the way to infinity. There are already a huge number of adapters that allow mounting just about any lens you can think of on the a6400, if you're willing to accept manual focus and, usually, a ring on the adapter that's used to stop down the "adopted" lens to the aperture used to take the photo.

You can find these from Novoflex (www.novoflex.com), Metabones (www.metabones.com), Fotodiox (www.fotodiox.com), Rainbow Imaging (www.rainbowimaging.biz), Cowboy Studio (www.cowboystudio.com), and others.

Some adapters of certain types and brands sell for as little as $20 to $30. With many of them you should not expect autofocus even if you're using an AF lens from some other system; as well, many of the camera's high-tech features do not operate. However, you can usually retain automatic exposure by setting the a6400 to Aperture Priority, stopping down to the f/stop you prefer, and firing away.

The ultra-high-grade Novoflex and Metabones adapters for using lenses of other brands sell for much higher prices. I found only two that are said to maintain autofocus with a lens of an entirely different brand. The Metabones Canon EF–to-Sony Smart Adapter (Mark V) and their similar Speed Booster model ($400 to and $650, respectively) maintain autofocus, autoexposure, and the Canon lens's image stabilizer feature when used with a camera. The "Speed Booster" part of the name comes from the adapter's ability to magically add one f/stop to the maximum aperture of the lens (thanks to the adapter's internal optics), transforming an f/4 lens into an f/2.8 speed demon.

The Metabones Smart Adapter V has been taking the Sony world arena by storm, thanks to the ability to use AF-C with Canon's EF or EF-S lenses and your camera's hybrid phase detect/contrast detect autofocus system. Reports are that autofocus with these lenses is equal to or superior to that of the same lenses when mounted on their native Canon camera bodies. The Canon lenses' in-lens IS also works. The Metabones Smart Adapter V is well made, with brass components, and costs a hefty $399, but if you are switching over from a Canon system, the ability to use your existing lenses is priceless. Other vendors are working on adapters, both for Canon and Nikon AF lenses, but I have not had the chance to evaluate them.

Other vendors are working on adapters, both for Canon and Nikon AF lenses. The first Nikon adapter I have had a chance to evaluate is the FotodioX Fusion Smart AF Adapter for Nikon F lens to Sony E-mount cameras. The reason Nikon AF adapters have been slow in coming is that Canon stops down its lens from wide open to the "taking" aperture (used to expose the image) electronically, whereas Nikon, which has used the same basic mount design since 1959, relies on a lever in the camera body to physically move a matching lever in the lens to stop down the lens. Commlite, which developed the technology used in the FotodioX adapter, had to include a motor *in the adapter* itself to adjust the f/stop at the moment of exposure, based on signals from the Sony camera.

The Fusion adapter works amazingly well and, in my case, allows me to use my dream lens, a Nikon AF-S Nikkor 105mm f/1.4E ED lens on both my a7R III and a6400. Because both have fast phase detect autofocus, the lens focuses extremely fast. I use it as a portrait lens on my full-frame camera and as a sport lens on the a6400, as it provides the equivalent of a 158mm f/1.4 lens on the APS-C camera. Those who do own Nikon lenses will want to know that the adapter requires a Nikon lens with a built-in autofocus motor (AF-S or AF-I) and will not autofocus with Nikon AF lenses, which lack the motor. (See Figure 11.8.)

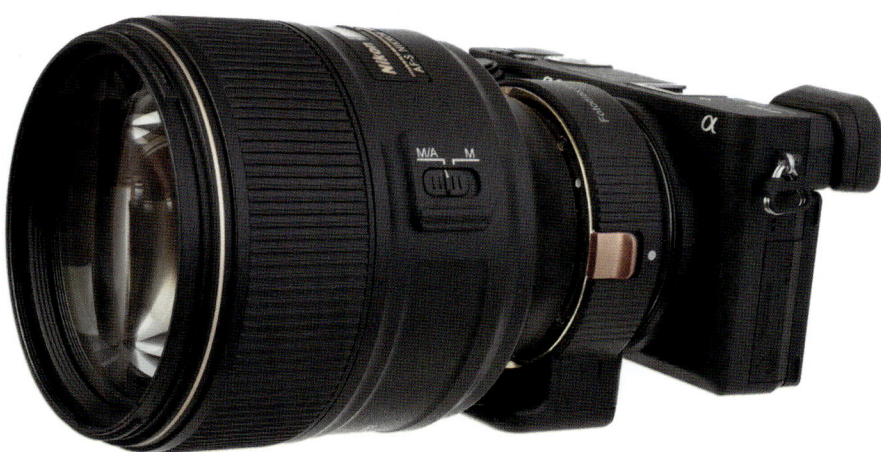

Figure 11.8
Sony a6400 with
Nikon 105mm f/1.4
lens attached.

Using the LA-EA Series Adapters

Sony makes four A-mount-to-E-mount adapters, which allow using Sony/Minolta A-mount lenses on an Alpha E-mount camera such as the a6400. Why four different adapters? All four, the LA-EA1, LA-EA2, LA-EA3, and LA-EA4, allow connecting an A-mount lens to an NEX/Alpha-series camera. The two odd-numbered adapters use *only* contrast detect autofocus with lenses that have built-in AF motors and are compatible with them. The two even-numbered adapters have built-in SLT-like phase detection AF systems for fast focusing with lenses that use the original screw-drive AF system. The LA-EA1 and LA-EA2 are designed for APS-C cameras, while the LA-EA3 and LA-EA4 shown in Figure 11.9 are intended for full-frame models like the a7 III series (but they will also work just fine with the a6400).

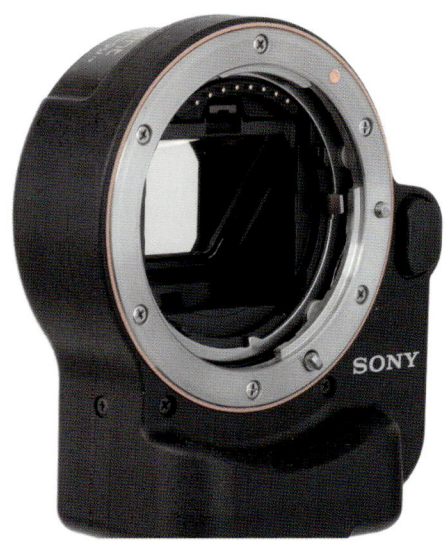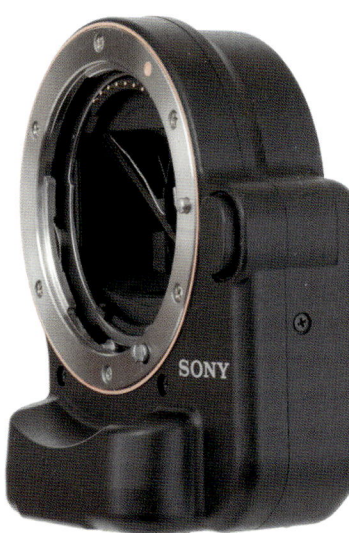

Figure 11.9
The LA-EA3 (left)
and LA-EA4 (right)
adapters allow using
A-mount lenses on
the a6400.

To make sure you are buying the right kind of adapter, it's important to keep in mind the difference between the two types:

- **If you are using newer A-mount lenses.** Most newer Sony-designed lenses have AF motors built into them, which you can tell from the SSM or SAM indicators in their product names, such as the Sony 300mm f/2.8 G SSM II (SAL-300F28G2). Such lenses receive autofocus instructions electronically from the camera through their contacts and use their internal motors to adjust focus. These lenses make the best use of the LA-EA1 and LA-EA3 adapters, because they utilize the a6400's native sensor-based AF system. Autofocus is fast and accurate.

- **If you are using older Sony or Minolta A-mount lenses.** These lenses *do not* have AF motors inside, and focus must be adjusted using a screw drive motor *built into the adapter*. Therefore, you must use the LA-EA2 or LA-EA4 adapters, which, as I've noted, incorporate their own SLT-type translucent mirror autofocus systems, including a motor. While focus is slower, you may find it eminently acceptable with many lenses. I get great results from my 100-400mm f/4.5-6.7 APO Tele-Zoom (pictured in Figure 11.10).

Figure 11.10
A Minolta 100-400mm zoom mounted on the a6400.

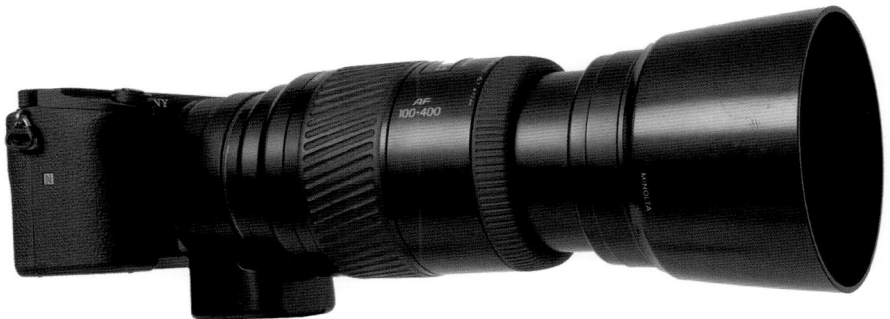

The LA-EA3 adapter and LA-EA4 adapters are the most versatile, as they work with full-frame and APS-C cameras like the a6400. Choose one or the other, depending on the type of autofocus used in your A-mount lenses. I own both, because I have a mixture of SSM, SAM, and screw-drive lenses. The LA-EA2 and LA-EA4 are clever because both involve, basically, building a version of Sony's Translucent Mirror Technology, found in the SLT cameras, into an adapter, as you can see in the exploded diagram shown in Figure 11.11. (In actual use, the lens must be physically mounted to the adapter; and don't worry: this configuration does not actually explode.)

If you're not familiar with the SLT cameras, light from the lens reaches a semi-silvered non-moving mirror, with 70 percent continuing through the mirror and adapter to the a6400's sensor. The 30 percent of the light reflected downward by the mirror is directed through a lens and another mirror to a 15-point AF sensor with three extra-sensitive cross-type sensors. The camera magically gains the same on-screen AF point selection options and high-speed phase detection autofocus in both Continuous AF and Single-shot modes as its SLT stablemates, and an electronic aperture drive mechanism allows full autoexposure functions with all A-mount lenses (except those used with a teleconverter). Virtually any Sony/Minolta A-mount lens can be used.

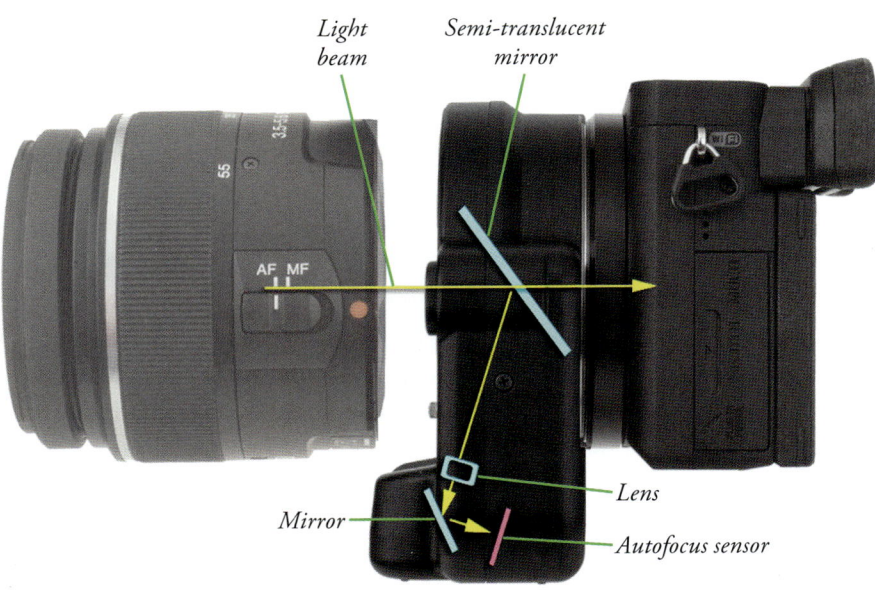

Light beam

Semi-translucent mirror

AF MF

Mirror

Lens

Autofocus sensor

Figure 11.11
The design of the LA-EA4 adapter looks like this.

While the LA-EA2 and LA-EA4 adapters are large at 3 1/8 × 3 1/2 × 1 3/4 inches, they each have a built-in tripod mount, so you can use them with bulky, heavy lenses that don't have a tripod mount of their own. For a few hundred dollars (plus the cost of your A-mount lenses), you can convert your a6400 mirrorless camera into a camera with a mirror! I'm glad Sony has made these accessories available for the a6400, but I find it amusing that such a petite camera can be fitted with pounds and pounds of adapters, lenses, and viewfinders that transform it from a compact model to a model that's easily the same size—or larger—than the SLT and dSLR alternatives. Table 11.1 summarizes your options concisely.

Table 11.1 LA-EA Series Adapters

Adapter	Autofocus	Format
LA-EA1	Contrast detect with lenses that have built-in SSM or SAM AF motors. Lenses using a screw-drive motor in the camera body will not autofocus.	APS-C
LA-EA2	Phase detect using Translucent Mirror technology.	APS-C
LA-EA3	Contrast detect with lenses that have built-in SSM or SAM AF motors. Lenses using a screw-drive motor in the camera body will not autofocus.	Full Frame and APS-C
LA-EA4	Phase detect using Translucent Mirror technology.	Full Frame and APS-C

WATCH THAT WEIGHT

Be aware than the a6400's lens mount isn't constructed to support the weight of very large lenses, such as the ones you might attach using either A-mount adapter. Support the lens by placing your hand under it (the tripod mount shown in Figure 11.12 is a good choice), and if using the setup on a tripod or monopod, attach the device to the tripod mount on the adapter, and not to the a6400's own tripod thread.

You'll find that these adapters give you access to some excellent lenses, such as my prized Minolta AF Reflex 500, a 500mm f/8 catadioptric (mirror) lens that folds the light path back on itself to provide a remarkably small and light super telephoto. This lens is remarkable as the first (and only) mirror lens with full autofocus capabilities. (See Figure 11.12.)

Figure 11.12
Minolta AF Reflex 500 super telephoto autofocus mirror lens.

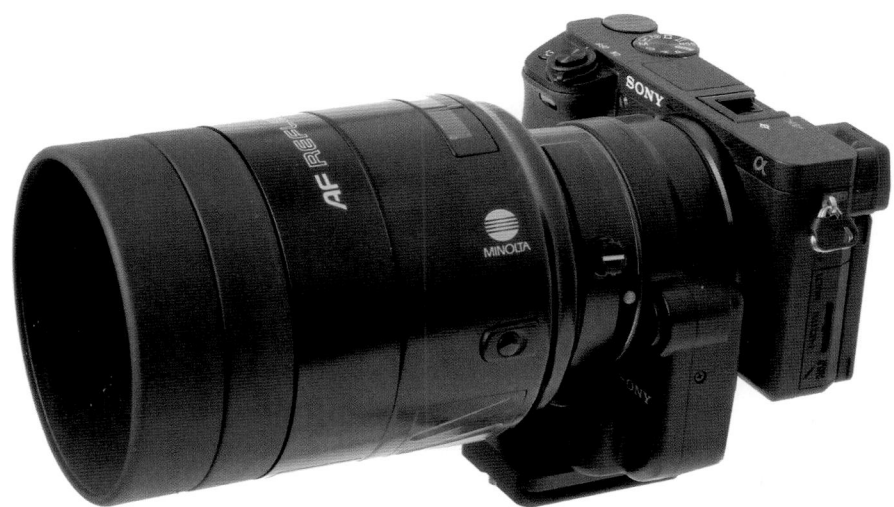

AF Micro Adjustment

The AF Micro Adj setting in the Camera Settings I-07 menu is the key tool you can use to fine-tune your A-mount lens used with the SLT-style adapters. This entry can be manipulated *only* when you're using a Sony or a Minolta Maxxum/Dynax A-mount lens with the EA-LA2 or EA-LA4 adapters. It is not available when using the LA-EA1 or LA-EA3 adapters. (The micro adjustment may work with an A-mount lens of another brand, but Sony warns that the results may be inaccurate.) Millions of A-mount lenses have been sold over the years, and the adapter is not terribly expensive, so I will assume that many readers will eventually want to consider the fine-tuning feature.

If you do not currently have such lenses or the adapter, you cannot use AF Micro Adjustment feature. But if you do own the relevant equipment, you might find that a particular lens is not focusing properly. If the lens happens to focus a bit ahead or a bit behind the desired area (like the eyes in a portrait), and if it does that consistently, you can use the adjustment feature.

Why is the focus "off" for some lenses in the first place? There are lots of factors, including the age of the lens (an older lens may focus slightly differently), temperature effects on certain types of glass, humidity, and tolerances built into a lens's design that all add up to a slight misadjustment, even though the components themselves are, strictly speaking, within specs. A very slight variation in your lens's mount can cause focus to vary slightly. With any luck (if you can call it that) a lens that doesn't focus exactly right will at least be consistent. If a lens always focuses a bit behind the subject, the symptom is *back focus.* If it focuses in front of the subject, it's called *front focus.*

You're almost always better off sending such a lens in to Sony to have them make it right. But that's not always possible. Perhaps you need your lens recalibrated right now, or you purchased a used lens that is long out of warranty. If you want to do it yourself, the first thing to do is determine whether or not your lens has a back focus or front focus problem.

For a quick-and-dirty diagnosis (*not* a calibration; you'll use a different target for that), lay down a piece of graph paper on a flat surface, and place an object on the line at the middle, which will represent the point of focus (we hope). Then, shoot the target at an angle using your lens's widest aperture (smallest available f/number) and the autofocus mode you want to test. Mount the camera on a tripod so you can get accurate, repeatable results.

If your camera/lens combination doesn't suffer from front or back focus, the point of sharpest focus will be the center line of the chart, as you can see in Figure 11.13. If you do have a problem, one of the other lines will be sharply focused instead. Should you discover that your lens consistently front focuses or back focuses, it needs to be recalibrated. Unfortunately, it's only possible to calibrate a lens for a single focusing distance. So, if you use a particular lens (such as a macro lens) for close-focusing, calibrate for that. If you use a lens primarily for middle distances, calibrate for that. Close-to-middle distances are most likely to cause focus problems, anyway, because as you get closer to infinity, small changes in focus are less likely to have an effect.

You'll find the process easier to understand if you first run through this quick overview of the menu options:

- **AF Adjustment Setting.** This option enables AF fine-tuning for all the lenses you've registered using this menu entry. If you discover you don't care for the calibrations you make in certain situations (say, it works better for the lens you have mounted at middle distances, but is less successful at correcting close-up focus errors), you can deactivate the feature as you require. You should set this to On when you're doing the actual fine-tuning. Adjustment values range from −20 to +20. **Off:** Disables autofocus micro adjustment.

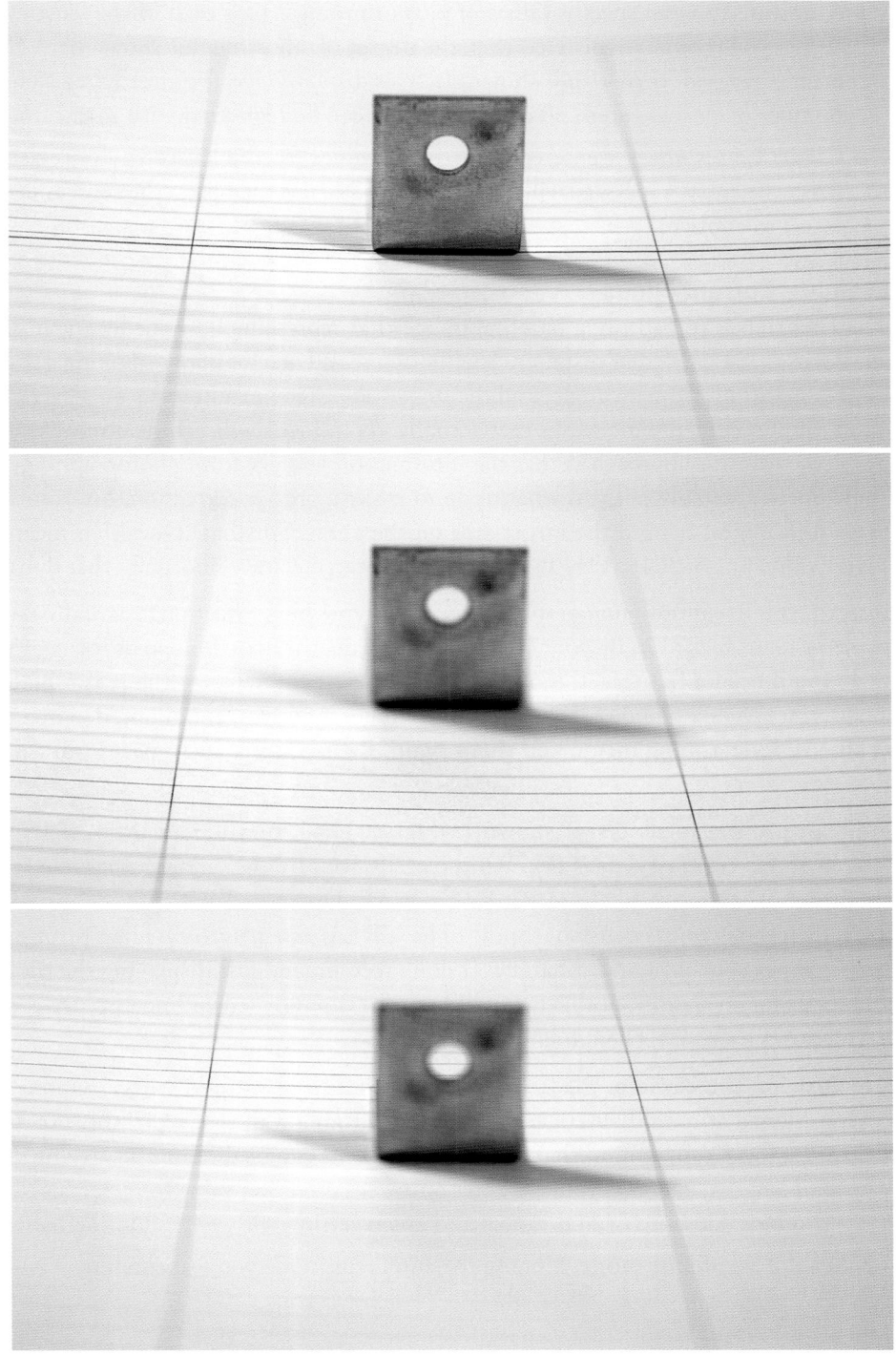

Figure 11.13 Correct focus (top), front focus (middle), and back focus (bottom).

- **Amount.** You can specify values of plus or minus 20 for each of the lenses you've registered. When you mount a registered lens, the degree of adjustment is shown here. If the lens has not been registered, then +/-0 is shown. If "-" is displayed, you've already registered the maximum number of lenses—up to 30 different lenses can be registered with each camera.

- **Clear.** Erases *all* user-entered adjustment values for the lenses you've registered. When you select the entry, a message will appear. Select OK and then press the center button of the control wheel to confirm.

Evaluate Current Focus

The first step is to capture a baseline image that represents how the lens you want to fine-tune autofocuses at a particular distance. You'll often see advice for photographing a test chart with millimeter markings from an angle, and the suggestion that you autofocus on a particular point on the chart. Supposedly, the markings that actually *are* in focus will help you recalibrate your lens. The problem with this approach is that the information you get from photographing a test chart at an angle doesn't actually tell you what to do to make a precise correction. So, your lens back focuses three millimeters behind the target area on the chart. So what? Does that mean you change the Saved Value by –3 clicks? Or –15 clicks? Angled targets are a "shortcut" that don't save you time.

Instead, you'll want to photograph a target that represents what you're actually trying to achieve: a plane of focus locked in by your lens that represents the actual plane of focus of your subject. For that, you'll need a flat target, mounted precisely perpendicular to the sensor plane of the camera. Then, you can take a photo, see if the plane of focus is correct, and if not, dial in a bit of fine-tuning in the AF Fine Tuning menu, and shoot again. Lather, rinse, and repeat until the target is sharply focused.

You can use the focus target shown in Figure 11.14, or you can use a chart of your own, as long as it has contrasty areas that will be easily seen by the autofocus system, and without very small details that are likely to confuse the AF. Download your own copy of my chart from www.dslrguides.com/FocusChart.pdf. (The URL is *case sensitive*.) Then print out a copy on the largest paper your printer can handle. (I don't recommend just displaying the file on your monitor and focusing on that; it's unlikely you'll have the monitor screen lined up perfectly perpendicular to the camera sensor.) Then, follow these steps:

1. **Position the camera.** Place your camera on a sturdy tripod with a remote release attached, positioned at roughly eye-level at a distance from a wall that represents the distance you want to test for. Keep in mind that autofocus problems can be different at varying distances and lens focal lengths, and that you can enter only *one* correction value for a particular lens. So, choose a distance (close-up or mid-range) and zoom setting with your shooting habits in mind.

2. **Set the autofocus mode.** Choose the autofocus mode you want to test.

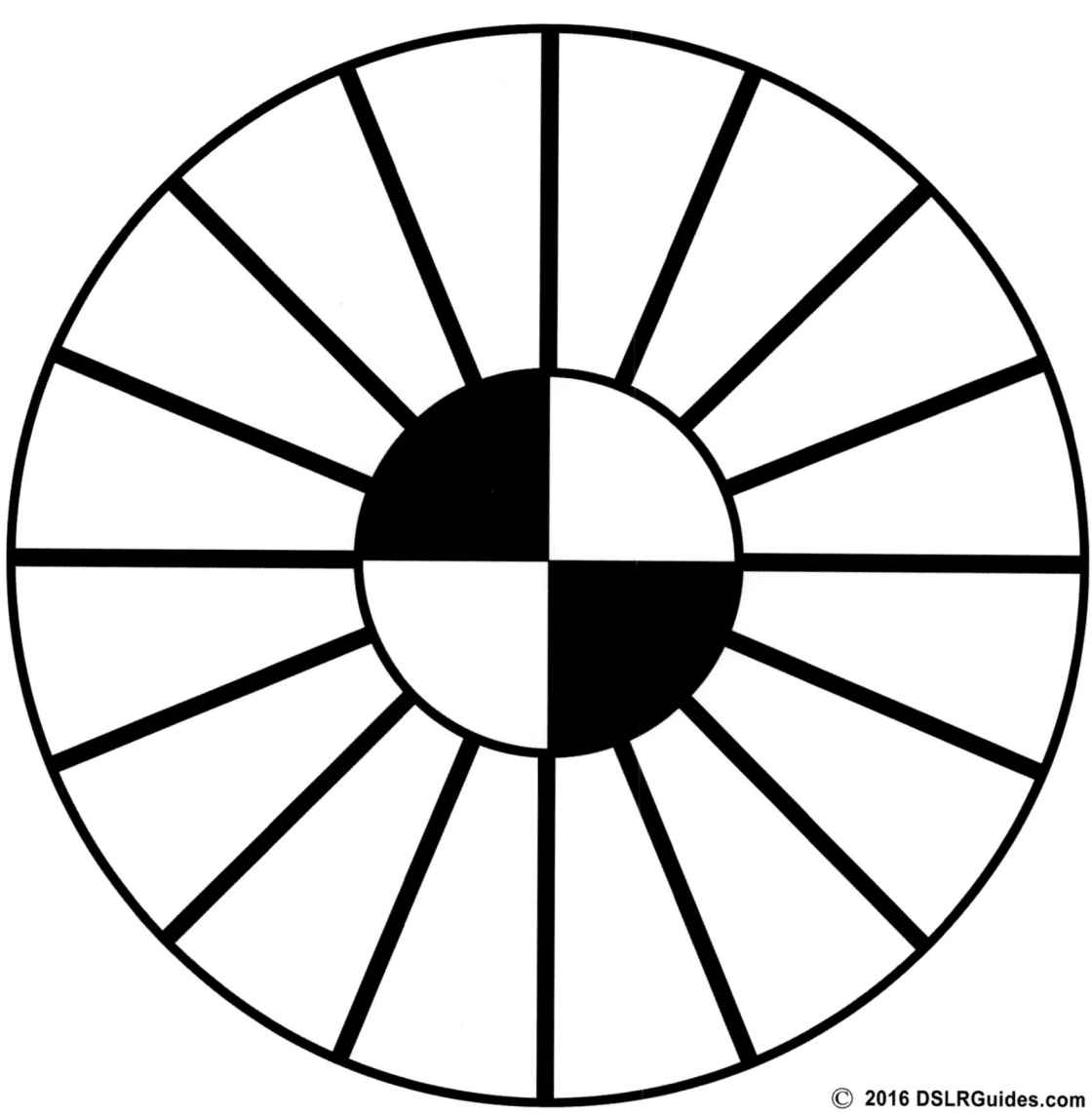

Figure 11.14 Use this focus test chart, or create one of your own.

3. **Level the camera (in an ideal world).** If the wall happens to be perfectly perpendicular, you can use a bubble level, plumb bob, or other device of your choice to ensure that the camera is level to match. Many tripods and tripod heads have bubble levels built in. Avoid using the center column, if you can. When the camera is properly oriented, lock the legs and tripod head tightly.

4. **Level the camera (in the real world).** If your wall is not perfectly perpendicular, use this old trick. Tape a mirror to the wall, and then adjust the camera on the tripod so that when you look through the viewfinder at the mirror, you see directly into the reflection of the lens. Then, lock the tripod and remove the mirror.

5. **Mount the test chart.** Tape the test chart on the wall so it is centered in your camera's viewfinder.

6. **Photograph the test chart using AF.** Allow the camera to autofocus, and take a test photo using the remote release to avoid shaking or moving the camera.

7. **Make an adjustment and re-photograph.** Navigate to the Custom Settings menu and choose AF Micro Adj. Make sure the feature has been turned on, then press down to Amount and make a fine-tuning adjustment, plus or minus, and photograph the target again.

8. **Lather, rinse, repeat.** Repeat steps 6 and 7 several times to create several different adjustments to check.

9. **Evaluate the image(s).** If you have the camera connected to your computer with a USB cable or through a Wi-Fi connection, so much the better. You can view the image(s) after transfer to your computer. Otherwise, *carefully* open the camera card door and slip the memory card out and copy the images to your computer.

10. **Evaluate focus.** Which image is sharpest? That's the setting you need to use for this lens. If your initial range doesn't provide the correction you need, repeat the steps between –20 and +20 until you find the best fine-tuning. Once you've made an adjustment, the camera will automatically apply the AF fine-tuning each time that lens is mounted on the camera, as long as the function is turned on.

MAXED OUT

If you've reached the maximum number of lenses (which is unlikely—who owns 30 lenses?), mount a lens you no longer want to compensate for, and reset its adjustment value to +/-0. Or you can reset the values of all your lenses using the Clear function and start over.

12

Working with Flash

Photography is a form of visual art that uses light to shape the finished product. The photographer may have little or no control over the subject (other than posing human subjects) but can often adjust both viewing angle *and* the nature of the light source to create a particular compelling image. The direction and intensity of the light sources create the shapes and textures that we see. The distribution and proportions determine the contrast and tonal values: whether the image is stark or high key, or muted and low in contrast. The colors of the light (because even "white" light has a color balance that the sensor can detect), and how much of those colors the subject reflects or absorbs, paint the hues visible in the image.

As a Sony photographer, you must learn to be a painter and sculptor of light if you want to move from *taking* a picture to *making* a photograph. Most of the time, you'll be working with available or ambient light, perhaps with reflectors or other modifiers, or even some additional continuous light sources, such as incandescent or fluorescent lamps. But at times you'll want to turn to one of the most versatile sources of illumination you have available, the brief, but brilliant snippets of light we call *electronic flash.* This chapter will show you the differences between working with continuous illumination and working with flash, and explain how to use the flash capabilities of the a6400.

Why Flash?

Flash sometimes gets a bad rap, but that's usually prompted by photographers who make poor use of the capabilities electronic flash offers. In some respects, working with continuous lighting instead is easier and more predictable. Conventional lighting is exactly what you might think: uninterrupted illumination that is available all the time during a shooting session. Daylight, moonlight, and the artificial lighting encountered both indoors and outdoors count as continuous light sources (although all of them can be "interrupted" by passing clouds, solar eclipses, a blown fuse, or simply by switching off a lamp). Indoor continuous illumination includes both the lights that are there already (such as incandescent lamps or overhead fluorescent lights indoors) and fixtures you supply yourself, including photoflood lamps or reflectors used to bounce existing light onto your subject.

On the face of things, electronic flash may be uncomfortably *different* from what we are used to, and sometimes considered difficult to use. In practice, you can use flash in all the same ways you use continuous lighting to shape your images, and, in some cases, take advantage of its special properties, such as its action-freezing short duration. Electronic flash is notable because it can be much more intense than continuous lighting, lasts only a brief moment, and can be much more portable than supplementary incandescent sources. It's a light source you can carry with you and use anywhere.

Of course, your a6400 has a small, underpowered built-in flash. There are several reasons for that. The company wanted to make the a6400 exceptionally compact, and a larger built-in flash would have added bulk. In addition, as you are undoubtedly painfully aware, the a6400 is equipped with undersized 1020 mAh batteries, with less capacity even than those found in some point-and-shoot cameras. I estimate that with heavy flash usage drawing power from an NP-FW50 battery, you would scarcely get 50 shots from a single charge. So, your best bet, if you're serious about flash photography, is to purchase an external unit, which slips right into the a6400's multi interface shoe on the top panel.

Before moving on to discussing flash in detail, here's a quick comparison of the pros and cons of continuous illumination versus flash:

- **Lighting preview—Pro: continuous lighting.** With continuous lighting, such as incandescent lamps or daylight, you always know exactly what kind of lighting effect you're going to get. If you're using multiple lights, you can visualize how they will interact with each other. With electronic flash, the general effect you're going to see may be a mystery until you've built some experience.

- **Lighting preview—Con: electronic flash.** Compact portable flash units often do not provide a "modeling light" function, although studio flash typically do.

- **Exposure calculation—Pro: continuous lighting.** Your camera has no problem calculating accurate exposure for continuous lighting, because the lighting remains constant and can be measured through built-in light meters that interpret the light reaching the sensor. The amount of light available just before the exposure will, in almost all cases, be the same amount of light present when the shutter mechanism is opened to take the shot. The Spot metering mode can be used to measure brightness in the bright areas of the scene and the dark areas; if you have a bit of expertise in this technique, you'll know whether it would be useful to bounce some light into the shadow areas using a reflector panel accessory.

- **Exposure calculation—Con: electronic flash.** A flash unit provides no illumination until it actually fires so the exact exposure can't be measured by the a6400's exposure sensor before you take a photo. Instead, the light must be measured by metering the intensity of a *pre-flash* triggered an instant before the main flash, as it is reflected back to the camera and through the lens.

- **Evenness of illumination—Pro/con: continuous lighting.** Of continuous light sources, daylight, in particular, provides illumination that tends to fill an image completely, lighting up the foreground, background, and your subject almost equally. A sunlit scene may have shadow areas too, of course, so you might need to use reflectors or fill-in light sources to even out the illumination. Barring objects that block large sections of your image from daylight, the light is spread fairly evenly. Indoors, however, continuous lighting is much less likely to be evenly distributed. The average living room, for example, has hot spots and dark corners. But on the plus side, you can *see* this uneven illumination and compensate with additional lamps.

- **Evenness of illumination—Con: electronic flash.** Electronic flash units, like the continuous light provided by lamps, don't have the advantage of being located 93 million miles from the subject as the sun is. Because of this factor, they suffer from the effects of their proximity.

The *inverse square law*, first applied to both gravity and light by Sir Isaac Newton, dictates that as a light source's distance increases from the subject, the amount of light reaching the subject falls off proportionately to the square of the distance. In plain English, that means that a flash or lamp that's 12 feet away from a subject provides only one-quarter as much illumination as a source that's 6 feet away (rather than half as much). (See Figure 12.1.) This translates into relatively shallow "depth-of-light."

- **Action stopping—Pro: electronic flash.** When it comes to the ability to freeze moving objects in their tracks, the advantage goes to electronic flash. The brief duration of the emitted light serves as a very fast "shutter speed" when the flash is the main or only source of illumination for the photo. In other words, this effect is possible when shooting in a dark area without much. if any, lighting provided by ambient sources but assumes that the subject is not beyond the range of the flash.

In flash photography, your camera's shutter speed (called *sync speed* in flash photography) is set to 1/160th second, but when flash is the primary light source, the *effective* exposure time will

Figure 12.1

A light source that is twice as far away provides only one-quarter as much illumination.

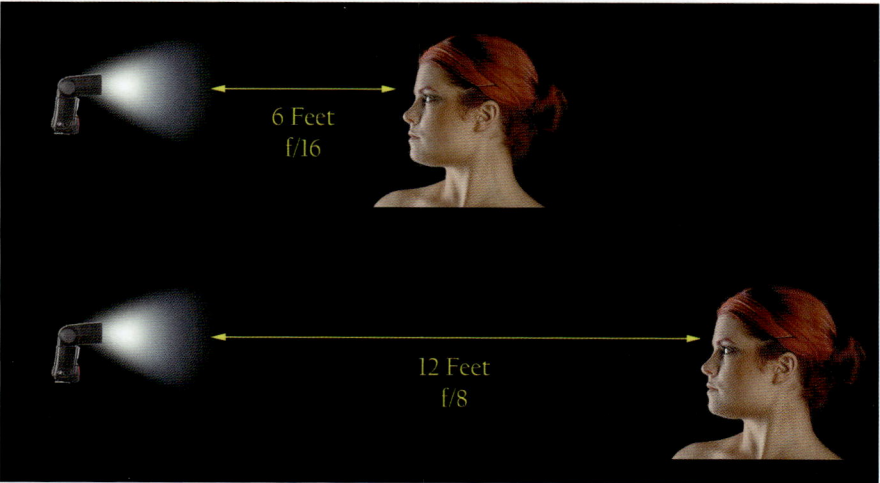

6 Feet
f/16

12 Feet
f/8

be the 1/1000th to 1/50000th second or less; this is the actual duration of the flash illumination. As you can see in Figure 12.2, it's possible to freeze motion with flash of very short duration. The only fly in the ointment is that, if the ambient light is strong enough, it may produce a secondary "ghost" exposure, as I'll explain later in this chapter.

- **Action stopping—Con: continuous lighting.** Action stopping with continuous light sources is completely dependent on the shutter speed you've dialed in on the camera. And the speeds available are dependent on the amount of light available and your camera's ISO sensitivity setting. Outdoors in daylight, there will probably be enough sunlight to let you shoot at 1/2000th second and f/6.3 with a non-grainy ISO of 400. That's a fairly useful combination of settings if you're not using a super-telephoto with a small maximum aperture.

But indoors, the reduced illumination quickly has you pushing your a6400 to its limits. For example, if you're shooting indoor sports in a dark arena, there probably won't be enough available light to allow you to use a 1/2000th second shutter speed unless you use a lens with an extremely wide aperture, such as f/1.8, with, say, the Sony Sonnar T* FE 55mm f/1.8 ZA. You can also specify a very high ISO setting, and accept that image quality may suffer. (In truth,

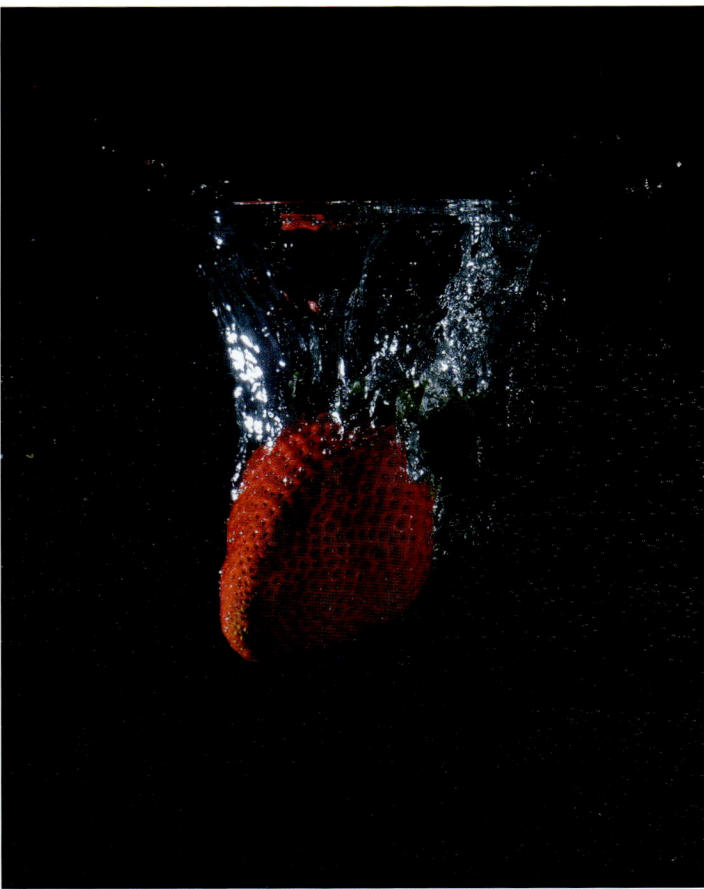

Figure 12.2
Electronic flash can freeze almost any motion because of its extremely short duration.

the gym where I shoot indoor basketball allows me to do so at 1/500th second at f/4 using ISO 1600.) In many indoor sports situations, you may find yourself limited to a shutter speed of 1/500th second or slower.

- **Flexibility—Pro: electronic flash.** The action-freezing power of electronic flash, at least for nearby subjects in a dark location, allows you to work without a tripod; that provides extra flexibility and speed when choosing angles and positions.

- **Flexibility—Con: continuous lighting.** Because incandescent and fluorescent lamps are not as bright as electronic flash, the slower shutter speeds required (see "Action stopping," above) mean that you may have to use a tripod more often, especially when shooting portraits. The incandescent variety of continuous lighting gets hot, especially in the studio, and the side effects range from discomfort (for your human models) to disintegration (if you happen to be shooting perishable foods like ice cream).

Electronic Flash Basics

Until you delve into the situation deeply enough, it might appear that serious photographers have a love/hate relationship with electronic flash. You'll often hear that flash photos are less natural looking, and that on-camera flash in most cameras should never be used as the primary source of illumination because it provides a harsh, garish look. Some photographers strongly praise available ("continuous") lighting while denouncing electronic flash.

As I noted at the beginning of this chapter, that bias is against *bad* flash photography. Indeed, flash—often with light modifier accessories—has become the studio light source of choice for many pro photographers. That's understandable, because the light is more intense (and its intensity can be dialed up or down by the photographer), freezes action, frees you from using a tripod (unless you want to use one to lock down a composition), and has a snappy, consistent light quality that matches daylight. (While color balance changes as the flash duration shortens, some Sony flash units can communicate to the camera the exact white balance provided for that shot.) And even conservative photographers will concede that electronic flash has some important uses as an adjunct to existing light, particularly to fill in dark shadows.

How Electronic Flash Works

The electronic flash you use will be built into the unit, as with the a6400's pop-up flash, mounted on the camera by slipping it onto the hot shoe, or linked by a cable connected to an adapter mounted on the shoe. In all cases, the flash is triggered at the instant of exposure, during a period when the sensor is fully exposed by the shutter.

The a6400 has electronic shutter options, which I'll describe later, and a conventional vertically traveling physical shutter that consists of two curtains. The front curtain opens and moves to the opposite side of the frame, at which point the shutter is completely open. The flash can be triggered at this point (so-called *front-curtain sync,* which is the default mode), making the flash exposure.

Then, after a delay that can vary from 30 seconds to 1/160th second, a second *rear curtain* begins moving across the sensor plane, covering up the sensor again. If the flash is triggered just before the rear curtain starts to close, then the optional *rear-curtain sync* is used. In both cases, though, a shutter speed of 1/160th second is (ordinarily) the *maximum* that can be used to take a photo, because that's the speed at which both the front and rear curtains are tucked out of the way, leaving the entire full frame exposed to capture the flash burst.

Figure 12.3 illustrates how this works, with a fanciful illustration of a generic shutter (your a6400's shutter does *not* look like this). As an exposure is made using the conventional (non-electronic) shutter, the curtains move as follows:

1. Both curtains open. With a mirrorless camera like the a6400, the sensor remains completely exposed, so that the image that's being captured can be viewed on the electronic viewfinder and LCD monitor.

2. Front curtain closes. As the exposure begins, the front curtain rises to cover the sensor.

3. Prior image is dumped. When the sensor is completely covered, the preview image is dumped, resetting the pixels so that the exposure can begin.

4. Front curtain begins to descend. As the front curtain drops, the sensor is gradually exposed to light, and the *ambient* exposure (using the available light in the scene) begins.

5. Front curtain continues to descend. More of the sensor is uncovered, and the ambient exposure continues.

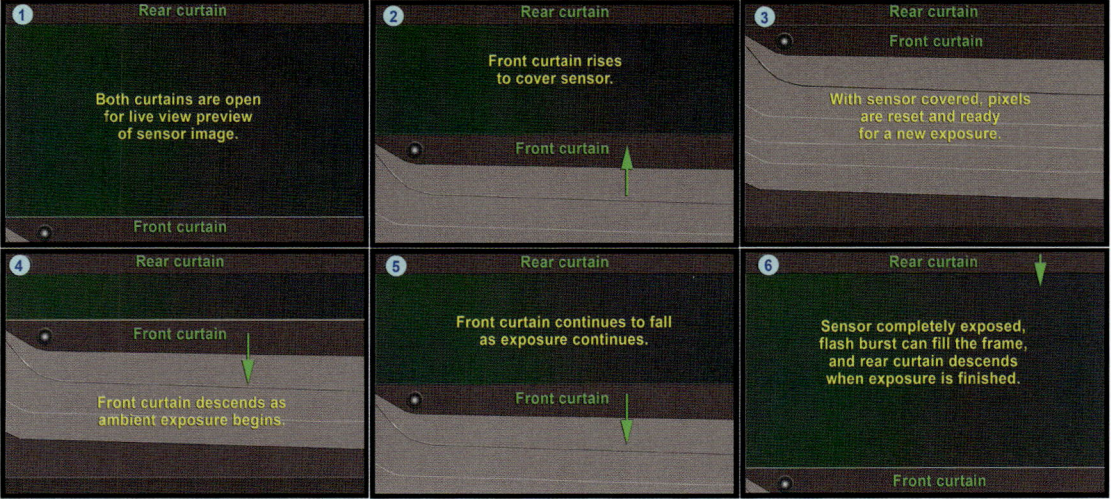

Figure 12.3 A focal plane shutter has two curtains, the lower, or front curtain, and an upper, rear curtain.

6. Both curtains open. With the sensor fully exposed, the electronic flash's brief burst can fill the frame.

- If this burst takes place as soon as the curtains are fully open, then *front-curtain sync*, which is the default, has been used. Following the flash, the sensor continues to be exposed for the length of the exposure, which can range from 1/160th second to 30 seconds (or longer, with a Bulb exposure).

- The burst can also take place *at the very end* of the exposure, just before the rear curtain starts to descend. This is called *rear-curtain sync*.

- When the exposure is finished, the rear curtain descends and the captured image is conveyed off the sensor to the camera's internal buffer, and thence to your memory card. The rear curtain then ascends to the top of the frame, exposing the sensor again and a preview image for the next picture appears in the EVF and LCD monitor.

Keep in mind that the a6400 *always* defaults to front-curtain sync unless you explicitly select another sync mode using the Fn button or Flash Mode entry in the Camera Settings menu.

And Now for Something Completely Different...

If you've absorbed that, things are about to get *really* interesting. The a6400 has special modes available from the Camera Settings II menu, in which either the physical front curtain or both the physical front curtain *and* the rear curtain are simulated electronically. Only one of the two modes can be used with flash. Here's the difference:

- **e-Front Curtain Shutter.** Recall that the sensor of a mirrorless camera is always exposed and feeding its image to the EVF and LCD monitor; in order to capture an image within a specified period of time, the sensor needs to *stop* collecting the image so the exposure can begin. In normal operation, as described above, when you press the shutter release down all the way, the shutter closes and the camera dumps the image you were previewing, resetting the pixels and leaving the sensor blank and ready to capture an exposure. When the e-Front Curtain Shutter is enabled, the physical front shutter doesn't close: the image is dumped *electronically*, and then the sensor immediately begins capturing an image. The physical rear curtain shutter then closes at the end of the exposure.

The advantages of the electronic front curtain are that the camera can respond more quickly with less shutter lag, there is no possibility of vibration caused by the physical front curtain shutter bouncing at the end of its travel, and an electronic front curtain shutter is quieter. As the a6400 is mirrorless, these cameras are already quieter than dSLR models, which have a mirror flapping about before and after the exposure.

However, an electronic front curtain shutter can exhibit problems with certain lenses and very fast shutter speeds. In such cases, when you are using an unusually wide aperture, such as f/1.8, some areas of the photo may exhibit a secondary (ghost) image. The aperture of an affected lens requires the "leaves" to travel a greater distance, and there may simply not be enough time. An overexposure may result. If you encounter that problem, turn the e-curtain option off; otherwise, you can do as I do and leave it on all the time.

■ **Electronic shutter.** The a6400 has an all-electronic shutter that can be activated by selecting Silent Shooting in the Camera Settings II menu. In that case, both the physical front and rear curtains are replaced by electronic equivalents. Exposure is started and stopped electronically, with no curtains at all. Silent Shooting is indeed silent; I've had other photographers watching me snap away in that mode ask me whether I was really taking pictures at all. It is an excellent mode for religious ceremonies and other events where even the quiet click of the e-Front Curtain might be intrusive.

As I described in Chapter 10, silent shooting's rolling shutter captures the image line by line (as opposed to a global shutter that grabs the image in one fell swoop), and is subject to the same unwanted side effects found in video cameras, including wobble/Jell-O effect in hand-held shots, diagonal skewing, smear, and other defects. But the most important complication, in terms of the subject of this chapter, is that the electronic shutter cannot be used with flash at all. If you have a flash mounted and powered up and press the shutter release, it won't go off when the electronic shutter is active. Indeed, the Flash Mode options in the Camera Settings II-10 menu are grayed out and unavailable.

Avoiding Sync-Speed Problems

Using a shutter speed faster than the maximum sync speed can cause problems. Triggering the electronic flash *only* when the shutter is completely open makes a lot of sense if you think about what's going on. To obtain shutter speeds faster than 1/160th second, the a6400 exposes only part of the sensor at one time, by starting the rear curtain on its journey before the front curtain has completely opened. That effectively provides a briefer exposure as the slit of the shutter passes over the surface of the sensor. If the flash were to fire during the time when the front and rear curtains partially obscured the sensor, only the slit that was actually open would be exposed.

You'd end up with only a narrow band, representing the portion of the sensor that was exposed when the picture was taken. For shutter speeds *faster* than the top sync speed, the rear curtain begins moving *before* the front curtain reaches the bottom of the frame. As a result, a moving slit, the distance between the front and rear curtains, exposes one portion of the sensor at a time as it moves from the top to the bottom. Figure 12.4 shows three views of our typical (but imaginary) physical focal plane shutter. At left is pictured the closed shutter; in the middle version you can see the front curtain has moved about 1/4 of the distance down from the top; and in the right-hand version, the rear curtain has started to "chase" the front curtain across the frame toward the bottom.

If the flash is triggered while this slit is moving, only the exposed portion of the sensor will receive any illumination. You end up with a photo like the one shown in Figure 12.5. Note that a band across the bottom of the image is black. That's a shadow of the rear shutter curtain, which had started to move when the flash was triggered. Sharp-eyed readers will wonder why the black band is at the *bottom* of the frame rather than at the top, where the rear curtain begins its journey. The answer is simple: your lens flips the image upside down and forms it on the sensor in a reversed position. You never notice that, because the camera is smart enough to show you the pixels that

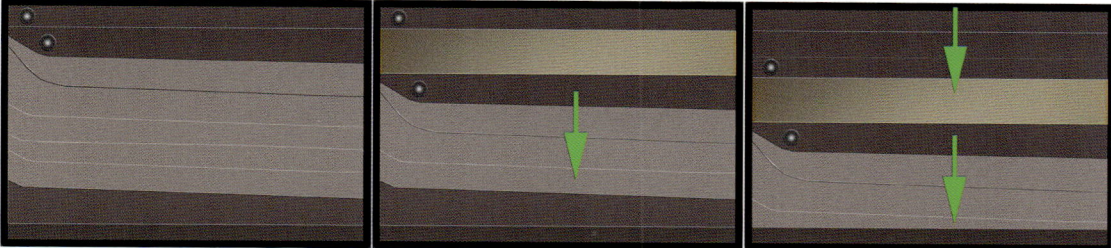

Figure 12.4 A typical exposure using the conventional physical shutter.

Figure 12.5
If a shutter speed faster than 1/160th second is used with flash, you can end up photographing only a portion of the image.

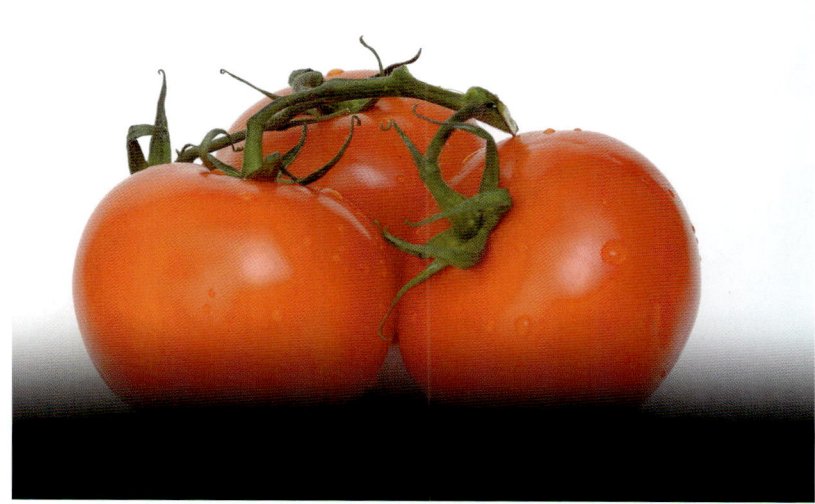

make up your photo in their proper orientation during picture review. But this image flip is why, if your sensor gets dirty and you detect a spot of dust in the upper half of a test photo, if cleaning manually, you need to look for the speck in the *bottom* half of the sensor.

I generally end up with sync speed problems only when shooting in the studio, using studio flash units rather than my Sony dedicated unit. That's because if you're using either type of "smart" flash, the camera knows that a strobe is attached, and remedies any unintentional goof in shutter speed settings. If you happen to set the a6400's shutter to a faster speed in S or M mode, the camera will automatically adjust the shutter speed down to the maximum sync speed as soon as you attach and turn on an external flash (or prevent you from choosing a faster speed if the flash is powered up). In A or P, where the a6400 selects the shutter speed, it will never choose a shutter speed higher than 1/160th second when using flash.

But when using a non-dedicated flash, such as a studio unit plugged into an adapter attached to the accessory shoe, the camera has no way of knowing that a flash is connected, so shutter speeds faster than 1/160th second can be set inadvertently.

Note that the a6400 can use a feature called *high-speed sync* that allows shutter speeds faster than the maximum sync speed with certain external dedicated Sony flash units. When using high-speed sync, the flash fires a continuous series of bursts at reduced power for the entire duration of the exposure, so that the illumination is able to expose the sensor as the slit moves.

HS sync is set using the controls that adjust the compatible external flash units, which include the HVL-F60M/RM, HVL-F58AM, HVL-F56AM, HVL-45RM, HVL-F43AM/HVL-F43M, HVL-F32M, and HVL-F36AM. (Note that all flashes ending in AM use the older Minolta-style foot and cannot be mounted on the a6400 without an inexpensive Sony ADP-MAA adapter.) High-speed sync cannot be used when working with multiple flash units. When active, the message H appears on the LCD panel on the back of the flash. You'll find complete instructions accompanying those flash units.

Ghost Images

The difference might not seem like much, but whether you use front-curtain sync (the default setting) or rear-curtain sync (an optional setting) can make a significant difference to your photograph *if the ambient light in your scene also contributes to the image.* At faster shutter speeds, particularly 1/160th second, there isn't much time for the ambient light to register, unless it is very bright. It's likely that the electronic flash will provide almost all the illumination, so front-curtain sync or rear-curtain sync isn't very important.

However, at slower shutter speeds, or with very bright ambient light levels, there is a significant difference, particularly if your subject is moving, or the camera isn't steady. In any of those situations, the ambient light will register as a second image accompanying the flash exposure, and if there is movement (camera or subject), that additional image will not be in the same place as the flash exposure. It will show as a ghost image and, if the movement is significant enough, as a blurred ghost image trailing in front of or behind your subject in the direction of the movement.

As I mentioned earlier, when you're using front-curtain sync, the flash goes off the instant the shutter opens, producing an image of the subject on the sensor. That happens whether you're using the mechanical shutter or the optional electronic Front Curtain option from the Camera Settings II-04 menu. Then, the shutter remains open for an additional period (which, as I've noted, can be from 30 seconds to 1/160th second). If your subject is moving, say, toward the right side of the frame, the ghost image produced by the ambient light will produce a blur on the right side of the original subject image, making it look as if your sharp (flash-produced) image is chasing the ghost. For those of us who grew up with lightning-fast superheroes who always left a ghost trail *behind them*, that looks unnatural (see Figure 12.6).

So, Sony provides rear (second) -curtain sync to remedy the situation. In that mode, the shutter opens, as before. The shutter remains open for its designated duration, and the ghost image forms. If your subject moves from the left side of the frame to the right side, the ghost will move from left to right, too. *Then*, about 1.5 milliseconds before the rear shutter curtain closes, the flash is triggered, producing a nice, sharp flash image *ahead* of the ghost image. Voilà! We have monsieur *le Flash* outrunning his own trailing image.

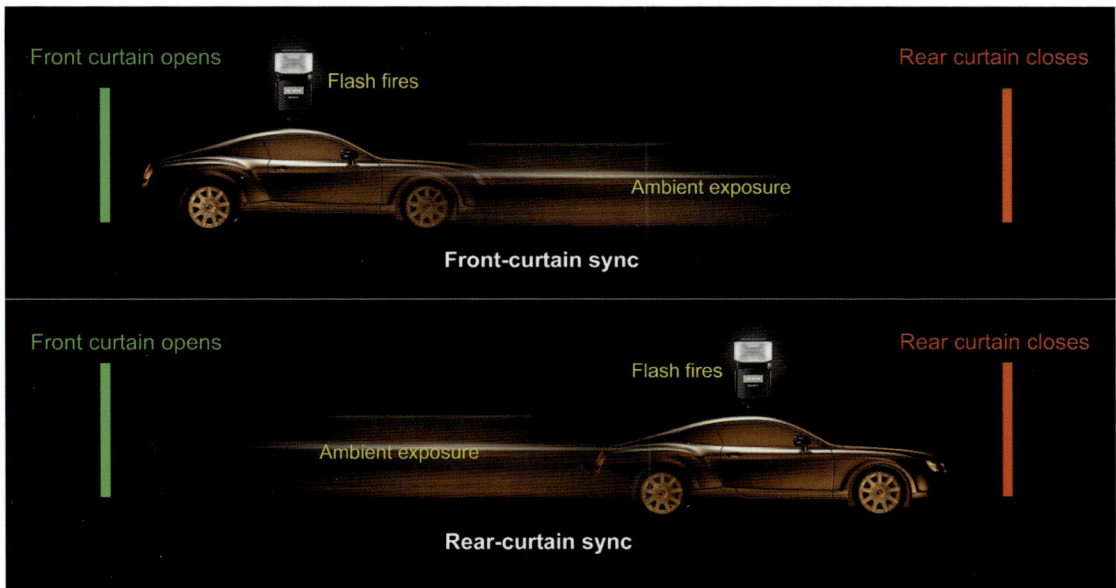

Figure 12.6 Front-curtain sync produces an image that trails in front of the flash exposure (left), whereas rear-curtain sync creates a more "natural-looking" trail behind the flash image (right).

EVERY WHICH WAY, INCLUDING UP

Note that although I describe the ghost effect in terms of subject matter that is moving left to right in a horizontally oriented composition, it can occur in any orientation, and with the subject moving in *any* direction. (Try photographing a falling rock, if you can, and you'll see the same effect.) Nor are the ghost images affected by the fact that modern shutters travel vertically rather than horizontally. Secondary images are caused between the time the front curtain fully opens, and the rear curtain begins to close. The direction of travel of the shutter curtains, or the direction of your subject, does not matter.

Slow Sync

Another flash synchronization option is *slow sync*, which is actually an exposure option that tells the a6400 to use slower shutter speeds when possible, to allow you to capture a scene by both flash and ambient illumination. To activate Slow Sync, press the Fn button, navigate to the flash options, and choose Slow Sync. Or, make the same selection from the Flash Mode entry in the Camera Settings I-10 menu.

Then, the exposure system will try to use longer shutter speeds with the flash, so that an initial exposure is made with the flash unit, and a secondary exposure of subjects in the background will be produced by the slower shutter speed. This will let you shoot a portrait of a person at night and, much of the time, avoid a dark background. Your portrait subject will be illuminated by the flash, and the background by the ambient light. It's a good idea to have the camera mounted on a tripod or some other support, or have SteadyShot (if available) switched on to avoid having this secondary exposure produce ghost images due to camera movement during the exposure. See Figure 12.7.

Because Slow Sync is a type of exposure control, it does not work in Manual mode or Shutter Priority mode (because the a6400 doesn't choose the shutter speed in those modes). It is not disabled in those modes: you can still select it using the Camera Settings menu or Function menu, but your shutter speed will not be changed.

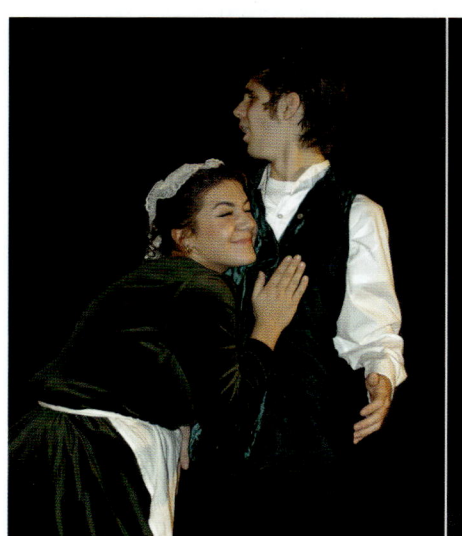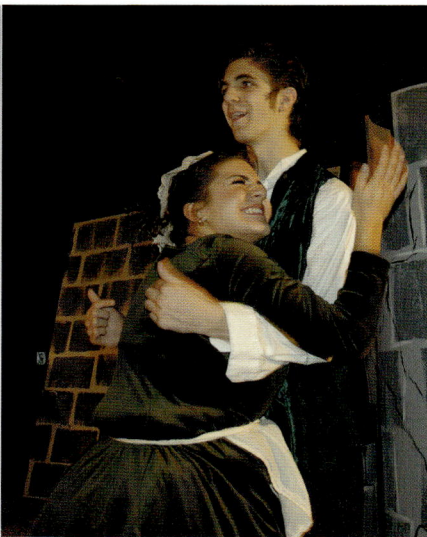

Figure 12.7
Without slow sync, ambient light may not be sufficient to balance with the flash exposure (left). When slow sync is activated, longer shutter speeds are selected, allowing the ambient light to register, too (right).

Determining Exposure

Calculating the proper exposure for an electronic flash photograph is a bit more complicated than determining the settings by continuous light. The right exposure isn't simply a function of how far away your subject is, even though the inverse square law I mentioned does have an effect: the farther away the subject is, the less light is available for the exposure. The a6400 can calculate distance if you're using lenses with a *distance encoder chip,* which detects the position of the focusing mechanism as focus is locked in just prior to exposure. The component transmits this information to the camera, which can use it to determine the distance to the subject, and, therefore, much flash output is required to illuminate the scene. This Advanced Distance Integration (ADI) delivers high-precision flash metering that is unaffected by the reflectance of subjects or backgrounds.

But, of course, flash exposure isn't based on distance alone. Various objects reflect more or less light at the same distance so, obviously, the camera needs to measure the amount of light reflected back and through the lens. Yet, as the flash itself isn't available for measuring until it's triggered, the a6400 has nothing to measure.

The solution is to fire the flash twice. The initial shot is a pre-flash that can be analyzed, then followed by a main flash that's given exactly the calculated intensity needed to provide a correct exposure. As a result, the primary flash may be longer for distant objects and shorter for closer subjects, depending on the required intensity for exposure. This through-the-lens evaluative flash exposure system uses distance information, and it operates whenever you have attached a Sony-dedicated flash unit to the a6400 or use the built-in flash, and a lens that provides the necessary distance integration information.

The built-in flash is a handy component because it is available as required, without the need to carry an external flash around with you constantly. Elevate it by pressing the flash button (on the center edge of the back of the camera). Use the P, A, S, or M mode to ensure that all flash features will be available.

BOUNCE FLASH

Although the built-in flash doesn't have detents to allow variable angles, you can easily tilt it with the tip of your index finger while shooting to provide additional flexibility. For example, you can carefully angle the flash downward when shooting close-ups (perhaps with mixed results), or tilt it backward to bounce it off a ceiling or other diffusing surface. Of course, the light may not actually reach the subject; you would need to use a high ISO (to increase sensor sensitivity) for this technique to provide any effect. Of course, if the ceiling is low or you're bouncing the light off a large white sheet of cardboard—and the subject is close to the camera—it may work well when using ISO 800 or higher.

Flash Modes

There are several flash modes available in the Camera Settings I-10 menu:

- **Flash Off.** The flash never fires; this may be useful in museums, concerts, or religious ceremonies where electronic flash would prove disruptive. This option is not available in P, A, S, or M mode; if you do not want flash to fire, keep it stowed within the camera body.

- **Auto Flash.** The flash fires as required, depending on lighting conditions. Not available in P, A, S, or M mode because flash *always* fires in these modes if it's attached and powered up, in the up position.

- **Fill-Flash.** When this option is set, the flash will always fire when set to P, A, S, or M modes, using one of the two Auto modes or in SCN modes where flash is not disabled. The camera balances the available illumination with flash to provide a balanced lighting effect. (See Figure 12.8.)

- **Slow Sync.** The camera combines flash with slow shutter speeds; the nearby subject can be illuminated by flash, but during the longer shutter speed, there's enough time for the darker surroundings (lit by ambient light) to record on the sensor.

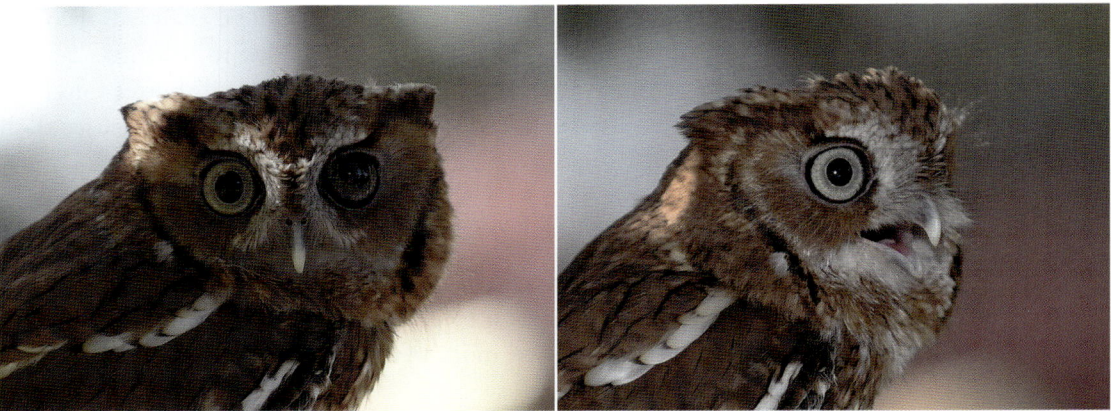

Figure 12.8 The owl (left) was in shadow. Fill flash (right) brightened up the bird, while adding a little catch light to its eye.

- **Rear Sync.** Fires the flash at the *end* of the exposure time, after the ambient light exposure has been made, producing more satisfying photos of moving subjects when using a long exposure; light trails will be behind the "ghost" image, as illustrated earlier in Figure 12.6.
- **Wireless.** Allows an optional external flash mounted on the camera's multi interface shoe to trigger one or more external flash units that support wireless off-camera flash; there's no need for any cable connection between the camera and the remote flash unit. This option is grayed out unless you have an external flash mounted and powered up; the a6400's built-in flash cannot be used to trigger other units wirelessly.

Flash Exposure Compensation

This is a feature discussed previously in Chapter 3. It's important to keep in mind how the camera's exposure compensation system works when you're using electronic flash. To activate exposure compensation for flash, visit the Flash Comp. item (see Figure 12.9) in the Camera Settings II-10 menu or use the Function menu, and set the amount of plus or minus compensation you want. This function is not available when using Auto or SCN modes or Panorama mode. When you find that your flash photos are too dark even after you have set +3, then the flash simply cannot provide more power; you must move closer to the subject, or use a wider aperture, or set a higher ISO, or take all of these steps. Note too that when a subject is extremely close to the camera, even a –3 setting may not prevent an excessively bright image. You'll probably have to *reduce* your ISO setting in that case.

Flash exposure compensation affects only the amount of light emitted by the flash. If you want to adjust the brightness of the ambient light exposure, you would also need to use the conventional exposure compensation feature. In fact, you can use both features at the same time, to get a brighter subject and a darker background, or vice versa. Let's say you're taking a photo of a friend posing against a light-toned background such as a white cabana on a beach. A plus exposure compensation setting (perhaps +1 when using multi-segment metering) will ensure that the cabana won't be

Figure 12.9
Set flash exposure
compensation.

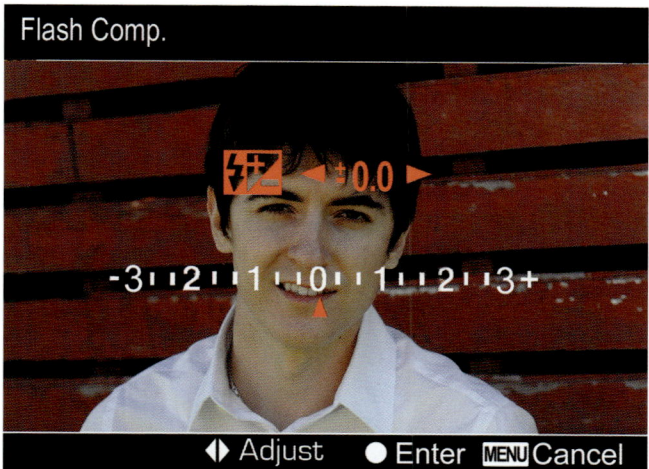

underexposed while a –1/3 or –2/3 flash exposure compensation will ensure that shadows on your friend's face will be lightened by a very gentle burst of flash. This is an advanced technique that requires some experimentation but can be valuable when used with some expertise.

Red Eye Reduction

When using semi-automatic or manual exposure modes (or any SCN mode in which flash is used), red-eye reduction is available if Red Eye Reduction is On in the Camera Settings I-10 menu (as described in Chapter 4). (You cannot be using rear-curtain sync, however.) The flash will fire a burst before the photo is actually taken as you depress the shutter release button. That will theoretically cause your subjects' irises to contract (if they are looking toward the camera), thereby reducing the red-eye effect in your photograph.

Using an External Electronic Flash

As I write this, Sony offers six accessory electronic flash units that are compatible with the a6400's new-style multi interface shoe: the HVL-F60M, its radio-wireless capable sibling the HVL-F60RM, and the HVL-45RM, HVL-F43M, HVL-F32M, and HVL-F20M. These external units can be mounted on the camera, connected to the camera's multi interface shoe with a cable (I'll detail how later) or (except for the HVL-F20M) used off-camera with wireless connectivity when triggered by another external flash used as a controller/master. Each can also function as the controller/master mounted on the camera to trigger other flash units wirelessly.

In addition, there are earlier Sony flash units designed for the older Minolta/Sony proprietary hot shoe. They can be used with the current cameras if you purchase an inexpensive adapter, such as the Sony ADP-MAA (about $25). Or, you can skip the adapter and use wireless-compatible legacy flash units off-camera in wireless mode, triggered by an on-camera master/controller. Although they are discontinued, I'll describe some of these earlier flash units because you may already own one or can find one used at a price that's hard to resist. I don't recommend the legacy flash/adapter approach, because older units operate using a more limited communication protocol, which I'll describe later. But because some of you may have an older flash or can pick one up used at a decent price, it doesn't make sense to pretend that these discontinued models don't exist, because they still can work with your a6400, especially as remote/slave units.

LET'S BE FRANK...

Although one of my jobs is to show you how to get the best from your wise decision to purchase a Sony camera, I'm not a cheerleader for the company. It's done a great job in responding to customer requests for features and upgraded gear, but Sony is still playing catch-up in the flash arena. It's been especially slow in providing affordable radio control flash options (as I'll note later in the chapter). The introduction of the HVL-F60RM in February 2018 added options, but at $600, many will not find it affordable.

The sheer volume of third-party options for gear makes it impossible to cover all of them in detail. So, I have generally devoted the available space to Sony products in this book, with the exception of a discussion of additional lens options. In terms of full-featured TTL-compatible third-party electronic flash units for your a6400, there are a number of excellent third-party products you should check out. Godox, in particular, makes good Sony-friendly flash which are marketed under the Godox name as well as rebranded for other vendors. Although I own Sony flash units, more often than not I use my Godox flash setup (which includes two Godox AD200 battery-operated studio monolights with TTL exposure metering).

Guide Numbers, Hot Shoes, and More

Before I describe the flash units themselves, there are a few aspects you need to understand in order to compare electronic flash. If you're a veteran Sony (or Minolta) shooter, you can skim over this section, or skip it entirely. Those new to photography or the Sony realm should find this information useful.

Guide Numbers

The first thing you need to learn when comparing flash units is that Sony incorporates the Guide Number (GN) of each flash in the product name. So, what's a Guide Number? The GN designation derives from the good old days prior to automatic flash units and through-the-lens flash metering, when flash exposures had to be calculated mathematically. Those days are very long ago, indeed, as Honeywell introduced Auto/Strobonar flash units way back in the 1960s.

Guide numbers are a standard way of specifying the power of a flash when used in manual, non-autoexposure mode. Divide the guide number by the distance to determine the correct f/stop to use at full power. With a GN of 197 at ISO 100, you would use an aperture of around f/19.7 for a subject that's 10 feet from the camera (197 divided by 10), or around f/9.5 for a subject at a distance of 20 feet. Because most countries in the world use metric measurements, guide numbers are given using values for both meters and feet. Thus, Sony's HVL-F60M unit has a guide number of 60/197 in meters/feet, and the 60 GN is incorporated into the unit's product name.

The Guide Number data is most useful for comparing the relative power of several flash units that you're considering. According to the Inverse Square Law, a flash unit with a GN of 200 (in feet) puts out four times the amount of light as one with a GN of about 100. If your accessory flash has a zoom head, which can change coverage to match the focal length setting of your lens, the GN will vary according to the zoom setting, as wider zoom settings spread the same light over a broader area than a telephoto zoom setting.

Hot Shoes

Starting in 1988, Minolta phased in a proprietary hot shoe, the so-called *iISO* shoe, which was supposedly more rugged and secure than the original ISO 518 shoe, based on a design that dates back to 1913, when it was used to attach viewfinders to a camera (electronic flash hadn't been invented yet). No other vendors, including Canon and Nikon, embraced Minolta's design and continued to use the industry-standard shoe. The ISO 518 standard doesn't specify any electronic connections between camera and flash, other than the "dumb" triggering circuit, so when sophisticated electronic flash units with TTL metering and other capabilities were developed, each vendor created their own hot shoe version with the necessary electrical contacts for their cameras and flash units. The chief consequence for non-Minolta/Sony shooters was that you could mount dedicated flash units from one brand onto the ISO 518 shoe of another vendor's camera, and trigger that flash in manual, non-TTL mode.

When Sony purchased Konica Minolta's camera technology it began redesigning legacy features, and the old iISO hot shoe came under scrutiny. In 2012, Sony introduced a 21+3-pin hot shoe which it dubbed the *multi interface shoe*, which resembles a standard ISO 518 hot shoe with its "dumb" contacts. However, tucked away at the front of the shoe are additional electrical contacts that allow intelligent TTL flash metering communication between the camera and flash, and much more. (See Figure 12.10.) For example, a whole series of stereo microphones from Sony and others, designed to plug into the multi interface shoe, are available. As I noted earlier, you can purchase adapters that allow you to connect older iISO flash to the a6400, or to attach new-model flash units to a camera that has the original iISO hot shoe.

Figure 12.10
The foot of current Sony flash units and other accessories is designed to fit the Sony multi interface shoe.

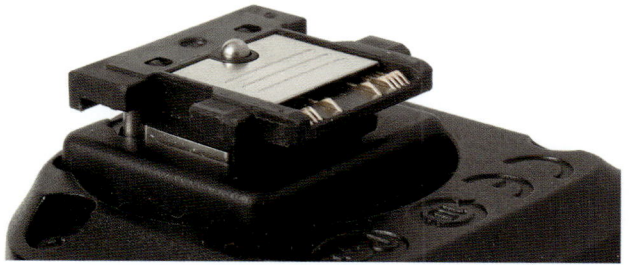

Cable Connections

In some cases, you can get your external flash off the camera without using a wireless connection by linking an HVL-F60M and a6400 with a physical cable. The gear needed for the hook-up can be costly, so I don't recommend it, but if you want to go that route, here's the way to go. Purchase the Sony FA-CS1M multi interface shoe adapter (about $40). It slides to the a6400 camera's multi interface shoe, and has a four-pin TTL socket on the front. Connect that socket to a matching four-pin outlet located on the underside of the HVL-F60M, beneath a protective terminal cap, using a 4.9-foot FA-MC1AM cable ($60). If you need more length, the FA-EC1AM extension cable ($60) adds another 4.9 feet to your connection. The HVL-F43M does not have the four-pin socket, and connecting it to a cable requires some additional adapters, so you're better off not going that way.

HVL-F60M/RM Flash Units

Sony now has *two* top-of-the-line flash units, the HVL-F60M, which uses optical triggering only, and the HVL-F60RM, which is compatible with both optical and radio control. The F60M version is currently listed at $550, but the price will probably come down a tad now that its $600 radio-friendly sibling has been introduced to replace it. Other than optical/radio control, the two units are physically and functionally identical. The F60M model is shown in Figure 12.11. The duo are the most powerful units the company offers, with an ISO 100 guide number (GN) of 60 in meters or 197 in feet at ISO 100. As I noted earlier, the GN does not indicate actual flash range but it's useful when comparing several flash units in terms of their general power output.

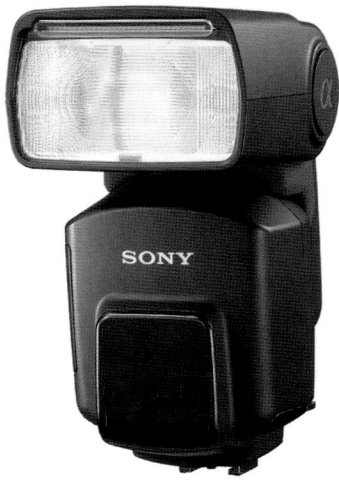

Like all Sony multi interface shoe flash units except the HVL-F20M, the F60M/F60RM automatically adjust the zoom head to vary the angle of coverage to suit the lens focal length in use. You can zoom the head manually instead, if you prefer. A built-in slide-out diffuser panel boosts wide-angle coverage so it's suitable for photos taken at short focal lengths with the 10-18mm zoom.

Figure 12.11 The Sony HVL-F60M is the top-of-the-line external flash unit and includes a bonus LED light for video.

There's also a slide-out "bounce card" that can reflect some light forward even when bouncing the flash off the ceiling, to fill in shadows or add a catch light in the eyes of your portrait subjects. This dust- and moisture-resistant 21-ounce unit uses four AA batteries but can also be connected to the older FA-EB1AM external battery adapter, which has room for 6 AA batteries for increased capacity and faster recycling.

You may find the FA-EB1AM available at reduced prices, as it was recently replaced by the FA-EB1 ($250). The new pack is compatible with both the F60M and F60RM units, and capable of accepting *either* four or eight AA batteries in replaceable magazines, for up to 660 flashes with speedy recycle times of 0.6 seconds. When connected to the flash, it becomes the unit's primary power source.

ANOTHER GOODIE

Along with the F60RM flash and FA-EB1 battery pack, Sony has introduced the FA-RG1 Multi Interface Shoe Rain Guard, which prevents water from seeping into the electrical contacts of the camera.

Regardless of power source, the F60M/RM automatically communicates white balance information to your camera, allowing the a6400 to adjust WB to match the flash output. It also offers a dedicated video light that can be useful for a bit of extra illumination if the subject is close to the camera. When you point the flash head upward, the trio of LED video illuminator lamps are revealed.

You can use this large unit as a main flash or allow it to be triggered wirelessly by another compatible flash unit. A pre-flash burst of light from the triggering master/controller unit causes a remote flash unit to fire. When using flash wirelessly, Sony recommends rotating the unit so that the flashtube is pointed to the location where light should be directed, while the front (light sensor) of the flash is pointed toward the camera. In wireless mode, you can control up to three groups of flashes, and specify the output levels for each group, giving you an easy way to control the lighting ratios of multiple flash units.

HIGH-SPEED SYNC

Those who are frustrated by an inability to use a shutter speed faster than 1/160th second will love the High-Speed Sync (HSS) mode this unit includes that allows for flash at 1/500th to 1/4000th second! (HSS is also available with the HVL-F43M, HVL-F32M, and the discontinued HVL-58AM and HVL-F36AM.) This is ideal when you want to use a very wide aperture for selective focus with a nearby subject with flash; HSS at a fast shutter speed such as 1/1000th second is one way to avoid overexposure. The Mode button on the back of the flash is used to choose either TTL or Manual flash exposure. You can then use the Menu button and plus/minus keys to activate HSS mode; HSS appears in the unit's data panel as confirmation of the mode.

Keep in mind that flash output is much lower in High-Speed Sync than in conventional flash photography. That's because less than the full duration of the flash is used to expose each portion of the image as it is exposed by the slit passing in front of the sensor. As a result, the effective flash (distance) range is much shorter.

In addition, HSS will not work when using multiple flash units or when the flash unit is set for left/right/up bounce flash or when the wide-angle diffuser is being used. (If you're pointing the flash downward, say, at a close-up subject, HSS can be used.)

This flash unit can provide a simulated modeling light effect at two flashes per second or at a more useful (but more power-consuming) 40 flashes per second for 4 seconds for 160 continuous mini-bursts. In wireless mode, the HVL-60M/RM can function as the main (on-camera) flash or it can be removed from the camera and used as a remote flash, triggered wirelessly by another compatible flash unit, as discussed earlier.

HVL-F45RM Flash Unit

If you want an on-camera flash capable of triggering external flash units optically *and* by radio control and are intimidated by the price of the HVL-F60RM, this flash is an affordable ($400) option. It also can be triggered wirelessly by an optical master, by another HVL-F45RM or an HVL-F60RM mounted on the a6400, or by the Sony FA-WRC1M Wireless Radio Commander mounted on the camera. When using radio control, it uses 14 channels to communicate with up to 15 flash units in five groups. It has a guide number of 45/148 (meters/feet) at ISO 100, and a fast 2.5-second recycle time. Its zoom head adjusts for the field of view from 24mm to 105mm (perfect for the a6400's kit lens) and has an LED video light.

HVL-F43M Flash Unit

This less pricey ($328) electronic flash (shown in Figure 12.12) shares many of the advanced features of the HVL-F60M/RM but has a lower guide number of 43/138 (meters/feet). Features shared with the high-end unit include HSS, automatic white balance adjustment, and automatic zoom with the same coverage of focal lengths and the slide-out diffuser, as well as a built-in bounce card. Its quick-shift function allows you to direct the flash upward or to the side by rotating the head. This unit also can be used in wireless mode as a master/controller or remote/slave, and it also offers the quick-shift bounce feature. The HVL-F43M is a tad lighter (at 12 ounces) than its bigger sibling and runs on four AAs. This flash replaces the similar HVL-F43AM unit, which uses the older iISO hot shoe.

HVL-F36AM Flash Unit

Although discontinued, you can easily find this versatile flash available online or in used condition. It uses the old iISO hot shoe, so you'll need an adapter. The guide number for this lower-cost Sony flash unit is (surprise!) 36/118 (meters/feet). Although (relatively) compact at 9 ounces, you still get some big-flash features, such as wireless operation, auto zoom, and high-speed sync capabilities. Bounce flash flexibility is reduced a little, with no swiveling from side to side and only a vertical adjustment of up to 90 degrees.

HVL-F32M Flash Unit

The $300 HVL-F32M is Sony's newest electronic flash unit. (See Figure 12.13.) It features a high-speed synchronization mode, wireless control, and automatic white balance compensation. In wireless mode, it can be used only on Channel 1 (as I'll describe shortly), but can function as both a

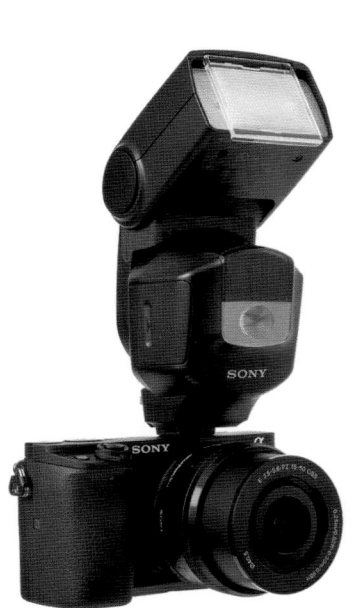

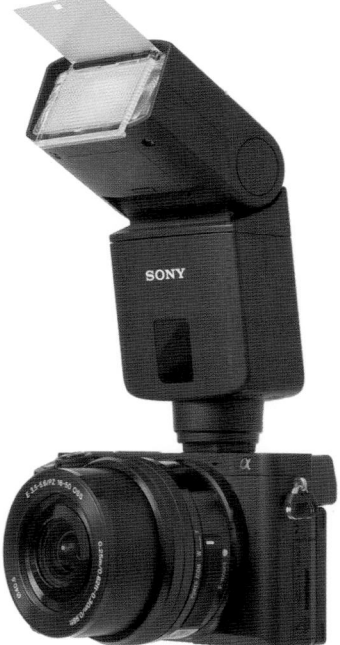

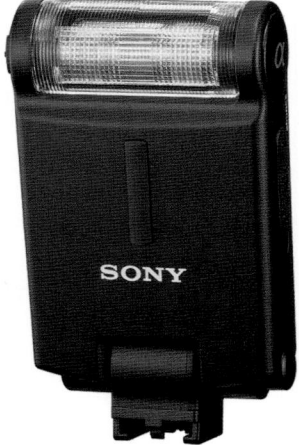

Figure 12.12 The Sony HVL-F43M is a more affordable external flash unit.

Figure 12.13 The Sony HVL-F32M is a more affordable external flash unit.

Figure 12.14 The HVL-F20M flash unit is compact and inexpensive.

master/controller and remote/slave. The flash is powered by a pair of AA batteries and it is resistant to both dust and moisture. Those who love to use bounce flash will like the built-in bounce sheet and retractable wide-angle panel that spreads the light to cover the equivalent of a 16mm lens.

HVL-F20M Flash Unit

The least-expensive Sony flash (see Figure 12.14) is the HVL-F20M ($150), designed to appeal to the budget conscious, especially those who need just a bit of a boost for fill flash, or want a small unit (just 3.2 ounces) on their camera. It has a guide number of 20 at ISO 100, and features simplified operation. For example, there's a switch on the side of the unit providing Indoor and Outdoor settings (the indoor setting tilts the flash upward to provide bounce light; with the outdoor setting, the flash fires directly at your subject). This flash can serve as a master/controller on the a6400 to trigger off-camera flash units wirelessly, but cannot be used as a remote/slave flash. There are special modes for wide-angle shooting (use the built-in diffuser to spread the flash's coverage to that of a lens with a very wide field of view or choose the Tele position to narrow the flash coverage to that of a 50mm or longer lens for illuminating more distant subjects). While it's handy for fill flash, owners of an a6400 camera will probably want a more powerful unit as their main electronic flash.

BATTERY TIP

You may not use your flash very often, but when you do, you want it to operate properly. The problem with infrequent flash use is that conventional nickel-metal hydride batteries lose their charge over time, so if your flash unit is sitting in your bag for a long time between uses, you may not even be aware that your rechargeable batteries are pooped out. Non-rechargeable alkaline cells are not a solution: they generally provide less power for your flash, and replacing them can be costly. The Energizer Lithium Ultimate AA batteries last up to three times longer, but they sell for about $10 for four.

I've had excellent luck with a kind of battery available from Panasonic (and, in some countries, from Fujitsu) called *eneloop* cells. They retain their charge for long periods of time—as much as 75 percent of a full charge over a three-year period (let's hope you don't go that long between uses of your flash). They're not much more expensive than ordinary rechargeables, and can be revitalized up to 1,500 times. They're available in capacities of 1500 mAh to 2700 mAh. I use the economical models with 1900 mAh capacity.

Wireless Flash

In order to trigger flash wirelessly, you'll need to own at least two compatible flash units, such as the HVL-F60M/RM, HVL-F43M, HVL-F32M, or HVL-F20M. One flash will be connected to the camera through the multi interface shoe and serves as the master flash or controller. A second (and additional) flash unit can be triggered wirelessly, with full exposure control. It is a limited range (about 16 feet) but a useful unit if you want your primary illumination to come from the off-camera flash, and, perhaps, use a less powerful on-camera flash as the master. In that mode, the HVL-F20M makes a workable controller/master, especially since it is the least-expensive Sony flash unit. But keep in mind that it cannot be used as a remote/slave flash unit.

To use wireless flash with optical triggering just follow these steps (I'll address radio control later):

1. **Connect the controller flash unit to the a6400.** Slide it all the way into the multi interface shoe so the connection is solid.

2. **Position additional flash(es).** Sony flash units come with a mini-stand that lets you set the flash on a table or other surface. You can also purchase third-party adapters, so the off-camera flash can be mounted on a light stand or a tripod. In a pinch, you can press a helper into service to hold your supplementary flash units. The remote units must be able to "see" the master/controller's pre-flash signal, either directly or by bouncing off another surface in the room.

3. **Power up flash and camera.** Note that when you turn off the camera, the flash turns off as well; you don't need to manually turn both on or off simultaneously if you want to save power during a shooting session.

4. **Switch camera and attached master/controller flash to wireless mode.** Use the Camera Settings menu's Flash Mode option or select Flash mode from the Function menu. Select Wireless (WL). Once the camera is set to wireless mode, press the shutter release halfway, and the attached powered-up flash automatically shifts into wireless mode as well.

5. **Set one or more remote/slave flash unit(s) to wireless mode and choose options.** Turn on the unit and follow the instructions supplied with your flash unit to switch to wireless mode, then select either controller (master) mode or remote (slave) mode. Then, choose a group and channel, which I'll explain in the next section. An alternate way of setting your off-camera flash to remote mode is to mount them on the camera, power up, choose Wireless (WL) from the Camera Settings menu's Flash Mode entry and press the shutter release halfway to transfer the setting to the flash. You can then remove the flash and a red LED on the flash will start blinking to let you know the flash is ready to use in wireless mode.

6. **Test your connection.** Press your defined AEL button, and the controller will emit a burst, which the remotes will respond to with a flash of their own about half a second later.

Key Wireless Concepts

Here are some key concepts you must understand before jumping into wireless flash photography:

- **Controllers.** The flash that communicates with and triggers all wireless flash units is called the *controller* in Sony nomenclature. It's more common within the photographic industry to use the term *master,* however, so I tend to use both terms together to avoid confusion.

- **Remotes.** The flash units that are controlled wirelessly are called the *remotes* by Sony, or *slaves.* There can only be one controller/master flash, but you can have multiple remote/slave units. All the remotes triggered by a controller/master must use the same *channel,* but flashes using a particular channel can be divided into one of two *remote groups,* and their power levels specified by group.

- **Channels.** Sony's wireless flash system offers users the ability to determine on which of up to four possible channels (depending on the flash's capabilities) the units can communicate. (The pilots, ham radio operators, or scanner listeners among you can think of the channels as individual communications frequencies.) The channels are numbered 1, 2, 3, and 4, and each flash must be assigned to one of them. Moreover, in general, each of the flash units you are working with should be assigned to the *same* channel, because the remote/slave flash units will respond *only* to a controller/master flash that is on the same channel. Note that the HVL-F20M cannot be used as a remote/slave flash, and when used as a controller/master flash, you *must* use its sole channel, Channel 1.

The channel ability is important when you're working around other photographers who are also using the same system. Photojournalists, including sports photographers, will encounter this situation frequently as Sony cameras make in-roads in these pro arenas. Each Sony photographer sets flash units to a different channel so as to not accidentally trigger other users' strobes. (At big events with more than four photographers using Sony flash, you may need to negotiate.) I use this capability at workshops I conduct where we have two different setups. Photographers working with one setup use a different channel than those using the other setup, and can work independently even though we're at opposite ends of the same large room.

- **Groups.** Sony's wireless flash system lets you designate multiple flash units in two separate groups, dubbed RMT (which is selected for all flashes by default) and RMT2 (which must be specified explicitly to change individual flashes from the default RMT group). All the flashes in all the groups use the exact same *channel* and all respond to the same master controller, but you can set the output levels of each remote/slave group separately. So, flash in RMT might serve as the main light, while those in RMT2 might be adjusted to produce less illumination and serve as a fill light. It's convenient to be able to adjust the output of all the units within a given group simultaneously. This lets you create different styles of lighting for portraits and other shots.

Note that these two groups consist *only* of remote flashes. Your on-camera controller/master flash is effectively a third group. If the controller is a low-powered unit like the HVL-F20M, it may not contribute much to the exposure at all (or, perhaps just add a little fill if pointed directly at your subject); a more powerful unit can become a potential third group. You could, for example, point the on-camera flash at a ceiling or wall to provide additional diffuse illumination.

If you're using only one group, all the flashes in the RMT group are automatically adjusted based on the settings you specify for the controller/master, such as flash exposure bracketing and/or flash exposure compensation.

- **Flash ratios.** This ability to control the output of one flash (or set of flashes) compared to another flash or set in groups allows you to produce lighting *ratios*. You can control the power of multiple off-camera flash to adjust each unit's relative contribution to the image, for more dramatic portraits and other effects. Ratios are available with flash units that use the new CTRL+ protocol (described next).

- **Flash Protocols.** Older Sony flash units, including the HVL-F20M, used a particular protocol to communicate. More recent units, such as the HVL-F60M, HVL-F43M (with multi inter-face shoe), HVL-F58AM, HVL-F32M, HVL-F32AM, and HVL-F43AM (the last two equipped with the old-style shoe) have an enhanced protocol for communicating with compat-ible flash, called CTRL+, but can also revert to the older protocol (CTRL) to be compatible with older flash as well. Because the HVL-F20M uses the original Sony protocol, it cannot be used to adjust flash ratios, as described above.

- **Metering.** In wireless flash mode, advanced distance integration (ADI) is not used (the dis-tance between the flash and subject can't be determined by the off-camera flash), and Sony's P-TTL flash metering is used instead.

Setting Channels and Remote Groups

To specify the channels and remote groups used by each flash, you must use the flash unit's controls and menu system to do so. Here are the procedures for the HVL-F60M and HVL-F43M.

Setting the HVL-F60M/RM

To choose the group on the HVL-F60M/RM, just follow these steps:

1. Press the MODE button to display the Mode screen.
2. Rotate the control wheel or use its directional buttons to highlight WL RMT.
3. Press the Fn button and use the control wheel to select the group, either TTL Remote or TTL Remote 2.
4. Press the control wheel center button to confirm your changes.

To choose the channel on the HVL-F60M/RM, just follow these steps:

1. Press the Menu button. The Menu screen appears.
2. On Page 1, select the entry to change. Use the control wheel to highlight the entry you want to adjust.
3. Select the wireless channel by highlighting WL CH and pressing the control wheel center button. Then use the control wheel to choose Channel 1, 2, 3, or 4. Press the center button again to confirm your choice.
4. You can also adjust the protocol if needed. Highlight the WL CTRL entry and press the control wheel center button. Use the wheel to select CTRL+ if you are using only compatible flash units (HVL-F60M/RM, HVL-F43M, HVL-F32M, HVL-F58AM, HVL-F32AM, or HVL-F43AM) or CTRL if you are using other flash units in your setup. Press the Menu button again to confirm your choice.

Setting the HVL-F43M

To choose the group on the HVL-F43M, just follow these steps:

1. Press the Fn button. CTRL or RMT will be blinking.
2. Press the right directional arrow on the flash as needed to highlight RMT or RMT2.
3. Press Fn to confirm your choice.

To choose the Channel on the HVL-F43M:

1. Hold down the Fn button for more than three seconds. The first Custom Setting item (CH01 HSS) is displayed.
2. Press the flash's left/right directional buttons to change to C02: Wireless Channel.
3. Press the up/down buttons to select the channel 1, 2, 3, or 4.
4. Press the Fn button again to confirm your choice.
5. You can also adjust the protocol, if needed. Hold down the Fn button for more than three seconds and use the left/right buttons to select C03: Wireless Controller Mode. You can choose 1 (CTRL, the old protocol) or 2 (CTRL+, the new protocol). Press Fn to confirm your choice.

Setting Ratios

Once you've set up one or more flash for the RMT group, and more for the RMT2 group, you can adjust the ratio used between them.

Ratios with the HVL-F43M

Just follow these steps when using the HVL-F43M as the controller or remote/slave. Remember that all flashes in all remote groups must be set to the same channel, as described previously:

1. The easiest way to set ratios is to mount the controller/master and remote/slave units on the camera in turn. With each flash mounted on the camera set to Wireless Flash as described earlier, press the MODE button on the flash to display WL.

2. Press the Fn button, then press the left/right directional buttons until CTRL and RATIO are *both* blinking.

3. Press the Fn button again. The line at upper right will display (see Figure 12.15):

   CTRL RMT RMT1

   1 : 1 : 1

4. Use the left/right directional buttons to move the highlighting to CTRL. When CTRL is highlighted, you can press the up/down buttons to choose the relative power of that flash, compared to the others, from 1, 2, 4, 8, 16, or - - (the latter disables the flash). For example, a setting of 16:1:4 would specify that the flash mounted on the camera has 1/16th the power of the RMT group, while the RMT2 group would have 1/4 the power of the RMT group. Selecting - - disables that flash or group. You might want to do that so that the on-camera flash doesn't contribute to the exposure, even though it will still fire a pre-flash to trigger the remote/slave units.

5. Press the TTL/M button to display TTL.

6. Repeat for each flash.

Ratios with the HVL-F60M/RM

Just follow these steps when using the HVL-F60M/RM as the controller or remote/slave. Again, all flashes in all remote groups must be set to the same channel, as described previously:

1. You can mount each flash on the camera and set the ratios. Press the Mode button to produce the Mode screen and select WL CTRL.

2. Press the Fn button to access the Quick Navi screen and use the control wheel to highlight WL CTRL. Press the control wheel center button to access the dedicated settings screen.

3. Use the control wheel to highlight RATIO. Press the center button to access your choices, Ratio: Off (the controller flash does not contribute to the exposure), TTL Ratio, and Manual Ratio. You can highlight TTL Ratio and use the control wheel to choose ON.

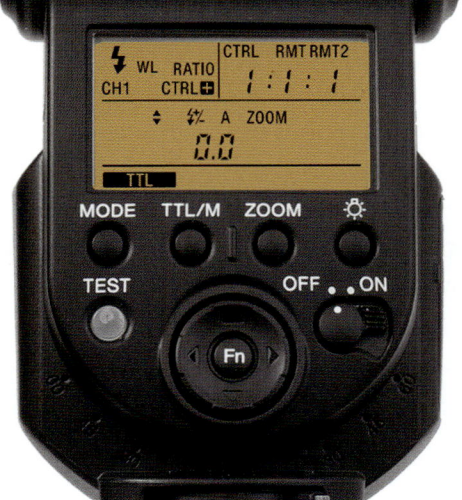

Figure 12.15 Set ratios on the HVL-F43M.

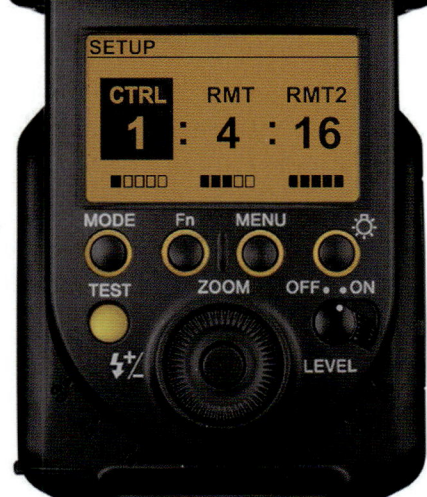

Figure 12.16 Set ratios on the HVL-F60M/RM.

4. Press the center button to return to the indicator screen.

5. Press the Fn button to display the Quick Navi screen and choose the Wireless Lighting Ratio control indicator located at middle left of the screen. Press the control wheel center button, then use the control wheel to change the lighting ratio of each group. Rotate the control wheel to choose the relative power of each flash, compared to the others, from 1, 2, 4, 8, 16, or - -. The - - setting disables that group. (See Figure 12.16.)

6. Press the center button when finished.

Radio Control

Your Sony electronic flash communicate with each other using optical control, via the pre-flashes emitted before the actual exposure takes place. That type of linking requires line-of-sight communication between master and remote units and works only over limited distances. Early in 2016 Sony introduced its wireless radio commander/receiver duo, which gives you a much greater range, many more channels to work with, and more control. Unfortunately, Sony's radio control solution is expensive, making it impractical for all but the most avid (and well-heeled) shooters. I expect it will be more popular among professionals who can justify the expense, and those, such as photojournalists, who need the flexibility of a larger number of channels to avoid conflicts with other photographers covering the same event.

To properly equip yourself, you'll need:

- **Commander.** You'll need one HVL-F60RM flash, HVL-F45RM flash, or FA-WRC1M wireless radio commander ($349) for every camera you want to equip with radio control. The radio-compatible flash or commander reside in the hot shoe of the a6400 and are used to trigger the off-camera electronic flash.

- **Flash units.** You must have at least one Sony flash from those listed above for the wireless commander to trigger. Ideally, you'll have several to allow you to configure multi-light setups, so plan on spending $250 to $600 for each remote flash.

- **Receivers.** As I write this, only the HVL-F60RM and HVL-F45RM can be triggered by radio controls. So, if you're using any other wireless-compatible (optical only) flash, it must be connected to a FA-WRR1 wireless radio receiver ($198). The flash units are *not* sensitive to radio controls on their own.

- **Light stands or an assistant.** The wireless commander generally resides on the multi interface shoe of your camera, so you'll need light stands to accept each receiver, which has its own hot shoe your flash is attached to. Alternatively, you can enlist the aid of an assistant to hold the receiver/flash in proper position.

- **VMC-MM1 Multi Terminal cable (optional).** This $28 cable allows you to connect another one of those $149 wireless receivers to a second (or third…) *camera* so the auxiliary cameras fire in unison with the flash and main camera. This very cool feature will appeal to sports and news photographers covering events.

Each commander transmitter can support up to 15 receivers in any combination of flash units and slave cameras, with your choice of 14 different channels (reducing those conflicts at the next presidential convention you cover in 2020). All the devices on a particular channel can be divided up among as many as five different groups, so you could conceivably have a dozen or more flash units spread among all those groups to provide very sophisticated lighting effects, over a range of more than 98 feet (30 meters).

But wait! There's more. The HVL-F60RM, HVL-F45RM, and FA-WRC1M wireless radio commanders give you Manual, TTL, and Group control of flashes, and power adjustment from full power (1/1) to 1/256th power in 1/3-stop increments. The 3.3-ounce commander and 3-ounce receiver each run on two AA batteries. While I don't expect to see many a6400 owners springing for this system, it's nice for ambitious photographers to know that these capabilities are there for them to grow into. Eventually, Sony will introduce additional radio-capable flash units and commanders, probably at more affordable prices.

Index